Trevor Anthony Lewis

The Influence

of

Social Institutions

on

Black Aspiration

Copyright © 2021 by Trevor Anthony Lewis

All rights reserved. No part of this book may be reproduced or used in any manner without written permission of the copyright owner except for the use of quotations in a book review.

Typeset by PublishingPush.com

Paperback: 978-1-80227-188-1
eBook: 978-1-80227-189-8
Hardback: 978-1-80227-190-4

Contents

Acknowledgements 10

Preface 12

Chapter 1: Tracing Black Aspiration and Illuminating Achievement ... 28

    Black African civilizations 33

    Africa before the Slave Trade 39

    Reparations and the British Government 42

    African culture and civilization 47

    Black Scientists and Inventors 51

    Imhotep 52

    George Washington Carver 53

    Jan Ernest Matzeliger 55

    Elijah McCoy 59

    Garrett Morgan 60

    Granville T. Woods 60

    Lewis Temple 61

    Castigated, seldom praised and chided the most 67

The Black studies dialectic 69

Summary and conclusion 75

Chapter 2: Policy Responses to Mass Immigration 78

Racism as riots 82

Consolidated state racism 84

The Origin of Humanity 98

Early Human Culture 110

Summary and Conclusion 119

Chapter 3: The Education System 122

The expectations, assumptions and practices which fail young Black people 122

Education Policy 123

The significance of 'Race' and other factors 127

    In Exclusion from School 127

The Significance of Education Policy 131

Racism in Contemporary Classrooms 132

The issue of Black hairstyles 157

Who's afraid of the big 'White oppressor' 161

Sources of Disaffection 163

Prejudice and Patronization 181

The influence of low Teacher expectation on the Child 182

Some factors to account for educational inequality 188

Ethnicity and policy ideology 188

Conclusion 197

Chapter 4: Institutional Racism in Higher Education 207

A Case Study 207

Owning up to Institutional Racism 211

Defining Institutional Racism 213

The Unravelling of Institutional Racism 214

The Emergence of a Concept 216

The adversarial nature of racism 219

The adversarial nature of institutional racism 221

Higher education's response to race 225

Understanding Institutional Racism 228

Why the need for recommendations? 239

Higher Education Institutions and Black Exclusion 240

Towards explaining the exclusion of minority ethnic people 244

Equal Opportunity Issues in Higher Education 245

Confronting Reality 250

Degrees, destinations and career progression 256

Research into Institutional Racism 257

Indirect Discrimination: Do Black and Asian students enjoy a service that compares favourably with that enjoyed by White students? 259

Employment Practices 260

Staffing Structure 261

Lack of Positive Action 262

Management and Leadership 263

Occupational Culture 265

Lack of information 270

Consultation 271
Professional Expertise 271
Training 273
Conclusion 276

Chapter 5: The Function and Rise of English Racism 279
The origins of English racism 293
Conclusion 311

Chapter 6: 'Draft' FAO Editor for Sociology 320
The influence of the media industry 320
Immigration 331
Powell's dystopian picture 331
Law and Order 334
Reports of 'horror' 338
Scarman accuses media 343
Racist attacks 347
Black video group 352
Investigative work into employment 354
Establish Black media 355
Researching the media as a service 355
The process of news-making 358
Perspectives on the media 360
Producing and reproducing racism 362
Ownership, control and partisan alliance 366
News values 371

Countering racism 377
THE RIGHT OF REPLY 378
The National Union of Journalists 379
The Press Council 380
Direct action 380
Conclusion 382

Chapter 7: Black Politics and the Campaign for Equality 389

Political participation and exclusion 392
Early minority activism 396
Voting behaviour 397
Minority ethnic political affairs... 401
The push for Labour Party Black Sections... 402
Minority ethnic parliamentary representation 407
Antiracist clamour and political alliances.. 412
Politics, pressure groups and reform.. 420
Race and class 422
Conclusion 424

Chapter 8: Racial Discrimination in Employment................................ 428

Racial Discrimination in Britain... 428
Three fields of investigation 429
Controlled actor testing 432
Findings of the actor tests 435
Summary of main findings 437
Direct racial discrimination.. 437

Indirect racial discrimination 440

Conclusion.. 442

Chapter 9: A Black Underclass in Millennium Britain - Myth or Reality? 443

The British Angle on the Underclass Thesis 447

Marxist Critique of the Underclass Theory.. 449

Social Factors that Determine the Underclass... 453

Conclusion.. 456

Chapter 10: Conclusion 457

Oxbridge; still too elitist.. 462

Facing the Facts... 467

Prospects for the Future... 475

Will the Press ever change? 479

Food for thought.. 480

The first pictures of Christ resoundingly portray him as Black 481

An ancient Roman coin illustrates Christ's African identity................. 482

Christ's Mother, "The Black Madonna" is worshipped throughout Europe, of all places... 483

The Turin Shroud, a Hoax.. 484

Black aspiration and parent power.. 486

The West and the rest 488

Division versus unity.. 492

Will change always prove elusive?... 495

Is Black aspiration a chimera?.. 511

Addressing tolerance 514

Moral values... 520

British culture 526

Focusing on colour prejudice 530

Managing diversity 532

Signs of the times, prospects and futures................................. 536

Saying no to reparations now 543

Etymologies and definitions 546

Affirmative Action as Compensatory Opportunity 548

Affirmative Action as Legal Remedy.. 552

Justifications and Criticisms.. 558

    Fairness 558

Legitimations and Counter-arguments.................................... 563

    Merit 563

THE INTERNALIZATION OF INFERIORITY 567

The challenges facing Black aspiration 572

Bibliography.. 584

Acknowledgements

They say, or it is rumoured, that no product of the mind or intellectual fare is solely attributable to its author and it is particularly true of the compendium construct such as that which follows below. I am indebted to those whose research has been central to the book's development. I am most grateful to Junior Paul Shand for his encouragement, support, advice, and friendship, and for sensing the potential in me, as I had no pretensions of writing an artistic work of this length without the guidance of university supervision. It is probably fair to say that, had it not been for Mr Shand, I may never have been inspired to write this book and it demonstrates what can be done through the power of positive thinking. Once my imagination had been fired by the initial stimulus input and positive regard of my friend and ally, I did not for one minute wish that I had never started the project, or that the job was beyond me, hard and challenging though it proved to be. Before this initial prompting, my inchoate thoughts of writing a book-length project extended only as far as to assume that in any event, such a book would be a non-fiction work.

In addition, I express my gratitude to friends and family members for their support throughout the laying down of this opus; their contribution has been invaluable in making the seemingly insurmountable possible. One does not know whether one can climb a mountain until at first one tries. A special note of thanks and indebtedness is extended to Mom for her support, guidance and wisdom, and in particular, that she taught me to think for myself. Also, over the years, she has proved a staunch and stalwart ally offering positive response bias when required.

Finally, an important component of the textual analysis is taken from a dissertation that first underwent scrutiny as part requirement for my Master of Arts degree in Sociology at the University of Worcester in 2009. I look back at the time spent at Worcester and the early supervision of tutors, Dr Mehreen Mirza and Dr Alan How 'with the pleasure derived from worthwhile achievement'. This book-length project is the culmination of over four years of primary and secondary research into the influence of social institutions on Black aspiration, which unwittingly began in academia although the conceptual picture for the book came much later. I take full responsibility for any imperfections and shortfalls in this volume, and, at the end of all practical matters, the verdict of its material content merit lies with the readership audience with whom I attribute collective arbiter of its usefulness.

Preface

This book is about Black aspiration and shall look to examine the influence of social institutions on Black aspiration. This work has been planned to illustrate and point up how Black ambition and aspiration continues to be silently blighted and to show that racism, in all its forms and disguises, is alive and unwell, but ultimately, the leaves of this volume aim to contribute to the cause of racial justice and equality for non-white people and to the amelioration of contemporary British race relations. Racism need not play a role in individual and institutional affairs, and to this end, the book seeks to capture the nub of what is really going on here, so that the pragmatic lessons of history can be learned and used to realize progressive future outcomes that celebrate and respect cultural diversity and full acceptance in society's mainstream institutions. This research attempts to incorporate an account of the Black British struggle for equality.

Built into the majority of chapters is a component part that aims to explore the influence of adverse fortunes in the lives of Black and minority ethnic people. To all intents and purposes, the chapters are about the Black and minority ethnic presence and the questions that it raises in Britain as a condition of residence and legal and moral obligation. The opening chapter attempts to explode some of the myths concerning the Black man/woman, by whom I mean the African and his Black antecedents, including mixed-race people, though this is not to say that South Asian people are not regarded as Black, but they prefer to assert their own particularity. For all minority groups, I use the terms people of colour, minority groups, non-white people and minority ethnic groups to distinguish all peoples that are not White. A quick note on non-white - it seems to suggest something lacking or a deficiency so I shall keep its use to a minimum. To pick up the threads, this is approached by examining and exploring the Black man's/woman's culture to reveal his/her contribution to civilization and this is quickly followed up with more recent Black-inspired inventive innovations in modern-day world culture. Beyond what has been said, the outcome of such an exposition reveals and exposes the modern-day contradictions and tensions concerning the Black man/woman.

For example, we are made aware that the African man has no history to speak of, and as recently as the year 2000, Black History is reported as not assuming a place on the curriculum in some British schools, reinforcing this idea (Parekh, 2000: 144). Such an idea was put before the public by the famous Oxford University historian Professor Hugh Trevor-Roper. In a 1965 publication, he wrote: "Perhaps in the future, there will be some African history to teach. But at present, there is none, or very little: there is only the history of Europe in Africa. The rest is largely darkness like the history of pre-Columbian America, and darkness is not a subject of history". Declarations of this nature actually diminish Trevor-Roper's standing to the semi or quasi-educated (Walker, 2006: 12). The history of Black people constitutes far more than just the Atlantic slave trade, the missionary expeditions and colonialism. If we trace history back to before the coming of the Europeans and beyond, as the opening chapter illustrates, an illustrious and magnificent African past and African-descended achievements can be found.

We learn that very different from being inferior, the Black man/woman has not only demonstrated inventive genius and pioneering skills and abilities, but also has a logical and rational mind; all the qualities English racism informs us s/he is deficient of, and unendowed with to achieve and succeed. Just as Macpherson judged all major British organisations to be characterized by institutional racism, and this was suspected and came as no surprise to the Black and South Asian community, so also did they suspect that the Europeans had falsified the truth and proliferated a colossal and incontrovertible misrepresentation regarding the man/woman of colour. A current government publication, 'McGregor-Smith Review: Race in the Workplace', reports that Black and minority group individuals are being stymied from progression in the workplace simply because their skin colour does not correlate – incurring a cost to the UK economy of an estimated 24 billion – roughly the same as 1.3 per cent of gross domestic product (GDP) per annum. Such a cost to the economy is significant, but the personal inflicted effect of racism and lived-through impact of racial discrimination on individuals' incomes, living standards, welfare and security is immeasurable (Mills, The Voice Newspaper, April 6-12, 2017:21). Ergo, White racism is an enduring and persistent problem and as for their part, overwhelmingly, Black people constitute not one iota of the social problem they are purported or propounded to represent.

Although African people have a long-established settlement history in Britain extending back as far as before the English came here, and then, in Septimius Severus' time, when he was the African Emperor over the Roman imperial army, ever since, post-war mass immigration research studies have shown that Black and South Asian groups have been subject to differential treatment at the hands of White British people and the country's kindred institutions. The South Asian presence in Britain also has a long history and can be traced back to the year 1505 (Fryer, 1984; Sewell, 1993). This work examines a range of sectors in social life, such as the institution of government, the mass media, compulsory schooling, higher education institutions, the labour market, the class system and how Black and minority ethnic people have contributed to mainstream British politics in order to effect social and political change for the amelioration of social conditions and for the upliftment and betterment of race relations in this country. The influence of these institutions with their own contributory net effect and brand of discriminatory practices are what the research illustrates and brings to the fore, suggesting something of what it is to be non-white in a social and political order of changing demands and circumstances.

As already mentioned, the Black and minority ethnic experience is coloured or characterized by prejudice, racial discrimination, racial disadvantage, and racism on an individual level and institutional racism at a structural level. Because these phenomena are all but invisible does not mean that they are not real and material aspects of the social composition that makes up the vibrant and diverse cultural tapestry that is the United Kingdom. Racism is doubtlessly among the most divisive and pernicious features of modern social organization, yet, by the same token, it is one that those endowed with sight cannot easily detect as visible (Lacey, in Mac an Ghaill, 1988). Our current system of government incorporates no formal framework of discrimination, no segregated public transport travel and no laws prohibiting inter-racial marriage. However, the unseen forces of discrimination are tangible enough. They pervade the labour market, they determine residential formations and they silently have an effect upon the operation of all major government institutions.

The education system is especially subject to racism. It is, conceivably, at a *prima facie* glance, difficult to understand the reason behind this situation. Whether education rests on developing the abilities of young impressionable people, increasing their understanding and skills and extending their knowledge of the world, it follows that surely this is a sphere of social life in which racism can be combatted, recognized and ousted from the minds of single individuals. Unfortunately, life takes a more complex and not so straightforward turn. Schools make up society and they mirror its structure (Lacey, in Mac an Ghaill, 1988).

Education's characterization, as in the above, cannot develop since the space and vitality it would necessitate has been seized by an incalculable competitive structure where 'understanding' is perceived as subversive if it stands in the way of achievement and examination's proud outcome. Consequently weakened, 'education' lacks the ability to combat and challenge racism (Lacey, in Mac an Ghaill, 1988). In the first place, does Lacey (1988) have an axe to grind by neglecting to mention the racist immigration laws incorporated in our government's formal framework and, therefore, is he also in denial? Since there is a proverb which states, where there is a will there is a way, it behoves education to not be unwilling and unable to confront and challenge racism wherever it lurks. Is Lacey (1988) not excusing the education system for not executing and exercising its duty and moral obligation to our children? The fact that Black Caribbean children are more likely to be seen as subversive supposedly makes the education system fair, or is it somehow skewed in favour of White English children? Has Lacey (1988) glossed over the detail that school processes, often the reason why school pupils rebel, interfere with achievement and examination success? Lastly, is Lacey (1988) not institutionalizing the very idea that education cannot change the situation of racism in the British education system?

It is an uphill struggle for education to do an about-turn, to consider and begin to deal with the problems that progressively challenge our society and to contribute to extending to young people a new intelligence. But part of that struggle is to make learning relevant to the Black and minority child by integrating Black history into the curriculum in all schools where there is an apparent need for it. At the time of writing, Lacey (1988) expressed pessimism regarding this struggle, however, some schools, by no means all, do now teach Black History in some form; so, there is scope for a fervent optimism that the tide of Black underachievement in British schools will be stemmed, if not now, then it's possibly a forthcoming future prospect.

The chapters on education provide important insights including analyses of major problems that one might hope are thought-provoking, challenging and comprehensive, though not exhaustive, since the debate moves on surrounding schools and higher education and, in the latter case, is an under-researched subject area. Despite over 50 years of race equality legislation in Britain, progress continues to be pedestrian and the emerging current and present wave since the British referendum to exit the European Union in June 2016 indicates that the lived experience of racially motivated diatribe, broadsides and thuggery are on the increase (Mills, The Voice Newspaper, April 6-12, 2017:21).

The subtext of this work is that because Black and minority ethnic people, in the modern era, live in a country of predominantly White citizens who have long negotiated their terms of social conditions and seek to maintain their position of social privilege and advantage, this is compounded by the collective consciousness or hangover from colonial times, otherwise known as the 'colonial mentality'; however, there is an underlying struggle to redress the balance of second-class citizenship and structured social inequality. This begs the question, can minority groups be truly considered and recognized as part of the working and middle-classes as opposed to the underclass given their second-class structurally subordinate status position? In response to this question, I would suggest that occupation tends, first and foremost, to determine social position whether working-class, middle-class or celebrity status, but unfortunately, aside from and underlying this, inequality exerts an influence in the equation rendering minority ethnic group members separated, disjointed and detached from true class membership position, potentially occupying a subordinate rung within their lived existence and in economic activity. Inequality serves to signify that non-white class membership position is undermined at every turn, and on many levels, as they apparently fare less well in society generally and appear to accept jobs in the secondary labour market or jobs that the British find undesirable, and which are of lower status; this would certainly suggest that some non-white working-class employees, or those who are under the illusion of being working-class, do not share the same platform as their White working-class equivalents.

The material detail that White groups are highly resistant to change in their hearts and minds and that their institutions function to maintain the status quo is central to the underlying dominant theme of the research and what confronts Black and minority groups in their struggle for racial justice and equality. Rangasamy (2004) puts forward the suggestion that the only effective instrument against institutional racism, by which Macpherson deemed all major organisations to be characterized, is for there to be a shift in the domestic institutional culture. (See Parekh, 2000: 71-75).

The self-same language used to designate and denote race relations in the United Kingdom is a root cause of considerable abstraction and political obfuscation (Parekh, 2000). The terms 'minority' and 'majority' describe immutable cadres and obscure the variability and heterogeneity of real practical matters. Such an expression as 'ethnic group' traps the appropriate group into its ethnicity and inhibits both its multiple personas and its volition of self-government. The language unit 'integration' is even more prone to lead one astray, as it implies a unidimensional process where 'minorities' are acculturated into the fabled homogeneous customary structure of the 'majority'. We are alive to these and other constraints of the prevailing vernacular of debate. Dreaming up a complete new dictum does not help, as such a language risks being too highbrow, unnatural and detached from the idioms of daily life to be intelligible, much less provide a conveyance for substantive discussion. Accordingly, therefore, the research determined to steer clear of, and give a wide berth to, the current vocabulary when it was convenient to do so (Parekh,2000).

Although progress in race relations seems painfully slow, each generation owes it to themselves and to posterity to improve the country in which they live and to leave a lasting legacy. This work offers to contribute to the debate and is a method by which I can exercise that momentous historical duty and responsibility.

The structure of the book is outlined below. Chapter 1 reflects on Egyptian civilization as the first and oldest recorded in history, indeed, the cradle of civilization, suggesting that Africans were the first to become civilized, proving beyond doubt that inferiority is a social myth. The picture the schools and the media paint gives one reason to doubt whether this is true at all, as White society extends a quite different view as seen in the portrayal of the British character in Margaret Thatcher's 'swamping' statement. Schools have a Eurocentric curriculum so that the truth about civilization is concealed among a raft of European endeavour and achievement, leaving one with the impression that anything good and important was invented by Europeans.

Preface

Chapter 1 interrogates whether Margaret Thatcher's 'swamping' speech was in any way racist or new. The wonders of Egyptian civilization and building techniques and masonry are discussed, revealing that some techniques were never surpassed – albeit realized on a grander scale. What is also revealing is that the Egyptians understood "pi". Egyptian innovation incorporated buildings sculpted downwards out of a mountain using a hammer and chisel. Before the slave trade, Africans manufactured soap, worked metals and precious metals and, among other things, tanned and worked leather. The British government's position on reparations is reported and African culture and civilization are considered, alongside a litany of Black contributors to world civilization in science and invention. On top of schools failing Black children, there appears a reluctance to place Black History on the school curriculum. This chapter establishes the parameters of the book.

Chapter 2 examines the inextricably associated experience of Black and minority ethnic migrants seen through the prism of government policy responses to mass immigration. The decade 1961-71 saw the introduction of three major laws which sought to exclude African-Caribbean and South Asian 'immigrants' from British shores. The 1971 Act phased out the legitimacy of Commonwealth 'immigrants' taking up permanent abode, and so represented an important intervention in the institutionalisation of racist legislation. The arrival of the SS Empire Windrush was a ripple in the wave of African-Caribbean migration – the large majority of migrant flows into Britain from 1945 and 1954 came from other European nations. This raised no discursive struggle concerns. But when the tide changed to Black and South Asian inflows from the colonies and former colonies, concerns were raised at the heart of British government circles, one which revealed a habitus to 'surrender to racism' over principles around nationality but also its indecision to enshrine racism in law.

The chronic labour shortage experienced in the post-war years saw the Labour administration encourage European men to come and take up employment here. Government recruitment policy did not include locating labour from among British subjects found in the colonies. However, employers cared less about religion and 'race' in the 1950s. Despite the Royal Commission's ruling that African-Caribbean and South Asian 'immigrants' were unwelcome and unwanted as a remedy for Britain's labour shortage problem, mass immigration followed because production targets in certain sectors of industry could not be achieved without it. The British Nationality Act (1948) encouraged employers to recruit from the Caribbean and Asian subcontinent throughout the 1950s. The failure of the Royal Commission to acknowledge these British citizens as an untapped labour source suggests that African-Caribbean and South Asian people were deemed as not 'of good human stock' (Miles and Phizacklea,1984:23). Both government administrations during this period held an anti-immigration stance and, as a result, legislation followed. This chapter investigates the notion of superior versus inferior races and separates it into its component parts to put the world into its proper perspective; i.e., the African was first to become civilized and all human beings are intelligent.

Chapter 3 attempts to consider the whole system of teacher effects in schools and their impact on students of African-Caribbean and South Asian parentage. Teacher effects are one thing but this does not mean that some pupils are not entirely responsible for temporary or permanent exclusion rates in British schools. Secondly, this chapter explores the policy responses to the Black and minority ethnic presence in British schools. Education policy has not helped since the progression of education policies extending from the 1980s has coincided with growing rates of school exclusions. Education policy rules and procedures have frequently had unintended consequences for Black and minority ethnic students and there is substantial resistance to change. Universal opinion sees the rise in exclusions as dovetailing with changes in the running of the education system which the late 1980s period ushered in. The 1988 Education Reform Act insisted on radical reorganization of British Education, which had polar opposite effects on the rate of exclusions.

Although it may be problematic to establish a direct correlation between education policy since the late 1980s and secondary school exclusions, it is feasible to draw on the divergent influences of the 'market system' of educational policy regarding how children from certain backgrounds are dealt with in the school *mise en scène*. A more recent piece of education legislation speaks to the experiences of minority ethnic children, including their educational failure and marked show in exclusion figures. Despite this, no targeted measures are put in place to address these matters. It has been determined that African-Caribbean males are 4-5 times more likely to be excluded in contrast to their White peers. Disruptive and aggressive behaviour patterns were among the reasons why young Black people were excluded. African-Caribbean students are liable to be selected for criticism when engaging in the same activity as their White counterparts. That this chapter attempts to consider the whole system of teacher effects in schools also summarizes five ethnographic studies to this end, focusing on the processes existing in and inseparable from teacher-pupil relationships.

Chapter 4 discusses higher education, a sector in crisis. Higher education remains unchanged by policies developed in other sectors to tackle racism and foster ethnic and cultural diversity. Studies have shown that White society cannot afford to be complacent. Emanating from such studies and other explorations is a conceptual picture of ethnic disparities for student and staff personnel. Important social research by the Association of University Teachers (AUT), which reflected on race and staffing issues in the old universities, also stressed a chapter of accidents and accepted that institutional racism exists in the workplace milieu.

In 1999, Carter, Fenton and Modood saw it necessary for what they coined an 'institutional antiracism'. Their analysis suggested a targeted approach to combatting institutional racism through a series of proposals. These proposals had the effectiveness of race equality strategies in mind where targeted action would transcend mere tweaking with entrance policies or engagement practices. But, then, it appeared that institutions of higher education were deficient of the ideational and analytical means to posit a strategy for dealing with racism across organisational boundaries and were unable to meet their new race equality function subject to law (following the passage of the Race Relations (Amendment) Act 2000). In this chapter, among other things, I aim to consider and show the adverse impact higher education institutions sometimes reeks on the Black and minority ethnic panoply of experience and how the ubiquitous role and presence of language and culture assumes a clearly defined shape and form in higher education institutions, which, to some extent, regulates things, usually to the advantage of the dominant groups and the disadvantage of the subordinate groups and to succinctly show how equal opportunity structures are marginalized. Also in this chapter, I intend to critically analyse the role and function of higher education in maintaining the status quo both from the standpoint of students and higher education staff personnel. Also, the chapter draws on autobiographical material to draw attention to Black exclusion in higher education as a case study.

Chapter 5 explores the function and rise of English racism. The focus is to outline the function of English racism, the main function of which is to conceal and legitimise the unfair use of Black labour, with the assumption that Blacks are innately inferior. The maintenance of White social status appears important in the role of racism. Equality has so far not been granted because it appears to be a 'threat' to White stewardship, dominance and hegemony. The chapter's main focus will be to outline how English racism took its rise once the floodgates had been breached and had a snowball-like effect in its intensity.

English racist ideology assumes that White Europeans are superior and Black Africans and people of colour are inferior. Once this view became public knowledge, the number of authors who championed this general belief system gathered apace adding to a substantial body of work on the subject. The reason behind this development was to excuse slavery and the slave trade and the literature surpassed earlier belief that all things black were bad or had negative connotations. The ground had been well-tilled or prepared before the first author came out as racist. This chapter provides a critical assessment of racist ideology as a counter-narrative that corrects matters. For instance, I argue that racist ideology has no foundation to the claim of White supremacy and is based on shameless lies, opprobrious slanders and is an egregious obscenity to all humankind. Race prejudice is an insanity of sorts that corrupts public morals and, above all else, is profoundly wrong, and incredibly racist to boot.

Chapter 6 reports on how 'race' is reported in the tabloid and 'quality' newspapers. White people who have little or no contact with Black people have their attitudes and opinions shaped by newspaper representations and, as opinion-formers, newspapers not only inform, they influence. The chapter opens with illustrations of what a powerful influence newspapers can be on public opinion. In this chapter, I aim to show the role of the media against Black and minority ethnic groups and how the media reproduce the mainstream ideology. I take the opportunity to look into and offer a potted history of press antagonism and bias in the press's campaign against Black and South Asian people. Instances of this kind of news reporting are documented in the text. I also take a look at how the riots of 1981 and 1985 were reported, paying particular attention to the political role of the media. To give due parity to the press reports of these developments would require a tome or volume of its own but in this chapter, I follow just some of the prevalent features of such coverage.

Racist attacks tend to be ignored or represented lightly by national newspapers and press treatment of news items is consistent with the underlying assumption that White life matters more than Black and South Asian life. Some examples are offered of how newspaper stories on race can appeal to 'popular' prejudices and fears and can compound and inflame racist sentiment, contributing towards and perpetuating racial attacks. Most British newspaper groups are bent on legitimating racism by encouraging racist beliefs and by attacking attempts to remedy racism. I show and identify the media industry's role as an employer from the viewpoint of the Black Media Workers Association (BMWA). This chapter also includes the research of the media as a provider of services. In a further section, I show the nature of newspaper journalism and how the press promotes racism. For instance, it would appear that consequent to press coverage, 'Black Hostility' is regarded as germane to, and gravely affecting race relations, though 'White Hostility' and the 'National Front' are not. A study by Hartmann and Husband concluded that media-powered perceptions of Blacks were 'more conducive to the development of hostility towards them than acceptance' (Hartmann and Husband, 1974:208 in Troyna, 1981:11). The issue of news values is covered, as in news publications, 'race' is consistently advanced as a 'hot' or volatile issue, and volatile issues promote newspaper sales. Newspapers sell not necessarily because of racist reporting but owing to sensationalism around race. The available infrastructure for press complaints and grievances precedes the chapter's conclusion.

The arrival and presence of Black and minority ethnic communities have seen a growing concern over serving minority community interests and chapter 7 is an attempt at chronicling the nature and influence of their development and the direction in which political interplay has taken matters. The main aim is to incorporate the fundamental modes of Black and minority ethnic mobilisation, the role of antiracist political organisations, the relevance of race and class, minority political participation and how minority politics feeds into local political agendas. Before concluding this chapter, we shall consider what the future chances are for Black and minority politics hitting their mark, particularly from the standpoint of social change, that are unfolding within minority communities in the contemporary political climate. Prior to engaging with the particulars at the heart of this chapter, however, it is *sine qua non* to broach certain general contentions about political participation and modes of mobilisation.

The emergence of the Labour Party Black Sections owed itself to some extent to the 1981 riots, but more specifically, it countered the frustration Black people encountered within the political system and was a clarion call for greater representation. The early signs were promising since the party already countenanced women's sections and youth sections; Jewish Party members also have an organised pressure group. The impetus for the campaign was, ergo, that the Black vote represented equal importance, and that the Party ought to align and orient itself to their needs. The central concern of the LPBS was to acquire constitutional recognition by the Party coupled with the same freedoms and accoutrements had by the Women's and Youth Sections. This came alongside a number of other stipulations, one being racial exclusivity. Black Sections' activists, amid accusations of 'apartheid', argued that Black representatives can best articulate the concerns of Black people. The Labour leadership failed to capitulate on LPBS demands but instead, formally sanctioned the Black Socialist Society (BSS) in 1993.

Chapter 8 aims to offer an overview of the main findings of studies carried out with minority ethnic groups in employment. What will be shown is the extent and nature of racial discrimination in the labour market and I will attempt to update this evidence by considering more recent data in this specific field of enquiry. In chapter 8, following a series of controlled experiments conducted in late 1973 and early 1974, it was found 'that there is still very substantial racial discrimination against South Asians and West Indians when seeking manual jobs, and that discrimination is worse for non-skilled than for skilled job applicants' (Smith,1977:104). The discrimination against South Asians and African-Caribbeans was principally predicated on colour prejudice and the extent of discrimination against African-Caribbeans, Indians and Pakistanis is similar.

In more recent research, Daniel found the Caribbean or South Asian 'immigrant' was much more likely to experience higher levels of discrimination. Despite subsequent laws aimed at combatting racial discrimination, the studies done since show a continued trend towards the considerable and based mainly on colour. While, for Smith, the extent of discrimination had diminished between 1967 and 1973, Brown and Gay found no evidence to indicate that the extent of racial discrimination (ascertained in 1984-85) had shown a reduction since 1973. A baseline one-third of employers remained among those choosing to reject African-Caribbean or South Asian job applicants on grounds of colour (Pilkington,2003:44). The most up-to-date tests of discrimination at regional level (CRE 1996; Simpson and Stevenson,1994) continue to signpost racial discrimination. Moreover, the finding that discrimination is a powerful controlling force that affects the life-chances of minority ethnic groups and that penalties impact upon successive generations just as much as the first, comes as no surprise.

Chapter 9 will consider the validity of the underclass concept in light of conflicting theory. By considering the structure of society, it begins to become easier to see that a substratum may exist beneath the working-class and that the social class scale is not all that we thought it was. Among those who contest the idea that an underclass exists are Pilkington (2003), who cites two PSI surveys, the Census and the LFS, to challenge the notion that minority groups comprise a racialised underclass. Again, Moore (1999) examines the evidence which also indicates the existence of an underclass but he rejects the very idea out of hand. Marxists, Castles and Kosack, also dismiss Rex's view that minority ethnic groups constitute an underclass. The underclass theory is fundamentally a Weberian one and Weberians would take issue with the Marxist critique of the underclass theory.

Marxist and Weberian theory differ in that the latter detect a minority ethnic underclass in Britain whereas Marxist theory finds that they constitute either a lower formation of the working-class or a 'fraction' of the working-class, but there are similarities between the two analyses (Sarre,1989; cited in Pilkington, 2003:63). They see eye to eye on four key questions. Firstly, they appreciate that the economy produces low-level jobs in the class system, and racial discrimination enforces the continued minority ethnic restriction to such market positions. Secondly, they converge in regarding racism as extremely pervasive, influencing the position of the minorities both in the occupational sector and also elsewhere, particularly in housing. Thirdly, they agree that in locating minority groups in the social hierarchy, due regard must be paid to their subordinate labour market status position. Finally, they are as one in recognizing that the unique position of minorities tends towards their development of unique consciousness levels and action (Pilkington, 2003:63). In this chapter, I critically analyse Marxist critique of the underclass theory to detect that White British people facilitate the creation of an underclass, and, when sociologists like John Rex point it out, they find it very hard to accept. I argue that a Black and minority ethnic underclass is not a myth but is reality.

Chapter 10 picks up the threads and strands of previous chapters, it looks at Oxbridge's still too elitist status, often not including enough Black and minority ethnic students among its roll. The failure of Oxbridge to admit sufficient numbers of Black and minority ethnic students is part of the complex structure of what is meant by higher education functioning and operating to maintain the status quo. In this chapter, I consider prospects for the future and describe and evaluate (a) whether Black aspiration is a chimera, (b) whether reparations is the *quid pro quo* way forward, and (c) whether the press will ever change, and I deal with the prospect that social reform change in the lives of Black and minority ethnic people is not necessarily inevitable but suggests that Martin Luther King's dream was not misplaced. Central to this chapter is the section on food for thought as it highlights Black ability and potential. Therefore, the obstacles which litter the path and sully the way for Black aspiration are social institutions or White society. A significant proportion of the chapter will focus on recommendations for the elimination of racial inequality and the chapter concludes with a brief look at the challenges facing Black aspiration.

Chapter 1: Tracing Black Aspiration and Illuminating Achievement

This book seeks to address and is geared and directed towards responding to the question of how society's institutions influence Black aspiration. Secondly, this book attempts to incorporate an account of the Black British struggle for equality. I must also acknowledge that society's institutions also influence White aspiration and thus it is not only Black aspiration that is embattled. Also, the bilateral relationship between them in terms of a universal aspiration is to prosper and thrive. By focusing and concentrating on institutions such as the British government, compulsory education, higher education, the labour market and the media, I shall attempt to systematically analyse how the effect against Black aspiration is so firmly entrenched and built into the social and moral fabric that is modern-day contemporary Britain.

The dawn of civilization was the product or the accumulation of knowledge that was Black African led and Black African inspired (Diop,1974:22). The Egyptian civilization, the oldest recorded civilization, was a Black African civilization that is testament to Black African accomplishment and testament to Black yearning and longing to develop, grow and create lasting extensions of themselves that can stand the test of time. Egyptian scholars, Herodotus and Manetho place the origin of the Egyptian civilization at 17,000 B.C. and by 4245 B.C., the Egyptians had proceeded to invent the calendar (which as an indispensable condition requires thousands of years to pass (Diop,1974:22). In those days, Black Africans were the masters of all they surveyed and their aspiration was not consistently and systematically undermined or encroached upon. The struggle for equality was a much later development that emerged with White stewardship (see Chapter seven). The fact that Africa is the cradle of civilization speaks volumes. It says much about African endeavour and the African character not to mention African determination to rise, grow and develop beyond humanity's circumstances (Diop,1974; Walker,2006;2008).

This is entirely contrary to what one can sense living in contemporary Britain. We are inculcated with the counterclaim that the British explored new territories and spread civilization throughout the globe. This misrepresentation is a product of the media and British schooling; in particular, I refer to the issue of immigration and Margaret Thatcher's famous 'swamping' statement to illustrate how the British character is portrayed. It was February 1978, and in a televised statement about immigration, Margaret Thatcher argued that immigration at its then present rate would, by the year 2000, mean an increase of people from the New Commonwealth and Pakistan to the order of four million in Britain (Solomos,1989). To this, she responded as follows:

That is an awful lot, and I think it means that people are really rather afraid that this country might be swamped by people of a different culture. The British character has done so much for democracy, for law, and done so much throughout the world that if there is any fear that it might be swamped, then people are going to be rather hostile to those coming in (Solomos,1989:129).

Here we have an intriguing and prime example of that which has been defined as the new racism. However, at what level is it actually racist? Or new?

In addressing this question, we embark on a course of explanation of some of the complexities of modern-day discussions on 'race', hence the difficulties of attaching clearly defined epithets such as 'racist' and 'non-racist' to personalities or personal statements.

The sense in which Mrs Thatcher's remarks qualify as not racist are a moot point. The position she takes has no immediate truck with 'race' and nor to any 'racial' marker evidently linked with historical racism, like skin shade, size of brain or physical appearance of the nose. In fact, the language used seems devoid of all biological pointers and, therefore, appears very different from any semblance of what Rattansi (2007) nominates as classical or 19th-century and a fair proportion of the 20th-century racism.

Also, there are no clear pointers to superior and inferior groups, especially with an implicit biological determinism, a chief component of classical racism. Put in place, however, and what is above all else ostensibly new, is the stress on cultural difference and the bona fide apprehensions of indigenous people that their national being and, by inference, culture may be in danger of being overwhelmed and made light of.

On the other hand, British national culture is strongly pitted against the nature of outsiders from geographic and political boundaries inhabited by non-white peoples. The 'New Commonwealth', in British cultural ideology, has consistently functioned to identify non-white populations by being set against the largely White Old Commonwealth of New Zealand, Australia and Canada (Rattansi,2007).

What is more, Mrs Thatcher identifies the British Isles as a unique cultural development. The racial import of this passing mention is crucial (Rattansi,2007). In former times, the concepts of race and nation have perpetually been joined together since the 18th century. Ideas surrounding the 'nation' have always coalesced in cultural, geographical, and biological proto-racial aspects. Ideas inseparable from Anglo-Saxon, Slavic, Gallic, Germanic and additional racial cultures have evidently had an effect upon notions of unique British, French, German and Russian national states of being.

Also, colour and culture bear a strong relationship through connections forming connections in Mrs Thatcher's discourse. There is some weight attached to the idea that the Black and brown New Commonwealth people fell short of a commitment to democratic ideals and the legal rule to which everyone is subject. Further, they are presented as failing to play a role in world history and global artistic successes.

So, implications of biological, colour-originated, nationally restricted cultural superiority and inferiority are evidently conveyed by the reference that democracy, the governance of law, and additional contributions to world civilization have been engineered by British, and in particular, White – not 'New Commonwealth'- peoples (Rattansi, 2007).

Needless to say, the White/non-white dichotomy and its linkage with democracy and additional aspects is achieved by advancing a highly condensed and ideological antecedent of British colonialism in which brutal land and resources acquisition took place; slavery, exploitation and wholesale slaughter of non-white 'natives' in Africa, the Caribbean, and the Indian territorial region are whitewashed out of the entire mental image. Not that the British character has not been influential throughout the world, but what she does not say is that Black Africans were internationally influential myriad years before. They played a pivotal role in the early history of Arabia, India, Palestine, Pakistan, Iran and Iraq (i.e., Phoenicia, Arabia Felix, Sumer, Elam and Indus Valley (Walker,2008:8). Africans also featured in the ancient and medieval history of Central America. Primevally, Blacks spread civilization all the world over as shown by Kamit (ancient Egypt), Canaan, Kush (Ethiopia), Sumer, Babylon, Indus Kush and Harappa (ancient India), the Shang of ancient China and the Washitaw and Olmecs (ancient America) (Suzar,1999:59). Further, great African civilizations encompassed the kingdoms of Mali, Benin, Songhai, Ghana and Zimbabwe, and the Moors, who presided over southwest Europe for 700 years. Africans had a civilizing influence everywhere around the globe. They left proof positive of this in the far distant regions of the planet. Civilization has undergone global destruction on many occasions from cataclysmic forces such as pole shifts. On every occasion this transpired, it was Black Africans – the Parents of humanity – who re-established and assembled anew and redistributed human social development and advanced organisation everywhere on Earth again (Suzar,1999). "We have found the Black complexion or something related to it whenever we have approached the origin of the nations" (Godfrey Higgens in Suzar,1999:59).

Above all is the fact that the independent situation was furthered to the non-white colonies (and the USA), hastened alone by violent conflict, and Democracy, directly and ineffectually instituted prior to a –well-timed exit is also ignored. So, also, is the crackdown on the extension of democracy by White minority hardliners of the period, such as Southern Rhodesia (Zimbabwe) and apartheid South Africa (Rattansi, 2007:98).

The prevalence with which Mrs Thatcher's comments belong to a deliberate, clear-sighted incomprehension to mask possible racism is the opposite of plain simple to interpret, and this type of question throws into confusion discussion of racism. Intentionality is a matter we shall now broach.

Expressions of racism do not prove that the individual or group concerned intended the remarks to be perceived as racist and would cause offence to those on the receiving end (Rattansi, 2007:112). Such remarks also do not mean that the individual or group concerned will necessarily and involuntarily carry out other sorts of discriminatory practices or has a history of such behaviour.

This matter serves as more than just a concern with learning or research interest. It can emerge as a crucial issue when judgements are pending about racist behaviour. A noteworthy incident that came to light in the prosecution case against the white youths for the racially motivated killing of Black teenager Stephen Lawrence in London appropriately and tragically points out the importance and not infrequent intractability of this issue (Rattansi,2007).

To build a case against the five White youths facing legal proceedings for murder, police secretly managed to acquire film footage of them at home. The covert surveillance shows the young men loudly vocalizing racist profanities and making stabbing actions with knives. However, the film was not submitted as evidence. It would not have taken much for the youths to assert in court, as they had already openly done, that they were merely 'fooling around' or 'messing about', and that the incidents prove little concerning their intentions or their culpability in actually carrying out the murder of Stephen Lawrence (Rattansi,2007). Charges have been brought against two White men concerning the killing (Pilkington,2011).

The matter of the relationship extending across from speech practices and other kinds of discriminatory behaviour fulfils a problematic role, and inferences need to be drawn with caution and near-complete attention to circumstances and additional behaviour. A point that might seem credible at a common-sense degree does not necessarily hold sway when judgements of proof allowing no uncertainty have to be adjudicated upon (Rattansi, 2007).

Black African civilizations

What do we mean by Black African civilizations? And what are the productions of Black aspiration? North African countries like Egypt are presently held as integral to the Arab world (Walker,2006). In such countries, power has been in the hands of the Arabians since their successful jihad of 639-708 AD. Until North Africa had been conquered, it was basically Negroe, like the remainder of the African continent. Monuments that date back the furthest in this region were erected when North Africa came under native African rule (Walker,2006).

'Pharaoh Djoser, the second king of the Third Egyptian Dynasty, ruled between 5018 and 4989B.C.' (Walker, 2006:20). He constructed the first monument in world history still revered today. Annually, thousands of holidaymakers seek out his Funerary Complex in the Saqqara city location. Imhotep, his widely regarded Prime Minister, engineered the Complex. A perimeter wall, now primarily in ruins, encircles the whole structure. It was built to a rectangular plan specification running to a length of one mile and with one entrance. A series of columns greets the eye on entrance, the earliest stone-built columns acknowledged by historians. Adjoined to walls, they are aesthetically pleasing having been fashioned on plant stems in close proximity to each other. The North House also has aesthetically pleasing columns integrated into the walls that bear papyrus-like capitals. Furthermore, the Ceremonial Court is found within the complex. Characteristic of everything else, these structures are solid and are therefore distinctive. The Court comprises of limestone blocks taken from a quarry and then shaped. Occupying centre stage in the complex is the Step Pyramid, the earliest of 90 Egyptian pyramids (Walker,2006). Comprising of limestone blocks, it stands 197 feet high (Walker,2006). Differing from subsequent pyramids, this structure is built on a rectangular design specification measuring 345 by 414 feet – approximating a ground coverage of 14,000 square yards. It comprises 6 steps and may symbolize a stairway. The building incorporates a sloping angle of 72x30' (Walker,2006:21). Beneath the pyramid lay a range of rock-hewn rooms and corridors. They are decorated with panels of brightly coloured tiles. In these subterranean quarters, Djoser and eleven individuals are stated to have been buried (Walker,2006). Concerning just what the Djoser complex means, Dr Charles Finch, a prominent African American scholar, intimated that: "[It] was humanity's first great architectural triumph. It established architectural forms, styles, and canons still in use today. The practical building technique and masonry evident in the entrance temple were never surpassed, though ... they were realized on a grander scale" (Walker,2006:21).

Examples of building work on such a scale include the monuments completed by the Fourth Dynasty Pharaoh – 'the Step Pyramid of Meidum, the Bent and Red Pyramids of Dashur, and the three Great Pyramids of Giza' – monuments completed between 4872 and 4615 B.C. (Walker,2006:

21). Among these, the initial Great Pyramid of Giza stands out the most. Its recorded height is 481 feet, approximating to the height of a 40-storey building. It comprises 2.3 million rocks of limestone and granite, certain of them weighing 100 tons (Walker,2006). The precision of the building work is staggering. Dr Alfred Russell Wallace, a renowned British scientist, spoke about this over a century ago in the course of addressing the British Association for the Advancement of Science:

- That the pyramid is truly square, the sides being equal, and the angles right angles;

- That the four sockets on which the first four stones of the corners rested are truly on the same level;

- That the directions of the sides are accurate to the four cardinal points [of north, south, east and west];

- That the vertical height of the pyramid bears the same proportion to its circumference at the base as the radius of a circle does to its circumference [i.e., the Egyptians understood "pi"] (Walker,2006: 21)

Located in a more southerly direction is the network of temples in the Waset city province. The Luxor and Karnak temples, presently in partial decay, had taken many years to complete with contributions from a number of pharaohs of the Twelfth, Eighteenth, Nineteenth and Twenty-fifth Dynasties (3405-664 B.C.) (Walker,2006). The Karnak temple was a mecca of business and culture. According to Walker, it should be seen as an abbey, for people not only lived but worked there and the premises were self-contained. The riches of the ancient world flowed through its passageways; gold and valuable woods from Kush, payment from Syria, and vessels from Crete. A succession of sphinxes lined the approach 'to the outer pylon, itself 370 feet across, 143 feet high, and 49 feet thick at the base', but tapering at the top (Walker,2006: 21). Beyond the pylon lay the temple of Amen, which initially had colossal doors to prevent access to outsiders. A place of incredible opulence, the Hypostyle Hall, representing one of any number of temples, 'was 171 feet long and 338 feet wide, covering an area of 56,000 square feet' (Walker,2006:22). There was none other to rival its scale of enclosed space in Egyptian building practice, beating Durham Cathedral into second place by 5,000 square feet. It accommodates 134 sandstone columns, bedecked with bas-reliefs and hieroglyphics. An architect forms a mental picture of the hall as follows:

No language [says Fergusson] can convey an idea of its beauty, and no artist has yet been able to reproduce its form so as to convey to those who have not seen it any idea of its grandeur. The mass of its central piers, illuminated by a flood of light from the clerestory, and the smaller pillars of the wings gradually fading into obscurity, are so arranged and lighted as to convey an idea of infinite space; at the same time the beauty and massiveness of the forms, and the brilliancy of their coloured decorations, all combine to stamp this as the greatest of man's architectural works...(Walker,2006;22)

Some of the huge obelisks the Egyptians built were placed in front of the Luxor and Karnak temples (Walker,2006) They consisted of a single block that was excavated from a quarry and then transferred to the required site. Pharaoh Hatshepsut commissioned one such obelisk to be built. It rose to a height of 90.2 feet and weighed a staggering 302 tons. An enormous and incomplete obelisk that is 41.78 metres in length was abandoned at Aswan, supposedly because it failed to measure up to existing levels of accuracy (Walker,2006). The high esteem in which these monuments are held has led one authority to argue the typological and symbolic connection between the obelisks of olden times and skyscrapers of the present day. As Elleh states: "Several texts exist of Pharaohs boasting that they erected obelisks which reached, pierced, or mingled with the sky" (Walker,2006:22).

Pharaoh Hatshepsut (1650-1600 BC) of the Eighteenth Dynasty is credited with having built one of Egypt's most celebrated monuments (Walker,2006). Senenmut, the Overseer of Works, carried out the necessary graft on her temple in the location presently called Deir-el-Bahri. Instead of being built upwards from a foundation, the Mortuary Temple was constructed downwards, being hollowed out of a mountain. The entire building was cut from the rocks using a hammer and chisel. The finished product is a pillared terrace construction that rises to three levels with 2 central ramps, also hand worked and handcrafted. The ramps cover much ground and climb gently to a higher standpoint. Their chosen design feature shows a two-part symmetrical divide in the temple. Hallway passages of limestone columns are followed by the interior chapels devoted to the deities Osiris, Hathor, Anubis and Ra. Along the colonnade, the interior displays wall reliefs that portray Hatshepsut's seafaring travels to Punt (i.e., Somalia), showing, in addition, the roundhouses associated with that country. 'There were over 100 limestone sphinxes, 22 granite sphinxes, 40 limestone statues of Hatshepsut, and 28 granite statues of Hatshepsut' (Walker,2006:23).

Rameses II of the Nineteenth Dynasty also constructed a temple fashioned out of a hill. The temple of Abu Simbel, in Nubia, is of astonishing proportion. The front of the building is 108 feet wide and comprises four enormous statues of the pharaoh, individually 66 feet high. Worth noting here is the organisational accomplishment involved. The scale of Rameses' images is such that each builder/sculptor would be close enough to their work for none of them to be able to see the overarching picture as they laboured. That being so, accuracy was vital and not only for artistic purposes. The structure was directed towards the east to capture the initial rays of sunlight that light up its idols at the extreme of a 208 feet passage. Visible on entry to the temple are representations of the deity Osiris. This was followed by a smaller hall that was, in turn, followed by an inner chamber (Walker,2006).

Further south, the Kushites (of southern Egypt, and northern and central Sudan) had an extremely long and ancient history (Walker,2006:23). In their initial stages, they pioneered a pharaonic culture, resembling that of ancient Egypt but having a genesis preceding that of the Egyptians. Five thousand objects of historical and cultural value were reclaimed from a succession of early pharaonic burial sites in Qustul

(Walker,2006). Other periods of greatness were accomplished in cities like Naqa, Gebel Barkal, Meroe and Kerma.

The Sudanese city of Naqa comprises three important temples, the Temple of Amen, the Lion Temple, and the Kiosk. They were built between 1 AD and 20 AD. Pharaoh Natakamani and Queen Amanitore erected the Temple of Amen and the Lion Temple. The Temple of Amen consists of a columned hall followed by an inner sanctuary similar to other Egyptian Temples. And also, 12 sculpted rams graced the approach to the entrance. The Lion Temple was given over to Apedemak, a local deity. The monumental gateway is a true likeness to Egyptian form with the King and Queen portrayed as conquerors putting paid to the heads of their adversaries. The portrayal of the Queen acting likewise may represent a dominant social role for the Queen Mother or may just as well represent matriarchy. Behind the monumental gateway is a single room structure, a design original to Kush. Lastly, the Kiosk is an unusual building that seems to have subsumed many cultural forms. The structure incorporates arches, possibly representing Roman involvement, and the uppermost part of the columns show vestiges of Greek involvement. Certain writers depict them as "pseudo-Corinthian". It is worth taking note, however, that no evidence supports the notion that the Romans (or Greeks) erected this temple. Numerous writers have suggested this possibility, but where there is a lack of solid evidence, we must come to the finding that this is a Kushite monument erected by Kushites (Walker, 2006:25).

There is a minimum of 223 pyramids in Kush within the cities of Nuri, Al Kurru, Gebel Barkal and Meroe. They are mostly 20 to 30 metres high with perpendicular sides, sloping at around 70 degrees. The blocks used to build these were smaller than their Giza equivalents. Customarily, pyramids are royal burial sites and were accessed via underground stairways from the eastern side (Walker,2006:24). The city of Meroe assumed central prominence in the Kushite Empire from approximately 590 BC until about 350 AD, a period supported by monuments. This city by itself contains, for example, 84 pyramids or so, many incorporating their exclusive miniature temple. Also, there are remains of a bath house bearing similarities with those of Roman renown. Two noted Africanists, Professors Roland Oliver and Brian Fagan, proffer their backing that:

Even today, the ruins of Mero[e] make an impressive sight. Six low hills of iron slag mark the southern and western perimeters of the town, bearing witness to what must surely have been the main industry of its inhabitants [i.e., iron smelting]. To the east, the main housing areas are the ruins of a whole series of temples and cemeteries, while the burial pyramids of the royal family crown the summit of a low ridge overlooking the site. Only a small part of the town has so far been cleared and excavated - the royal cemeteries, some scattered temples and the so-called Royal City, which extends along the banks of the Nile near the main landing stage. Here, the Temple of Amun [sic] was found to be 450 feet long, built of brick and sandstone blocks, and forming a series of courts and halls enclosing a central shrine (Walker,2006:24).

Musawarat in Sudan contains the largest complex, covering extensive grounds. The curious structure is known as the Great Enclosure. Built around 220 BC, it contains a succession of walled enclosures and building constructions that encircle a central temple, itself erected on an elevated platform. A colonnade surrounds the central temple. Outside is a succession of ramps and passages connecting the different sections of the building and also linking two further temples. The construction work is decorated with elephant motifs (Walker,2006:24; Walker,2008:16). Dr Davidson, an English Africanist floated the idea that the building served as a centre to train, and therefore tame, African elephants. Other learned individuals, just as convincingly, perceive it as a religious place for housing pilgrims.

Africa before the Slave Trade

On 11 May 1790, the testimony of Charles Berns Wadstrom (otherwise known as Carl Bernhardt Wadstrom) was published in a report headed 'Minutes of the evidence taken before the Select Committee on the Slave Trade' (Walker,2007:36). On the subject of how slaves were procured and in large numbers, the Select Committee questioned a number of seasoned witnesses who had had practical experience of enslaving Africans. Mr Wadstrom was sufficiently knowledgeable of the West African regions today known as Senegal, Gambia and Goree Island. Of Swedish origin, Wadstrom's initial interest was in plans to settle and administrate in West Africa using agricultural enterprise rather than to trade in human beings. An expedition had sailed to West Africa under his leadership with this venture at issue in 1787, hence his authority on this region in Africa. Details of his testimony, forwarded on 29 April 1790, were as follows:

The Select Committee was eager to learn about the manner of culture in that corner of Africa. They enquired of Wadstrom: "Have they any manufactures amongst them?" Wadstrom's reply was immeasurably informative:

I have been surprised to see with what industry they manufacture their cottons, their indigo, and other dying articles, as well as several sorts of manufacture in wood; they make soap; they tan leather, and work it exceedingly well, and even with good taste... they work bar iron... into several articles, as, for instance, lances, instruments for tillage, poniards, etc; they work in gold very ingeniously, and so well, that I never have seen better made articles of that kind in Europe; a great number of articles for ornaments of gold, silver, brass, leather, etc. Wadstrom added that: Their cloth and their leather they manufacture with uncommon neatness; and I have samples with me to shew [sic] in case it should be desired (Walker,2007:36).

Wadstrom's testimony disclosed further pieces of evidence. The Monarch of that region went by the name of Dalmanny. An erudite man, he had attained Grand Marabout status before his election to Kingship. The people over whom he reigned were very honourable and friendly and showed Wadstrom "all civility and kindness" (Walker,2007:38). Curiously, they also owned a "materia medica" of about 2,000 or nearer 3,000 plants. King Dalmanny "had entirely prohibited the slave trade throughout his whole Kingdom" (Walker,2007:38). He also placed alcohol sales under a blanket ban. While the Senegal Company, a French cohort, initially attempted to corrupt the King to revise his thinking on the traffic in people, he declined their presents. Therefore, the Senegal Company offered financial inducements to the lighter-skinned Moors to invade and snatch Dalmanny's subjects and issued the Moors with the requisite military hardware to execute the raids. The effect of the aggression, as Wadstrom believed, was "the chief hindrance to the improvement of the cultivation; in so far as the Negroes never venture to go out into the fields unless very well armed" (Walker,2007:38).

Therefore, the Select Committee enquired: "Do you mean to say that if the slave trade was abolished, they would extend their cultivation and manufactures?" (Walker,2007:38). Wadstrom responded: "Yes; particularly if some good European people had enterprising spirit enough to settle among them in another way than is the case at present" (Walker,2007:38).

Charles Wadstrom's eyewitness account is extremely important. What proportion of people appreciates that Africans once manufactured soap? What proportion of people recognizes that Africans had arrived at a manufacturing standard in gold articles that far outstripped anything the goldsmith's craft had to offer in Europe? (Walker,2007:38).

This passed as evidence that the idea of Africa being primitive and backward was NOT credible in the eyes of the British Government. They knew otherwise. It is worth noting and ironic for they were the prime movers behind the processes that led to the mass enslavement of Africans! (Walker,2008:7). The British Government allowed inflexible ideas about Africans to flourish and influential British people like John Stuart Mill, in his treatise "On Liberty", described Africans as being in their "nonage". Charles Darwin, in his book, "On the Origin of Species", depicted the African by use of the word "savage" and David Hume and many others propagated and disseminated woefully disreputable and unfounded ideas to a nation and the world. All of this has an effect that militates against Black aspiration – making Black people think and feel that they do not have what it takes to succeed – seeds of doubt are sown, even though there are those who have overcome disadvantage and discouragement. And the Select

Committee were privy to exquisite examples of African manufacture that almost certainly are STILL under the control of the British Government or its inextricably interwoven institutions (Walker,2008:7).

Reparations and the British Government

Historically, the British government doled out 20 million pounds in pecuniary resources to slave owners and, to this day, successive governments have followed the trend to not even extend so much as an apology for slavery and the slave trade to the Black diaspora (a play staged at the Black Country Living Museum entitled "No dogs, No Irish, No Blacks", October 27, 2016). Then-Prime Minister Tony Blair expressed "deep sorrow" for the British government's involvement in the trade, but gave no formal apology. "It is hard to believe that what would now be a crime against humanity was legal at the time" he exclaimed (Lammy, 2012:152). As recently as 2007, the British government has been uncommitted to calls for reparations to the descendants of slaves. To more recent calls for an apology and reparations, the British position was as follows:

This is a longstanding concern of theirs and there is a longstanding UK position, true of successive governments in the UK, that we don't think reparations are the right approach.

The PM'S point will be he wants to focus on the future. We are talking about issues that are centuries old and taken under a different government when he was not even born. He wants to look at the future and how the UK can play a part now in stronger growing economies in the Caribbean (Campbell and Pears,2015:2; in The Voice newspaper).

This is how the British government parries, dismisses and repudiates calls for reparations. Most importantly, here we see how the British government doubles down on a double standard. Why when it comes to a moral obligation, are the British government so dispassionate? It is hardly a surprise because what would make Black people might break the dominant group. The British government maintain that it is in the past and we should let bygones be bygones. Yet, pecuniary resources – from slavery and the slave trade and the subsequent government pay-out to slave owners – has been passed down through the generations and manifests as the benefits of the past being utilized and enjoyed in the present. Moreover, let's not forget that the world is structured in the manner that it is because of history, so one can appreciate the call for reparations – as a redistribution of wealth – and an apology for slavery as reconciliation. This is a longstanding concern because successive British Governments have allowed matters to lapse and have refused to capitulate to the call for reparations. Another British Prime Minister, David Cameron, distances himself from history or Britain's part in slavery and the trade in slaves and looks to the future; yet, the past is bound up in the present and the future and is why the world is so profoundly unequal; so, therefore, history should not be dismissed as irrelevant because it is as relevant as the contribution the past makes to shaping the present and the future. What successive British governments have dismissed out of hand is a legitimate proposal.

It suits the British government's purposes to look to the future as it tries desperately to ignore the consequences of the past and would incline towards stating that reparations are impractical and unrealistic and would also much rather take a dim view of uplifting and improving the material conditions of descendants of slavery. A true meaning of justice would serve the interests of Black aspiration rather than, at every turn, experiencing a strong and adverse reaction from the prevailing order. The British government's line on reparations and apologising for slavery and the slave trade reflects a large public backing, if truth be told; usually, charity begins at home is the rallying cry of the White British populace.

Part of the response to Jamaica's concerns came from David Cameron himself who offered a 25-million-pound prison-building programme funded by the overseas aid budget. In addition to the prison deal, Cameron caused widespread anger when he implored the Jamaican parliament to "move on" from the disheartening legacy of slavery. The controversial deal would mean Britain would advance 40 per cent of the cost to raise a new 1,500-bed prison where Jamaican nationals doing stretches in British prisons would be deported without consent. Jamaican nationals are the third largest group of foreign nationals in British jails, with seven in ten doing stretches vis-à-vis drugs or violence. Together with the proposal to repatriate something in the region of 300 Jamaicans by 2020, the Jamaican government will have to shoulder the remaining 60 per cent responsibility of the building costs (£37.5m) (Onibada,2015).

The Cabinet Office added, Cameron's visit was to "reinvigorate ties between the countries", and involved putting forward a planned £300m development fund for the Caribbean region.

"I believe this money would help to unleash trade across the region with new roads, new bridges, and new port infrastructure to help speed up freight movements," Cameron said (Onibada,2015:3; The Voice, October 8-14).

He said, the matter arising, to be financed in the Caribbean, had the potential to benefit British businesses that have the know-how and high proficiency in infrastructure improvements. The PM also committed himself to ensuring that Jamaica obtains some of the $ 9 billion promised by the UK for climate change extending across the forthcoming five years. His comments overlapped with the inception of Britain's Black History Month.

It is, in actual fact, Cameron's suggestion to Jamaica to forget about slavery, to say nothing about airbrushing out history; so, is there little wonder that reparations campaigners accused him of "historic amnesia"? (Onibada,2015). Conservative party acolytes are ideologically backwards-looking though their indelible obligations around this chapter in history remain, just as sure as the historical event itself remains. Reparations would not erase history but would create a healthier climate, allowing and permitting people to move on from the painful legacy of the transatlantic slave trade. After all, slave owners were allowed to move on from their loss of human property but they seemed to do it at the expense of the slaves, who were the real victims, being left to beg on the streets. British bias towards their own kind and British bias against slaves and their descendants accounts for the lack of balance here. The need to be compensated was greater in the case of the slaves as opposed to the slave owners, and in the modern era, Black people, as a result of slavery and the European plunder of African resources, are situated within the lowest social strata in contemporary British society, and Jamaica, unlike Britain, is not a first but a 'Third World' country (Cashmore and Troyna,1990). Thus, in both the past and the present, the need for compensation or *quid pro quo* is more legitimate and more important.

British plans to construct a multi-million-pound jailhouse in Jamaica is a distraction or manoeuvre to put the reparations debate into the shade as far as a Voice poll can tell. The online poll petitioned the paper's readers. 'How do you feel about David Cameron's plans to use £25 million of the overseas aid budget to build a prison in Jamaica?' (Onibada,2015:3). The findings demonstrated that 58 per cent of informants proffered their consent to it being a distraction. However, 24 per cent of participants welcomed the British Prime Minister's proposal. But an additional 16 per cent declared that the proposal was embarrassing and considered that Jamaica should decline the money.

Responding to the plan, Diane Abbot, the newly installed Shadow Secretary of State for International Development, berated it as persistently incorrect "in principle and in practice". (Onibada,2015:3). She argued:

"I do not believe aid money should be spent on building prisons merely as an adjunct to the British criminal justice system.

If David Cameron is really interested in seeing a decrease in the levels of criminality in Jamaica, he should be investing more in education projects, and helping to promote local agriculture and manufacturing, which would provide legal employment for young Jamaicans," Abbot maintained (Onibada,2015:3).

She portrayed the proposal as a "superficial public relations initiative that does not begin to deal with underlying issues" and suggested that Britain was laying itself open to human rights wrangling from prisoners if transferred against their volition (Onibada,2015:3).

Jamaica's former Prime Minister Bruce Golding attacked the British government for trying to 'bully' Jamaican taxpayers into picking up the bill for what he considers is Britain's responsibility (Onibada,2015:3). The Voice newspaper headlined the story on its front page describing the plan as a 'slap in the face'. In a similar vein, the Gleaner's Andre Poyser reports a journalist and political commentator's take on Cameron's attitude around the question of reparations: "What Cameron said was an insult. It was an insult to the nation of Jamaica and it was an insult to the entire Caribbean and Black people around the world", Rojas maintained (quoted in The Weekly Gleaner, October 8-14, 2015).

Drawing parallels with the Jewish case for reparations, Rojas maintained that Cameron could not address that matter with the same limited ethics that he summoned up to the Caribbean in respect of its calls for reparations.

Think about if Cameron had said to a Jewish organisation, 'Forget about the Holocaust, let's get over the Holocaust....' It is Germany paying reparations, because of their crimes perpetrated against the Jewish people, that created the financial basis for the state of Israel to be established. Germany paid reparations to Israel for 10 years uninterrupted, billions and billions of dollars, to establish today what is the most powerful and the most modern state in the Middle East, he asserted (Poyser, October 8-14, 2015).

Historically, the interests of slave owners were clearly a higher priority to the British government than to value and bestow deference to the Black diaspora at the time. What effect must this have on Black people considering that they are not valued by the contemporary British government as much as slave owners were by past governments? In order to elucidate on this, immigration legislation of successive British governments, in the past and also the present, worked against Black people and can, in a nutshell, be described as a wholly unequal state of human affairs rendering African Caribbean and South Asian people second-class citizens. Mass immigration and government policy responses to it is a topic we shall consider in a later chapter.

African culture and civilization

Witnesses appearing before the Select Committee made reference to the very many Africans who were trilingual – that is, conversant in English, French and Portuguese – not to mention being speakers of their own languages, Mandinga, Wolof, etc. This degree of mastery with language occurs again and again in African history (Walker,2008:7).

Mr Wadstrom delivered his testimony in 1790. The enslaving process of Africans was of course underway by then; indeed, the tale of this sordid episode in world history actually began in 1441. At that period in time, Antam Goncalves, a young mariner, introduced the opening slave raid campaign and such raids came of age with mass enslavement. This begs the question, was African culture and civilization, just before that period, a complete mystery? And is there any extant evidence of what was occurring there? (Walker,2007:38)

In 1441, West Africa was regulated by the Mali Empire. Its imperial sweep comprised of regions now called Mali, Mauretania, Senegambia and also Guinea. Whereas the empire was in decline and unstable, forfeiting its fourteenth-century place as the world's wealthiest state, it remained impressive. Consisting of four hundred cities and significant towns, three were especially important - Timbuktu, Djenne and Gao. Timbuktu had commodious houses built with clay bricks, wood and plaster (Walker,2007:38). It boasted three illustrious temples whose minarets marked the Timbuktu skyline. The grand Malian King, Mansa Musa, developed the Djinguerebere Mosque in the fourteenth century. It was a mysterious nine-aisle structure looking rather like a fortress. The built environment included the Sankore University Mosque where 25,000 students studied. The third major institution was the Oratory of Sidi Yahia. Timbuktu Koran schools exceeded 150 where twenty thousand pupils were instructed. The city populace numbered 115,000 – over five times the size of fourteenth-century London (population 20,000) (Walker,2007:38). Leo Africanus, the city's early historical observer (who wrote a portrait of Africa in 1526) saw "numerous judges, doctors [i.e., of letters], and clerics, all receiving good salaries from the King" (Walker,2007:38). The same focal lenses noted that "more profit is made from the book trade than any other line of business" (Walker,2007:38). Educated conjecture suggests that 700,000 manuscripts, many of them surviving from this period or predating this period, are treasured by Timbuktu families and repositories.

Djenne was an eleven-gated city surrounded by a defensive wall. Its buildings were pleasing to the eye with villas two floors high, usually with toilets and internal drainage systems. The Grand Mosque was spectacular. It was a colossal structural triumph, then more than two hundred years old. Its form resembled that of a fort with obeliskoid pillars integrated into its walls. Djenne also had its own University. In its medical department, cataract surgery on the eyes was instrumental to learning (Walker,2008:10).

Gao, too, was an impressive city though it had since disbanded from the Mali Empire. Al Idrissi, a medieval geographer (who wrote The Book of Roger, 1153) portrayed it as a "populous, unwalled, commercial and industrial town, in which were to be found the produce of all arts and trades" (Walker,2007:38-39). A major find of royal graveyard inscriptions has come to light, the earliest dated to the eleventh century AD. In recent years, a group of archaeologists from the University of Cambridge conducted ground-breaking excavations in Gao. Among their finds were important pieces that were exhibited at the British Museum in 1998. Of great interest was a discovery labelled "Fragments of alabaster window surrounds and a piece of pink glass, Gao 10th – 14th century" (Walker,2008:10).

Leaving behind the Mali Empire and approaching the West African shore was the Yoruba civilization, administration centred in the city of Ife. The civilization of Yoruba has drawn much acclaim from many scholars. One writer commented: "It is impossible to describe here all the riches of the civilization of Ife" (Diop,1974:158). An additional scribe offered even higher praise: "Modern ethnologists" a German scholar asserts, "have found the art of the Yorubas so astonishingly high in quality that they did not [at first] ascribe it to a Negroe race".

Chapter 1: Tracing Black Aspiration and Illuminating Achievement

He elaborates further:

The Yoruba empire consisted of city-states similar to those of ancient Greece...[S]ome of these states had a hundred and fifty to two hundred and fifty thousand inhabitants. Art objects of the highest quality were found in their ruins – glazed urns, tiles with pictures of animals and gods on them, bronze implements, gigantic granite figures. The Yorubas introduced the cultivation of yams, the preparation of cheese and the breeding of horses into West Africa. They had outstanding artists in metal, gold-casters, cotton-weavers, wood-carvers and potters. The professions formed themselves into guilds with their own laws, their children were brought up in educational camps, their public affairs were directed by a courtly aristocracy and an exuberantly expanding bureaucracy [It began in Babel, pp.213-14, Herbert Wendt, cited in Walker,2008:11].

Nearer the Central African interior of 1441 extended the Empire of Kanem-Borno and eastwardly lay the Sudanese territory of Alwa. Sir Richard Palmer, an Englishman, waxed learnedly and lyrically on the Kanem-Borno Empire. Once he had done the research, he intimated that: "[T]he degree of civilization achieved by its early [rulers] would appear to compare favourably with that of European monarchs of that day". He was at pains to point out the fact that this paralleled a time when "the Christian West had remained ignorant, rude, and barbarous" (cited in Walker,2006:92).

The Sudanese civilization of Alwa had a capital that was called Soba. Of this city, Ibn Selim el-Aswani, a medieval eyewitness, described, "fine buildings and large monasteries, churches rich with gold and gardens: there is also a great suburb where many Muslims live" (quoted in Walker,2008:16). Its ceremonial area was a building built on two levels out of clay brick. More recently, archaeologists enquiring into this lost city have salvaged segments of ceramic grilles for windows. What remained of window glass panes were also located nearby (Walker,2008:16).

The east coast, from the Horn of Africa to Mozambique, has remnants of more than fifty towns and cities. They grew and prospered between the ninth and the sixteenth centuries. Among these cities was Kilwa, a strategic former seaport situated on a small island set off the Tanzanian coast, and currently a UNESCO World Heritage site. During the fourteenth century, Ibn Battuta (writer of Travels in Asia and Africa) declared Kilwa as "one of the most beautiful and well-constructed cities in the world" (Walker,2007:41).

"Today", states Basil Davidson, who penned A Guide to African History, "only a shabby village stands there". The eminent British authority elaborates:

> Yet beyond the village can still be found the walls and towers of ruined palaces and large houses and mosques, which is what the moslems call their churches. A great palace [the Husuni Kubwa] has been dug out of the bushes that covered it for hundreds of years. It is a strange and beautiful ruin on a cliff over the Indian Ocean. Many other ruins stand nearby. But the strangest thing about Kilwa and other towns nearby is that there is little to be found about them in the newer history books. Even when the cities are described, they are said to be not African, but the work of people from Arabia and Persia. History books saying this are out of date, and they are wrong. (cited by Walker,2006:39).

In 1961, British archaeologists investigated this "strange and beautiful ruin" – the royal palace of Kilwa (Walker,2007:41). The building itself was magnificent with in excess of a hundred rooms, comprising an entrance hall, hallways, enclosures, terraces and a swimming pool. The interior décor was ornate and included vaulted roofs. The second level to the building had a roof inventively consisting of barrels, domes and conical forms, all composed of concrete. During the night, oil lanterns, amounting to thousands, illuminated this marvellous monument (Walker,2007:41).

Gedi, near the shores of Kenya, is also a ghost town. Its remains date back to the thirteenth or fifteenth century AD - other authorities say earlier - and include the city rampart, the palace, private dwellings, the Great Mosque, seven minor mosques, and three obeliskoid tombs. The defensive walls are nine feet tall and had a minimum of three gates. The mosque had a washing pool immediately preceding it so the believers could perform ablutions. It had a cleansing mechanism made of limestone so that water could be reused. The dwellings at Gedi tended to have a court, leading onto the principal room, and following that was the private chamber. Also, there were smaller connecting rooms, like the bathroom, the toilet, kitchen, bedroom and storeroom. The royal palace was designed along similar lines as a large arrangement of these houses but put together with an entrance hall. The palace showed evidence of piped water regulated by taps, bathrooms and additionally, 6 indoor toilets (Walker,2008:22).

The British *hoi polloi* have never been made aware of Africa's standing before the onslaught, the snatching of people, and the mass enslavement. Therefore, this has contributed to the unhealthy idea that these atrocities were far from criminal offences committed against genuine people, but instead, against faceless and uneducated savages. The British government has been in the position to dispute these anti-African machinations since 1790 at the minimum but has clearly elected not to raise a finger to repudiate them. (Walker,2007:41). In a later chapter on immigration, we shall see how the British government tends to be supine if it suits their purposes, and the British government also plays to the gallery when it comes to assisting in the promotion of Black interests. Gilroy (2002) judges the country to be racist and the evidence in favour of his claim is incontrovertible and overwhelming.

Black Scientists and Inventors

Since we have dealt with African civilizations, we now turn to focus our attention on exactly what are the productions of Black aspiration. In schools and in the media, when it comes to inventions and who invented what, the emphasis tends towards white inventors, to the extent that one assumes that White people invented and originated most everything that is important and valued in contemporary society. However, this reflects media bias and is a failure to credit and recognize the creative genius of Black individuals. We hear of Thomas Edison's light bulb, George Stephenson's Rocket and the

Wright brothers' flight across the channel, to name just a few, that are learned through the British schooling system and the British media. But unto this world, there are unsung heroes and internationally, Black inventors throughout time abound.

Imhotep hailed from Kemet, (Egypt) Africa and was born there on the 21st May 2980 BC. His mother went by the name of Khreduonkh and his father Kanofer, was a recognized architect and master builder. The name Imhotep is the equivalent of "I come in peace" (Williams and Henry,2003:5).

Imhotep

Imhotep had many strings to his bow. He was a top-flight official, a lawyer, an author, an architect, a principal lecturer, a philosopher, a mathematician, a magician as well as a physician (Williams and Henry, 2003:5). In his role as architect, taking his tutelage from King Djoser, Imhotep drew up the papers for the step pyramids of Saqqara on Cairo's boundary perimeter. These pyramids are 195 feet above ground level, each with a base of practically 374 feet wide. Many sightseers from all corners of the world visit Africa to see them. A large number of contemporary scientists from places as technologically advanced as Japan and the USA have endeavoured to erect replica pyramids. They have employed the theory and the practices they suppose the ancient Africans applied, but have thus fallen far short of reproducing the pyramids. In addition, Imhotep drew up the papers for The Great Temple located within the Saqqara structure, which was finished in 57 BC (Williams and Henry,2003:5).

In the capacity of physician, Imhotep was worshipped across Kemet to Greece as the god of medicine (Williams and Henry,2003:5; Sertima,1991:184). The ancient Greeks designated him Asclepios and powerful thinkers like Hippocrates and Galen, who existed long after Imhotep's time, studied his writings extensively. Over the course of time, Hippocrates was awarded the title Father of Medicine, so much so that when doctors graduate, they bind themselves through the Hippocratic

Oath. Any number of proponents would maintain that it is to his predecessor, Imhotep, by a long margin, that they swear, for he is the first Father of Medicine. It was Imhotep who coined the phrase "… eat, drink and be merry for tomorrow we may die" (Williams and Henry,2003:5).

George Washington Carver

George Washington Carver came into this world in 1860 in Missouri, U.S.A. Both he and his immediate relatives were slaves on the Moses Carver estate. Throughout slavery, slaves were divested of their African names and customs; instead, they had little alternative but to adopt the European appellation of their owners. During George's early childhood years, he and his maternal parent were kidnapped from the Carver estate by night riders. Night riders were individuals who kidnapped slaves and the slaves changed ownership for monetary gain. Moses Carver regained possession of George in exchange for a racehorse (Williams and Henry,2003:15).

George was spared the hard graft in the fields because he was a sickly child. He found working in the garden satisfying and became enormously interested in plants and the reason they grow. He also found drawing and painting flowers intrinsically satisfying. George did not receive money for services rendered as he was a slave and so did not have the means to purchase paints. He rose above this obstacle by finding out how to formulate paints from flowers. He had the good fortune, however, of receiving some schooling. On finishing high school, he processed papers to be educated at Highland University but was turned down on the grounds of skin colour. He was allowed through the doors of Iowa State University where he showed proficiency in art and science. George graduated from the University having gained two degrees. His destination, on leaving University, was as a university lecturer and research scientist (Williams and Henry,2003:15).

His excellent work attracted many job offers, among them one from Thomas Edison, the American who gave us the light bulb. He opted for a post from the prominent Black educationalist Booker T Washington, at the Tuskegee Institute, a well-known Black college.

George Washington Carver supplanted King Cotton's reign in the American South with the peanut. His experiment bore success, in some appreciable measure due to the boll weevil, King Cotton's great adversary (Rogers,1996:464). Carver illustrated the many unimagined uses the peanut could be put to. He formulated over 250 products from it, among them milk, peanut sauce, bisque for ice cream, flour, ink, face cream, breakfast foods, oleomargarine, wood stains, and a separation active in infantile paralysis. He derived over sixty articles from the pecan nut and derived seventy sweet potato products, among which were shoe blacking, flour and rubber. Carver transformed native wild berries into tasty sweetmeats and from the contrasting clay formations he produced dyes. He found a way around the paint problems of the rural South by combining these products from clays with unwanted motor oil. In 1917, when war with Germany put an end to supplies of aniline dyes, he produced dyes of any number of colours from adjacent clays, which, when applied to leather, linen, silk, cotton and wool, lost none of their colouring to washing or sunlight. In a word, he illustrated, as none other before him had done, that practically everything concerning man could be brought into his service. The fruit of his endeavour was displayed across the Deep South and to the Ways and Means Committee of the House of Representatives, causing people to re-evaluate their own preconceptions of the Black man amid popular amazement. Representative John N. Garner of Texas, later Vice President, referred to it as "a most wonderful exhibition" (Rogers,1996:465).

This man, who came from the lowest echelon of society and was invariably subject to the contempt and diatribe of the commonest Southern White, had international recognition and admiration showered on him (Rogers,1996:468) Scientists from all sides and corners of the planet visited his workplace and great industry leaders, such as Henry Ford of the Ford Motor Company, not infrequently asked him to indicate ways to manufacture better cars. He was the recipient of many prizes in his lifetime; nevertheless, his aim remained the same. He is quoted as saying, "...My life goal is to make useful products from simple things" (Williams and

Henry,2003:15). On departing this life, he endowed every penny he had saved to the advancement of scientific research.

Jan Ernest Matzeliger

Despite the disadvantage which assails oppressed people everywhere, there are always Black individuals in the United States who would rather not settle for the accepted job conventions for their colour but would rather strive to make a contributory achievement, regardless of all that assails them. Such individuals have a place or station in virtually every field, even among the very problematic one of scientific invention (Rogers,1996:350).

In certainly one sector of industry, American supremacy can be traced directly to a Black man, Jan Ernest Matzeliger. A trailblazer in the enterprise of shoemaking, he boosted the American economy, and others, to the tune of billions of dollars, made a dozen or so millionaires, engineered hundreds of thousands of jobs, and contributed significantly to what is considered one of the defining characteristics of civilization, viz; the wearing of shoes. Massachusetts, heart of the world's footwear industry, has been a distinct beneficiary of his ingenuity (Rogers,1996:350). Matzeliger hailed from Dutch Guiana, South America and was born there to a Dutch father and a Black mother. Mechanically minded as a child, in his first decade of life he was introduced to the government workshops of the colony as an apprentice. Having an eager urge to find out more, he set off for New York City once his apprenticeship finished. Disadvantaged by his colour and his shortage of pecuniary resources, he still managed to learn a great deal about machinery.

Five years into his second decade of life, he ventured to Lynn, Massachusetts, and owing to the more liberal social setting there, he secured employment on the factory floor of M.H. Harvey, where he used a McKay machine for turning footwear. In this environment, his attention was of course directed towards shoe-making machinery. Recognizing how time-consuming a procedure lasting of shoes by hand was, he determined to invent a contraption to do it, the like of which had been the esteemed dream of many an able youth eager to become prosperous. Inventors had spent time, effort and energy in this pursuit and promoters had expended hundreds of thousands of dollars in striving to transform the lasting of shoes from time-consuming to time-saving methods, as Blake and McKay had transformed the stitching of the uppers (Rogers,1996:351).

When Matzeliger made his intentions known, his White fellow workers laughed him to scorn. The suggestion that a Black man should succeed where a number of the best White minds had failed seemed absurd. They insisted, moreover, that whatever was to come in mechanized form, nothing could ever replace hand-lasting. The lasters were convinced that their position was unassailable. These expert craftsmen were the crème de la crème of the footwear industry, earning from $20 to $40 a week, a handsome wage in those days (Rogers,1996:51).

Finding a room above the historic West Lynn Mission on the corner of Ann and Charles Streets, where he was hidden from view and also the prospect of too curious eyes, Matzeliger burned the midnight oil studying, experimenting and drawing (Rogers,1996:351).

Constrained by what he could afford from his meagre wages, he opted to utilize any material he could lay his hands on. Primarily, he used sections of wood and unwanted cigar and packing boxes. After six months of doing his utmost and pushing the boundaries of physical limitations, he produced a model which, however crude, gave him the incentive that he was working towards winning ways.

Even though he tried to keep his work secret, the hand-lasters found out about his efforts and sometimes put in an appearance to laugh at the peculiar-looking system of sticks in the guise of a machine. One of their number, in racial contempt, decided to call it "the niggerhead machine", the appellation by which it was widely known later (Rogers,1996:351).

For the same purposes, Matzeliger's friends tried to persuade him to accede to what seemed in their eyes like an unwise pursuit and argued that the days at work were hard and long and therefore should be followed by rest and recreation. One particular individual, however, could see something he valued in the combination of sticks and suggested he take it off Matzeliger's hands for 50 dollars. But Matzeliger considered that if someone was prepared to part with $50 at the first offer, it was likely to fetch an even higher figure elsewhere, so he declined his offer.

He now decided to move to the next stage and make a metal replica. Bringing together an assortment of iron pieces, he worked indefatigably, filing and installing the parts unassisted. Four years on saw the finished article that would work. This time, $1500 was offered for his invention enabling the attachment of leather around the toe, which figure he again declined. Significantly encouraged by the popular interest his model attracted, he began building a more improved version; he aimed for perfection. For a further six years, he laboured on his invention to the point where he had devised a more refined machine (Rogers,1996:352).

An especially good feature of the invention was that its pincers for pulling the upper closed were sufficiently effective and did not damage even the most paper-thin leather.

Nowadays, experts all agree that no better technique for handling loose tacks for securing the upper to the sole bears any precedent. The particular fashion and action of the pincers replicated exactly the unusual and practically unique mastery with which skilled hand-lasters treat awkward upper leather in their construction of shoes. The shoe-making industry has seen no other invention capable of giving form to a shoe on all types of lasts, and it is almost impossible to make shoes to satisfy commercial standards without accessing Matzeliger's machine (Rogers,1996:352). His twelve-year journey in pursuit of a single dream had been manifestly successful.

In the hands of the United Shoe Manufacturing Company, this new invention soon saw the competition fall by the wayside until, some years later, it monopolized 98 per cent of the footwear machinery business.

Thereafter, the shoe industry expanded many times over. Shoe stocks returned very high yields for investors. Earnings improved by more than 350 per cent, though wages improved by only 34 per cent and the charge levied on footwear fell (Rogers,1996:353; Suzar,1999:40).

The invention was established in factories but there were obstinate and protracted strikes by the hand-lasters in opposition to it. One experienced laster said, "The machine revenges Matzeliger by singing as it works: I've got your job! I've got your job!" (Rogers,1996:353).

F.A. Gannon notes:

Sales of shoes abroad increased by approximately $16,000,000 annually. United Shoe Machinery Company machinery and shoe experts were sent around the world and American shoe-manufacturing methods were adopted farthest north in Norway, in tropical Central America, in England and all the countries of Europe, in Africa, Australia and even in China, Japan and the Philippines (quoted in Rogers,1996:353).

The United Shoe Manufacturing Company built an exemplar manufacturing complex in Beverly, Massachusetts. It was composed of reinforced concrete and engaged 5000 individuals at a substantial average wage. Adjacent recreational buildings, among which were a country club, a motorboat club and a gun club, were erected, and a band and a sports team was assembled – all for the employees to use and access. The general well-being of shoe workers subject to the working arrangements improved considerably, and tuberculosis, their most destructive plague, was hugely curtailed.

A single stockholder, Colonel McKay, endowed $5,000.000 to the engineering department of Harvard University.

And how did Matzeliger fare? The astonishing young genius was destined not to enjoy his achievement. Close confinement and excessive work had militated against his health. He was struck down by tuberculosis and passed away two years on, in September 1889, several years shy of his fortieth birthday (Rogers,1996:353).

In his will, Matzeliger named as beneficiary of a number of shares of his stock, the North Congregational Church, a White congregation that had shown him favour. In subsequent years, this church, falling upon hard financial times, invoked the bequest and let the stock go for $10,860. A plaque in this church immortalizes the inventor.

The Consolidated Hand Lasting Machine Company, in its newsletter, said of him:

The conviction is forced upon us that this man of iron will, this man of nerve, who could not be turned from his course, knew whereof he spoke and built better than he knew, very much better than his most sanguine friends hoped for. Such men do away with old methods and institute new and better ones. Such men make missionaries and martyrs. Without such men, we should be without material progress. (cited in Rogers,1996:354).

What Edison is to artificial illumination, Matzeliger is the equivalent to footwear. This great Negro genius will be remembered for almost every shoe produced and worn by contemporary human beings.

Elijah McCoy

Elijah McCoy gave us the lubricating cup that supplied oil to machinery while it maintained operation mode. The industry that could apply this invention was the locomotive industry. McCoy was Canadian by birth, of runaway slave parents, and arrived in the United States following the Civil War. His fundamental discovery, a "Drip Cup", ended untold complaints of waste and expense by making it needless to stop and restart engines so as to lubricate them. McCoy launched the Elijah McCoy Manufacturing Co. in Detroit, Mich., with the aim of developing and placing on the market his innovations, working with such industry that from 1873 to 1899, he obtained 25 patents for distinctive types of lubricators. The certainty awakened by the repute of his lubricating products was such that the idiom "the real McCoy" was coined in relation to machinery that bore the McCoy product, and this idiom became common currency in our language (Sertima,1991:220).

Garrett Morgan

Garrett Morgan, inventor of the first traffic light system, was born in Paris, Tenn., in 1875 and relocated to Cleveland, Ohio, in 1895 where he invented a belt fastener for sewing machines in 1901 (Sertima,1991:222; Bubeula-Dodd,2004:52). He also invented the gas mask which won first-class acclaim at the Second International Exposition of Sanitation and Safety (1914), and two years after, wearing his gas mask, he dramatically rescued twenty workmen trapped in a tunnel under Lake Erie, and a gold medal for heroism was bestowed on him by the City of Cleveland. He patented his traffic light in 1923 and later sold the patent rights to the General Electric Company for $40,000 (Sertima,1991:222).

Granville T. Woods

Granville T. Woods, also known as the "Black Edison", received over 35 patents on electro-mechanical products which he sold to Westinghouse Air Brake, General Electric and American Bell Telephone (Sertima,1991:220). His life spanned the years 1865 and 1910. Over twelve inventions by Woods upgraded the electric railway systems. As well as his electric railway works, Woods attached other electrical inventions to his name. They incorporated improvements in telegraphy, electric motor regulators, telephone mechanisms and automatic cut-offs for electric circuits (Sertima,1991:220-222). His single most important electrical invention came to be his induction telegraphy. This device was designed to send and receive telegraphic messages from a moving train. His work drew universal awareness from technical and scientific journals not only in America but also worldwide.

Two other inventors that I would like to share with the reader that should not escape our compass are Lewis Temple and Norbert Rillieux.

Rillieux's invention changed how sugar was processed. In 1846, he obtained a patent for a "multiple-effect vacuum evaporator" that transformed sugar cane juice into a granular consistency of white sugar crystals (Sertima,1991:222). Rillieux's modus operandi was better at achieving the desired effect and economy than all other methods and fundamentally, his modus operandi is seen in industry-wide use today.

Norbert Rillieux inherited the status of a slave in 1806 in New Orleans. He was educated in Paris, France where he practised teaching and published a number of articles concerning the steam engine and steam economy. On returning to Louisiana, he amassed a reputation as the most well-known engineer in the State on account of his invention. Rillieux's way of working was used all over Louisiana, subsequently embraced in Cuba and Mexico, and, in due course, was embraced in Europe when it was brought on board for the sugar beet industry (Sertima,1991:222).

Lewis Temple

Lewis Temple lived in New Bedford, Massachusetts between 1830 – 1854 and worked as a blacksmith. As a job of work, he crafted 'whaling harpoons for the 19th-Century New England whaling industry and he invented a harpoon that revolutionized whaling' in America (Sertima,1991:224). Prior to Temple's invention, the spiked head of the harpoon proved inadequate for the thrash and roll strength of a whale. Not infrequently, whales broke free from the sharp end of the harpoon. Temple crafted a flexible harpoon head - one that gripped at right angles to the parallel pole and "locked" into the whale's tissue. Temple's toggle harpoon came to be the universal harpoon and it continues to be used today in certain regions of the Caribbean.

In 1926, Clifford Ashley, an expert on whaling, stated – "It is safe to say that the 'Temple Toggle' was the most important single invention in the whole history of whaling. It resulted in the capture of a far greater proportion of whales that were struck than had before been possible" (Sertima,1991:224).

When taken together, the part played by Black Americans concerning science and inventions is such that it is not feasible to live a complete day in any region of the United States, or across the world, without partaking in the legacy of their contribution. Even so, the resourcefulness of the African American imagination, which exerts a major influence on life in the United States, is principally unknown to the large majority of Americans, and it would appear that this story is replicated in the UK. The life of Lewis Howard Latimer (1848 -1928), lending to a long line of Black pioneer inventors, is a model example of the point I look towards highlighting (Sertima,1991:229).

Lewis Latimer was born on 4th September 1848 in Chelsea, U.S.A. He was the fourth descendant of Rebecca and George Latimer. Virginia was home to his father who was a slave but managed to escape and made it as far as Boston where abolitionists Frederick Douglass and William Lloyd Garrison came up with the money in exchange for George Latimer and his family's freedom (Williams and Henry,2003:1).

When only 16 years old, he signed up for the naval army where he participated in armed combat during the American civil war. Once the war had ended, he returned to Boston and accepted employment with the Crosby and Gould company as a draughtsman.

To fast-track his knowledge, Lewis purchased second-hand tools and read all the books on draughtsmanship that came into his possession. He became adept at the art and grew to be an excellent draughtsman.

Latimer and Alexander Graham Bell, the inventor, became friends. Bell was piecing together a device for the hearing-impaired, now referred to as the telephone. Bell required someone to draw pictures of the way in which his device worked so that it could be patented. He was cognizant that Latimer had an ability for technical drawings, so Bell petitioned Latimer to draw up the papers. This was far from easy since every single component required a drawing and Latimer had to describe the way in which each electrical and mechanical device ran. In 1876, thanks to Latimer's detailed diagrams, Bell received a patent for the telephone (Williams and Henry,2003:1).

Latimer also worked in close association with another inventor, Thomas Edison. Edison developed an electric light bulb in 1874, however, it was scarcely viable as it did not maintain luminescence for long. In 1881, Lewis Latimer developed an electric incandescent light bulb with a carbon filament. This was an enhancement on Edison's light bulb. He also invented an inexpensive process for mass-producing the carbon filaments. Latimer fashioned a wooden socket into which the light bulb would fit, which was the precursor to the plastic and metal formulated ones used today. His new ideas and lighting caused quite a stir for his day and a number of his inventions are now exhibited at the Smithsonian Institute in Washington, D.C. (Sertima,1991:234).

In the 1870s, Hiram Maxim of Weston Electric Light Company invited Latimer to London, England, to facilitate the setting up of the early electrical industry in the UK. Latimer lived in Lewisham, London along with his wife Mary, from 1870 until 1882 (Williams and Henry,2003:1).

Latimer returned to the USA in 1883 having received an invitation from Thomas Edison to join his distinguished group of pioneers. Out of his high estimation for Thomas A. Edison and his tutelage and ability in the electrical arena, Latimer wrote a 140-page textbook on the incandescent lighting system, a first of its ilk in 1890 (Sertima,1991:234; Williams and Henry,2003:1).

Throughout his life, Latimer always recalled the struggles of people of colour. He was always mindful of the help the abolitionists bestowed on his father. He continued to cultivate his friendship with Frederick Douglass and fully backed the cause of freedom and justice for his people. Facts about Lewis Latimer that also escape attention are that he was also a poet, artist, musician, writer and civil rights spokesman (Williams and Henry,2003:1).

I would like to convey to you certain particulars of the lives and endeavours of two more contemporary, 20th-Century inventors – Meredith Gourdine (1929-1998) and Frederick McKinley Jones (1893-1961).

Physicist and energy system engineer Meredith Gourdine has led in the evolution of electrogasdynamic systems and the 'practical application of the energy conversion process' (Sertima,1991:226). In 1966, the U.S. Department of the Interior, Office of Coal Research, granted Gourdine over $600,000 to fine-tune a model generator that used a poor-quality coal to instantly generate 80,000 volts of electricity. The generator neither used steam nor did it have any moving parts.

Gourdine came to be in Livingston, N.J. in 1929 and collected his Doctorate Degree in Engineering Science from the California Institute of Technology. In 1952, while settled as a physics student at Cornell University, Gourdine left to attend the Helsinki Olympic Games and received a silver medal in the long jump.

After obtaining the Doctorate at Caltech in 1960, Gourdine joined the Aeronautical Division of Curtiss-Wright Corp. and it was in this place that he rediscovered an 18th-Century energy conversion process and, from it, developed his imaginative innovations in the area of electrogasdynamics. Unsuccessful at trying to sell his invention to his employer, he amassed $200,000 and established his own research and development company, Gourdine Systems, Inc.

He has invented certain products and processes that rest on the application of electrogasdynamics technology – a process to do with 'the interaction of charged particles with a moving gas stream' (Sertima,1991:227). By means of this interaction, extremely high voltage can be generated from the low voltage initially produced. The fact has been recognized by scientists since the late 1700s. The problem was that no one individual could fathom out how to apply the technology to generate sufficient electricity to make it viable – especially for modern requirements.

Gourdine Systems has shifted from research and development in electrogasdynamics to four important application areas: paint-spraying systems, air pollution control, energy conversion and printing (Sertima,1991:227).

The Gourdine non-stop high voltage energy generation exploiting 'pulverized coal and air in a combustion chamber' situated at the opening of a coal mine could denote a new source of low-priced electrical power (Sertima,1991:227).

Environmental pollution control in built-up areas using the general rules of the Gourdine non-stop energy conversion method has been invented. Basically, spots of dust are ionized and conveyed by an advancing air stream to a storage point. The company, at the present moment, has developed procedures for control of industrial, residential, diesel and automotive exhaust emitting into the environment (Sertima,1991:227).

In printing, Gourdine's electrogasdynamics principles have been applied to deal with difficulties regarding non- contact printing methods.

The Gourdine painting system, or 'electradyne coating', utilizes a gun to release particles charged by a useful potential of 6KV. A fraction of the kinetic energy in the flowing air stream or within the particles per se is used to increase the particles to optimum potential. The charged particles adhere themselves to the closest ground plane which is the component part to be coated.

The uses to which electrogasdynamics have been put by Gourdine have the prospect of exerting a long-lasting effect on the lives of humankind for some time to come. Moreover, as we struggle to find sources of renewable and affordable energy, the enterprise of Meredith Gourdine can scarcely be forgotten.

Frederick McKinley Jones invented the first viable truck refrigeration unit that caused a shake up in the food transport line in the United States and, in turn, the world. A handheld refrigeration unit developed by Jones was a feature of the battlefields of Europe throughout World War II and it caused many lives to be saved because blood serum for transfusions, food items and medicines could be stored for the future beneath a cooling system (Sertima,1991:225).

Jones was born in 1893 and orphaned for the majority of his formative years, never having had anything above an eighth-grade education. His economic activity as a teenager was as a car mechanic, building racing cars, and he helped in World War I where he undertook electricity and electronics instruction. He went to Hallock, Minnesota following the war and came to be employed initially as a farm machinery mechanic and subsequently as a technician for a firm that made motion picture film paraphernalia and other cinema accoutrements.

In the first half of the twentieth century, news came to Jones one day that a friend of his employer who was in the transport business had lost a consignment of poultry when the ice blocks melted short of reaching the marketplace. Jones directly commenced working on an air-cooling system for trucks. His challenge succeeded and, in 1949, he collected a U.S. patent for his air-cooling system.

For his inventions, Frederick Jones received over 60 patents: 40 were for refrigeration appliances alone. Further patents were for portable X-ray units and sound equipment systems for motion pictures. In addition, Jones patented most of the special components of his air-cooling units; the automatic gasoline engine that switched his cooling systems on and off, the reverse cycling device for emitting heat or cold, and mechanisms for regulating air temperature and moisture (Sertima,1991:225).

The resolution of difficulties in any social organization is a task both of accumulating knowledge and of innovative thinking on the part of particular individuals. It is central that people draw upon the wealth of tradition as a catalyst for inventiveness in the numerous sciences and technologies.

If it were not for the life of Black men of genius, the human family in modern-day society would fare less well, whether viewed in terms of pure physical well-being or more loosely expressed of expanding horizons which render any society a place that augurs well for the future. Blacks are extending the frontiers of knowledge in almost every new discipline of the sciences and technologies, from fresh new approaches to engineering science to never before ways of understanding our past. The ability of Black men is now being adopted by the National Aeronautics and Space Administration, with three Blacks presently receiving call-ups to the Space Shuttle Program, and by such humanitarian formations as the World Health Organization (Sertima,1991:228). Blacks are contributing to the great circulation of learned information and completing exciting new research at both largely White and largely Black colleges and universities.

Activity of this nature, as can be expected, is not a new thing. The large majority of people have linked the Black man's genius with the practical advancements of George Washington Carver (whose enterprise with the peanut, sweet potato and soybean made so significant a contribution to agriculture and industry) or with the medical advancements of Dr Charles Drew, a leader in the line of blood plasm preservation. Unfortunately, there is a substantial gulf in public perception between the few apparently knowing that Carver and Drew are just two of what is a lengthy inventory of Black scientist-inventors and intellectuals whose genius has actively played a part in our society as we see and experience it (Sertima,1991:228).

Castigated, seldom praised and chided the most

Because British schools tend to focus and concentrate on British/European themes and predominantly White contributions to civilization, they deliberately fail to inspire Black children to take particular interest in the learning process. However, the Black boys who do endeavour to gain academic credentials and abide by behavioural codes set out by the school authorities have invectives levelled against them of being 'batty' (gay), 'acting white', or being 'pussies' (girls) (Rattansi,2007:158). And a peer pressure group of Black boys operates that participates in forms of 'street culture' which unfurl into hedonistic, violent, marijuana-smoking, and principally anti-school transgressions which make it harder for more educationally minded boys to retain credibility and withstand accusations that they are reneging on their communities (Rattansi,2007:158).

Black children fail to see the relevance of Henry VIII and his many wives, (short of imparting in them a sense of reverence for the institution of monarchy), as taught in British schools, and they wonder what purpose it serves in relation to preparing them for the workaday world. It may be that this works at a subliminal level where their respect for monarchy translates into a more amenable outlook when it comes to paying their taxes. If anything, Black children wonder why people like themselves do not feature in school history books and this may give rise to a source of frustration. Schools service the myth that Africa is without a history because no attention is paid to highlighting African achievements and contributions to civilization, and schools thoughtlessly feed into the myth of Black inferiority by refuting it only informally and not generally.

Moreover, it is little wonder, with all the processes children are exposed to in schools, from low teacher expectation of pupils' academic outcome, to teacher practices that favour White British pupils but affect people of colour, that Black pupils tend to underachieve in British schools. If Black pupils were taught about how full a history Africa holds, that is to say, that it is the birthplace of humanity, the cradle of civilization, that writing and language emanated and started there, this would bolster and boost Black children and inspire them to learn and take pride in their identity and education. Learning about Black scientists and inventors would further explode the myth of inferiority and would instil a sense of pride born of self-belief and lead to a growth in self-esteem. The belief in themselves would be a belief in their own resource.

Schooling appears to be many different things to many different people, including inspiring children to learn and the form and content of the curriculum can either maintain enthusiasm or result in distraction or disruption in the classroom. And, all too often, Black children are distracted away from learning mediated by the curriculum format and teacher racism, consequently engaging in resistance to schooling strategies although not entirely rejecting the idea of education per se (Wright, Weekes and McGlaughlin,2000:39). If school curricula focused on certain of the topics covered and discussed in this text, Black underachievement would move towards being a phenomenon that happened then, but not now. The Egyptian civilization, and before that the earliest recorded Nile Valley civilization, was Ta-Seti of Nubia, which may carry the tenor of either "Land of the bow" or "Land of Set", is proof positive of how far back Black aspiration can be traced and is capable of, when, rather than being systematically undermined or subordinated, it is uninterrupted by progress (Finch,1999, pp.96-7). Certain of the themes on education shall be discussed at length and in more detail in Chapter three.

The Black studies dialectic

However, in response to supplementary schools that teach Black studies and the proposal of Black studies in British schools, Cashmore and Troyna (1982) are not entirely convinced and argue that the real issues are left untouched and could further alienate and add to the polarization of Black youths. To be sure, is not the crux of the matter the White rejection of the facts and White British rejection of Black youths? The emphasis of differentness that Black studies might engender, Cashmore and Troyna (1982) say, 'can be divisive' when associated with certain postures and attitudes. Division is woven into the very fabric of society, is it or is it not? For example, there is nothing more divisive than racism, which Black youths will undoubtedly face. Why not prepare our children for society as we live and experience it and should that not involve some form of Black history in the school curriculum? The ideation of instilling a sense of identity in young Black people and the investment of time and energy by its architects, Cashmore and Troyna (1982) seem to think would be 'destructive to relationships between young Blacks and the rest of society in the longer term' (p.24). Instilling a sense of pride in one's identity is more productive and less harmful than the racism they are likely to experience in the wider scheme of things. And they add in their conclusion that Black studies, in their opinion, is, 'cosmetic in function and their masters myopic' (Cashmore and Troyna,1982 p.24). Black studies deal with difficult issues more likely to ground Black youths and that can hardly be taken as perfunctory; Black interests are central here and the counter-argument is anything but flexible. Is this about why White institutions should change things to accommodate the Black child?

The whole idea of the above format is to present a balanced view. Cashmore and Troyna's argument, however, is indicative of a dominant culture perspective because if you show me a Black Parent who does not want their children to learn about Black history, then I will show you a Black Parent that does not have his or her children's best interests at heart. What Black Parent would not want their children to know that they descend from a long line of genius? Because for a people to survive the long dark deadening night of the soul that is slavery, and soon after slavery and the slave trade had ended, for many to then receive academic degrees and some did not stop at one degree, from distinguished universities, one ultimately has to draw the conclusion that more is possible from a people of indomitable spirit and this is partly where the construction of the Black man as a 'threat' is derived from.

It is quite possible that this spectre of a 'threat' is why British schools have long been failing African-Caribbean children so that they are only fit for manual or menial-type work which White British working-class people fight shy of (Coard,1971:35). African-Caribbean students are invariably over-represented in exclusion figures (Sewell,1997, p.xiv). "Exclusions are to education what stop-and-search is to criminal justice" (Ojo,2007:7). The 1985 committee of inquiry underlined 'that West Indian children, as a group and on average, are underachieving' (Swann 1985:81; quoted in Pilkington,2003:134). The lexicon has transmuted over time, with the 1996 OFSTED report privileging the term 'African-Caribbean' and eschewing the term 'underachieving', but the same weight is evident. 'Recent research tends to show African-Caribbean pupils as relatively less successful than their "Asian" and White peers' (Gillborn and Gipps, 1996:29; cited in Pilkington,2003:134). That which came before, however, warrants alteration taking into account Pilkington's analysis of further recent research, which incorporates nationally representative samples and involves dividing ethnic groups by gender and political and geographical boundary origin. Although there are certain differences in the findings of research that centres on the performance of children in schools and the findings of studies that examine young people's highest qualifications, cumulatively they make known that it is African-Caribbean young men and not young women who are underperforming and that the hierarchical order of Pakistani and Bangladeshi groups is most favourably not noticeably better and may be worse still (Pilkington,2003:134). Consequently, African-Caribbean young men tend not to acquire the qualifications and credentials for upward social mobility in the occupational structure and there is firm and resolute resistance to promoting Black people in the workplace environment anyway.

Underachievement does not come by way of exclusions alone; it may also be the outcome of rebellion, institutional and individual forms of racism and language comprehension problems. Furthermore, the stress of life in a social system that devalues African-Caribbean people – of which schools are a part – is perhaps another factor in this equation (Gibson and Barrow,1986). The application and suitableness of the word 'underachievement' are held to be problematic. A number of writers have pointed out that there is a risk that the term 'underachievement' has become accepted as a beyond question truism 'rather than as a problem that requires sensitive and systematic integration' (Troyna,1984; cited in Wright,1992:91). Accordingly, it is likely that African-Caribbean students' underachievement turns out to be a self-fulfilling prophecy. It could comprise a negative ideological framework which teachers, administrators and prime movers may use to designate pupils and exonerate themselves of blame (Wright,1992:91).

The then Conservative MP for Wolverhampton, Enoch Powell, in his notorious 'Rivers of Blood' speech in April 1968, appealed to popular desires and prejudices and by declaring that, 'In fifteen years' time, the Black man will have the whip hand', thereby alerted the White British public to the potential rise to prominence of the Black man if left unchecked, and if the numbers of those who have seen their aspirations thwarted or dashed in British schools is anything to set store by; Enoch Powell's legacy is being played out in schools up and down the country and often unconsciously so, in order to prevent vast upward social mobility among young Black people taking place.

A decade or so later, then British Prime Minister Margaret Thatcher emphasized the 'British way of life', which she claimed was threatened by 'aliens' with being 'swamped' and this coincided precisely with Powell's 'Kitsch jeremiad' ten years earlier, reinforcing the message that Black people are not welcome in this country (Warmington,2014:33). More recently, David Cameron has slapped the Black diaspora in the face after calls for reparations and instead, offering a prison-building scheme in Jamaica; playing to the gallery of fears and prejudices among the White British public. Immigration is also a popular Conservative Party theme to rouse and rally popular support among the British voting public, consistently then, appealing to these national characteristics. On the question of reparations, there appears to be a consensus across all three major UK political parties.

Hence an upward struggle for social mobility is made that much more intensely difficult by the barriers that the Black population face since Black people are seen as a 'threat' and unwelcome to boot. And, Cashmore and Troyna (1982) are informed by, and appealing to, a predominantly White readership's fears, desires and prejudices in much the same way that politicians appeal to White British people as a media-consuming public who notice these news items and events in public life. Bound up in the image of the Black man as a 'threat' is the construction of us as 'problems' and Black studies refute negative constructions of Black self-image and has a way of turning them into positive affirmations. Just how ethnocentrism turns the tables on Blacks and South Asian groups, knowledge of social history can right that picture.

A well-rounded education is essential to growing children, not purely a whitewashed and 'white-biased' one because such an education will serve them for life in the knowledge that they have learned the truth and not simply believing speciously in the myth about Black people. This integrated programme of study will also encourage Black students to knuckle down and make the 'cultural impact' Cashmore and Troyna (1982) make mention of, and the teaching of Black studies in schools would make significant headway in tackling the root of the problem of transforming the thinking within schools. The dominant culture perspective seems to have rubbed off on Cashmore and Troyna (1982) who appear to not go the whole hog in dismissing the idea of Black children learning about their cultural heritage, but clearly, they do dismiss the idea, albeit not initially, because, in the final analysis, they reject it as having only a sticking plaster effect on a serious social issue, and of those who implement it engaged in a short term fix arguably unaware of its debatable desirability and implications; clearly then, to reveal a dominant culture orientation and an ideological axe to grind. The debatable desirability and implications of Black studies does not detract one iota from it as sine qua non despite all Cashmore and Troyna's (1982) apprehensions and concerns.

Learning about Black studies forms a connective link with life in contemporary Britain in that it can be seen as a coping mechanism for the buffeting effects of life in everyday Britain which, I am not going to deny, tend more often than not to be due to the colour of Black people's skin. However, the debate does not end there. Cashmore and Troyna (1982) point out some further weaknesses: that they must be seen as dangerous since the formation of pride in being Black and the solidarity associated with it, each, in turn, can have a polarising effect; and Black studies neglect broader issues and provide children with a history rather than a present. According to Cashmore and Troyna (1982), diverted intellectual energies may well cause further alienation from a world Black youths feel ambivalent towards. The inclusion of Black study programmes alongside existing curricula, they add, does not necessarily mean an increased inherent similarity with the components of education which are taken for granted, the understanding of which we are inclined to consider is a prior requirement for some degree of substantive headway to be made through life, whether occupationally or educationally.

There are high and low-status subjects but to suggest that Black studies may be a low-rank status subject merely because its focus is Black people-centred and the unfortunate link to Black subordinate status does not necessarily mean that the subject should be seen as a low-status category. That this is even an issue suggests that culturally, Black studies have struggled to gain parity against other subject areas and it should be of the same status as History, if the playing field is seen to be level. Cashmore and Troyna (1982) shift on a two-dimensional plane from attributing a problem to Black people and ignoring the influence of White British people in this equation, to devaluing the subject at the centre of the problem. What is more, history has an influence on the present or is why things are organized the way they are at present. Therefore, the necessity of learning history defies any critical opposition and without knowledge of their history, Black people are like a tree without roots. That the implication of teaching Black history spells polarisation and alienation for Black youth is no falsification, but their polarisation and alienation can scarcely get any worse than they already are. However, learning history is necessary if the myth of Black inferiority is to be addressed at all and it has, therefore, germane connection with life in early twenty-first-century Britain for people of all nationalities in this respect, and regarding the debatable desirability and implications, Black youths will have to live with polarisation and alienation and how that impacts on their relationships with others in contemporary British society, though to further add, Black youth need a sense of identity which Black studies can help to provide.

The persistence of differential treatment of Whites towards Blacks, historically the source of bad 'race relations' situations, does not help matters and therefore Whites can be seen to engage in racism for the benefit of all White people, i.e., providing 'colour constitutes a basis for community' (Carter and Williams,1987; quoted in Troyna,1987:174). Black people have to do their utmost to survive "the slings and arrows of outrageous fortune" on a quotidian basis (Shakespeare,1980:66). Cashmore and Troyna (1982) make it sound like Black studies teach Blacks to hate Whites; if that was the case, how is it that '55 per cent of all African-Caribbean males and 35 per cent of all Caribbean females in the UK have White partners'? (John, G., 2005; quoted in Richardson,2005:99). Is it a case of Cashmore and Troyna (1982) seeking to turn the tables as Whites have done historically in order to maintain the advantage? In addressing Cashmore and Troyna's (1982) concerns and apprehensions, the focus has been on the indispensable condition of the teaching of Black studies in British schools, and since the debatable desirability and implications stem from a sceptical position of what such a programme of study can hope to achieve (i.e. Black pride and an altered sense of awareness in which things are put into their proper perspective and brought into sharp focus), this suggests that it is with the greatest regret that Cashmore and Troyna (1982) envisage that people of African descent have a history worth discovering, exploring and celebrating. Cashmore and Troyna (1982) insist on discouraging the teaching and imbibing of Black studies/Black History because it shows Europeans in a bad light as amoral, ruthless and rapacious and because the British government declines to apologize for the slave trade and slavery. The British government's refusal to pay reparations is, on so many levels, tantamount to and consistent with keeping Black people down and Cashmore and Troyna (1982) would appear to countenance such a governmental policy.

Summary and conclusion

In this chapter, I have discussed Egyptian civilization and its architectural and design achievements in a historical context and, in so doing, exploded certain myths – some of its architectural forms, styles and canons are still in use today. The Egyptian building innovations and techniques led the world, and indeed, although Ta-Seti, a Nubian civilization, was established prior to the Egyptian civilization, it is better known as the oldest recorded and a Black African civilization into the bargain. The British government was privy to the achievements of African culture by at least 1790 but chose to do little or nothing to dispel the myth about the African because it served their purposes. It is difficult to overstate how important it is for young Black people to learn about African history and culture before, during, and after the slave trade and slavery.

Given that White slave-owners were handsomely compensated for loss of human property, it begs the question, how long will the British government continue to historically devalue a part of its citizenship composition or people of African descent and refuse to redress the balance for slavery and the slave trade? I suggest until kingdom come. Why should it be only White people who can be shown some human compassion for loss of human life or serious maltreatment? For the Jews, it was a 6-million death toll and during the age of slavery, the toll was over 10 million (The Voice, March 19-25, 2007), as many lives were lost traversing the middle passage (the Atlantic crossing from Africa to the Americas), and slave-owners employed ever-inventive and extremely punishing ways to kill slaves. Yet, as this work confirms, the Jews were compensated by the German authorities. Why, then, should Black people continue to be cold-shouldered by the powers that be on the issue of reparations? Slavery is the biggest ever holocaust known to man, significant for bridging approximately four centuries, yet the latest British government rebuttal on reparations simply illustrates that the British government does not have atonement and reconciliation on its political agenda. An examination of the reparations debate saw a further British government dismissal of the calls for an apology for slavery and the slave trade. The reparations debate was floated in March 2007 and saw a resurgence in October 2015.

Illustrations of the Black man's genius showing the productions or fruit of his labour and aspirations were outlined through such people as Imhotep, George Washington Carver, Jan Ernest Matzeliger, Elijah McCoy, Garret Morgan, Granville T. Woods, Lewis Temple, Norbert Rillieux, Lewis Howard Latimer, Meredith Gourdine and Frederick McKinley Jones, each of whom are notable by their absence as household names. In Chapter Two, we consider the experience of Black and South Asian people as seen through the optic of the host community backlash and policy responses to their arrival and settlement in the UK. Black studies/Black History ought to be put on the school curriculum, if not already, and if Cashmore and Troyna (1982) cannot countenance this, then, they are part of the problem that stymies Black forward movement in Britain today. This chapter is put forward to illustrate that despite racist ideology and government inaction around race, the Black man/woman has always been proficient and competent and no counterpoint nor counter-narrative to this truth, the whole truth and nothing but the truth will hold water indefinitely.

Chapter 2: Policy Responses to Mass Immigration

This chapter aims to focus on the history of mass immigration and the inextricably associated 'immigrant' experience will be captured through the spectacles of government policy responses to African-Caribbean and South Asian migrants alighting on British shores. In outline, the decade 1961-71 saw the implementation of three major laws to serve the purpose of excluding African-Caribbean and South Asian 'immigrants'. The 1971 Act phased out the legitimacy of Commonwealth 'immigrants' taking up permanent abode, and so represented an important intervention in the institutionalisation of racist legislation (Solomos,2003). Aside from this is the subordinate and underlying theme to contradict widely held but false notions through systematically considering a number of different routes.

Economic opportunities offered few openings for the populations of Caribbean Islands to be able to sustain themselves and consequently, many Caribbean people turned to considering the alternatives of emigrating to America or Britain as a means through which their circumstances could be improved (Fryer,1984; Phillips and Phillips,1998; Pilkington,2003). Underdevelopment in the Asian subcontinent was also a concern but was in part facilitated by British decimation of the region's textile industry which was thought to rival the Lancashire-based one. Such economies were subjected to satisfying British interests and because investment was rare and clearly insufficient, these countries have failed to emerge above the precipice of poverty in terms of creating jobs for their people so they see migration as a way of changing their economic fortunes. Migration to Britain deserves to be seen amid this background (Pilkington,2003).

Within the first post-1945 decade, war-shattered Britain underwent a process of sudden economic growth. However, not unlike other Western European nations which were also enjoying this 'boom', Britain sustained a chronic shortfall in labour (Cashmore and Troyna,1990). Despite the arrival of the SS Empire Windrush in 1948 carrying some 500 passengers from Jamaica, there was no significantly substantive immigration from British colonies and ex-colonies at this stage – the majority of migrants entering Britain from 1945 and 1954 came from other European nations (Fryer,1084; Phillips and Phillips,1998; Solomos,1993). In the interval between 1945 and 1951, between 70,000 and 100,000 Irish people crossed over into Britain. While concern was very much an afterthought about Irish migrants entering the country, the issue raised nothing remotely resembling a debate at this stage (Solomos,1993). This period is important for two reasons. It highlighted that most migrants to Britain were identifiably White people rather than African-Caribbean and South Asian people. It also signposted a decisive turning point: during these passing years, where we witness the first signs of a transformation from logistical migration flows issuing from European locations to flows originating in the colonies and former colonies, this transformation was juxtaposed by a crisis at the heart of British government circles, one which revealed not only how inclined it is to 'surrender to racism' over principles around nationality but also its indecision to enshrine racism in law (Fryer,1984; Miles,1993).

The shortage of labour experienced during the post-1945 labour administration was a problem the state attempted to alleviate by encouraging European men to come and work here (Miles,1993). Government action was marked by a steadfast refusal to adopt an inclusive recruitment policy by locating labour from among British subjects found in the colonies. There has been insufficient take-up on this point in recent historical investigations of the period (Miles,1993). Against recruiting from the colonies, a number of independent and state-run schemes to recruit migrant labour were initiated (Miles and Phizacklea,1984). The European Volunteer Workers scheme saw the introduction of 77,000 displaced individuals from Europe to jobs in British industry where there were labour shortages. An additional 8,000 Ukrainian prisoners of war were also found work and approximately 88,000 Polish Armed Forces personnel who wished to settle here were assisted and found employment between 1946 and 1950. Although further attempts to secure other foreign workers (mostly Italians and Germans) were much smaller in scale, the number of aliens granted work permits between 1946 and 1950 equalled 136,000, including dependants (Miles and Phizacklea,1984).

The general welcome extended to the European migrants to put down roots in Britain was paralleled by state concern with the overall ramifications of a comparatively smaller group arriving from the colonies in this period (Joshi and Carter,1984; Solomos,1993). Recent research tells us that irrespective of this embryonic development, African-Caribbean and South Asian migration and settlement make for nothing like the same political response as European migration. Secretly, the government was pondering on how best they could impede or thwart the migration flows of African-Caribbean and South Asian people from the colonies (Joshi and Carter,1984; Solomos,1993).

However, employers cared less about religion and 'race' in the 1950s (Miles and Phizacklea,1984). 'Large-scale immigration' followed despite the contents of the Royal Commission's report which ruled that African-Caribbean and South Asian 'immigrants' were unwelcome and unwanted as a solution to Britain's labour shortage problem because certain sectors of industry felt that production targets could not be met without it. The Royal Commission wrote:

Immigration on a large scale into a fully established society like ours would only be welcomed without reserve if the immigrants were of good stock and were not prevented by their religion or race from intermarrying with the host population and becoming merged in it' (cited in Miles and Phizacklea,1984:24).

Although it appears that economic priorities had been overriding, backing from officialdom was anything but withheld. The British Nationality Act (1948) advanced the notion that the Commonwealth was an untapped labour source by describing all Commonwealth residents as British citizens, entitled to enter and live in Britain. This was not lost on those employers who placed recruitment advertisements in the Caribbean and Asian subcontinent throughout the 1950s. The failure of the Royal Commission to acknowledge these British citizens as an untapped labour source suggests that African-Caribbean and South Asian people were deemed not to be 'of good stock' (Miles and Phizacklea,1984).

It is often reported that a laissez-faire period operated between 1948 and the early 1960s, with both parties maintaining the outward appearance of opposition to an outspoken backbench fringe who held an anti-immigration stance (Pilkington,2003). The availability of government papers intimates, however, that both government administrations throughout this period privately were of the same persuasion as the anti-immigration lobby. 'The set of the official mind was always opposed to the permanent settlement in Britain of South Asian and African-Caribbean communities' (I Spencer 1997:19, cited in Pilkington,2003:213). Attitudes differed markedly between the arrival of European and Irish aliens because they were regarded as of good stock whereas fears were articulated about the problems large numbers of African-Caribbean and South Asian people arriving in Britain presented for assimilation. In light of these concerns, state policy endorsed during the inter-war period 'to exclude and control Jewish and Black migrants' (Solomos,1993:52) was adhered to in the post-1945 period for African-Caribbean and South Asian subjects. In fact, changes in government administrations during the 1950s saw each party consider legislative controls. Intentions such as these were briefly halted because 'there was a widespread recognition within ruling circles that while any controls on immigration had to be racial in form, the government could not be seen as openly espousing discriminatory controls' (Malik,1996:21, cited in Pilkington,2003:213). A sufficient case had yet to be built, considering the lack of identifiable public anxiety, the need to fill jobs and the international position in terms of the Commonwealth (Pilkington,2003).

Racism as riots

By 1958, the case had moved up a level to see indigenous public ill will turned on African-Caribbean and South Asian residents resulting in 'white riots', and in Nottingham and Notting Hill, youths carried out attacks on African-Caribbean and South Asian citizens (Pilkington,2003). The disturbances stimulated one of two responses from politicians across political parties. The first view considered that the riots typified racism. White working-class individuals had worked out frustrations on a minority group held to be inferior. To bring about racial harmony, governments needed to construct policies to counter racism and to eliminate the disadvantages felt by White and Black groups. The second view considered that the riots demonstrated that liberal attitudes towards 'immigrants' had been pushed to their limits. Large scale immigration had caused resentment. To minimize people's anxieties and thus further racial harmony, governments could do no less than restrict the flow of New Commonwealth migrants and urge those settled here to assimilate (Pilkington,2003). 'A solution that ignored their attempts to do so by attending dance halls, from which they were banned' (Miles and Phizacklea,1984:34)

The minority that already advocated this second action plan had by this time begun to grow in number (Cashmore and Troyna,1990) However, Ceri Peach shows that immigration controls were unnecessary, arguing that migration from the Caribbean was dependent on economic need; it 'rose and fell to the demand for labour from year to year' (1968:93; quoted in Cashmore and Troyna, 1990:58; Miles and Phizacklea,1984:41-42). In a similar vein, Vaughan Robinson has demonstrated a link between South Asian migration to, and recession within, the UK (1980; cited in Cashmore and Troyna,1990). Also, long-term unemployment was an uncharacteristic feature of the British economy around that period, so the likelihood of recent 'immigrants' becoming benefit dependent was quite low. Yet, the government failed to act to allay these and other anxieties, the outcome of which was the riots in Nottingham and Notting Hill (Cashmore and Troyna,1990).

As it transpired, the standing Conservative government avoided the more constructive and more rational step of targeting social problems through state measures to improve the circumstances of inner-city inhabitants (Cashmore and Troyna, 1990). On the obverse, it credited the racist interpretation of the situation, viz, that the uncontrolled entry of African-Caribbean and South Asians had led to these problems, therefore requiring limits to the numbers admitted to the UK. Attempts to resist the clamour for immigration control lost out in a climate of open season on African-Caribbean and South Asian people (Solomos,2003). The Commonwealth Immigrants Act of 1962 was the first legislative step to limiting the numbers allowed into Britain by asking New Commonwealth migrants to satisfy entry conditions. In contradistinction, not one finger was lifted to impose restrictive controls over the numbers hailing from the Republic of Ireland, despite the Republic not being part of the Commonwealth. The reason for and the upshot of this legislation were unambiguous and against this background, we can appreciate why authors Ann and Michael Dummett remember it as a 'policy of surrender' to racist scaremongering (1969; cited in Cashmore and Troyna,1990).

The 1962 Act signalled the dawn of 'the numbers game' in Britain and from this point on, the foremost concern in the British collective consciousness has been with the numerical quantity of African-Caribbean and South Asian migrants entering or having the right of free entry to the UK (Cashmore and Troyna,1990). Dating from 1962, then, efforts to control the numerical migration flow has assumed greater importance in the province of race relations policy. The act paved the way for a succession of progressively restrictive and, in fact, racist measures to be implemented in 1965, 1968, 1971 and 1981 and more followed (Cashmore and Troyna,1990).

Consolidated state racism

Consent to turn over administrative controls on New Commonwealth migration to legislative action was officially approved in October 1961 when the Conservative administration called public attention to the Commonwealth Immigrants Bill (Solomos,2003). The barriers the Bill erected were backed by the contention that it was necessary to bring African-Caribbean and South Asian immigration to an end because of the near inability of the host community to assimilate them. The Bill was not welcomed in certain quarters as a way of managing the movement of Black migrants, and the Labour Party and media groups saw it as yielding to crude racist agitation. Labour Party leader, Hugh Gaitskell, had his day in parliament when he expressed particularly strong opposition to the Bill and its unqualified conflating of immigration and race (Solomos,2003). This 'race/immigration' coalescence was used to satisfy or mean, in coded language, the Black man (Castles and Kosack,1985; Miles and Phizacklea,1984: 38, 41, 45). One has to question what is meant by the 'Black man' because African-Caribbean people were not the only people of 'colour' entering the UK. This characterization obscures the fact that according to Castles and Kosack (1985), nearly two-thirds of 'immigrants' in the UK are White.

While the Act was strenuously criticized by the Labour Party, the 1964 general election victory of the Conservative Peter Griffiths in Smethwick influenced the party to accept the racist ideology of the day (Pilkington,2003). The fall of the Smethwick seat to the Conservatives rested on an 'anti-immigration' platform alongside an openly racist campaign slogan which stated, 'If you want a nigger for a neighbour vote Labour' (Solomos,2003:60). The Labour Government did not fail to appreciate or realize the lessons. Under Labour, the 1962 Act not only stood but further restrictions were introduced in its 1965 White Paper and were justified by the racist argument that the African-Caribbean and South Asian presence presented a problem and ending all future New Commonwealth immigration provided the solution and contributed to better 'race relations'

(Bourne and Sivanandan,1980; Pilkington,2003). 'Without integration', asserted Labour spokesman Roy Hattersley, 'limitation is inexcusable; without limitation, integration is impossible' (Bourne and Sivanandan,1980: 335). This 'syllogism' stands as the bipartisan joined-up thinking on immigration and 'race relations' from then onwards. Though it seemed as if Labour had lost its moral direction, there was no doubting that political advantage was what was at stake (Bourne and Sivanandan,1980; Miles and Phizacklea,1984: 47-58).

As state racism escalated, attacks on African-Caribbean and South Asian residents followed suit, mounting year on year (Fryer,1984) But more violent than anything else, since the broadside affected every African-Caribbean and South Asian settler, was their descent as 'immigrants' to the lower rank position of second-class citizens, a relegation for which the 1962 Act was responsible. Blackness was paralleled with second-class citizenship, with the standing of undesirable 'immigrant'. E.R. Braithwaite, author of 'To Sir with Love', outlined in 1967 his sentiment on being a second-class citizen:

> In spite of my years of residence in Britain, any service I might render the community in times of war or peace, any contribution I might make or wish to make, or any feeling of identity I might entertain towards Britain and the British, I - like all other colored persons in Britain – am considered an 'immigrant'. Although this term indicates that we have secured entry into Britain, it describes a continuing condition in which we have no real hope of ever enjoying the desired transition to full responsible citizenship (Fryer,1984:382).

Two developments in 1968 ensured that the second view specified above (namely that liberal attitudes towards 'immigrants' had been pushed to their limits) had won out (Pilkington,2003. They included the enactment of laws designed to restrict the flow of East African Asians into Britain and what Paul Foot (1969) had designated 'the rise of Enoch Powell' (cited in Pilkington, 2003:215). Both developments will be considered in turn.

Part of the detail of the 1962 Act allowed British citizens residing in independent Commonwealth countries free entry provided they were in possession of a British passport (Solomos,2003). This brought a significant number of European settlers and a considerable number of Asians in Kenya and Uganda into the equation. A proportion of these people entered Britain between 1965 and 1967 and, as a direct result of late 1967 calls for immigration control by media groups and politicians, a heated discursive struggle was sparked (Solomos,2003).

The climax of this discursive struggle came in February 1968 (Solomos,2003). As already indicated, the Labour Party had recognized the electoral expediency of immigration controls and so there was little surprise when it favoured this political campaign by calling attention to the second Commonwealth Immigrants Act in 1968. This Act was designed to control the number of East African Asians by subjecting them to immigration control. The Act ruled British passport holders out of immigration and settlement in Britain except for when they could demonstrate 'close connection' with the political and geographical boundary, defined as a parent or grandparent having Britain as his or her birthplace (Pilkington,2003). The circumstances surrounding the Act's passage left government open to the charge of a 'colour bar' and 'probably the most shameful measure that the Labour members have ever been asked by their whip to support' (The Times, 27 February 1968; quoted in Solomos,2003: 60).

Harold Wilson's insistence that 'the criteria for exemption' from the 1968 Act 'were geographical, not racial' was considered spurious by critics of joined-up thinking on immigration and 'race relations', and also by the African-Caribbean and South Asian populations (Cashmore and Troyna).

The 'race/immigration' equals problem theme received further input between the 1968 Act and the 1970 election (Solomos,2003). Although it was difficult to imagine even tighter controls than the 1962 and 1968 Acts, this general subject area was allowed to assume even greater discursive struggle proportions. It was in this context of increasingly broad resentment and animosity aimed at African-Caribbean and South Asian settlers that these groups, over a three-year period, were twice asked to accept the implications of the Labour Party's law, the idea being: our anti-discrimination laws or 1968 Race relations Act indicate our efforts to ensure that you enjoy equal citizenship rights in the UK, nevertheless, our immigration laws are patently transparent – we don't want people like you to continue coming here! (Cashmore and Troyna,1990).

In this climate, the Labour government found itself on the defensive against Enoch Powell's notorious 1968 speech in Birmingham, which assisted in spreading the message that a further tightening of immigration controls would not be sufficient to resolve the 'race problem' (Solomos,2003). The content of this and a series of other subsequent speeches, warned, as he envisaged, of (a) a future changed by immigration, and (b) the extended risk of racial tension rivalling that of America surfacing in Britain. The pre-eminent section of Powell's speech is where he infamously said:

> As I look ahead, I am filled with foreboding. Like the Roman, I seem to see 'the River Tiber foaming with much blood'. The tragic and intractable phenomenon which we watch with horror on the other side of the Atlantic, but which there is interwoven with the history and existence of the states itself, is coming upon us here by our own volition and our own neglect (Enoch Powell,1968, quoted in Solomos,2003:61).

Powell believed that the long-term response should surpass immigration control and involve the repatriation of immigrants who had made Britain their home, thus offering up repatriation for political discussion. In his notorious speech, Powell waxed lyrical to create an image of indigenous Britons becoming 'strangers' in their 'own country':

> They found their wives unable to obtain hospital beds in childbirth, their children unable to obtain school places, their homes and neighbourhoods changed beyond recognition, their plans and prospects

for the future defeated (Enoch Powell,1968, quoted in Solomos, 2003:61).

According to Powell, the two-party system of government had failed to deliver on bringing immigration to an end causing the situation to develop and requiring more draconian measures to resolve the problem (Solomos,2003).

The speech stirred such a furore that it resulted in Heath eliminating Powell from the Shadow Cabinet (Solomos,2003). However, the attention the media gave to his apocalyptic cataclysmic bombshell throughout 1968 and 1969 and the time-space beyond in the run-up to the 1970 general election was considerable. This concentrated the attention of those firmly behind Powell's spearheading rallying cry to repatriate African-Caribbean and South Asian 'immigrants' who had taken up residence in Britain (Solomos,2003).

Legislators had, however, only partially surrendered to racism (Fryer,1984). With the newly installed Conservative government came the Immigration Act of 1971, directly representing three years of unrelenting pressure by Powell, who had proceeded to call for a 'Ministry of Repatriation'. The Act itself, which was not imposed until 1973, put an end to all primary immigration. This closed the door on African-Caribbean and South Asian people entering Britain save for those under a contract labour scheme, who were shown in to do a particular job for a certain length of time: no longer than one year to start with. Immense power was entrusted to police and immigration officers: they could arrest whoever they thought were illegal 'immigrants' without a warrant. Based on the Home Secretary's judgment, an immigrant worker could be expelled if that was held to be 'conducive to the public good' (Fryer,1984:385) The number of dependants coming in was further curtailed. Every assistance would be extended to 'immigrants' who preferred to be repatriated (Fryer,1984).

The African-Caribbean and South Asian communities were now subject to all manner of abuse, harassment, imprisonment without trial, separation of kinship units, 'fishing raids'-to every kind of personal indignities, degradations, and misery, from the examination of female genitalia to determine whether women were virgins to the derisory laughter of British officials when an 11-year-old girl became violently agitated on being informed that an entry certificate would not be awarded to allow her to join her mother and siblings in Britain (Fryer,1984).

In closing this chapter, I shall consider some of the themes which appear recurrent in this work. The race/immigration equals 'problem' seems to have been constructed by the government and one of the aims of this chapter has been to demonstrate its resilience.

The response to mass immigration has been an 'immigrants as threat campaign'. How can African Caribbean and South Asian people be a 'threat to the material security of Whites' or a 'threat to the British way of life' or 'British culture' merely by their presence when they themselves are victims of structured inequality, racial prejudice, racial discrimination and persistent and systematic racism and are subject, de facto, to multiple deprivations? (Devine,1997; Joshi and Carter, 1984; Solomos,2003). This is not to say that African-Caribbean and South Asian people are not in competition with indigenous White people for scarce resources such as jobs and housing, but often, they find themselves either unemployed or in possession of the worst kinds of jobs and housing. In short, how can a relatively small group of people be a 'threat' when they are systematically dominated and prodigiously regulated by White society? This indicates that White British people are not so tolerant a group after all. African-Caribbean and South Asian people often do not compete with or pose a 'threat' to White people on the same terms. The African-Caribbean and South Asian presence does not appear a problem but their presence did create problems; however, prejudice and discrimination are also problems (Bourne and Sivanandan,1980).

Let's not forget that White people maliciously act on their prejudices and African-Caribbean and South Asian people are merely trying to obtain the same rights as other citizens (Sivanandan, cited in Fryer,1984). Moreover, the number of African-Caribbean and South Asian people against the host community amount to about 5 per cent of the population, therefore, things are being blown right out of proportion and Black and minority ethnic people can hardly be seen to represent a 'threat'. Historically, the real problem has been prejudice, discrimination and racism that threatens African-Caribbean and South Asian people and still continues to date.

That White people regard African-Caribbean and South Asian people as a 'threat' to the 'British way of life' is a form of cultural imperialism because White people are really rather afraid that there may come a time when African-Caribbean and South Asian people rise to prominence economically and politically and White people, *en masse*, are on their guard against Black aspiration ever amounting to much and seek to frustrate, thwart and impede it at every turn; or this is more identifiably the survival strategy of systemic power at work and in progress.

The reason for these social problems is deeply rooted in history and all sections of British society are affected by these problems which, to some extent, capitalism facilitates (Cashmore and Troyna,1990). Bipartisan government could have taken a better lead as their actions and beliefs percolate down to the general population and are internalized. From the very genesis, the government defined colour as the 'problem' thus encouraging prejudice and discrimination and the British media were equally responsible. Government allowed public resentment of the African-Caribbean and South Asian presence to dictate proceedings or govern responses over principle. The principle was around nationality and African-Caribbean and South Asian people were British passport-holders but, the bipartisan government surrendered to racism rather than targeting inner-city disadvantages of 1980's Britain which both Black and White people faced (Cashmore and Troyna,1990). Two-party government and sections of the media share the onus of creating a racist Britain and the British people played their part by expressing resentment towards the African-Caribbean and South Asian communities and voting for the party that had the hardest line on immigration. In 1989, the Runnymede Trust made the following statement:

Chapter 1: Tracing Black Aspiration and Illuminating Achievement

Black people are a problem and unwelcome here. That is the message which is restated and reaffirmed every time immigration policy is made more restrictive. It is a message not lost on 'our people' in Britain – on the employers who can ask, with reason, why they should have 'them' in their firm if the government does not want them in the country, on the tenants who do not want them in 'their' streets or housing estates, on the parents and pupils who do not want them in 'their' schools, on the 42 per cent of young White people who, according to the *British Social Attitudes survey*, will now willingly admit to racial prejudice (Gordon, 1989:13; cited in Skellington, 1996:64).

Robert Moore (1999) implies that racial prejudice and discrimination are so far entrenched that they are very nearly impossible to reverse. Just as government, parliament, the media and political parties racialised African-Caribbean and South Asian people as 'problems', so too can they initiate positive opinion-forming steps to reverse the prevailing trend – but the political will does not appear to be present and entrenched racist attitudes are. Government endorsement of racist immigration controls to minimize numbers has a negligible effect on 'race relations'; it simply panders to and appeases the fascists and who is to say that immigration laws, the latest of which was passed in 2002, will put an end to racist attacks (Solomos,2003)? The Royal Commission defined South Asian and African-Caribbean people as inferior and the UNESCO Statement on Race refutes all such claims and also was formulated because of the destructive nature of organizing 'races' into hierarchical systems (Miles and Phizacklea,1984:14-15). The following pages aim to contradict the Royal Commission.

In the first place, if we look into the idea of superior versus inferior 'races', we find that White people were designated as superior in order to excuse slavery and colonial exploitation (Fryer,1984; Fryer,1988:27; Hartmann and Husband,1974:22-23). Britain's grip on the empire has been diminishing since the late eighteenth century. However, the consciousness it gave rise to is often more difficult to dislodge than the structures of which it was originally a part and rode tandem with. More to the point is that while the empire per se may have passed into dissolution, the consciousness concomitant with that empire has undergone tortuous changes from one generation to succeeding generations and remains largely undisturbed. And nowadays, the idea that White people continue to believe in superior and inferior 'races' does not exist in a vacuum, but is a hangover or legacy of the colonial era (Cashmore and Troyna,1990:53). This is what Cashmore and Troyna (1990) call the 'colonial mentality'.

Numerous White individuals disseminated and propagated literature that subordinated and was highly critical of the man and woman of colour and the enterprise which had its own financial reward – receiving widespread acceptance in Europe. The distribution of the print media attacking the African and people of colour eventually acquires a pseudo-scientific mantle that papers over its irrationalities and allows it to assume intellectual respectability. According to Cashmore and Troyna (1990), assimilation is a key factor in rendering old myths and ideas about White superiority redundant (pp.22-23).

In the second place, if one undertakes to cross-reference the word superior, we find that, in fact, it can be seen to mean the same as the term, able. The need to consult a dictionary serves only to confirm accuracy; here, the term calls to mind the common-sense defining characteristics of better, more important or higher in rank or quality, but, when cross-referenced, the term superior reveals that it has close association with, or is a synonym of the term, able, and South Asian and African-Caribbean people, are, if anything, endowed with intelligence. Also, the literary paroxysm on the African and people of colour was promoted and fostered because White people were inclined to favour their own kind and this preference appears to have dictated proceedings, in addition to justifying racist exploitation.

Thirdly, the theory that organized 'races' into hierarchical systems and resulted in the slaughter of over 6 million Jews by supposedly 'superior' Germans was of concern to the United Nations Educational, Scientific and Cultural Organization (UNESCO) and, in 1949, it established an appointed group of experts with the aim of outlining a scientific statement about the reality of 'race'. Their findings were made public in Paris in July

1950. What was later acknowledged as UNESCO's 'First statement on race problems' made important claims as detailed below (Cashmore,1988:309). One, it found that all human beings belong to the same genus and are originated from one stock. Biological variances between groups of humans were acquiesced as extant, but these were noted as being the development of evolutionary variables and not as unchangeably immutable attitudes. Two, it was found that what separates diverse peoples biologically is differences in how often a small number of specific genes occur, but that genetic homogeneity is more common than genetic heterogeneity between groups. Therefore, they distinguished a 'race' as a human group with a distinct but mutable gene formation.

Fourth, they found that these genetic variances have no causal link to cultural variances or to intelligence. They challenged the idea that there is any demonstrable proof that different human groups differ in their inherent characteristics and that IQ tests fall flat in distinguishing between what might be inherent ability and environmental variables in the assessment of intelligence. Lastly, they found that 'race' was, above all else, a social myth and not a biological fact, identifying that in the case most people apply the term colloquially, they do not allude to different formations of gene manifestation.

In the wake of the UNESCO statement came three subsequent statements in the 1950s and 1960s. All of these involved development around the subject matter and what was missed out of the first statement, but also, on one occasion, a split in opinion (Cashmore,1988). The disagreement was made manifest in the second UNESCO statement, printed in Paris in July 1951, a statement whose context comes out of the reaction to the first by a collective of geneticists and physical anthropologists who made representations against some of its draft decisions. While this collective group of scientists scarcely railed in principle against any of the above litany of claims, they did seek to develop the formal definition of 'race' to subsume more than statistical variances in population gene occurrences. Focusing on this group's purpose, 'race' alluded to population groups identified by inherited physical differences. Through this means, they were adding scientific integrity to the banal, common to all notion of 'race' which is implicated upon such variances as skin colour, hair texture, etc., a notion far removed from the first statement (Cashmore,1988).

The third 'UNESCO statement on race' was formulated in Moscow in August 1964 and constituted a review of the earlier two statements (Cashmore,1988). It recognized and restated the main findings of statement number one and presented a major condition to the key claim of statement number two. Concerning the latter nexus, the Third statement advanced that classification founded on hereditary physical features is unable to set forward distinct categories and bears little scientific interest or usefulness.

The Fourth UNESCO statement was consigned to paper in Paris in September 1967 and concentrated on the various systemic causes of racism (not race) and projected a set of recommendations aimed at how racism might be more deliberately militated against (Cashmore,1988). Therefore, when the Royal Commission asserts that African-Caribbean and South Asian people are inferior, it is the biggest imaginable lie, utter nonsense and completely unfounded; not to mention very definitely racist. Therefore, superior and inferior 'races' do not exist in reality but they are socially constructed.

Finally, there is an aspect of jealousy surrounding racial prejudice that is part of everyday discourse, though the topic is often not broached outside of that informal social context which is more prevalent during the summer months in the UK; here I refer to suntans (Willis,1977:153; Mac an Ghaill,1994: 87; Sewell,1997:177). Paradoxically, racist ideology suggests that White people are fiercely proud of their possession of White skin covering, however, it would seem that this assumption is not without its tensions and contradictions since a significant proportion holiday in sunnier climes, generally because the warmth of the sun is healthy and a tan is part and parcel of the circumstances if holidaying means White people lounge for long periods in the sun. Others fast-track this process by darkening their skin by using spray-tanning techniques, yet, at the same time, may buy into or subscribe to notions of White privilege and dominance juxtaposed with

Black disadvantage and subordination. It is clear to see, therefore, that there is a double standard and reversed logic to the propounded intellectual superiority of Whites because many White people so want to look like the very people they despise, and this runs deeper than mere skin colour. White intellectuals, Cashmore and Troyna (1982) maintain that 'there is something special about the experience of being Black and that this experience structures the position of Black youth' (pp.25-26). Norman Podhoretz (1963) in his treatise 'My Negro Problem – And Ours' waxed mellifluously on White male obsession with Blackness, and the Black male form:

> Just as in childhood, I envied Negroes for what seemed to me their superior masculinity, so I envy them today for what seems to be their superior physical grace and beauty. I have come to value physical grace very highly and I am now capable of aching with all my being when I watch a Negro couple on the dance floor, or a Negro playing baseball or basketball. They are on the kind of terms with their own bodies that I should like to be with mine, and for that precious quality they seem blessed to me (quoted in Sewell,1997:178)

Conversely, the very fact of being White and indigenous to the country tends to bestow certain freedoms, within reason, without the injurious consequences of their actions. This is the prevailing condition and reality of a liberal democracy that enshrines ethnocentric beliefs and values whereas Blacks – through the struggle for equality – are attempting to redress the balance alongside the dominant group.

On the other hand, it would appear that the vast majority of Black people are equally proud of being Black but, as a result of powerful forces in the mainstream of society that unfavourably impacts against them, they sometimes experience despair and wish or wonder, what if they were White, to escape all the disadvantages of being Black and enjoy all the freedoms associated with being White (Coard,1971:28-33). Now, there are those who might argue that the freedoms enjoyed by Whites are precisely and directly because their descendants have fought in world wars and other conflicts around the world. Yet, the descendants of African-Caribbeans and South Asians who have been called upon for four centuries to assist Britain in campaigns of war and have fought and died for this country, are denied the same freedoms and humanity as Whites today. (A play entitled, "No dogs, No Irish, No Blacks" staged at the Black Country Living Museum near Birmingham, 27 October 2016).

If we are to get caught up on origins, most, if not all White people would find that if they were to trace their ancestry far enough back in history, they would find, no less, a Black individual and, if this is a staggering conclusion, then even the out and out racists among White people should begin questioning their motives or even protesting vigorously at the treatment of Black people in modern-day Britain and seeking a radical transformation in attitudes and the social structure. The fact that this does not happen suggests that Whites cherish the preservation of the status quo or that the above fact is not widely acknowledged. And, the above conclusion by itself invalidates all contentions justifying why Whites enjoy certain freedoms stemming from their ancestors fighting and dying in wars for the body politic. That the fabric of Black origins is interwoven biologically and historically with White people generally might be intriguing and astonishing, but equality for Blacks still seems, incalculably, some way off and a far cry from being realized.

Atmospheres within public houses frequented by a mainly White patronage undergo a transitional shift of focus when a Black presence is introduced to the mix, all at once becoming the centre of attention, and is perhaps one reason why racial prejudice and discrimination are additional, as to why Black people are not genuinely permitted to feel Black and Proud.

The wearing of straight hairstyles by Black females is not only *de rigueur* but also satisfies a wish to be like White people and skin bleaching is also a noted activity among Black female and male circles so, all told, we have Blacks on the one hand and Whites on the other hand, emulating one another's physical characteristics. The very act of transforming one's appearance from curly to straight hair suggests that one thinks and feels that straight hair is better. In comparative and contrasting terms, this occurs for different reasons. Whites feel that they look better or healthier with a tanned complexion and are jealous of the rich vein and range of Blackness Blacks collectively possess, or are motivated by freedoms whereas Black females are motivated by the mood and spirit of the age and factors at various levels of society that work against them but, in addition, there is the wish to satisfy attention-seeking behaviour mainly towards the opposite sex, and in so doing, experience what it is like to have fairer skin and lank hair. However, there is the prospect of hair management issues associated with going natural since African-Caribbean hair needs an abundant amount of care and attention on a day-to-day basis. So, because straight hairstyles do come with an easy to manage daily regime that is to some extent life-changing, this is another reason for the adoption and sustained use of such styles frequently seen in contemporary British and American society. Rawles (1978) accentuates the proposition that "identifying with the image of White femininity is an exercise in self-hate for Black women" (p.245; cited in Katz and Taylor,1988:214). The Black person's wish to be White, or feeling that there is a lack of balance, may include male as well as females and is purely related to the effects of inequality at the micro and macro levels of society.

By the selection of teaching resources, the society highlights who and what it considers as significant – and by a priori reasoning, by deliberately neglecting to include who and what it considers as insignificant, infinitesimal, irrelevant (Coard,1971:31). South Asian people occupy white-collar positions in the labour market partly because their features are closer to White European characteristics and they tend to be better qualified than African-Caribbean individuals. It is not peculiar, however, for South Asian children to have a false or distorted self-image as being that of wishing they were something other than their true colour because of the British school system (Coard,1971).

The Origin of Humanity

Further research reveals that Africa has a critical function in the ancient history of humanity. It was, in fact, the place where the human race was born (Walker, 2006, 2008; Diop, 1974:262; Suzar, 1999:47; Massey, 2007:599). Diodorus Siculus, a prodigious Greek historian of antiquity, wrote a comprehensive study on world history in the first century BC. These volumes illustrate the shape of historical knowledge in Diodorus' time. The following is an excerpt on human origins:

> Now the Ethiopians [i.e. Africans], as historians relate, were the first of all men and the proofs of this statement, maintain, conceded by practically all men; furthermore, that those who dwell beneath the noon-day sun were, in all likelihood, the first to be generated by the earth, is clear to all; since inasmuch as it was the warmth of the sun which, at the generation of the universe, dried up the earth when it was still wet and impregnated it with life, it is reasonable to suppose that the region which was nearest the sun was the first to bring forth living creatures (quoted in Walker, 2006:130).

Charles Darwin, the Father of Natural Selection theory, penned *The Descent of Man*. This 1871 treatise comprised the first known endeavour to apply natural selection speculation to the origin of humanity. Among the questions Darwin discussed was *On the Birthplace and antiquity of Man*. This selection takes its rise as follows:

> We are naturally led to enquire where was the birthplace of man... In each great region of the world, the living mammals are closely related to the extinct species of the same region. It is therefore probable that Africa was formerly inhabited by extinct apes closely related to the gorilla and chimpanzee; and as these two species are now man's nearest allies, it is somewhat more probable that our early progenitors lived on the African continent than elsewhere (cited in Walker, 2006:130).

The savant Albert Churchward, author of the excellent *Signs and Symbols of Primordial Man*, devised a theory of the beginnings and evolution of humanity and culture in 1910. The investigations of this great English thinker advanced the speculations of Darwin as well as those of his guide, Gerald Massey:

> [R]esearch has led us to bring forward such evidence, as furnished by the records and monuments of the country or nations of the world, where we find the same myths and legends, the same sacred ceremonies and identical religious beliefs, which, when correctly interpreted, proves that only one conclusion can be definitely arrived at, which we have set forth in this work – viz. the first or Palaeolithic man was the Pygmy, who was evolved in Central Africa at the sources of the Nile, or Nile Valley, and that from here all originated and were carried throughout the world (cited in Walker,2006,pp130-131).

In 1961, Robert Ardrey, an American scholar, wrote an important august study on evolution entitled *African Genesis*. This book introduces itself in a wonderful rhythmical cadence where it is clarified that:

> Not in innocence, and not in Asia, was mankind born. The home of our fathers was that African highland reaching north from the Cape to the lakes of the Nile. Here we came about – slowly, ever so slowly – on a sky-swept savannah glowing with menace (cited in Walker, 2006:131).

In his dual volume work called A *Book of the Beginnings*, Gerald Massey assures us that:

> It is suggested that the black race was first, and that equatorial Africa was the birthplace, not only of the human being, but of the original modes and types of expression which have more or less persisted from the beginnings of human utterance to the present time. Inner Africa was the land of the earliest namers of things and acts, who were therefore the creators of nouns and verbs which constituted the main stock of language before the descent into Egypt and the dispersion, on the way to developing the thousand dialects of the world from the one mode and form of speech evolved at starting (Massey, 2007:600).

The archaeological discoveries broadly underpin the ideas posited by Diodorus, Darwin, Churchward, Ardrey, and Massey. The oldest recorded skeletal remains of identifiable modern humanity (homo sapiens sapiens) were unearthed at four distinct places in Africa. Human remains found at Omo in Ethiopia were calculated at 195,000 years old (Walker,2006:131; Walker,2008:24). Skeletons have also been discovered at Laetoli in Tanzania, Klasies River Mouth in South Africa, and Border Cave in South Africa. These discoveries have been calculated at between 130,000 and 110,000 years old (Walker,2006:131). The oldest homo sapiens Kasie's remains unearthed in Asia were calculated at 95,000 years old. The oldest discovered in Europe were calculated at 39,000 years old. Lastly, the oldest discovery in Australasia was calculated at 32,000 years old while it is credible that humans have occupied that continent for 70,000 years. Human skeletons beyond Africa are, thus, much younger than the oldest African discoveries. This evidence buttresses the belief that humanity was founded in Africa and intermittently dispersed over the globe.

All of the discoveries discussed thus far, among which are the Asian, the European, and the Australasian discoveries, were of the Negroid type (Walker,2006:131). The oldest recorded skeletons of non-Negroes that have to date been unearthed include the Cro-Magnon remains discovered in both southern France and the Caucasus province of Russia. These discoveries, certain of which are Caucasians or anyway ancestors of Caucasians, have been calculated at 20,000 years old. The oldest recorded remains of the Mongolian type (Chinese, Japanese, Malaysian, etc.) are even younger (Walker,2006:131)

In 1974, a noteworthy fossil was found in Ethiopia alongside the shores of the Awash River. The collection of bones was of a prehistoric ancestress of humanity akin to a species labelled Australopithecus afarensis. Her posture was determined as upright-walking, measuring under four feet tall, and weighing in at 60 pounds. She incorporated a comparatively small brain and inherited skull features that could be likened to an ape. Her legs, pelvis and teeth, nonetheless, were much more approaching a modern human. Calculated at 3.5 million years, the find suggested that the ancestry that produced humans stretched back over a greater expanse of time than previously thought. What nomenclature should we adopt in the case of this ancestress? Professor Donald Johanson of the US Institute of Human Origins suggested we call her 'Lucy'. Because the discovery took place in Ethiopia, however, others think it more appropriate that she be given an African name. Ethiopians name her 'Dinquinesh' which means 'thou art wonderful' (Walker,2006:73).

During the 1980s, scholars, under the leadership of Rebecca Cann of the University of Berkeley, carried out pioneering work with contemporary human DNA. Their conclusions, found in a 1987 issue of Nature magazine, indicated that all contemporary humans have an ancestral line traceable to a single female forebear. Her thinking is an instance of monogenesis – the notion that all human groups derive from the same parent population. Professor Cann's paper was entitled *Mitochondrial DNA and human evolution*. The contents of the abstract reveal and disclose the following news item:

> Mitochondrial DNAs from 147 people, drawn from five geographic populations, have been analysed by restriction mapping. All these mitochondrial DNAs stem from one woman who is postulated to have lived about 200,000 years ago, probably in Africa (cited in Walker, 2006:73).

Dr Cann reached conclusions on the way in which her team's findings ought to be viewed on account of the fossil data information:

> We infer ... that Africa is a likely source of the human mitochondrial gene pool ... Our tentative interpretation...fits with one view of the fossil record: that the transformation of archaic to anatomically modern forms of homo sapiens [i.e., homo sapiens sapiens] occurred first in Africa ... and that all present-day humans are descendants of that African population (quoted in Walker, 2006:73).

Newsweek, the universally read weekly journal, proved highly effective in popularising the new DNA research founded at the University of Berkeley. Regarding the African ancestress, they edify us thus:

> Scientists are calling her Eve, but reluctantly. The name evokes too many wrong images – the weak-willed figure in Genesis, the milk-skinned beauty in Renaissance art, the voluptuary gardener in "Paradise Lost" who was all "softness" and "meek surrender" and waist-length "gold tresses". The scientists' Eve – subject of one of the most provocative anthropological theories in a decade – was more likely a dark-haired, black-skinned woman, roaming a hot savanna in search of food (quoted in Walker, 2006:74).

In the UK, the time-honoured Conservative newspaper, the Daily Mail, made these research findings part of the consciousness of their readership. They also perused *River Out of Eden*, a new tome on the theme by Oxford University professor Richard Dawkins:

> Just imagine this: you, me and every man, woman and child who walks the Earth is descended from the same African woman. Genesis gave us a version of the story with the Garden of Eden, as do most religious and tribal legends. But what if the existence of a shared ancestral mother could be scientifically proven, a matter of fact rather than faith? ...In his new book, River Out of Eden, the zoologist Richard Dawkins, author of The Selfish Gene, sets out to achieve this mind-boggling goal. His compelling conclusions are rooted in Darwin's theory of natural selection. Dawkins does not just content himself with taking us, step by step, back to our common ancestor; he goes much further, giving her an identity. She was a [B]lack woman who lived a quarter of a million years ago and we can trace our way back to her only through the female line (quoted in Walker, 2006:74).

The suggestion has been forwarded that *homo sapiens sapiens* developed from earlier hominid types in East Africa extending across an estimated time span of five million years (Walker, 2006:133). New research is even now beginning to question this position. Certain quarters claim that hominid remains stretching back seven million years were excavated in the Sahara. We therefore call on the reader to recognize that new discoveries will instantly make the archaeological material put forward herein out of date. Furthermore, each discovery will spark discursive struggles concerning whether the hominid exhibited is in fact a human forebear or an evolutionary blind alley. No matter which alternative, the main point remains ineluctably in place. The roots of humanity's family tree are African in origin and the forebears of humanity are equally of African origin. The details alone will change as fresh discoveries are uncovered and discussed.

According to the literature, humanity, which was Black African from the very beginning, evolved and passed through various stages of development, the details of which are recounted by Robin Walker (2006) and Cheikh Anta Diop (1974) confirms the evolution theory as does Gerald Massey (2007). The evolutionary type *homo erectus* emerged about 1.7 million years ago. Of the ancestors of humanity, these were the first to travel outside Africa's boundaries. Skeletal remains of them were uncovered in Asia, exemplified by Java Man and Peking Man. Those that belonged to this species most closely look like modern humans. The tallest among them measured six feet in height. While smaller than contemporary human skulls, there is a degree of overlap in size with the not so large contemporary skulls. The principal difference was that homo erectus skulls were lower, flatter, and the brow-ridges were more prominent. As regards their culture, they were first to mastermind fire and were advanced in the art of toolmaking. In addition, the consensus of thought vouches for them as having been forebears of the contemporary human type that came after them about 195,000 years ago (or 200,000 years ago where DNA evidence is concerned) (Walker,2006:134).

The White people of Europe came forth about 20,000 years ago. They were derived from African migrants to Europe who accessed the continent 39,000 years ago. These migrants, named Grimaldis or Cro-magnons in textbooks, left an important civilizing influence generally accepted as the Aurignacian Culture. Mr Legrand Clegg, a noted feature writer to the

Journal of African Civilizations, educates us on the significance of the African migration:

> One can state without exaggeration that the Grimaldis [referring to the early Africans] brought "civilization", such as it was, from prehistoric Africa to prehistoric Europe. Their invention of sculpting and their general contribution to the field of art were universally recognized by scientists until the modern Grimaldi "blackout", which occurred because of the need of some Western authorities to deny "the area over which [N]egroids were scattered on the face of the globe". In addition to their invention of pendants, stone implements, certain styles of dress, an advanced symbol system, and perhaps even musical instruments, the Grimaldi were undoubtedly the first homo sapiens to bury their dead and they may have introduced to the world the use of the bow (quoted in Walker, 2006:134).

The African migration can be evinced through the early art from Europe. This early art, in practically all instances, portrayed individuals that were not dissimilar to the Bushman and Hottentots. These are the Black African indigenous groups from south-western Africa who are more accurately called Khoisan (Walker, 2006:134).

Artwork from this early social period is largely thinly distributed. A mere twenty pieces have survived to the present – fifteen portraying females and five portraying males. The females are manifestly characterized as fat, steatopygous (i.e., possess large buttocks), and with peppercorn hair. Professor Ernest Albert Hooton, a Harvard University anthropologist working in the first half of the twentieth century, stated that: "It is interesting to note that the clearest cases of steatopygia occur in the representatives of females from the Aurignacian period of the European cave-cultures and among the modern Bushman-Hottentots [i.e., Black South-West Africans]" (Walker, 2006:75). Dr Charles Finch, a leading scholar of our times, notes that:

> These figurines are almost certainly mother figures modelled on the African Grimaldi woman, the standard-bearer of Aurignacian culture in

Europe. In non-Western traditional cultures, particularly in Africa, obesity is often the mark of beauty and whenever an obese female is figuratively represented, she is invariably a mother figure (Finch, 1999:61).

It is common knowledge that a small section of all the world's population is affected by albinism. Present among these early Black migrants were small numbers of albinos who, over an interval of thousands of years of severe climatic pressure, would slowly have become the largest group in Europe. The continuum of skin intensity among albinos, the hair colours, and finally the eye colours, correlate well with those of present Europeans. As Dr Charles Finch clarifies, "Thus, a mutation, deleterious in one environment, confers a distinct advantage in another and swiftly propagates for that reason" (Finch,1999:35). In closing his analysis, Dr Finch advances:

> that the Homo sapiens sapiens population that survived the last glaciation… was largely a group of albinoids who were better adapted to the ecology than their darker relatives who had originally colonized the area. These latter were gradually replaced by albinoids, though small groups of African aboriginal types long persisted on the North Atlantic seaboard because of the availability of Vitamin D-rich salt-water fish (Finch,1999:35).

Apart from White skin colour, further traits concomitant with Caucasians like lank hair and narrow facial features, came about to fit with the environment. Dr Finch set out how this operated:

> Eighty-five per cent of the heat loss from the human body comes from the head and face. In equatorial Africa, the kinky, and particularly the peppercorn, hair of the early human types would expose more of the scalp to the atmosphere and so promote heat loss. The typical Negroid broad nose and flaring nostrils would enhance the loss of moisture, and therefore heat, during respiration. The thick Negroid lips would increase the surface area of the face and further facilitate heat loss. Bodily leanness, so characteristic of the East African Nilotic types,

would also promote heat loss. Among Caucasians of the frigid north, by contrast, body heat would have to be conserved. The characteristic Caucasian narrow nose and thin lips, by reducing surface area, would help preserve heat. The narrowed nostrils would also aid in warming inspired air. Caucasian straight hair, falling down on the back of the neck, would help preserve heat in the head and neck region. The tendency in the male Caucasian to have more profuse body hair may have also been an aid to heat preservation on the hunt away from his campfires. We have already noted that hominids, like other warm-blooded animals, are regulated by the effects of Gloger's Law, which states that the closer an animal is to the equator, the darker his coat; the closer to the Arctic Circle, the whiter his coat. The polar bear, the arctic fox, and the snowshoe rabbit are all examples of winterized white-coated Arctic animals who illustrate Gloger's Law. The Caucasian phenotype among Homo sapiens also follows it (Finch,1999:36).

The Mongolian peoples of Asia (the Chinese, Japanese, Malaysian, etc.) probably emerged as a result of miscegenation between Black and White (Walker, 2006:136). The likeness in appearance of the Mongolian peoples to certain of the indigenous southern African Negroes (the so-called Bushman or Hottentot type) is somewhat dramatic. Both groups are low on body hair, short in stature and with epicanthic folds over their eyes, probably the single most generally accepted stereotype of the Mongolian face. The Japanese scholar Dr Nobuo Takano devised a contention that the South African strain of Negro crossbred with Europeans to bring forth the Mongolian strain. Considering that "Bushmen and Hottentots" were accessing and exploring prehistoric Europe, as confirmed by the Aurignacian art, it is not unlikely that they also settled in Asia. The union with the newly emerged Caucasian reduced the shade of the people and straightened their hair. This must have happened within the last 20,000 years (Walker, 2006:134). A number of these peoples, several thousand years on, migrated from Asia to America crossing the Bering Strait. They came to be the first humans to live in North, South and Central America –

the Native Americans. Therefore, the indigenous peoples of the Americas, and the Mongolians, are from the same stock.

In all other parts of the planet where there were neither Caucasians nor Mongolians, the populations remained entirely Negro. This was so of prehistoric western Asia, southern Asia, Australasia, and also Africa. Moreover, a surviving trace of these early Negro inhabitants is still extant this contemporary day in Asia and Australasia. Making reference to the wide dispersal of the Blacks in prehistoric years, Professor Chancellor Williams of Howard University asserts that:

> This fact alone indicates the great tasks of future scholarship on the real history of the race… How do we explain such a large population of Blacks in Southern China, powerful enough to form a kingdom of their own? Or the black people of Formosa, Australia, the Malay Peninsula, Indo-China, the Andaman and numerous other islands? The heavy concentration of Africans in India [sic] … opens still another field for investigation … The African population in Palestine, Arabia and Mesopotamia [i.e., Iraq] are better known although the many centuries of Black rule over Palestine, South Arabia, and in Mesopotamia should be studied and elaborated in more detail. All of this will call for a new type of scholarship, a scholarship without any other mission than the discovery of truth (Walker, 2006:137).

The above data has met with many and various objections. In Europe and North America, many people are raised on the Genesis narrative of human origins from the Book of Books. Despite today's levels of awareness, the Bible story feeds and supplies the 'common sense idea' that the Middle East was the site of humanity's beginnings, which was, no doubt, where the apocryphal Garden of Eden was ostensibly located. Also, ideas drawn from the book of Genesis, in particular the Semitic race and the Hamitic race, still informs modern linguistics (Walker, 2006:137). In 1650, the Irish cleric, Archbishop James Ussher, intimated that the creation of the world took place in 4004 BC, grounding his conclusion on a reading of the *Holy Bible*. A number of years later, Dr John Lightfoot, a former Vice-Chancellor of Cambridge University, provided even greater accuracy. He advanced that the creation occurred on 23 October 4004 BC at 9 AM! (Walker, 2006:137).

More significant, however, is the opposition from a school of anthropological thought known as Polycentrism. This school, while conflicting with each other over the details, acquiesce that the human race has various disparate origins, not just a single one. Certain nineteenth-century scholars were of the opinion that 'the Africans evolved from the gorilla, the Europeans from the orang-utan' (Walker,2006:137). This detritus won over no one, not even the most conservative, and it was time to start all over again with a new approach. In the 1930s, Franz Weidenreich, himself a convert of racism, put forward a more nuanced understanding of the nineteenth-century system of ideas. Approximately thirty years later, his student, Professor Carleton Coon, was able to gain favour for Weidenreich's ideas. Professor Milford H. Wolpoff, of Michigan University, revised Coon's ideas into a theory called multiregional evolution. This concept proposes that the diverse human groups in the world, in particular Africans, East Asians, Europeans, Australo-melanesians (i.e., Black people of Asia and Australia), Mongolians, etc., each developed distinctly from diverse man-like apes. Herein the logic follows that the racial diversity between peoples is greater than initially apparent because each race included a distinct evolution.

To demonstrate Professor Wolpoff's ideas, it is edifying to take as an example the development of the Europeans. It has already been highlighted that a number of homo erectus ventured outside of Africa's boundaries around 500,000 years ago and made extensive explorations of the world. In Europe, certain of these developed into Swanscombe Man in Britain, and Steinheim Man in Germany, both about 300,000 years ago. Neanderthal Man succeeded these types about 80,000 years ago and this type, it was maintained, developed into the modern European. Accordingly, Wolpoff and his acolytes can inculcate that Europeans are not from the same lineage as anatomically modern Africans but instead from Neanderthal Man (Walker,2006:138).

This hypothesis, however, does not hold any amount of water. Firstly, Walker (2006) argues, the spread of ancient *homo sapiens sapiens* remains found around the globe show that there is a paucity of Caucasian remains comparable to 195,000 years old. The known facts indicate that the earliest Caucasian skeletons, even when the most generous dates are applied, are merely 20,000 years old. Although unexpected in Europe, there are older remnants dated at 39,000 years, but these we know as Negroes, not Caucasians. Secondly, he maintains, African *homo sapiens sapiens*, emerging some 195,000 years ago, is far more ancient than Europe's Neanderthal Man, emerging a mere 80,000 years ago. According to Walker (2006), recent attempts have been made to bring Swanscombe Man and Steinheim Man into line as Neanderthals. In regard to this, Walker (2006) further asserts his view that this is false information designed to trick the unsuspecting into thinking that the Neanderthals are far older than modern humanity, whereas actually, they are younger. Finally, Walker (2006) holds up research from the University of Munich that scotched the Wolpoff School claims. A Washington Post staff columnist adequately set out this data information as follows:

> Neanderthal – the brawny enigmas who mysteriously disappeared 30,000 years ago after coexisting with modern humans in Europe for tens of thousands of years were not close relatives or even ancestral forms of existing people, a new study has found. Instead, unprecedented DNA tests on a famous Neanderthal skeleton indicate that the creatures were almost certainly a separate species that contributed little, and probably nothing, to the present human gene pool. The finding, by veteran ancient DNA researcher Svante Paabo of Munich and colleagues, could help bring down the curtain on one of the longest-running and feud-prone disputes in anthropology; whether Neanderthals disappeared after nearly 300,000 years [sic] because they evolved gradually into modern humans, or whether they were abruptly superseded by an evolutionary upstart that left Africa only a few dozen millennia ago and from which all people now alive are descended (Walker, 2006:138).

The article closes with the following information:

> Although the recent out-of-Africa hypothesis is now the predominant theory among experts, the debate will continue, and Paabo's lab is looking for other DNA sequences. Meanwhile, DNA specialist Tomas Lindahl of Britain's Imperial Cancer Research Fund observes in a companion article in Cell: "the present recovery... represents a landmark discovery, which is arguably the greatest achievement so far in the field of ancient DNA research" (Walker,2006:139).

Early Human Culture

The emergence of a revolution in human culture, from hunting and gathering to farming, took place earlier than 10,000 years ago (Sertima,1991:58). Professor Fred Wendorf et al determined that between 17,000 and 18,500 years ago – while ice continued to grip much of Europe – Africans were the first to raise crops. They did it in the floodplains of the Nile, now encompassing Egypt's Western Desert region. The people of Wadi Kubbaniya established crops of wheat, barley, capers, dates, lentils, legumes and chickpeas. In addition to what was left of various crops – principally seeds – were found grindstone, milling stones, engraving burins, hide scrapers, mortars and pestles and cutting blades. In ancient times, the level of the Nile was higher than at present. Each year before the Aswan Dam was established, the Nile would burst its banks, flooding into the Wadi Kubbaniya region and depositing rich silt. As the overflow of water ebbed away, catfish were left without any escape route from the ponds that were due to depressions. Seeing that a great deal of ash and charcoal were found, it appears that the shelf life of fish was prolonged by smoking (Sertima,1991:58).

Once the fish stocks were exhausted, the people took full advantage of the conditions to plant crops. Following the planting, there was a return to hunter-gathering activity, that is, if the recovered bones were anything to go by. The Kubbaniya people hunted wild cattle, hartebeest and the odd hippo. When December or January was upon them, this was the season for gathering in the crops. The cereals as well as perhaps the chickpeas were ground to provide flour. Gazelles were the staple food source of the people after harvest. Also procured by hunting were ducks, wild game and geese. In the summer months, the river would rise and overflow again. As the waters receded, the annual cycle would begin again (Sertima,1991:61).

In 1980, Dr Charles Nelson, an anthropologist at the University of Massachusetts, announced through the organ of the *New York Times* news of a significant phenomenon (Sertima,1991:20). Empirical evidence suggests that Africans were domesticating cattle 15,000 years ago. Dr Nelson's colleagues detected teeth and cattle bones ranging over a small area indicating that the animals were domesticated. If the cattle were wild, the remains would have been spread much further over a larger area (Walker,2006:141). And evidence indicates that tsetse flies would have wiped out any wild cattle. The dominion territory where the cattle remains were found was generally not plagued by flies, thus safeguarding them from this peril. Dr Nelson found the cattle bones at three places in the Lukenya Hill District of the Kenyan highlands. The territory was about 25 miles from Nairobi (Sertima,1991, pp.65-6). Bayard Webster, in a piece intended for the *New York Times*, explained Dr Nelson's take on the outstanding nature of these two remarkable archaeological discoveries – agriculture and animal husbandry:

> He said that such findings suggest that many of the elements necessary for the development of civilization – agriculture and animal husbandry and their accompanying technologies – may have originated in surrounding areas and were exported to the Middle East through trade and cultural diffusion of information and ideas (Sertima, 1991:65).

The earliest known human culture was established in Katanda, a province in north-eastern Zaire (now Congo). Alison Brooks of George Washington University and John Yellen of the National Science Foundation encountered the find in 1988 (Walker,2006:139). From a site in the Congo region, they recovered a finely crafted set of harpoon points, all carefully polished and barbed. Furthermore, a tool was uncovered, of comparable quality, considered to be a dagger. The foregoing pointed to there being an early fishing-based way of life. The Katanda people coordinated annual fishing trips during the rainy seasons. They netted catfish. "What's exciting is that we're seeing strategic planning for subsistence by people who lived so long ago," says Brooks. "Humans in Africa invented sophisticated [tool] technologies long before their European counterparts, who have often been credited with initiating modern culture" (Walker,2006:139). At first, Brooks and Yellen calculated the artefacts at 70,000 years old. Then, they reviewed the dating of the Katanda way of life to 90,000 years old (Walker,2006:139).

The ancients made other significant strides forward that have become knowledge. In 1964, a hematite mine was encountered in Swaziland at Bomvu Ridge in the Ngwenya mountain range (Walker,2006:139). The mining industry, quite by chance, first encountered the find. Professor Raymond Dart, a scholar at the University of Witwatersrand in Johannesburg, made a thorough search of the site. His colleagues found a large collection of ancient mining tools in addition to tunnels and adits. This intimated that early humanity in this region had been involved in systematic mining. Over time, 300,000 artefacts were found together with thousands of stone-made tools. Adrian Boshier, an archaeologist assigned to the site, calculated the mine to an astonishing 43,200 years old, within an error margin of plus or minus 1,600 years. The earliest miners dug for a resistant material called specularite. This is a form of hematite, an iron-bearing ore. Specularite occurs in two separate colours – red and black. It was pressed into use as a body dye and a cosmetic, and may also have found use in funeral rituals (Walker,2006:139).

Dr Raymond Dart is linked with another important find. In the first half of the twentieth century, his archaeological team found a manganese mine at Chowa in Zambia. They discovered thousands of early manganese tools, in particular grindstones, hammers, choppers, wedges, chisels and axes. The Chowa mine was found to be 28,000 years old. The manganese may have been used as a cosmetic on account of the blackish hue of its ore. Another use to which it was put is tool-making.

Chapter 1: Tracing Black Aspiration and Illuminating Achievement

The earliest evidence of any arithmetic system we have on record is made manifest in the Ishango bone. It is a tool handle with notches arranged in certain formations and a piece of quartz inserted in a narrow hollow in its head. Jean de Heinzelin, a Belgian archaeologist representing the Royal Institute of the Natural Sciences, discovered it in the late 1950s. Its every detail has been studiously covered by both its discoverer, Jean de Heinzelin, and the archaeologist Alexander Marshack. After de Heinzelin unearthed the hoard of extremely old tools at Ishango in Congo near Lake Edward and encountered the bone, he was instantly taken by the not uninteresting formation of horizontal notches carved into it. He realized straight away that these notches were neither by chance nor by accident, but were symbolic of a number system. The notches were organized in three ascending columns on the artefact - two columns cover one side and a single column covers the reverse side. The single column of closely approximated notches was organized in the following order from the top downward: 3-6, 4-8, 10, 5-5, 7 displaying a pairing of 3-6, 4-8, 5-5. Notches appearing in pairs like these seemed, in de Heinzelin's view, to have been associated with the practice of addition and multiplication by doubling.

On the counterpart of the bone, two columns are visible, one showing a number pattern arrangement from the top downward of 11, 21, 19, 9. In de Heinzelin's opinion, this arrangement was brought about by the subsequent operations: 10+1, 20+1, 20-1, 10-1. On the obverse vertical edge of the self-same side, the arrangement from the top read 11, 13, 17, 19. This arrangement appears to represent each and every prime number between 10 and 20. De Heinzelin's assessment of the bone suggests that the artefact could well have belonged to a people who understood a system of numbers based on ten, (decimal) system, and who possessed some awareness of prime numbers, and multiplication by doubling. Also, in two of the columns, the sum total arrived at after addition is sixty, indicating that the ancient East African people were *au fait* with a number system based on sixty, widely regarded to have been devised earlier by the Babylonians. The understanding of base 60 which Dr Finch propounded is, *en passant*, the mathematical linchpin upon which modern-day timepieces are based. To illustrate the point, on a modern timepiece 60 seconds =1 minute, and 60 minutes = 1 hour.

Experts are not in universal agreement over the markings on the Ishango bone. Alexander Marshack, who has placed the notches on the artefact under close microscopic scrutiny, argues:

> It represents a notational and counting system, serving to accumulate groups of marks made by different points and apparently engraved at different times. Analysis of the microscopic data shows no indication of a counting by fives and tens but that the groups of marks vary irregularly in amount. That this is an early system of notational counting is clear; however, this does not necessarily imply a modern arithmetic numerical system. I have tracked the origins of such early notational systems back to the Upper Paleolithic cultures of about 30,000 B.C. (Cited in Sertima,1991:111).

In The Roots of Civilization, Mr Marshack offers his assessment:

> When I examined this tiny petrified bone at the Musée d'Histoire Naturelle in Brussels, I found that the engraving, as nearly as microscopic examination could differentiate the deteriorated markings, was made by thirty-nine different points and was notational. It seemed more clearly than before, to be lunar (Cited in Sertima, 1991:112).

De Heinzelin initially dated the age of the Ishango artefacts at 8,500 years, transporting them back to 6,500 B.C., consequently classing the culture as "Mesolithic". However, more sensitive radiocarbon dating techniques have been applied to the site by Alison Brooks and has called attention to a rethink over the age of Ishango to 25,000 years, catapulting it back to 23,000 B.C. This places Ishango in the Upper Palaeolithic period, forcing us to profoundly overhaul our outlook on when and where humanity first immersed himself or herself in formal scholarly, indeed "scientific", inquiry. "Upper Palaeolithic proto-mathematics and calendars in East Africa are consistent with the Upper Palaeolithic evidence (41,000 to 28,000 B.C.) for systematic iron ore mining in south-east Africa, revealing the presence of a "protoscience" and a "prototechnology" in Africa older than 20,000 years" (Finch, 2007, pp. 56-7). This modus vivendi savoire-faire, launching Africa on the threshold of social organisation tens of thousands of years anterior to our wildest imaginings, again depicts Africa as the birthplace of techniques that slowly percolated to other global territories (Finch,2007:57).

Another marker of cultural progress relates to a mummy discovered in southwestern Libya. Approximately five decades have passed since the finding of a mummified infant under the Uan Muhuggiag rock shelter. The infant was committed to the ground in the fetal position and mummification was conducted using a level of sophistication that ultimately suggested centuries in its coming of age. The technique is older than any of Ancient Egypt's earliest mummies by a minimum of 1,000 years. There are questions surrounding carbon dating but the mummy may date from 7438 (+/-220) BC at the earliest, to 3500 BC at the latest (Walker,2006:142). The significance of the mummy along with the culture that spawned it is not lost on Dr Savino di Lernia of the University of Rome. He is of the opinion that historically, large parts of Africa shared an overarching culture that encircled the regions now known as Mali, Sudan, Algeria, Niger, Chad, Libya and Egypt before this landmass became a desert. The rock art, as such, shows elephants, lions, crocodiles, giraffes and hippopotami – most of these animals, if not for savannah regions, would not survive. A selection of the earliest pottery connected with this culture is traced to around 7000 BC. Within this overarching culture, cattle bore a mythical and sacramental significance. The building of circular temples served for the sacrifice of cattle. Also, cattle feature in around 50% of the rock art. And there were religious ceremonies where humans wore jackal-headed masks portrayed in the rock art. The tendency was also for humans to be buried in the fetal position. At first, Italian archaeologists considered that this way of life was unique to Libya however French archaeologists showed a similar way of life obtained in Niger 500 miles southwards. Dr Joann Fletcher, the eminent English Egyptologist, is of the view that the mummification handling process of this culture fed into later Egyptian mummification. In addition, she believes that its cattle veneration fed into Egyptian religion's thinking of a later era. Lastly, she thinks that its jackal mask ceremonies fed into the Egyptian idea of Anubis, the god of embalming – shown to represent a jackal in Egyptian art. Furthermore, according to Walker (2006), archaeological evidence can be evinced that Uan Muhuggiag-decorated pottery subsequently emerged in the southern Nile Valley area. Dr di Lernia indicates that the Uan Muhuggiag people moved to the Nile Valley after the region turned to desert and they became an essential component of the Ancient Egyptian way of life. Dr Fletcher briefly outlines the significance of these findings accordingly:

> I find it quite extraordinary that this central Saharan civilisation shows all the features we generally associate with later Egyptian pharaonic culture and mummification is a prime example. There are definite links between the two cultures (Walker, 2006:142).

The building of the Great Sphinx of Giza near Egypt's capital Cairo signifies a further marker of cultural progress. One of the great monuments of early African technology, this mighty structure was constructed with the head of a man together with the body of a lion. To begin with, the builders shaped the head and the front part. Time was allowed to lapse before the builders fashioned the body, in particular the back part. As a monument of great historical interest, an important question it raised was: How ancient antiquity is it?

In October 1991, Professor Robert Schoch, a geologist from Boston University, showed that the Sphinx was crafted between 7000 BC and 5000 BC, dates that he felt were conservative. He reached this conclusion by inspecting how much erosion rainwater had caused to the body of the statue. Egypt is an arid country where there has been very sparse precipitation for thousands of years. The Sphinx, however, shows signs of partial disfigurement through rainwear. Dr Schoch took it that the rain damage could only have taken place many thousands of years ago when Egypt underwent frequent rainfall. Collaborating with the seismologist, Thomas Dobecki, Professor Schoch was able to reach solid but conservative age ranges for the construction of the edifice (Finch,2007, pp.18-23). How this data was received in Egyptological cohorts, however, was not favourable. On the pages of the *International Herald Tribune* of 25 October 1991, we read the subsequent lines:

> The research findings were announced Wednesday at the annual meeting of the Geological Society of America in San Diego. They immediately drew fire from Mark Lehner, an Egyptologist at the University of Chicago who is a leading expert on the Sphinx (Walker,2006:143).

To date, Professor Lehner's emotional paroxysm has become the common reaction to this data by Egyptologists whereas no reliable evidence to the contrary has in any instance been lodged by them in dispute of Professor Schoch's findings. Dr Schoch's dating consequently stands unchallenged. Baron D.V. Denon, a French traveller, made a noted sketch on the location of this statue in 1798 AD. He also remarked upon it: "The character is African... the lips are thick...Art must have been at a high pitch when this monument was executed" (Walker,2006:143). African civilisation, the earliest in world history, was set in stone with the construction of this design and artistic wonder some 7,000 years ago. Civilisation was a full 1,000 years in the making in Asia and 4,000 years in the making in mainland Europe.

Mr Peter Eckler, an American publisher, aptly summarised the significance of this remarkable feat. In 1890 he released an English language version of *The Ruins or Meditations on the Revolutions of Empires and the Law of Nature,* by Count De Volney, one of the marvels of enlightenment literature. In the publisher's preface, Mr Eckler stated that:

> We are in reality indebted to the ancient Ethiopians, to the fervid imagination of the persecuted and despised [N]egro, for various religious systems now so highly revered by the different branches of both the Semitic and Aryan races. This fact, which is so frequently referred to in Mr. Volney's writings ... may even suggest a solution to

the secret so long concealed beneath the flat nose, thick lips, and [N]egro features of the Egyptian Sphinx (Cited in Walker, 2006:145).

Count De Volney himself wrote a superb outline of the complex changes that humankind traversed on the long journey from savagery to civilisation. We pass the rubric of the last word on this theme entirely over to him:

Formed naked in body and in mind, man at first found himself thrown, as it were by chance, on a rough and savage land: an orphan, abandoned by the unknown power which had produced him ... Like to other animals, without experience of the past, without foresight of the future, he wandered in the bosom of the forest, guided only and governed by the affections of his nature. By the pain of hunger, he was led to seek food and provide for his subsistence; by the inclemency of the air, he was urged to cover his body, and he made him clothes; by the attraction of a powerful pleasure, he approached a being like himself, and he perpetuated his kind. Thus, the impressions which he received from every object awakening his faculties, developed by degrees his understanding, and began to instruct his profound ignorance: his wants excited industry, dangers formed his courage; he learned to distinguish useful from noxious plants, to combat the elements, to seize his prey, to defend his life; and thus, he alleviated its miseries. Thus self-love, aversion to pain, the desire of happiness, were the simple and powerful excitements which drew man from the savage and barbarous condition in which nature had placed him ... Wandering in the woods and on the banks of rivers in pursuit of game and fish, the first men, beset with dangers, assailed by enemies, tormented by hunger, by reptiles, by ravenous beasts, felt their own individual weakness; and, urged by a common need of safety, and a reciprocal sentiment of like evils, they united their resources and their strength; and when one incurred a danger, many aided and succored him; when one wanted subsistence, another shared his food with him. Thus, men associated to secure their existence, to augment their powers, to protect their enjoyments; and self-love thus became the principle of society ... And men, aiding one another, seized the nimble goat, the timid sheep; they tamed the patient camel, the fierce bull, and the impetuous horse ... When, therefore, men could pass long days in leisure, and in communication of their thoughts, they began to contemplate the earth, the heavens, and their own existence, as objects of curiosity and reflection; they remarked the course of the seasons, the action of the elements, the properties of fruit and plants; and applied their thoughts to the multiplication of their enjoyments. And in some countries, having observed that certain seeds contained wholesome nourishment in a small volume, convenient for transportation and preservation, they imitated the process of nature; they confided to the earth rice, barley and corn which multiplied to the full measure of their hope; and having found the means of obtaining, within a small compass and without removal, plentiful subsistence and durable stores, they established themselves in fixed habitations; they built houses, villages and towns; and formed societies and nations (Cited in Walker, 2006, pp.145-146).

Summary and Conclusion

It is not too difficult to see the assault that African-Caribbean and South Asian aspirations came under as a result of immigration legislation aimed at people like themselves, yet nearly two-thirds of 'immigrants' were White, but just to recapitulate and reiterate.

British Government policy responses to mass immigration was a response to people of a different skin colour and culture coming to these shores. That is to say, the debate initiated and aroused by the African-Caribbean and South Asian presence called attention to concerns regarding race relations, 'integration' and 'assimilation', and it was about managing and controlling a growing number of non-White people. It is, at this stage, important to look closely at the notion of integration. Does 'integration' denote a process through which subject racial groups come to acquiesce as above board the authority and privilege of the White majority in society? Or does integration mean a situation where groups come together culturally and economically by way of a process of adaptation, strife or competition? Maybe it is possible that 'integration', if there is a circumstance in which it occurs at all, involves a coalescence of each of these processes (Bilton et al,1989:140). Maybe African-Caribbean and South Asian groups should accept that it is a 'White man's Country' but, integration should mean that we can enjoy the same freedoms as Whites currently do, in order that peace and unity can stand a chance.

White people entering this country did not raise the same concerns and were therefore accepted as desirable and of a good stock, unlike African-Caribbean and South Asian people. The increasingly restrictive policy responses to mass immigration caused by mass public resentment operated to make African-Caribbean and South Asian people feel unwanted, unwelcome and second-class citizens to boot. This may have contributed to African-Caribbean and South Asian people lowering their expectations of life in Britain, whereas they came with quite high hopes. Moreover, it is not improbable that the chief source of inequality – unfavourable life-chances – is likely to give rise to resignation instead of aspirations for status elevation among Blacks; where this acceptance occurs, the true degree of the structural limitations on Black life-chances continues to be hidden (Bilton et al,1989:140). On the contrary, research shows that whether Black people are resigned to disadvantageous life-chances or not, this does not mean that the true degree of the structural limitations on Black life-chances remains hidden because it does not; the true picture cannot be any clearer than that the true degree of the structural limitations on Black life-chances is massive to substantial or according to other research, large in extent (Smith,1977; Mac an Ghaill,1988). However, it is so well hidden that many people are not aware of the existence of such historical research documents.

Both the Conservative and Labour Parties surrendered to racism over principle because political expediency was at stake and African-Caribbean and South Asian people were classified as 'problems'. That African-Caribbean and South Asian people were also seen as a 'threat' to the British way of life just adds to the general antagonism and unreasonable hostility shown towards African-Caribbean and South Asian people in Britain, and could ironically be viewed by people of colour as grist to the mill. Also, the increasingly restrictive immigration laws served to undermine, to a greater extent, the welfare and security of this country's African-Caribbean and South Asian populations. Schools play their part in creating an impact against individuals of colour, but more frequently, against African-Caribbean pupils' aspirations, and we shall consider in the next chapter the role they play. British government policy responses to mass immigration saw racism directly enshrined in British law.

Superior versus inferior 'races' do not exist in reality but they are socially constructed. Some might argue that the freedoms enjoyed by Whites are precisely and directly because their descendants have fought in world wars and other conflicts around the world. Yet, although African-Caribbean and South Asian people have been called upon for four centuries to assist Britain in campaigns of war and have fought and died for this country, their descendants are denied the same freedoms and humanity as Whites today.

First to occupy and populate the planet was Black African homo sapiens sapiens and they were the first to establish a civilization; civilization was 1,000 years in the making in Asia and 4,000 years in the making in mainland Europe, succeeding this first and oldest recorded event. The fact that Black African individuals were the first on the face of the earth suggests that all other types of human beings derive from African stock.

Chapter 3: The Education System

The expectations, assumptions and practices which fail young Black people

The ultimate effect of adverse schooling outcomes, no doubt, is exclusion from school but the effects of school exclusion protrude significantly beyond the arena of schooling (Wright, et al,2000) to involve aspirations, unemployment and the likelihood of becoming involved in criminal activity. Although school exclusion is the ultimate effect in the relationship between school and pupil, other effects, and let's call them teacher effects, can tend to lead up to or cause exclusion. This chapter attempts to examine the whole system of teacher effects in school and their impact on Black students of African-Caribbean and South Asian descent. While teacher effects are influential, this does not mean that some pupils are not entirely responsible for temporary or permanent exclusion rates in British schools. Secondly, this chapter explores the policy responses to the Black and minority ethnic presence in British schools.

The growing indication of students being temporarily and permanently excluded from school causes a sense of unease among the public, professional and government sectors (e.g., Social Exclusion Unit 1998)

(Wright et al,2000). Despite the contention that the subject of exclusion is intricate and the problem wide-ranging, what becomes clear is the convergence of the progression of education policies extending from the 1980s and the growing rates of school exclusions. It can be asserted that these categories are closely linked. Therefore, it will be stipulated that each is alternately the cause and the effect of the other.

Education Policy

> Black minorities have frequently been casualties of rules and procedures which may not have been intended to discriminate against them but which, in effect, do so and there is considerable resistance when hitherto taken-for-granted procedures are brought into question (Rattansi, 1992:23; quoted in Wright, Weekes and McGlaughlin, 2000:4).

There is widespread agreement that the rise in exclusions is closely connected to changes in the administration of the education system which emerged in the late 1980s. Much of what literature there is within the sphere of exclusions has centred on connections between this and the development of a 'free market' in education, succeeding the 1988 Education Reform Act (ERA) (Wright et al,2000:4). The literature in question indicates that most of the fundamental tenets laid down in the 1988 ERA, in particular those which pertain to scholastic achievements (the circulation of examination outcomes in school league tables), and parental selectivity (the dictate in schools in the direction of open enrolment), have produced a climate which stresses individualism and competitiveness. In the light of this ethos, some parents and children will find it much easier to compete than others. The 1988 Act recommended radical changes to British education, which had divergent effects on the essential character of exclusions. A major recommendation was the inception of a national curriculum, along with a process of assessing its efficacy, with the aspiration of enhancing the status of British children compared with their European counterparts. In addition, the Act sought to diminish LEA regulation of schools by giving local authority-funded schools the green light to 'opt out', transferring responsibility for money management decisions to separate schools. Further, it proffered the idea of 'parental choice' in the election of schools, initially proposed in the 1981 Education Act, through commending the notion of 'open enrolment' (Wright et al,2000:5). This, consequently, did away with the LEA's ability to impose restrictions on the number of children given access to each school, whilst permitting parents to seek learning opportunities for their children outside the periphery of catchment areas and even local authorities. The conclusion has also been drawn by some researchers and learned experts within the discipline of education, that the ideation of 'parental choice' and 'opting out' plays a role in the production of an education system characterized by racial segregation since they empower some White parents to eschew schools with a perceived roll of more than the desired number of Black pupils.

As much as it may have been problematic to establish the immediate effects of educational policy since the late 1980s in relation to the exclusion of students from secondary schools, it is feasible to outline the differing influences of the 'market system' of education concerning the ways in which children from cultural groups are responded to in the school setting.

Looking at Hayden's (1995) comments concerning the 'quasi-market' system existing within recent education policy, it is feasible to notice the process by which children are constructed as 'marketable' or something divergent in outcome and which could influence their educational careers (Wright et al,2000:5). The 'market' *weltanschauung* within education is predicated upon a need to raise efficiency, cost consciousness and ample utilization of resources. But parents are situated differentially within this consumerist background. Therefore, social divisions of race and class have an effect upon parents' selection of school, and the same applies in reverse. This then influences the overall marketability of children from disparate class and racial contexts. This point becomes highly relevant when we bring to mind that children from working-class and minority ethnic backgrounds come into view disproportionately in exclusion statistics. Not straying from the context in which this contention is set, exclusion has been enforced as a form of control and selection where 'the difficult pupil must either be seen as an object of punishment or a drain on resources' (Cohen et al,1994:2; cited in Wright, Weekes and McGlaughlin,2000:5).

The transformed financial arrangements stemming from Local Management of Schools (LMS) and realized by the 1988 Act, has signified that each school is now responsible for funding professional services for children going through emotional and behavioural difficulties. In light of cost, and the market cultural characteristic spirit of efficiency, the extension of these services may not any longer be thought of as a priority within the majority of schools and, as it transpires, is limited. Therefore, the privations of such children will meet with a shortfall notwithstanding research which has revealed that the problems of children who have learning and/or emotional difficulties not infrequently show themselves in disruptive behaviour.

On account of diminished resources in schools for the nurturing of pupils with behavioural difficulties, and the operationalization of the national curriculum, teaching staff have limits placed on time expended with individual pupils displaying these or other problems inside the classroom. The national curriculum has also compounded the already high incidence of stress among teaching staff, as it decreases flexibility and autonomy existing in teaching and raises the accountability of institutions through the gauging of performance. Seen through this optic, it has affected the net teacher/pupil interplay which again does not produce a climate responsible for the privations of children (Wright et al,2000:6).

The idea of 'choice', which educational policy brought about for parents, became especially problematic for certain groups of parents and children. Choice both attached itself with the marketability of the child, and also had racialized ramifications, e.g., the disproportionate representation of Black pupils in exclusion data. The reality of racialized stereotypes, intersecting with the antagonistic nature of relationships surrounding Black male pupils and white teaching staff is a well-recorded body of evidence (Mac an Ghaill,1988; Sewell,1997; Gillborn,1990;

Pilkington,2003). Consequently, ideation of 'choice' raised concerns in relation to 'choices' extended to Black parents of children who are vulnerable to or at a high susceptibility of being excluded.

A recent piece of education legislation is the Standard and Framework Act 1998 (Wright et al,2000). The key part of this reform is the *raison d'être* to improving education standards, lowering school exclusions and amplifying the participation of parents in children's education. What is more, there has been a review of the open enrolment policy and the grant-maintained schools and city technology allocation. But the marketization of schooling evidently remains, with no change to the local management of schools and the yearly publication of performance tables predicated on national assessment tests (alternatively alluded to as 'league tables').

The Act reflects upon the experiences of minority ethnic children within the British system, in particular as concerns their comparative poor academic performance and their over-representation within the exclusion figures. Despite this, there is a failure to put strategies in place for addressing these issues. Therefore, one commentator has indicated that the cartesian mind has little option but to draw the following conclusion concerning the recent reform: "initiatives relating to effective schools, improving schools, value-adding schools, and all the rest of them, are, for the next five years at least, to be colour-blind, culture-blind, racism-blind' (Richardson, 1998:23, quoted in Wright, Weekes and McGlaughlin,2000:7).

The Social Exclusion Unit (1998) recently produced a report that has established national objectives for the minimization of exclusions: 'that by 2002, there will be a one-third reduction in the number of both permanent and fixed-term exclusions' (Wright et al,2000:7). However, notwithstanding the report's acceptance of the unconscionable exclusion of young people from ethnic minorities, the 'race' component scarcely features in the target set for lowering exclusions. Put differently, the first hitherto national target for lowering exclusions is 'colour-blind'.

By failing to stipulate a specific target for a reduction in the exclusion of Black children, the way is left clear for the situation to persist or even worsen. Previous research suggests that Black children are unlikely to share equally in any improvement, and that by 2002, therefore, we would be in a position where the relative over-representation of Black children has actually grown (Majors, Gillborn and Sewell,1998; cited in Wright, Weekes and McGlaughlin,2000:7).

The significance of 'Race' and other factors
In Exclusion from School

The previous section looked closely at the ways wherein education policies have afforded a context inside which school exclusions have found their own level. The object of this section is to determine how policy interconnects with experience inside the classroom to result in rising exclusion rates. In the process, it explores ethnicity, gender and cultural dimensions within exclusion from school. As already mentioned, statistics show that certain groups of children and adolescents are at a more significantly increased danger of exclusion than others. The research data information suggests that those in disproportionate danger of exclusion are African-Caribbean males of primary and secondary school age category (Wright et al,2000). However, this is not a picture in sharp focus because some LEAs fail to record the ethnic origin of excluded pupils. The disproportionate representation of Black pupils among those excluded from mainstream education is not new (Coard,1971). Recent DFE statistics indicate that boys account for the very large majority of all exclusions (83 per cent of permanent exclusions in 1995-96) (Wright et al,2000). But as part of this grand total, OFSTED and the DFE have demonstrated that African-Caribbean males are 4-5 times more likely to be excluded than their White peers. Even more closely, the present exclusion statistics show that in certain areas, African-Caribbean boys were almost 15 times as likely to be excluded from school as their White classmates. Disruptive and aggressive behaviour patterns were at the forefront among the reasons submitted for the exclusion of young Black people.

More widely, any careful scrutiny of African-Caribbean students in the exclusion process has signified that other minority groups' familiarity with the process has been mirrored in the published work to date. South Asian students have been historically under-represented in the school exclusion figures. Recent numerical data analysis, however, is indicating that exclusions of South Asian students are on the rise in certain local authorities, particularly amid Pakistani boys. A recent exposition in Birmingham for the academic period 1994-95 and 1995-96, attested that African-Caribbean males are unconscionably over-represented in the permanent exclusion figures but also reveals a rise in the permanent exclusion of South Asian students from secondary school, particularly Pakistani males. This buttresses the conclusions of an earlier OFSTED survey which announced that: 'An increasing number of LEAs are aware of, and concerned about, the disproportionate number of minority ethnic pupils, in particular boys of Caribbean and African heritage (but increasingly also boys of Pakistani heritage) being excluded' (OFSTED,1996:27, Cited in Wright, Weekes and McGlaughlin,2000:8).

The uppermost aspect of this tendency in exclusions is the seeming interconnection between culture, ethnicity, gender and inferior social status. Most important to an insight into the reason why some ethnic minority groups appear disproportionately in exclusion figures is an analysis of the institutional processes which give rise to exclusion.

There exists a growing number of research studies that urges that the exclusion of Black students reflects, on one side of the coin, the essential character of teacher-pupil relationships – described by complex, divergent expectations and presuppositions, and on the obverse, Black students' response to how they encounter schooling. Researchers (e.g., Gillborn,1990; Mac an Ghaill,1988; Wright,1992; Sewell,1997) have examined the processes which result in the *ne plus ultra penalty* of exclusion and each one has found that interaction between White teaching staff and Black students is characterized by conflict. Wright, in particular, suggests that notwithstanding intentions and obligations to equality, White teachers as a collective apprehend and reciprocate to African-Caribbean pupils in ways that give them no just cause. African-Caribbean students are liable to be selected for criticism when engaging in the same activity as their White counterparts. To underpin this observation, their fellow pupils, of all ethnic descriptions, judged the treatment handed out to African-Caribbean students to be not only unequal but also unfairly harsh (Sewell, 1997; Gillborn,1990). To offer an explanation, Wright (1987) indicates the latent expectations and assumptions that White teachers hold concerning their Black pupils, notably an understanding that African-Caribbean culture is marked by a general disavowal of authority. Disciplinary measures were founded on the need to directly destroy at source and respond harshly to whatever problem may arise. This unequal approach became the datum point of much confrontation between pupil and teacher. African-Caribbean students who contested or challenged the teachers' unequal management of affairs were considered as exhibiting authority-rejection behaviour and deemed to be problematic. Wright (1987) also discovered that while teachers were inclined to coalesce education and schooling in the process of evaluating pupils, the pupils themselves made no such crossover (Wright, et al,2000:8-9).

The notion of 'resistance' in reference to schooling has been used by a number of authors keen to look at how certain groups of students negotiate and respond to their secondary positions in schools, whilst refraining from the doctrine that schools have little choice in the matter of their ability as schools to duplicate these cultural and social inequalities. Research completed by Paul Willis (1977) endeavoured to look into the dichotomy between structure and agency that former social reproduction narratives had broached. However, Willis's research has been disparaged as dualistic and determinist.

Additional research on the subject of resistance has pointed out that pupil interaction with the schooling process can be construed in ways not similar to those of Willis (1977). Working-class students are not the only category of pupils seen to resist schooling. Class does not necessarily have a bearing on pupil resistance. The idea of particular student groups being necessarily anti-school in their orientations has been demonstrated to be facile since research has shown, for instance, that African-Caribbean male students present orientations that are mutually exclusive; pro-school and anti-school sentiments (Gillborn,1990; Sewell,1997). Findings of this nature are a contrasting theme to that research which centres on discontented African-Caribbean pupils (Mac an Ghaill,1988; Cashmore and Troyna,1982). Research is also accountable for showing that it is the apprehension of teachers' authoritarian positioning that disdain is shown towards and not education per se (Sewell,1997). Former research showed that it is the forms of discrimination that pupils discerned in their teachers that they show disdain towards and not the primacy of education. Curiously, the sense and awareness of inferiority influenced a child's motivation to learn and lowered personal ambition (Cook,1988; in Katz and Taylor,1988).

Students carry into schools their racialized and gendered backgrounds and these interchange with their tendency towards power. Bourdieu (1977) points out that pupils have a package of dispositions towards power that are in a state of continuous flux and are primarily inseparable from social class. Race and class are the warp and weft in matters of how pupils are inclined to the power relations they face in modern schooling. The way in which 'race' determines the educational experience is apparently related to class position and is also delineated in contrast to the numerical sway of the White middle-class culture of education professionals (Wright et al, 2000).

That said, 'race' in itself and of itself impacts on the experience of students in school. Work by Horvat (1997) has revealed that 'race' alone has the capacity of moulding and shaping school experiences. Hence:

> Often, this racial influence functions most effectively as a marker of class membership and position (Horvat,1997:13; quoted in Wright, Weekes and McGlaughlin,2000: 9).

Further research also insists on the relationship of race and gender in the enquiry into the Black experience (Wright, 1992).

The convoluted manner in which gender and race interrelate in how Black pupils fare does call for further examination. The male/female differences operating among Black pupils has *de facto* been used to define the differing orientation of pupils and incidence of academic achievement.

To be subsequently shown, resistance often resided in pupils' racialized and gendered social stations as seen in the wider sphere. Non-standard speech patterns, dress and styles of walking not infrequently smack of displaced resistance and these outlets possess greater cultural capital when used in a domain (school) where Black students are at a numerical and power-related disadvantage.

The Significance of Education Policy

This chapter seeks to provide an outline of the conditions in which the increase in school exclusions precipitated in the 1990s has found its own level. It has made efforts to locate the rise in exclusions within broader concerns of educational policy, especially the marketization of schooling. Whereas education policy has tended over time to de-emphasize racialized positions as a noteworthy element of the education process, inside the background of school, exclusion and discipline have become more and more racialized such as by the disproportionate rate of exclusions of African-Caribbean students. Policy has worsened the issue of exclusion: there has come to be a strengthening of the idea of the 'ideal' student by stressing cost-effectiveness, examination prosecution and marketization in schools. Ergo, disruptive pupils are perceived as costly in both pecuniary and league table position terms. Against this backdrop and atmosphere, schools may be discouraged from seeing their purpose as being inclusive, i.e., education for all. They may regard certain pupil groups with a cross to bear approach. Following on from this, the contemporary educational climate, with its stress on elevating standards and running a tight ship, will ever increase the school's power to apply stricter penalties to pupils (Wright et al.2000).

Racism in Contemporary Classrooms

We turn now to examine ethnographic research studies that have investigated teacher-pupil relationships in multi-ethnic schools and their influence on Black female and male youth of African-Caribbean and South Asian parentage. Why elect to look at ethnographic studies? This is because ethnographic research studies explore the process at the heart of teacher-pupil relationships (Pilkington,2003:146). Our focus below will be on five such expositions. Research of this type that investigates schools concerns itself not so much with the differences restricted to individual schools as the dimensions that schools share. Certain writers inform us that schools are informed by ethnocentric values. The dominant monocultural curriculum extols the virtues of one culture and in particular is biased against young people from minority ethnic groups, who realize that cultures outside the mainstream, if not ignored, are belittled.

Certain commentators inform us that the bias against African-Caribbeans is rather alarming and assumes a racist form. A former work that involved 510 teachers from 25 schools from different parts of the country revealed 'a high degree of consensus of opinion concerning the academic and social behaviour' of Caribbean young people, with over two-thirds of teachers accepting in essence that such students are less able and constituted an increase in disciplinary problems (Pilkington,2003:145). Because the teachers showed a much greater propensity to accept negative generalisations about students of Caribbean origin as compared to Asian or European heritage, it does certainly seem 'that there is large scale stereotyping of West Indian pupils' (Brittan,1976; quoted in Pilkington,2003:145). Meanwhile, contemporary evidence is sadly lacking as concerns questionnaires on teachers' attitudes towards minority ethnic students. Professor David Gillborn, however, can draw on international studies that suggest White teachers tend to envisage Black students in disproportionately negative ways – for example, that young Black people tend to be regarded as a potential behaviour problem, not as a potential achiever of five A* GCSEs (TES), 19 February 2016). This is borne out by what young people say about people like teachers; 'Middle-class people and people in authority don't understand young people and regard youth culture – our clothes, music and daily struggles – as negative, (Richardson,2005:161). And also, he can draw on qualitative studies with students, teachers and parents that attest to these processes. Furthermore, Gillborn can show statistically how Black Caribbean over-representation in permanent exclusions has increased and decreased but never disappeared, despite what policymakers resolve to do, and he can point out how these issues mediate with wider racist processes throughout society.

However, he faces a shortfall in proving a shred of this to anyone, not infrequently White people who negate the interpretation that racism is a phenomenon that suffuses society and tends towards being invisible or subtle.

Research has also found that constantly telling boys that they are underachieving – in comparison with girls – can lead to an implicit bias in boys directed inward at themselves. Racial bias operates in the same way. Black boys are expected to underachieve, but some Asian cultures – e.g., Chinese and Indian – are associated with higher achievement levels and this positive bias also creeps in (TES,19 February 2016:29).

Whereas race and gender appear to capture a large proportion of media coverage in the UK, global location and the demographic structure of local communities can give rise to additional types of bias.

Social class bias, for example, might play a bigger role in schools where there are few minority groups but larger differences in socioeconomic status – working-class pupils are implicitly seen as 'less able', with the danger that they will be treated in such a way that impacts on how the pupil sees herself or himself, leading to a self-fulfilling prophecy (TES, 19 February 2016:29).

To what extent is bias a feature in UK schools? To date, no one has been able to quantify the true prevalence of the problem, asserts Dr Sally Palmer, lecturer and department equal opportunities liaison officer at the UCL Institute of Education.

It is difficult to know the exact prevalence of bias within primary and secondary schools in the UK, partly as there is no systematic approach to recording it, but also because children and adolescents can be shy or worried about reporting these incidents, she explains (TES,19 February 2016).

A further question is what yardstick can adequately measure something that large numbers of teachers aren't so much as aware exists. Gillborn situates the problem in the framework of the "decades of research" pointing out that teachers do not expect Black Caribbean students to achieve much in comparison with their White and South Asian peers. "It works through the everyday routines of schooling – who is encouraged, who is told off, who is placed on the 'top table' or in the top set", Gillborn declares.

The teachers doing this are usually completely unaware of their behaviour and are often horrified when it's pointed out. The cumulative effects on achievement are devastating. But how many teacher education courses cover this at all? Very few. How many schools routinely interrogate the ethnic make-up of their GCSE tiering decisions? (TES,19 February 2016).

He doesn't consider that enough time and money are being targeted at confronting the issue of unconscious bias in education. Actually, he argues that in the mandatory schooling system, subsuming teacher education, the action being implemented to challenge bias today is a percentage of what was carried through a decade ago, and in all sincerity that was "wholly inadequate".

For example, research on both sides of the Atlantic demonstrates that significant race inequalities occur whenever students are separated into different teaching groups based on any notion of their ability, potential, attitude – this happens regardless of the system, Gillborn declares. We've known this for decades. And yet still, many schools, teachers and policymakers say that setting by ability is good for everyone (TES,19 February 2016).

The majority of teachers alongside their trade unions think of themselves as liberals on race questions and they respond truculently to any insinuation that they are falling short where Black students are concerned. The 1985 Swann Report, however, signposted that: 'Teacher attitudes towards, and expectations of West Indian pupils may be subconsciously influenced by stereotyped, negative or patronising views of their abilities and potential, which may prove a self-fulfilling prophecy, and can be seen as a form of unintentional racism' (Abbot cited in Richardson,2005:110). The overwhelming majority of Black parents in 2001 would maintain that there has been no significant change in the intervening years since 2001 because schools are a microcosm of society and thus reflect society's value system. We can conclude that in over a decade, teachers' attitudes have undergone little in the way of change towards Black students since 'no government has seriously addressed racism in education for over a decade' (TES,19 February 2016).

The mental picture gleaned from Coard's pamphlet is the suggestion that the policy and practice of a high proportion of teachers might be racially biased and (unintentionally) discriminatory or insufficiently oriented to the problem. This was far from being well-received by various teacher unions in the 1970s.

The strides forward have been significant in not only the policy but also practice since then but the knee-jerk reaction to defend teachers regardless of the price to be paid remains strong. Hence the leader of a large schoolteacher union argued that the definition of institutional racism hosted in the Macpherson Report was 'gobbledygook' and pertains little to education. An attack on the terms of the Macpherson Report is one thing but to utterly deny that institutional racism exists in the education system is quite another. Other organisations have also learned that the lessons take some stomaching. When cornered and with nowhere else to turn, some have summoned Bernstein's cry from the heart that 'education cannot compensate for society' (Mackney,2005; cited in Richardson,2005:222). Doesn't accepting this premise admit to there being something inherently wrong with society and that schools are inextricably linked to that problem?

The material detail that the Stephen Lawrence inquiry featured in the world's news media, and that new race relations legislation has been introduced, means nothing if the initiative to learn lessons by the powers that be is lost. It is worth calling attention to the inquiry's statement of institutional racism:

> The collective failure of an organisation to provide an appropriate and professional service to people because of their colour, culture, or ethnic origin can be seen or detected in processes, attitudes and behaviour which amount to discrimination through unwitting prejudice, ignorance, thoughtlessness and racist stereotyping which disadvantage minority ethnic people.

It persists because of the failure of the organisation openly and adequately to recognise and address its existence and causes by policy, example and leadership. (The Macpherson Report, cited in Richardson,2005:95).

Recent evidence indicates that the education system has come short of learning from the sadness of Stephen's murder and in the wake of the inquiry. Schools are judged to be pedestrian in waking up to their new responsibilities and most appear satisfied to initiate no further steps. On a domestic scale, in the education department's 'Five Year Strategy' for root and branch educational reform, the matter of institutional racism is conspicuous by its very absence. There are but a few possible explanations arising: one, the education department may take it that institutional racism has been jettisoned from the system (even given the continued underachievement and even given the consistent over-exclusion of young Black people); two, the department might suppose that this is entirely an issue for schools that it can turn its back on; or three, possibly the Department for Education is merely content to not pay the issue any attention (Richardson,2005:95).

Having considered the Lawrence inquiry correlation towards the back end of this brief update sketch – despite the paucity of recent evidence from questionnaires – on teachers' attitudes towards minority ethnic students, a succession of research studies in schools tend to confirm the foregoing picture that 'African-Caribbean and South Asian pupils can be subject to different expectations' Gillborn and Gipps,1996: 54; quoted in Pilkington,2003:145). A research investigation into a boys' comprehensive in the first half of the 1980s noted, 'There was a tendency for South Asian male students to be seen by the teachers as technically of "high ability" and socially conformist. African-Caribbean male students tended to be seen as having "low ability" and potential discipline problems (Mac an Ghaill,1988:64).

Mac an Ghaill empirically researched a boys' secondary school and a sixth form college in the first half of the 1980s. Most White teachers locate responsibility within the Black youth's community itself for the 'problems' they face and consider that Black youth should adapt anew to suit the school's demands, and in turn, the students attribute racism as the primary problem, as well as the teachers' racist practices and the solution, therefore, being in the schools radically transforming to live up to their expectations, this suggests that conflict was evident. Mac an Ghaill (1988) admit that the main problem in the teaching and regulating of Black youth is not that account should be taken of their culture but rather that account should be taken of racism. He continues, there may be no deliberate intention to manage Black youth any differently to White youth, but the inadvertent teacher effects lead to differential responses which militate against Black youth. Different action plans, that are enlightened by class and gender, are taken up by different elements of the youth in their opposition to a racially organized society, Mac an Ghaill notes. These shared responses which derive from the broader expanse of the Black community can be understood as clearly defined strategies of survival, he asserts. The above reinforces the notion of there being conflict in schools which exists as well in the wider society for Black youth and tends to colour their response to schooling as simply a way of surviving, Mac an Ghaill argues.

Conflict could more clearly be understood when an examination was taken of teacher ideologies and practices. Mr Fleming, a former history teacher at 'Kilby School', used racist stereotypes in his explanation of the 'problem Black population' and these were not just lying dormant in individual teacher's heads. In the final stages of the 1960s, they were changed into social and specific responses. First, gradually perfected among the staff was a social acceptance of a serious level of overt racism. Mr Dempster, a senior teacher, outlined the context during this epoch:

> People, teachers were much more openly prejudiced. The West Indians were talked about as belonging to the jungle and all that sort of thing. Remember, it's often forgotten but in schools, things like size are important. First years are easily, more easily controlled than fifth formers. Well, then teachers were confronted, it was always thought of as confrontation with big West Indians. They were challenged, so they resorted to derogative labelling. It was a kind of defence mechanism. And with Indian kids when they first arrived, there was a lot of talk about them being sly, pretending they couldn't understand you if they got in trouble (Mac an Ghaill,1988:42).

'Kilby School' operated a regimented system of streaming, with the method for allocating pupils to different streams resting not on cognitive ability but on subjective behavioural criteria, meaning African-Caribbean pupils who were of 'higher ability' than their South Asian or White counterparts being placed in the lower streams. One teacher legitimated the unequal streaming practice in the following passage:

> There are boys of relatively higher ability in the lower sets, especially among the West Indians. I've told you before, Johnson and Brown were marvellous at Maths, especially problem-solving. But it's their, it's the West Indians' attitude and that must decide it in the end. You can't promote a boy who is known to be a trouble-maker, who's a dodger. It will look like a reward for bad behaviour. We've always got to be looking behind our shoulder and asking ourselves what effect will this move have on the other boys? (Mac an Ghaill,1988:81-2).

The African-Caribbeans not infrequently met this challenge with resistance, through the forging of distinct subculture alliances, the 'Rasta Heads'. In addition, Caribbean rebellion can be seen through the prism that things were stacked against them since the teachers' negative approach towards them tended to encompass most things; not only was Creole or patois described as sub-standard speech but also as 'aggressive, babbling, loud, meaningless, argumentative and jabbering', whereas some South Asians also resisted; however, their subculture – 'the Warriors' – assumed a minor visibility level (Mac an Ghaill,1988:55). Against high-status subjects like European languages, South Asian languages were viewed negatively and African-Caribbean students were encouraged to use their languages in the classroom on the grounds that 'this will increase their motivation to work' (Mac an Ghaill,1988:57).

In reality, the teachers' negative assessment of Black youth's language functioned primarily to hamper them from attaining effective and expansive oral and written techniques. The Liberal teachers in principle argued for the recognition within the curriculum of the African- Caribbean students' languages. But, in reality, this has given rise to the enforcement of a pluralist perspective for 'low-ability' pupils and this linkage has contradictorily tended to strengthen the critical assessment of Creole.

At 'Kilby School', racism was extensive across the White staff, including the upper echelons of the school hierarchy, the teachers and the executive and auxiliary workers. Many of the staff had worked at the school for a significant number of years yet they did not side with the Black community. Their unsympathetic attitude towards them was shown in ways unbecoming (Mac an Chaill,1988). The school was society in miniature and the racist stereotypes lying beyond the school gates were what teachers came with to the teaching environment. Mr Barlow calls to mind his first thought patterns regarding his redeployment at the school:

> I didn't want to come here. I tried to find other places, anywhere. I'd heard all about the area, not the school itself really but about the problems of coloured kids, about the reputation of the West Indians.

You would read about them mugging old ladies round the place in the papers, but, and then the thought of having to teach them (Mac an Ghaill,1988:64-65).

Such inflexible representations of the broader expanse of society were also a determinant factor in the racial ordering of the nature of being at the school.

There is more to teacher practices than meets the eye as the following example illustrates. Mr Young was at odds with the teachers' powerful social image of African-Caribbean students. He was thought of by his colleagues as a successful school teacher who had minimal disciplinary problems and was good at dealing with trouble-makers. Mr Young was under the pretext that Mac an Ghaill (1988) was helping a number of students with language issues and so was unaware that Mac an Ghaill (1988) was observing his classroom interplay with the students. Mr Young was astounded when Mac an Ghaill (1988) pointed out to him how he had reciprocated to a number of occurrences involving pupils who had 'interrupted' the lessons. While there were, *in toto*, 34 in a class, just 5 African-Caribbeans, they had been witnessed about twice the number of times, relative to the 27 Asian pupils and 2 Whites, to have caused an interruption. Most tellingly, as Mr Young discloses below, was his mental picture of the South Asian and African-Caribbean youth, which intersected with the measuring rod he used to determine what constituted a 'classroom interruption'.

I see, I would, I did come away, well, I would've come away thinking that I was not working with the stereotypes, at least not those ones. It's amazing, really; Jasbinder turning around for a ruler is legitimate, is seen as O.K. Richard [African-Caribbean] doing the same thing is regarded as interrupting and his behaviour is good generally. I don't think of him as one of the problems. I bet he's noticed that I treat him differently (Mac an Ghaill,1988:66).

Mr Young was alive to working with stereotypes that were part of something Lacey (1976, p.60) designates as the teachers' 'crude conceptual picture of the class', in which he sorts the students into groups that correlate with "the bright boys", "the conformists" "the troublemakers", etc.' (Mac an Ghaill,1988:67). These crude general headings are drawn on as coping mechanisms in the structuring of classroom interaction. Something Mr Young was not alive to, he argues, was how for teachers at 'Kilby School', this ideological framework formed the foundation upon which rests the racist stereotypes that they made use of within the school. Mac an Ghaill (1988) believed that at this point, the racist stereotypes performed the strategic role of teacher survival. This example of a Liberal teacher goes to show that racist practices are not uncomplicated. This is of some significance, he adds, to those who are inclined to read these practices as the preserve of a far-right political persuasion.

The sub-culture group, the 'Rasta Heads' drew inspiration from Rastafarianism, an ideology of resistance that assisted in identity formation but, the 'Kilby School' authority figures were successful, among the staff, at blowing the 'Rasta Heads' behaviour out of all proportion. For the large majority of teachers, this group was identified in wholly negative terms as a destabilizing influence on the school authority.

A clearly defined system of racist stereotyping which incorporated a polar opposite dimension for the two youth groups, was fully functional at 'Kilby School'. Teachers from two different schools of thought acted explicitly within this context, whereas most of the Liberals acted implicitly within it. The prevailing social image of the male pupils to emerge was on one hand the 'high-achieving conformist' South Asian, and on the other, the 'low-ability truculent' African-Caribbean. But this is not to maintain that the teachers designated students exclusively in those stereotyping terms (Mac an Ghaill,1988:72-73). Notwithstanding, these racist cartoon outlines, which were often kept under wraps, were of most significant value in sensing how White state professionals experience Black and South Asian youth. Moreover, these racist social perceptions were of major importance to the tiering system in place at 'Kilby School' which will briefly be examined.

South Asian students tended to be over-represented in the top stream whereas African- Caribbean students were over-represented in the lower streams and not entered for examinations, this was justified in terms of the Liberal teachers' acceptance of the' common-sense' educational heading of ability, aptitude and attitude (Mac an Ghaill,1988:77). While the Liberals were at variance with the stratification system, he suggests, they could not see that their adoption of its theoretical support, i.e., the idea of the scarce resource of intelligence, served to replicate, uphold and one-sidedly legitimate a strict categorization of 'academic' and 'non-academic' students. The connective link between racism was made through this extant framework, he adds. In relation to 'Kilby School', this division and the division between the South Asian and African-Caribbean students was little different. For example, then, Mac an Ghaill (1988) adds, the insufficient numbers of African-Caribbean pupils in the top streams and selected for O-level examinations resulted in a simplistic social image of African-Caribbeans as a whole, as largely non-academic, and their ethnicity as being the primal cause.

The reasoning of this sub-culture did not incorporate failure or inability to complete examinations, nor did it incorporate cultural deficiency, but it incorporated questioning the validity of scholastic achievement and qualifications vis-à-vis the requirements of the local economic structure. The 'Rasta Heads' rejection of modern forms of employment was their guiding principle for life at 'Kilby School'. The subordinate labour market position of Black employees' was openly associated with British imperialism and teachers were historically seen to represent what the 'Rasta Heads' interpreted as the existing state of affairs between Blacks and Whites (Mac an Ghaill,1988:90).

The 'Rasta Heads' resistance to schooling was often directly expressed through their disengagement from the formal activity of schooling into the informal activity of their sub-culture (Mac an Ghaill,1988:86). The 'Rasta Heads' practised late arrival for lessons, unsettled other students by insisting on back row seats of the classrooms, constantly interrupted teachers, attempted to sow discord, talked persistently throughout lessons and found sleep preferable to the demands of completing written work. They rarely satisfied homework demands, never studied for school tests and failed to sit annual examinations (Mac an Ghaill,1988:99).

The Asian sub-cultural youth group, 'the Warriors' responded similarly to their experience of racism. Because the teachers were mindful of and distracted by the 'Rasta Heads', the Warriors not infrequently tended to be overlooked, though elements of the group were considered as disciplinary problems. Their consensus on the school was one of collective hostile authority and pointless work demands. Being an African-Caribbean and a disciplinary problem, as teachers viewed it, brought African-Caribbeans as a whole into disrepute, whereas South Asian transgressions were seen in terms of personal deviancy and South Asians as a social group were not typecast. 'The Warriors' relentlessly interrupted lessons by arriving late, dragging chairs, acting altogether mirthfully and verbally opposing teachers (Mac an Ghaill,1988:129).

South Asian students often resisted schooling through language use. Languages such as Punjabi, Hindi, Urdu or Gujarati were employed to rile and exclude teachers. Even the 'Rasta Heads' defiant language was adopted against authority. 'The Warriors' erection of barriers to schooling was articulated through their avoidance of written work. The methods devised to achieve this were considered proudly; for example, turning up late for lessons to miss the outline plan, failing to equip themselves with a pen, rendering the pen the teacher provided unworkable, claiming to have injured their hand or simply falling asleep. Group members determined to navigate an entire term without processing any written work. 'The Warriors' erection of barriers to schooling was also articulated through a high level of absenteeism (Mac an Ghaill,1988).

Whereas the 'Rasta Heads' defied the teachers by not producing a parental letter explaining their absence, 'the Warriors' were inclined to produce a forged letter and so letting them off the hook. Consequently, the 'Rasta Heads' faced an increased incidence of suspensions for failure to attend. The disproportionate representation of suspended African-

Caribbean students then functioned to strengthen the unequal teacher stereotype of the 'rebellious' African-Caribbean and 'passive' South Asian student (Mac an Ghaill,1988:132).

As I have already shown, the 'Rasta Heads' and 'the Warriors' assumed an anti-school position that developed into a disregard for formal education, while the 'Black Sisters', coming together as friends in a sixth form college, adopted a strategy of 'resistance within accommodation'. On one level, they negate the racist curriculum; on another level, they keep their eyes on the prize of academic credentials. Not unlike other young Black women in a similar context, theirs is a culture defined as anti-school but pro-education (Mac an Ghaill,1988:11; Pilkington,2003:147).

The 'Black Sisters' intimated that racism affects the lives of Black people and the three schools they attended and the sixth form college showed strong evidence in support of such a claim. Their collective response of resistance, which was seldom overt, incorporated such behaviour as collective late arrival for lessons, overshooting homework deadlines, refusing to take part in group discussion, and engaging one another in their mother tongues and other behavioural manifestations that conflict with the schools' and the college's day-to-day life and regulations.

Why African-Caribbean females succeed where African-Caribbean males often fail academically was broached by the 'Black Sisters'. Their take was the increased 'visibility' of the latter to the teachers in relation to other anti-school pupils in their form of resistance. The South Asian females concurred that the African-Caribbean males were 'most likely to get picked on' due to the system of racist stereotyping operational in schools, with African- Caribbean males being seen as the chief troublemakers. The African-Caribbean young women maintained that many boys often directed the dominant racist perception inwards at themselves. Consequently, they excelled in sport and music but met low teacher expectations of their intellectual performance leading to a self-fulfilling prophecy. The 'Black Sisters' explained that the dynamics of the boy's peer group led to a stronger and lasting effect while they were less affected and so had increased autonomy in how they reciprocated at school (Mac an Ghaill,1988:33).

Gillborn (1990) researched an English comprehensive that he called 'City Road Comprehensive' in the mid-1980s. Although the great majority of teachers seemed authentically faithful to principles of equality of educational opportunity and would reject ideologies that insist on the inherent differences between the 'races' and embraced fairness for all, they widely believed 'in an African-Caribbean challenge to authority' which they held to be 'qualitatively as well as quantitatively more serious' than their classmates of heterogeneous ethnic origins (Gillborn,1990:38). 'The myth of an African-Caribbean challenge' was an article of faith which the teachers strove to suppress at the earliest stage. Consequently, African-Caribbean pupils were proportionately subject to greater amounts of punishment, and even more significant perhaps 'was the fact that they were often singled out for criticism even though several pupils, of different ethnic origins, were engaged in the same behaviour' (Gillborn,1990:30). A clique of three African-Caribbean boys was formed in response and there was a high level of antagonism and conflict between White teachers and African-Caribbean pupils. Unlike the counter-school culture of Paul Willis' 'lads', resistance to their differential treatment embraced the attainment of academic qualifications. Though they would react angrily to perceived unfair treatment, while in contradistinction, one individual recognized and rejected the negative image and criticism of the teachers and succeeded against the odds, in a strategy of accommodation (Willis,1977:94). Resistance was a path that some pupils followed and accommodation was a path that other pupils followed, although some pupils fell somewhere in between the two, highlighting the complexity of pupil adaptations to the school's dominant value system. Crucially, the experiences of African-Caribbean students in 'City Road' corroborated the complex and obviated nature of student adaptations, and emphasized the vital function which ethnicity played with reference to their educational life-chances. While the teachers were, on the whole, 'liberal' in their conscious effort, their good offices tended more frequently to have racist consequences (Gillborn,1990).

The material detail that South Asian males were of a different ethnicity impinged on the way they experienced school, especially in relation to those they chose as friends, and contact with racial harassment. As regards their social interaction with teachers, however, the South Asian students did not consistently undergo any ill effects as teachers internalized certain stereotypes of their students. Therefore, African-Caribbean and South Asian students encountered 'City Road' in ways that were worlds apart (Gillborn,1990:202). The conclusion Gillborn draws from his research is that 'race' matters. To gainsay that the demography of minority ethnic communities within the social environment has any implications regarding the educational system is where error intersects with ignorance, Gillborn argues. In addition, Gillborn argues, the truism that ethnicity does affect how pupils encounter school has enormous consequences in respect of the educational system in the UK.

Wright (1992) researched four inner-city primary schools between 1988 and 1990. In this case, using observation and interview techniques which were the major sources of data collection, it was evident that, 'teachers tended to treat 'West Indian' boys in a more restrictive way than others, issuing orders rather than encouraging them to express their feelings and ideas in the class' (Wright,1992:14). By contrast, South Asian children were treated more favourably than their African-Caribbean peers but frequently were treated less favourably than their white classmates' (Wright,1992:42). The African-Caribbean presence in the classroom was observed to elicit control and criticism from White teachers and they were the single most penalised social group. Furthermore, African-Caribbean male children were not infrequently singled out by some teachers for reprimand even when the same behaviour was being committed by other children in the classroom. What follows below is a series of events in a classroom context of four-year-olds illustrating the above negative teacher effects experienced by Marcus.

Chapter 3: The Education System

TEACHER:	Let's do one song before home time.
PETER:	[white boy] Humpty Dumpty.
TEACHER:	No, I'm choosing today. Let's do something we have not done for a while. I Know, we'll do the Autumn song. What about the Autumn song we sing? Don't Shout out, put your hand up nicely.
Mandy:	(Shouting out) Two little leaves on a tree.
TEACHER:	She's nearly right.
Marcus:	[Afro-Caribbean boy with his hand up] I know.
TEACHER:	(talking to the group) Is she right when she says 'two little leaves on a tree'?
WHOLE GROUP:	No.
TEACHER:	What is it, Peter?
PETER:	Four.
TEACHER:	Nearly right.
MARCUS:	[Afro-Caribbean boy, waving his hand for attention] Five.
TEACHER:	Don't shout out, Marcus. Do you know, Susan? [white girl]
SUSAN:	Five.
TEACHER:	(holding up one hand) Good, five, because we have got how many fingers on this hand?
WHOLE GROUP:	Five.
TEACHER:	Okay, let's only have one hand because we've only got five leaves. How many would we have if we had too many? Don't shout out, hands up.
MANDY:	(shouting out) One, two, three, four, five, six, seven, eight, nine, ten.
TEACHER:	Good. Okay, how many fingers have we got?
MARCUS:	Five.

TEACHER:	Don't shout out, Marcus, put your hand up. Deane, how many?
DEANE:	Five.
TEACHER:	That's right, we're going to use five today. What makes them dance about, these leaves?
PETER:	(shouting out) The wind.
TEACHER:	That's right. Ready, here we go.

Teacher and children sing, "Five little leaves so bright and gay, dancing about on a tree one day. The wind came blowing through the town, whoooo, whoooo, whoooo, one little leaf came tumbling down.

TEACHER:	How many have we got left?
DEANE:	(shouting out) One.
MARCUS:	(raising his hand enthusiastically) Four.
TEACHER:	(to Marcus) Shush. Let's count, one, two, three, four.
TEACHER:	How many, Deane?
DEANE:	Four.
TEACHER:	Good, right let's do the next bit.

Teacher and children sing the next two verses.

TEACHER:	How many have we got left, Peter?
PETER:	Don't know.
MANDY:	Two.
TEACHER:	I know that you know, Mandy.
MARCUS:	Two.
TEACHER:	(stern voice) I'm not asking you, I'm asking Peter; don't shout out. We'll help Peter, shall we? Look at my fingers – how many? One, two. How many, Peter?
PETER:	Two.

TEACHER:	Very good. Let's do the next bit.

Teacher and children sing the next verse. At the end of the verse:

TEACHER:	How many have we got left, Susan?
SUSAN:	One.
TEACHER:	Good, let's all count, one. Let's do the last bit.

Teacher and children sing the last verse; at the end of the verse:

TEACHER:	How many have we got left?
All Children:	None.
TEACHER:	That's right, there are no leaves left. Marcus, will you stop fidgeting and sit nicely? (Wright, 1992:19-21).

During an exchange between Wright and the African-Caribbean child, a care assistant based at the unit, about what was witnessed above, commented,

> Marcus really likes answering questions about things. I can imagine he's quite good at that because he's always got plenty to say …, but they [white teachers] see the black children as a problem here (Wright, 1992:21).

Black and minority ethnic carers forming the nursery unit staff membership at 'Bridgeway School' also expressed disquiet about the postures of White co-workers towards African- Caribbean males in particular. Most teachers seemed unconscious of their unconscionable criticism and controlling directives levelled at African-Caribbean students in the classroom. In point of fact, most of the episodes observed in the classroom were far removed from the ones referenced above (Wright,1992:27). Nevertheless, the contour of teacher-pupil interplay did not escape the mental acuity of the White children.

The African-Caribbean gripe about unfair treatment suffered through the leadership of their teachers was frequently vouched for by their White classmates:

SUSAN: [white, 11 years old] Teachers, they're prejudiced against blacks, especially Mr M.

INTERVIEWER: In what ways would you see prejudice happening?

SUSAN: Because sometimes if there's a black and white fighting in the playground, he'll [the teacher] bully the black and not the white. If whites bully black, the Black will get done for it.

INTERVIEWER: Why do you think that the black child will get done, as you say?

SUSAN: Because Mr M and some of the other teachers are prejudiced. They don't like blacks against whites ....In assembly, if a black [child] and white [child] are talking, he'll [Mr M.] shout at the black, and tell him [pupil] to come out to the front (Wright, 1992:27).

During a verbal exchange between Wright and two White children (Ricky and Neil, both in the seven-year age bracket at 'Bridgeway School'), both remarked upon the unequal treatment of their sable contemporaries and what they believed to mediate between black children's management and the school's staff composition:

RICKY: There's all white teachers here.

NEIL: Except some people that come to help [the non-teaching staff].

RICKY: All the teachers are white. It's only black people who help. Everyone else that's White is a teacher

	here ... There should be black teachers because there's more black [pupils] and they won't get picked on so much.
INTERVIEWER:	Are you saying that the black children are picked on?
NEIL:	Yeah, they get done a lot in class for messing about ... and being 'cock of the School'.
INTERVIEWER:	What's 'cock of the school'?
NEIL:	Tough and all that (Wright, 1992:27).

It is patently transparent, therefore, that an understanding of teacher's persistent criticism and control of African-Caribbean and Rastafarian children was not limited to support staff, African-Caribbean and Rastafarian children themselves or to their White contemporaries. As in the above portrait, support staff and pupil declarations were underpinned by classroom observation (Wright, 1992).

Tony Sewell (1997) studied two secondary schools, one mixed, and the second a boys' school. 'John Caxton School' was the starting point leading into the main ethnographic research focus at 'Township School'. Like Mac an Ghaill (1988), Gilborn (1990), and Wright, (1992), Sewell (1997) found in his John Caxton teacher survey that teachers issued greater control and criticism to African-Caribbean boys than to other ethnic groups. Sewell argues that, in addition, it would suggest that teachers respond negatively to many overt signs of ethnicity from these boys. Mindful that a small sample cannot lead to general claims, however, Sewell also discovered that teachers attribute the complex exchanges with African-Caribbean boys to failings to do with their home and culture. Sewell noted that lying behind the negative attentions of the teacher was the inference that African-Caribbean popular culture was a crucial destabilizing challenge in school. According to Sewell, there were boys who did assume the traditional Black girls' strategy of being, on one level, pro-education and, on another level, anti-school. However, they found equilibrium too difficult to maintain in the light of teacher and peer network negativity. Sewell also adds that there is a social cost of self-sacrifice to academic success in school. Individuals felt that integration concessions were required to fit into the white mainstream and key aspects of the Black community and sub-culture if they were to eschew negative teacher discipline.

The number of exclusions indicates a high degree of conflict between teachers and African-Caribbean males (Sewell,1997:30). The destinations of those leaving school showed a high proportion of African-Caribbean boys compared to White boys moving into the further education sector. The figures reveal that despite the exclusion rate, education continued to be an important vehicle to economic and social advancement for African-Caribbean boys (Sewell,1997:30).

The pattern of teacher response to African-Caribbean sub-culture within the school can be divided into three general categories: 'supportive', 'irritated' and 'antagonistic' (Sewell,1997). For the most part, teachers in 'Township School' were certain that the cultural forms that flowed from the most committed of boys to this sub-culture unfavourably affected their schooling. Sewell (1997) qualifies his three categories outlined above as mere generalizations which assist in understanding teacher attitudes to African-Caribbean male culture.

Teachers who were supportive of African-Caribbean sub-culture number ten per cent (Sewell,1997:34). Supportive teachers strived to obtain the best results from their relationship with stigmatised students and were *au fait* with and critical of teacher racism. The high African-Caribbean exclusion rate is seen by Mr Lewis as bad classroom management and not the cultural affiliation of the boys. The fact that these teachers had empathy for disaffected Black boys was where they think their strength as teachers lie. Sewell (1997) describes further sub-categories for supportive teachers as he develops his analysis, making this category more and more complex.

Teachers who formed the irritated category constituted 60 per cent (Sewell,1997:36). These teachers are frustrated with the school and its pupils, who they blame for the school's behaviour problem. They have mixed feelings for African-Caribbean norms and they tend to favour an assimilationist approach and doubt whether teacher racism entered into matters. Their single biggest concern is 'discipline'. The behaviour of the Black boys caused problems because the school did not assert its authority. The influence racism can have on a child's academic performance is something these teachers tend not to accept. The high ratio of Black students is instead mentioned or they assume that things are rosy in a multicultural school. They found too much about the boys' culture anathema to be supportive – occurring along a continuum from sexism through to an interpreted challenge to authority (Sewell,1997). Importantly, Sewell distinguished irritated teachers as those who are 'cynical'. Such teachers evenly apportion blame to the school's leadership along with the boys' culture for the issues confronting the school. They seldom lay the blame at their own door – instead, they see themselves as the innocent party in an unpredictable world. What defines these classroom managers is that they see the positives and the negatives in the boys' cultural norms and are not altogether antagonistic (Sewell,1997:137). The teachers forming the 'irritated' category firmly believed that the students were to shoulder most of the responsibility for the disproportionate exclusion rates.

Dividing into two groups and accounting for 30 per cent of the staff are antagonistic teachers (Sewell,1997). A proportion of these are openly racist and regard the cultural expressions of the boys as an unacceptable distinguishing feature of all Black people. For example, some African-Caribbean boys became aggressive due to school lunch deprivation and a teacher uttered, 'Well, Black kids tend to worry about their food more than white ones' (Sewell,1997:37). The second group feels, on moral, political and cultural levels, that the African-Caribbean sub-culture undermines their personal development. And some teachers claim to have identified aspects of the *modus vivendi* of these boys and perceive it to pose school authority problems.

Sewell noted that certain teachers, with interests in the Antagonistic and Supportive camps, tended to view South Asian students as being of high ability and socially conformist. African-Caribbean boys, on the other hand, were seen in contrast with their perception as hostile to the school power structure rather than of lower ability. This is a significant assertion because, according to Sewell, at 'Township' as quite distinct from the studies of Wright (1987) and Mac an Ghaill (1988), no evidence was present to suggest that White teachers believed in a less able Black student population. The large majority of teachers, however, had a firmly held belief that African-Caribbean boys were inherently anti-authority while South Asian boys were quite the reverse. While South Asian students were perceived as passive, Sewell questions this by arguing, what about the conformist African-Caribbean student and the rebel Asian boys?

Sewell's (1997) major survey of an inner-city boy's comprehensive school saw African-Caribbean pupils display a range of responses to schooling which he describes as: 'conformists', 'innovators', 'retreatists' and 'rebels'. The conformist students constituted 41 per cent of the study's participants and they formed two categories at 'Township School'. Group A was the elitist student, for whom academic success was seen to represent a departure from the group identity of the Black community. Despite this, they did not entirely reject Black identities but would sometimes enter into a 'racist discourse', for example, by stereotyping their fellow African-Caribbean students. Group B was viewed in terms of the word 'accommodation'. This was the individual endeavour to, first, remain a pro-school character while being up against negative power structure mentalities that liken all African-Caribbean students to philistines and, second, to 'accommodate' the negative input by the anti-school sub-culture that perceives academic success as being effeminate. Mediating between these two sub-categories is the Conformist students' wish to distinguish academic success as quite separate from the collective and more in tune with the individualistic (Sewell,1997).

Out of the 100 African-Caribbean boys surveyed, 35 per cent were classified as innovators (Sewell,1997). This group were pro-education thanks mainly to their parents but the schooling process was something they rejected. Many of the innovators ideated the schooling process under the

Chapter 3: The Education System

umbrella terms of repressive, exclusive and racist. African-Caribbean students who come under the 'retreatist' category number 6 per cent. As students, they reject education and the process of schooling but have no dealings with the sub-culture. In practice, no significant alternative to schooling is found; their aim is to not entertain work. Sewell subdivides this category into 'invisible resistance'. It directs itself to the chief cultural accord in the way classroom authority figures saw White and minority ethnic response to schooling. But as a strategy of resistance, it was difficult for these boys in this school category to achieve the desired effect. The 18 per cent that remained were designated rebels, but, to themselves and others, were known as 'the Posse'. Because children resist school in ways that need unravelling, Sewell undertook to split 'the Posse' into two branches: 'the Black nationalists' and the 'hedonists'. Children from 'the Black nationalist' wing rejected school through racialized notions that see White racist teachers and a dominant culture curriculum operate in opposition to Black interests. The 'hedonists' are those who stand against education and the schooling process preferring instead to replace them with the music, style and clothes of the sub-culture. A significant number of African-Caribbean students across all categories remonstrated that the biggest issue in 'Township' was not first-hand teacher racism predicated on the perception of a mythic challenge to authority by the students but rather a dereliction of authority (Sewell,1997).

Sewell (1997) and David Gillborn (1990) both feature pro-school boys who do relatively well in a sea of ethnographic studies that focused on apparent 'Black underachievement' and Black counter-school culture. Stephen appeared in Sewell's study school and was similar to Paul Dixon from Gillborn's study in that they were both pro-school, absorbed negative criticism from teachers and distanced themselves from peers that they thought were misguided. They both identified the influences which might impede upon their academic performance and determined to avoid them despite the cost. Paul concluded his pro-school career at 'City Road' by collecting 'O' level certificates in six different subjects: the greatest accolade of any African-Caribbean male in his school year (Gillborn,1990:63).

Stephen, a Black year 10 student, was strongly against any association with an exclusively Black gang called 'the Posse' but his teachers felt that no such separation could be made in regard to punishments. Stephen would all too frequently be identified with the anti-school pupils, despite his attempts to assert individual particularity. This stance was also attacked by his fellow students and, most vehemently, by the year 10 gang:

"TS: What do the 'Posse' think of you?

Stephen: I think they think I'm part of them, even though I'm doing my own things now. When I go to my class and they bunk off, they will say to me I'm a goody-goody. But I turn to them and say that when I get in my flash car and you're begging for money, then you'll wish you had behaved like me.

TS: What do they say when you tell them this?

Stephen: They call me a pussy" (Sewell, 1997:87).

The sting that the invective 'pussy' conveys is Stephen's ultimate penalty for school compliance, which is a contention against his masculinity. Deferential school behaviour is incompatible with male subculture attitudes. Mac an Ghaill (1994) talked about how some anti-school Black boys have linked academic success with being womanish or gay:

> The Black Macho Lads were particularly vindictive to African-Caribbean academic students, who overtly distanced themselves from their anti-school strategies. In response, the Black Macho Lads labelled them 'batty men' (a homophobic comment). As Mercer and Julien (1988:112) point out, a further contradiction in subordinated Black masculinities occurs, 'when men subjectively internalise and incorporate aspects of the dominant definitions of masculinity in order to contest the conditions of dependency and powerlessness which racism and racial oppression enforce'. Ironically, the Black Macho Lads, in distancing themselves from the racist school structures, adopted survival strategies of hyper-masculine heterosexuality that

threatened other African-Caribbean students, adding further barriers to their gaining academic success (1994, p.87-88).

The important distinction dividing the rebels from the conformists was the power of the conformists to speak in 'good' standard English (Sewell,1997:81). The measure of a rebel was the inability or unwillingness to converse in the elaborated code of their teachers. Conformists tended to select their friends from an admixture of heterogeneous ethnic origins, unlike the cohesive band of Black cohort rebel members. Fordham (1988) describes the element of collective identity that conformists tended to resist as 'fictive-kinship' (Sewell,1997:82). The contestation of the 'fictive-kinship' system operating within the Black community was expressed epistemologically, not of 'acting white' but rather of 'acting elite'. While these boys ostensibly accepted the dominant school ethos, which was anti-Black unity, many were still seen to represent a general African-Caribbean challenge. A departure from the fictive-kinship of the Black community did not mean that conformist students concurred with Fordham's idea of 'racelessness' considering that they did not wholly disavow Black identities.

The issue of Black hairstyles

The new Black head of 'Township', Mr Jones initiated his hegemonic role by excluding ragga culture from the school with the controversial banning of patterns in the hair. This created an uproar, with many Black boys protesting that the ruling was racist because it lacked universality across the student composition. The hairstyle was fashionable when Mr Francis (White) was headmaster yet he elected not to raise a finger. What made matters even worse was that it emerged that teachers were not clear on the ruling – it was open to interpretation. The ambiguous cultural investment of laying down the law on hairstyles left many classroom authority figures having to take interpretive decisions which lay them open to the charge of cultural bias. When asked to comment on banning the boys from wearing patterns in their hair, Mr Jones argued:

What I am trying to do is to get them to create an atmosphere and image in the school which is not like anywhere else. We live in a society, whether you be White or Black, where certain dress styles are stigmatised or certain types of behaviour will be associated with that dress code. Whether it's right or wrong, it's there. I want the kids in this school to use me as an example. I want to equip them with skills to manoeuvre their way through society and get to the pinnacle. As far as I am concerned, it applies to their outward image as well as what comes out of their mouths. To me, the whole thing comes as a package so [what I am saying to them is] use me as an example and I'll guide you through so that you can get on in society (Sewell, 1997:92-93).

The policy confused teachers, as in the case of Mr Cole, who took the directive to mean any hairstyle that looked 'ethnic', which targeted and disproportionately affected African-Caribbean boys. Sewell's contention is that Mr Jones is engaging with Black culture by endorsing a racist discourse: his assumption that his way of life is superior is an unconscious bias against African-Caribbean pupils, even though he shares the same reality as them. Far be it from me to argue that Sewell's contention is flawed; his logic and reasoning can scarcely be critically assessed as unsound nor picked to pieces. The contention that the school cultural characteristic spirit is about uniformity needs no justification here, but the ruling meant different things to different teachers and was viewed by the boys to be racist. White contemporaries in 'Township' were left alone to develop their own culture. The cultural expression of a group of White boys, was, for instance, to wear ponytails, yet Mr Jones did not envisage this as impacting negatively upon their schooling and future prospects. Also, the hairstyle was a fad, and as we all know, fads change, and this hairstyle is something the boys would grow world-weary of sporting. Moreover, Mr Jones should lead by example but he should, like his predecessor, let boys be boys.

On the other hand, his discourse falls short of being completely racist. He highlights the 'weakness' in a number of the boys' cultural lenses of academic attainment as a White person's entitlement. This thread of Mr

Jones' standpoint attacks the boys' dismissal of Black academic achievement, which he imagines to act against the fulfilment of an aim.

Teachers in 'Township' tend to gravitate towards a total rejection of the policy that states that Black kids cannot have patterns in their hair. Ms Allen is reported to say: 'I agree with the boys; it makes no difference to their education or behaviour; it is the headmaster being trivial and even racist' (Sewell,1997:136). A coalescence of such opposing emotional attitudes as antagonism and approval to the sub-cultural African-Caribbean practices is elucidated upon by Ms Williams (Irritated):

> Ms Williams: I totally disagree with the rule. I think something like hair, particular for Black people, is an expression of their identity. We live in a society where if you're not as White in looks and so-called attitude then you're marginalised. Particularly for Black males, there is something about that style which is about them. It's been copied all over the place. This rule is a total intrusion on a person's freedom to express themselves (Sewell,1997:136).

In the main, the substantially White staff were not wedded to pre-empting boys from sporting patterns in their hair. It was scarcely on the former (White) headteacher's agenda and the numerically larger proportion of them regarded the new head's directive petty. On the other hand, they upheld the assertion that the crucial logic behind African-Caribbean boys bearing unconscionable exclusion levels was their sub-culture. Even though Black hairstyles constitute a major ethnic/cultural marker, why did an overwhelming number of White teachers regard them with indifference? (Sewell,1997). Black hairstyles elicited two basic attitudes from the teaching staff. One attitude rested on ignorance. Sewell was bystander to an incident involving a PE teacher where that teacher issued an instruction to a pupil who had finished dressing and was attending to his hair to hurry up as he had little hair to comb. The concept that curly Black hair requires no uplifting or attention smacks of ignorance, thus, understanding that Black men require the least possible grooming.

The second attitude, shared by practically all the Black teachers, considered that the patterns were admirable as an art form and improved the boys' self-esteem.

The axe Mr Jones has to grind concerning his opposition to patterned hairstyles of African-Caribbean boys is complex (Sewell,1997). He is considering the wider cultural and political implication, wanting to impress upon the boys a more valorised system of grooming which will be of benefit to them as an acceptable style for a career on leaving school. It expresses highly critical sentiment on what he takes to mean the shortfall in African-Caribbean status group culture in Britain to arm young men with enterprise and an iron will to succeed educationally and occupationally. As part of his duty to assist in securing the material well-being of African-Caribbean boys, Mr Jones was frequently witnessed by Sewell instilling an African-Caribbean boy with the message 'smarten up and look to me as a role model of how to make it' (1997, p.166). It is open to the interpretation of a racist discourse considering that he threatens the cultural norms of African-Caribbean boys while leaving those of White contemporaries untouched. However, it could be seen as offering up some fatherly advice to children who need to be led. Also, the opportunity Mr Jones has lost is that classroom managers at 'Township' still warranted exclusions of African-Caribbean students founded on small-minded explanations and their own failings – the fundamental explanation to account for why conflict and alienation characterize the relationship between more African-Caribbean boys and their teachers. Black stylised haircuts, therefore, had a twofold influence. They assisted in the creation of an ethnic identity stronghold but were also an essential factor in the manifestation of an African-Caribbean male sub-culture that turned into another version of schooling (Sewell,1997).

Instrumental to the ways the 'rebels' in 'Township School' expressed their resistance was to contravene the rules on haircuts with patterns, whereas 'conformists' steered clear of stylised haircuts or just sported (agreeable) short back and sides. The 'rebels' also had a greater propensity to have Funki-Dreds or designs that mimicked rap and ragga musicians.

Black boys who fell foul of adhering to the requisite short back and sides convention were frequently ridiculed for saying no to or ignoring school rules. The essential features of this taunting often took on racial/sexual forms, with epithets like 'nappy head', 'nigger head' 'batty man' (homosexual) and 'pussy' (Sewell,1997:165).

Who's afraid of the big 'White oppressor'

American scholars Fordham and Ogbu (1986) examined the fear of 'acting White' as a salient influence upon the ways of thinking and attainment of African-American students. They suggested that 'one major reason Black students do poorly in school is that they experience inordinate ambivalence and affective dissonance in regard to academic effort and success' (Quoted in Sewell,1997:109). As Fordham and Ogbu postulate, African Americans experience a collective identity or fictive kinship with fellow African-Americans. An element of this collective identity is that fellow group members pull together in an oppositional mutual distinctiveness that is partly explained as not partaking in things that are linked with White Americans, who are seen as their traditional oppressors. Fordham and Ogbu (1986) took issue with the 'cultural discontinuity theory' of minority achievement, which asserts that a major explanation for underperformance of minority students is that they are outside the cultural backgrounds, understandings and readings of time, space and raison d'être with those who instruct them and evaluate them (Sewell,1997:110).

Key pointers to 'acting White' were identified by African-Caribbean boys at 'Township School'. These extend across speech, dress, acting all stuck up and, in relation to schooling:

You suck up to the teachers

Grovelling to teachers

Get good grades

Always do your work

Bunk off lessons

(Sewell, 1997:185)

Curiously, those which occur above the last point are not only incongruous to it, but they also encapsulate qualities that Mac an Ghaill's (1994) group of Academic Achievers thought were employed as markers of femininity or homosexuality. In fact, Sewell cites one of his respondents as saying that: 'The White boys are just pussies; they haven't got the balls like a Black man; most of them go on as if they are batty men [homosexual]' (1997, p.xii). This response was met with general approval from the group of boys attending the interview. However, when Sewell remarks that, 'they are active agents in discourses which appear to be seductively positive but are in essence racist', he is perhaps referring to this universally sanctioned statement made by the group of African-Caribbean boys (Sewell,1997:177).

The matter of acting White is connected to matters of ethnic identity. Conceptual frameworks of ethnic development indicate that subjecting someone to the charge of acting White may be part of ethnic identity formation where the individual feels significant attachment with his or her own group and insignificant attachment with or even opposition towards the majority group (Sewell,1997). For instance, Sewell cites Cross (1991) to have mentioned the 'Blacker-than-thou' syndrome as encompassing being at the stages of being in the throes of Black identity formation. Phinney (1990) notices that the moment of pondering over one's ethnicity may 'involve rejecting the values of the dominant culture' (Cited in Sewell,1997:110).

Both scholars have not ventured to explore and develop the various ways gender engages with the condition of acting White. The literature (Fuller,1980) and the data information from the Innovators at 'Township' show that acting White intersects with the mode of how these boys develop their masculinity (Sewell,1997). In relation to Black girls, although not secure against the syndrome, traditional scholastic knowledge is associated with power. This knowledge base meant little to the male innovators as to its linkages to power in the labour market and was also pigeonholed as feminised and consequently lower than the higher knowledge of the street whose custodians were the anti-school sub-cultural group.

This contradiction was one decisive factor in explaining the discontentment prevalent among significant numbers of 'Township' students with school (Sewell,1997). However, before floating the idea that this is a simple truth, Sewell makes some qualifications. On the authority of Bergen and Cooks (1995), apparently, the students who were hardest hit by the allegation of selling out or acting White were the proportion in schools with equal racial distribution. Students in schools with equal racial distribution seemed more sensitive to the sharp contrast between the 'races', so the pressure to take sides was greater and/or to choose the company of White students alongside their own ethnic group (Sewell,1997).

The innovators at 'Township School' were in a largely Black social setting and their cross to bear was, to a lesser extent, acting White but acting as 'a Black hyper-heterosexual male' (Sewell,1997:111). This demanded disavowing some ideas that could be traced to the White Western world. But, the White profile in 'Township' was insufficient to necessitate this anxiety. Instead, the 'surveillance' from their Black contemporaries was identified as giving the most cause for concern.

Sources of Disaffection

Many African-Caribbean boys felt that they were at the mercy of the schooling process and many who were members of the school gang 'The Posse' felt aggrieved about teacher racism (Sewell, 1997:169-170). The fifteen-year-old gang members all considered that 'Township School' had contributed to the problem of their school failure. Moreover, the schooling process assailed their most precious attribute – their 'manhood'. Teacher power was integral to this process where their ability to put pupils down was the root cause of many conflicts. Manhood in this sense also interconnected with the widespread fear teachers had regarding the 'size', 'presence' and 'styles of walking', of individuals from 'The Posse' (Sewell,1997:122). They felt that this explained the repression at 'Township' and they countered with their own hyper-heterosexuality.

A significant proportion of the African-Caribbean boys in 'Township' were excluded, not for contravening expressed directives but for 'crimes' that were contingent on interpretation, as exemplified by violent and disruptive conduct (Sewell,1997:186). What stood out in the conceptualization of many classroom managers was that African-Caribbean students were in the frame as school rule-breakers or were so inclined to do so. The paradox applicable to nearly all of these boys was that they were seldom condemned for contravening any 'explicit' rule. Such boys were entangled by mechanisms of authority that had controlling consequences.

In other words, African-Caribbean boys were in an ineluctable context of conflict that chiefly involved their leading classroom authority figures and their classmates. They sustained an unconscionable measure of regulating influence, which their teachers (psychiatrists, prison guards, courts, police) legitimated by their mental pabulum of Black masculinity (Sewell,1997:186).

Wright (1987) conducted an ethnographic and statistical study of two multi-ethnic comprehensive schools during the periods 1982 and 1984. The study concentrated on boys and girls in their penultimate and final years at school. Wright observed the quality of classroom relations between the teacher and the African-Caribbean pupil as not infrequently defined by confrontation and conflict. The relationship between the teacher and these pupils often adopts the form and function of the teacher imposing classroom discipline and/or meting out criticism. Furthermore, the detail of classroom life which gives rise to conflict between the classroom manager and the African-Caribbean pupil was witnessed by Wright to often be extraneous to the essential matter of teaching. For example, Wright observed some teachers too frequently punctuate their lectures with comments or jokes referencing the African-Caribbean pupils' ethnicity and physical attributes. Such behaviour by the teacher was observed to be a source of considerable distress to these pupils.

Indications are that behind the calibre of interplay between the classroom authority figures and their African-Caribbean pupils were the wholly unfavourable attitudes and expectations associated with teachers concerning these pupils. This is no hollow claim, Wright presents field notes and discourse from two lessons to sustain the allegations (Wright,1987:111). Verbal exchanges with the African-Caribbean males and females from both schools, in an endeavour to determine their outlook on school and social reality and their response to their lived experiences, indicate that these pupils repeatedly wonder whether classroom life extends any further for them beyond disrespect, directives and criticisms (Wright,1987:116).

The African-Caribbean female who declared that, 'if the teachers have no respect for you, there's no way I'm going to respect them', demonstrates the extent to which misfortune experienced through actual means of certain teachers comes to be firmly established cerebrally in these pupils and inform their conceptualization of schooling (Wright,1987:118). The African-Caribbean girls and boys had cause for complaints and dissatisfaction concerning their teachers' attitudes and conduct towards them. Both genders were prepared to openly challenge and tackle the teachers through the medium of Jamaican patois in their interaction with the teacher. However, because their complaints were couched in patois, teachers felt threatened as their culture did not usually include such a repertoire and so this contributed to an amplification of the teachers' negative attitudes and conduct towards exponents of Jamaican patois. In relation to the African-Caribbean students, the endorsement of codes outside of teacher understanding is a deliberate piecemeal deconstruction of the teachers' authority. According to Wright, this strategy was seen to achieve the desired effect. In this way, and by collectively baiting teachers at break times with a Jamaican patois rant, African-Caribbean students actively engaged teachers to 'get our own back for what they [teachers] do to us' (Wright,1987:122). And, this behaviour saw the African-Caribbean students become embroiled in a self-fulfilling prophecy, which tended to complement the teacher's perception of them, namely expulsion or suspension.

An offshoot of African-Caribbean students being denied educational opportunities owing to adverse relations between them and their classroom managers stemmed from the finding that their teachers falsified assessments of their abilities and academic attainment. Data information indicates that in their evaluation of the African-Caribbean pupils, the teachers allowed behavioural criteria to dominate their thinking over cognitive ones. Put differently, the allocated assessment would most likely be a reflection of the teacher's non-objective involvement with the knotty behavioural situations of school life. This consequently led to a context where African-Caribbean students, far more than any other ethnic groups, were inclined to be allocated to ability bands and examination sets significantly below their real scholastic achievement and ability. This demonstrates that in their evaluation of the African-Caribbean pupils' ability, the teachers were less inclined to administer professional judgement (Wright,1987:123).

Wright (1987) was also able to prove statistically that more than any other student group, African-Caribbean students appear more to have the odds favouring them being allocated to examination sets below their ability (i.e., African-Caribbean student 'D' having achieved eighty-two per cent in French, is assigned to a CSE set) than is evident for White and South Asian student groups.

The flagrant misallocation of the African-Caribbean students on grounds of their potential would clearly indicate that within this institution, openly discriminatory practices were carried out against the African-Caribbean students, an indication which is possibly supported by what one of the teachers had to say regarding the allocation of African-Caribbean student 'D' to a CSE set: 'This student has been on the fringe of trouble all year; her attitude to the teachers is not at all good and she can be a nuisance in class' (Wright,1987:124).

This teacher's statement sends out the message that some teacher's view ability as an admirable trait, but it is only admirable when demonstrated by a White, and perhaps a South Asian student.

Among a plethora of issues that the research findings bring to light is that of the perception of Black students' (particularly those from African-Caribbean extraction) educational achievement in the British school system (Wright,1987). In recent memory, the educational effectiveness and proficiency levels of African-Caribbean students have hitherto been perceived in terms of 'underachievement' (e.g., TES, Friday 19 February 2016, pp.28-9). The theory of underachievement of African-Caribbean schoolchildren has certain implicit understandings. A particular understanding is founded upon the liberal *weltanschauung* of equality of opportunity and meritocratic principles, that is, the existing in and inseparable from assumption that schooling functions as a forum for self-realization/actualization, honing, sharpening and polishing abilities, and for the improvement of society's skill set. A further understanding renders the experiences of distinct student groups within the education system as roughly identical. The African-Caribbean child's experience of school laid down by Wright (1987) clearly brings these understandings into question.

Wright concludes that because of complex school processes which impact unfavourably upon African-Caribbean children's experience of schooling, it may fundamentally be better appreciated by using terminology like 'inequality' or 'educational disadvantage' rather than being seen as 'underachievement'. Structural and institutional phenomena are drawn on for why such an assessment has been forwarded and Wright emphasizes that the circumstances of the Black child within the British school system require the foresight to be seen in this light.

Prior to providing an interpretive analysis of the foregoing five ethnographic studies, one further exposition conducted by Peter Foster (1990) between 1985 and 1987 in a multi-ethnic secondary school threatens to throw out the baby with the bathwater and cast doubt on the credibility of our research findings. In sharp contrast to the above studies, the protagonist found no suggestion that the students felt that racism was a problem within the school, save for three students who, when interviewed, 'complained, without being asked, about what they felt was racism from their teachers (Foster, 1990:134). But Foster extends short shrift to these claims, situating them instead as bound up in the Black students' far-reaching, *ne plus ultra* sense of alienation from the institution of school. He closed the matter in the statement that follows:

> Occasionally, the hostility of Afro-Caribbean students was expressed using the vocabulary of 'racism', but such accusations rarely specified incidents that were racist in terms of the definition I have used (Foster, 1990:136).

Another way to view this sees Foster taking as watertight the heavy reliance placed upon the students' responses as instances of boys undergoing racist/sexist discrimination at the hands of their teachers. It remains to be seen for certain that we are obtaining an accurate picture from these students. When all is said and done, they are simply reiterating what most students sense concerning school regardless of racism (Sewell, 1997).

Curiously, Foster (1990) himself is responsible for the practically inadvertent case building for race and gender inequality by not weighing observations critically (Sewell,1997:12). For instance, he asserts that:

> There was a tendency for Afro-Caribbean boys to be less likely to be placed in the top sets than would have been anticipated given their numbers in the school (p.174).

> Afro-Caribbean boys were somewhat more likely to be seen as poorly behaved (p.146).

> Interestingly, Afro-Caribbean boys were more likely to be seen as anti-school than might have been expected given their numbers in the year (p.131). (Quoted in Sewell,1997).

This litany of specific information is wholly beyond Foster's ken as clear evidence of racism however it masquerades. Foster is compelled to account for these differences with reference to their bearing as facts ('this may have been because Afro-Caribbean boys, on average, in this particular year had less ability') (p.174) or because 'Afro-Caribbean boys were somewhat more likely to present behavioural problems to the teachers' (p.143). Foster found it necessary to retreat from addressing the issue of the education system to disproportionately claiming that Black students are at fault, an analysis that heads in a racialised direction (Sewell,1997).

The deep sense of alienation of a cadre of children delineated by 'race' requires some elucidation. It is not sufficient to express that the ultimate responsibility lies with society, not school: is school not the very fabric of society? Does not society have bound up within its ranks people who perform roles as teachers and/or parents of children? Therefore, if 'society' is responsible, it is important to recognize how that society locates itself in school. Foster's perspective on racism is reductive in that he would simplify to matters of contempt or direct discrimination, whereas racism as an exclusionary practice shows itself in many and multitudinous ways. The duality of the institutional and the personal is material enough though at the level of the school it is part of the complex system or web of assumptions about class and gender (Sewell,1997).

'Milltown High' was a site in which conflict pervaded the school day, though Foster is at pains to state that conflict did not characterize every particular aspect of school life. To this end, he notes, 'there were times when relationships between teachers and students were extremely co-operative and friendly' (Foster,1990:27). However, at 'Milltown High School', the degree of conflict that defined schooling was far more pronounced than in other schools Foster had come into contact with. According to Grace (1978), schools in working-class catchment areas have tended to be places not only of institutional and age-related conflict but also of class conflict (cited in Foster,1990). In point of fact, the position has been taken by some (Willis,1977), which others (Wright, Weekes and McGlaughlin,2000) argue to be more complex, that schools such as these are key sites where working-class groups redefine a culture of resistance.

Despite this, 'Milltown High' was distinct from the other schools in so far as being located in a social *mise en scene* where cooperation between diverse ethnic groups stretches back over a long period of time. Secondly, students who held racist beliefs were extremely reluctant to voice their views in the school for fear of their personal safety. African-Caribbean students dominated peer group cultures and enjoyed a slight numerical advantage. Thirdly, the teachers appear to have been successful in promoting an anti-racist agenda. Some of the students Foster conversed with were clear on the majority staff position on racism and concurred with it, sometimes admonishing their fellow students for their racism. To this extent, then, the teachers appear to have been behind good social relations within the institution of school.

However, in other respects, 'Milltown High', to whatever extent, resembled the other schools we have looked at, in that student attitudes and behaviour towards their teachers was at variance with classroom control; their friendship network modus vivendi was often anti-academic, underlining instead an orientation towards being a 'hard knock', non-conformity, verbal dexterity, and 'havin' a laugh'. In this way, students caused staff undue pressure and stress; classroom control was often contested, sometimes with hostile and aggressive behaviour patterns, and the school was seen to process teachers, who drew on all their powers of control and survival rather than learning to remain in or be forced out of the job, as school processed students. The level of students' hostility and at best ambivalence to schooling was so great that Foster reiterates that it was far worse than any other school he had come into contact with.

To broach the theory once again that society itself is situated in school, Foster is opposed to the re-education of teachers because it may elicit hostility and alienation and even advances the notion that the vast majority of teachers do not subscribe to views that disadvantage minority ethnic students. Yet, some teachers at 'Milltown High', in any case, considered all White teachers as inevitably racist because of their background and 'mono-cultural' upbringing. So, if a school can implement a multicultural and anti-racist programme and its teachers have a high level of racial and ethnic awareness as a result, even though teacher training devotes little attention to 'race' awareness, the point is that hostility and alienation can only be provoked if teachers entertain beliefs that run counter to the fair and just treatment of minority ethnic students. Re-education is an important point here because inevitably, racist teachers sometimes behaving in unintentionally racist ways without even realizing or being consciously aware that they are doing so, is a significantly large barrier to radical social progress and a non-racist society in which all can aspire to reach their full potential. Foster's apology of schools, and within-school processes and teachers, his rapid and unsympathetic dismissal of racism awareness training for all teachers, raises serious concerns as to whether he would espouse such ideals as he essentially seems to endorse a message that at best, says more research should be done and at worst, that racism via teachers or through school processes at 'Milltown High School' is not the question but minority students are disadvantaged by attending 'low achieving schools' that restrict their chances of educational success, and by the ability of economic and cultural groups to manipulate the system and optimize capital usage to other neighbourhoods where alternative and 'better' schooling is made available for their children to advance in the field of educational opportunity. Foster's treatise is a claim dropped into a sea awash with counter-claim and, how can the sway of so many counter-claims be unfounded? Is it at all likely that, in the long periods Foster spent with 'Milltown High School' staff members, he lost sight of his ability to function in a detached and objective manner and therefore became partisan?

It is all well and good for teachers to have lofty cultural norms founded on White middle-class values of the 'ideal client', but it is another thing when it disadvantages minority ethnic boys leading to problems of motivation, academic progress and ultimately 'underachievement', it flies in the face of equal opportunities, privileging income groups and resource repositories, and is an ideological paradigm to beat the working-class with and thus helps to reproduce society's social characteristics. As teachers at 'Milltown High' had somewhat adjusted their conceptions of worth to be more inclusive of certain minority ethnic cultural signifiers, this idea of them being at a disadvantage does not appear to be the case. The fact that African-Caribbean students outperformed their White peers at 'Milltown High' militates against the trend but, on the other hand, what chance have minority ethnic students if, as in other schools, a multicultural and anti-racist programme is not in place and White middle-class conventions predominate? For Marx, 'the ideas of the ruling class are the ruling ideas in every epoch', and this assertion encapsulates Foster's angle on ruling class ideas gaining the ascendancy in terms of how student worth – informed by wider social perceptions – is evaluated, and the pitfalls this view offers invite divisive processes and by giving them the nod, Foster lacks originality and completeness (Bilton,1989:44).

While Foster was aware that the unique qualities of his study school may have been critical in him arriving at conclusions that diverge from the other ethnographic explorations, he has, in a concerted effort with Gomm and Hammersley, subsequently attacked the validity of these studies. A collection of writings has snowballed in a book weighing into ethnographic and other research work which purport to point to school processes being conducive to educational inequality (Pilkington,2003). It is *sine qua non* that their conclusions are cited. Regarding studies claiming to indicate that schools are discriminatory in the process of student allocation to different types of course, they conclude: 'Taken overall, this body of research fails to establish that discrimination against working-class and Black students occurs on any scale in the allocation of students to courses or through the effects of this allocation' (Foster et al,1996:105). Regarding studies claiming to show inequalities in classroom treatment, they conclude:

> There are also some serious problems with the evidential base on which descriptive claims about differential treatment rely. Sometimes no evidence at all is presented, even though the claims are sufficiently plausible to be accepted at face value. And when evidence is provided, it is often of a kind that cannot effectively support the sort of claim made: for instance, one or two examples are offered to establish the different frequency of particular sorts of teacher action in relation to different categories of student. Moreover, many of the interpretations

made of data are questionable (Foster et al,1990:138; cited in Pilkington, 2003:150).

Providing such cynicism towards evidence which signposts discrimination at the level of the school and in the classroom, their overarching conclusion pulls little by way of any real punches: 'There is no convincing evidence currently available for any substantial role on the part of schools in generating inequalities in educational outcomes between social classes, genders or ethnic groups' (Foster et al,1990:174; cited in Pilkington,2003:150).

In what way does this critique stand up when ethnicity is the issue, where the central focus has related to the performance of Caribbean pupils? Our approach follows the line of scrutinizing the evidence on discrimination in assigning individuals to different types of course (Pilkington,2003). In this connection, there is substantial evidence that Caribbean students are thinly distributed in top sets and thickly distributed in bottom sets. Out of all conceivable possibilities, the 1992/3 report of HM Chief Inspector of Schools recognized that they, together with other minority ethnic students, were on the whole 'under-represented in the top sets' (Pilkington,2003:150). Material evidence also suggests that placement is repeatedly not predicated on merit per se and that this puts Caribbean pupils at a disadvantage. We noted earlier the existence of evidence from Wright (1992) and Mac an Ghaill (1988), which points up that behavioural criteria rather than cognitive ones alone were employed in the allocation of students to different types and levels of learning and that this practice discriminated against Caribbean students in particular. Moreover, there is further evidence running on a parallel trajectory. For example, an analysis of one local education authority indicates that:

> When there was a mismatch between the VR [verbal reasoning] band in which a pupil had been placed by teachers and that based on test performance, Caribbean pupils were more likely to be placed in the lower VR band ... while ESWI [English, Scottish, Welsh and Irish]

pupils were more likely to be placed in a higher VR band than their test scores would suggest (Kysel,1988:88; cited in Pilkington, 2003:151).

Foster himself recognized that behaviour and not ability-affected allocation in his own social research. He saw it in the following terms:

> The behaviour of older Afro/Caribbean boys tended to be regarded less favourably. In a sense, their youth cultural norms conformed less closely to their teachers' conceptions of the 'ideal' and as a result, they seemed somewhat more likely to be allocated to lower-status groups in the school's system of differentiation (Foster,1990:181; cited in Pilkington,2003:151).

Also, emerging from a telling footnote to their highly critical diatribe of knowledge of discrimination, Foster et al further recognize themselves that 'it may be of significance that the departures from what would be expected on the basis of measured ability that have been found within and across studies, while small, tend to be always in the same direction. This indicates that more thorough investigation is justified' (Foster et al, 1996:81; cited in Pilkington,2003:151). We should certainly consider that, this too, signposts that indirect discrimination is most likely occurring since allocation via behavioural criteria has been proven to have, however inadvertently, an unfavourable effect against Caribbean students.

What of the effects of streaming? Mac an Ghaill (1988), Wright (1992) and Gillborn (1990) do indicate a move towards the systems of thought of different streams to differ widely, with those occupying the bottom streams gravitating towards involvement in resistance, and at certain stages in their treatise, Foster et al, also give credence to 'the operation of a differentiation – polarisation effect' (Foster et al,1996: 103; quoted in Pilkington,2003:151).

We now turn to examine the evidence on discrimination in the classroom. The value of Foster et al's critique lies in alerting us to the dangers of not interpreting ethnographic studies with a critical eye. While they can bring a colourful understanding of classroom life, there is the risk of selective perception, where observations tend to be read through the lens of already existing theory. Alternate readings are invariably feasible. Consider the extract above regarding Marcus. We are prevailed upon to suppose that Marcus is especially subject to censure because of his ethnicity. Could other reasons not warrant acceptance? Is it Caribbean individuals in particular who are subject to censure? As part of this particular research, Wright (1992) does in fact present evidence to show that White teachers, in particular, discriminated against Caribbean males, in particular (Pilkington,2003), and this is all-important. Because it is only when different strands of evidence are utilized which corroborate one another that ethnographic studies carry efficacy. The social research we have focused on is like Shakespeare's Hamlet in character on this issue, but all employ an admixture of methods to triangulate their final outcome. Further, they unanimously indicate a comparatively serious level of conflict between White classroom authority figures and Caribbean students. What distinguishes Foster from the others lies in seeing staff responding appropriately to the conduct of Caribbean students and playing an indeterminate role in generating conflict (Pilkington,2003).

In a quite distinct publication, Foster maintains that teacher stereotypes are founded on observations of students' conduct and academic proficiency in the classroom (cited in Pilkington,2003). He may present a high degree of accuracy here. But observations are not value-free and may be informed by prior typification. At this juncture, is a student undergoing teaching practice in a boys' comprehensive taking on new knowledge from school management:

> I was told that I had to look out for the West Indians and what to do. If they went mad, one just had to leave them alone to cool down. There was nothing we could do, and things like that if they swore at us in their own language, we must report it. They had trouble from them in the past.

The student subsequently secured a school position. Here he is, 12 months later:

The West Indians are tough. I tried not to let anyone influence me in how I treated them but they look at you with wild eyes if you tell them to sit down. They are looking, expecting trouble. They are more prejudiced than white people. The Asians are better, you tell them to do something and then meek an [mild] they go an' do it (Mac an Ghaill,1988:64-5; quoted in Pilkington,2003:152).

Further to evidence that experienced professionals may inform teacher typification, there is, in addition, evidence from the expositions by Wright (1987) and Gillborn (1990) and, nearer the present from OFSTED (Smithers, 2001) that the equivalent behaviour may be responded to differently by teachers. The foregoing is especially disturbing if it leads to Caribbeans being especially at risk of censure in their formative educational career, as was the case for Marcus, because Smith and Tomlinson (1989) suggest that students who are under the cosh of constant criticism tend to underperform (cited in Pilkington,2003).

To identify evidence which indicates that Caribbean students are occasionally at risk of unfavourable treatment in the classroom context does not necessarily signify, however, that Foster's research study and in its wake Foster et al's critique of ethnographic research in this field should be rapidly dispensed with. A substantial school of thought exists that says, at least in the last two years of schooling, the conduct of some Caribbean students is not described by classroom authority figures as deviant but is *de facto* deviant (Pilkington,2003). The point at which Foster and his critics essentially disagree is on the subject of their logic of 'bad behaviour'. For Foster, priority is laid at the door of extra-school factors. 'There may be a general tendency for Afro-Caribbean students on average to be less well behaved in schools' (Foster,1990:168; quoted in Pilkington, 2003:153) because of their induction to a distinctive subculture resulting from a realization on their part of scarce post-school opportunities and rejection of racism beyond the school gates. For the others, priority is laid at the door of school processes, with certain Caribbean pupils conceptualized as having recourse to a distinctive subculture so as to withstand their unfavourable treatment in schools. The vexed question between Foster and his critics calls to mind the vexed question on the subject of the criminalisation of Black people. For certain commentators, the increased participation of Caribbean young men in public order offences is largely to blame for their increased criminalisation; for others, racial injustice in the criminal justice system is largely to blame for their increased criminalisation. More concurrently, however, there have been strains by some criminologists 'to move beyond the either/or of racist criminal justice v black criminality' (P Taylor et al. 1995:486; quoted in Pilkington,2003:153) to identify that both 'reinforce and feed off one another in a vicious circle of amplification' (Reiner, 1993:14; in Pilkington,2003:153). The juxtaposition we venture to say is that in schools, both unfavourable treatment and 'bad behaviour' may engender the creation of a vicious circle.

The foregoing statement has been adopted by some contemporaneous ethnographic studies which attempt to show how wider social meanings of both ethnicity and gender influence the schooling affairs of Black pupils and contribute to a vicious circle. Connolly puts forward an instance of this in his multi-ethnic primary school study. In this connection:

> The over-disciplining of Black boys tends to construct an image of them, among their peers, as being 'bad' and quintessentially masculine. This, in turn, provides the context where Black boys are more likely to be drawn into fights and to develop 'hardened' identities, which then means they are more likely to be noticed by the teachers and disciplined for being aggressive. The cycle is thus complete (Connolly,1998a:114; quoted in Pilkington,2003:154).

Although Connolly apportions a substantial amount of the blame for the development of this cycle to staff, Sewell, in his boys' secondary school study, disputes the notion that teacher racism alone' leads Black boys 'to adopt a culture of resistance to schooling' (Sewell, 1997:170; in Pilkington,2003:154). Although he recognizes that teachers are inclined to give the nod to what Gillborn (1990) designates 'the myth of the African Caribbean challenge' and pictures boys in particular as putting their authority at risk, he also underlines the function of the Black students' subculture which 'helps to feed the stereotype that African-Caribbean boys are more openly aggressive/rude than their "weak" white counterparts' (Sewell,1997:104; in Pilkington,2003:154).

Teachers, as well as pupils, are envisaged as informed by cultural forms of Black males received outside the classroom. The teachers are inclined towards holding ethnocentric presumptions of the broader expanse of people and places and presume 'that African-Caribbean boys were instinctively against authority while Asian boys were the complete opposite' (Sewell,1997:61; in Pilkington,2003:154). The consequence was that African-Caribbean boys incurred an undue measure of control and criticism relative to other student groups. Simultaneously, the Black subculture within the school confines made connections in relation to an external street culture and laid emphasis 'on a Black collectivist anti-school ideology, on pro-consumerism and phallocentrism' (Sewell,1997:108; in Pilkington,2003:154). Although this subculture empowered the boys to withstand the racism outside the school and retain a vibrant Black identity, its assumption of a machismo male paradigm fell short of producing academic success. The balancing act, for a number of boys, of academic attainment with being gay or womanish was apparent here and erected barriers to pupils attempting to secure educational credentials.

At the centre of conflict between teachers and Black pupils were frequent expressions of ethnicity from the boys. Black hairstyles were grounds on which a stand was often made amid rampant dispute within the boys' ranks. The new Black head issued an edict banning the boys from wearing patterns in their hair while the ban left untouched White boys who wore ponytails. The outcome saw Black hairstyles assume 'a key factor in the display of an African-Caribbean masculine subculture that became an alternative to schooling' (Sewell,1997:166; in Pilkington,2003:155). This leaves the way open to the generation of a vicious cycle, in which what is seen as a gesture of disrespect from teachers is greeted by aggressive behaviour patterns from pupils who are subsequently penalized for their behaviour.

A cycle of this nature can, as was ripe to happen in this school, have devastating consequences leading to 'black young people [being] proportionately more likely to be excluded than members of other ethnic groups' (Gillborn and Gipps,1996:52; in Pilkington, 2003:155). As sanctions obtain, permanent exclusions are the single most severe penalty schools can discharge. The sanction is now equally being more widely applied for insubordination of various kinds and is also being applied disproportionately with Black pupils, particularly Caribbeans.

David Gillborn et al. (2016) have been conducting a two-year research programme that looks at the effects of the vicissitudes in education policy and practice in the wake of the murder of teenager Stephen Lawrence in 1993. The study's initial findings are outlined in the following. Generally, there is a meaningful reduction in the probability of permanent exclusion juxtaposed with the situation in the late 1990s (TES,2016). Largely, this appears to date back to the expressed initiative to reduce figures (directed by central government) between 1998 and 2001. Generally, a student in 1997 was nearly three times more at risk of permanent exclusion than they are in 2014. But, in relation to the unequal opportunities of permanent exclusion where Black Caribbean children are concerned, the news is not good. Compared with their White counterparts, Black Caribbean students' chances of being permanently excluded have established relative unchangeability (dwarfing the White rate by about three to four times over the 18-year period). Over-representation (compared to the White rate) has not fallen below [a multiple of] three for more than a decade (since 2004). Over-representation (compared to the White rate) has never fallen below [a multiple of 2.9 during the 18 years of national data availability (TES,2016).

To recognize that the data for indirect discrimination at the institution of school level and to recognize that the data for differential treatment at classroom context level are more apparent than Foster et al. indicate does not necessarily follow that schools are a major gateway 'in generating inequalities in educational outcomes between ... ethnic groups' (Foster et al,1996:174; in Pilkington, 2003:155). Foster et al. are only too right in refreshing our memories along the lines that we cannot generalise from specific schools and specific classrooms to every classroom. In fact, it is doubtful whether the principle behind ethnographic research is to create generalisations at all (Pilkington,2003). And although there are across-school processes – as advanced by the converging picture transmitted by the main body of ethnographic studies – we cannot arrive at an informed judgement regarding the 'causal efficacy' of school processes without a comparison being drawn between the input of extra-school factors. The research around school effectiveness, which does attempt to control factors like previous achievement and social class, intimates that variation between institutions does make an impact but that extra-school dimensions are generally far more significant in deciding student progress (Pilkington,2003). While this research is interested in the differences between schools but does not discount putatively common discriminatory practices across schools and therefore can serve to confirm the implication that racism in schools is a significant factor in accounting for differences in ethnic attainment, however, Pilkington's approach endorses extreme caution before reaching a final conclusion.

A cautious approach is given added force when we recall the complexity in levels of ethnic educational attainment, which indicates that, although certain minority ethnic groups are outperforming Whites, Caribbean male pupils are underachieving and the Pakistani and Bangladeshi groups are also failing to meet the challenge (Pilkington,2003). It is difficult to disentangle the role of racism in this complex picture but some important insights can be gained from the Caribbean experience of education. The Black child expends energy in the exercise of learning under three very important handicaps: (1) Low expectations on discharging his obligation to perform in a white-governed middle-class educational establishment; (2) Low motivation to reach his true academic potential because he feels that he does not have an equal chance of succeeding; and lastly, (3) Low teacher expectations which may influence the amount of application exerted for his benefit by the teacher, and also have an effect upon his own self-image and his abilities (Coard,1971:25). When the system functions and operates against you and when everyone looks to you to fail, the probability is you will contemplate failure too. Whenever you anticipate failure, the odds are you will, Coard (1971) maintains.

The above reinforces the idea that most teachers absorb the indoctrination that every single person in the society undergoes - that Black people are inferior, are less intellectually able, etc. than White people. Moreover, the notion is corroborated by the evidence that Caribbean boys are often overrepresented at the lower end of the educational hierarchy, set or stream, where they are expected to do less well in school and placement tends to be on the basis of behavioural rather than cognitive criteria (Wright, Weekes and McGlaughlin,2000:130).

Prejudice and Patronization

There is a multitude of reasons to account for Black underachievement levels, and we need to establish what they are in order to advance recommendations to change the prevailing trend. The three principal ways in which a classroom authority figure can seriously impede u the performance of young Black people are (1) by being overtly prejudiced; (2) by being patronizing; and (3) by being host to low expectations of the students' abilities. Each one of these attitudes is part of the mindset of teachers in the UK. To be sure, these three attitudes are pervasive (Coard,1971). How such sentiments affect the Black child is substantial and devastating.

Coard (1971) reports having conversations with numerous Black teachers whose encounters with some White teachers leaves much to be desired. Two African-Caribbean teachers in South London relayed to Coard the news of White teachers who passed time in the staff-room smoking and refused to extend their service to a class of predominantly Black students. On the occasion they were challenged by one of the Black classroom teachers, they expressed that they drew the line at teaching 'those niggers'. These developments were something the headteachers of the schools were notified about, who lodged no penalty against the teachers in question. In fact, these schools' leading figures had been seeking to prevail upon the students to abandon their studies on reaching the school-leaving age, although their parents were all for their continued tenure in education, in some cases to gain qualifications, and in alternate cases, because they felt that another year's general education would be decisive for their children's future. In this case, then, the teachers colluded to thwart these young Black students from improving upon their education by simply reneging on their obligation to teach (Coard,1971).

There are numerous other classroom managers who are patronizing or condescending where Black children are the issue (Coard,1971). Such individuals are the type who consider a Black child much like a prized pet animal. Coard has often been in earshot of teachers uttering: 'I really like that coloured child. He is quite bright for a coloured child'! (Coard,1971:19). One classroom authority figure actually once said to him, in a bona fide and good-natured tone of voice: 'Gary is really quite a nice boy considering he is Black' (Coard,1971:19). Further data highlights other teachers who avoid putting the Black child under too much pressure academically, as 'he isn't really up to it, poor chap' (Coard,1971:19) Children penetrate these hypocritical and ignominious statements and attitudes more frequently than adults give them credit for, and they feel profoundly affronted when anyone treats them as if they were inferior, which has patronization written all over it. They amass resentment and develop deep-seated psychological blocks to learning.

The influence of low Teacher expectation on the Child

The IQ tests which are placed before the Black child, consisting of inherent cultural bias, afford him a negative rating only too frequently. The teacher assessment criterion for the prospective proficiency of the child rests on this IQ test. Once in the teacher's possession, the IQ test results are assumed to count as 'objective' confirmation of the 'colonial mentality' operating not only at a subliminal level but sometimes openly expressed: that the Black children, in general, have lower IQ than their White counterparts, and must therefore be expected to underachieve in the classroom. The ignominious

Professor Jenson, the Enoch Powell of the academic community, has lent support to so-called Black inferiority by overtly disclosing that Black people are innately less able than Whites, and hence Black children should occupy a separate teaching environment (Coard, 1971).

In this context, is there little wonder that most English teachers have lower expectations of the Black child than the White child? That teachers expect less has profound consequences on the child's veritable performance and will now be inflected from two studies conducted on both sides of the Atlantic.

In research conducted in London, 118 epileptic students were requested to sit an IQ test. Those charged with teaching them, unaware of the test results, were then petitioned to give their judgment of the students' intelligence by indicating if a student was 'average', 'above average', 'well above average', etc, from their value judgment of each student (Coard,1971:21). Worth an important mention here is that epileptic children experience considerable prejudice levelled against them by society at large, matching that which Black children face – but patently not as severe. Classroom managers also tend to regard them as being subnormal to ordinary children – reinforcing the correlation between the circumstances of the Black child.

'In twenty-eight cases, the teachers seriously underestimated the child's true ability' (Coard,1971:21). Put in slightly different terms, a quarter of the students were wrongly evaluated! A case in point is that of a thirteen-year-old female who acquired an IQ of 120 (i.e., university level!), had fallen at her 11+ examination and was seen to occupy the 'D' stream of a secondary modern establishment. Her classroom manager felt that she was of 'below average' ability! (Average ability=100). One other child with family issues and poor material resources obtained an IQ score of 132 (which is exceptionally high). Her classroom managers, however, all surmised that she was nothing other than 'low stream' material! (Coard,1971)

Evidence of this calibre is staggering because now that schools are mainly comprehensive, with some 163 selective grammar schools, it is the rough calculation of the teachers and leading authority figures which determines what stream a minor is allocated to – which in turn, affects the level of expectation accorded him academically. In the event that these teachers whose business it is to know the young people in *loco parentis* make serious errors in a quarter of the cases to do with epileptic children, against whom vestiges of prejudice exist, can one ideate how many errors of judgment are made by classroom managers when young Black people are implicated?! (Coard,1971:21-22).

Two American specialists in education completed IQ tests on the students in a particular institution in San Francisco. They concealed the true test results from the teachers. Rather, they haphazardly selected twenty appellations of students from the school and informed the classroom managers that these were the intelligent students, despite the fact that they were not. Before the year had ended, the children were quizzed again, and the class authority figures were asked a multitude of questions concerning them. The score of children who the teachers regarded as the most intelligent did very much better than their contemporaries. They achieved higher ratings than the other students in the IQ test. The classroom teachers considered that they were 'happier', more 'curious' and 'interesting' than their peers, and 'more likely to succeed in life than the others' (Coard,1971:20). In Grade 1, the students whom the teachers believed were intelligent achieved 27.5 points (on average) in their IQ scores, contrasted with an average of 12 points for those outside the twenty students, a difference of 15.5 points! In Grade 2, the discrepancy and variance was 9 points (Coard,1971:20).

These ratings can make every difference in the race for a child to secure a grammar school place or not; or which type or level of course a child is allocated to in a comprehensive; or whether, in fact, a child is withdrawn from an ordinary school and dumped in an ESN school. Also, these attainment patterns on the initiative of the children were merely the outcome of how much the teachers expected from each individual. They had little at all, if any, special attention paid to a single group, and the authority figures and minors were told nothing concerning the experiment.

According to what the experts indicate: 'In our experiment, nothing was done directly for the child. There was no crash programme to improve his reading ability, no extra time for tutoring, no programme of trips to museums and art galleries. The only people affected directly were the teachers; the effect on the children was indirect' (Coard,1971:21). Nevertheless, they registered these significant differences in performance inextricably linked to how much the class manager expected of his or her charge. This illustrates why biased IQ tests are no longer compulsory, conducted under entirely biased contexts; for the teacher places confidence in these quizzical examinations, and the teacher's expectations influence the child's academic advancement (Coard,1971).

Material information of racism in schools appears stronger than Foster et al. point out since we cannot underestimate or overlook the effects of racism on the Black child both inside and outside the school. For example, the over-representation of Caribbean children in lower streams in schools could reflect unfair discrimination by teachers (Troyna,1987). And, it may reflect the teacher's failure to inspire groups of pupils to persevere with schoolwork; it may be on account of a misallocation of cultural capital dating back in the pupil's school career; it may be an individual response to racism within and beyond the school, resulting in a rejection of school in relation to which the teacher has no alternative course of action. Once placed in lower streams, groups of pupils are subject to low teacher expectations and are less likely to be entered for a higher GCSE system of assessment no matter how well they do. In short, the ineluctable and inescapable prospect is that low teacher expectations could be the contributing factor in accounting for patterns of ethnic educational underperformance (Coard,1971; Mac an Ghaill,1988:3; Wright, Weekes and McGlaughlin,2000:130; Warmington,2014 pp.136,150).

Teachers, both in America and Britain, tend to attribute primary responsibility for underachieving and struggling Black young people to the "home culture" and parenting background style of the students concerned and are inclined never to bring the legitimacy of "classroom culture" into question (Mac an Ghaill,1988; Stoll,2013:87). Mac an Ghaill (1988) argue that the main problem in the teaching and regulating of Black youth is not that account should be taken of their culture but rather that account should be taken of racism (p.3). This simulacrum is corroborated by Wright (1987) who observed that behind the calibre of interplay between the classroom authority figures and their African-Caribbean charges were the wholly unfavourable attitudes and expectations associated with teachers concerning these pupils.

More recently, Gillborn has emphasized the disproportionate representation in permanent exclusions from school of Black Caribbean youths and suggests that this illustrates systemic institutional racism, but others contend that it simply defines Black children as less well behaved (Creasey,2016). Gillborn recognizes how racism in schools affects Black boys; the notion that they are expected to underachieve is internalized and that some Asian cultures – e.g., Indian and Chinese - are stereotyped as high-ability material that delineates a positive bias which such students are receptive to, and although Asian groups are expected to do well, we cannot uncomplicate the picture by putting ethnic differential attainment levels down to the teachers' attitudes and expectations since Pakistani and Bangladeshi categories are on equal terms with Black kids when it comes to academic performance levels. Gillborn concludes that the problem of unconscious bias in schools is getting worse rather than better (Creasey,2016). The education system intersects with a wider set of constraints which, often inadvertently, contributes to the maintenance of Blacks emerging from a background of structured inequality (Mac an Ghaill,1988).

The angst-ridden question, which has come under our examination, concerning the cumulative effect which school processes impart in explaining Caribbean underachievement mediates with a wider debate concerning the objects of educational inquiry. Foster et al, assume a 'methodological purist' standpoint, emphasizing that 'the purpose of research in this area should be to produce knowledge relevant to public debates, not to eradicate inequality' (Foster et al,1996:40 in Pilkington,2003:157). By contradistinction, Troyna and acolytes adopt a partisan, or that which Gillborn (1998) privileges to coin a 'critical' position, seeing the object of sociological inquiry as that of taking stock of what is currently occurring in order to tackle injustices (Pilkington,2003). The methodological purists argue that researchers who assume an avowedly anti-racist standpoint too readily acknowledge evidence in the direction of differential treatment and indirect discrimination. The foregoing adherents retort that, if nothing else, they are explicit regarding their guiding principles, while the methodological purists, by importing extremely rigorous criteria to estimate studies signposting differential treatment and indirect discrimination, are *in toto* concerned to champion teachers. Notwithstanding variance between those who assume a methodological purist and a partisan position, both, in reality, are opposed to 'falsifying data and suppressing "unhelpful" findings' and both acknowledge the necessity for 'assessment of factual claims in terms of logical consistency and empirical adequacy' (Foster et al,1996:40; quoted in Pilkington,2003:158). A situation in which methodological purists and partisan sociological inquirers differ is on the subject of whether the research around school processes squares with these criteria. The anterior adopt extremely rigorous criteria, argue that extant studies do not persuade them 'beyond reasonable doubt' and, for that reason, conclude that 'it seems unfair and unwise to criticise current practices' (Foster, 1993: 551; in Pilkington, 2003: 158). By contradistinction, the posterior show that it is invariably feasible to challenge researchers' understandings, argue that their social research advances convincing interpretations and, for that reason, conclude that it is urgent and pressing on schools to look again at their current practices. The ideological ramifications of the standpoints adopted by the dichotomous camps are clear. The first tends towards a conservative preference of modern practices; the second points towards a radical challenging of modern-day practices. To be sure, given the explicit commitment of methodological purists to a scientific system of approach, it is the 'critical' researchers who are more attentive to a Popperian worldview of social science because, if nothing, else they do lay down a theory to explain Caribbean underachievement. By contradistinction, the methodological purists cover themselves in critiques 'mostly constructed in negative terms' (Gillborn,1995:56; in Pilkington,2003:158) and do not in the least, through their combined organ, propagate any theory whatever.

Some factors to account for educational inequality

The ways all children respond to schooling are multiple as the African-Caribbean boys in Sewell's study illustrate but do the reasons Caribbean children underachieve also correspond as multiple? Since we have explored different accounts for ethnic educational attainment levels, of which Caribbean children's underachievement has been the major focus, we venture into fiercely contentious political ground. While sociologists are presently less likely to fall prey to the fallacy of a unidimensional view and often recognize that a range of variables engaging in a not uncomplicated manner are needed to reason why there is Caribbean underachievement, there remains a tendency to mainstream some factors and to sideline others. More specifically, we have noted the leaning of some towards the rejection of cultural factors while others dismiss the contribution of school processes. Blazing a trail through these turbulent currents, we can identify that intelligence is not a key factor but that evidence exists to indicate that a miscellany of social variables are salient: economic deprivation, which alone derives at least in some measure from racial discrimination; cultural variables, which require a measured contextualisation to abstain from 'blaming the victim'; failing schools, which are often situated in disadvantaged provinces; and (the often unwitting) racial discrimination in compulsory state educational institutions (Pilkington,2003).

Ethnicity and policy ideology

The post-war period has been marked by a perennial concern with assimilation but different policy phases can be distinguished despite this preponderance. To be sure, it is not unusual to notice three such phases – 'assimilation, integration and cultural pluralism' (Troyna and Carrington, 1990:20; quoted in Pilkington,2003:159). James Lynch (1986) has defined

Chapter 3: The Education System

the period advancing from the emergent post-war years to the 1960s as an age of 'ignorance and neglect' (p.42; quoted in Gillborn, 1990:143). Come the latter half of the 1950s, however, there was increasing resistance to immigration endemic to the White British population. While immigration had been actively encouraged as a way of meeting Britain's demand for labour, the acquaintance with racism in the employment and housing sectors was mirrored in physical assaults on African-Caribbean and South Asian people. As 1958 drew to a close, a series of onslaughts by White youths snowballed into 'riots', first in Nottingham and thereafter in Notting Hill, London. Whereas many contemporary portrayals clearly recognized the 'immigrant' population as the innocent party and not aggressors, sections of the popular news media and parliamentarians (including those of different political hues) strived to justify and rationalize unwarranted action on the part of convicted Whites (Gillborn,1990)

After the 1958 riots, demand for the door to be closed on immigration rose to unprecedented levels. The logic was that as 'immigrant' numbers increased, so would the 'friction' increase. Following from this, 'the colour problem' would be managed by restricting the numbers of Black people: a firmly held belief which the Conservative Party gives credence to in debates around immigration today (Gillborn,1990). This organising principle was expressed in the 1962 Act to restrict the immigration of individuals from the Commonwealth – the fledgling of a succession of initiatives and adaptations to immigration legislation which have systematically stripped away the rights of 'immigrants with dark skins. White Australians, Americans and Germans are never defined as a problem' (Dickinson,1982:75 cited in Gillborn,1990:144).

On account that the above run-down accords, from the late 1950s onwards, the political Zeitgeist changed from one of laissez-faire to one of enforced initiatives and measures to assimilate citizens of the Commonwealth into British society (Gillborn,1990). The assumption was made that once they had overcome the language barrier, mores and conventions, 'immigrants' would be incorporated into White society with no further hostile episodes. The Department of Education and Science

(DES), for instance, collected statistical evidence on 'immigrants' on the basis that individuals had resided here for less than ten years, clearly working along the guidelines that in a decade, sufficient time had passed to be absorbed into 'British' culture (Gillborn,1990).

Throughout this period, then, 'immigrants' from Caribbean Islands and the Indian geographical and political region were seen as a problem to which the remedy was assistance to become adapted into the existing (White) order. In the sphere of education, the assimilationist posture led to a commitment to teaching English as a second language (E2L) to South Asian people and promoting middle-class values. To serve as an illustration, Williams (1967) relayed that teachers in Sparkbrook garnered their reason for being as 'putting over a certain set of values (Christian), a code of behaviour (middle-class), and a set of academic and job aspirations in which white-collar jobs have higher prestige than manual' (p.237; quoted in Gillborn,1990:144).

So, the main purposes of educational policy in this period were to secure that the existing educational superstructure remained afloat and to shield the (often racist) attitudes of White heads of family units; in no other place was this more evident than in the plan of dispersal. In November 1963, a central government official moved to argue that 'as the proportion of immigrant children increases, the problem will become more difficult to solve, and the chances of assimilation more remote' (quoted in Pilkington,2003:160). In reciprocation, the LEAs were given approval to disperse 'immigrant' children 'between different schools in an attempt to "spread the problem" and avoid any school becoming predominantly 'immigrant' in character' (Swan, 1885:192; quoted in Pilkington,2003:160). Hence the image of minority ethnic children as something of an educational problem moved towards being institutionalized. Since it underpinned the very basis of the dispersal guideline, a guideline that panders to the line of reasoning and baser instinct of White parents.

> It will be helpful if the parents of non-immigrant children can see that practical measures have been taken to deal with the problems in their

schools and that the progress of their own children is not being restricted by the undue preoccupation of the teaching staff with the linguistic and other difficulties of immigrant children (DES Circular 7/65, quoted in Gillborn,1990:145).

The dispersal plan was met with opposition from many quarters. According to Farrukh Dhondy's observation, by 'bussing' minority ethnic children beyond their own communities and into 'White' districts, dispersal policies furthered pupils' liability to racial harassment – not excluding physical attacks, which played a role in at least one loss of life (Dhondy,1982:36; cited in Gillborn,1990:145).

The assimilationist phase was effective until the late 1960s. It rested on certain highly debatable assumptions: that the bare minimum of changes applies to the education system; that the profile of 'immigrants' gave rise to problems; that the difficulties encountered by 'immigrant' pupils derived mainly from lack of English-speaking ability; and that assimilation, was largely contingent on a changing minority ethnic group, which was not only feasible but desirable. A number of these assumptions came under not infrequent criticism throughout the 1960s (Pilkington,2003). Although 'busing' of minority ethnic pupils no longer persists, it is perhaps that much more noteworthy to point out, as Mullard (1982) has underlined, assimilationist policies was the vehicle used to convey a 'belief in the cultural and racial superiority of the "host" metropolitan society', a view which still carries even among apparently 'erudite' scholars (p.125).

Set against the model from which it emerged, the integrationist perspective attempts to be anodyne. In 1966, Roy Jenkins' address as then Home Secretary, is frequently interpreted as the tide turning on the assimilationist model spelling a departure towards what appeared a more liberal integrationist phase. Jenkins promoted 'not a flattening process of assimilation but equal opportunity, accompanied by cultural diversity, in an atmosphere of mutual tolerance' (quoted in Mullard,1982:125). Put differently, and on a superficial level at least, the notion of cultural superiority, which had upheld the early and remaining influence of those who argued for assimilation, should be superseded by the fundamentally more liberal and egalitarian ideal of cultural tolerance. Jenkins' address was an important move away from earlier beliefs; this interpretation of integration acknowledged that equal opportunities did not already exist, that racist assumptions and procedures, institutionalized or alternately, had, in reality, inhibited the advancement of equal opportunity arrangements and the genesis of harmonious 'race' relations and an equal society. In addition, it sought to shift the focus of attention and process away from social and cultural requisites and privileging political integration. Having floated the idea of equality which, in succession, would be achieved by extending equal educational, social, and economic life chances, minority ethnic groups, or so it appeared, would be free to renegotiate their status in society with all the dominant group categories (Mullard, 1982).

Educational answers to this period in British 'race' relations were defined by the visibility of various teaching resources and courses which strived to examine the dissimilarities between different minority groups and raise awareness of minorities' cultural norms and historical contexts. Sadly, the material was not, to a great extent, fit for purpose and frequently transmitted and maintained crude stereotypes of minority ethnic groups as, most favourably, exotic and strange, and least favourably, as backward and primitive. James Lynch (1986) alluded to the closing stages of the 1970s as the 'deficit phase' in the evolution of multicultural education, an age when the 'emphasis was on lifestyles rather than life chances' (p.41; quoted in Gillborn, 1990: 147).

A number of important gains were made in this period, notably vis-à-vis the authorized conclusion of dispersal policies and the introduction of limited legal safeguards in the Race Relations Act (1976). The Act itself paved the way for the Commission for Racial Equality (CRE), an organisation no stranger to criticism that has actually achieved important successes in many instances of individual and institutional discrimination (Gillborn,1990). Notwithstanding these marginal signs of progress, however, the dominant values and beliefs and the way the integrationist model proceeds is not by any stretch of the imagination different to those of its assimilationist predecessor. Notwithstanding the wording of 'tolerance' and 'diversity', the fundamental purpose of educational policies continues to be the protection of the status quo.

By allowing limited diversity in respect of religious beliefs, customs, dress and even language, it is assumed within the framework of the [integrationist] model that blacks will be more likely to accept than to reject outright those [values and beliefs] which actually shape our society (Mullard, 1982:128).

Policies founded on the values and beliefs of assimilation/integration were, then, ill-judged, ideological and often racist. The assumptions of such policies undervalued minority ethnic people, subtracting from them and rendering them a problem that would ultimately peter out as they became an additional part of society. A strategy of this kind was destined to fail.

The modus vivendi hodgepodge, social solidarity and spirited resistance of minority ethnic groups secured the misfortune of the 'flattening process' (quoted in Gillborn,1990:147). However, the education system underwent increasingly intractable concerns regarding 'race' and achievement, with the Select Committee on Race Relations and Immigration finally advocating the establishment of an official 'inquiry into the causes of the underachievement of children of West Indian origin' (Swan,1985:216; quoted in Pilkington,2003:162). In 1989, an inquiry was set up with the general instruction to document findings on the education of young people from minority ethnic categories which signalled the, albeit short-term, downward spiral of integrationism.

While assimilationist and integrationist perspectives proceeded along the assumption that minority groups were a 'problem' and simultaneously sought to protect the existing system, cultural pluralism struck a somewhat different tack. Given a pluralist society implies one 'which enables, expects and encourages members of all ethnic groups, both minority and majority, to participate fully in shaping the society as a whole within a framework of commonly accepted values, practices and procedures, whilst also allowing and, where necessary, assisting the ethnic minority communities in maintaining their distinct ethnic identities within this common framework' (Swan,1985:5; quoted in Pilkington,2003:163). There remains an apparent assimilationist motif here and therefore, some consistent follow on from the two earlier phases even though the model has been revised. Rather than pose the question of whether Britain fits the description of a plural society, it seems the priority should be the question of its pertinence in relation to multiracial education.

In this context, the dominant idea of multicultural education is 'acculturation', 'a process of mutual and pluralist acculturation for children and teachers' (Lynch,1986:178; quoted in Troyna,1987:186) targeted at 'releasing our education system from its monocultural prison and opening it up to the liberating influences of other cultural perspectives (Parekh,1986:26; quoted in Troyna,1987:186). Operationalized at the classroom level, racism in the curriculum is conceptualized as being chiefly due to 'a process of omitting any significant knowledge about Black people ... from the normal curriculum' (Davis, 1986:16; quoted in Troyna,1987:186).

In a nutshell, multiculturalism is not antithetical to antiracist education; 'antiracism is implicit in multiculturalism' (Grinter,1985:9; quoted in Troyna,1987:186).

Mullard (1982) suggests that cultural pluralism can mean different things to different people. He argues that for certain individuals, it can mean faithfully observing a policy of complete cultural segregation which could give way to calls for political segregation; for some other group it could connote a guideline plan of revised integration predicated upon a more equal distribution of power; and still further, for other people, it could be applied to justify and encircle more educational advancement, curricular improvement and educational compassion. Assuming there is this awkward concern with the concept and the nascent way it is coming to be used in Britain – as a renewed policy of integration – it seems far more beneficial presently to view it not as approaching a distinct model but more

Chapter 3: The Education System

rather than less liberal and potentially progressive incarnation of the integrationist model (Mullard,1982).

While this understanding can be viewed as a neat process of eliminating it altogether, it does, on the other hand, present the opportunity, firstly, to deal briefly with a common underlying supposition of the two principal models, and secondly, tentatively to reach a shared perception on the significance of multicultural education. In connection with the first point, one of the prime problems concomitant with the pluralist assumption in general and pertaining to cultural pluralism being a multiracial education paradigm, in particular, stems from the angle of focus on the dissemination of power in contemporary society (Mullard,1982). On paper, at least, it views power as a resource base held by the culturally diverse groups that account for a plural society. Not least, then, all groups hold power; all groups hold approximately equal lots of power; or, whether doubting the prospect of precisely equal lots, all groups acquire sufficient power to see to the preservation of a high level of cultural independence and uniqueness; and all groups are apt equally to exercise pressure on the existing state and parley with its agencies to ensure that a certain level of cultural stability is maintained. Not accounting for the highly problematic matter of the actual 'socio-cultural' demography of the ruling class and the still more difficult matter of the character of state power as opposed to that held by affiliate cultural groups, the problems arising out of this perspective are, however, quite obvious (Mullard,1982:129). Equitable dissemination of power will not hypothetically only rest upon group numbers, the economic base of the distinctive groups, history, the mobilizing capacity of each group, and a range of other factors, but more importantly, in a dualistic intercontinental and interconnected economy contingent on two adversarial political and economic doctrines, it will rest on at least three further factors:

1. The not inexact relationship maintained between the plural state and the international economy.

2. The association the plural state establishes with socio-economic and ethnic-based affiliate groups.

3. The associations that are constructed among the affiliated groups themselves (Mullard,1982:129-130).

In relation to the British context, it is materially difficult to substantiate that a plural society correlates to society as we know it in the broadest sense of the concept. No constituent minority group, be they African-Caribbean, Indians, Pakistanis, Africans, nor Blacks considered collectively, possess anywhere near the equivalent amounts of power as the indigenous White 'British' group. Therefore, no matter whether we accept and ask no questions about cultural pluralism as a multicultural education paradigm, breaking with that of integration, it is transparently evident that the admixture of Black groups to a White society and to White schools denotes that cultural traditions are not allowed to flourish without the expressed permission, approval and cultivation of White society in general and of White indigenous power groups more especially. All told, then, this indicates that the power assumption resting at the pedestal of the cultural pluralism model as construed by its largely White British proponents – as a culturally outlined version of integration – and at the pedestal of the already-introduced models of assimilation and integration is practically one and the same thing (Mullard,1982).

One headteacher came within an inch of the point when she set out rhetorically:

Is (Britain) a society into which immigrants are gradually absorbed into English culture? Is it a society in which the best is taken from, say, West Indian, Asian and English culture to form a basis for a new culture? Is it a society in which the English culture must adapt itself to new and increasingly powerful voices of the different cultures? Are immigrant cultural forces sufficiently powerful to encourage the indigenous population to change its cultural heritage? Will a 'ghetto' situation contain immigrant cultures and cause the indigenous population to ignore and disregard immigrants, causing a multiracial society to remain really a racial one (with the same power structure)? (Townsend, H.E.R and Brittan E.M. 1973; quoted in Mullard, 1982:130).

The point of the matter is, of course, that all three models assume some levels of cultural change in terms of Black groups in compulsory state education and society without any such change in terms of White groups in compulsory state education and society (Mullard,1982). White groups are in a position of power; White groups and schools are able to dictate that Black groups and students assimilate or integrate. Legitimate power in a free market economy and a racist society cannot be distributed. However disguised and masquerading in platitudes or goodwill, the three multicultural education perspectives are in fact power perspectives. They constitute power models established by leading White figures for the preservation of the authority of White groups, for the maintenance of our society in terms of how it is essentially viewed by those groups (Mullard,1982).

Conclusion

This chapter has concentrated on evidence emerging from ethnographic studies of schools and multi-ethnic classrooms. More so than anything else, the sociology of education has meant society's acculturation of 'immigrant' groups, without disruption, while that society seeks to preserve social inequality and an apparently unchanging and esteemed set of core values, beliefs and institutions (Mullard,1982). Although this research appreciates the differences between schools, as Foster's (1990) study pointed out, the features that schools share appear significant as they emerge to shape society. The dominant monocultural curriculum extols the virtues of one culture and in particular is biased against young people from minority ethnic groups, who realize that cultures outside the mainstream are, if not ignored, certainly belittled. To receive the message, however tactfully and diplomatically, that your culture and history are of no consequence is to engender responses that extend from low self-worth and the absence of confidence to disaffection and resistance. To receive the message that your culture and history have some meaning only within the science of teaching confines of the school curriculum and not beyond the school perimeters in the White regulated world of economic activity and politics is to encourage the response of a 'blacks-only for the black studies class' (Mullard,1982:131). Black studies not only address racist ideology, but it also helps dispel the root of prejudice and intolerance which is where the vital inclusion of White pupils is *sine qua non* (Pilkington,2003). What follows below is a brief consideration of the link between ethnic origins and education.

Our survey of the evidence indicates that, although those from Asian cultures, namely, Indian and Chinese, tend to outperform those from Caribbean origins, there are also divisions observable within both these groups. On scrutiny of the South Asian group, we discover that the underperformance of Pakistani and Bangladeshi students is covered over by Indian and other South Asian students' goal achievement. On subjecting the Caribbean group to a similar approach, we find that it is boys in particular who are underperforming. The attainment of Indian, Chinese and African Asian students is more consonant with the meritocratic thesis whereas the attainment of Pakistani/Bangladeshi students and Caribbean boys is more consonant with a reproductive framework (Pilkington,2003).

In turning to account for such underachievement, we venture into fiercely contentious political ground, with proponents of competing meta-narratives often at crossed swords with one another. Although dubious of IQ being a key factor, it is contended that a series of social factors are salient: economic deprivation, which derives at least in some measure from racial discrimination; cultural variables, which require a measured contextualisation to abstain from 'blaming the victim'; failing schools, which are often situated in disadvantaged provinces and (the often unwitting) racial discrimination in compulsory state educational institutions (Pilkington,2003).

Education policy has made things worse not better regarding the problem of school exclusion and particularly attributable are issues surrounding the marketization of schooling (Wright, Weekes and McGlaughlin,2000). According to Sally Tomlinson (2008), the structural examination of racial inequality came in submerged beneath the agenda to wider reconfigurations in domestic politics. 'The Conservative government', she maintained, had, 'between 1990 and 1997, virtually removed issues concerning racial and ethnic inequalities in education from political consideration' (Tomlinson,2008; quoted in Warmington,2014:128), stipulating rather on a colour-blind perspective of fairness. The then Blairite government, which succeeded the Conservatives in 1997, oversaw continuity with many of the existing market reforms in education, though being keen to express a greater pledge to social justice and human difference. The upshot, Tomlinson asserted, was a painfully diminished framework for tackling racial injustice in education:

> [A] continuation of Conservative market policies of choice and diversity in schooling and a targeting of 'failing' schools exacerbated school segregation and racial inequalities. Policies intended to improve the achievement of minority groups have had some success, but the higher achievements of Indian and Chinese groups have led to facile comparisons which further pathologise young people of African-Caribbean and Pakistani origin. Failure to develop a curriculum for a multi-ethnic society has contributed to an increase in xenophobia and racism, and there were no educational policies to deal with increased hostility towards young Muslims. Home Office policies targeting refugees and asylum-seekers have encouraged racial hostility towards their children despite amended race relations legislation.

Tomlinson (2008:153), quoted in Warmington,2014:129).

The diminution of discourses surrounding race, racism and education was summarized by Archer and Francis:

> [I]ssues of race/ethnicity are really only acknowledged by or addressed by education policy within the context of 'underachievement' ... issues of race have been subject to a pernicious turn in policy discourse which removes the means for engaging with inequalities, naturalises differences in achievement between ethnic groups and places the responsibility of achievement differentials with minority ethnic individuals. This discourse denies racism as a potential cause of

differences in achievement and hides inequalities within congratulatory public statements

(Archer and Francis,2007:1; quoted in Warmington,2014:129).

In brief, by fighting shy of the structural – the racialized magnitude of resources, curriculum, certification, teacher training, labelling of students, disciplinary systems – and gravitating to individualized interpretations of underachievement – conduct, aspiration, family backgrounds – the achievement rhetoric provided an opportunity to standardize racial inequalities and to revisit the pathologization of certain Black groups, students and parents, albeit dressed up in neo-social-democratic terms (Warmington,2014). The above was evident notably in what Tomlinson (2008) and Gillborn (2008) have defined as the exegesis of model minorities. If racism was consistently cropping up in education, so the implication unfurled, why did Chinese students achieve where primarily African-Caribbean boys failed? What is the reason for Indian student success where Pakistani students failed? Hence the scenario that Black parenting, academic aspirations, youth subcultures, spiritual foundation and self-segregation again came to represent the common or garden questions in debates on the subject of Black underachievement (Warmington,2014).

Although assimilationist underlying principles have tended to predominate in the post-war stages, there have been separate policy phases: assimilationism, integrationism and cultural pluralism (Pilkington,2003). Occurring briefly in the 1980s period, cultural pluralism led those taken up with 'education towards racial equality' to believe that headway was being forged, but since then, *weltschmerz* has become more common as assimilationist and integrationist underlying principles have reclaimed their dominance. Clearly, what multi-cultural education, as seen in British schools, is informing Black pupils is the invariable continuity of a blot on their escutcheon that is second-class citizenship; and paradoxically, so that it is possible to survive or live as Blacks, it is incumbent to counter racist authority within and outside school (Mullard,1982). As apprehended and implemented by many, multi-ethnic schooling has appeared to become a means of control and equilibrium instead of one of reform, of the subordination instead of the autonomy of Blacks in compulsory educational establishments and society at large.

In the absence of a radical review of multi-ethnic education analysis and praxis, our society's acquisitive and racist culture will perpetually be spread by all schools: in the absence of a radical reorganization of our society, holistically speaking, and of the significance and praxis of multi-ethnic education especially, we shall, for the foreseeable future, continue to refer to Black kids in White compulsory state educational establishments, instead of simply children in schools (Mullard,1982:131). This indicates that race matters, and that due to conditioning, White teachers stand on a continuum between teetering on the brink and being very definitely averse and reluctant to teaching certain types of pupils, which somehow explains the high exclusion rates of Caribbean boys, sometimes in circumstances where White pupils emerge free and untouched by such consequences. Chapter four will explore the context, processes and influence of institutional racism on the Black and minority ethnic population in higher education.

Secondary school pupils are at a stage in their lives where they are inclined to respond to schooling in unexpected and complex ways, such as the range of responses displayed by Sewell's (1997) Caribbean Black boys. Of course, if a child decides to rebel, there is little a teacher can do, but, subjecting a child to constant censure from an early age, such as in the case of Marcus, can lead to underachievement and Marcus was not even rebelling (Pilkington,2003). This analysis suggests that Marcus is not the only Black boy whose experience of school is damaging and enormously devastating on their academic progress and will to succeed. I have argued that low, or in fact, racist expectations and assumptions could be the contributing factors in accounting for patterns of Black educational underperformance.

Paul Willis's lads rebelled because schoolwork was anathema to them, but rebellion in Black boys can take the form of being pro-education but anti-school processes. Schools are producing disproportionate numbers of rebellious and underachieving Black boys, and teachers, for their part, should cease treating students differentially, conceptualizing them in terms of negative stereotypes and picturing Black Caribbean students as discipline 'problems' and as a 'threat' to the smooth running of things, and begin to be motivated by human educational sensitivity towards all students. Student behaviour should not govern allocation to bottom sets over ability entitlement to top sets even though it may look like rewarding bad behaviour. Social justice is at stake here and nothing else besides. African-Caribbean students should be seen as potential five GCSE A* students by virtue of the fact that low teacher expectation tends towards a self-fulfilling prophesy and gives rise to racial disadvantage. The likelihood that these guidelines will be heeded, taken seriously or followed is remote and therefore the mitigation of school exclusion is unlikely because schools are being granted ever-increasing powers to sanction and discipline students who, particularly in the lower streams, are responding to their experience of schooling.

This chapter has presented a portrait in which Black and South Asian children are seen to live out their formative years into adolescence in an environment that consistently undermines their aspirations and culminates predominantly in massive underachievement. There are some exceptions, such as the Paul Dixons of this world, who tend to be overlooked and one can understand why, when the number of academic success stories of Black Caribbean boys is considered (Gillborn,1990). The result of failing Black aspiration is a community that languishes in the bottom stratum of the British social hierarchy faring equally less well generation after generation. What awaits those who achieve and progress through college and then onto higher education and what this involves and the involvement of non-white staff will be the subject of the next chapter. If we trace the educational progress of schoolchildren, it may be discerned what tends to transpire.

African-Caribbean children start their school careers at five with no appreciable difference in standard to the national average. However, the age of ten sees their educational progress dip behind their peers (Parekh,2000). The gap is wider in arithmetic than in English. In their sixteenth year, the number of African-Caribbean students living up to five higher-grade GCSE passes (grades A*-C) is far short of half the national average. The government's own statistics do not paint as bad a picture, based on the National Youth Cohort Study (Parekh,2000).

At Key Stage 2 (age 11) in English and Arithmetic and at GCSE (16) typically, Gujarati and Punjabi (i.e., 'Indian') pupils achieve outcomes that exceed the national average. The variance at GCSE is even greater than at Key Stage 2.

Pakistani and Bangladeshi students perform beneath the national average, but gradually narrow the difference between themselves and others during the active life of their education. In certain localities, they fulfil expectations or exceed the national average at GCSE (Parekh,2000).

Averages manage to mask substantial diametric opposition. To illustrate, young people of Pakistani and Bangladeshi heritage register favourable proportionate levels in terms of access to university, particularly in London and Scotland, yet are also proportionately represented among those aged 16 with dismal qualifications.

Individuals from Gypsy and traveller backgrounds are especially at risk. While some make a perceptibly positive start in primary school, when they reach secondary stages, their generally woeful attainment levels raise serious concerns. In 1996, intelligence established a rough ballpark figure of as many as 10,000 Gypsy and traveller children of senior school age who were apparently not signed up for education in English schools (Parekh,2000). 'Often schools do not want them', so it is expressed and 'often Gypsies themselves do not want the schooling that is on offer' (Parekh,2000:146).

'The key question in education,' a respondent said, 'used to be, "What can a school do for its pupils?" Presently, the key question is, "What can pupils do for their school?" (Parekh,2000:156). Pupils selected and streamed into top-flight sets and thus seen as likely to secure the much-sought-after A-C grades at GCSE are earmarked, and in effect, bestowed unconditional positive response bias, sometimes spanning a two-year period before they take the exams. Social investigative research has evinced that this disadvantages Black pupils and those for whom English is an adjunct language, and that a proportion of the vexed question is that schools apply racist stereotypes and rationale when trying to hypothesize those who are and those who are not likely to add to the school's reputation by way of the league tables (Parekh,2000). The tiering of GCSE exams denotes that pupils taking the same subject are submitted for disparate examination papers, each with a limited scope of possible grades. For pupils submitted on the lowest tier, the highest level they can usually aspire to is a grade C – though the situation is that much worse in mathematics, in which the bottom tier is capped at grade D.

State primary school pupils can traverse through their primary school careers and, in particular, Black pupils, without ever being encouraged to push for a grammar school place where they may be exposed to elite subjects not covered by the Secondary Modern school curriculum. Instead, teachers fail to spot the potential of the Black child and see them not as an academic success but as a source of trouble and factory fodder. Black pupils, sometimes because of unambitious parents, tend to be left to progress through to Secondary Modern school where they are exposed to factory life in woodwork and metalwork while Grammar School pupils are exposed to non-menial more noble activities leading to commercial life and elite careers. Moreover, Black pupils are not exposed to the idea of a university, or what one might look like and the occupational outcomes and advantages linked to university attendance. On a personal note, I remember my English teacher telling the entire class, of which I was a member, not to use the word 'and' at the beginning of a sentence and not to use the word 'nice' at any point. Some years later, I found university books and articles that use this exact practice and I see no reason why the word 'nice' cannot be used appropriately. The colloquial use of the term 'nice' can seem to be

Chapter 3: The Education System

mundane but when one considers its word association linkages, such as good, superior, and, among other things, agreeable, one comes to understand that it is a word pregnant with meaning, as is the term 'and'. The obvious influence upon the class was for impressionable children not to use university writing skills and parlance conventions.

With few exceptions, the destination of the Black child is low-grade menial work, usually in factories, whereas grammar and public schools offer higher-level opportunities. If a Black pupil in a Secondary Modern school states that s/he wants to become a Barrister s/he is more likely to be derided and discouraged and directed to lower his or her sights (Briscoe, 2006: 186-189) whereas the opposite would apply at grammar or public school. Grammar and public schools encourage high aspiration levels while the same levels of aspiration in a state Secondary Modern school are seen as too ambitious and unrealistic. White pupils, however, are less likely to be discouraged and told to aim lower when they express high aspiration; so, what we can see emerging is that teachers and schools stereotype pupils as achievers and underachievers, winners and losers.

In an anecdotal vein, to show that academic performance does not always transfer into educational or occupationally commensurate rewards, here is an example; an African-Caribbean friend of mine told of how he outperformed most of his peers at the eleven-plus (attaining third place overall in his class) and was not offered a grammar school place and soon became aware that friends placed beneath him were offered and took up grammar school places. He recounted how his mother complained but to no avail and that he thought the system so unfair. He described the way in which his long-term classmate worked in his family's vehicle tyre retail outlet after attending grammar school and how he would have taken full advantage if he had attended grammar school. The same individual told of a Windrush generation Black male accountant from Jamaica who was confronted with barriers in the process of transferring his skills to Britain and was directed by someone to work as a bus conductor. He subsequently found work in this field and prosecuted his duties for many years. Although he was educated in Jamaica, he was forced to lower his expectations in Britain and stories like this one abound among post-war migrants.

Anecdotes such as the above suggest that Black academic performance is underrated and undervalued and that Black people are damned if they do and damned if they don't perform academically. Black girls tend to fare better in schools than Black boys because they knuckle down and apply themselves whereas Black boys tend to adopt a cavalier approach to schooling and are sometimes failed by the school. It may be that, in some cases, this cavalier approach is arrived at independently, but we cannot rule out the influence of the subculture or peer group culture that tends to assume that schoolwork is either womanish or gay.

Chapter 4: Institutional Racism in Higher Education

A Case Study

Higher education has hitherto operated in a climate unaffected by change in the form of policies developed in schools, the health service, local authorities and the police to combat racism and foster ethnic and cultural diversity (Law et al,2004). Higher education institutions primarily function in a 'colour-blind' fashion and seldom admit that beneath the façade of the liberal academy there are underlying issues. Contemporary sociological inquiry has, however, pointed out that White society cannot, in all earnest, rest on its laurels. For example, Sarah Neal's (1998) study of equal opportunities policies in universities, John Bird's (1996) exposition of the participation of Black students within the academic community and Carter, Fenton and Modood's (1999) quantitative and qualitative assessment of ethnicity and employment in higher education all point up problem areas. Following on from these and other explorations, a mental image appears of ethnic disparities in student access, racial discrimination prosecuted by admissions tutors, the racialised experiences of Black and South Asian students on initiating their journey through higher education institutions, dissatisfaction with the deficit of diversity in the academic environment, racist discrimination in grading and assessment, racism while on work placements and race discrimination in the graduate pathway to employment (Law et al,2004:93). Important social research by the Association of University Teachers (AUT), which cogitated over race issues and postures among academics and ancillary staff in the old universities, also indicated that racialised malaise is prevalent in higher education institutions, in which Black and minority ethnic authority figures may well encounter racist harassment, feel unduly dealt with in job applications, and accept that institutional racism exists in the workplace milieu (Law et al,2004).

In 1999, Carter, Fenton and Modood singled out a necessity for what they termed 'institutional antiracism'. Their analysis suggested certain specific approaches to combatting institutional racism, including:

- The notion that institutions need to acknowledge racism as a structural problem for the institutional unit and not only for Black and minority staff and student population;
- Commitment needed a top-downwards approach;
- Groups and individuals beyond the institution itself should be allowed to participate in bringing racial equality policies into effect and the recording of progress;
- Interview panels need to reflect the population more fully and should therefore include Blacks;
- Curricula need to undergo revision so that Black histories, cultures, perspectives and aspirations could enjoy more appropriate inclusion;
- Higher education financial support agencies should consider releasing funding only when ethnic minority employment targets are met;
- Higher education should never be insular and should be guided by good practice in other quarters, e.g., local authorities (Carter, Fenton and Modood,1999:56-7).

The overarching thrust was that for race equality strategies to be sufficiently effective, this would mean direct attention beyond mere tinkering with admissions policies or employment practices. However, it was evident that institutions of higher education mainly lacked the ideational and analytical tools to posit a strategy for addressing racism across organisational boundaries and were incapable of seeing through their new race equality requirements subject to law (following the passing of the Race Relations (Amendment) Act 2000 (Law et al,2004:94). Guidance on how to initiate an antiracist institution is available but, because it is a web-based resource "(http://www.leeds.ac.uk/cers/toolkit/toolkit.htm)", shedding light on how a higher education institution functions, it will therefore need no further mention here (Law et al,2004:94).

In this chapter, among other things, I intend to consider and show the adverse impact higher education institutions sometimes deposit on the Black and minority ethnic range of experience and how the ubiquitous role and presence of language and culture assume a clearly defined shape and form in higher education institutions, to the advantage of the dominant groups and the disadvantage of the subordinate groups, and to briefly show how equal opportunity structures are marginalized.

The concept of institutional racism was brought to our attention and the forefront of our consciousness by the murder of a young man. Stephen Lawrence was slain on April 22nd, 1993 while awaiting the arrival of a bus in south-east London alongside his friend, Duwayne Brooks. The matter that motivated a group of young White men to launch an attack on him was Stephen's skin colour. Stephen was the victim of a fatal stabbing because he was Black (Pilkington,2011).

Incidents premised on racial hatred are not a new fact of life in British society. 'Violence has been an enduring feature of the White British reaction to the presence of 'blacks', 'Pakis', and Jews who have settled on this island' (Pilkington,2011:1). Racist murders occur infrequently, but the assumption that the racist murder of Stephen Lawrence was unprecedented is mistaken. And it was also not the last. The Institute of Race Relations has established that over 65 racially motivated murders have been committed since 1991 (Pilkington,2011). More recently, the murders of Zahid Mubarek and Anthony Walker have made media headline news. Asian teenager Zahid Mubarek was fatally assaulted, while detained in prison in 2000, by a racist inmate who had nothing but good things to say about Stephen Lawrence's assailants and Anthony Walker, an African-Caribbean teenager, was killed in strangely similar circumstances to Stephen Lawrence, by White racist co-conspirators in Liverpool in 2005 (Pilkington,2011).

While the racist murder of Stephen Lawrence is far from being unparalleled, it greatly exceeds other cases as having made the most media headline news items and resonated greatest with people across ethnic distinctions. This is, for the most part, attributed to Stephen's parents, Doreen and Neville Lawrence, who demonstrated remarkable tenacity in prosecuting justice for their son and made a concerted effort towards that end aim. Although they confronted countless barriers, even *inter alia* a flawed police inquiry that has meant Stephen's murderers have escaped successful prosecution, their poise and determination did ultimately pay dividends. They prevailed upon the then Labour government in July 1997 to establish a judicial inquiry looking closely at the police investigation into their son's murder. Charges have been brought against two White men in connection with the murder (Pilkington,2011).

The inquiry fell to a former High Court judge, Sir William Macpherson of Cluny. The public hearings commenced on March 24th 1998 and the eventual report went to print on February 24th 1999. The essential conclusions are concisely summarised: 'The conclusions to be drawn from all the evidence in connection with the investigation of Stephen Lawrence's racist murder are clear. There is no doubt that there were fundamental errors. The investigation was marred by a combination of professional incompetence, institutional racism and a failure of leadership by senior officers. A flawed MPS review failed to expose these inadequacies. The second investigation could not salvage the faults of the first investigation' (quoted in Pilkington,2011:2).

Owning up to Institutional Racism

Chapter six, entitled racism, grossed or outflanked all other chapters in the report. It considered and dealt with what Jack Straw, the then Home Secretary, in the chair to table the report to Parliament on February 24th 1999, admitted being 'the central and most important issue for the inquiry' (quoted in Pilkington,2011:2). Curiously enough, the chapter found that institutional racism was prevalent in British society. While the inquiry's central angle of focus was the police, the report indicated that all major establishments in British society are defined by institutional racism. 'Racism, institutional or otherwise, is not the prerogative of the Police Service. It is clear that other agencies, including, for example, those dealing with ... education, also suffer from the disease' (Pilkington,2011:2). This was a remarkable and strange admission because 'for 30 years, British officialdom had consistently denied that it had any meaning when applied to Britain' (Pilkington,2011:2).

The sole alternative judicial inquiry established under the Police Acts was Lord Scarman's focusing on the 1981 Brixton riots. Enclosed in the pages of his report, Lord Scarman, in his ultimate finding, explicitly rejected the idea that the police and further structures in British society are defined by institutional racism: 'Institutional racism does not exist in Britain' (Pilkington,2011:2) The tenor of institutional racism supporting this claim is set out initially in the report: in Britain, he advocates, the police and major organisations do not 'knowingly, as a matter of policy, discriminate against black people' (Pilkington,2011:2). Scarman recognized, on the other hand, that 'racial disadvantage and its nasty associate racial discrimination have not yet been eliminated (Scarman,1981: para 9.1; quoted in Pilkington,2011:3) and 'that practices may be adopted which are unwittingly discriminatory' (Scarman,1981: para 2.22; quoted in Pilkington,2011:3).

The Macpherson report adds to these suggestions. It approves of the initial report that there is insubstantial evidence that the action plans of the police and major organisations are racist but disavows what Scarman accepts as a natural follow-on, not least that they are not defined by institutional racism. Macpherson believes that the concept of institutional racism negates implying whether the action plans of organisational structures are racist. Rather, the concept is defined as 'the collective failure of an organisation to provide an appropriate and professional service to people because of their colour, culture or ethnic origin. It can be seen or detected in processes, attitudes and behaviour which amount to discrimination through unwitting prejudice, ignorance, thoughtlessness and racist stereotyping which disadvantage minority ethnic people' (Macpherson,1999: para:6.34; quoted in Pilkington,2011:3).

The report met with welcome-sounding noises in Parliament. The then Prime Minister Tony Blair struck a chord during his weekly session of question time: 'I am proud that it was this Government who set up the Lawrence inquiry. I am happy to accept its judgement ... The publication of today's report on the killing of Stephen Lawrence is a very important moment in the life of this country. It is a moment to reflect, to learn and to change. It will certainly lead to new laws, but more than that, it must lead to new attitudes, to a new era in race relations, and to a more tolerant and inclusive Britain' (Hansard,1999: col380-381; quoted in Pilkington,2011:3). In placing the report before Parliament, Jack Straw went further still. He unconditionally accepted the indictment of institutional racism, holding culpable 'both the Metropolitan Police Service and other Police Services and other institutions countrywide' and directed the government to action the entire report's recommendations: 'The inquiry's assessment is clear and sensible. In my view, any long-established, white-dominated organisation is liable to have procedures, practices and a culture that tend to exclude or to disadvantage non-white people. The report makes 70 wide-ranging recommendations, and I welcome them all' (Hansard,1999: col 391; in Pilkington,2011:3).

The sheer remarkableness that surrounds government willingness, and indeed, numerous other institutions, to own up to the indictment of institutional racism is not just the material detail that the state had steered an unflinching course till February 1999 to have no concomitant link with the concept, but in addition, that the concept was available and existed because it was the brainchild of two Black power acolytes in the US.

Defining Institutional Racism

The following overlapping questions are of some concern to me as a Black African-Caribbean individual who has had first-hand experience of institutional racism and is partly why I have been prompted to write this book. Is it ever appropriate to designate public organisations and, more specifically, universities as institutionally racist? In what way have these organisations and, more precisely, universities interacted with the indictment of institutional racism? To what extent has a government, which took a dim view of the widespread existence of institutional racism, taken measures to counteract institutional racism and foster racial equality in social organisations and especially universities? (Pilkington, 2011:10) Such questions do not necessitate that a definitive analysis be made at this point in the exercise as to how best to ascribe a meaning to institutional racism and the usefulness of the concept. Such concerns could, as the phenomenologists would have it, be categorized and Macpherson's usage assumed. Whether or not we adopted this position, we could subsequently decide if it was a discriminating concept that served to illuminate our examination of higher education or obversely, whether it was a befuddled notion that was shown to be of infinitesimal analytical value. Despite everything, Pilkington (2011) considers that it is useful at this juncture to make available a working definition even though the issue of its analytical usefulness ineluctably needs to be considered and dealt with later.

The concept flags up, in particular, the processes in organisations which, however inadvertent, involve disadvantaging individuals from minority ethnic groups. Evidently, there are the likes of these processes and prevailing race relations legislation recognizes their prevalence in the practice of rendering illegal indirect racial discrimination. The problem is whether or not we are assisting in matters by delineating the likes of these processes as institutional racism. Institutional racism can be defined at this point as pertaining to 'those instances where a racist discourse has become embedded in certain institutional [processes]' (Singh,2000:38; in Pilkington,2011:11). It is not enough to signpost an inequality in experience or consequences among people, that is, the dichotomy of the White British and minority ethnic groups (Pilkington,2011). It is *sine qua non* to show that this inequality has its origins in racist discourse, and therefore, demonstrates how 'exclusionary practices arise from, and therefore embody, a racist discourse' (Pilkington,2011:11). Two interconnected processes especially tend to be emphasized in a significant amount of the research: the 'institutional culture', which 'is racist if it constitutes a climate of assumptions which are hostile to outside groups, racially or ethnically defined' and 'routine practices', which are racist if they involve unfair treatment of people from minority ethnic communities (Pilkington,2011:11). It is appropriate, however, not to portray individuals as *modus vivendi* ignoramuses whose behaviour is shaped by such processes. Although institutional processes represent structural conditions for the behaviour of individuals, and therefore, both restrict and assist what is accomplished, individuals are also free agents having ultimate responsibility for their actions.

The Unravelling of Institutional Racism

What, then, has been the correlation between colonialism and racism in the post-cold war/ post-colonial epoch of the 20th century's close? (Hesse,2004). Established European and American social science schools of thought have not regarded racism as a central component of western societies either throughout or following colonial *ancien régimes*. Western intellectual activity has primarily perceived colonialism via metaphors of law and legislation rather than culture and regulation especially where the formal parting of the ways of colonial orders and the racisms they articulated are concerned. In sociological theory, for example, the disestablishment of European empires and American racial segregation are conceptualized as identical disconnected legal terminations of supplanted historical epochs.

Racism is explained with reference to the 'residuum' and 'exceptionalism' rather than continuity and normality (Hesse,2004:141). This is, in part, because of the failure to apprehend the western cultural system of colonialism, equally its antecedent continuities and concurrent specificities. To illustrate the point, what is understood as the issue of cultural diversity, or the problem of multiculturalism in Europe and America, originates its unsettling connotations from western colonial and imperial objects in which so-called non-European/non-white/non-Christian others were represented as being lower in the hierarchy of human species in western political units (Hesse,2004:142) The key western motif to the multicultural, considering its racialised sphere of knowledge, has never been bereft of colonialism. The colonial intervention involved western powers issuing direction over culturally diverse 'non-European' otherness by enforcing or enticing its acceptance of the normality of White hegemony, which implied their subordination to western rule, symbolism, stratifications, epistemologies and controls. Though western states were compelled to initiate engaging changes to their imperial focus, considering the development of liberal-democratic social organisation in the post-war era, this has not injured the cultural characteristic spirit of colonialism which has come to be as complicit with western ontology as secularism, humanism or English pronunciation (Hesse,2004).

In western Europe, migrants (and their progeny) from Africa, Asia and the Caribbean saw their historic background of dependency and subordination altered when entering the landscape of the European geographic and political boundary: the 'classic postcolonial' transition. How, then, is the coloniality of racism as much maintained as negated in Western democracies? (Hesse,2004). Firstly, in the wake of formal decolonisation, racial relations were still under a cloud of coloniality, though not infrequently represented in culturally divergent ways and fresh political insights, and so entirely westernised as to seem uninteresting or unsurprising (e.g., references to racial harmony or favourable and unfavourable race-relations). Secondly, instituted was a socially constructed process of colonial dislocation and counterclaim (i.e., colonialism is considered an anachronism of past history, not the present day), marked inescapably by a 'collective amnesia about and systematic disavowal of empire' (Hesse,2004:142), leaving the social mores of coloniality ubiquitous in social artistry (e.g., immigration measures) but muted in social symbolism. Thirdly, in connection with the newly democratically engaged citizens, the migrants hailing from the former colonies, the encounter was seen as a fresh start. Indigenous Europeans began to view these 'children of empire' as if they had come from somewhere other than a hot climate or wonder what had possibly caused them to be here in a European nation. The European nation came to be a legendary community with an influential nationalist antecedent and a far-removed colonial past. But what consistently disrupted the suggestion of a successful postcolonial transition in places such as Britain was the force and numbers of complaints, charges and organized protests against racism. In the place at which the frequency of racism could not be effectively represented by the establishment in Eurocentric terms, in the place at which these terms were rejected by critics, the mutual toleration of racism and liberal democracy was uncovered, if not accounted for (Hesse,2004).

The Emergence of a Concept

At polar ends of the Atlantic, this begged the question, to what extent could the concept of racism be derived from these inconsistencies and conundrums of western democracy's withdrawal from and yet clearly defined deep knowledge of coloniality? (Hesse,2004). This issue engaged the writings of W.E.B. Du Bois (1947), Aime Cesaire (1955), and Frantz Fanon (1956) throughout the late 1940s and 1950s in the interchange between the exigency of the post-World War II phase and the imperative of the anticolonial and civil rights offensives. Reviewing their critical assessments of western democracy, taken from this historical way away, implores us to cast doubt on whether it is *passé* to discuss coloniality after the dismantling of empire and racial segregation. Does the need arise to dismiss 'the assumption that the world has been decolonised'? (Hesse,2004:143). This type of inquiry first saw the emergence of the concept of institutional racism as a courageous consignment to paper in the writings of Stokely Carmichael and Charles V. Hamilton in the late 1960s. The most curious and generally left unnoticed in Carmichael and Hamilton's famous treatise *Black Power: The Politics of Liberation in America* is the disbelief of the introduction which sets up the premise for the interrogations which ensue. They commence by petitioning:

> What is racism? The word has represented daily reality to millions of black people for centuries, yet it is rarely defined – perhaps just because that reality has been such a commonplace. By racism we mean the predication of decisions and policies on consideration of race for the purpose of subordinating a racial group and maintaining control over that group (Carmichael and Hamilton,1967:3; quoted in Hesse, 2004:143).

What rendered this exposition so challenging was their stipulation, twenty years after the inception of the United Nations and the Universal Declaration on Human Rights and after the enactment of the 1964 US Civil Rights Act, that racism was a phenomenon that still demanded a definition. The traditional ongoing nature of American racism and the customary ways it has been omitted from definition gave rise to the idea that institutional racism 'has another name: colonialism' (Carmichael and Hamilton,1967:5; quoted in Hesse,2004:143). This is a crucially perceptive and radical departure from the Eurocentric notion of racism.

Since the circumstances in which Carmichael and Hamilton's initial concept of institutional racism was that of activist political struggle, in which that work was laid down and that conceptual analysis was scarcely the angle of approach to their intervention, it is understandable that cynical commentators would not view their treatise as foundational or even original. Even so, it has profound consequences for the examination of the concomitant link surrounding western racism and western democracy which numerous supporters and antagonists have, in a few special cases (e.g., Blauner,1972; Goldberg,2002), generally fallen short of developing (Hesse,2004). They apprehend institutional racism as highlighting practices of racial dominance, not the ideological system of race that occupies time and space in the Eurocentric trajectory. In giving the impression that racism comprises a system of practices, they situate the underlying principle and consistency of that system in the colonial interlinking between White and Black (i.e., non-white), west and non-west, European and non-European, as opposed to in the domestic relation between majorities and minorities, or nationals and 'immigrants'.

Carmichael and Hamilton are referring to a 'liberal-democratic/colonial assemblage' that is consistent in relation to its continuities, yet historically repudiated and unscrutinised in western cultural structure (Hesse,2004:143). Bound up with that is the orthodox context as opposed to the so-called exceptionalist circumstances of lawful racial segregation that gives us to understand that racism tends to be both 'overtly' individual (e.g., racist attacks) and 'covertly' institutional (e.g., racist exclusion from higher education). Whereas how to comprehend the relation between the dichotomy is not in every instance clear, it is propounded that 'institutional racism relies on the active and pervasive operation of anti-black attitudes and practices', in which a 'sense of superior group position prevails' and it is taken as read that 'blacks should be subordinated to whites' (Carmichael and Hamilton,1967:5; quoted in Hesse,2004:144). The point at issue here is whether we grasp the subtext of institutional racism in the lexicographic language of ideological discourse or in the conventional no-nonsense sense of racist governance. On Carmichael and Hamilton's part, the concern is substantially with racist praxis and their hegemonic conventions. The value of their approach revolves around what meaning we assign to 'covert' with regard to these institutional social mores. The less powerful sense of the term regards covert as indirect, adumbrated, understated or possibly unwitting; however, therein lies the danger of diluting the institutional aspect; it lacks a well laid out approach and is loaded with a singularly individual and peculiar orientation. The more powerful sense of 'covert' directs itself more institutionally inwards and can be characterized by terms such as hidden, disguised, concealed, unacknowledged and negated but which is inexorable in its outcome or tactical resolve. Under the pretext that it is the colonial aspect of the 'liberal democratic/colonial assemblage' that has a concealed institutional presence, underpinned by a 'hidden transcript', substituted by the 'official transcript' (Hesse,2004:144), institutional racism, dissimilar to the ideological allied with so-called 'overt racist regimes' (Hesse,2004:144), is framed by liberal-democratic mores; it 'originates in the operation of established and respected forces in the society and thus receives far less public condemnation' (Carmichael and Hamilton,1967:5; quoted in Hesse,2004:144). That constitutes a momentous challenge that has a past antecedent and continues to confront us in the present day.

The adversarial nature of racism

Racism, in the first place, was defined as a system of ideas, and, in its main usage, alluded to the theory of race. This particular definition was the one that gained international centrality and was spread by the United Nations. Whereas in the period following the war, such an interpretation of racism was widely held, it has thereafter become axiomatic that the concept is, to all intents and purposes, contested. In the years following the holocaust, what has become evident is that people now tend to shy away from advancing the theory of race and make patently transparent references, at least not in the broad public sphere, to the racial inferiority of non-white groups. This material detail has drawn forth two responses. In the opinion of some sociologists (Banton,1985), diminishing belief in the theory of race suggests that racism is on the wane, but for others (Rex,1970), it signposts the need to rethink our understanding of racism. The second proponent has met with more widespread approval, with revision generally taking two distinct forms (Pilkington,2011).

In one instance, it has involved protracting the significance of the term in a specified way as to incorporate both beliefs and practices which cause racial disadvantage and actually even to subsume racial disadvantage itself. This trajectory is the one privileged by those who openly accept the concept of institutional racism and recognize that this is a crucial feature of the existing social order.

In the second instance, racism has continued to touch on beliefs and not practices or outcomes. Rethinking has involved lengthening the understanding of racism in a specified way as to incorporate not only the theory of race but also other beliefs which justify racial inequality. Although a discourse which makes patently transparent reference to race and stratification is less common in the post-war stage, in its place has emerged another discourse 'whose dominant theme is not biological heredity but the insuperability of cultural differences', a discourse 'which at first sight does not postulate the superiority of certain groups or peoples in relation to others but 'only' the harmfulness of abolishing frontiers, the incompatibility of lifestyles and traditions' (Balibar,1991:21; quoted in Pilkington,2011:6). This discourse functions in a corresponding role to the preceding one in justifying racial inequality and so can be described as racism of sorts – cultural racism. Although this discourse fails to fall on 'new' pastures (Barker,1981) since Muslims have, for a substantial period, been liable to this discourse, and whereas it has not completely displaced one which centres on race and class, (Mason,1995) its proliferation suggests that one can desist from entertaining the idea that racism goes under one guise (see Pilkington,2011). However, prior to us concluding that there are separate racisms, not least scientific and cultural racisms, it is incumbent on us to identify the central features of racism.

The definition of racism we will outline here is that of 'a discourse which involves four features: identifying groups, which reproduce themselves over time, on the basis of physical markers; seeing essential differences between them; associating others with negative characteristics; and visualising the dissolution of boundaries as undesirable' (Pilkington, 2003:189; cited in Pilkington, 2011:7). Scientific racism in this mental image centres on race and class, while cultural racism centres on fundamental cultural differences.

The adversarial nature of institutional racism

What, then, does this mean for the concept of institutional racism? Whether the concept of racism is still to all intents and purposes contested, this is perhaps more evident in the instance of institutional racism. In the view of many commentators, the concept is analytically significant in bringing into focus the way widely held social values and routine structural practices generate racial disadvantage. Instead of supposing that racial disadvantage is the outcome of direct discrimination and that that discrimination, as is mutually supposed, is, in succession, the result of racial *parti pris*, the concept of institutional racism lays open the prospect of more complex causal processes at work. While the principle that everything has a cause may periodically be operative, with individuals exacting their subjective prejudices in overt exploits of discrimination which lead to racial discrimination, the ideation of institutional racism prompts us 'that, to thrive, racism does not require overt racist individuals, and conceives of it rather as arising through social and cultural processes' (Parekh,2000:71; quoted in Pilkington, 2011:7).

The actual basis of differential treatment in relation to race may not depend on a few unsavoury characters who bring the organisation into disrepute, but may be the result of a widespread occupational culture or taken-as-read organisational practices which, though unintentionally, cause racial disadvantage. Hence the debacle of the police inquiry into the killing of Stephen Lawrence was not, in Macpherson's view, attributable to overt exploits of discrimination by uniformed officers exacting their subjective prejudices, but derived instead from the occupational ethos of the police where 'both negative racial categorisations of black and the apparent irrelevance of race to incidents that require its recognition are features' (Holdaway,1999, para 8.2; quoted in Pilkington,2011:8).

We outlined Macpherson's interpretation of institutional racism in the foregoing text. It is extremely far-reaching covering a continuum of (conscious and unconscious) attitudes and (intentional and unintentional) practices, which are reported as leading to racial disadvantage. It is perhaps more far-reaching than at first apparent since it encircles inaction as it does action. As part of the same paragraph in which the above quote appears, the report continues: 'It [institutional racism] persists because of the failure of the organisation openly and adequately to recognize and address its existence and causes by policy, example and leadership. Without recognition and action to eliminate such racism, it can prevail as part of the ethos or culture of the organisation. It is a corrosive disease' (Macpherson,1999, para 6.34, quoted in Pilkington,2011:8).

The Macpherson Report caused an upsurge in enthusiasm for institutional racism with the concept gaining renewed confidence among some academic researchers to account for racial disadvantage (for example, Gulam,2004). In fact, a decidedly seminal report emphasized the significance of institutional racism and further elaborated to identify 'various interacting components of institutional racism' (Parekh,2000:73; cited in Pilkington,2011:8). Are there any traces of 'indirect discrimination' in the services made available to people from minority ethnic communities? Do 'employment practices' operate against minority groups? Does the 'occupational culture' leave scope for ethnic inclusion? Can the 'staffing structure' be considered one where senior staff are unconscionably White? Can there be a 'lack of positive action' in making members of minority ethnic groups part of the decision-making process? Are 'management and leadership' disposed to the question of combating institutional racism as a major concern? To what degree is 'professional expertise' pervasive in communication between different cultural groups? Are there any vestiges of germane high-quality 'training'? To what extent is there 'consultation' with agents from minority groups? Can there be a 'lack of information' on the organisation's effect on minority communities? (Pilkington,2011:8).

Whereas such questions warrant an organisation's attention if it is to make inroads into seeking racial equality, it needs to be recognized that they deal with issues that should be conceptually distinguished. Therefore, they concern, *inter alia*, beliefs which justify racial inequity ('occupational culture'), racially discriminatory practices ('indirect discrimination') and forms of racial disadvantage ('staffing structure'). It is debatable that defining each of these as aspects of institutional racism papers over important demarcations and is not serviceable in identifying the convoluted processes which give rise to racial disadvantage. Although the ideation of institutional racism is perhaps a politically expedient support mechanism to encourage venture enterprises to rethink their practices and adopt positive measures to facilitate racial equality, 'we must also be aware of the dangers of using such terminology very loosely and rhetorically' (Pilkington,2011:9).

'In the aftermath of the publication of the Scarman Report, there was a wide-ranging discussion about both the concept of institutional racism and its various meanings, as well as the way in which it could be applied to specific institutions' (Pilkington,2011:9). Learned experts identified that the ideation was not only used to mean all things to all people but also that, in respect of certain proponents such as Sivanandan, its meaning changed without legitimation from work to work. To the concept's doubters, institutional racism constituted a kind of 'conceptual inflation' (Pilkington,2011:9); the concept of racism haemorrhages any specificity and its significance as an analytical device declines as important dividing lines, such as those separating beliefs that support racial inequity (both biological and cultural), racially unequal practices (both intentional and unintentional) and forms of racial disadvantage are blurred (Pilkington,2011).

The claims levelled at preceding usages of the ideation have also been left at the altar of Macpherson's inordinately far-reaching usage. Certain critics have pointed out a very real risk in this usage of 'allowing the phrase to mean all things to all accusers' (Pilkington,2011:9). The most scathing exponents have gone still further. They have pictured the Macpherson take as a maladroit concept which papers over major distinctions (Dennis et al,2000) and as 'an unsystematic jumble of defining elements: impersonal processes, conscious attitudes and behaviour, and unwitting or unintentional prejudice' (Rattansi,2007:134). The fact that remains true is that its focus on single institutions threatens the very basis of Carmichael and Hamilton's original immersion with 'the systematic interconnections between discrimination in institutions such as housing, education, policing, and employment which create processes of cumulative disadvantage (Pilkington,2011:9). Moreover, this particular commentator goes so far as to argue that the concept of institutional racism itself should be discarded, yet he subsequently valorizes its important insights; not only is the latter a flat contradiction of the former but also, by definition, he could be seen to be sitting on the fence or avoiding commitment (Rattansi,2007:137,139).

Far from being at all surprising that Macpherson's understanding of institutional racism has been lambasted, even by those in favour of anti-racism, as ambiguous, inflated, and unsystematic, since it 'was the product of a 'power game' between the inquiry and the police ...it was a political necessity for the inquiry to define institutional racism in a way that would convince and be acceptable to the then commissioner of the Metropolitan Police, who had publicly opposed it' (Pilkington,2011:9).

The ultimate phrasing of the definition was, as Richard Stone, one of three expert aides to Macpherson, pronounces, the outcome of an extended process of negotiation: 'You look at our definition; it was going to be one line, one sentence, that was it. Then all of us felt that there were certain words that were not in, which is why we had the second paragraph. Then we had to work out how you're going to typeset it so [that] the second paragraph doesn't get lost in the first paragraph ... that's why you've actually got two paragraphs looking as if they're two ... And a typical sort of bartering goes on ...The prime example is that I went to Bill Macpherson one day and said, 'Bill, this unwitting prejudice, very unhappy about unwitting because I think it's very often witting [racism]. Ah, but he said, you do not understand, Richard, this is a judicial inquiry and we have to rely on precedent. There is only one precedent and that is Scarman. Scarman used the word unwitting and I think that it is very important we put it in so that people can see that we are not ignoring our precedents. And anyway, he said, you asked for racial stereotypes [to be included in the definition] yesterday and you got it.' And that completely undermined my challenge' (Stone quoted in Pilkington,2011:10).

Higher education's response to race

Although the police have re-evaluated their approach to race, particularly since the early 1980s, a similar message cannot be proffered on behalf of the academy in terms of their response (Pilkington,2004). More recently, no association was made between the shift from an elite to a mass-oriented higher education system which produced a progressively diverse student cohort, with growing numbers from minority ethnic communities. Evidence suggests that minority ethnic groups, on the whole, are disproportionately represented among admissions set against their numbers in the 15-24 age category (Pilkington,2004). Although it is true that, after regulating for differences in attainment, socio-economic and other contextual dimensions, certain minority ethnic groups, not least Black Caribbeans, Bangladeshis and Pakistanis, remain significantly less likely to gain admission to university, minority ethnic groups are, in the main, disproportionately represented in higher education and constitute an increasing component of the student population. In particular, this can be found in the new universities, partly on account of the ethnic bias evident in 'old' universities (Modood and Ackland,1998; Pilkington,2004,2011)

The expansion in the volume of pupils from minority ethnic groups began before the commencement of the 21st century in schools, generating in succession a series of policy responses and a salient research programme, specifically into the underachievement of Black Caribbean pupils (Rampton, 1981 and less pointedly Swann,1985 and recently Gillborn and Mirza,2000 but in addition see Pilkington,1997 (references cited in Pilkington,2004). While schools have issued a variable response, what is indisputable is that equally practitioners and prime movers have identified the need to begin thinking about and starting to deal with issues pertaining to race and schooling. Academic researchers have not eschewed the arising discursive struggles and, in some instances, 'passionate disagreements in the wider society' on race and schooling have been 'replayed inside the academy' (Pilkington,2004:21).

The decisive point at issue here is the extraordinary dearth of activity centred around race and ethnicity in connection with higher education (Bird,1996; Neal,1998; Law et al,2004). The principal policy response in this sphere has involved the advancement of equal opportunity policies. A modern-day study finds that 'it would be fair to say that higher education has not been in the forefront of moves to tackle equal opportunities in the last two or three decades' (Pilkington,2011:11). Equal opportunity policies were originally introduced during the 1980s, chiefly in certain of the polytechnics, in response to a modicum of power and influence exerted by local authorities (Pilkington,2004). Concerning the Committee of Vice-Chancellors and Principals' (CVCP's) instalment of the Commission on University Career Opportunity (CUCO) in 1994, a fresh external impetus was injected into ameliorating policies in both the 'new' and 'old' universities. What followed was that, by 1996, the upswing in equal opportunities policies culminated in a more or less even distribution across the sector (Pilkington,2004). The crux of the matter, however, is that these policies fall far short of observing questions concerning race and ethnicity as compared to gender, their more or less single concern with staffing issues and their finite impact (Neal,1998; Pilkington,2004,2011). A late twentieth-century study corroborated that racial equality policy developments still lagged behind those policy developments related to gender, with around a third of institutions acknowledging that their equal opportunities policies in no specific sense began to tackle racial equality concerns (Carter, et al,1999).

Familiar with the constraints of equal opportunities policies in confronting racial disadvantage, the then Commission for Racial Equality, renamed the Equalities and Human Rights Commission (EHRC), sent out a leadership challenge in 1997. The CVCP and the Standing Conference of Principals (SCOP) were quick to respond as signatories. Constituting a share of their interaction to this challenge, research was contracted on ethnicity and employment in higher education, flowering in a report for public consumption in June 1999, which signposted disadvantages undergone by academic members of authority from minority ethnic groups

(Carter et al,1999). This report, in addition to the conclusions of the Bett Report (1999) which had pointed to the disadvantages encountered by female academics, contributed to raising the contours of equal opportunities inside higher education. Further, the availability of the Macpherson Report earlier in the year saw to it that the question of racial equality received particular high-level positioning. While it concentrated on the police, the report indicated that all major enterprises in British social life were characterised by institutional racism and so it was therefore pressing on all enterprise organisations and encompassing higher education institutions to look closely at their practices and procedures to facilitate racial equality.

A lively spell of activity broke forth. The leading figures of the main academic unions (Paul Mackney of the National Association of Teachers in Further and Higher Education (NATFHE) and David Triesman of the Association of University Teachers (AUT) openly accepted the claim that the higher education sector was characterised by institutional racism (Pilkington,2004). An important conference was staged by NATFHE in partnership with other bodies to discuss future action plans within the framework of and in relation to the final solutions of the Stephen Lawrence inquest and the Carter Report. The CVCP, SCOP, the Universities and Colleges Employers Association (UCEA) and CUCO, alongside the unions, acceded in their official reciprocation to the Macpherson Report to a collaborative approach whereby separate institutions would be sanctioned to overhaul their equal opportunity policies on account of the advisory statements of the Bett, Macpherson and Carter Reports and fashion concrete cultural change. Prevailed upon by the Secretary of State for Education and Employment in his fiscal letter to the Higher Education Funding Council for England in November 1999, CVCP, SCOP and UCEA subsequently promised to endorse equal opportunities by placing the joint approach within a new domestic framework agreed with the HEFCE. This framework is referred to as the Higher Education Equality Challenge Framework and was introduced in 2001 (Pilkington,2004).

The aforementioned analysis signposts not only the enhanced momentum being given to equality policy developments within the sector but also widely interpreted that, in themselves, equal opportunity policies have not impacted to bring lasting and enduring social change. Further, this fails to be the only occasion on which unions have voiced concern regarding race equality and this fails to be the only occasion when managers have foregrounded race issues as constituting a general equal opportunities agenda (Pilkingtion,2004).

Prior to the Race Relations (Amendment) Act, the two main mechanisms called on by the government to precipitate change in higher education institutions involved monetary incentives to encourage an increase in student participation and also to effectuate the crucial aspects of the Equality Challenge with regard to staff. The agency that funds the sector, HEFCE, reduced the block grant so as to allocate specific funds to institutions relating to expanding participation and the establishment of a human resources policy process. While the government is interested in steering higher education institutions in a specific direction, neither pays attention to race. Evidence that other government initiatives for higher education are of greater importance is apparent in its 2003 White Paper, *The Future of Higher Education,* in which race is conspicuous by its absence (Pilkington,2004).

Understanding Institutional Racism

At source, institutional racism is firmly entrenched in and mediates with cultural history. It represents clear evidence of essential dysfunctions in the interplay between culturally and ethnically heterogeneous beings. This section is inspired by research and documentary evidence in the sector but also by a common cognizance of the troubling concerns that British non-white intellectuals face at present. According to Rangasamy (2004), the various theoretical stances and discursive struggles that discourse is generating deserve appropriate academic scrutiny. Then, and only then, can the profusion of good endeavours and well-meaning tendencies be founded on an apprehension that effectively considers and begins to deal with the cultural issues that lie behind institutional racism.

Statistical evidence relating to career advancement and promotion, instructional equipment, student performance and subject specialism provide key pointers to the magnitude and site of institutional racism inside the educational sector. Qualitative and quantitative data are useful guides for organizing realistic timescales and streamlined priority programmes for change. However, statistical evidence indicates the signs or consequences of institutional racism; this must undergo careful assessment with qualitative material to generate the kind of revelatory evaluations capable of discerning, and eventually abrogating, the hidden disparities in forms of structural racism. It would appear necessary to unravel the often masked and therefore elusive obstructions to career advancement and to the deflation and disincentive they produce and draw from. In reality, discrimination on any basis is an affront to the goodness of one's professional stature and can have devastating effects. It may elicit a defensive, brunt-stricken attitude that can weaken the positive expectations that fuel high performance within competitive situations (Rangasamy,2004).

Speculation can construct forms of substantive connections between statistical and material evidence on institutional racism. Accordingly, it can generate critical analysis adept at ensuring fair and equal judgement in the establishment of people-centred and professional relationships and their denouement. However, speculation that arises from interpretative observation is also a kind of good vigilance, which the reality of racism in academic circles makes desirable, perhaps even essential. Similar to a virus that the environment has denied independent life but which gains a common existence when carried by an appropriate living organism, intellectual racism can change from a correspondingly containable concept and become a predominant feature in the functioning, identity and scope of agency of institutions. Precisely as a virus can thrive and flourish in the face of the adverse conditions put in place to neutralise its effects, institutional racism not infrequently survives and becomes well-adjusted to antiracist measures. It then emerges anew in subtler and stronger strains to suit the demands of a changing environmental milieu (Rangasamy,2004).

The desired exegesis for institutional racism is often isolated bureaucratic malpractice or amoral understandings of institutional rules and conventions. However, the magnitude of such 'innocent thoughtlessness' calls for deeper reflection and careful examination. The insidious *parti pris* operative in the allocation of life chances and career rewards also shapes the labour force and its operational nature for reduced functioning. This prevents the institution from delivering its true achievement potential. High threshold levels of discrimination institutionalise a crisis situation and this, by itself, begs urgent attention (Rangasamy,2004).

As stated by Rangasamy (2004), the inception and development over successive generations of ingrained patterns of inequity suggest that institutional racism attributes its persistence to the bigoted design, overt or subtle, that underscores every single act of discrimination. The deliberate ploy, with its embedded typifications and biases, often emerges in interactive situations like job interviews, promotions and condemnation hearings, when there is a degree of control over the fortunes of non-white staff. Depracatory and critical assumptions, stated or unstated, concerning the skill levels of non-white staff, are permitted to shape judgement and procedural end results. By themselves, such assumptions are frequently too absurd to escape critical analysis. However, the conventions of collective decision-making make for effective cover for bigotry.

For Rangasamy (2004), the typifications and biases beneath institutional racism are traditional and cultural constructs. These typifications and biases comprise the attitudinal legacy of the colonial past, so are firmly established in the collective consciousness. On the structural level, they are inclined to fashion the vitality and attitudes of other generations and order forms of internal professional associations. In certain contexts, people and institutional racism call upon reciprocal early influences. Institutional racism stops at being the metaphorical obstruction in the works that conventional agendas of race awareness training can resolve. Instead, it is dynamic in nature and role activity and grows in guile and resilience with every challenge it successfully negotiates. Possibly the only effective approach to dislodge or disengage institutional racism is to supplant the institutional culture. In order for this to transpire, institutional racism must be situated within its broader cultural and historical background. Panacea strategies must likewise be gauged to accommodate the being of scope and related cultural warp and weft of the problem. In addition, they must possess the transferable intellectual skills and energies, otherwise, they may assist in the scope institutional racism has accrued over decades to withstand change, and would consequently contrast with the desired effect (Rangasamy,2004).

The analogy of an institution is a collective mind involved in and concerned about a range of professional issues. Not unlike the human mind, institutions factor in reality, express their mores and reflect their collective and autocratic thinking through language. Moreover, they apply language to modernize policies and streamline their thinking. However, more significantly, just as language primarily defines the horizons of cognition and implementation, so organisations rely on their institutional terminology to configure their structural appellation and public face, and they can revise it periodically to the requirement of contemporary circumstances. Hence the institutional rhetoric is prone to generate objective and subjective significance capable of articulating and legitimating the patterns of inequality embedded in institutional daily affairs (Rangasamy,2004).

Because the prevailing political/social order and its essential institutional functions rest on the discharge of power, institutional language extends interesting parallels with political modes of expression. Also, the form and content of rules and regulations that drive the institutions are imbued or precipitated by political agendas. The work of Maurice Bloch (Bloch,1997) has particular pertinence here (Rangasamy,2004). He noted that political speech-making, especially the institutionalised articulation of reverence for tradition and chief spokespersons, configures the moral and conceptual framework for the captive audience to accept dominance by the powers that be and the system, unquestioningly and often subliminally. Within Bloch's wider orientation of analysis and also within the boundaries of institutions, language proceeds into the often-private discursive struggle between individual questioning and group compliance. Group acceptance changes the institutional systems of thinking and action into a powerful and, in most cases, irresistible current that inhibits or makes professionally calamitous the critical antagonism from lone individuals. Bloch pointed out that formalised speech limits the range of feasible questions and feasible answers. The language the institution finds favour with often structures its processes in ways that restrict freedom of expression and neutralize any significant resistance to authority. The myopic adherence to institutional rules can create a smokescreen for individual and group aversions. This can be seen in some instances where institutions comply with the protocols that govern recruitment and progression but highlight the negative aspects of non-white candidates and make light of their positive aspects while working counter-clockwise for White candidates. These processes, which are adversely routine, cartoon outline the skills of both Whites and minorities, and breach confidence and faith in the system (Rangasamy,2004).

But, as Bakhtin has noted, verbal rhetoric is not neutral; it possesses the right characteristics or qualities for private use and is in line with the wishes of the speaker. There is no doubt that language is permeated with the goal objectives of others (Bakhtin, et al, 1983; in Rangasamy,2004). People in favour of institutional racism first acquire ownership of the institutional *lingua franca* and of the corpus of guidelines and directives which channel its very expression. Given that their watchword incorporates spoken language, they expropriate institutional language beyond how it informs socialisation and use it to circulate and celebrate their particular experiences, but also and seriously significant, to negate the experiences of others. In educational institutions, sustained and enduring denial undermines the *amour propre* and professional status of the precluded group and effectively causes pernicious effects for them. The employment of discriminatory institutional terminology to praise and reward the accomplishments of some while denigrating and downgrading that of others constituted a key colonialist device for subordinating colonised entities. What is paradoxical is that supremacist Eurocentric antecedents inform the curricula of the educational establishments of former colonies to date (Rangasamy,2004). However, it is also illustrated in most universities' stand against consulting Black staff substantively as part of their moral encumbrance towards the Race Relations (Amendment) Act 2000.

Verbal in addition to institutional languages are employed for 'race making'. In verbal language, it is explicit, as used by certain newspapers and screen and stage artistes. However, it is also employed ambiguously, to keep alive, to exist with and to excuse the racial contradictions and ironies inseparable in culture (Hymes,1971: 51; cited in Rangasamy,2004). The rhetoric of certain institutions generates and underpins systems of cultural conduct suitable to the formation of diversity, but on an equal footing with the dominant sphere, using its unidimensional culture of the White, male and bourgeois notion of social justice to defend its interests. So, communicative proficiency, which in respect of institutional language comprises a thorough understanding of institutional guidelines and directives, does not automatically certify everyone for career advancement – as non-white personnel in British universities know only too well. The regulation over promotion and additional rewards of advancement is contingent on ownership of the institutional rhetoric and of the prevailing political/social order (Rangasamy,2004).

Such rhetoric is an effective means of exclusion. Minority ethnic personnel have noted that those who own the institutional language, as a function of their will and for their particular private inward satisfaction, place career development life-chances at the crossroads of certain individuals and tune up their skills to the requirements for organisational promotion and progression. Skill levels in institutional as in verbal expression determines not only the speaker's expressed content but also the tone in which s/he delivers it. Given that there is a noble aspect to speaking that could have socio-political ramifications – Martin Luther King springs to mind – so also is there a way of expressing institutional language to enable the realisation of something breaking through with particular effect. Very different from being the institutional guidelines and directives that determine end results, but the personalities that make sense of these guidelines and directives (Rangasamy,2004).

The emphasis on skill levels highlights the role and contribution of the audience in the formation of messages and their significance. The institutional rhetoric and the racism it may circulate is effectively the overlap of many mentalities, conceptualizations, ways of working, and particular kinds of conservatism. Therefore, does the institutional rhetoric articulate the culture of the organisation? Associated with that culture is a kind of knowledgeability, a tacit understanding that its established and clearly evident ways of coming to a settlement and conducting procedures are necessary for the health and smooth running of the institution. Also, the culture codifies the recognized criteria and provisos that regulate access into the visceral existence of the institution, and admission to the privileges of advancement, that follows from a proper sense of camaraderie. Institutional cohesion requires accepting this culture and its taken-for-granted knowledgeability without question. Presenting opposition to this is a frightful prospect, even for claimants of discrimination and harassment. Their automatic and unthinking compliance serves to support, though inadvertently, the institutional bigotry that preyed upon them to begin with (Rangasamy,2004).

Rangasamy's experience of over three decades extends the idea that the myopic characterisation of institutional racism creates a controlled environment for those responsible for it. It serves to preserve and guard against the psychological, ethical, political and other interests of the dominant group for the dominant group. Hence it is construed as elevating, morally rewarding and intrinsically satisfying. It consolidates the belief that the extant relationships of power are immutable and indispensable. Beyond what has been said, it constructs a representation of non-white personnel as pathologically in need of suitable professional duty and managerial adequacy. Most favourably, they have ape-like intelligence (Rangasamy,2004:33).

Towards the intersection of the institutional availability of guidelines and directives with individual perceptions and proclivity for action, there comes into focus institutional common sense. Institutional knowingness neutralizes the acquiescence that confirms archetypical thinking and agency. It renders it unnecessary to consider or question the problems that counteract institutional interests (Pcikering,2001; cited in Rangasamy,2004). This manner of working, common between language and institutional frameworks, has been allowed over time to become the norm and thus embedded in everyday work patterns. Institutional racism and the intellectual and moral canons of many higher education institutions have become interwoven (Rangasamy,2004). Having said that, the institutional language even bears conduits that convey and applaud the experiences of minority group members and overseas staff and students.

The modus vivendi of a university is distinct in the way it communicates and interprets its institutional guidelines and directives as equally determined by the nature and standard of its pedagogy and research. Because the latter incorporates inspectors, funders and commissioning groups for research, in addition to students, the interpretation of guidelines and directives necessarily touches on several more operations, like self-critique and valuation, the contextualising of professional praxis, inspection and answerability (Rangasamy,2004:31). The expert responsible for certain interpretative operations has been the topic of a selection of studies. Charles Goodwin's (1994) offering (in Rangasamy,2004) is of specific pertinence. Goodwin examines three practices that aficionados use in what he designates the development of professional vision, and these procedures are well suited for defining the processes that render institutional racism and additional types of discriminatory practices possible.

Goodwin defined the initial practice as 'encoding', a process by which all qualitative data affecting the institution are codified into items of information that revive the discourse of the employment category

(Rangasamy,2004:31). In the course of action, institutional racism and additional forms of private *bête noire* may also be arranged in code. This divergence from the standard in the understanding of the rules rests on stereotypes for its rationalization and critical limiting factor. Stereotypes already conform to encoded systems of belief and modes of thinking. Such attitudes associate the institution with recent or past mental images like colonial form, nationalism and patriotism out of which divisive constructions can be rendered. The connective link between typifications and institutions is an insidious but far from dull one. The institution improves and conceals the partisan background of stereotypes to which it participates as host, it rationalizes its racist, xenophobic, sexist and further unsettling additional meanings. Plus ca change, plus c'est la meme chose, or in other words, 'the more it changes, the more it stays the same'. In exchange for this extension of residence, the stereotype adds to the institution its representative and critical motor. The witting or unwitting use of stereotypes allows institutions to undertake strategies of symbolic repression of individuals, ideas and courses of action that they deem threats or a liability to the status quo. Typifications also help single out and encode the goal objective, in addition to the processes entangled in them-and-us contexts.

An added process Goodwin pointed up was 'highlighting', which involves marking and emphasizing particular phenomena and character attributes for the object of categorisation and compartmentalization (Rangasamy, 2004:31). Institutions see fit to celebrate the accomplishments of certain individuals, for instance, while losing sight of or dismissing those of others. Rendering career-enriching life-chances available to favoured individuals is a further device. Universities have progressed spanning several centuries predicated on the assumptions that White heterosexual men from the privileged middle and upper strata were naturally equipped for university training. Therefore, the socio-economic and national culture that govern the system of running and authoritative direction of universities, specifically the older ones, are originated from those social categories. Given the tone and inflection of Ann Bishop (1997), university values comprise a 'complex set of interlocking systems, assumptions, principles and practices' that can be effectively levelled to frustrate the advancement of once-excluded groups who had resisted the restrictions of the academy (Rangasamy,2004:32). They continue to be dormant caveats dominating the sense of institutional *esprit de corps* beneath a layer of seemingly democratic conventions. However, these caveats are re-enlivened to legitimate the exclusionary and punitive measures doled out to certain of the once-excluded groups who confront 'professional difficulties' in their quest to acculturate themselves to something many of them see as a strange and professionally alienating social setting.

Goodwin determined the third procedure as presenting and expressing material portrayals of people and circumstances. The aforementioned engages the negative stereotyping of unwelcome groups, often 'from the motive to restore a threatened self-image' and concomitant self-esteem (Rangasamy,2004:32). Non-white professional experts in British institutions are not infrequently wrongly indicted of (stereotypic) aggressiveness and arrogance at any time that they confront discrimination and unbalanced judgement in promotional and associated matters. Despite the justified intense irritation that such inequitable rejections stir up, non-white professional experts feel that they should take into account the fragile establishment of the Whiteness of some of their governing heads. In processes that think about and begin to deal with incidences of inequality, the primary concern is often devoted to not alienating or inflaming White sensibilities. A certain number of White managers use 'playing the race card' as a defence mechanism for professional ineptitude and evidence in support of their stereotypic estimation.

The three-pronged processes work together to create the background for the material and inner life and perpetuation of the institution, which would find articulation through the institutional language. A concise study of key aspects of this situation may suggest remedial action against institutional discrimination:

1. The processes contribute toward a particular perception of the actual physical geography of the institution, including the extended demography and intellectual realities in which it is situated and to which it has aligned its loyalty. This self-image, a key component of an institutional badge of office prized and treasured over years, often functions as the first frontier of resistance against changes enforced from outside. The self-confidence this creates can trap the institution in its self-image and dislodge its synchronization with evolving social class and political trends.

2. However, the essential purpose of the preceding self-image is to preserve the conservatism that maintains internal organization and the accompanying power structure while supporting particular sets of investments and the existing state of affairs in the process. That said, crucially, it can help order the internal animation of the institution to reciprocate to perceived and actual threats internally and externally.

3. The vitally important desideratum to survive often inhibits flexible cognition and results in enforcing controls on opinions instead. And it rationalizes the institution's control over the materials for processing qualitative data and research. Certain Black professional intellectuals have complained that they have been left out of the Research Assessment Exercise schemes. Different ones have experienced an oversight for PhD supervision despite their accomplishment and specialism.

4. Essentially, therefore, behind a perfunctory of homogeneity and equality, institutions often camouflage administration of decision-making processes and discrimination that might contravene the law, but that justify their code towards particular sets of personnel and students.

5. Domestic institutions, with their sovereign charters and perennial histories, accede to and maintain mastery of the outside world founded practically on the colonialist model. Thus, they put before

the public their institutional perception and the racism that it ventilates as a system of super-morality instead of a deficiency in sagacity (Rangasamy, 2004:32-33).

Interrogating factual and statistical information, as this chapter urges, would help develop the professional skeleton for processes of 'imaginative identification' that Chinua Achebe, in his opus 'The Truth of Fiction' (1978), describes as the reverse of indifference (Rangasamy,2004). This identification is the element in human relationships that promotes self and mutual awareness, self and shared actualisation. In addition to professional development, it would convey the egalitarianism of the institutional language and would pave the way for natural justice. However, there must first be in place a dynamic, enlightened and compassionate hegemony by institutional management in facilitating, initiating, influencing and monitoring the changes very directly required in institutional culture and language (Rangasamy, 2004).

Why the need for recommendations?

The rubric of equal opportunities and race equality policy are of interest and concern to policy-makers, managers, professionals, teachers in higher education and academics, and can be seen as forming part of the solution to what can be described as institutional racism being embedded in the structure of higher education institutions. While it is legitimate and justifiable to speak to the Black and minority experience – upon which this work reflects – however, would policy-makers, managers, academics and professionals be lost in the absence of solutions and recommendations? Solutions and recommendations are an open declaration or acknowledgement that all is not well, and such policy initiatives are necessary if we are to begin to work towards an antiracist college/university.

Higher Education Institutions and Black Exclusion

Despite the enactment of the Race Relations (Amendment) Act 2000, higher education institutions in contemporary Britain appear to function in a critical role that is not conventional or predictable where Black and minority ethnic groups are concerned. For example, one would expect that an institution whose mantra alludes to high academic standards, without those standards impacting negatively upon the person, would honour its ideals and live up to its principles. However, in practice, the author can indeed vouch for the fact that this particular higher education institution requires an upper second-class degree award at Bachelor level before an individual can be considered eligible for admission to pursue a PhD career. Holding a Master of Arts degree warranted little consideration for admission to a doctoral programme at this specific institution who made a mockery of, and was openly in defiance with, their motto and consequently did not go anywhere near being fair and equitable and was seen as unfairly discriminatory and elitist. The telephone conversation that conveyed this news suddenly became silent on hearing me say, "That is elitist and you as an institution claim not to be". The call ended with me not having obtained another word from the institution's representative; the line just seemed to become inactive.

The author can also vouch for the veritable fact that the 'old' universities in Britain appear to be far from without blemish on this count, or are not immune from the practice of denying access no matter what the standard of the application for admission and, in particular, one such institution does so by reference to their national and international desirability, effectively taking cover behind the ancient university cachet which, of course, is the Holy Grail and aspired to by many, but does this really make the pill of rejection any less unpalatable to swallow in the knowledge that they have attempted to sweeten the pill by foregrounding their popularity and prestige as the reason for operating a closed-door policy on hopeful candidates despite their competence and specialism? This institution also claims that the "high volume of applications" was the reason for denying access, therefore, concealing the very real possibility that social institutions have a tendency to skew the rules firmly towards the dominant group, both nationally and internationally, and where economic priorities win the day, much to the detriment of Black and minority ethnic candidates.

The results of a further application to the same institution yielded another rejection letter which asserted that "the graduate application process is extremely competitive" suggesting that the application of yours truly did not have any force or effectiveness and was unable to compete under adversarial conditions, which verges on an affront. The use of the term "competitive" is to state the obvious, so why use it at all other than to make the not-too-dissimilar point to the one referred to above? Once again, in the employment of the word "competitive". the institution alludes to the spectre of its national and international popularity and prestige which it so often hides behind.

Britain's most cherished and revered educational institutions win the right to that reverence only because it is the accepted norm and venerable by dint of age-old centuries of time, but, in certain quarters, that reputation is tarnished and not beyond or above reproach. In the author's particular case, this institutional exclusion was a way of excusing exclusion and hiding behind university cachet. Such institutions ensure that intelligence is no guarantee to success but instead is a barrier, and they, in turn, reinforce inequality, waste resources and exploit the power relations that exist between non-white people and the dominant group. The power vested in these institutions is, for the most part, exploitative power as they exploit subordinate groups with impunity. It does not escape the author's attention that this latest exclusion is not only an affront but it is also patronizing, given the fact that I already knew that the graduate application process is extremely competitive.

One can always console oneself with the adage that 'it is their loss, not mine', but while this is glorying in self-belief and holding oneself up in high esteem, at the same time, it is inertia and a fool's paradise since this is the cry of someone resigned to their fate. Some would argue that this outlook is the only way to confront reality and then move on. But if one thinks that highly of oneself, they should try, try again, as I did, because maybe, just maybe, one will succeed with another blow. The notoriety that these institutions carry for excluding people who hail from backgrounds such as mine, saw me initially write a marathon research proposal to challenge and convince them of my far from dilettante approach to the cause and to try to dissolve and melt their hard ice-cold exteriors, but their callous rejection and opposition only confirmed and corroborated how resolute such institutions are, when faced with serious potential, to exploit and subjugate. Such social exclusion leaves one in a state of nothingness, in limbo, without purpose and unrewarded for one's effort, only to pick oneself up from off rock bottom level to muster one's designs once again in another direction – having been not entirely astonished – and to form a queue elsewhere.

Frustration, alienation, disaffection and disconsolation are all words that describe how the decision impacted upon me; it is utterly devastating that they can just turn around and with the flick of a pen or turn of mind, deny access and, in the process, offer inadmissible grounds for their action. It is not that difficult to see that episodes like this and other institutional exclusions, in addition, lead to the formation of an underclass that is not entirely of an individual's or collective group's own making. To state that the world is an unfair place does not overstate the case in relation to this particular institution, and British higher education in general.

Black social reality is not something on which to base a study, as such institutions are simply not interested, and suggests that they exist largely in denial that racism is prevalent. Black social reality is only controversial because White people cannot relate to it or imagine the anxiety it causes, which is why they often end up disputing or denying the resilience and persistence of racism owing to the fact that they do not have the first idea nor any clue concerning the plight of Black and minority ethnic people. And, this is how the truth becomes controversial because White groups cannot share Black social reality.

For an institution to exclude an applicant on the basis that it lacks the staff profile required to supervise a doctoral research project suggests, at best, an under-funded institution and, at worst, inadequate staffing levels, and frankly, a higher education institution whose reputation is in tatters, or so it appears because, for staff research interests and knowledge base to be found wanting in any subject area, this admits to an institution that is failing in the one defining quality that all universities pride themselves on: professional expertise. This was in addition to being informed, on a visit to the institution under discussion, that there had recently been a staff profile enhancement that incorporated the author's particular research interest and that this new addition would add something to the supervisory input of the author's proposed research area. On the other hand, the above-outlined incidence of exclusion may have been a poor excuse to avoid doing something that they ought to do and, again, this underlines the perception that higher education institutions cannot be taken at face value or relied upon to see policy through to practice. With other institutions, one hits a cold and unfeeling brick wall barrier stating that the university cannot offer one a place, indicating an indifference to say any more than that or to account for why such is the case. One can only assume that the reason for such a cold and heartless response was because the institution suspected that the applicant was a person of colour and felt that it was beneath their dignity to impart a second-class citizen with a credible explanation as to why the closed door. The idea that an institution responds inflexibly demonstrates blatant defiance to an open-door policy and suggests that evasive action is being taken to thwart and frustrate a prospective student batting for the Black struggle rather than the seemingly favoured White homogeneity. Higher degree research proposals tend to indicate the ethnicity of the applicant: an interest in Second-World-War poetry might smack of a White person, or the relationship between African-Caribbean boys and schooling might be indicative of a Black individual; but to make sure, higher education institutions ask for the ethnicity profile of the applicant and do not respond in a uniform capacity but apply the institution's own brand of access denied default message if need be.

On the other hand, White students may be inclined to explore subjects considered the province of Black students and vice versa. Yet, whereas White students are allowed to search into Black social issues, prospective Black students are turned away. Research proposals are a requirement of doctoral applications to higher education and advise institutions regarding the subject area of interest of the prospective student candidate; institutions then tend to determine the ethnic origin of the applicant and decide whether to apply the ethnic penalty or so it would seem to appear. It follows, therefore, that White students can study whatever subject area they please whereas the same sentiment cannot be echoed for Black and minority ethnic students. Institutions can accept the truth as seen through White students' eyes but find it very difficult to accept from a Black perspective. Freedom of information is enshrined in this country's democratic ideals but it is revealing as to how undemocratic higher education institutions are at the present time. Although this does not demonstrate the extent, it demonstrates the nature of higher education institutions' facility to maintain and reinforce the status quo of White privilege and minority ethnic disadvantage.

In the author's experience, higher education institutions can hardly claim to be an environment in which discrimination absents itself, and therefore, staff in higher education can take little comfort in arguing that documented evidence of discrimination mainly emanates from schools and further education establishments (Bird,1996:88). The subsequent passage goes some way to offering an explanation as to why admission to higher education for a doctoral research study was not realized, though there can be no excuse.

Towards explaining the exclusion of minority ethnic people

Firstly, on an analytical level, equal opportunity for everyone can only take its march in a social order where there obtains, *inter alia*, widespread regard for the prevailing values and beliefs (Mullard,1982:128) When this is not the case, equal opportunity is contingent on the extent of mutual tolerance in evidence. However, considering the need initially of depending on mutual tolerance – that racism has an entity – it is quite likely that the extent of equal opportunity to be obtained at any particular time by any particular group will dovetail very closely with that group's leaning towards a society's prevailing attitude and standpoint position. Whether it disavows this attitudinal structure, equal opportunities of entry to key stations in the power structure where socio-political change can be enacted will be denied; whether it accedes, equal opportunity of admission will possibly be extended with the conceptualization that the extant cultural beliefs will be maintained. In slightly different terms, given that minority groups share a different sense of reality linked inextricably to structural inequality operating at different levels of society, equal opportunity in effect means equal opportunity only if one subscribes to the dominant ideas and values that govern White middle-class culture (Mullard,1982:128).

To clarify things further, now, had I been White, these institutional doors that remained tightly shut, doors that by rights should be open anyway, would, as a matter of course, be open and staff be ready to facilitate one's academic progress for an allotted timespan; thereafter, White people go on to perpetuate the dominant values and beliefs whilst being aware that the system is skewed in their favour but needs to be more equitable. However, built into White systems of belief is an unwillingness to change things, so things remain as they are, whilst Black and minority ethnic people, on the other hand, are seen as a 'threat' to the undisturbed functioning of society precisely because they may want to effect change for the better.

Equal Opportunity Issues in Higher Education

Black and minority ethnic students and professionals are a casualty of higher education not following through equal opportunities policy into practice and the perception of higher education being unconventional and unpredictable where Black and minority ethnic students are concerned is justified, in that, the willingness of institutions to deliver on equal opportunities can become removed from the doubtfulness of social justice and become enmeshed with public relations, marketing issues and the preoccupation with cultivating a picture of the model institution (Neal,1998:72). Any form of unfair discrimination in this context, according to Neal (1998), is quite simply a waste of human resources. The tendency for higher education institutions not to be committed to equal opportunities issues and to depart from issues of social justice can be evinced in the following quote by a senior lecturer in an institution's Social Science faculty:

> When these places [new universities] were trying to expand, they made wonderful, high-sounding noises about equal opportunities, but as soon as they feel they have to compete and they're called universities and they want to look good, then they'll throw it all out the window (Neal,1998:70).

Carter, Fenton and Modood's (1999) discussion group circulated the view that equality policies within universities made for infinitesimal effect on recruitment trends and adduced the scarcity of minority ethnic academic staff at senior levels as validation of their failure.

> The issue of equal opportunities is very often paid little more than lip service and coexists with patterns of discrimination and disadvantage that are deeply entrenched.

> Most universities have an equal opportunity policy but in practical terms, it doesn't mean very much. White staff always seem to do better than ethnic minorities even when their qualifications are the same (Carter et al,1999:53).

Members of the discussion group also alluded to 'old-fashioned attitudes and ignorance about equal opportunities' in high places within the academic field, which was considered to counteract the appointment and upward mobility of minority ethnic people.

There is a problem with this university about the perceptions that white staff have of ethnic minority staff. There are some staff members who have been in post for a long time and, to all intents and purposes, they are in a time warp with their attitudes; there are also professors and heads of departments who have got jobs on the strength of the 'old boy' network and the idea of equality of opportunity is something which is beyond their experience (Carter et al,1999:54).

Certain discussants vigorously argued that minority personnel should be employed on the grounds of individual merit not out of 'political correctness', and articulated considerable concerns about policies which fostered, for example, quotas:

In the final analysis, the most important thing about recruitment is that it must be down to the quality of the applicant. However well-intentioned positive action or even positive discrimination might be, it will always lead to accusations of tokenism, which makes the job harder (Carter et al,1999:54).

From their standpoint, the aim of equal opportunities policies was to raise, not reduce, the meritocratic level in higher education. And some had reservations that positive discrimination policy procedures would engender the charge of tokenism and resultant White backlash. Certain among them reflected that some colleagues had already come forward telling them, in effect, that 'you got the job because you are black' (Carter et al,1999:54).

With this end in mind, the enhancement of the meritocratic ethos of academic institutions, two policy procedures were agreed upon. Firstly, the idea was advanced that all interview panels should comprise at least one minority ethnic individual. Discussants accepted that this would serve as a safety measure against the likelihood that panels may intentionally or unintentionally discriminate against minority ethnic candidates. Secondly, the idea was advanced that the appointments procedure should be technically more 'transparent'. In the large majority of cases where people had sought promotion, they were not relayed a reason for why their application was not successful, and this also left room for discrimination and doubtless allowed the notion that discrimination has an entity (Carter et al,1999). In her case study of four universities, Neal (1998) found evidence that equal opportunities structures were made light of which attests to the uncommitted rather than the democratic position universities ought to take on equality initiatives.

The occasions on which marginalization took place were within those equality structures that complement each case-study university's main equal opportunities committees (that is, those structures where senior management heads were not physically on hand). For instance, in 'Russell College', an organic process whereby all faculties acted in unison to elect a member of staff to Equal Opportunities Consultant had taken effect since 1986. This collection of consultants convened three-yearly group meetings and filtered news through the Equal Opportunities Officer that would find its way onto the Equal Opportunities Committee (Neal,1998:78). When senior management were not directly on hand, there was apparent marginalization of equal opportunities structures and the people placed in positions within them. Equal opportunities structures had the prospect of being marginalized, then, through the especial low status of equal opportunities activity, there was a shortage of disposable time to devote to equality-related activity and an uncertainty as to how to go about the job of work. In 'Northfield University', marginalization mechanisms had their origins in the historic background of the institution – the antagonism and suspicion shown towards the Section II-resourced racial equality initiatives. Although these initiatives had undergone transformation and change, the vilification and suspicion remained, and therefore, continued to isolate those people responsible for putting the initiative into effect (Neal,1998:81). The remaining two universities in Neal's (1998) case study were 'Castlebrook University' and 'People's University'.

In her recommendations for change, Neal (1998) argues that marginalization may not occur if the managerial regulation or devolved hierarchical paradigm of equal opportunities that operated in the case studies is reconstructed and replaced with a system involving a far higher degree of coordinated, transparent and wide-ranging discussion and discursive struggle throughout the institutions. In addition, she argued that this needs to coalesce with a centralized but egalitarian process of continuous policy generation. She notes that the spin-offs in regard to having a wider deliberative system for policy generation would carry forward and be seen in the wider colonization of, and thereby obligation to, equality policies. She suggests that covering a greater breadth of policy ownership would help to expand both perception/awareness of the policies and intensify their endorsement within the institutions. Although it is essential to retain management approval wherever possible for equality work, a much less intimidating management culture, with less masculine ways of working than was demonstrated among the four case studies, would warrant a proliferation of involvement, and more favourable policy acceptance, within the institutions, Neal (1998) adds.

Connected to this is the call for more prudent 'public relations' work in all aspects of equality-related initiatives (Neal,1998:122). Fuller explanations of the logical basis for such initiatives are needful. Such formulation also needs to marry up with the sine qua non guidelines on how to bring the initiatives into operation with a view to widening support for equality policies at the point of production. While the foregoing measures may set policy processes back, however, this delayed progress in itself may be more successful in augmenting the colonization of equal opportunities policies while, simultaneously, it would avail space for a higher level of reflexive, evaluatory and self-critical direction in terms of addressing the specific equality questions that need to be dealt with. Together with such changes is the indispensable condition to appreciate equal opportunities policy processes as perpetual. Conventional wisdom dictated that the four universities and the AUT and NATFHE (academic trade unions) tended to imagine the policy process as anchored. Put in a different way, once policy formulation had taken place and procedures set up to operationalize that policy, then beyond this, the process extends no further. The comparative lack of evaluatory paperwork or exercises was an evidential basis of this. It is not well judged to see equality policies as complete, but instead, should be made accountable to perpetual, self-critical practices of review (Neal,1998:122).

Confronting Reality

The findings that emerge in this chapter only serve as confirmation of what the Black and minority ethnic communities already suspected and comes as no surprise to say the very least. Denials of the accusation that institutional racism exists in higher education suggest that this negative influence is beyond their experience and plays no part in the lives of those who deny the charge, and so, they cannot share the reality of those the charge in question affects. As I have already mentioned, institutional racism in higher education resonates with yours truly, having faced multiple doors slammed shut before one – post Master of Arts degree – and if the prevailing wind is anything to go by, there can be no doubt that I am not alone in having faced such deep reverberations. The material detail that the author is among those who have been excluded from higher education is a travesty indeed and indicates that even when one plays by the rules, there is no guarantee of success as the warped and whimsical nature of White society and social institutions sets glass ceilings for minority ethnic individuals and is intent on barring advancement and is how we come to know that White society oppresses those unlike themselves. One has to question whether the rules change legitimately or are a device to exclude certain groups.

In 2012, the coalition government headed by the then Conservative leader David Cameron and the Liberal Democratic leader Nick Clegg introduced tuition fees for higher education in England and Wales; students will now face catastrophic debt on leaving university and for this reason, the prospect of university tuition fees will deter those from low-income and working-class families, including Black and minority ethnic people. It seems that since higher education was once the preserve of the rich and well-heeled and was effectively elite, the government has ushered in a new era of elitism throughout higher education in England and turned it back to what it once was. Nick Clegg, incidentally, had formally declared that he would not introduce tuition fees - an election pledge - prior to coalition power-sharing, thus consolidating the image of the untrustworthy and disingenuous politician. Notwithstanding government loans that are repayable once a graduate finds work, the new changes can only seem to mean fewer Black and minority ethnic students seeking admission to higher education and consequently access to upward social mobility. Nick Clegg later apologized profusely after protests and public ire over tuition fees but the damage had already been done and there was no possibility of an about-turn.

I have argued that higher education institutions show a tendency to fail in implementing equal opportunity policy procedures into practical conditions and this can be seen in the action of exclusionary policy initiatives adversely affecting Black and minority ethnic candidates. According to Paul Allen (1998), evidence on the attainment of racial equality indicates that institutions of higher education, even in the present climate, have considerable ground to make up and a growing number of minority students are calling institutional commitment into question, whilst undergoing institutional indifference.

A higher education system that works in the best interest of minority groups must openly acknowledge the barriers a White society throws up and give due regard to the strife and adaptations that minority group students have to adopt in order to survive. Of course, the decisive point at issue for Britain's Black and minority ethnic student population at present is to open existing educational power structure doors, but, ultimately, it is not that simple transforming them so that they develop a way of seeing, knowing and feeling akin to the Black perspective, which is also crucial if there is to be a demise of the ivory tower (Allen,1998:94-95).

I have briefly elucidated something of my experience and will give further details below of the processes of higher education, the influence of which fed widespread disillusionment, disaffection and frustration with the system in itself and of itself which put an end to my hopes, dreams and aspirations after multiple applications, of one day teaching in a university and becoming a much-needed role model for Black and minority ethnic learners and that, to some extent, constitutes a brief and individual case-study sketch to illustrate a principle. The experience in aggregate diminished my faith in the offer of British educational institutions being genuinely and realistically a vehicle for minority group upward social mobility but, to compound this, there is no guarantee of graduate labour market success in a society whose values are dead set against positive Black role models and Black images, whether rhetorical or real.

Most of this was at a time when the government was threatening tuition fee payment for higher education, which then, when it transpired, resulted in a tripling of the then-current fees to nine thousand pounds per academic year, edging the likes of myself out of the running – through lack of funds – for higher acclaim and glory in the form of a Doctor of Philosophy research award. While it led the author to question the value of higher education, it did not succeed in dampening one's unflagging and unwavering optimism and hope in humanity. The long deadening night of the soul that was slavery and the slave trade was eventually abolished amid recalcitrant resistance on all sides; so, maybe everything has its time and season to flourish, giving way to brave and burgeoning new eras and although it seems a long way away, there may come a time when Doctor Martin Luther King's dream of freedom and justice may break out into a glorious reality and it is for the powers that be to take note that there is no time like the present and that the time is ripe for change. Doctor King professed, 'I have a dream my four little children will one day live in a nation where they will not be judged by the colour of their skin but by content of their character' (cited in Washington,1986:219). The tokenistic nuggets of freedom and justice or the morally reprehensible constraints of discrimination for people of colour may be understood and discussed as the 'new racism', but there is nothing new about it; however, it can be considered the 'new slavery' having coherent continuity with something old or the new colonialism and these chains must, one joyous daybreak, be broken! If it is possible to break the chains of slavery, then there is always hope that one day, freedom and justice will rain down like a mighty torrential flood of cascading waters and in the words of Doctor King people of colour will be able to congregate and cry out as in the old Negro spiritual, "Free at last, free at last; thank God Almighty, we are free at last" (Washington,1986:220).

This is King's abiding hope and it is the author's also and institutions of higher education demonstrate a tendency to function – so far as Black and minority ethnic students are concerned – in contradiction to and making a nonsense of King's great everlasting and abiding hope. One institution, in its application form, required to know the year my mother entered the country and I had to consult her with this immaterial detail in order to make a university application. Such a question only creates an open window to discrimination and has nothing whatever to do with my ability, competence and specialism and is extraneous and impersonal to boot. However, it also informs the admissions officer that the applicant is post-immigration wave generation and if anything, is revealing of one's ethnicity, and as it transpired, ineligibility to attend that particular institution. The question itself was an isolated incidence but the scale of the question warrants that institutions of higher education are a law unto themselves and should never be permitted to ask such an outlandish and preposterous question. The indifference the author experienced at the hands of admission officers in higher education institutions was quite staggering; it was literally as if one had come up against an insurmountable barrier in which these institutions were completely uninterested in taking one any further forward. It is altogether shameful, ignoble and wholly disgraceful of the higher education system that one's research area gave the clue of one's ethnicity or non-English status so, therefore, the author can summarily conclude a case of blanket institutional racism across the board of all the institutions concerned. The solitary institution that showed an interest was not a university of choice but was a last resort because of the scale of exclusion. At first, showing a *prima facie* reluctance to reciprocate and stating that they did not provide PhD courses, they made a note of one's contact details and responded subsequently with further interest. However, by that stage, the tripling of the then fees had been introduced and aside from not being able to afford the fees, what little interest one had nurtured was by then lost and the opportunity lapsed. What is worth noting, however, is that the institution waited until the higher fees had been introduced before making the offer. It appears, therefore, that this institution was, and is, mercenary because it is no coincidence that their offer intersected and dovetailed with the increase in tuition fee payments.

Data collection techniques have negated the widely reiterated assumption that minority ethnic students are inadequately represented in higher education given the tenor that their numbers in higher education are beneath their numbers in the wider community (Modood and Acland,1998:96). In the early stages of recent times, minority ethnic groups by then consisted of 16 per cent of the undergraduate community in England as against 9 per cent of the working demography (Pilkington,2011). The increased incidence of involvement of students from minority ethnic extract juxtaposed to White students derived from 'their higher occupational aspirations and high levels of parental support' (quoted in Pilkington,2011:16).

Before we grasp the nettle, there is an issue with under-representation. In general, the figures conceal gender differences. Once proper consideration is taken of these, there is information that the higher education involvement rate of Bangladeshi women falls beneath that of Whites and that the higher education involvement rate of Caribbean men is just slightly raised above that of Whites (Pilkington,2011). Also, in general, the figures paper over significant status distinctions between higher education institutions. Regulating for these intimates that, 'with the exception of Chinese applicants, ethnic minority candidates are concentrated in new universities (Pilkington,2011:16) and are relatively less likely to be encountered in the old universities, out of which employers show a propensity to recruit (Parekh, 2000), and medical schools (Pilkington,2011).

The most disturbing aspect is 'strong evidence that minority candidates face an ethnic penalty [when applying to old universities]. Institutions in this sector are more likely to select White and, to a lesser extent, Chinese candidates from among a group of similarly qualified applicants. Although ethnic minority candidates may be admitted to old universities in reasonable numbers, they generally have to perform better than do their White peers in order to secure a place' (Pilkington,2011:16). This penalty was something the author encountered on his quest for further study in the old universities, and what he found was an insurmountable barrier that refused to take one any further forward, and all because admissions officers knew or suspected my ethnic origin. In destroying the author's hopes and dreams, they have no qualms as ultimately, people not unlike themselves benefit from the undisturbed status of the existing state of affairs, and the difference I would have made was abrogated because only minority ethnic group members are classified as a 'threat' to the smooth running order and control of things. Also, for the author to confound the educational stereotype and present a positive social image to many, is something admission tutors and academic professionals least welcomed, or so it would appear. The charge of institutional racism seems a damning indictment on the institutions in question, but, at the same time, appears far too lenient because what these institutions exacted was illegal under the Race Relations Amendment Act 2000 and admissions officers were allowed to continue their everyday affairs not having incurred punitive measures for their actions, and being at liberty to commit and perpetrate further acts of discrimination. The likelihood that new universities house and accommodate minority group members goes some way in the exegesis as to why, at least, to begin with, they do less favourably in the labour market and sustain an increased likelihood of continuing after degrees to further academic exposition or training (Pilkington, 2011).

The author's journey entailed a frenetic flurry to beat the introduction of catastrophic tuition fee payments for higher education, applying all of nine times in total and applying on two separate occasions to two particularly favoured institutions no less. There are token Black intellectuals who, of course, have not experienced the glass ceiling of higher education institutions, however, the same cannot be said for the author and concrete ceiling is closer to the mark when faced with multiple institutional exclusion.

Degrees, destinations and career progression

The evidence indicates that Black and minority ethnic groups experience educational disadvantage and then occupational disadvantage. Although token Black academics may not experience institutional entry difficulties, this is not the plight of the general minority ethnic population; the Black experience is characterised by racism and racial discrimination in accessing higher education. Research shows that minority group graduates submit more applications than their White equivalents and yet secure fewer interviews. They suffer a reduced likelihood of realizing their preferred occupational destinations and are more likely to be in a job where they feel overqualified (Allen,1989:93). Occupational progression is a further consideration, in that Black and minority ethnic staff tend not to obtain their promotion entitlements and because of their contract of employment, they experience job insecurity and may not get the appropriate pay scale conditions they deserve.

Research pointed to the difficulties of minority ethnic people in obtaining promotion as the single most important grievance to emerge in discussion groups and achieved an overwhelming consensus. The group's participants maintained that for minority ethnic candidates to be approved for promotion, the prerequisite is that they accumulate twice as many publications, qualifications and experience to rival their White counterparts (Carter et al,1999:53). Also, participants pointed out the sheer weight of numbers of minority ethnic academic staff on short-term contracts and they chewed the fat concerning the insecurity concomitant with short-term contracts. One participant illustrated the point thus:

> It is a gamble; you never know if your contract will be renewed or not. It is hard because there is my family to consider. I would prefer to stay here for their sake, but it means that I have to go on getting short-term

contracts renewed and you can never be certain that this will happen (Carter et al,1999:53).

Research into Institutional Racism

It appears that higher education institutions function to maintain and reinforce the status quo and schools operate along similar lines (Van Dyke,1998:132). Secondary schools stymie Black aspiration through the process of streaming Black kids into bottom sets based primarily on behaviour rather than cognitive ability. African-Caribbean children are structurally allocated bottom-of-the-heap status and are disproportionately excluded from schools prior to making their way in the world - *en masse*, acting to undermine their sense of self-worth - reflecting society's hierarchical structure.

Higher education institutions stymie Black aspiration through marking and assessment of written work. This is also a characteristic of schools where it takes the form of downgraded essay work and persistent low grades, and this tends towards the achievement of a mediocre or third-rate honours degree award, the action and result of which is an oppressed individual. (van Dyke,1998:121-122). Persistent low grades over a prolonged and sustained period in the same environmental milieu can undermine an individual's self-esteem and can affect academic performance levels, in turn, ultimately undermining and thwarting ambition. For students, satisfactory rewards in the currency of grades are paramount to academic career progression and finally job prospects but the influence of higher education institutions raises concerns as to whether the academy is really institutionally racist. For when higher education institutions are not stymieing Black aspiration through marking and assessment of work, *inter alia*, such as the use of institutional language by trusted and respected White, middle-class, male institutional representatives who uphold and safeguard the interests of the institution and the status quo; that the academy is preventing Black applicants from accessing opportunities to better themselves is a moral outrage. This is a catch-22 situation whereby even if one collects a Master's degree award, eligibility to proceed to a doctoral degree is sometimes thwarted by the academic world's insistence upon a good honours degree, thereby undervaluing the Master's degree prerequisite to pursuing academic career progression. Elitism is one way to exclude Black applicants; seemingly plausible but feeble excuses are another, all of which play into the hands of institutional racism. Collecting the passport to proceed is one thing but there is no guarantee that further educational opportunity will be granted as barriers and obstacles can be thrown up and the way barred, which is the nature of the beast that often rears its ugly head in academia ultimately to the detriment of Black aspiration.

At every turn and on many levels, it appears that all sectors in society operate, with few exceptions, to maintain the pre-existing political/ social order. Because Black and minority ethnic groups are concentrated in *ci-devant* Polytechnics and employers prefer to recruit from what they see as a two-tier system of higher education, where older universities are seen as more prestigious, the job prospects of Black and minority ethnic graduates, therefore, suffer disproportionately compared with their White graduate counterparts (Parekh,2000:148).

The significance or true nature of the above is continuity over change (Pilkington,2011). Yet, despite the inexorable ethnic turnabout of fortunes in higher education that are adversely germane to minority ethnic groups, the lack of direct attention given to addressing the issue is telling. According to how the author of research conducted in 2003 to investigate the obeisance of the academic community with the indispensable conditions of the Race Relations (Amendment) Act articulated it, 'Given the inertia that accompanied the RRA 1976 and the performance of the sector on 'race' issues prior to the RRAA 2000, it is obvious that self-regulation cannot be depended upon to deliver equality and social justice to marginalised groups' (quoted in Pilkington,2011:121). This floats the question considering whether the lack of apparent headway in race equality signals that the academic community is institutionally racist. We now turn to focus on research conducted by Pilkington (2011) to see if we can find which of the components of institutional racism discerned by the Parekh report 2000:74-75 continue to be manifest:

Indirect Discrimination: Do Black and Asian students enjoy a service that compares favourably with that enjoyed by White students?

On the one hand, substantial progress has been made. On Pilkington's (2011) authority, there is now much more reliable intelligence as to how students from various ethnic backgrounds are faring. Such intelligence demonstrates that students belonging to different ethnic groups are inordinately represented in the academic composition corresponding to their numbers in the population, both domestically and regionally.

Quantitative factual evidence has, since 2004-2005, been generated yearly on student admissions, enrolments, sources of anxiety or worry, retention and good degrees (Pilkington,2011). Such evidence bases have of late been enhanced by additional reports on degree failure frequencies (Pilkington,2011). These unfold certain relentless ethnic differentials: undue and unfavourable offer rates to candidates of Black African background; a shortage of minority ethnic students attending part-time courses; an excess of Black and Asian students indicated by tutors as a 'cause for concern' (with a third of Black and Asian first-year students positioned accordingly); a higher incidence of withdrawal of Black students on full-time courses and minority ethnic students on part-time courses; an unfavourable difference in the numbers of minority ethnic students collecting good degrees, 'twenty percentage points difference for Asian students and a ten percentage points difference for Black students'; and minority ethnic students are more likely to fail their degrees, with the difference between Asian and White students increasing over a 48-month period from a fraction below 1 per cent in 2004 to more than 13 per cent in 2007 and that separating Black students and White increasing over the equivalent time from 1.9 per cent to 3.7 per cent (Pilkington,2011:121-122). While these ethnic differentials are, by themselves, not sufficient to render the university guilty of indirect discrimination, however this possibility can scarcely be abandoned and indeed a comprehensive impact assessment picked up some practices to do with course selection that were discriminatory (Pilkington,2011). In his research university, Pilkington (2011) found it extremely difficult to present incontrovertible material information of discrimination and whereas he also found its extent impossible to determine, he concluded that there is scarcely any doubt that students attending the university are not cushioned from exposure to it.

Employment Practices

Are Black and minority ethnic staff being dealt with equitably as concerns recruitment, promotion and staff development?

Pilkington (2011) reports that significant progress in the area of statistical reports on students has been made, but there is a reluctance to process statistical data on staff applications, shortlisting and appointments. The negligence of HR to provide such reports and to carry out initial equality impact assessments on HR procedures was put before the Equality and Diversity working group. Although this was first actioned in May 2007, there was hesitation to make mention of this in successive minutes. Despite that, a paper put forward by an Equality and Diversity official to the May 2008 conference suggested that 'the university is in breach of its statutory duties as regards its employment-facing functions and activities (i.e., availability for analysis monitoring data, implementation of EIAs)' (Pilkington, 2011:123).

In the period straddling 2002 and 2008, no reports were generated which provided coherent material information on applications, shortlisting and appointments (Pilkington,2011). Consequently, evidence from the reports in 2001 and 2008 will have to be examined to identify the virtue of employment practices.

The indication of the 2001 report was that ethnic differentials were apparent in the dual aspects of shortlisting and appointments. The odds between Black and White applications were assessed, as also was that between Asian and White candidates. The prospects were against the two non-white group candidates being shortlisted and appointed and favoured White candidates (Pilkington,2011).

At present, there is little information to suggest whether unfavourable ethnic differentials remain particularly noteworthy. However, what is striking as both Equality and Diversity Officers relate is that individuals from Black and Asian backgrounds continue to have the odds stacked against them when it comes to being recruited to practical vocations like cleaning, catering and security than would otherwise be expected from their profile level in the immediate labour market. A current report, predicated on evidence for 2005-2006 and 2006-2007, corroborates the precision of this feeling, with 'the proportion of minority ethnic candidates applying for posts (20% and 14% respectively) equating to 7 per cent and 8 per cent of successful candidates respectively' (Pilkington,2011:124).

The matter that is alarming is not only persistent evidence of unfavourable ethnic differentials but also the absence of monitoring and the failure to act to address such differentials. Notwithstanding the duty and responsibility in accordance with the Race Relations (Amendment) Act to not infrequently put into the public domain relevant intelligence on how different ethnic groups are faring, appropriate surveillance reports are not coming to light on appointments and also retention, upward mobility, staff enrichment and complaints, grievances and chastening incidences. Outside the limits of what has been said, even when reports have come to light, invariably, they do not result in appropriate a priori reflection.

Staffing Structure

Do Black and Asian people have a favourable profile level in senior management?

Senior management posts remain unconscionably in the hands of White people. The Vice-Chancellor and Pro-Vice-Chancellors remain, in most instances, to be White. It is also a similar story for Heads of Support Departments. A different case arises when it comes to Dean/Heads of Schools in which there has been a breakthrough to this unidimensional model and that was for a brief period in history: a single individual Head of School was Black. A Black African professional academic scholar whom Pilkington (2011) interviewed, while inclined towards reluctance to challenge the level of adherence of the institution to race equality, perceived the homogeneous likeness of senior management as a difficult situation:

Here, I am not saying that no support has come from the institution that no matter where you come from, the move for equality means that you can get anywhere. [But] people look at and don't see people present at senior level, and there's a perception that ... nobody's going to speak for me. The institution needs to be proactive, ensuring equality at all levels (Pilkington,2011:129).

Lack of Positive Action

Is sufficient energy being expended on recruiting Black and Asian people to senior posts?

Little or no energy has been expended on appointing Black or South Asian people to senior posts. The one departure to this was the Governing Council in which two people from different ethnic backgrounds have been recruited. The (ex) Chair remarked in Pilkington's (2011) earshot, 'That's more than enough; we have now a higher representation than their proportion in the general population warrants' (p.129). Whereas some positive measures have been taken concerning gender, and progress fashioned as expressed by access to senior posts, an equivalent assertion cannot be made of race where the monochrome picture of senior staff is accepted without question.

Management and Leadership

Is the advancement of race equality a central first concern?

Thinking about and beginning to deal with institutional racism has not been held as a central first concern for managers or academic governors (Pilkington,2011). The importance of the Macpherson Report escaped the attention in 1999 at Governing Council or Senate, or more remarkably, the Equal Opportunities Working Group (EOWG).

At different points in time, the focus on race equality has ebbed and flowed. There have been times when the university acted on a high-watermark initiative to address the subject of race equality. On other occasions, the matter has not even been in the institution's eyeline. The push for equal opportunities policies in the late 1980s onwards finally led to the establishment of policies for different aspects of equality. Pilkington's (2011) case study university oversaw race equality plans that were launched in 1996. However, the plans were no sooner launched than directly forgotten, to the extent that talks were staged at EOWG in 1999 concerning the need to introduce an action plan policy. The obligation as provided for by the rules of Race Relations (Amendment) Act to introduce, by May 2002, a race equality guideline and practical procedure was not suitably met. The guideline and procedure were awarded baseline points scores by the Equality Challenge unit; it was deemed 'not yet to be aligned with the requirements of the RRAA [and] in need of urgent revision' Pilkington,2011:130. The institution was then required to submit again its guideline and practical procedure to HEFCE within a recommended period. This afforded the leeway for race equality partisans inside the institution to develop a coherent guideline and practical procedure and prevail upon senior management to make provision for appropriate resources to underpin the guideline and procedure.

Race equality has subsequently enjoyed greater prominence within the institution, with the quantitative reports on students presently feeding into mainstream committees and decision formation. Notwithstanding this, there are more and more indices of some antithetical platitudes to the equality and diversity programme of action. Consider, for example, the quantitative reports on students. In terms of how an Equality and Diversity officer viewed it:

> People's response to the data is interesting. It is essentially either the numbers are too small ... so that is one way in which it is dismissed or minimised; the other is to say, well, it is too big, we recognise that this pattern exists but society is at fault, you know, this is not something to do with [Midshire]. And that is another way you dismiss it (Pilkington, 2011:130).

Such responses are not out of the ordinary. Social enquiry in institutions other than 'Midshire' also picks up on 'attitudinal barriers' when staff are confronted with evidence revealing the true nature of ethnic differentials. These barriers represent 'obstacles in terms of getting staff members to take issues of racism and race equality seriously and to act accordingly and appropriately' (Pilkington,2011:130). Illustrations of such barriers are highlighted in the following: dismissing the likelihood that a serious issue exists ('Let's face it. The university is a liberal environment'); viewing the issue as not anywhere as bad as elsewhere ('I'm sure that race equality is less of an issue in a university than other work places'); displaying the onus ('The difficulty is that we can't get any ethnic [sic] people to apply'; and casting doubt on the fitness and properness of any conventional measures ('The trouble is that we don't know who we should be comparing ourselves with') (Pilkington, 2011:130).

While the primacy is to examine statistical evidence critically, the predominant interplay of staff when petitioned to reflect on evidence revealing the true extent of ethnic differentials has been guarded defensiveness. Numerous staff reject the evidence without pausing for thought and challenge the fitness and properness of entry quotas. The matter that is clear at 'Midshire' is a *ne plus ultra* reluctance even existing between senior staff like Heads of School, to devise recruitment or other quotas as concerns any of the equality strands. Although the institutional language continues to point towards mainstreaming, the actual true nature is all of a piece with mundane, including no change for the better established, for example, in the involvement of race equality quotas into the strategic agenda (Pilkington,2011).

Occupational Culture

Is it not the case that racism is tolerated and diversity celebrated?

It is informative to draw parallels between the interviews completed with police officers from Black and Asian heritage and those completed with fourteen scholastic and support human resource figures from minority ethnic groups. The first explicitly recounted the extent and nature of the racism encountered by police officers from both the wider social element and from their White opposite numbers. Racism, as it turns out, was not an unusual phenomenon but a daily event. In juxtaposition, the second group were much more unwilling to report coming into contact with racism. A UK-born female lecturer articulated it thus: 'I am often reluctant to revisit my experience of racism in academia largely because, 1, I don't want to be couched as a victim, 2, academia is in many ways a positive space for me, and 3, I think negative moaners are a bore' (Pilkington,2011:125).

This contact with racism not infrequently had to be extrapolated from extraneous material information and, for all, that these were primarily less patently transparent than the lived trials minority ethnic police officers redefined. A young Indian female minimum contact lecturer reflected, 'I don't think I've acknowledged this before, even to myself or someone else, but I do think I get patronised a bit ... it's like, look at this Indian girl ... she's relatively bright and she's doing so well for herself, kind of thing, let's all look after her, kind of thing, let's help her along. It works to my advantage most of the time but I would sometimes not have that. I would rather like just be like everyone else ... A lot of time people just say, oh you know, she might have an interesting point because she's the Other ... It's just stuff like that, and I think that patronising attitude is a bit irritating at times' (Pilkington,2011:125). This particular intellectual did not have recourse to the concept of racism to put her experiences across. Some staff did, but more frequently than not this was only following a protracted period of apprehending matters with the mind and through the senses in terms appropriate to themselves.

Minority ethnic human resources did not involuntarily conceptualise unfortunate circumstances in racist dialogue but instead, learned to face facts. A Black British female associate of the support staff team, who was brought to account for moving outside the range of her remit, learned to see in her mind's eye her lived trials as racist only after having dealings with a trade union:

> At first, I thought it was just a case of conflict between myself, my colleagues and the department, you know. I was getting too, I was getting above my station. You know, this is your job, all we want you to do, and you're now getting above your station. So I thought, you know, it's just a conflict. The more I became angry about it, because I didn't see I was doing anything wrong ... I was just signposting people and, you know, I thought that instead of being congratulated for that, I was being penalised. That made me angry and after a while, I'm thinking, you know, why should I get a slap on the wrist for doing my job? I started internalising it; I was comparing myself to other departments that I was pointed out to by the Union and I started to formulate that it might be an issue of race. I was saying, had it been my White colleague, that they were doing the same [to], there would not have been a problem. So I started, my mind started turning around thinking, oh well, let's look at this objectively, and I thought it was race. It was race (Pilkington, 2011:125-126).

Her adverse circumstance was not by any stretch of the imagination unique. A Black British female associate of another support team in a more senior role also came to see the union as a highly esteemed support mechanism: 'What I have done is work quite closely with the trade unions – that is how my role has received some measure of support and a level of awareness' (Pilkington, 2011:126). In most compartmental divisions (both scholastic and support), White personnel are preponderant and minority ethnic personnel feel like 'space invaders' (Pilkington,2011:126). They are incisively alive to being 'the only Black person sitting in that room' (Pilkington,2011:126). In view of this, there is some data information that manpower from minority ethnic backgrounds experience hyper-surveillance. A learned expert elucidates on this: 'Because they are not the natural bodies of academia, Black academics have to endure a burden of doubt from those around them. And it comes with a high level of hyper-surveillance, giving a feeling that colleagues and students are more likely to pick up on any mistakes and see them as signs of misplaced authority.'

A UK-born Asian female lecturer outlines her lived trial with her Head of Department as furthered below:

> I felt like I was being watched. Every time I marked an essay ... she'd come in and look in and look at, you know, have you marked it? Can I have a look at your comments? So any little opportunity she had to exercise discipline, she would use it ... And one day ... she said to me, I'm coming into your lecture (Pilkington,2011:126).

Examples of racial stereotyping were something that Pilkington (2011) did not come into direct contact with but interviews with three minority ethnic personnel in a support department proved to be unexpectedly enlightening. That which follows are examples they sketched out. On Black and South Asian people: 'They have got a chip on their shoulder because they are Black ... Every Asian or Black or every ethnic minority, because they have the [race relations legislation] protection, will go out and look for these things.' On Muslims: 'If you are brown, Asian, coloured skin, or a Paki, or whatever, obviously you are Muslim ... Within the Muslim community ... the tensions that are going on at the moment, you will get, they are recruiting for suicide bombers and things like that'. On international students: "If I can't understand the student, they are not worthy of my time, should be able to speak English ... It's like, well, if they can't speak English, they shouldn't be here. I can't spend my time trying to understand these people' (Pilkington, 2011:127).

It is easy to make the mistake that only junior members of staff are prone to expressing racial stereotypes. On the say-so of a minority ethnic individual who was part of another support department, a well-established senior manager dismissed claims that few minority ethnic candidates took up positions in the following terms:

> They lack the education, qualifications and experience that White applicants have, and that is the reason why they are not successful because they are ignorant and not experienced – that's what I derived from these comments, which of course I challenged ... It was said in an open-plan office as a throwaway comment, with sideways glances at me as if, aren't you going to say something? That is hugely insulting, particularly because I was aware that I was, and still am, the most senior support Black person here. I don't know any other in the entire institution at my grade and I find that odd in an institution of this size that only one Black person would be academically or equivalently qualified to occupy a position as a principal officer ... [This] says more about the institution than the applicant, in my view (Pilkington,2011:127).

Examples such as these may be an exception to the general rule since often, one does not come across occasions when they are circulated for the consumption of others. This is perhaps the case, because of the feeling, evident in equal opportunity training, that political correctness holds sway and that one might find oneself openly accountable. A White respondent to a focus group rendered a pertinent observation with this in mind:

> What happens over and over again in an organisation that claims to be committed to equal opportunities is that people stop learning. I'm not ready and I am going to be so PC. That is the biggest problem because you can't ever learn. You are always either right or accusing someone of being wrong. Unless we approach it as a learning process, we'll get the same thing: people keeping their heads below the parapet so that they can't get it wrong (Pilkington,2011:127).

It is not clear whether there is one occupational culture in universities. While distinctions may be evident in how racism manifests itself in universities as compared to the police, there are clearly noticeable cultural differences extending across from academic schools to support departments. On all too many occasions, we overlook this because we suppose – wrongly – that academic employees comprise the large majority of the gainfully employed when, in reality, they comprise a noticeable minority. Although it is important to observe differences extending across from individual academic schools and from individual support departments, there appears clear evidence at 'Midshire' that racism and racial stereotyping occur more frequently in (certain of) the support departments (Pilkington, 2011).

The most scathing attack on the institution emanated from a comparatively senior Black female who worked in the support department though had recently taken her leave of the post. When asked to consider the five years spent at the university, she responded:

> So, does racial discrimination exist? It's alive and well here! It's painted over ... and how shall I put it? As a colleague put it to me, they don't overtly discriminate against you; they just move you around and unsettle you and don't give you the products you need to do your job. That's how they discriminate against you. But they don't call it that; it's just seen as restructuring, moving you around and that's what has happened to me since day one (Pilkington, 2011:128).

Evidently, there are times when minority ethnic staff sense that they do not truly belong and where their cultural characteristics are not openly welcomed. From 2004, however, attempts have been made to culturally highlight a transformed and more inclusive university environment. The chaplaincy is currently multi-faith; facilities are spread across campuses for Muslim cultural rituals and different seasonal traditions are celebrated. An Equality and Diversity discussion scheduling is organised each year and annually, an Equality and Diversity week; and activities are staged to recognize Black History Month and Holocaust Memorial Day. Such growth and expansion engender both the celebration and administration of cultural differences (Pilkington,2011). The chaplaincy may presently be multi-faith but Christianity is hegemonic. Hence a multi-faith debate, where Pilkington (2011) was present, included representatives from distinct faiths, but aside from the Hindu, they were all White and they had all been screened by an advisory panel to the local Bishop. Although this type of multiculturalism does not escape criticism (Sharma,2004; cited in Pilkington,2011) and scarcely lets us lose sight of the overarching picture, it does portray official recognition of identities that are vital to people, and viewed from this angle, is a progressive development.

Lack of information

Is the university able to gauge the effective influence of its policies and practices on minority ethnic communities?

'Midshire' University has made headway in completing equality impact assessments. An introductory assessment schedule has been given the go-ahead and some key guidelines and plans have been analysed for suitability. Although all new guidelines and plans are, as a point of regular procedure, expected to be analysed before being accepted, this requirement is not consistently being satisfied. Headway has been spasmodic and many new HR guidelines have been accepted without first being analysed (Pilkington,2011).

The knowledge at the fingertips of the University in terms of students has immeasurably improved and this has permitted the University to make progress in assessing the effective influence of its guidelines and plans on Black and South Asian communities. A similar statement cannot be made of knowledge related to staff. The knowledge at the fingertips of the University has withered on the vine, with the outcome that it finds itself unable to undertake a coherent examination of the effective influence of its guidelines and plans on Black and South Asian communities (Pilkinton,2011).

Consultation

Are Black and South Asian people's views sought and considered on central concerns?

Infinitesimal targeted attempts have been made to come across and confer with Black and South Asian personnel specifically. The evolution of the race equality guideline and procedure involved infinitesimal consultation inwardly with Black and South Asian personnel and none outwardly. And on the subject of a recent institutional rethink of arrangements to underpin the equality and diversity programme at the university, of the 25 people conferred with, only a solitary individual was from a minority ethnic community and she was sought out to enter into discussions because of her occupational position as an Equality and Diversity Officer (Pilkington,2011:133).

Professional Expertise

Do staff possess expertise in intercultural problem areas?

Hardly any members of the University staff possess expertise in intercultural ways of knowing and interactive exchange. In regard to one support development, this scarcity has entailed repeated shortfalls in defusing problems while tension had a life source. Further, this has, in succession, resulted in the forfeiture of very able personnel. The compartmental division is, by sheer weight of numbers, White and has only historically appointed four minority ethnic members to the staff profile. (Pilkington,2011). All have vacated their post and one remains, in their view, pushed by an impossible situation as opposed to being pulled by opportunities becoming available elsewhere. The first asserted that she had been robbed of the corresponding support systems for staff enrichment as her White counterparts and lodged her complaint of racial discrimination against the university with the assistance of an industrial tribunal; the second claimed that a senior internal position was not posited on the labour market and that she had consequently been deprived of the prospect of applying for occupational mobility; the third posited a remonstration against her Head of Department for neglecting to respond to justifiable concerns that she brought to the surface and for neglecting to treat her even-handedly.

Each of these three examples provides case study lines in which equality and diversity guidelines seemed to be intentionally contravened and overturned by White staff indifferent to the equality and diversity programme of action. Racist activity rates were, in some instances, deliberately left unrecorded:

> If you look at the incident reporting form ... there is a little bit on the back that says, if it is a racist attack ... It's on the reporting form, but one of the staff actually openly said, oh no, we don't fill that bit in because we have been told not to ... We don't want to show ... that sort of thing happens (Pilkington, 2011:131).

In further instances, there was obstinate resistance to filling out equality monitoring forms:

> I do equality monitoring for the department to see, Is our service meeting ... the needs of students from different countries ... ethnic groups and so on? People don't want to know about ethnic equality monitoring. They don't want to know about equality full stop. It's not in their remit ... They are supposed to give them [equality monitoring forms] to the students. The form goes to the student with the pack; say they are going for, for example, funding ... And some people aren't sending them, aren't giving the student the equality monitoring forms ... They don't want to know ... [Eventually] management will have a word with them. Nothing is still being done. They are saying I am not following what the management are saying (Pilkington,2011:131-132).

This department had a culture that was host to a widely held belief that management lacked resolve and was therefore reluctant to set staff straight when they flagrantly disregarded institutional and departmental guidelines.

Each and every minority ethnic staff member in the department extended material information that their Head of Department had shown a reluctance to guide and direct in ensuring obeisance with equality and diversity guidelines. Support for this view was offered by a number of White department members. One told Pilkington:

> You will get lip service. They [management] will tell me what I need to hear and then they won't act on it ... It's not personal. It's just some people are not confrontational or they don't, they can't, they are more indecisive about, okay, how do I take this decision? Why can't they just deal with the problem because then little things get bigger and bigger, and bigger and bigger, and then there is a point that people will say, I am not having that anymore (Pilkington, 2011:132)?

Questioned as to whether he perceived that staff had skills in intercultural matters, one of the Equality and Diversity (EDO) Officers remarked: 'Most staff do not have a clue' (Pilkington,2011:132). He supported his viewpoint with allusion to a hate episode that arose in the inter-faith chaplaincy. The detail of this incident was that some anti-Christian source information was discovered which happened to have been deposited in the facility by a Muslim cleaner. The reaction of the Head of Department under whose authority it fell was initially to disregard the incident. His inaction was broken only after being resolutely directed by the PVC at the EDO's awakening to fill out a hate activity rate report form, see the cleaner responsible and place documentary evidence on her file. In opposition to letting the matter rest, the Head of Department then informed the local Special Branch of the incident (which had instructed senior management in the interim). Subsequent to initial inaction, he went to the opposite end of the continuum, thus potentially inflaming intercultural tensions (Pilkington,2011).

Training

Is there high-calibre training available that allows individuals to understand the way in which they can endorse race equality?

The delivery of high calibre training has improved with the progression of time and the number of those receptive to training has significantly widened. Before the race equality guideline and procedure was developed and enshrined into an equality policy and procedure, training was much of a muchness and up to the individual. From then on, different brands of training (counting bespoke training have been in place for different groups and an optimistic target has been determined for staff to acquire training in equality and diversity. Whereas significant progress has been achieved, the University falls some way short of satisfying this 100 per cent target of personnel being trained, with a broad range of staff from the top on down being stubbornly resistant to grace training sessions with their presence. The responses from those who have presented themselves at recent training have been favourable with most acknowledging their obligations in accordance with the race relations legislation. Evidence has emerged, however, that the drive for staff to undergo training has degenerated and that for many social forms it has again become up to the individual (Pilkington,2011).

The academy and institutional racism: continuity or change?

Having now looked closely at the components of institutional racism highlighted by the Parekh Report, we can see elements of continuity and also of change at 'Midshire' University. Our attention will first focus on the changes before moving on to focus on the continuities.

Evidently, certain changes were made extending across from 1999 and 2008. The institution has ameliorated its monitoring by group affiliation of the student experience; it has set in motion a more inclusive way of looking at things that displays public recognition of different identities; it has an equality policy and procedure that does deal with race; equality and diversity training has been scaled up, with more staff currently conscious of their obligations in accordance with the race relations legislation; and intelligence on the effective influence of institutional guidelines and plans on Black and South Asian groups has improved (Pilkington,2011).

Continuities or continuing phenomena tend to overshadow the above changes as there remains much more work to be done. These are manifest in: enduring ethnic inequalities in the student conscious awareness of events that adversely impinge on minority ethnic students and indicate probable indirect discrimination; ethnic inequalities in staff appointment that adversely impinge on Black and South Asian applicants and indicate probable indirect discrimination; some minority ethnic personnel experience racism and some White staff are derogatory regarding political correctness; an unconscionably White senior staff network, who appear quite the reverse of being at pains to change the situation; low primacy given to putting in place a race equality policy; few staff are disciplined in intercultural matters; a high level of staff absenting from equality and diversity training and infinitesimal targeted attempts made to confer with Black and South Asian communities.

On a scale of ten possible dimensions, 'Midshire' University scored only four points registering any apparent progress. Small wonder, then, in this connection, that a senior Black female representative of the support staff passed judgment on what had happened spanning the preceding five years as follows:

> On the face of it, there have been improvements because we have nice policies now and we write nice statements and we are going to consider the equality impacts. Fine. But what does that look like? We have not moved further than changing the curtains, but behind the windows, the grime still exists (Pilkington,2011:136).

A brief deconstruction of Pilkington's concluding points is as follows. Because Pilkington's research University is not a paradigm case of institutional racism, unlike the police, and is seen as a liberal academy, Pilkington is unwilling to undertake or become involved regarding 'Midshire' University as institutionally racist, yet, he conveniently confirms that the police are; while being fully aware of two overwhelming factors: firstly that the two institutions bear some significant similarities below the surface and secondly, he may well have been aware that the Macpherson report found all major institutions in British social life to be characterized by institutional racism. Pilkington (2011) presents before the eyes the evidence and is surprised at the results that there were extraordinary similarities extending across from 'Midshire' police, 'with the University having comparable or worse scores in the case of six components' (Pilkington,2011:138). Given the overwhelming proportion of White senior staff networks and the Macpherson report, in addition to, what Black and South Asian employees have recounted, should Pilkington indeed be surprised at his findings even though he thinks that they are not conclusive? The case for the University is that it recognises the significance of race equality and has taken steps to address it, but only because it has been goaded into a renewed effort to change. Are these steps just a cover to show those from the outside looking in that change is afoot, when, in reality, little real and substantive change has occurred? For example, little attention is paid to transforming the overwhelming Whiteness of the University and how White privilege is couched within it: and staff and learners from Black and South Asian heritage continue to undergo disadvantages paralleled with White staff and learners; and yet such racial inequality remains submerged beneath competing issues for senior managers and scholastic governors.

Conclusion

What does seem apparent is that no institution openly welcomes the label 'institutionally racist' and Pilkington is alive to this axiomatic truth and is swayed by it in terms of 'Midshire' University. Pilkington spares White sensibilities rather than alarming and inflaming them even though his judgement might contribute to the university redoubling its efforts to prove its accusers wrong. Clearly, 'Midshire' University is not alone in failing to dispel the claims put forward by the Macpherson Report and we have to question whether domestic institutions really have, as their ultimate goal, a truly inclusive and democratic sector of society. It seems the case that all universities function to maintain and reinforce the status quo and reflect society's hierarchical structure.

The fact that race equality keeps slipping down the priority list is testament to a reluctance to move beyond merely 'changing the curtains' and the material detail that race equality is no longer a priority confirms and reinforces this outlook. That institutions of higher education still discriminate against Black and minority ethnic groups in the light of recent legislative changes to protect this group, and in this enlightened and technologically advanced day and age, of course, speaks to the Black experience, and demonstrates that institutions are only interested in creating a favourable impression that turns out to be illusory, misleading and bogus. What we need to see are changes overshadowing continuities and these changes making a positive difference to people's lives, both staff and students alike, so that designated attachments and appendages – as is currently applicable – do not have a place to reside.

A preference for business as usual and merchants who consider that, if it is not broke why fix it, should think again, as this approach inclines towards a tendency to do nothing or to remain unchanged. The 'old' and established universities are the worst offenders here as Black and minority ethnic groups tend to be concentrated in the new institutions. Pilkington's results were somehow unanticipated and suggest that they pointed to the pervasiveness of institutional racism, and for all that has been said and done, Pilkington is perhaps instrumental to its gainsaying. The pervasiveness of institutional racism compares with the popular antipathy of political correctness in workplace cultures and within this antipathy, informal network norms influence decision-making on recruitment of staff, helping to make the workplace environment overwhelmingly White and contributing to a lack of acceptance and tactful sensitivity towards the Other, causing, in some cases, workplace complaints and grievances (Parekh,2000:226-227).

In the next chapter, we look at the rise and function of English racism in the lives and lived experiences of Black and minority ethnic people and how its curving trajectory has spanned any number of years. In the final analysis, what does seem significant is that Pilkington (2011) stands up for Macpherson's concept of institutional racism in the face of scathing criticism from Rattansi (2007) and like-minded commentators, yet, abandons the concept as too broad or as 'conceptual inflation' which ultimately leads to an analysis which obviated and eschewed designating 'Midshire' University as institutionally racist. It is easy to be ambivalent about the sector when it is considered that racism is likely to co-exist together with a broad range of reformist, antiracist, multicultural and minority-welcoming systems of belief, programmes, procedures and projects (Law et al,2004).

Stephen Lawrences' life, legacy and memory will be honoured and recognized nationally on Stephen Lawrence Day and become enshrined in national history which is the result of what Doreen and Neville Lawrence fought for and spearheaded. Stephen Lawrence Day will be marked for the very first time on 22 April 2019.

Chapter 5: The Function and Rise of English Racism

This chapter aims to show how English racism has dogged and incriminated the image of people of colour and offers a counter-narrative by way of redress, but, firstly, we will interrogate the function of English racism. As we have already seen, White collective consciousness has, for centuries, viewed people of colour as inferior to themselves and that appears, just as in the days of slavery, to have consequences for Black and minority ethnic people. These consequences impact adversely on the lives of Black and minority ethnic groups and have the effect of blighting lives and to understand why this is part of the existing conjuncture, we need to consider the historical relationship between Black and minority ethnic groups and White people. White stewardship has meant that Black and South Asian people have been subordinated during slavery and the slave trade and also colonialism, often forced to labour serving the interests of slavocrats. Indian industries were decimated during imperialism and since the British were disgorging Africa of its material wealth, namely, its people, it led to the underdevelopment of places collectively known as the Third World. Slavery and colonialism saw the brutal and inhuman treatment of non-white peoples and English racism came as a handmaiden to the structured organization of the 'races'.

Goodhart (2013) detracts from this harsh and uncomfortable reality and adds a comfortable twist for a largely White audience whose antecedents, in the initial stages of the twentieth century, thought of the empire in terms of 'the white Dominions' – New Zealand, Canada, Australia, giving secondary consideration to South Africa – with whom they shared an identity, and, in some ways, a culture. This throws up the question of whether the rank-and-file British people were unaware of the broad sweep of the Empire which consisted of vast global territories and huge numbers of Black and South Asian people, and by side-tracking and diverting the gaze away from this uncomfortable fact, Goodhart (2013) minimizes its effect and validity on the reader. *The British Dream*, as Goodhart's treatise is entitled, seemed to align itself with the White British, and as it unfolded, it revealed a steady inculcation of a Eurocentric character and perspective that remained true to the book's title throughout.

In July 2018, we celebrated the 70th birthday of the National Health Service and we can also look to other national institutions such as the Monarchy and the mother of all parliaments with some semblance of pride. National sporting events like the World Cup, Wimbledon Tennis Tournament, the Olympics and the Ashes cricket test series all nurture a sense of pride in being British. On the other hand, because the past is bound up in the present, it can be considered controversial to glory in national fervour, aside from national institutions and national sporting events because the 'Great' was put into 'Great Britain' through the misery and suffering of a myriad Black and South Asian people during the age of slavery and the slave trade as well as colonialism. Furthermore, national pride is, in a sense, to condone the savagery, tyranny and oppression that prevailed during these chapters in history, and how can one be jingoistic knowing that the 'Great' in 'Great Britain' was put there through Black and South Asian misery and suffering and loss of life? The British National Party, for example, is extremely patriotic and one has to question what they are being patriotic about because the historical dimension leaves very little to be proud of. The intense passion of national pride can be seen as a double-edged sword as, on the one hand, it can be seen as innocuous and, on the

Chapter 5: The Function and Rise of English Racism

other hand, it can be seen as dangerous. While the White British are inclined to argue, that we should not read too much into things, this is convenient dominant ideology rhetoric that marginalises, discounts and dismisses legitimate concerns and is indifferent to the sensibilities of this country's Black and minority ethnic communities. It is of the utmost importance that White British people apprehend with the mind through the faculties that there are technical approaches to being proud of indigenous cultures without entangling the whole imperial, nationalistic and racist detritus into the bargain. The wealth of this nation has literally been contingent on human misery, suffering and high mortality rates sustained during the triangular trade and the Indian economic and industrial exploitation and colonialism which subsequently led to the financial backing, inter alia, of the Industrial Revolution (Fryer,1984,1988).

Some of the profits were frittered away on sumptuous living by the absentee planters who returned to Britain with their entourage of Black household slaves.

A proportion was used to support the pro-slavery West India lobby, perhaps the first official parliamentary lobby in history (Fryer,1988). This was the fulcrum by which the 'West Indians' imposed their mettle on British politics, on the legislative process, on the judiciary and through the fourth estate, on public perception. The lobby's vitality, as The Cambridge History of the Empire outlines, became 'a dominant factor in the control of colonial policy' (Fryer,1988:15).

A share of the profits followed a cycle of reinvestment into the colony trade and these were used, viz, to purchase the manufactured goods required to run the plantations. This provided an additional spur for British industry: by 1784, the equivalent of half of Britain's exports were directed to the colonies (among which were the newly independent United States).

Finally, and most crucially, some of the profits provided a cash injection to British industry. Pecuniary funds amassed from the triangular trade financially facilitated 'James Watt's steam engine, the South Wales iron and coal industries, the South Yorkshire iron industry, the North Wales slate industry, the Liverpool and Manchester Railway, and the Great Western Railway' (Fryer,1984:16; 1988:15-16). In 1765, Anthony Bacon MP was allowed a contract to provide 'seasoned, able and working negroes' to the islands of Dominica, Tobago, St Vincent, the Grenadines and Grenada, and the British polity paid him nearly £67,000 for these slaves. The money flowed directly into industrial development across Merthyr Tydfil, then an undeveloped hamlet. Bacon accepted a 99-year lease on 4,000 acres of unspoilt mineral land, established coal mines and iron foundries that at some point became known as 'Bacon's mineral kingdom', and he found his fortune through this course of action (Fryer,1988). The burgeoning origins of the British banking system, from the early country banks and Barclays through to the Bank of England, bear close association with the triangular trade, along with the embryonic origins of British insurance. Gradually improving British capitalism had an infinite money supply, a boundless mechanism with three links: sugar husbandry, manufacturing industry and the trade in Africans. Beyond what has been said, the trade in Africans was the 'essential link' (Fryer,1984:16). The system in toto 'was frankly regarded as resting on slavery' (Fryer,1984:16). Subsequent to the abolition of slavery, the British government allocated a 20-million-pound one-off compensation payment to slave owners and the slaves were left with nothing. This, in itself, tells us what the then British government thought about Black people. The debate on reparations sees an enduring reluctance to bestow upon Black men and women their just rewards and suggests that successive British governments are loath to formally accept that they owe a great debt to Black people whose ancestors' blood helped build this illustrious nation; instead, they worry and concern themselves that there may be disproportionate numbers of Black people in the country and seek to prevent more of their like from entering. This illustrates the British government's marginalization of Black people and it is an invidious set of circumstances because slave owners were compensated for their loss of human property whereas the real victims in all of this, the Black Africans were left in need, and, in want of subsistence, often had to beg on the streets.

It's time that the British government, whose legacy, I might add, is steeped in inequality, redress this imbalance. The benefits of this imbalance are, as I have already mentioned, being enjoyed at the present moment by many and it is almost as if the British government, by not conceding in the debate, are complicit in keeping Black people subjugated and showing an unwillingness to enact a turn of events in the socio-economic fortunes of Black people. Here, we are looking at the issue of the rightful entitlement or birthright of Black people and there is no getting away from or compromising this crucially important fact. Government is driven, among other things, by popular desires and prejudices and, therefore, behind the British government's rebuff on reparations is the fear that the British public may revolt at such a decision to pay out – as is paralleled by the general public influence driving government opinion on immigration. After all, and in so many words, the British government reflects the opinions of the British populace.

The main function of prejudice towards Black and minority ethnic workers is to mask and legitimate the unfair use of their labour by claiming that they are innately inferior. Along these lines, prejudice clearly serves to benefit the ruling class. But this does not unavoidably suggest that prejudice is wittingly produced and deliberately created in the present era (Castles and Kosack,1985). While certain ruling class group members do agitate for an increase in hostility towards people of colour, other group members publicly counter such agitation. To be precise, prejudice arises from concrete associations in a given past context, and agitation geared towards changing attitudes can yield but a marginal effect. However, prejudice is not just a preconceived notion of the concrete past association. For the whole time that it has been, prejudice can itself serve to determine the course of social relationships. Here, Rex reflects on racialism; it 'has a double significance as part of the total situation and as having an independent causal role in the dynamics of stratification and race-relations structures' (Castles and Kosack,1985:458). In a similar manner, prejudice against minority workers acts like a self-fulfilling prophecy: the group being taken advantage of is discredited as biologically inferior so as to justify its allocation to a subordinate place on the wealth and status scale. When indications bear witness to such a societal location, this is, in time to come, used as a measure of the groups' inferiority. This cyclical pattern serves to impede the group from changing its circumstances and achieving equality with White society.

An added function of prejudice relates to the attitudes of White British workers towards the system of free-market economy. It comes to the attention that prejudice is especially common among workers, as an outcome of the undemocratic socialization process at the one end, and of their unease and fear of being pitted against others at the other end. Customarily, the root causes of this enmity towards minorities come under impercipience as regards the proletarians that are the subject of discussion. Rather they support their feelings by suggesting that minorities are sullied, bring in disease, pursue women, and initiate skirmishes. So much as when the spectre of rivalry for employment and accommodation is identified as one of the issues coupled with immigration, this most likely leads not to finding fault with the capitalist social order which generates such insecurity, but instead, to resentment levelled at people of colour themselves. Black and minority ethnic workers, therefore, assume the role of scapegoats for the inadequacies of the capitalist status quo, which fails to deliver adequate housing stock and an assurance of security to every single member of the working population. Due regard is averted from the social system which devalues all workers into rivals in their dependent orientation as breadwinners and tenants. Hostility is directed at people of colour rather than at the privileged elite. And so, prejudice towards Black and minority ethnic groups is a powerful device in maintaining the existing conjuncture (Castles and Kosack,1985).

A further function of prejudice is a close cousin of the aforementioned one. It's about the composition of the proletariat and the class consciousness of the host community. If workers carry vehement prejudice against their minority ethnic colleagues (and particularly if there is anxiety regarding competition), they, more often than not, back discriminatory measures adopted by employers and the state to see to it that minority ethnic workers remain in the bottom stratum of the social and economic hierarchy. The considerable extent to which minorities are exploited is not viewed as feeding into solidarity, but as serving the interests of the indigenous workers. The actual schism in the working class, therefore, finds its subjective opposite number: there is a schism in proletarian consciousness. Native workers often fail to support minorities when the latter engage in industrial action to ameliorate their conditions. The historic class consciousness resting on collective principles and processes tends to be supplanted by a factional consciousness of the dominant workers. In fact, the change may advance even further: the positioning towards collective action geared to improve the status of all workers may be supplanted by objectives for subjective advancement without any alteration in the unequal structure of society. Along these lines, prejudice against minorities deals a debilitating and damaging blow to both the solidarity of the labour organization and working-class consciousness.

The triumvirate functions of prejudice are directly in line with the concerns of the ruling elite. They serve to conserve the societal conjuncture by firstly rationalizing the exploitation of minorities, secondly, averting workers' gaze from the real causes of their precarious position, and thirdly, dividing the labour movement and undermining class consciousness. But these triumvirate functions run counter to the long-term concerns of the proletariat. Still, as is evident, many workers harbour prejudices against minorities. Recognized or partially recognized programmes, contingent on liberal – humanitarian principles, can scarcely be expected to deliver a change in this situation. Conversely, the ruling class benefits from prejudice and so can hardly be expected to endorse effective measures to deflect it. On the obverse, as Cox has identified; 'We cannot defeat prejudice by proving that it is wrong. The reason for this is that race prejudice is only a symptom of a materialist social fact' (quoted in Castles and Kosack,1985:460). If this conception can be taken as the origins of prejudice, then quite different steps are to be taken to eliminate it. B. Bettelheim and M. Janowitz have put forward such an approach for the United States:

The economic goals of such action are thus clear; an adjusted annual wage to do away with fears of seasonal unemployment and an extension of social security. In the absence of comprehensive and successful attempts to move in that direction, it remains doubtful whether programmes orientated specifically towards interethnic issues are at all relevant for changing ethnic relations (Castles and Kosack,1985:460).

On the condition that prejudice is an outcome of socio-economic circumstances, then it can only suffer the death knell through an alteration in these circumstances, pre-eminently by the eradication of the fundamental insecurity which colours the conjuncture of the proletariat in the capitalist social order.

So long as White people feel superior to Black and minority ethnic groups, it appears that there will always be social and economic consequences that manifest themselves in racial hatred, racial abuse and racial attacks. Racism confirms and reinforces the idea that Black and minority ethnic groups have not been granted full citizenship rights of equality with the White British general population. The social consequences of a White population which feels superior to Black and minority ethnic people is that White people align themselves with the right to dominate, a modicum of which seems benevolent; but, in the presence of minorities, a White person will, given half the chance, issue an edict and, of course, this is one way White dominance expresses itself. At best, White dominance can be shown in the issuing of an order and at worst, discord and racism. And further consequences are that Black and South Asian people are under-represented in senior positions in the workplace; career progression and promotion represent a stumbling block for minority professionals; employment contracts for minority ethnic groups tend to fuel job insecurity and so on.

In the face of racism and racist acts, first, we are confronted with the idea that Whites view what takes place in Britain as part of their freedom, in their own country – although Africans were here before they came – to dominate over so-called inferior groups of people that threaten British culture; secondly, racist deeds may operate out of resentment to the competition Black and minority ethnic people represent in housing, employment and the provision of available services and through which frustration and anxieties are vented, when, in their own country, things are not working in their favour and when White people perceive that minorities are getting ahead in whatever respect that might happen to be.

The function of racism, then, is that Britain is a predominantly White country and White people desire that they gain the ascendancy over people of colour and attempt to establish the age-old colonial relationship of authority and subordination to maintain an edge, as indigenous to the land and in their own country, over Black and minority ethnic people despite the obstacles in the way and whatever the cost. The maintenance of White social status appears important in the role of racism. The master/servant relationship of colonial times is constantly played out by White authority figures instructing and directing minority groups as to how affairs must be conducted, but it is also commonplace for ordinary White people to issue directives to those they feel are beneath them and to whom they feel superior. Equality has so far not been granted because it appears to be a 'threat' to White stewardship, dominance and hegemony.

Racism is also part of the fabric which ensures that White dominance is perpetuated and stands the test of time. One only need cast one's historical memory back to the rise and fall of the Roman Empire to see that the British Empire is no longer, and so this country, alongside other territories, is the last bastion of British political, economic and social power and racism can be seen as the nation and its people being consistently on guard, like an army garrison against a perceived 'threat'. The notorious Enoch Powell, in his 'rivers of blood' speech, altered irretrievably the perception of the British people to immigration as a 'threat' to the British way of life and therefore implying that the nation must mobilize and be on its guard and operate a partisan policy towards White people otherwise outsiders or strangers will have the 'whip hand'. Racism is a by-product of White survival strategy and in the allocation of scarce resources, it usually chimes with Malcolm X's expression 'by any means necessary'. Powell's dystopian vision attracted many supporters both inside and outside parliamentary politics and he was indeed a call to arms for the British populace. Powell wanted immigration stopped and in 1974 the new Labour administration (again) made no attempt to cancel immigration legislation enacted by the Tories (Goodhart,2013). The mood of rank-and-file Conservatives was shown 'in 1969, 327 out of 412 Conservative constituency associations wanted all 'coloured immigration' stopped indefinitely' (Goodhart,2013:146). To be sure, British immigration legislation was, and is, racist because it did not apply to White people from Europe, Australia, New Zealand, Canada, America and Ireland. On the other side of the coin, between 1971 and 1983, more people had vacated Britain than had entered it. Also, Britain was hostile to Caribbean and South Asian 'immigrants' while welcoming Polish and East Europeans.

Powellism captured the Zeitgeist of the late 1960s and lit the blue touchpaper for a renewed surge and impetus in racial hostility. Since the murder of Stephen Lawrence in 1993, there have been almost a hundred more such murders to date, all in the name of 'keeping Britain White' (Goodhart,2013; Perry,2015). These are apparent consequences of a nation on guard against a perceived 'threat' and it is not far from conceivable that Powellism lies beneath it. This is not to say that racial hostility did not exist before Powellism but Powell the demagogue appealed to the basest instinct of the people and gave racism a shot in the arm. At the contemporary level, it manifests itself in many ways and is pervasive at all levels of society. White 'Race' membership almost certainly means that life's turn of events is likely to treat one more kindly in some way. In other words, White privilege has its advantages. The outcome of the function of racism among African-Caribbean males is that they will experience higher unemployment, harsher sentencing and differential treatment at the hands of mental health services. In all probability, the well-educated Black man will encounter a British university system where "70 per cent of the professors" are simultaneously both White and male (Evaristo,2017:12, The Times Literary Supplement). That universities seem to think that professors should have a White face is a sorry example of what universities deem as the colour of intelligence.

According to the facts or exact meaning, Powell's speech did little more than explain the reasons for the controls on immigration as espoused by Conservative Party policy. A point that is not in question is the sympathy with which the speech was met. A nationwide survey following the speech found as little as 15 per cent at odds with it and 74 per cent at ease with it. The statistics in the West Midlands may have been more emphatic and Clem Jones, the then editor of the Wolverhampton Express and Star, acceded that the flood of mail he received concerning the speech was, by force of numbers, pro-Powell (Goodhart,2013).

Even with Powell's sacking by the Tory leader, Edward Heath, support for him redoubled. Dockers organized protest marches in favour of him and 69 per cent of public opinion was in conflict with his sacking. He threw reticence to the wind for mainstream anti-immigration sentiment and has lurked and lingered over UK domestic politics and the immigration debate more so than elsewhere, from April 1968 to the present (Goodhart,2013:143; Eddo-lodge,2017:118-119).

The initial effect of the speech was to bring about an increased feeling of discomfort for Britain's obviously identifiable minorities. The nation's people appeared to witness overt hostility and violence stepped up in the following weeks and months. This climate was confirmed especially in Powell's Wolverhampton local province, which, by 1968, had a minority contingent of about 15,000 (out of a population that spanned approximately 150,000), half of whom were Caribbean and half were Asian, chiefly Sikhs and Hindus whose former homeland was the Punjab (Goodhart,2013).

When Powell uttered, 'In this country, in fifteen or twenty years' time, the black man will have the whip hand over the white man', he deliberately chose not to say the less emotive phrasing 'advantage over' (Eddo-lodge,2017). Whip summons up a normalised picture of punishment for trifling offences arising out of forced labour and wretchedness, of subjugation and complete and utter dominance evocative of slavery. It has been pointed out that Enoch Powell's speech bears all the hallmarks of a speech so racist the like of which startles British memory, but his language carried the same racial overtones as Britain's link with Blackness spans the centuries (Eddo-lodge,2017). For Powell, the only alternative method to hand to maintain power in Britain was through the subjugation of a people, for that is the way Britain has held onto and kept hold of its power historically.

Underlying Powell's speech is what Eddo-Lodge (2017) calls 'fear of a black planet' (p.118). It's a fear that the underprivileged 'other' will take command of the helm. Enoch Powell's fears of a role reversal have assumed a prominent place in the modern-day ideological discourse on immigration. During the time, running up to the 2015 general election, the Labour Party issued official merchandise which incorporated a mug that was inscribed 'controls on immigration'; they subscribed to that fear. Elements of the British population stipulate that we inhabit a tiny island and the time has come to bar access. People are concerned that the ever-diminishing British national character is being slowly undermined by 'immigrants' whose only object is not to leave behind war and poverty but to extirpate the material fabric of the country.

The fear surfaces on many different levels. It reaches us through the form of 'concerns about' immigration, expressed by political parties in general elections of late. It reaches us through the form of 'preserving our national identity' (Eddo-Lodge,2017:118). Central to the fear is the assumption that anything not operating for White homogeneity exists solely to expunge it. To such a degree, multiculturalism is the thin end of the wedge towards the obliteration of Western civilisation.

Over half a century on from Powell's speech, and the 'fear of a Black planet' refuses to go away quietly (Eddo-Lodge,2017:119). The term multiculturalism has become a euphemism for a considerable number of British anxieties concerning immigration, 'race', difference, illegality and peril. It has now become a dirty word, an anterior word for fears relative to Black and Brown and overseas people posing a peril to indigenous British citizens. If your status is that of an 'immigrant' - in spite of whether you're second or third extraction – this is to be taken to heart. Outsider groups are multiculturalism. Those who are afraid of multiculturalism are afraid of outsider groups. Moreover, in the mood of 1980s-style political Blackness, 'immigration concerns' are not so much about who is Black, but, to a greater extent, relative to who isn't White British (Eddo-Lodge,2017).

Despite the successes of Wolverhampton in practically every other respect, Powell and Powellism signalled a retrograde step for Britain (Goodhart,2013). At the moment when a dialogue should have been initializing relative to integration, racial justice and discerning the plausible from the racist gripes of the White British whose communities were undergoing transposition, he diametrically shifted the argument and shut it down. He delayed, by upwards of a generation, a systematic discursive struggle about the positive results and the negative results of immigration. In addition, Powell did not make it any easier for liberal and centre-left mainstream politics to start patterning ideas relative to a modern, post-imperial patriotic cohesion which could sow solidarity among the majority and the rest in a revised and unified outlook of the country.

The emphasis on populism in terms of race became a point that sat uneasily with the leaders of the two main political parties who had determined not to steer a collision course; it was circulated that a few 'immigrants' would do little to change things substantially and the focus on race was, in practice, averted from national politics (Goodhart,2013).

Various though the historical reasons may be for Britain's flippant stance on minority integration, yet, Enoch Powell undoubtedly consolidated it by making it seem somewhat wrong to think logically about boundaries, immigration, 'race', integration and social cohesion (Goodhart,2013).

It would be remiss not to exercise caution in attributing disproportionate power over events at the door of one man. However, Powell can be said to have been largely responsible for the election of Margaret Thatcher, the emergence of the multiculturalist left in the 1980s and 1990s and perhaps, indirectly, Labour's new immigration commencement in 1997 – following Powell, the one principle that Liberals and the left found common ground on was that they disagreed with Powell and were pro-immigration and 'immigrants' (Goodhart,2013).

Powell and Powellism may well have contributed to both political parties adopting a more restrictionist stance on immigration. Since Powellism veers towards far-right politics, it is only fair that right-wing extremism should feature in accounts of post-war immigration, as was particular to the decade after 1968. Moreover, because Powellism represented a more pressing concern to politicians, this does not mean far-right extremism can be discounted out of the equation, even though the large majority of the electorate chose not to vote for a far-right party and they needn't, as the major political parties, especially the Conservatives, serve their interests. However, in recent years, members of the far-right British National Party (BNP) have been elected in some of our cities (Bhavnani et al,2005:33). Powell's influence is still as potent as it ever was over democratic politics and in particular, the immigration debate, from the day of his speech to the present, so how can Britain be consistently shown, in Eurobarometer opinion polls, from the 1970s into the twenty-first century as occupying middle ground among Europeans on approaches to race and immigration? If Britain is genuinely moderate on attitudes to race and immigration among Europeans, it is only because they are being compared to places such as Germany, Italy and Spain where fascist movements have attained power, and so put Britain in the European political middle ground.

Margaret Thatcher's three terms in office are, needless to say perhaps, concomitant with the free-market restructuring of Britain, laying low the predominance of the unions and the introduction of growing inequality. Many seem to forget that Mrs Thatcher had, at some stage, been a peer acolyte of the Powellite wing of the party and triumphed in the 1979 election owing to the utility of certain Powellite themes. Once elected, she made every effort to deliver on immigration, though she seldom spoke about the issue. The proportion of work permits issued was cut further (they evened out at 10,000 to 20,000 a year from 1973 to 1989), and remarkably so, the automatic entitlement to introduce an incoming spouse was curbed by the 'primary purpose rule', wherein the prospective husband or wife (chiefly from South Asia) had to show that the marriage was grounded in other reasons besides that of gaining access to Britain (Goodhart,2013:150). We now turn to focus on the historical function of English racism which can be seen in slavocracy or plantocracy racism.

The origins of English racism

Christianity and its basis, the Bible, coexisted with the Church of England's official view that Africans are human, yet, at the same time, turning a blind eye to slavery. 'Christianity and the embracing of the Gospel does not make the least difference in civil property,' argued Thomas Sherlock on the subject of the slave trade in 1727 (Fryer,1984:146). Sherlock was, in succession, Bishop of London, Salisbury, and Bangor, and he was declaring the Church of England's formal position. The planters in the West Indies were of the common opinion that if they allowed their Black slaves the autonomy to take on Christianity and be baptized, this would mean opening the door to their freedom. The Church went all out to allay the planters' fears on that count; on the question of slavery, it so much as offered its support. Nonconformist Christians were also, but for the odd exception, less agitated by the institution of slavery in the literal sense than by the planters' conflict with the crossover to and baptism of their slaves into Christianity. In the strong exchange of words that ensued, the planters maintained that Black people did not qualify as human beings but were animals bereft of souls to save; 'What, such as they?' they rallied. 'What, those black Dogs be made Christians? What, shall they be like us?' (Fryer,1984:146). In addition, they demanded reassurance as to whether the clergy would begin baptizing horses. At this point, English racism essentially took its rise, and we find it expressed or documented in centuries-old religious tracts. Such tracts make curious discovery today, for, in the main, their authors contend that Africans are human short of the slightest raised eyebrow as to them being slaves.

The anterior tracts of this ilk suggest that even prior to the mid-seventeenth-century, race prejudice was reifying into a verbally articulated racism that was, by then, leading in effect to first-degree murder by members of the preponderant group of human beings. 'The primary functions of race prejudice are cultural and psychological. The primary functions of racism are economic and political' (Fryer,1984:134). Some of English racism's proponents such as John Locke, David Hume, Edward Long and Philip Thicknesse had the economic and political function of justifying the institution of slavery, each of which we shall look at in turn. Racist ideology did not appear in print until mid-way through the eighteenth century, and already, the landscape had been well-tilled for racists by three seminal thinkers who, in and of themselves, helped to make credible the suggestion that Africans were mentally inferior to Europeans (Fryer,1984).

Appearing as early as 1677, Sir William Petty, founder of modern political economy was among the founding members of the Royal Society, and, in a paper entitled 'The Scale of Creatures', expressed the opinion that Europeans were different entities to Africans not only in hue, hair, contour of face, symmetry of nose, lips and cheekbones and specificity of skull: 'They differ also in their Naturall Manners, & in the internall Qualities of their minds' (Fryer,1984:151).

Petty's living and breathing compatriot, John Locke, who apparently had a £600 stake in the Royal African Company, not only managed to square an acquiescence in the sacrosanct rights of man with the approach that Black slavery was subject to the apologist, but also rendered a substantial if (as some credit it) unintentional contribution to the approach that Africans were, in certain respects, inherently inferior to Europeans (Fryer,1984). Locke's *Essay concerning Human Understanding* (1690), regardless of its philosophical reasonableness as the primary reference point of systematic empiricism, opened the door to the contention that Africans and humanity are indivisible but nevertheless had an intellectual competence level comparable to that of the animal world. Casting doubt on the Augustinian perspective that human intellectual faculties are distinguished by supernaturalism, Locke underscored the vacuous mind's reception of 'sensations' from the external environment and understood mental faculties as devices for interpreting sensations. Locke's epistemology created the circumstances to enable a mechanistic organization of faculties which, 'by rendering the concept of mental ability less amorphous than previously ... helped channel much of the debate on the Negro towards the gratifyingly specific question of whether or not he was the mental equal of the White man' (Fryer,1984:151). So, therefore, the father of English empiricism and foremost systematic advocate of liberalism in political theory served to construct a respectable basis for the racist theory of cognitive hierarchical system. Clearly, Locke was not immune from racial prejudice. 'The Child certainly knows', he wrote, 'that the nurse that feeds it, is neither the Cat it plays with, nor the Blackmoor it is afraid of'. And once more:

> A child having framed the idea of a man, it is probable, that his idea is just like that picture, which the painter makes of the visible appearances joined together; and such a complication of ideas together in his understanding, makes up the single complex idea which he calls man, whereof white or flesh-colour in England being one, the child can demonstrate to you, that a Negro is not a man, because white colour was one of the constant simple ideas of the complex ideas he calls man: And therefore he can demonstrate by the principle, it is impossible for the same thing to be, and not to be, that a Negro is not a man (Fryer, 1984:151).

'Whatever may be the early thoughts of an English child', vapidly remarks Leon Poliakov, 'those of Locke betray an unconscious prejudice' (Fryer, 1984:152).

While the outlined representation may be embarrassing for historians of western philosophy, worse is on the horizon. Following Locke came the great empiricist David Hume, who, without much ado, revealed himself as a racist. European people, he declared, were innately superior to each and every other race. He stated this in a footnote as part of the 1753 reprint of his treatise 'Of National Characters', first published in 1748. Turning a blind eye to the welter of evidence that disclaimed his prejudices, Hume wrote:

> I am apt to suspect the negroes, and in general, all the other species of men (for there are four or five different kinds) to be naturally inferior to whites. There never was a civilized nation of any other complexion than white, nor even any individual eminent either in action or speculation. No ingenious manufacture amongst them, no arts, no sciences. On the other hand, the most rude and barbarous of the white, such as the ancient GERMANS, the present TARTARS, have still something eminent about them, in their valour, form of government, or some other particular. Such a uniform and constant difference could not happen, in so many countries and ages, if nature had not made an original distinction betwixt these breeds of men. Not to mention our colonies, there are negroe slaves dispersed all over Europe, of which none ever discovered any symptoms of ingenuity; tho' low people, without ingenuity, will start amongst us, and distinguish themselves in every profession. In JAMAICA indeed they talk of one negroe as a man of parts and learning; but 'tis likely he is admired for very slender accomplishments, like a parrot, who speaks a few words plainly (Fryer,1984:152).

This citation by the Scottish savant Hume, with its disreputable reference to the classical authority Francis Williams, was not the onset of racism to appear in the printed form. That badge of notoriety belongs to the author of a short piece of written work placed in the public arena in the London Magazine in 1750. Professing to precis Buffon, the writer – who thought better of signing his name – described 'the people called Negroes' as 'the most remarkably distinct from the rest of the human species' (Fryer,1984:152). In the wake of certain remarks about the differences extending across from 'Hotentots' and 'Caffers', including differences in the exterior female genitalia, this commentator added his distinctive input to the debate by insisting that 'a great difference between Negroes and all other

Blacks, both in Africa and the East-Indies, lies in this, that the former smell most abominably when they sweat, whereas the latter have no bad smell even when they are sweating' (Fryer,1984:153).

The gates admitting entrance to racism were by now well and truly open, and a substantial amount of detritus worked its way into cultural literary forms over the decades that followed. The epitome, worth quoting extensively as it is one of Edward Long's two main sources, is to be located in the *Universal History* (1736-65). Two of this colossal compendium's 23 folio tomes contained page-turning high-flown abuse of Africans, who 'are now everywhere degenerated into a brutish, ignorant, idle, treacherous, thievish, mistrustful, and superstitious people' (Fryer,1984:153). Many Greek and Roman commentators were cited for the approach that Africans were:

> proud, lazy, treacherous, thievish, hot, and addicted to all kinds of lusts, and most ready to promote them in others, as pimps, panders, incestuous, brutish, and savage, cruel and revengeful, devourers of human flesh, and quaffers of human blood, inconstant, base, treacherous, and cowardly; fond of and addicted to all sorts of superstition and witchcraft, and, in a word, to every vice that came in their way, or within their reach ... It is hardly possible to find in any African any quality but what is of the bad kind: they are inhuman, drunkards, deceitful, extremely covetous, and perfidious to the highest degree. We need not add to these their impurities and blasphemies, because in these they outdo all other nations, Africa being known to have been ever burning with innumerable impurities; insomuch that one would rather take it for a volcano of the most impure flames, than for a habitation of human creatures ... St. Austin, who was a native in that country, scruples not to confess, that it is as impossible to be an African and not lascivious, as it is to be born in Africa and not be an African ...

> Thus, much shall suffice for the general character of the native Africans ... it is so far from being either unjust or exaggerated, with regard to the far

greater part of them, that in many instances, they deserve, if possible, a much more odious one; they being in many parts so utterly void of all humanity, and even natural affection, that parents will sell their wives and children, and vice versa, for slaves into the American colonies ... even for so small a matter as a gallon or two of brandy ...

If we ... take a cursory view of their manufactures and mechanic arts ... we shall find the spirit of indolence running through them all, even the most necessary of them ...

If we look into those few manufactures and handicrafts that are amongst them, we shall find them carried on with the same rude [i.e., ignorant] and tedious stupidity (Fryer,1984:153-154).

So much as where the *Universal History* forgoes generalizations and privileges a detailed consideration of a specific African political unit, the same enduring prejudice stamped its damaging evaluation. And so, the section on Benin stipulated that 'In general, the negroes of this country are libidinous, and much addicted to venery' (Fryer,1984:154).

Galvanized by the result of the Somerset case, and also the perceptible beginning of a groundswell of public opinion opposing the institution of slavery, these colonial partisans were now working beyond the bounds of customary limits. Samuel Estwick is an important figure in the understanding of Edward Long as he informed and inspired Edward Long's writings. Samuel Estwick, assistant representative for Barbados, passionately advanced the demand for legal action to safeguard racial purity by excluding the arrival of Black people into Britain. The progeny of a Barbados planter, Estwick took as his wife the female offspring of a governor of Barbados, acquired 'very large possessions in the West India islands', became representative for Barbados and paymaster-general, and occupied a position in the House of Commons for 16 years (Fryer,1984:156). In his broadside on the Mansfield verdict, *Considerations on the Negroe Cause* (1772), Estwick urged that legislation to exclude Black people would 'preserve the race of Britons from stain and contamination' (Fryer,1984:156). And in a subsequent edition, made available the following year, he expanded upon his racist views, maintaining that Blacks did not have the same claim to humanity as Englishmen. Animals are differentiated by many kinds, 'each kind having its proper species subordinate thereto' (Fryer,1984:156). Therefore, it is a lot to digest that humanity was not also divided in that way:

> Does this not seem to break in upon and unlink that great chain of heaven, which in due gradation joins and unites the whole with all its parts? May it not be more perfective of the system to say, that human nature is a class, comprehending an order of beings, of which man is the genus, divided into distinct and separate species of men? (Fryer,1984:157).

On citing both Locke and Hume, and transmitting a brief account of African barbarity and endemic moral depravity ('Their barbarity to their children ... Their cruelty to their aged parents'), Estwick determined that Black people were 'filling up that space in life beyond the bounds of which they are not capable of passing; differing from other men, not in kind, but in species' (Fryer,1984:157). Put in slightly different terms, Black people were incontrovertibly and perpetually sub-human. All of this then meant that the plantocracy which Estwick was paid to represent was only exercising its right to deprive them of autonomy and extract unfairly the utmost labour from them.

This booklet of Estwick's was a very close first principal source for Edward Long's racist tirade against Black people. Born in Cornwall in 1734, Long had a Jamaica planter as a father whose family connections with the island had residential roots sometime after Jamaica became a colony of Britain in 1655. Long arrived in Jamaica as a young man of 23, took the hand of a Beckford heiress in marriage, distinguished himself in property ownership and was privileged to occupy the position of justice of the Vice-Admiralty Court. He embarked on a journey back to Britain in 1769 and put his *History of Jamaica* out for public consumption five years later. However, as if to sort of test the water for the *History*, first came a pamphlet called *Candid Reflections Upon the judgement lately awarded by the Court of Kings Bench ... On what is commonly called the Negroe-Cause* (1772). The most felicitous term in the modern era to come to recollection would not, perhaps, be candour for that fluent and persuasive passage in which, subsequent to designating Black people in Britain as 'a dissolute, idle, profligate crew', Long unwittingly showcased his most ruminated and deep-seated reverie:

> The lower class of women in England are remarkably fond of the blacks, for reasons too brutal to mention; they would connect themselves with horses and asses if the laws permitted them. By these ladies, they generally have a numerous brood. Thus, in the course of a few generations more, the English blood will become so contaminated with this mixture and from the chances, the ups and downs of life, this alloy may spread so extensively as even to reach the middle, and then the higher orders of the people, till the whole nation resembles the Portuguese and Moriscos in complexion of skin and baseness of mind. This is a venomous and dangerous ulcer, that threatens to disperse its malignancy far and wide, until every family catches infection from it (Fryer,1984:157-158; Rattansi,2007:31).

Long makes no bones about his political, social and sexual anxieties. He notes that if the rights of Englishmen were conferred upon people of colour, they might just become MPs or men and women of property. For such to ensue would be neither politic, useful nor advantageous. Blacks were unable to contribute, at whatever level, towards the status and upkeep of the kingdom: 'They are neither husbandmen, manufacturers, nor artificers. They have neither strength of constitution, inclination, or skill, to perform the common drudgeries of husbandry in this climate and country' (Fryer,1984:158). What is more, Long set a precedent both in the tone and the material pabulum of modern-day racism with his adage and mantra 'the public good of this kingdom requires that some restraint should be laid on the unnatural increase of blacks imported into it' (Fryer,1984:158).

The above illustrates the savage art and practice of blaming the victim, which, throughout time and space, has been the distinguishing mark of those who oppose the African race (Shyllon,1977). In the piece above, we are exposed to West Indian moral principles that marshal the language of indecency through one of their most notable exponents. For a fuller citation of Long which is complete with the most out of the ordinary statements and contradictions, see Shyllon,1977. The sable-complexioned individuals are 'a dissolute, idle, profligate crew', yet the prospect 'of their becoming landholders in the Kingdom is not to be denied'. Black people lacked intelligence but in the same way 'they are remarkably acute and dextrous'. Blacks are not half as 'useful in menial employments as our White servants', but they 'debar our own poor from access into families for their livelihood'. The 'renegado blacks' are slothful and complacent, but they are ready and 'glad to serve for less wages' (Shyllon,1977:99).

Emerging on the market some two years later was Long's *History of Jamaica* trilogy. The book itself is an unsystematic mishmash, the leaves of which contain observations of varying gradations of merit on meteorology, climatology, zoology, medicine, botany, geography, history, law, commerce and government – and an enthusiastic tirade against colonial governors, whom Long appears to have disliked almost to the same extent as he disliked Blacks, charging them with 'artifice, duplicity, haughtiness, violence, rapine, avarice, meanness, rancour, and dishonesty' (Fryer,1984:158). However, the matter that is of interest to us here is the longwinded section which, comprising Long's theory of natural Black inferiority, may be deemed the classic study of English racism. What has already come to our attention are the two immediate sources that Long places under consideration without actually allotting written acknowledgement. There is little doubting that he had, within easy reach as he worked, those leafy tomes of the Universal History portraying Africa and Africans in highly critical and damaging terms and Estwick's booklet, from which he transcribed, more or less verbatim, the passage about the humble standing of Africans in 'that great chain of Heaven' (Fryer,1984:158). Reference to Long at excessive length need not be necessary to expose both his poisonous ill-will and his uninspired rhetoric.

'For my own part', he wrote, 'I think there are extremely potent reasons for believing, that the White and the Negroe are two distinct species'. Rather than hair, Black people had 'a covering of wool, like the bestial fleece'. Black lice littered their bodies. Their 'bestial or fetid smell' was so pungent that 'it continues in places where they have been near a quarter of an hour' (Fryer,1984:158). They had no strategic forward-thinking or basis of morality. They behaved like monsters towards their children. Black men had strong feelings only for women, and over-indulgence in food and drink; no motivation only to be idle. In Africa, 'their roads are mere sheep-paths, twice as long as they need be, and almost impassible'. All commentators have remarked that Blacks were 'the vilest of the human kind' (Fryer,1984:158-159).

When we reflect on ... their dissimilarity to the rest of mankind, must we not conclude, that they are a different species of the same genus? ... Nor do [orang-utans] seem at all inferior in the intellectual faculties to many of the Negroe race; with some of whom, it is credible that they have the most intimate connexion and consanguinity. The amorous intercourse between them may be frequent ... and it is certain that both races agree perfectly well in lasciviousness of disposition (Fryer,1984:159)

To be sure, Long continued, the orang-utan was much closer in form and resemblance to Blacks than the second bore to Whites. There was a continuum of intellectual hierarchy, too, from monkeys preceding through to varieties of Blacks, 'until we mark its utmost limit of perfection in the pure White'. The table manners of Black people left much to be desired 'eating flesh almost raw by choice, though intolerably putrid and full of maggots'. They divide the meat up with their 'talons' and 'chuck it by handfuls down their throats with all the voracity of wild beasts'. They had no concept of shooting birds in flight, 'nor can they project a straight line, nor lay any substance square with another'. In sexual behaviour (a topic to which Long made reference again and again), they are libidinous and shameless as monkies, or baboons' and 'the equally hot temperament of their women has given probability to the charge of their admitting these animals frequently to their embrace'. To put it succinctly, Africa was the 'parent of every thing that is monstrous in nature' (Fryer,1984:159).

The matter that is not plagiarism specifically is mere small-minded prejudice, commensurate with planters' dinner-table palaver. Also, the plagiarism draws on sources that, as it appears apparent, were themselves far from original. Long's idiosyncratic flair lay in associating a 'scientific'-sounding declaration of Black inferiority – he set a pseudo-scientific racist precedent – with an excuse of Black slavery that is represented with far more credibility than any prior assertion of the slave owner's position. As a 'scientist', he is utterly execrable but otherwise occupying very good offices; as a pro-slavery advocate, he occupied somewhat less good offices but, paradoxically, requires that more serious attention be attributed. What follows is the handy overview of Long's perspective on Black slavery supplied by the editor of the 1970 recast of the *History of Jamaica*; it reflects adequately how the racist abuse links into, and is useful to the role of, the overarching economic contention:

> That the trade in slaves and in goods produced by slaves was immensely profitable, not only to the West Indies, but to Britain itself and that it greatly enriched Englishmen in all walks of life; that West Indian slavery was, on the whole, a mild and benevolent institution and that slaves were better off than the lower classes in Britain; that negro slavery was inevitable and necessary in certain regions of the world; that the slave trade benefited and helped to civilise Africa; that virtually all the slaves were originally convicted criminals; that in every mental and moral way negroes were absolutely inferior to white men, and that the most constructive thing which could happen to them was to be compelled to work productively (Fryer,1984:160).

What is curious is that Long, in his apology and justification of Black slavery, fails to mention two of the pro-slavery contentions that had wide currency during his day. His book makes no reference to God's curse on Ham. Long had little to do with orthodox religion, and that contention evidently fell under his radar (though, in 1789, it emerged to take centre stage in a pro-slavery tract by the Tobago planter and West India Committee publicist Gilbert Francklyn) (Fryer,1984:160). In no part of Long's *History* is the contention that Britain could scarcely forgo the slave trade given that other European dominions would simply seize the opportunity and soak up the profit. This very same contention appeared in Hugh Crow's memoirs, *The Life and Times of a Slave Trade Captain* in 1830 in which he marshals a laissez-faire argument or apology for the slave trade and bemoans its abolition (Crow,2007; xii, 93, 117). Despite all indications and representations, Britain's greatest slave trader was for some the hero while for many others he was the villain, though no other designation but the latter matches or fits his actions, as his actions render his argument, in his personal defence, ridiculous and which speaks far louder than mere words could ever purport or hope to accomplish. Put in slightly different terms, Crow was a slave trader who railed against change and no amount of argument could subvert this material fact. Many people would recognize Crow's remarks as seriously flawed and there is no separating nor mistaking the man from his times. Long is known, in fact, to have been of the opinion that 'a total sacrifice of our African trade and American possessions' to a fantastic idea of English liberty' would downgrade Britain into 'the tributary province of some potent neighbour' (Fryer,1984:160). However, by the early 1770s, the abolitionist movement had only just begun to spawn a following, and Long was under no apprehension that the British were anywhere near as likely to relinquish the slave trade and slavery as to relinquish roast beef and beer. Thus, on this count then, the History is inaudibly speechless.

Such omissions render the economic main point of Long's contention much more significant (Fryer,1984). As an additional point and needless to say, in one important dimension, he was attesting to the truth. The institution of slavery had indeed proved hugely profitable to Britain and to any number of rapidly augmenting British enterprises. So, what then of Long's contention that slaves in the West Indies experienced better living conditions than the lower orders in Britain? That also rings true – for the smaller number who performed domestic chores on efficiently organized plantations. They travailed under infinite threat of a reduction in status to fieldwork in addition to an infinite threat of the lash. However, with regard to food, physical accommodation space and working conditions, their overall circumstances exceeded those of the men, women, and minors in small-scale and family-run businesses or the large ugly factories with their draconian, drastic discipline. This, then, was the second strand of truth within the substantial economy with the truth. Yet Britain's working classes, accounting for their extended hours, poor conditions, dismal wages, and unsanitary housing, were infinitely more fortunate than the aggregate number of plantation field slaves. To describe Britain's industrial base as 'dark satanic mills' is utterly accurate. However, within our geographical and political confines, the overseers thought better of flogging their workers, or depriving them of vitally important parts and limbs, or cropping their ears as a punishment (Fryer, 1984).

'We must not presume, 'admonishes David Brion Davis in *The Problem of Slavery in Western* Culture (1966), '… that Edward Long lacked a sympathetic audience, or was totally unrepresentative of his time' (Fryer,1984:161). Quite the opposite. He occupied good offices and his approach resonated with many. However, a logical and coherent argument employing tender feeling and humanity, has scarcely been the linchpin for a consummate demagogue (Shyllon,1977). Recourse to the crude and basic tendencies in man, however, and the purveyors of supremacist thinking and racial purity are definitely unassailable and successful.

In the very year that his *History of Jamaica* surfaced, none other a figure than Oliver Goldsmith, author of *The Vicar of Wakefield* (1766), *She Stoops to Conquer* (1774), and other lasting additions to English literature, characterized the physical 'deformities' and 'insupportable' odour of Black people in language dramatically not dissimilar to Long's. 'This gloomy race of mankind,' he furthered, in his *History of the Earth*, 'is found to blacken all the southern parts of Africa'. Their cerebral hemispheres were 'incapable of strong exertions'. As a whole, the Black race was 'stupid, indolent, and mischievous'. And, once more, in the exact same year, a British 'lady of quality' on a sojourn in Antigua, astonished by the 'dreadful' scars linked to punishment beatings to the slaves' backs, consoled herself with the thought that 'when one comes to be better acquainted with the nature of the Negroes, the horror of it must wear off. After all, the Blacks were 'brutes' whose natures seem made to bear it, and whose sufferings are not attended with shame or pain beyond the present moment' (Fryer,1984:161).

What is clear is that by the 1770s, racism had become established, uninspired, intellectual fare in Britain. More specifically, the dystopian cloud of racial intermarriage and 'contamination', consistently summoned by the West Indians' agents, was hanging over England. A year on from the release of Long's *History*, the novelist Charles Johnstone, better known for his outrageous chronicle *Chrysal, or the Adventures of a Guinea* (1760-5), asserted in his book *The Pilgrim* that the prospect of miscegenation between English people, Jews and Blacks suggested 'their progeny will not much longer have reason to value themselves on their beauty, wit, or virtue' (Fryer,1984:161). A decade later, James Tobin of Nevis was declaring his warning that 'the great numbers of negroes at present in England, the strange partiality shewn for them by the lower orders of women, and the rapid increase of a dark and contaminated breed, are evils which have long been complained of and call every day more loudly for enquiry and redress' (Fryer,1984:161-162). The response to this statement came from Olaudah Equiano, who demanded, 'Can any man less ferocious than a tiger or a wolf attempt to justify the cruelties inflicted on the negroes in the West Indies?' Equiano confronted Tobin in a competent and direct manner. Some of the most affluent planters, he indicated, had sired children for their Black slaves, and were accountable for infanticide, abortion, 'and a thousand other horrid enormities'. Why then should two people who love each other not commit themselves to each other in marriage? 'Why not establish intermarriages at home, and in our colonies? And encourage open, free and generous love, upon Nature's own wide and extensive plan, subservient only to moral rectitude, without distinction of the colour of a skin?' (Fryer,1984:109).

Alarm bells ring and one shudders to see the way in which prejudice can so far eclipse all fellow human feeling resulting in lines of thought in men that are unconscionable, and to produce such base and sordid thoughts, such blunt and degenerate sensibilities, this meeting of corrupt minds twisted by their idee fixe around the Black man as a phallic symbol (Shyllon,1977).

Pointing to the fact of the matter, at the time when Long and Tobin were writing, 'the middle and higher orders' of Englishwomen were far from unattracted to black human beings (Shyllon,1977:105). Kitty, Duchess of Queensberry, Countess of Bristol, Duchess of Kingston and Elizabeth Chudleigh, and the Suffolk lady who would scarcely permit King, William Franklin's Black, to return to his master, were very different from the 'dregs' of time and social place, but its 'elite'. The polluted propaganda and fraudulent misrepresentations that formally accused only the commonly designated lower classes of women of 'strange partiality shewn for' the Black is a complete and absolute fiction (Shyllon,1977:105). To this, one must also add O *tempora! O mores!*

Yet more virulent a racist than Edward Long – albeit anything but a fresh injection of originality –was Philip Thicknesse, who had lived in the English colony of Georgia for some years and then moved on to Jamaica for a few years' isolated warfare against the Black insurgents who had taken to the mountains. This encounter seems to have left him with a hostility towards Black people more violent still than his infamous hostility towards men midwives. He incorporated into the second impression (1778) of his book, *A Year's Journey through France and Part of Spain*, an unexpurgated chapter on his bête noire. Black people were:

> In every respect, men of a lower order, and so made by the Creator of all things ... Their face is scarce what we call human, their legs without any inner calf, and their broad flat foot, and long toes (which they can use as well as we do our fingers) have much the resemblance of the Orang Outang, or Jocko [i.e., chimpanzee], and other quadrupeds of their own climates. As to their intellects, not one was ever born with solid sense; yet all have a degree of monkey cunning, and even monkey mischief, which often stands them in better stead than sense. They are

in nature cruel, to the highest degree ... The frequent marriages of these men here with white women, and the succession of black, brown, and whity-brown people, produced by these very unnatural (for unnatural they are) alliances, have been better observed in France, than in this once country of greater liberty ... I laugh when I hear ... talk of the fidelity of those people. I never yet knew one who was not at bottom a villain ... They are a bad and gloomy-minded revengeful people, and in the course of a few centuries, they will over-run this country with a race of men of the very worst sort under heaven ... London abounds with an incredible number of these black men, who have clubs to support those who are out of place and [in] every country town, nay in almost every village are to be seen a little race of mulattoes, mischievous as monkeys and infinitely more dangerous ... A mixture of negro blood with the natives of this country is big with great and mighty mischief, and ... if they are to live among us, they ought by some very severe law to be compelled to marry only among themselves, and to have no criminal intercourse whatever with people of other complexions. There is not on earth so mischievous and vicious an animal as a mule, nor in my humble opinion, a worse race of men than the negroes of Africa (Fryer,1984:162-163).

This ungracious, unfounded and curmudgeonly invective comes across like an overblown and hyper-accentuated Long in scale and manner, whom Thicknesse had undoubtedly read and who (on the authority of Shyllon) perhaps was the 'Lover of Blacks' who commented with such serious inconsistency in the *World* newspaper three days before Wilberforce's due date to take his first Commons formal action against the slave trade.

The written address comprised a gloom-ridden prediction of what would transpire in Britain presupposing that the slaves in the West Indies were set at their liberty. Once ensconced in plantation ownership, they would conceivably live in Britain as 'a new tribe of West-India Planters' and many into the nobility: 'The breed of the inhabitants would be improved by the cross ... The British Ladies' noses ... would get a truss up ... It would save the expence of frizzing their hair, for their hair would friz of itself'. By then, Blacks in England had to some extent envisaged their future glory: 'Witness the great and tremendous tails they have affixed to their curly pashes [i.e., heads] ... This degree of vanity ... may be pardoned, considering the benefit that will arise from this ostensible method of shewing their parts; and how much sooner it will attract the notice of the Fair Sex, who are ever partial to parts and abilities'. One benefit of the 'blending of the breeds' would be 'the graceful air that the young bucks, our grandchildren, of the mixed breed, will have, in walking in St. James's and Bond-Streets; - the cross will give them the appearance of a swivel in the backside, or a circuitous motion of the podex' (Fryer,1984:163).

Taking this into account, including the strained sexual innuendo, it is representative of the strongly critical approach of the times, as is the thought-provoking and grudging practice that 'Civis', in the Morning Chronicle, had of disclaiming Black literary achievement: 'If I were to allow some share of merit to Gustavus Vasa, Ignatius Sancho, &c., it would not prove equality more than a pig, having been taught to fetch a cord, letters, &c. would shew it not to be a pig, but some other animal' (Fryer,1984:163).

Up to and including the 1790s, the frowned-upon prospect of intermarriage had become a major consuming concern with the proponents of racism. Black men taking the hand of a White woman in marriage formed the basis of Anglo-Saxon racism (Shyllon,1977). No particular concerns were raised towards the Englishman's propensity in Africa to proceed in raping and ravishing African women and girls, but when, in England, the Black man began taking White women through the process of courtship then marriage, an extraordinary level of sexual and social tension was aired. A glaring example of the perverse contradiction in White male cognitive systems of thought, that of his own volition enters the body of the Black women, and by the same token believes that his social order is going down the pan when the Black man takes the White women. It is fundamentally quite shocking and highly cheerless indeed that such aesthetic and functional human behaviour as coition, the process by which two human beings become one, either for the joy of bringing forth new life or as an affinity of love, affection, and a shared mortality, should have been and remains the source of so much pain, sadness, wickedness, and the vicious assault upon human life, particularly in the parallel universe that is the Anglo-Saxon kingdom (Shyllon,1977:3).

For the commercial agent John Scattergood, it was 'madness' to unleash Blacks to the freedoms of Europeans 'and treat them as our equals'. Were slavery abolished, 'the Negroes from all parts of the world will flock hither, mix with the natives, spoil the breed of our people, increase the number of crimes and criminals, and make Britain the sink of all the earth, for mongrels, vagrants, and vagabonds'. If Britain exercised wisdom, Scattergood added, she should exclude black people from her environs 'while it is yet in her power to hinder their migration hither' (Fryer,1984:164).

Edward Long, Philip Thicknesse and fellow exponents were not unrepresentative of their time and place and no innate tendency to paper over an uncomfortable subject can mask this phenomenon (Shyllon,1977). Nineteenth-century Britain's intellectual and scientific community were pretty much all convinced that only northern European people possessed the faculty for thinking and social organization, so much that the likes of distinguished ethnologist James Cowles Prichard, humanitarian and monogenist as so it appeared, decisively claimed a link extending across from the 'physical character' of West Africans and their 'moral condition' (Fryer,1984:169). The shared experience of either intellectual or informal contact with the most unjust fabrications and withering contempt concerning their race gave rise to that group affinity and group cohesion among Blacks which Sir John Fielding so greatly vilified (Shyllon,1977). The unavoidable truth is that racism stretches back as a way of life to when the first Blacks raised a profile in Britain. Scientific thought took race superiority and inferiority for granted until the twentieth century was well underway. The matter that lies unstated is that, when the influx of Blacks into England had risen and grown substantially, men were advancing the same measures as today to counteract the Black danger signs. Back then, as currently, the government was lobbied to put an end to further immigration, or more specifically, further inward flows of Blacks into the political unit.

Back then, and current in the 1970s, as can be traced to Powellism, the government was lobbied to introduce financial incentives to repatriate the Blacks already here, and restrict the inward pull into the country of those who remained outside (Shyllon,1977; Layton-Henry,1984). And in two instances during the scale of time, in 1596 and in 1786, Blacks were apparently removed from the country. Back then, as currently, it was assumed that Blacks were occupying stations which, by heritage, should be occupied by the indigenous population. Back then, as currently, the numbers game was engaged in. Back then, as currently, Blacks could not bear children in the absence of censure. Suffer the fledgling newborn to come unto me ... so long as they are White. Back then, though only privately today, the prospect of interracial union was raised (Shyllon,1977). Back then, as currently, White society has been hostile to Black aspiration. Back then, as currently, race matters. It has only been 60 or 70 years since racism lost intellectual credibility.

Conclusion

This Chapter deals with racial arrogance on a mammoth scale and at its most bitterly hostile and one can be forgiven for thinking that it was not the best or most comfortable of reading experiences. Nineteenth-century English racism depicts White Europeans at the top of the social and evolutionary scale and the African at the bottom. At the turn of the nineteenth century, White English people thought they were the top race (Fryer,1984). It is one thing to play host to firmly established ideas of uncompromising barbed critique of the African and people of colour, and quite another thing to judge favourably in the case of White people because one is biased, and not escape the charge of racism levelled squarely in the direction of White people who entertain such wholly unpleasant and destructive ideas. The social ill that is racism has devoured all traces of decency that remain of the mindset of Western man. The major destructive pest that is racism continues inexorably to undermine the vitals of the British island kingdom.

The justification of slavery and the slave trade was English racism's prime motive while the desire for dominance, control and imperial expansion was another. The low pitch and depths to which these writers plummet is truly devastating, not to mention totally racist and unsound. There is no length to which they do not traverse and moral principles go right out of the window in the vicious campaign, which does not even hesitate at criticizing the hot tropical climate of the life-giving sun of the African continent, over which the Africans have no mastery and which must surely be preferable to the inclement British weather. This just illustrates the great premium attached to racism by this venal breed of men. It also illustrates the grounding in history we should all have, so that this complete and utter stuff and nonsense and opprobrious slanders can be deflected and cast aside and consigned, once and for all, to the proverbial garbage receptacle.

However, this is precisely the point because extending far beyond the dissolution of the material conditions that ab initio gave rise to racist thought, these drowned ideas began to emerge to awareness again in the minds of those in contemporary times. The product or consequence was the engagement in various different kinds of racist practices on the part of a significant proportion of White people in Britain, subsuming White people in positions of authority. This chapter has a special place in the context of this book because racist ideology, peddled by the above advocates, not only influenced and shaped the life experiences of those in its immediate trajectory but also has an outstanding place in the lives of Black and minority ethnic people in Britain who have been, to a massive and substantial extent, poisoned over the last say 400 odd years. The broad categories under which nineteenth-century English racism can be summarized are Anglo-Saxonism, vulgar racism, anthropology, phrenology, trusteeship, social Darwinism, evolutionism and teleology (Fryer,1984:170). In the next chapter, we shall look at the role and function of the media in the lives and lived experiences of Black and minority ethnic people and as a provider of services and an employer. Pretty much all the work on English racism lacked originality and completeness and was selective information about the African that was not lost on the British public. Samuel Estwick's portrayal of Africans as morally depraved is much akin to the pot calling the kettle black. Hume's diatribe warrants that, oblivious to the facts, he dismissed the Benin Bronzes, the golden stool of the Asantehene, the Ife terracottas, the wonders of Zimbabwe, the precious artefacts of Tutankhamun, Black music, et cetera, et cetera (Shyllon,1977:199).

The malfeasance and graspingness of racists is, at times, too unacceptable for words. It is vital to recognize that racist ideology is page after page of high-flown unmitigated fictional storytelling or unabashed and slanderous lies in order to perpetuate the belief in racial superiority and racial inferiority. If White people believe that black lice litter the bodies of Black people then they will believe anything. Indeed, these writers do not seem to credit White people with the sense they were born with, and it is clear that in this vicious campaign against Africans, anything goes. Black people should be aware that race prejudice is insanity of sorts. The proponents of English racism can hardly bang on about Africans eating meat almost raw when even today, the British dine on meat in a similar fashion, that is lightly cooked or rare. To equate Africans with animals, reference was made to talons rather than hands, but, like Whites, Blacks are human beings too. Racists are irrational charlatans who fail to face reality, want others to do likewise, and are so warped and twisted that they would not know the truth even if it approached them and launched a scathing paroxysm against their integrity.

The exponents of English racism turn the tables on the victim making it seem as though Blacks are the miscreants and this is the distinguishing feature of those who oppose the African diaspora. Yet truth, compassion, rationality and humanity have never been the makings of a successful demagogue. By targeting popular desires and prejudices in man, however, the proponents of racial superiority and Whiteness carry the day.

Constant reference to miscegenation is the racist's bugbear of that and this age, yet it is essentially the White man's 'crime' (Shyllon,1977). There is nothing like miscegenation that so triggers indecent and crude emotions among Whites towards Black men as this morbid folly. What is menacing to know is that race prejudice destroys all feelings for humanity and corrupts absolutely the group members concerned, an example of which will be seen in the final chapter. There is no escaping nor avoiding the fact that racist ideology is mendacious propaganda and an exercise in denigrating, dehumanising and demonizing the African and people of colour, the consequences of which are still being felt today.

In a widely recognized passage in *Commerce of the Human Species*, Clarkson put Hume in the picture that, in subservience, the African race had brought forth Phillis Wheatley and Ignatius Sancho: 'If the minds of the African were unbroken by slavery, if they had the same expectations in life as other people, and the same opportunities for improvement, either in the colonies or upon the coast, they would be equal, in all the various branches of science, to the Europeans, and that the argument that states them "to be an inferior link of the chain of nature and designed for servitude", as far it depends on the inferiority of their capacities, is wholly malevolent and false' (Shyllon,1977:199).

Clarkson felt that it was not necessary to address Hume's assertions in relation to African capability. He left the matter on a quiet note, as they had been so elegantly overturned by the erudite Dr Beattie in his 'Essay on Truth'. Beattie concluded his much-vaunted artistic creation in 1767. Destroying the central pillar of Hume's racist ideology, he offered these words:

> It will be readily allowed that the condition of a slave is not favourable to genius of any kind; and yet the black slaves dispersed over Europe have often discovered symptoms of ingenuity, notwithstanding their unhappy circumstances. They become excellent handicraftsmen and practical musicians ... That a Black slave, who can neither read nor write, nor speak any European language, who is not permitted to do anything but what his master commands, who has not a single friend on earth, but is universally considered and treated as if he were a species

Chapter 5: The Function and Rise of English Racism

inferior to the human; that such a creature should so distinguish himself among Europeans, as to be talked of through the world for a man of genius, is surely no reasonable expectation. To suppose him of an inferior species, because he does not thus distinguish himself, is just as rational, as to suppose any private European of an inferior species, because he has not raised himself to the condition of royalty (Shyllon,1977:200).

The stimulus for this chapter emerged out of a reading of Goodhart (2013) who, in his book *The British Dream*, asserted that 'people had been encouraged to feel that they were superior to colonial people, albeit in a decent, Christian way' (p.139). This statement moved me to respond to this emotive topic which I thought worthy of investigation as something so central to the Black experience and its linkage with Black aspiration. Firstly, here, Goodhart (2013) is seen as an apologist for the British general public who largely hold misleading and distorted beliefs about Black and minority ethnic people. Moreover, it illustrates, secondly, that he is unaffected by racism because these ideas, however 'decent' or 'Christian', are anything but innocuous and have consequences for Black people and those of colour. Thirdly, Britain is not the Christian country it once was, and in fact, Christianity gave its approbation to slavery and the slave trade, and Christian people can reflect negative approval, therefore, the way in which the British public hold these views can be questioned. Fourthly, it shows that Goodhart (2013) will go to almost any length to defend the British public and is, indeed, not so much a truth-seeker but in it to fight the British corner. The above instance was not the only occasion on which he was seen to be championing the British cause and seemed bent on showing the British in a good light.

Reni Eddo-Lodge (2017) wrote about her frustration with how discussions on race and racism were being led by those who could not share the experience of racism themselves, and Goodhart's (2013) book echoes Eddo-Lodge's frustration. How does this apply to me and black aspiration generally? I emerged from a background where I was aware of racial superiority and inferiority but did not know whether such beliefs were valid or not. In fact, I railed inwardly and sometimes outwardly against such a proposal as I was growing up in my teenage years. This was a constant source of frustration and I suspected that Black inferiority was a falsehood. And, for example, in my school years, I found it difficult to make friends because of these conflicting ideas and wondered whether I was inferior to my White peers, and this extra psychological obstruction played havoc, undermining and inhibiting academic growth and development, and somewhere along the line, affected academic performance levels because of the constant mein kampf of whether I could succeed against the odds. This was compounded by racism at school and racism outside the school gates.

White students do not have this cross to bear and kind of obstruction that needs to be shrugged off and start more or less from a *tabula rasa* blank page, as it were, with few if any cares and a position from which it is easier to apply themselves. It is accordingly more of an achievement than the norm when a Black individual succeeds because s/he has had to overcome seemingly insurmountable barriers along the way. South Asians tend to succeed because they apply themselves and their stereotype is much more positive and they tend to be given positive response bias from their teachers that feeds into their collective reputations. Alternatively, Black kids are seen as a potential source of trouble rather than a possible five A* GCSE success. However, there are exceptions to the South Asian model I put forward; Shirin Housee's (2018) ethnocentric experience of schooling is a prime example. Even though racist ideology applies to South Asian students, their families tend to support them through difficult periods and give them every encouragement in the teeth of racist beliefs and practices. The long and the short of it is, ethnographic studies suggest that Black aspiration faces a battle that is entrenched and reflected in the society in which we live and is a deep uphill struggle that shapes and affects teacher-pupil relationships. (Wright,1987; Mac an Ghaill,1988; Wright,1992; Gillborn,1990; Sewell,1997).

During my school career, I was approached by a teacher who invaded my personal space and said, 'you can do it'. I walked away interpreting this to mean I can do anything I put my mind to, but it was not until I went to

Chapter 5: The Function and Rise of English Racism

university that I found out definitively the truth behind the shameless lie of superior and inferior 'races', spelling out the importance of Black History being taught in British schools. In this chapter, we have, firstly, forged an account of the function of English racism, secondly, touched on the significance of Powellism, and, finally outlined and debunked racist ideology or traditional myths and legends which currently have a life and are constantly being renewed in the minds of White British people, and are thus central and apposite to the experience of Black and South Asian communities. The importance of teaching Black History in British schools is that it gives students of colour an opportunity to advance in life less petulant and less surprised about widely held but false notions and present-day realities, which shape and influence the daily experience of Black people emerging to life's journey. Racist ideology can be seen as the corruption of public morals or the application of inaccurate, specious and propagandist material of the vituperative kind and typography, in the sense that this pertains to Black and minority ethnic people.

Originating at the historical reference point, racism presents itself initially as an unqualified scientific error (Fryer,1988). The actual concept of 'race' is an anachronism from the early history of the biological sciences. Geneticists and anthropologists, on the occasion when they are considering the differences in human physical characteristics, scrap the use of this archaic concept. They have abandoned it. They no longer continue to divide Homo sapiens sapiens House's into 'races' on the shallow basis of skin complexion or any other variation of sorts. They currently accept that the so-called 'races' only represent temporary compositions of genetic materials that are relative to all humankind. They currently accept that there is no scientific reason for dividing people into immutable biological categories called 'races' or for asserting that each of these categories possesses inborn, immutable cultural traits. They currently accept that physical differences can scarcely reflect underlying and salient intellectual differences and that it is misconceived to presume that they do (Fryer,1988).

However, these misconceptions are not only scientific errors. Constituting some 400 odd years, racism has conveyed a specific social function. The aforementioned phenomenon functioned as an ideology: a set of false ideas rationalising the exploitation and regulation of people with an identifiable degree of melanin in their pigmentation by people whose melanocytes are less active. The mental impression of 'race', removed from the lexicon of scientists, survives in familiar conversation as a political system: a system that helps to adjudicate who has dominion over whom. The attribution of individuals to ethnic groups is a political function. Racial markers are political weapons through which a dominant group can impose upon the subject group the spectre of subjection (Fryer,1988).

The fear that assumes that anything not operating for White homogeneity exists solely to expunge it, is a one-sided and ideological affair conveniently discounting and overlooking the fact that the world is seen through a White lens and exists, partially at least, to expunge Black and minority ethnic groups from parts of the British narrative and this finding is not the self-indulgent luxury of a fear but is reality (Olusoga,2016). It explains why Powell received the media attention he sought and is a fear born of paranoia. Black people can countenance pro-Black causes and be in a mixed-race relationship, as so many Blacks are and still have freedom, justice, and equality as priorities indivisible from love, emotional warmth and the quest to promote human welfare. Moreover, what this 'if you're not with us you're against us' White fear fails to perceive is that White homogeneity is part of the problem and as for a solution, from a White perspective, things can just as well stay as they are. White society shows a great reluctance to adopt change as the 'if it ain't broke, why fix it' syndrome applies, even though ultimately, society is broken and does need fixing. The problem is that White society is busy having it all its own way, yet, is still not satisfied, and enmeshed herein, Black and minority ethnic groups incur consequences and interact with these consequences from the social and economic bottom of the pile.

Finally, tethered to this fear is a myopic attitude that is in denial of growing inequality which essentially emerges as an epiphenomenon of Whites looking out for one another's interests and that inequality ineluctably may have to be approached from a counterpoint perspective involving, above all else, atonement. To bring things into sharp focus, it is important to note that exponents of English racism used their education to justify exploitative ends, regardless of the facts, making them seem impercipient, impervious and blind to understanding, judgement, or perception and is why Equiano is known to have exclaimed, "Oh, fool" when the African character and reputation was called into question. Ultimately, White people carry less melanin in their melanocytes, which is why their pigmentation is White, and so, the above advocates were not only justifying the purview of English racism but also can be seen to reflect White rage and even White men's jealousy, since White women tend to be drawn towards Black men and vice versa (Perry,2015:119).

Chapter 6: 'Draft' FAO Editor for Sociology

The influence of the media industry

If, according to McLuhan (1964) 'the medium is the message', then information and content are the tell-tale signs of journalistic commentary which coincides with journalists' thought-pattern frames concerning news values (p.287). But isn't the devil in the detail, because journalists seem not only to be extending the command of the English language in an insider group versus outsider group approach, but also, appear to be projecting on popular opinion the underlying idea that the English language, as an extension of the British body politic, or paraphrased interpretations of some functional part of them into diverse materials, should perpetually reflect indigenous prejudices, fears, and suspicions as a general rule of thumb when it comes to announcing news items about and concerning Black and minority ethnic people? Press power to practise dogma or, for that matter, discrimination against powerless minorities is in the very character of ownership and control of the English language and this group of professionals also owns and controls the mode of 'mental production' (Hall et al,2013:62).

In this chapter, our attention will be drawn to the role of the media in relation to Black and minority ethnic groups where, at first, the locus of concern concentrates on the lack of impartiality, objectivity and balance in media representations and how the media reproduce, amidst their seamless web of tensions, the exegesis of the notorious, of the dominant ideology. As a subordinate sphere of activity, in this chapter, I shall research the media as an employer and in its provision of a service. Thirdly, this account attempts to shed light on why newspaper coverage happens to be racist in so far as championing and perpetuating an unequal conjuncture in which people of colour are, in every respect, framed as second-class citizens, looking at the composition of the vested and controlling interests of the British press and what this means for the viewpoints offered by the newspapers, and at the material detail and framework of preponderant news values. Finally, it directs itself towards pointing out the infrastructure through which press racism can be disputed and focuses on ways in which media professionals have challenged the recurrent racism for which they exchange currency at their newsagents or of which they take doorstep delivery every morning.

Although the media can be seen to 'create' the news and can be seen to transmit ruling-class ideas, a conspiracy is not the founding cornerstone upon which it rests, though the following spokesmen seem to suggest otherwise (Hall et al,2013:62). "A newspaper," Lenin once revealed, "is not only a collective propagandist and collective agitator; it is also a collective organiser." Stalin touted it as "the most powerful weapon of our Party". For Khrushchev, it was "our chief ideological weapon" (Mcluhan,1964:232). It is no coincidence that each proponent emphasizes how powerful an influence the press is on public opinion. Indeed, the newspapers can be used for good or ill but some cannot bring themselves to accept that public organs of communication could be used with iniquitous intent. Hard though it may be for some to imagine, yet the unimaginable moral low point not only has its place but is frequently visited by the British press. Instead of discharging the functional capacity in the interest of the greatest good for the greatest number, newspapers act in the functional capacity of corrupting the greatest number (Mcluhan,1964:226). The media finds itself in a crucial position and in a crucial role in the public depiction of racialised inequalities and the renewed impetus of 'race hate' (Bhavnani et al,2005:37. For example, an important piece of research conducted in the 1970s illustrated how Black youth came to be criminalised in the media hyperbole surrounding 'mugging' (Hall et al,2013).

The media function in a key capacity within Britain's Establishment. Through directing their object at those in the lower stratum – often with coverage resting on distortions, myths and downright lies – they deflect critical attention away from the wealthy and powerful upper echelons at the apex of society. In no part whatever can this be seen as a surprise, given that those who own and control are themselves bound up with that elite, systematically given over to the maintenance of the status quo. Considering the way in which and who calls the tune, much of contemporary British media serves as an extremely robust champion with the cares and concerns of the rich and powerful at its heart (Jones,2015:88).

Such is the influence of the media that elections are almost won and lost at the behest of media campaigns against their opponents. Also, the media can make or break political careers. According to Jones (2015), there is no such thing as a free press in Britain: there is a press independent of direct government intervention, which is an entirely different thing. Alternatively, more so than not, the mainstream media is run by a very tiny minority of politically motivated proprietors, whose stranglehold over the media is one of the most consummate and devastatingly effective forms of actual polemical power and significant impact on public opinion in modern Britain. McLuhan (1964) puts it thus: 'Today's press agent regards the newspaper as a ventriloquist does his dummy. He can make it say what he wants. He looks on it as a painter does his palette and tubes of pigment; from the endless resources of available events, an endless variety of managed mosaic effects can be attained' (p.230-231). The vocabulary of received political debate is dispassionately enforced, especially by the tabloid print media; those who fly in the face of them can face the cleansing power of publicity. The media, expressed in a different way, is a support mechanism of the Establishment – despite however unpalatable a truth this may seem to many journalists (Jones,2015).

During World War II, the U.S.O. sent bespoke issues of the leading American magazines to the military services, without the ads being inserted. The men stipulated that the ads should be brought back, as perhaps one would expect, because the ads are by far the best aspect of magazines and newspapers generally. More care and attention, more wit and skill go into the construction of an ad than into each and every literary form of magazine or press. Ads are current affairs. The matter that is amiss with them is that they tend always to be good news. With a view to counterbalance the effect and to promote good news, it is *sine qua non* to have a significant amount of bad news. Also, the newspaper is itself a hot medium. It includes bad news in its battery in the interest of intensity and reader engagement. Real news happens to be bad news and as every newspaper from the onset of print can confirm, inundations, infernos and other communal catastrophes by land and sea and air outflank any kind of individual calamity or villainy as news. Ads, in striking difference, have to shout their happy message from the rooftops in order to compete with the penetrating influence of bad news (Mcluhan,1964).

The BBC is a favourable conveyance for the Establishment for it privileges the free-market social system to be presented as a detached, apolitical standpoint. Now a divergence from this would be seen as *parti pris* and needing to be resisted to preserve objectivity. '99 per cent of business coverage on the BBC has the subtext that "business is good",' opines the former BBC journalist speaking unofficially. 'They say "capitalism is good, capitalism is dynamic, the free market is delivering, it is making better lives for the people of the Global South". If you argue, "capitalism is bad, capitalism is not delivering, capitalism is ruining the lives of the Global South", that's read as ideological. In order to present a balanced view, both ideas should be recognized with equal vigour, but the BBC don't, as these are the wishes and desires of the elite (Jones,2015:120).

The right's inexorable criticism of the BBC for 'left-wing bias' is a canny pre-emptive strategy: it allows them to govern the material content outflow of the BBC. The *Daily Mail* is an especially vociferous critic having even accused the perennial TV series Sherlock of presenting 'more evidence for the BBC's 'left-wing bias' (Jones,2015:120). In February 2014, Conservative cabinet minister Chris Grayling indicated that the BBC was overrun by a 'left-leaning, metropolitan group of people who are disproportionately represented there' (Jones,2015:120). This mires the corporation in ever-present trepidation of providing material information of left-wing bias. On the occasion that the BBC stages the opportunity for more critical journalism, intimates the former BBC journalist, corporation managers seem to think 'they have to atone for it' with programming that produces the opposite effect (Jones2015:120). Aware of the pitfalls concerning matters such as immigration, BBC senior officials are psychologically unwilling to approach them through the optical lens of economic unease like declining wage values and a shortage of jobs. The hierarchical system of the BBC helps see to it that everybody plays by the rules. For the purposes of securing career progression, a journalist has to establish a friendship with his or her superior who can defend their interests in the event of something going wrong, and promote them on the occasion when things go right.

Moreover, the BBC has been inclined to report certain key events – events very much involving communal concern – with a very light brush stroke approach. At the time when the Conservative-led administration took office in 2010, it began a planned privatization of the NHS that had scarcely been put before the British public throughout the election campaign – the Conservative power-seeking pledge had stepped out of its comfort zone to stress its allegiance to the NHS. Yet it was almost beyond the leap of public imagination to learn about this privatization policy procedure by watching BBC news broadcasts because it scarcely bore a mention in them. At the time when the legislation was being approved by parliamentary officials in 2012, it received bottom basement coverage. At the time when it was finally enacted, news bulletins revealed 'Bill which Gives Power to GPs Passes' – a government slant on the legislation vehemently disputed by organizations acting on behalf of NHS workers, subsuming the British Medical Association that covers for GPs themselves (Jones,2015:121). Uniformly, cuts were ordinarily being defined as the sanitized 'savings'. Considering that the government restructured a well-loved national institution and thought little of whether they were treading on the public's toes beforehand, the BBC functioned akin to its press office.

The BBC reflects Establishment opinion equally on national and foreign matters alike. In January 2009, it refused to give air time to a petition by the Disasters Emergency Committee to raise funds for the benefit of those affected by Israel's armed takeover of Gaza. This specific gesture ran 'the risk of reducing public confidence in the BBC's impartiality', asserted the then Director-General, Mark Thompson (Jones,2015:121). The gesture caused general outrage, apparently accentuating a clear pro-Israeli one-sidedness in BBC coverage. At the time when some BBC journalists asked Thompson if they could individually sign up to a declaration in support of the DEC cause, they were told that going against the grain of the 'machinery of representation' would mean the corporation would no longer require their services.

Research with no axe to grind highlights the degree to which the BBC reiterates the outlook of the status quo. An exposition carried out by Cardiff University academics, published in 2013, looked closely at the BBC's coverage of a wide spectrum of issues. Their conclusions indicated an unsurprising bias in favour of the presiding government in office. But while appearances by Gordon Brown outflanked David Cameron in 2007 by no more than two to one, David Cameron outflanked Ed Miliband on news reports in 2012 by almost four to one. Also extant was a similar contrast in ratios extending across from Conservative and Labour ministers in 2007 and 2012. The exposition could also claim that the discursive struggle over the European Union was structured and dominated by those at variance with it, with few advocates in league with its defence. Business agents appeared on the BBC substantially more frequently than they did on advertisement-revenue-funded ITV news. In 2012, business agents outnumbered trade union agents on the BBC's News at six by upwards of nineteen to one, a striking amplification from five to one in 2007. Exponents from Britain's business capital – such as hedge-fund managers and stockbrokers – reigned supreme over coverage of the 2008 credit crunch and subsequent extended financial assistance to the banks. The BBC, to use few words, is an exit point that is firmly pro-business, biased in favour of right-wing adherents, and is a supporter of all those who wish to express Establishment perspectives (Jones,2015).

Impercipience occurs precisely when the focus is on the program "content" of our media while casting aside the form, whether it be the wireless, print or indeed, the English language (Mcluhan,1964:226). Because the press is a mosaic form, videlicet, it does not take a detached "point of view", and participation in process is precisely why it is so useful and conducive to democratic government and the defence and continuity of a social order of unequal power relations where Black and minority ethnic groups, are, on multidimensional levels, subordinated. Elsewhere, McLuhan (1964) details mosaic to mean, 'it is made into a communal image or cross-section' (Mcluhan,1964:230). Hardly ever has the media been known to adumbrate politico-social activities designed to combat racism and xenophobia (Bhavnani et al,2005), for the sham or bogus character has always pervaded the media, not only those of recent times (Mcluhan,1964). The proprietors of media consistently endeavour to avail the public of what it wishes for because they suspect that their good offices are in the medium rather than in the message or the agenda. The uniform demands of the academic community – that the newspaper plies its mosaic form to advance a definite point of view on a one-sided platform agenda – represent a failure to perceive the form of the press in any way whatever.

In Britain and across the Atlantic, research shows sharply defined underrepresentation and stereotypical portrayal in entertainment genres, unfavourable and problem-directed characterisation within factual and news discourse, and a tendency to set aside structural inequalities and perceived racism experienced by minority ethnic groups in both (Bhavnani et al,2005). A then CRE investigative inquiry into stereotyping in the media (1998) discovered that White respondents felt that Black and minority ethnic communities were soaking up resources - housing, education, health provision - which 'rightly' was the preserve of White people. Subordinate groups apprehended with the mind through the senses that the media profiled them in finite ways, as unidimensional characters or as problems, given to being pictured as criminals, drug traffickers and so on. A study of the 10 most popular programmes provided by each of the five major channels looked closely at the portrayal of minorities and found that there was a shortfall of minorities from TV drama serials and standard leisure programmes such as horticulture, culinary cuisine activity and other lifestyle pursuits. The viewing public from minority groups bleated about tokenism, stereotyping and an easy approach to encapsulate their communities (Bhavnani et al,2005)

The methods used to portray Muslims in the media have also undergone some scrutiny by Poole (2000) in Bhavnani et al (2005). Poole noticed that over a period of three years from 1993-1996 (before 9/11), Muslims were singled out as a liability to security owing to their ostensible participation in 'deviant' activities. The public face of Muslims was also held up as a liability to British core values, arousing concerns of the challenges they faced to integrate. Occurrent also were additional divisive representations of existing in and inseparable from cultural differences extending across from Muslims and non-Muslims in the UK which then led to problems in communication between people.

Needless to say, these views are not uniformly expressed. To illustrate the point at issue, young White people saw it as divisive to have distinct television programmes on different ethnicities, while some members of racialized groups stated a preference to be more differentiated as concerns their ethnicity (Bhavnani et al,2005).

British newspaper sales have fallen partly because the city of Liverpool rejected *The Sun* after it disseminated police lies about the context in which ninety-six football supporters of Liverpool FC perished in the Hillsborough catastrophe of April 1989: various Liverpool newsagents continue to boycott *The Sun*, and its latest circulation in the city is merely a quarter of the

55,000 print types it sold successively prior to the disaster (Jones,2015). However, Britain's love of the newspaper is significant and noteworthy as only Japan nudges it into second place in the ratings of newspapers purchased per head of population, and the popular tabloids chiefly target the working-classes, whereas the so-called 'quality' broadsheets are produced with professionals and business people in mind (Gordon and Rosenberg,1989). The argument could be put forward that the preconceived view of the established media is increasingly less important as newspaper sales decline, social media becomes more and more prevalent, and people access news from an ever-broader range of online sources (Jones,2015). However, the downward slide of the British press would tend to signify even less close attention being paid to elite groups at the vanguard of society. In this section, I aim to show the role of the media against Black and minority ethnic groups and how the media reproduce the mainstream ideology.

Among the issues of the day that have been taken up by the British press, few have come under the power of the press to influence and affect thinking as much as the subject of 'race' (Gordon and Rosenberg,1989). By far, the press has been responsible for drawing up a lineal account of the ontology of the 'race problem' in this sceptred isle. If, at this juncture, we take a detour to give somewhat of a potted history of press antagonism and bias, the nature of the 'race problem' as defined by the British press will be sketched out and the campaign the press has waged against Black and South Asian people will become clear in terms of examining the root of where the popular press is coming from and where it might be heading. Recurrent and popular themes are a window through which the popular press can be viewed and can be seen to represent the production and reproduction of a culture and the British way of life.

Research from the 1970s into press coverage of race relations reveals how media images of minority groups consistently stressed ideas that minority groups caused trouble and occupied jobs and homes that would otherwise belong to White people. These studies have documented the fixation of the press with the issue of immigration and with the quantitative quality of non-white people either here or descending onto these shores. Such investigative inquiries have argued that alternatively, the media could have presented images of the chauvinism, discrimination and deprivation encountered by Black and minority ethnic people. These considerations, whether of specific conjunctures or more general constructs, have shown how the press has functioned in a predominantly negative role. At its most favourable, this has made light of or marginalised the essential problems Black and South Asian people face; at its least favourable, it has deteriorated and aggravated racist moral sense in Britain with a powerful combination of the stereotyping of Black and South Asian people, salacious imagery, scaremongering and scapegoating.

Early research is unstinting in showing the way in which the press has transmitted an overwhelming mental pabulum to African-Caribbean and South Asian people, that there is limited space for them here, that their profile proportion levels are not gratefully received, their contribution to social organisation or the public good is insignificant and their troubles and strife are of little importance. Moreover, they have illustrated how non-white people are substantively under-represented as workers across the newspaper industry (Gordon and Rosenberg,1989). According to a 2014 government *report*, 54 per cent of the top 100 media professionals attended a private school – this is given that domestically, only around 7 per cent of pupils receive a private education (Jones,2015). High-ranking non-white journalists are very thin on the ground, while women are also seriously under-represented. Jones (2015) ventures to explore why there are so few women journalists higher up the food chain but is silent on why African-Caribbean and South Asians are under-represented, which brings us back to the findings of earlier research above. Even when investigating the Establishment, Jones (2015) fails to shrug off his own apathy and indifference to establishing why non-white people are edged out of labour market positions simply because their face does not correlate.

We do know that broadcasting also suffers from an under-representation of minority groups and women. Union employment practices tend to conflict with the interests of minority groups. Such practices include 'word of mouth' recruitment, in-house advertisement of vacancies and the stipulation of unnecessary credentials. For instance, a Thames TV consultant, modernizing job opportunities for women, came across the demand for 'O'-level physics and maths for camera operators (Curran et al,1986). However, many of the White employees stationed on the job themselves did not have such credentials. Also, it is said that too few African-Caribbean and South Asian people apply for jobs and those that are taken on prove to be not professional enough.

The subtle nature of institutional racism is put in the shade and is under wraps compared to the daily dose of overt racism experienced in the news media, and is responsible for declining able non-white workers' positions in the communications sector. Marc Wadsworth (1986), in Curran et al (1986), believes that the greater employment of Black and South Asian people is essential to erasing the White media values which give the lie to the claim that we live in a multi-racial, multi-cultural society. This can be contrasted with Stuart Hall's (1986) assertion that, despite its many shortfalls and its loss of ground under pressure, scope for minority and marginalized perspectives have widened not narrowed following the emergence of Channel 4. While he stands firmly behind that judgment, he further adds the following: All the same, regularly and routinely, day in, day out in the press, evening in, evening out on television, week in, week out in the journals, we come across uniform categories, a uniform range of images, uniform systems of representation, a uniform set of presences and absences, emphasis and weaknesses, uniform explanatory frameworks, uniform pictures introducing meaning to uniform connections of association, uniform schemes and narratives, uniform links and smooth interconnected developments, tending to replicate and recreate a certain interpretation of Planet Earth in and amidst the endless 'diversity' of our monumental British media institutions, easily and gracefully to time everlasting (Hall, 1986: 11; cited in Curran et al,1986). What Hall (1986) goes on to say is that he was referring to 'bias'. He continues, however; the concept is hopelessly inadequate and, on many levels, misleading. It suggests intentional and wanton self-conscious bending of the guidelines. It goes without saying that a significant amount of intentional, conscious 'bending' carries through all the time. A further point that Hall (1986) makes is that he is certain that if everyone in the industry desisted from 'bending' it at the drop of a hat, the emphases and systematic 'absences' in the media would persist.

The overarching strategy endorsed in British newspapers is to portray Black and minority ethnic people as a social problem (Gordon and Rosenberg,1989). African-Caribbean and South Asian people are depicted as posing a Black peril threat to White society; this is seen through the prism of their immigration to UK shores and then, when ensconced here, seen as tantamount to a law and order problem. The achievement of this effect is derived from a number of options: through the striking presentation of news items involving banner headlines and clearly visible positioning, stirring or incriminating quotations and platitudes from people presented as establishment-type figures, popular stereotypes, reiteration of unreliable news items, and the creation and massage of popular fears to suit their purposes. Here we look at a number of instances of this kind of news reporting (Gordon and Rosenberg,1989).

Immigration

Black and South Asian immigration to Britain has invariably been conceptualized by the press as posing a problem for mainstream British society and exponents at odds with such immigration could invariably be granted extensive and sympathetic newspaper incorporation.

Powell's dystopian picture

The soliloquies and pronouncements of Enoch Powell have consistently been given extensive coverage ever since his principal maiden speech on the question in April 1968. On that occasion, Powell declared that Britain was 'heaping up its own funeral pyre' by sanctioning the immigration of large numbers of Black and minority ethnic people. 'Like the Roman,' he stated, 'I seem to see the River Tiber foaming with blood' (Gordon and

Rosenberg,1989:3). As part of this and subsequent speeches, Powell warned of grave racial conflict and struggle if the immigration of African-Caribbean and South Asian people was not halted and minority ethnic groups were not urged to vacate Britain. Although he had been banished to Northern Ireland, seated in relative political no-man's-land, Powell could always be assured of a sympathetic press newspaper inclusion for his stance on 'race'. In April 1983, for example, 15 years after his 1968 address, the *Sun* featured a major piece, 'was Enoch right?', juxtaposing what Powell had 'predicted' with what in real terms actually happened (12 April 1983; in Gordon and Rosenberg,1989). Before the month had passed, the *Sunday Express* covered a piece by Powell which cast doubt on the sagacity of sanctioning African-Caribbean and South Asian immigration to Britain (24 April 1983; in Gordon and Rosenberg,1989).

Two years on, in the slipstream of the Handsworth riots, Powell re-emerged to his topic of urging Black and minority ethnic people to vacate Britain, declaring that the government should offer financial incentives for people to leave. The *Daily Express* covered the speech verbatim, while *The Times* printed a substantial extract. Papers not already mentioned reported the speech on lead pages or fully: 'Enoch: Pay blacks to quit Britain' (*Sun*), 'Powell says it again: Send them home' (*Daily Mail*), 'Powell in race speech storm' (*Daily Express*), all 21 September 1985; in Gordon and Rosenberg, (1989:4). While the speech received a critical reception in editorials and other written pieces, the lineal opinions of this backbench MP continued to receive extensive publicity. Also, the *Daily Mail* (21 September 1985) argued in an editorial that the conflict with Powell was not that he could be termed racist, 'which he is not', but that his demands were 'impractical'. By the same token, the *Sunday Express* condemned Powell's accusers who called him a racist and argued that it was doubtless that Britain was in the throes of a 'race problem' which had been 'swept under the carpet' for 30 years (22 September 1985; in Gordon and Rosenberg,1989).

In 1988, two full decades on from his 1968 speech, Powell was once more given extensive publicity in a number of newspapers. In the Independent (19 April 1988), Andrew Gimson maintained that the British public owed Powell 'a great debt for starting to think about and deal with the matter of national identity' (Gordon and Rosenberg,1989:4). Contained within the pages of the *Daily Mail* (22 April 1988), George Gale asserted that Powell's fears were not without foundation: 'The debt the country owes him can never be paid sufficiently' (Gordon and Rosenberg,1989:4). Powell was allowed a platform in *The Times* to cast his mind back on his address of 20 years ago. Revisiting it, he was 'struck by its sobriety' (Gordon and Rosenberg,1989:4). He had not instigated hyperbole nor had he instigated a moral panic as concerns the impact of immigration on the 'indigenous population' (19 April 1988; in Gordon and Rosenberg,1989).

Practically every word Powell had to say on 'race' or immigration was allowed to be given extensive publicity. Nevertheless, the press was not duty-bound to treat Powell along such lines; they chose to. Powell had no reason to expect the kind of treatment he received at the hands of the communications industry, as he was neither a major public figure nor was he a government statesman of any kind. It was not as if, for over 20 years, he was a high-ranking MP of any great note and when the 20th anniversary of his 'rivers of blood' speech came round, he was not, as matters stand, an MP. Nor did Powell's views correspond with public perception. Instead, he assisted in creating an unyielding resolve of racist opinion. While Powell alleged to be forwarding perennial concerns of his Wolverhampton voters, the actual fact was that immigration and inter-racial activity were not political priority areas in Wolverhampton until Powell broached them in 1968. What also emerged is that none of the 'ordinary' men and women, whose conscious awareness of events and attitudinal viewpoints he claimed to be drawing on, could ever be found. Furthermore, Powell himself did not see it necessary to table the motion until 1967 (Gordon and Rosenberg,1989).

Therefore, how do we justify the way in which the print medium responded to Powell's utterances? A unidimensional interpretation is that Powell was submitting things with which certain newspapers sided – that the immigration of African-Caribbean and South Asian people was not only damaging for the geographic and political boundary but also detrimental. A further interpretation is that they considered his doomsday prophecies as having some existing in and inseparable from 'news' value. Whichever of the two given alternatives is the case, Powell was promoted to the rank position of a national aficionado on inter-racial affairs and the effect that the viewpoints he transmitted might have on African-Caribbean and South Asian people and on race relations was, for the most part, ignored. Thus, not unlike Powell, sections of the British press failed to represent a significant section of popular opinion on the subject of 'race' and immigration. They were pandering to escalating racist tension, to bring about respectability and to fashion a racist public standpoint. They were spearheading the way in setting out a general position where the country was framed as being under threat from without.

Law and Order

Similar to how the newspapers have portrayed African-Caribbean and South Asian people as an immigration problem, so too have they often pictured them as a problem of 'law and order' (Gordon and Rosenberg, 1989:13). Such has been the case since the mid-1970s. Crimes ostensibly involving minority ethnic groups have frequently been accorded disproportionate news story coverage and the reporting has often connoted that the behaviour of single minority ethnic people is typical of all minority ethnic people – a generalisation they would hold back from suggesting of White Brits. Moreover, some newspaper feature stories have indicated that minority ethnic people generally are disproportionately involved in specific types of crime. An unambiguous example of this kind of news media practice can be evinced through treatment of crime figures emanating from the Metropolitan Police in the 1970s.

In January 1975, the 'mugging' panic picked up where it had left off. An entirely new chapter of the cycle took its rise. Derek Humphry introduced his work on Black crime in South London with the desire that the details he spelled out again would not be used to fan prejudice (Hall et al,2013). However, this was a desperate desire. The fundamental problems beneath the crime statistics, as Humphry saw them – 'poverty, poor housing, lack of jobs and broken families' – were not as vividly striking or quotable as the truism that street crime in Lambeth 'had tripled in five years and 1974 was the worst on record' or that 'of 203 muggings' in Lewisham in 1974,' 172 were committed by Black youths (Hall et al,2013:324). While cautiously worded, the article did encourage selective quotation by electing the highly contentious question of 'crime' as its main thrust of entry and in its shortcoming to identify the institutionalised nature of the chauvinism on which 'the fundamental problems' rest. At all events, the article aroused hostility amongst Blacks themselves, in part because of the way in which it was broached, because when the *London Evening News* incorporated the earliest of its four-day 'spreads' regarding the subject, the rhetoric and tone were much less guarded, and the legitimations less cautiously drawn. The earliest, on 12 January, was sensational enough: 'The Violent Truth of Life in London' (Hall et al,2013:324). It began with a well-known juxtaposition: 'You are more likely to be mugged in Lambeth than in New York' (Hall et al,2013:324). A litany of latter-day incidents followed, with a shortened account of the *Sunday Times* numerical quantities. In all sincerity, the Evening News coverage did not wholly corroborate with their headlines. While John Blake's treatise, on 12 January, focused on 'frightened local residents', it cited certain local officials who were apprehensive not to 'frighten people' and regarded and identified together this and other associated pieces, gave much greater emphasis than almost all features in the preceding phase of the rotation to 'environmental' causes: 'no play, no holidays, no presents, youngsters get off to a bad start'; 'the growing sense of isolation felt by Blacks'; 'trapped between an education system that seems unable to understand their problems and a white society that seems to thrust humiliating identities upon them' (Hall et al,2013:324). This transposed form was not across the board. Considering that, and within the same time frame, the *Birmingham Evening Mail* picked the theme up again – including two front-page leads extending across from December 1974 and January 1975 – its generalised application of the 'mugging' epithet was inseparable from the 1972-3 form: 'bullies, muggers, vandals and exhibitionists have made the subways their own' (Hall et al,2013:324)

However, in another place, there had been a salient shift in the form of labelling. The until-now obscure storyline of Black crime had been simplified and sharply defined. Its racial marker was now obvious: victims were middle-aged Whites; assailants were Black; locations were identified provinces of South London. Punitive procedure questions which regulated the first debate were predominantly omitted; a social-problem standpoint was almost universally taken up (Hall et al,2013).

This change in emphasis and interpretation must be followed back to its origins. The matter that had precipitated the Humphry account was a special adumbration (never fully available to the hoi polloi) on street felony in South London, made ready by Scotland Yard and distributed to the Home Secretary. Regarded and identified together, the panic at the escalating statistics for Black felony, and the social problem, environmentalist interpretations of felony, appear in this adumbration, and in the following judicial comments made regarding it. The statistics which Humphry and others drew on from the report unmasked first, (a significant but hitherto unaccepted fact about the crime figures), that the police presently documented the 'race' of those transgressed against and transgressors in such incidents for 'operational reasons'; second, scary comparative statistics. These floated the idea that street felony was nearly as high in neighbouring South London districts as it was in Lewisham and Lambeth; that '80% of the attackers are Black and 85% of the victims are white'; that 'theft from the person' felonies had now surpassed the 1972 zenith and a salient majority of these were perpetrated by Blacks (Hall et al,2013:325). However, the report is also claimed to have maintained that 'it is not a policing problem; soaring street crime is caused by widespread alienation of West Indian youth from White society' (Hall et al, 2013:325). In addition, when Commander Marshall, then head of the Metropolitan Police Community Relations Department, passed judgement on the figures, he made a special effort to point to urban pressures such as high unemployment, the generation divide, problems of diaspora identity and the impact of 'black extremist voices' as inclusive factors (Hall et al,2013:325). Humphry affirmed that his interviews verified this line of reasoning: 'Nowadays, they reason that there aren't many jobs available and the blacks won't get them anyway' (a quote from a Peckham youth worker, Norris Richards; in Hall et al,2013:325). The matter that is significant about this is that two separate and apparently conflicting perspectives are being adopted at one and the same time: a police-crime-management standpoint and a social-problem standpoint. Whether the remainder of the press focused first on the sensational figures, few neglected to say that 'For the first time, the police have put the population, housing, school and employment statistics alongside their crime data' (Hall et al,2013:325). The application of this dual standpoint as set against the different emphases of the 1972-3 time frame will remain unexplored as it loses the focus of what I initially set out to show.

At this point, I intend to concentrate on how the riots of 1981 and 1985 were reported, paying particular attention to the political role of the media. The stark depiction of an inherent 'black lawlessness' dominated media features of Britain's urban unrest from Bristol in 1980 up to and including Toxteth, Brixton and other places in 1981, to the 1985 disturbances in Handsworth, Brixton and Tottenham (Gordon and Rosenberg, 1989). To give due parity to the press reports of these developments would require a tome or volume to itself, but here I follow some of the prevalent features of such coverage.

The Bristol Evening Post of Thursday, April 3, 1980, contained the opening-page headline 'Violence Rules in Nine Hours of Siege Terror' in addition to smaller headlines, 'Now 300 police in riots vigil' and 'They just went wild' (Cohen and Gardner,1982:16). The second was linked to an interview with the proprietor of a café and his brother following the police drugs raid which triggered the remonstration but the headline makes no mention of this. No reference is made to the ferocious police dogs deployed in the raid and the material detail that the counsel of the Community Liaison Officer went unheeded. The feature coverage is presented as if no such police harassment of the people in St Paul's took place. If it had taken pains to investigate, *The Post* would have been informed by local Black residents how a number of their clubs had been shut down and how they viewed the raid as another further assault on what meagre community resources they had.

Reports of 'horror'

In the central feature item, St Paul's is labelled 'the immigrant district', and in an oratorical staging, Bristol's police chief states that on reflection, he should have pressed more men into service on the raid, not the reverse. In keeping with such oratorical instances, he argues that he was not *au fait* with any tension extending across from police and local people and does not believe the fighting 'typical of the people of St Paul's. I am sure most of them would abhor what happened last night' (Cohen and Gardner, 1982:17). Contained within pages two and three, we behold the headlines 'War on The Streets', 'Counting The Cost of Mob Rule' and 'Residents Tell Of Riot Horror' (Cohen and Gardner,1982:17). Only one feature item was headed 'We knew This Would Happen – Resident' with black commercial traders and community leaders resolutely pointing the finger at police action, and a succinct feature informing us that the then CRE chairman, David Lane, was expected in Bristol to 'try to piece together the reasons for the explosion of violence' (Cohen and Gardner,1982:17).

The overarching impression conveyed of the 1981 Brixton disturbances was that of criminal young Black people intent on attacking the police and pillaging from shops (Gordon and Rosenberg,1989). *The Sun*, in the Saturday, April 11 edition, leads with a substantial headline 'BATTLE OF BRIXTON – 100 black youths in clash with the cops' (Gordon and Rosenberg,1989:18). Its central feature item commences 'A mob of 100 black youths battled with police in a London street last night' and contained within its conclusion 'Brixton, the heart of Britain's West Indian community, is known to its inhabitants as 'The Front Line'. It is notorious for muggings, assaults and murders' (Cohen and Gardner,1982:17). This chimes with the racist detritus that the *Sun* throws up one day on from the next. It takes great pleasure in abusing Black people by ascribing them to mindless 'mobs' who have a propensity for violence. *Sun* reporters only find themselves in areas like Brixton on the occasion when there is a sensational 'riots' story for them, and of course they would have no insight into what 'The Front Line' is truly about, and no reason why local residents should tell them. Just as certain as when the clock strikes the hour its bell-tolling mechanism is directly synchronized, so too should one ask, why liaise one day with press agents who will abuse one in the next daily round?

The *Sun* transported headlines equivalent to 'flames of hatred that swept the streets of London' (Gordon and Rosenberg,1989:18). In the same vein, the *Daily Star* banded the words 'FLAMES OF HATE' and 'the weekend of violence that woke Britain up to the burning hatred smouldering in our streets' (Gordon and Rosenberg,1989:18). Singing from the same hymn sheet, the *Daily Express* articulated the words 'Bloody hatred in the streets (all 13 April 1981; in Gordon and Rosenberg,1989:18). The *Daily Mail* implored 'Who planned it – and why?', while an editorial put left-wing organisations in the frame that disparaged the law enforcement agencies and 'agitators' who had arrived at 'ample cannon fodder' in the unemployed and disaffected Black youth (Gordon and Rosenberg,1989:18). 'This is the new exploitation of the blacks of London', the paper suggested (13 April 1981; in Gordon and Rosenberg,1989:18). However, the truth concerning Bristol and Brixton was that the local residents revolted against oppressive policing in addition to other social and economic disparities (Cohen and Gardner, 1982)

The editorial discourse of most papers distanced themselves from their news reportage, and, while roundly condemning the violence, appeared to exhibit some cognizance of the fundamental basis of the unrest. In illustration of the fact, the *Daily Star* stated: 'As we condemn the senseless terror ... we also condemn the deep-seated social problems ... which spawned them. We must find the determination – and the money – to solve them' (13 April 1981 in Gordon and Rosenberg,1989:18). That very day, the Daily Express stated that the first priority was to control and neutralise the tension in the boundary confines, but elaborated further to contend that the inner-cities, with their poor housing, unemployment and ineffective community resources, were 'highly combustible' and the economic downturn had furnished the spark. Brixton highlighted and demonstrated the necessity for structural economic policies to be expanded to ameliorate social conditions and to hasten the course of events. The *Sun*, too, on its editorial page called on the police to ameliorate relations with the local community and urged the unemployed 'not to be led astray by rent-a-mob troublemakers' (13 April 1981; in Gordon and Rosenberg,1989:19).

These truisms were not significantly disparate from those of the 'quality' broadsheets. *The Times* editorial section, for example, said that while there is no justifying the violence, an investigation was necessary to focus on relations extending across from the police and Black folk and at the socio-economic situation of boundary confines like Brixton and at the interplay of central and local governing administration (13 April 1981; in Gordon and Rosenberg,1989). The Financial Times also stated: 'The fundamental problem is not to stop the rioting but to tackle the cause' (13 April 1981; in Gordon and Rosenberg,1989:19).

The Daily Telegraph for Monday, April 13 contained the front-page headline 'Looting Gangs Roam Brixton' and 'Teenage Mobs Pour Out To Bombard Police' (Cohen and Gardner,1982:20). Above a picture of an upturned car is the subsidiary heading 'The hellish sounds of riot – fire alarms, police sirens, breaking glass, the cries of "pig"' (Cohen and Gardner,1982:20). Sir David McNee issued a blunt warning that London confines would not be designated 'no-go' locations and he opined that police 'had put a lot of effort into race relations' in the locality – apparently not nearly enough (Cohen and Gardner,1982:20).

At no point in that interview is he prompted about Operation Swamp '81', the clandestine saturation policing practice by groups of plainclothes personnel which entailed stopping and searching hundreds of community-based people throughout the week preceding the riot. This was a further difficulty or annoyance that pushed race relations to breaking point as far as young Brixtonian's were concerned but Sir David escaped being quizzed as to why no community representative was made aware of the exercise at such an untimely stage in race relations.

Any legitimate and substantial effort made to explain what actually transpired by the media is noticeable by its absence – indeed, it is taken for granted that explanations are non-existent. According to how Fleet Street sees it, these 'disturbances' happen with no prior notification and have no antecedents. This happens to be why it is always crucial to establish Royal Commissions and tribunals to look into and 'discover' the symptomatic causes of such sudden outbursts. The idea that rioting is a way of taking long-held grievances or emotional outlets forward is discounted. Rather, media reporting insists on diversionary theories akin to the 'mob rabble', the 'criminal element' and the 'outside conspiracy' (Cohen and Gardner,1982:14). The last idea was incorporated shortly after the development (this was proof positive of Southall, April 1979, and Brixton, April 1981) simply to be discounted subsequently as having no basis in reality. However, it served the direct diversionary objective. An example of such journalism is expressed through Ronald Butt commenting in the *Daily Mail*, who argued that the ones to apportion blame to in the riots were, in the main, Black people and the assumption flowing from this was that White society was not culpable for the points of view that gave vent to young Black violent anger. He placed the blame firmly in the attitudes held by young Black people and with the agitators who orchestrated such points of view for their own purposes (Solomos,1989:106).

The contradictory message concerning whether the developments in Bristol had amounted to a race riot had been superseded by July 1981 by the mental picture that considering that a substantial number of those partaking in the riots were racial or anyway the result of bad relations extending across from the police and young Black people. However, racism in the exact sense of the word was seldom spoken about, for the riots were not appreciated as associated with real grievances but solely to the interpretation that young Blacks formulated of their place in the scheme of things, and to the broader processes which were threatening the role of law (Solomos,1989).

The meanings and sense which media reporting comprised were not uncomplicated and often ambivalent. But the law and order main thrust, the fear that unruly street violence was emerging as an established phenomenon of the English cultural heritage and the linkages made around Black youth as the main participants involved highlight the mirror image reflection of the reconfiguration of order as the principal priority of official political discourse during this periodic age (Solomos,1989:109).

To return to media diversionary theories, the real 'conspiracy' occurs between strands of the media and the police who effectively manipulate their own register of developments to suit their own ends. Here, as I have already indicated, Hall et al, (2013) are at pains to suggest that there is no conspiracy, only a tendency embedded 'in the very structures and processes of news-making itself, and cannot be ascribed to the wickedness of journalists or their employers' (p.68). It is left to the reader to make up his or her own mind but as we shall see, Cohen and Gardner (1982) appear to have reasonable grounds. They continue, journalists are willing associates aiding and abetting in this manipulation. The material detail that it is frequently crime reporters who are nominated to cover riots or 'race' news items conveys a great deal intrinsically on how news editors interpret their significance. Crime reporters depend greatly on Scotland Yard as an essential wellspring of news and knowledge catchment (many ply their trade by taking full advantage of the press room and access to press telephone resources at the Yard). To invariably display the inveterate habit of confirming validity across various sources - or being cynical about the police storyline – is to risk disapprobation from the Yard. To tend their 'hot line' to the police, press agents are forced to cultivate an unquestioning attitude towards police say-so and only maintain a sketchy balance with accounts across other sources (Cohen and Gardner,1982).

This way of working can be seen year on year in the gradual preparation coverage of the Notting Hill Carnival, in announcing the annual crime statistics, and during inquests into events such as the Deptford fire. A reporter for the *Times* told Cohen that Scotland Yard had remonstrated to her editor during a forum that her reporting style was disproportionately against the police. She was requested by him to 'correct' the balance next time and in perpetuity.

According to one civil rights solicitor who holds extensive knowledge of US riots, 'Fleet Street reporting reveals a sharpening edge of racism and a deeply incestuous relationship with Scotland Yard that proceeds unchecked' (Cohen and Gardner,1982:15). Alluding to the late *cause célèbre* over police crime scales, she asks 'Do the stories represent the independent judgement of reporters and editors or do they instead give prominence to officially sanctioned and judiciously-timed police leakages so that public opinion becomes, on examination, suspiciously close to other products of Scotland Yard's press office, providing its own justification for its own actions?' (Cohen and Gardner,1982:15).

Scarman accuses media

A further diversionary strategy is to accuse the media of exacerbating the riots, rather than analysing the detail of the way in which they report them. Such claims are intended for the TV channels carrying the clear meaning that images of anarchic street confrontations have a 'copycat' effect on the (usually young) viewing public. With no evidence to speak of, he maintains that 'the media, particularly the broadcasting media do, in my view, bear a responsibility for the escalation of the disorders (including the looting) in Brixton on Saturday, April 11 and for their continuation the following day, and for the imitative element in the later disorders elsewhere' (Cohen and Gardner,1982:15). He entreats editors and producers to go out of their way to achieve 'balance' in the news items of the riots while making an indirect reference to censure the fact that the media fail to report areas like Brixton 'fairly'.

This outlook on media onus and duty was trotted out by former Conservative Attorney General, Peter Rawlinson, in the Lords' wrangle on Scarman. He contested that the BBC in particular bore 'a substantial degree of responsibility' for intensifying the disturbances and that there was an obscuring of the separation between reporting and opinion-forming and a reduction in the quality of news reporting (Cohen and Gardner,1982:15). Since the material detail that Scarman's own order of events showed the rioting in an advanced state of progress by the time BBC cameras made their appearance in Brixton, a separate analysis from the British Film Institute Research Unit, authorized by the BBC and the IBA, illustrated that short of 10 per cent of young people watch any semblance of television news anyhow. Moreover, clusters of youths questioned in cities where the disturbances occurred said television had not impacted upon them.

More meaning, however, is enveloped in the affirmation by Eric Moonman, who provided a Contemporary Affairs updating on 'copycat hooligans', that 'the media must bear some of the responsibility for the prevalence of stereotyping, particularly of different racial groups and of the police, by the way in which they are portrayed in dramatic presentations' (Cohen and Gardner,1982:16). The plain fact seems to be that the media allocates far more time to reacting to events than to facilitating education and investigation into the roots of social tension.

The entire volley of strands can be seen extending across newspaper reportage of the St Paul's, Bristol disorder of April 1980, the Brixton disorders of April 1981, the disorders in Liverpool, Manchester and other places that followed in July and in news items of crime statistics in March 1982 which comprised a racial categorization of 'violent theft' (Cohen and Gardner,1982:16).

By 1985, Britain had experienced another spate of riots; however, the scant understanding shown by media groups of the context of Black and minority ethnic people had been cast aside. The riots in Birmingham's Handsworth district in September that year were imparted overwhelmingly with the mental representation of an eruption of criminal activity and nothing else – 'a criminal enterprise, executed for loot and arson' (*Daily Express* 11 September 1985), and 'an orgy of arson and looting' (*Daily Mail* 11 September 1985; in Gordon and Rosenberg,1989:20). Some weeks later, the *Daily Express* advanced in an editorial: 'Those who witter on about "inner-city deprivation" seem incapable of seeing that there are people who think of rioting as a form of fun and a source of profit' (30 September 1985; in Gordon and Rosenberg, 1989:20).

In the main, national newspapers also sought to point up that the unrest had been inter-racial, with African-Caribbean anger and hostility aimed at Whites and South Asians. According to the concise interpretation of the *Daily Mail*, it was 'tribal', and embroiled African-Caribbean covetousness of 'hard-working Asian shopkeepers' (Gordon and Rosenberg,1989:20). Reportage of this kind ignored the facts that South Asians and Whites had also presented themselves for street conflict alongside African-Caribbeans, that White and African-Caribbean trading places had also been targeted, and that the ratio of White people arrested was higher than that of Black people. Media groups also ignored the reality that Handsworth had had its unusual background of deep cultural malaise extending across from the police and the local resident population and that social circumstances were not considerably different from those arising in Brixton four years previously.

Like peas in a pod, many newspapers came to focus again on the presage foretold since 1968 by Enoch Powell, that racial strife was bound to occur if the immigration of Black and minority ethnic people were not put in reverse, as if to suppose that the Handsworth riot was the true reflection of a prophecy. Writing in the *Sunday Express*, John Junor questioned whether the script might not have been flipped if Britain 'today might not be a place in which old people in Handsworth and Brixton were not afraid to answer a knock on their doors at night if it had been not Enoch Powell but the then rest of the Tory leadership that had been chucked in the dustbin?' (15 September 1985; in Gordon and Rosenberg,1989:20). On the pages of the *Evening Standard*, former Labour MP Brian Walden asked his Liberal cronies to clarify why Powell's predictions were spurious (18 September 1985; in Gordon and Rosenberg,1989). And Powell, in the exact sense, was given a platform in the *Sunday Express* to declare, 'I told you so', arguing that possibly Handsworth had been a negative and a positive effect in that it might demonstrate that we could not 'conjure away disaster' as was thought following 1981. The riot defined things positively, Powell argued, that repatriation remains the only alternative measure available to 'stop the torch from being put to Britain's funeral pyre' (15 September 1985; in Gordon and Rosenberg,1989:20-21). Few media industry personnel might have given credence to Powell's universal medicine, but many felt that they could accept his hang-up with immigration and Black and minority ethnic demographics were a major reason for the disturbances. The matter was lucidly expressed in the *Sun* reporting on Britain's 'Biggest centres of immigration' under a lead headline, 'Cities in the front line, where the fear of mob war grips the streets' (11 September 1985; in Gordon and Rosenberg,1989).

At the time that the Tottenham riot broke out a few weeks after Handsworth and Police Officer Keith Blakelock being slain at Broadwater Farm, certain newspapers raised once more the idea of external agitators who had started the rioting. The *Daily Telegraph* attributed 'Trotskyites, Socialist extremists, Revolutionary communists, Marxists and black militants' (9 October 1985), whereas the *Daily Express* had it in mind that 'Street Fighting Experts Trained in Moscow and Libya Were Behind Britain's Worst Violence'. Such functionaries had been 'lying low under the umbrella of outwardly innocent racial pressure groups' (8 October 1985; Gordon and Rosenberg,1989:21).

Not many newspapers thought it necessary to seek out the causes of the Broadwater Farm disturbances. The *Daily Mail* simply gave notice to Britain's Black communities that they ought to 'forego the luxury of these orgies of arson, looting and murderous assaults' or they would evoke a 'paramilitary reaction unknown to mainland Britain' (8 October 1985; in Gordon and Rosenberg, 1989:21). In the weeks that followed, the *Sun*, whose editorials tend mainly to be short and snappy, carried a page-long editorial which acquitted the British people who 'are not, and never have been, racist' and denounced the 'black racists' who were 'creating an appalling danger for Britain' (24 October 1985; in Gordon and Rosenberg,1989:21).

Racist attacks

Notably, as the print medium has consonantly emphasized the alleged participation of Black people in unlawful activity and sensationalised incidents involving Black people at cross purposes with the police, in turn, it has in balanced proportion accordingly ignored the circumstances of Black and minority ethnic people as the injured party in racial violence. The prevalence of such violence waged against people of colour over a considerable time frame has been extensively logged in various accounts* but has been represented lightly by national newspapers.

*See, for example, Paul Gordon, *Racial Violence and Harassment* (Runnymede Trust,1986); Commission for Racial Equality, *Living in Terror* (1987) and *Learning in Terror* (1988).

The Asian-English-oriented newspaper, *New Life*, produces each week an account of racial attacks in its 'Score of Shame' section, but few, if any of these, are incidentally reported in the domestic press, save for the Guardian, Observer and the now-defunct Independent. This absence of mind in racial violence appears even in instances of very serious onslaught, arson and, at the extreme end of the spectrum, murder. To illustrate, in 1981, the anti-fascist publication *Searchlight* reported four supposedly racially inspired killings in 1980 and 1981 which were beyond the very mention in any domestic tabloid or broadsheet papers (Gordon and Rosenberg,1989).

On occasions when newspapers do report events that may have been racially inspired, the coverage tends to be one of two things; short-lived or distorted. For example, at the time that 13 young Black people died after the New Cross Fire in January 1981, from the onset, almost all the domestic press factored out the likelihood that the fire may have been the work of a racist attack. They followed this line despite the welter of evidence of racially inspired attacks both encircling the New Cross district and domestically. Alternatively, several newspapers treated the fire disaster in consideration of a noisy social gathering as the Daily Express recounted: 'noisy party that drove neighbour Ken to call the police' (19 January 1981) as though this in some way clarified or even justified the tragedy that unfolded (Gordon and Rosenberg,1989:22).

At the time when thousands of Black people paraded through central London in objection to how the fire was reported and the unsuccessful attempt by the police to unravel it, the corresponding action of the press was to portray the file past as a 'Rampage of the mob' (*Daily Express* 3 March 1981) and the 'Day the Blacks Ran Riot in London (*Sun* 3 March 1981; Gordon and Rosenberg,1989:22).

These limited news reports of racial violence sharply contrast with the news reports of incidents in which the victim is Caucasian and the professed assailant Black. The slaughter of Markland Chambers, a Black male individual in Swindon in April 1981, did not appear in the national press in any shape or form and the slaughter of Mian Azim in south London that year was covered in just four newspapers and then chiefly not making front-page news. On the other hand, the slaughter of White youth Terry May in south London by young Black gang members was given complete and detailed treatment under such news report headlines as 'Innocent victim of race hate' (*Daily Express* 3 June 1981), 'Black Vengeance Mob Kills Helpless Cripple' (Daily Star 3 June 1981) and 'Rampaging Blacks Kill Youth After Wrecking Pub' (Daily Telegraph 3 June 1981); cited in Gordon and Rosenberg,1989:22).

On a more routine footing, street robberies ('muggings' by name only), are still held by most media outlets as occupying priority over arson attacks and violent criminal acts against Black victims. In January 1986, for instance, the *Daily Star* covered a succession of 'muggings' in a geographical location of south London, a news story which included a sizeable map highlighting with easily discerned markers where the numerous deeds had been done. However, a replica map could have been developed vis-à-vis racial attacks in certain areas, both in London and outside its peripheries. Besides the fact that coverage like this never emerged in the *Daily Star* (or was common amongst newspapers), the paper (not unlike most others) has allocated just enough space to report the basic details of racial attacks. On occasions when newspapers do extend sympathetic understanding, as was the case in August 1985 when the circumstances in east London had deteriorated to such an extent that a blind eye could no longer be turned, the news reportage lasts for only a temporary phase. Stories emerge and admittedly editorials are drafted condemning the violence, yet, within a matter of two weeks, the novelty wears thin and the issue sees no further lifeline so far as newspaper activity is concerned (Gordon and Rosenberg,1989)

Following a spate of attacks (12 August 1985), they were said to "increase the fears that racial extremists are behind the recent spate of fires" and a statement from community leaders is reported as a "claim that there have been at least 20 attacks on Asian families" (Van Dijk, 2016:167). In the wake of so many attacks on South Asian families, Scotland Yard is attributed as saying "We have an open mind as to the motives, but so far, there is nothing to suggest that it was racist" (Van Dijk,2016:167). We see a defence mechanism synchronizing in with the denial of racism, which we become expectant of and used to hearing it being practised while inquiring into and reporting in relation to race, is even proposed to these incidences of vicious right-wing crime. From the perspective of the police and the conservative press association, the victim's race came maybe as mere coincidence.

The Times bore only a number of features on the attacks (Van Dijk,2016). Corresponding and dovetailing with the residual conservative press, generally these articles are not expansively developed and do not appear to sound the message that these attacks represent a serious threat and a community-wide scandal. There remains only one slightly longer contextual article by race relations columnist Pat Healy (13 August 1985), where a Bengali girl and a Bangladeshi man are directly quoted alongside Home Office and CRE spokesmen and a White pressure group. In the following two days, a call by 50 Asian community leaders and the Black Sections of the Labour Party is published in inexplicit statements, in conjunction with an explicit police statement claiming that the Asians "had been unwilling to listen to the police point of view" – that being that, the attacks are not easily searched into (Van Dijk,2016:167). There are no in-depth background exchanges with victims and limited descriptions of the violent extreme of the attacks.

We understand that even in the event of racial attacks, where the conscious awareness and the thought patterns of a large party of South Asians are palpable, generally, the conservative press either fails to pay particular attention to these kinds of racial crimes or is inclined to limit its coverage to "police and politics" news coverage, which highlights the mentality and the agency of the authorities (Van Dijk,2016:167-168). The critique of the victims around lack of substantive police attention is occasionally alluded to, but not documented further or inquired into. Practically no news items exist which only put forward the opinions or conscious awareness of South Asian people. Whether these views or experiences are delineated, they are mostly attended by comments from the police or the powers that be. The Guardian alone, though it also reflects the police standpoint, puts forward several larger background portrayals of the experiences and thought patterns of the victims. Following the racial attacks throughout the summer of 1985, any follow-up is almost non-existent. Evidently, as is true for the powers that be and the police, the matter has no primacy for the newspapers. If truth be told, the ones who experience distress are 'only Asians' while the attackers are White (Van Dijk,2016:168).

By overlooking the prevalence and the substantiveness of racial violence, the print media helps toward its perpetuation, but the print media can also help more explicitly toward racial violence (Gordon and Rosenberg,1989). An increase in racial violence took place in 1976 as a recurrent decline and regrowth of anti-immigration representation unfurled in the national press. With news features in the national media about 'race war' consciousness-raising by Enoch Powell, a destitute South Asian family put up in a hotel with public funds – **'4 star Asians run up £4,000 bill'** (*Sun* 7 May 1976), the alleged common occurrence of illegal immigration – **'Immigrant racket row'** (*Daily Express*, 25 May 1976) and related to the extent of expected Indian sub-continent inflow – **'New Asian invaders'** (Sun 17 May 1976), racial attacks spiralled upwards reaching new heights

(Gordon and Rosenberg,1989:23). The dwellings of Black and minority ethnic people were stoned and set alight and in Southall and east London, three Black youths were the victims of fatal knife crime. Fronting Granada TV's programme, 'What the Papers Say', then, Journalist Paul Foot floated the idea: 'Race hate and race violence does not rise and fall according to the numbers of 'immigrants' coming into Britain. It rises and falls by the extent to which people's prejudices are inflamed and made respectable by politicians and newspapers' (Gordon and Rosenberg,1989:23).

However, the contribution the press makes to setting the context wherein racial violence occurs transcends its action or inaction about racial attacks. More and more, the press in Britain (bar a few) has consciously decided on legitimating racism by encouraging racist ideas and by attacking efforts to address racism. It is not difficult to see that with this 'machinery of representation' in place, the press can be seen as an outlet that produces and reproduces racism.

I now turn to concentrate on the Black Media Workers' Association (BMWA) in order to show and identify the media industry's role as an employer from the perspective of the BMWA. The Black Media Workers' Association was formally introduced in February 1981, in line with its diverse and direct nature, at a forum attended by more than 150 people from occupations and professions far and wide. The Black Media Workers' Association is an independent organisation that pools the talents of people from an African-Caribbean, South Asian and African background. They have no alliance with any political party or pressure groups and follow an independent strategy and plan of action.

The establishment of the BMWA is not in any way dissimilar to an assumed group of individuals who arrive at a form and process of mutual interest. They were people who occasionally cultivated each other's friendship and who gradually came to see that the difficulties they encountered as workers, whether that be in the autonomous Black media, or the conventional White media, lend themselves to common expression. The experience of isolation, frustration and the ensuing alienation were transposed to such an extent as to become a central unifying feature for something greater than cooperative co-allegiance, later to prove itself crucial to the continuance of the association (Morris,1982).

Black video group

The activity of the BMWA might be said to span two separate aspects. One takes the title *concerns of the profession*, which start from items like developing the independent Black media, ending in the manner in which the press reproduces racism and imperialism – and introducing these issues for discussion with networks such as the media unions. The second sphere of activity might suitably take the title *concerns of the Black community*. Operationally, this has resulted in activities like establishing a video group, which was then involved in rendering a tape on 'Black people and the NHS' (Morris,1982). They also seek to give groups embroiled in policy activity access to not only the Black independent media but also the mainstream, in order to propagate an important perspective that would otherwise remain exempted from the formation of popular opinion.

The sphere of *Training and Employment* is, in their view, completely bound up with their commitment to the Black and minority ethnic population in that, people of colour expect to be privileged enough to seek and acquire employment in the media, and when gainfully employed, to have not dissimilar rights and conditions in the workplace as the next person. So, the BMWA has invested a great deal of time and resources into trying to remove the racism that leads to our under-representation in a large variety of jobs throughout the media industry – and causes the absence of wealth creation in the media generally.

On the occasion that they claim that racial discrimination is in all seriousness occurring, Morris and friends are usually faced with one of two main thrusts. The first disputes their ability to level such a charge at all on the basis that they can provide no definitive confirmation of racial discrimination. The second line of reasoning employed to rebuff their statements (and it tends to shift slightly) maintains that adequately qualified

Black and minority ethnic people are non-existent, or that their hard graft is unprofessional – and so they are unsuited for jobs or for upward social mobility. The controversy which surfaced over the programme *Black Londoners* is an example of why BMWA attaches the importance it attributes to the interconnected questions of employment and training (Morris,1982).

Around the mid-70s, BBC local radio phased in an airtime spot devoted to what was designated 'access' programming. The word 'access' simply meant that residents of the community were encouraged to make programmes that represented a community viewpoint, until now unincorporated in mainstream discussion. This process was how Black Londoners came to evolve. The programme had a monthly turnaround that changed to a weekly programme and directly rose to national and global prominence. They were never extended adequate resources to fund the manpower required to produce it, even given its noticeably advanced status in relation to identical (and unidentical) programmes. The men and women who laboured on the programme not infrequently gained their training 'on the job' (Morris1982:77).

This aspect of employment engendered two serious drawbacks. Firstly, their occupational prospects were restricted because they lacked the required conventional qualifications and training. Also, what was being accomplished by Black broadcasters was not, in many cases, introduced into mainstream programmes at optimal listening periods – partly due to the lack of conventional training, added to by racial chauvinism at the hands of the programmers. Allowances were made, however, for sudden eruptions of national tension, such as when the nation and its people collected themselves after frustrated and disaffected Black youths roamed the streets. These escalating dissatisfactions were why Black workers on Radio London came into conflict with the management, for they needed carte blanche over programme- production, and regarded themselves to be completely established professional broadcasters. The Black Londoners' instance clearly reveals the importance of the subject of employment and training, both in terms of career chances and on-air accomplishment (Morris,1982).

Investigative work into employment

The assignment of the BMWA has come to be one of reciprocating to these criticisms, in order to rid the employer of any further loopholes for not employing Black and minority ethnic people. Towards this end, BMWA has reached a settlement with the NUJ, ACTT and the ABS to make sure that research is conducted into the recruitment of Black and minority ethnic people across the entire media industry. This investigative work is being adopted with the hope of the possible bringing-in of quotas to put an end to the enduring under-representation of Blacks. In acting on the concerns of young people of colour, lamenting that they did not know how to access the media industry, the BMWA has issued a leaflet giving guidance on how to apply for specific jobs and what kinds of credentials are needed. Therefore, Morris et al have made significant headway towards firmly addressing the criticism vis-à-vis the lack of appropriately qualified job applicants, in addition to beginning to make sure that people of colour receive adequate training.

The employer is being called upon to engage with the publications that Black and minority ethnic people subscribe to and they are being invited to recruit by way of the independent Black press, so that suitably qualified non-white groups do present themselves. And, Morris et al have taken it upon themselves to sponsor a program of study on radio and print-journalism, together with the then Polytechnic of Central London, which started in the academic year 1982-83. The program of study bears some relevance to the viewpoint of the BMWA, for in it, Morris et al have sought to ensure that a replica of the White reporter is not forged by giving the program a Black perspective. According to Morris et al, training represents part of their onslaught on the White *parti pris* that is so firmly established in the mainstream media sector.

Establish Black media

In addition to assailing the established White media, the BMWA is also about consolidating the autonomous Black media, because it is among the small corners of the media sector as a rule over which Morris et al exert some effective regulation and are thus placed to make the most immediate progress. The instruction that is gained in the autonomous Black media is a feature that Morris et al would seek to advance, not only from the angle of making sure that there is adequate provision to learn from the existing array of skills in the different media but, to a greater degree, ensuring that employment possibilities are not restricted, should a person of colour wish to seek work elsewhere. Morris and other members of the BMWA plan to ensure that Black and minority ethnic staff, already employed in the autonomous Black-owned media, are qualified to cross over to White mainstream media or contribute towards it through independent productions. The BMWA then aimed to schedule a series of training programs, at weekends, in different aspects of the media industry, in order to aid this process. The social position of people who gain skills through this method was then a matter that Morris and friends had to follow up on with the employers and trade unions.

Researching the media as a service

With a view to discussing these overall societal aspects of racism, unequal power relations, the media and the contribution of ideology to the immediate social levels of news and news-making, we need access to further intelligence concerning the complex structures of media communication. In other words, we need to place under careful scrutiny the way in which the reproduction of racism on the part of the media at the large-scale level is, in reality, reproduced at the small-scale level of news-making and feature stories (van Dijk, 2016).

Social research on routine news-gathering coincides with earlier expositions of news values and indicates that the order of 'news-beats', in addition to the explanation of newsworthy occurrences, are determined by influential professional and social understandings and organizational practices. Therefore, powerful oligarchies and institutions, particularly in the corporate and ideological arenas, are in part able to regulate their access to, as well as their representation in the media. They have actively organized access via press offices, press publications and press conferences, and also, they have, to some extent but not entirely, control over news-gathering and representation by strategic leaks, private contacts, financial incentives, or heterogeneous forms of lex talionis against non-complying journalists or newspapers (van Dijk,2016).

Despite this, powerful elite groups are not always represented in a positive light. Yet, it is pertinent that they foreground news actors (partakers, including passive or impartial ones) prima facie, that their vocal articulation is heard, and that their views are presented as plausible and legitimate, even on the occasion when the Press may disapprove of the details of their procedures and guidelines. Seen from this angle, the part played by the oppositional Press – unrelated to the 'radical media' – is scarcely dissimilar from other opposed elite groups, like the parties of the legitimately declared opposition, the unions or certain sections of the metaphorical elites, as in education, learned inquiry or the arts. To be sure, some newspapers may position themselves as the vocal articulation of such oppositional forces, provided that they stay within the limits of an open but carefully guarded understanding of legitimate dissent. It may even claim to speak 'for the people' at a time that large sections of the general public are thought to oppose specific procedures or plans of certain elite groups (van Dijk,2016).

Such limits delineate rather specific aspects of news-making and news reports. They determine the tasks given to journalists, the selection of central spheres of interest, the nature of questioning sources, the strategies of 'checking out' details, the validity and hence the vicissitudes, or absence of them, in Press publications, and generally, the digressive 'work' of reporters. Constrained by this structure of news-making, oligarchies and their policies are, by definiendum, newsworthy. Their views will be requested and cited credibly, and their characterization will on the whole be respectful. Therefore, at all stages of news-gathering, described as a complex web of source information-processing, and at all stages of news report construction, the social, economic and political power relations may unwittingly become reproduced (van Dijk,2016).

The rhetorical patterns disseminated by mass media are, by definition, reproducible, that is to say, manifold copies may be generated or made available to a mass market (Thompson, 1997). The replication of patterns is generally regulated as strictly as can be by the media institutions since it is among the principal means through which rhetorical patterns come under economic valorization. Patterns are replicated in order to produce exchange value within a market system or by a controlled form of economic transaction. For this reason, they are commodified and thought of as objects with a selling point, as services for which to exchange payment or as media that can promote the sale of additional objects or services. At a first view, therefore, the media should be seen as a component of a collection of institutions concerned in fluctuating degrees, with the fixation, replication and commodification of rhetorical patterns. Fixation can tend to involve processes of encoding by which rhetorical patterns are converted into information that may be stored in a particular device or material foundation; the rhetorical patterns may be conveyed as data and then decoded for the object of retrieval or consumption. (Thompson,1997).

Pertinent to include in this study is the supposition that the elite interpretations of the 'facts', their characterizations of reality, will tend to tower over those of 'the other', non-white groups (van Dijk,2016). In our example, given earlier in this chapter, of the African-Caribbean 'rioters', we have seen to what extent such a dominant version of ethnic events is involved. Expressed in another way, it is germane at this stage that we point up White group power and the role ideologies play in their reproduction in and by means of the media (van Dijk,2016). Albeit an especially well-worn adage that 'you shouldn't believe everything you read in the newspapers or see on TV', most people perusing the newspaper or viewing a TV news bulletin anticipate that they will gain a grasp of what salient events are occurring the world over, of 'what's happening' (Bilton et al,1989:432).

However, as media analysts have increasingly witnessed, the news doesn't simply 'happen' – rather, it is generated, it is a socially generated product, the outcome of social practice with a separate structure to it. So, features contained in a TV broadcast or enclosed within a newspaper comprise only a partial reality of the day's new events, yet are designated as 'news' by the communication media. Expressed in another way, the news is not only a credible update of events whose value and meaning is indivisibly evident and not a point of issue, but it is a socially constructed form of data information resting on a whole host of determinants: media manpower notions of what is salient and informative; the background circumstances from which the news emerged and the origins from which it emanates, and so on. As Hall et al (2013:56) highlight:

> The media do not simply and transparently report events which are 'naturally' newsworthy in themselves. News is the end-product of a complex process which begins with a systematic sorting and selecting of events and topics according to a socially constructed set of categories.

This method of selection – or 'agenda-setting' – tends towards the opposite of taking place haphazardly: rather, it is the organized result of certain forces, as we shall soon see.

The process of news-making

The matter that becomes 'news' is formed not only by physical and pecuniary pressures, by cultural and prescriptive constraints, but also by 'internal' institutional pressures inside the media, which are homogeneously powerful agents in the reproduction of the dominant ideology. As Golding and Elliot (1979:18) in Bilton et al, (1989:432) maintain:

> The content of broadcast news portrays a very particular view of the world that we can label ideological … This is not the result of a conspiracy within newsrooms or of the inadequacies, professional or political, of broadcast journalists. It is a necessary result of the structure

Chapter 6: 'Draft' FAO Editor for Sociology

of news-gathering and production, and of the routines and conventions built into broadcasting practice.

To be specific, the basic structure underlying knowledge which media news applies to make sense of events and questions are partly 'internally' generated by way of editorial processes and procedures' technical constraints, professional ideologies relating to journalistic objectivity and neutrality, and so on. Certain practical constraints, such as prescribed deadlines (competing with the clock), the desire to create visually evocative material, pressures to acquire 'hot' news in addition to the conventional dimension of a newspaper or scope of a news transmission, marshal the demand for a constant stream of news to be frequently available, in almost constant portions (overseas news, sports, economic news, and so on) and not infrequently consigned to certain sections of the medium or broadcast. So, for these reasons especially, one cannot consider news reporting as merely relaying faithfully 'what happens in the world' (Bilton et al,1989:433).

Mass communication works with definitions of the matter that are significant and 'newsworthy, with 'a set of institutional definitions and meanings ... commonly referred to as news values' (Bilton et al,1989:433). News reporters claim that their specialized training, and expertly achieved 'nose' for a story, endow them with a special skill for identifying what events and people are 'news' as a result of their extraordinary or humanly interesting quality. So, for example, features affording the potential for the sensational and visually attractive (with appropriate photographs or film to hand), those which can be viewed in terms of people and personalities, those which are current and presentable as concluded accounts of separate events or questions, those which are allegedly entertaining, oddly distracting or tantalizing, or especially those which incorporate 'bad news' or when havoc affects the normal state of play are occasions on which news media professionals deem news newsworthy by news commentators.

Consequently, certain spheres of social activity are given prominence by the news media, and an especially crucial feature of this agenda-setting *modus operandi* is the propensity for those from elite and privileged backgrounds to be more freely consulted for quantitative and subjective readings. As Hall et al, (2013:61) suggest:

> This is what Becker has called 'the hierarchy of credibility' – the likelihood that those in powerful or high-status positions in society, who offer opinions about controversial topics, will have their definitions accepted because such spokesmen are understood to have access to more accurate and specialised information on particular topics than the majority of the population.

Albeit too straightforward to drive at a conscious process of conspiracy extending across from the news media and establishment type authority figures in society as giving rise to these circumstances, it is, nevertheless, the case that specific frameworks of perception are established which facilitate as given contexts within which problems can be 'naturally' brought to light. Competing perceptions have to be in a position where access to this framework is available or be faced with a tussle for recognition and justification with the odds stacked formidably against them. Although it is patently important to recognise the regulating effects and impact of technical and institutional aspects of media output on the quality of the finished article, we cannot lose sight of or minimise a basic material constraint that is the form of ownership and control to which we shall return later.

Perspectives on the media

We shall now explore the media as a provider of services which can be seen through the Marxist and pluralist prism of the media. The Marxist perspective on the media takes the opposite view to that of media manpower and the pluralist standpoint to which we have yet to turn, in stressing that the media and their artefacts cannot be seen beyond the background of the material involvement in a capitalist society, its mode of production, and power relations between different groups. According to the Marxists, the media represent a fundamental mechanism of control held by the dominant social category, who, aside from controlling material production, further control the mode of mental production through ownership of media organization outlets. The media benefit, alongside the family, the education system, religion, etc, as similar in kind to the ideological machinery used by the dominant social category to reproduce the framework of class imperialism (Bilton et al,1989).

The media, as Marxists believe, systematically replicate the ideology and therefore hegemony of the ruling class, and circulate these ruling ideas into the awareness of subordinate groups, so shaping the pattern and impact of the belief register of these groups. They make available justifications and legitimations for the ruling class and existing state of affairs, excluding alternative explanations and challenges to scarce resource arrangements and power imbalances. Therefore, the mental picture of an array of institutions, events and courses of action in society (for instance, forms of inequality and privation, deviants, women) is strategically distorted, because they take acquisitive capitalist society as their assumed criterion for making sense of social reality and for interpreting how social categories relate to one another within it (Bilton et al,1989:438).

The common perception of the communication media – especially of the press and TV – and one kept fluid by media staff themselves, has a patently transparent pluralist context about it. Seen through this prism, the media are major influences within the democratic system of a 'free society', ensuring an unbridled social expression of distinct opinions on matters of social interest and concern; provided that in the democracy all things remain the same, the opportunity for catholic elocution of a wide variety of voices and views is a fundamental prior requirement. As this pluralist view maintains, the media, on both sides of the Atlantic, comprise a diversity of viewpoint and information, are free-standing and not state-governed institutions providing a range of 'definitions of reality' (Bilton et al,1989:429).

Also, the media ostensibly act as objective independent servants of the masses: aside from providing entertainment, they influence and educate the masses and, more importantly, ask questions, act as guardians of the powerful and powerless, and as watchdogs of the public good against violation of widely held standards and courses of action, or misuse of power. The cross-examination of parliamentarians in TV question and answer sessions, the research activity of the investigative journalist, and the identification of alarming new 'problems' all ostensibly testify to the media's public service function in social critique and self-governing public awareness.

This view rests on the argument that the media defend, above all, the supreme power of the consumer seeking to deliver on consumer demand by 'giving them what they want', whether it be news, fiction or entertainment: the public's input is decisive and media owners and manpower respond to their requirements (Bilton et al,1989:429). Therefore, any claims that the media revert to a 'consensus' of how the world is presented are, as far as this view is concerned, fundamentally misconceived, as the media are held to be merely reproducing ideas extant in society among the majority of the population, independently reached and verified by them as 'sensible' (Bilton et al,1989:429).

Producing and reproducing racism

The newspapers are a source of information and a window on reality and the world, but we already have some idea of how Black Caribbean and South Asian people are portrayed. However, do the papers severely criticize far-right groups and individuals who display 'White hostility' or the reverse? According to Mooney (1986:70), 'papers do not tell the truth, they say, and all journalists are dishonest'. In this section, I intend to show the nature of newspaper journalism and how the press promotes racism. In support of Mooney's (1986) statement, he adds that in New York, the intelligentsia argued the pros and cons of the Alastair Reid case: the New Yorker writer acceded he frequently made-up quotes and manufactured stories. In 1981, a New York Times reporter was given his marching orders when it was found that he penned a 'composite' (i.e., untrue) feature about Belfast, and, that year, the *Washington Post* was required to return the Pulitzer Prize it was awarded for a manufactured piece on drug addicts. Thus, people treat what they read in the papers with a large pinch of salt while newspaper editors make their excuses for not adhering to good newspaper reporting standards in a move towards mere entertainment by maintaining that the public 'doesn't want to know' (Mooney,1986:70). The circular shape of deception is destructive. In Britain, as the *Sun* newspaper showed, Murdoch has no regard for the truth, buttresses the establishment, and its lies are the structure upon which the state rests. On the authority of Mooney (1986), the truth is what people want, as they deserve better than newspaper proprietors and personnel (and television moguls) credit them with.

What the press does cover and what the press does not focus upon are two sharply contrasting things. In the routine practice of reporting news where 'race' has a direct bearing on issues being considered, perennial tenets, myths and typifications are frequently reproduced. But the ground covered by press reporting transcends simply mirroring commonly held views. Newspapers make available an opportunity for furthering opinion. Newspapers are conscious of the fact that they are able to impinge on perceptions and lend credibility and respectability to stated viewpoints. Mainly, by way of editorials and 'comment' space, they prompt their readers to assume certain positions and make sense of events from a particular perspective. Newspapers' lifeblood, therefore, could be engaged to combat racial injustice, pressing into service editorials to mobilise public opinion away from racism and 'comment' space as an opportunity to attack the base of racist thinking, myths and stereotypes (Gordon and Rosenberg,1989).

Evidence also seems to point out that negative attitudes directed at the Black and minority ethnic population in the UK are influenced by the manner in which race-related information is expressed in the mass media (Troyna,1981). For example, it would appear that consequent to press coverage, 'Black Hostility' is viewed as germane to, and gravely affecting race relations, though 'White Hostility' and the 'National Front' are not (Troyna,1981:40). One exposition found that the media 'serves both to perpetuate negative perceptions of blacks and to define the situation as one of intergroup conflict' (Critcher et al,1977:173; in Troyna,1981:11). A further study, by Hartmann and Husband, concluded that media-driven understandings of Blacks were 'more conducive to the development of hostility towards them than acceptance' (Hartmann and Husband, 1974:208; in Troyna,1981:11).

David Dukes, John Kingsley Read and Robert Relf were the three foremost and widely reported transgressors of 'white hostility' during the period 1976-1978 (Troyna,1981). Dukes, a principal member of the Ku Klux Klan, received considerable coverage by his sojourn to Britain in 1978. Kingsley Read, a former associate of the NF and head of the splinter group National Party, achieved media attention for his comment, 'One down, one million to go' following the racial killing of Gurdip Singh Chaggar in 1976 (Troyna,1981:32). Of the three, Robert Relf drew the most attention for his calculated action to erect a sign putting his house on the market explicitly for an 'English Family'. During the publicity of Relf's trial, his subsequent corrective for contempt of court, and his forty-five-day starvation diet in jail, there was no attempt worthy of mention to background this event in the circumstances of Relf's steadfast and enduring racist activities. Rather, he was presented as 'a man of principles' -prepared for incarceration rather than back down on his racist assumptions. He was invariably portrayed as the 'Race Rebel', the 'Defiant' adversary of the recently introduced Race Relations Act. The *Daily Express*, for example, in its editorial of 22 June 1976, thought it more fitting to condemn this new 'Draconian' piece of legislation as opposed to Robert Relf himself. Under the banner headline, 'SELF-DEFEATING', the *Daily Express* maintained that Relf 'should never have been jailed in the first place' and that his instance showed 'the wrongheadedness of trying to outlaw prejudice' (Troyna,1981:32). That Relf was sentenced for contempt of court and not for infringing the new Act was only briefly alluded to in the editorial. Therefore, the *Daily Express* 'Whitewashed' over the matter that Relf was held under lock and key not for erecting the sign, but for taking exception to its removal. All the same, by focusing on the question of 'free speech' and Relf's 'democratic right' to articulate where he is coming from as regards Black and minority ethnic people, the *Daily Express* contributed to nourishing and strengthening

Relf's persona as the 'Lone Crusader' 'actively engaged in the battle against the attrition of freedom' (Troyna,1981:33).

What emerges from Troyna's analysis are certain continuities with and divergences from initial studies of press concentration on race-related news stories. Firstly, it is beyond question that the portrayal of Black and minority ethnic people as personae non gratae in the wider social sphere has been nurtured in the press throughout the 1960s and 1970s. For example, 'Immigration' is still seen in terms of regulatory control - that is, barring them from entry – whereas there are also signposts that the debate regarding race relations has shifted further still to the Right with earnest discussions about repatriation being undertaken within the parameters of mainstream late-1970s politics. Furthermore, this understanding of non-white people as a problem has additionally been confirmed by the prominence afforded the NF and other demonstrable forms of 'White hostility' in the local and national news media.

The coverage accorded to Robert Relf's recalcitrant resistance against 'the attrition of free speech' is a strong indication of how the communication media highlights the problems which it apprehends with the mind through the senses as originating solely from the numbers of Blacks settled in Britain. In the *Daily Express* editorial on Relf, to which we have already made mention, it was clear to see that 'a lot of people believe that Mr Relf should be free to sell his house to whoever (sic) he chooses' (Troyna,1981:33). In light of this, it was then pointed out that the development of a non-homogenous society should not inhibit free speech, no matter whether the expressed opinion is an affront to people of colour or likely to cause a detrimental effect on race relations: 'You cannot stop Mr Relf thinking as he does so why stop him saying what he thinks?' (Troyna,1981:33). A broadly similar argument had been raised two years previously by *The Observer* in its editorial statement on the Red Lion Square disturbances:

'However detestable in a multi-racial society the views of some extreme right-wing organisations might be, they are still entitled to the same freedoms as the rest of us' (23rd June 1974).

The reportage afforded to crime and certain 'Human Interest' features, on another level, suggests that the extent to which there are social problems has been worsened by the numbers of Black and minority ethnic people settled here. Moreover, the consistent use of 'Adjectival Racism' in these news items only emphasizes and consolidates this image (Troyna,1981:33). 'Adjectival Racism' is the unwarranted use of ethnic origin in reports. For examples of a broader tabloid and broadsheet newspaper range of racist reporting, see (Gordon and Rosenberg,1989).

Ownership, control and partisan alliance

There is good reason to suggest that newspaper proprietors are notorious when it comes to intervening editorially with their papers. Men like William Randolph Hearst (subject of the film Citizen Kane), Lord Beaverbrook, Lord Northcliffe and his brother Lord Rothermere were not given to deception or concealment regarding their desire to fiddle with the papers they owned and that they were at liberty to do so (Trowler,1996).

Contemporary media barons take on a similar mantle. They constructively dismiss editors with whose standpoint position they are in conflict. Mike Gabbert, editor of the *Star*, was dropped by Lord Stevens in 1987 for reducing it to a low-level market orientation. Its increasing priority and prominence to scantily clad females and its pet name of the Daily Bonk soon became more than enough for Lord Stevens. He considered that its 'girlie magazine' public perception was not congruent with his new appointment as a peer. The axe also allegedly fell on editor Eve Pollard for being overly critical of Lady Stevens' associate, Princess Diana. The late Robert Maxwell, then leading figure of Mirror Group Newspapers, who was putting Magnus Linklater through his paces for the position as editor of the *London Daily News*, was in the throes of spelling out that he did not meddle editorially when the editor of the *Daily Mirror* showed up with a lead page sample from that paper for Maxwell's approbation! Roy Greenslade, editor of the *Daily Mirror* extending across from 1989 to 1991, tells various anecdotes of Maxwell's alteration of that paper in his 1992 work, *Maxwell's Fall* (Trowler,1996).

Rupert Murdoch is widely recognized for interfering in editorial policy. He dispensed with Harold Evans' services as editor of *The Times*, and Stafford Somerfield, editor of the now-defunct *News of the World*, following conflict over policy. Frank Giles, erstwhile editor of the *Sunday Times*, has related that when Murdoch was in Britain's capital city, he would make every effort to stop by his office on Saturday evenings simply to look over the initial copies of the paper as Giles was taking delivery of them (Trowler,1996).

A prevalent aspect of media content within the media arena owned by media moguls is their lightweight material detail: girls, glitter, star prizes and the lionized tends often to be served up. This is the case with the News International newspapers and schedules in Britain and of Berlusconi's channels in Italy. Despite everything, *The Times* has shifted towards this trend:

> Before Murdoch took over the *Sunday Times*, the journalists defined a good story as one that someone, somewhere does not want you to read. This approach is incomprehensible to Murdoch. His journalism is about pap, dressed up as sensationalism. Why try to interpret and understand the world, when a good piece of fiction, a well-turned headline or a carefully cropped photo will do the trick?

(Trowler,1996:75)

It is a similar story abroad. The American magazine *TV Guide* tended to bring issues to light, ask why certain issues went ignored by the TV broadcast companies and include a raft of sober subject matter. The Murdoch hierarchy changed this arrangement once News Corporation's buy-out of the magazine was complete: 'They just wanted fluff', said one veteran journalist. The matter that had been to exercise the critical and investigative faculty became advertorials: an opportunity to advertise (Trowler,1996).

The circulation and availability as well as the output of the mass media rest in the grasp of a few elite personages. Newspaper availability is concentrated in the grip of two enterprises, TNT and Newsflow. News Corporation has a 12% dividend in TNT which makes available 40% of newspapers. Newsflow, an adjunct of the National Freight Corporation, makes available the remainder (Trowler,1996).

Three wholesalers – Surridge Dawson, John Menzies and WHSmith – regulate most newspaper circulation in the UK. Surridge Dawson have 19% of the newspaper circulation business, Menzies 28% and WHSmith 53% (Trowler,1996). Even the poster market sector is now markedly monopolized with a reduction from 20 to only four poster site contractors extending across from 1986 and 1990.

Support for government manipulation of the media lends itself well to easy discovery. Political journalists sense that prime ministers have invariably sought to exploit the media to consolidate their own position and to fortify the secrecy of government. 'Spin doctors', such as the Conservatives' Director of Presentation from 1986-91, Harvey Thomas, seek to make sure that stories emerge in the most favourable light (Trowler,1996).

Cunning plans are engaged in order to ensure that the media cover items with the desired motive. An example of this involves the use of sound bites in rhetorical addresses – short snappy wordplay that will contribute towards good public perception. An example of this is Mrs Thatcher's 'You turn if you want to. The lady's not for turning' (Trowler,1996:76). At the time when John Major stepped down from the pre-eminent position in the Conservative Party in June 1995, he saliently emphasized the phrase levelled at his critics; 'It's time to put up or shut up', indicating a phrase, strikingly apt in expression and manner, to the waiting reporters (Trowler,1996:76). In the everyday scheme of things, campaign reporters are served information that makes their assignment easier, given the caveat that they conceal the source's identity. The head of an elected government's press secretary tends to be designated as 'sources close to the prime minister', for instance (Trowler,1996:76).

In buttressing this right-wing prevailing established orthodox order, the press represents and legitimates its institutionalised inequalities consisting also of its racial inequalities (Gordon and Rosenberg,1989:60). One example, implicit within much correspondence news, is the one-sided weltanschauung that the essential nature of being of a non-white in Britain or overseas is subordinate in value to that of a White individual, and that, therefore, its deprivation has less news value (Trowler,1996:215). Non-white world views are given the green light of expression, but the 'establishment' view is highlighted, underlined and treated as more important (Trowler,1996:18). To be sure, allowing this apparent discursive struggle between, say, the opinions of minority ethnic communities and those of the dominant group helps to achieve consensus in society. But as a consensus, it is established and developed around the edifice of the dominant, hegemonic system of ideas. Certain opinions are rendered conventional, normal or sensible, while others are thought of as extremist, irrational, unsubstantial, utopian or unworkable (Trowler,1996).

However, the intersection between a predominantly right-wing press and a right-wing government does not mean that the press is directly governed and orchestrated by the authorities; neither do they explicitly champion the ruling elite (Gordon and Rosenberg,1989; Trowler,1996). More specifically, the tabloids put themselves forward as 'the voice of the people' or 'the voice of Britain' and still hold dear the distance and divergences between the state and single constituents (Gordon and Rosenberg,1989:60). The fact that news enters the media conveyance system as 'pure news' is stylistically fine-tuned some way further down the line and ends up as media 'bias' which rests with journalists and sub-editors who adhere to the first concerns and political standpoints of editors and proprietors (Gordon and Rosenberg,1989:60; Trowler,1996). Media journalists and editors seem to have little in the way of conflict between them in the manner in which they view matters of 'race'. There are obvious differences throughout the hierarchical chain and levels in newspaper media but the absence of clear-cut conflict indicates that editors and media magnates do not just have a bearing on things through the exercise of their power. Rather, the fundamental value system lying beneath reporting and assessment of events regarding minority ethnic people sufficiently permeates throughout the newspapers as a commercial enterprise. The considered news values of a given newspaper are accepted and respected at every level through which news is channelled. Journalists employed at a particular media institution will have some idea how they will cover a story and know the form and format their paper likes to put forward, what it will highlight and what its 'approach' will be. They may also recognize what their paper requires, and have ideas consistent with what their paper sees as news and how that news should be transmitted and packaged (Gordon and Rosenberg,1989:61; Trowler,1996:78-80).

The everyday context in which media professionals operate is hierarchical and has resolute agency through strong workplace cultures. The various interplay of values and ego common sense that occur simultaneously in the workplace must be seen in isolation as the emergent construction units of institutional racism. Ethnically similar workgroups are hardly helpful in keeping alive workplace ways of working consistent with depicting a multi-ethnic reality. While codes of practice are logical contentions for controlling conduct, it would be foolhardy to accept that they are effectuated and negotiated in operational settings completely defined by logicality. Media professionals of whatever description have a robust in-group affinity and are extremely resistant to external inquiry and regulation. Therefore, in total, whilst it is entirely rational to believe that many media personnel are entirely sincere in their support of codes of practice, it is childlike to suppose that they are structurally equal to implementing them. It is understandable that it need not take the presence of functional unchanging racists within the newsroom, or another place within the institutional media structure, in order to explicate the abysmal record of the communication industry in promoting ethnic diversity, or in assuring equity and entry of people of colour to the media (Downing and Husband,2005).

News values

Journalists are keenly observant of 'news values' – material that flags up as merging with professional baseline criteria which aid the process of what issues and events will grab the public's attention. Race has been the tool of analysis that 'explained' and legitimated Britain's colonial world power past. The overriding view of world pecking order position placed White nations uppermost, at the apex of social organisation, and distinguishing Black nations as 'savages' or 'barbarians' destined not to make advances other than through the tutelage and dependence of those White nations (Downing and Husband,2005:32; Gordon and Rosenberg,1989:62). Since the disbandment of Britain's colonial empire and the introduction of extensive Black and South Asian immigration to Britain, race has once more emerged at the forefront and is applied to 'explain' contemporary social tensions. 'Race assumes a central position in public discourse concerning the many Gordian knots of deprived inner cities, falling academic achievement, economic decline and a significant number of other factors, with communities of colour increasingly subject to censure for the self-same problems that cause them the most serious consequences. In press publications, 'race' is invariably advanced as a 'hot' or volatile issue, and volatile issues promote newspaper sales. Those papers that dominate the overall newspaper sales picture frequently enmesh the word 'race' with adjectives or verbs to reflect this volatile quality. Hence, we hear of 'race storm', 'race row', 'race riot', 'race fury', 'race battle', 'race war' (Gordon and Rosenberg,1989:62).

Hartmann and Husband (1974) describe the inveterate ingestion of news as 'conflict, tragedy and deviancy' (p.154). News of this kind is clearly functional to the effect that conflicts within the wider social sphere and deviation from social norms are of essential relevance to the perpetual seamlessness of a state. Also, news of this kind is often enticing to the audience for its human interest or dramatic effect. In focusing attention on race relations, the news value of negativity, however, has a veritable potential for ill effects. This signifies that positive anecdotes of harmonious race relations stand less chance of being carried than anecdotes of racial strife, and the negative conduct of minority groups comes to be more newsworthy than their positive accomplishments. That the majority population can be seen in the same light does not detract from how serious a bias this is. Since the representation created of the minority group is likely to be consistent with extant stereotypical viewpoints about them, the propensity to perceive selectively has the potential to amplify the unfavourable quality of the image advanced in the mass media. It remains to be said that sections of the majority ethnic public may be predominantly or absolutely reliant on the media for their data on the minority group, and considerable emphasis on negative anecdotes will inevitably give rise to a distorted mental image (Hartmann and Husband,1974:154-155).

The habitus towards the more 'unambiguous' matters to become public knowledge may have similar negative consequences for the documented announcement of race relations, for certain of those matters which have an obscure significance to the journalist may well be the exact matters that have real meaning to the minority population; but because of their nebulosity, they stand less chance of being reported. Below is an example of such an occurrence. In January 1971, a number of petrol bombs were hurled through the window of a London residence where some Black party-goers were in attendance; several people were burned, some very severely (Hartmann and Husband,1974:174-175). This event received very little attention in the national press. In all honesty, could this incident, causing serious personal harm to Black individuals, tangibly be as inconsequential as the documented announcement it was given indicated? The dastardly deed and its scant coverage were clearly of consequence to the Black community. There is the possibility that it was cast in reduced significance in case reporting it would initiate further violence. It may even be that sensational coverage could have led to that effect, but here was a chance for the press to explicate clearly, and with care, the ontology of racism and link it to this fearful example of racism's latent possibility. The event passed virtually ignored by the press and, rather than banish racism, they tended towards maintaining the ban on discussing it. This is tantamount to a mutually dependent habitus for the media industry to project a dominant interest in the general scheme of global affairs from which minority interests become left out in the cold.

An associated factor that makes matters newsworthy is their capacity to be explained within a familiar structure or in terms of obtainable images, stereotypes and outlooks (Hartmann and Husband,1974). The structure and the outlook may derive from the prevailing culture, or they may derive from the news itself and become part of, and indistinct from, the culture. The state of affairs is one of seamless interaction between events, cultural significations and news structures. The manner in which events are made public knowledge helps formulate the outlook on how minority communities will behave or in what way race-relations situations evolve. Succeeding events that are in line with the outlook have a greater likelihood of emerging as news than those that fail to, and new matters arising may be interpreted as expressed by available images even if the available image is not *de facto* the most apt. (The application of the image of racial strife sourced from the American unrest of the sixties as the structure for announcing the British situation serves to illustrate the point being discussed.)

'The news media respond quickly and with keen interest to the conflicts and controversies of the racial story, but, for the most part, disregard the problems that seethe beneath the surface ...' (Hartmann and Husband,1974:159). Discord and rivalry are the basis of 'newsworthiness' and their import as criteria in public awareness selection is as transparent in the documented announcement of sport as in the case of politics and 'race'. The personal skills of the journalist when applied to the coverage of 'race' create an emphasis on discord, negativity and the unconventional that again sets 'newsworthiness' in conflict with reporting underlying currents and existing knowledge. In the instance of the freestanding event, the increased potential to capture the elements of discord and sanguinity can be compressed into a seminal news story. The concealed but detectable processes of inner-city dwelling and the reasons for *parti pris* and resentment are, on these measures, less agreeable to manipulation into favourable news column inches than are representations of violence, crime, and human tragedy, which assume greater visibility as symptoms.

In explicating the treatment of race in the American public announcement industry, it is sometimes helpful to cite the private prejudices and racist assumptions of individual reporters, just to show that prejudiced and racist journalists unmistakably do exist. The same norms and values which lie beneath news preparation would appear to represent a concatenated propensity to provide an inaccurate overview of race relations. Scrutiny has been levelled at the potential inadequacies of the media industry and at the role contributed by news values in creating these shortcomings. Professional standards exist that guide news output and these do afford protection against overly biased and reckless reporting (Hartmann and Husband,1974). However, the matter that we have been advocating is that substantially, the journalists' proficiency is subjective, and that risk factors underlie the news values which govern his or her conduct. Interest in responsible journalism does not necessarily or inescapably produce adequate reportage of race-related subject matter.

Racial prejudices and stereotypes are very different from natural. Such values are acquired, largely through text and talk. It is crucially important to recognize and appreciate that the media contribute a vital function in this reproductive procedural action. A substantial body of research shows that journalists repeatedly use racist stereotypes to represent and define Britain's minority communities (Cottle,2000; Hartmann and Husband,1974; Gordon and Rosenberg,1989; van Dijk,2016; Hall et al,2013; Richardson, 2004). Fowler (1991) advocates that the pattern of news scenarios is "a reciprocal, dialectical process in which stereotypes are the currency of exchange" (p.17; in Richardson,2004:49). Accordingly, his interpretive explanation of a stereotype "is a socially constructed mental pigeon-hole in which events and individuals can be sorted, thereby making such events and individuals comprehensible: 'mother', 'patriot', 'businessman', 'neighbour', [for example] on the one hand, versus 'hooligan', 'terrorist', 'foreigner' on the other" (Fowler,1991; in Richardson,2004:49). Expanding on this contention, Fowler illustrates that in news dialogue, stereotypes and their equivalent stereotypical antithesis are both integrated and integrative of the news value 'meaningfulness', as suggested by Galtung and Ruge (1965):

'Meaningfulness', with its subsections 'cultural proximity' and 'relevance', is founded on an ideology of ethnocentrism, or [...] more inclusively, homocentrism: a preoccupation with countries, societies and individuals perceived to be like oneself; [... and] with defining groups felt to be unlike oneself (Fowler,1991:16; in Richardson,2004:50 emphasis added).

Through the manner and means of this process, the stereotypical imagery of 'Others' may be one (unfavourable) aspect of news dialogue promoted and argued through the same values news construction rests.

Superficial and prejudicial sweeping statements reside safely in a press that feeds on dramatizing discord and simplistically presenting the facts of a matter, the drama that surrounds it and the shallow explanation for it. Newspapers sell not necessarily because of racist reporting but owing to sensationalism around race (Gordon and Rosenberg,1989). Additionally, at the time that an issue is developed, or more regularly distorted, into squaring with these guidelines of news values, its outcome can be very detrimental, especially as strong feelings piqued on 'race' themes have found translation in racist onslaughts on diasporic groups and their property.

Given the likelihood that sensationalism sells newspapers, it remains a prospect without the racism. At times when other news media have highlighted controvertible race issues below lurid and provocative headlines, the *Daily Mirror* and the then *Today* have held firm refusing to surrender to such racism and causing no ill effects to their kudos. They appear to feel duty-bound to cover these bones of contention in an equally competitive style but minus the racist constituent (Gordon and Rosenberg,1989).

The tabloid lexicon has also been taken up by the smaller market share Black and minority ethnic community newspapers like *New Life*, *Caribbean Times* and *Asian Times*, which have provided evidence of the inequalities experienced by Black and South Asian residents and their responses in a conventional news medium. Although recognizing that differences in scale negate direct comparison, such mediums have nevertheless shown that conventional news values could add colour to struggles for equality between ethnic groups rather than be applied to provoke racial tensions.

Therefore, no inherent link exists between news values, other values and racist public announcing and commentary (Gordon and Rosenberg,1989). Prevailing tabloid news values do not on their own sufficiently explain racism in the press, whereas in the organisation of the press industry, its present structure, composition and prevailing perspectives, the way 'race' is dealt with in relation to tabloid news values has regularly served to consolidate racism and it remains to be the case (Gordon and Rosenberg,1989).

With some exceptions, the variables examined thus far – composition of the newspaper industry, ownership and control, news values – come to be seen to throw into the hat of racism in a progressively harsh environment of race relations and a proportion of people indicate how and why the fourth estate means to articulate a racist outlook. However, they do not furnish a complete picture of press racism and the way in which it is replicated. Any one of these variables does not in itself contribute towards a racist press (Gordon and Rosenberg,1989).

An indispensable variable spreading throughout all these elements of the link extending across from the press and racism, which adds to the latter potency and continuity, is with clarity of the dominant cultural expectation – an expectation firmly established in the financial, ideological and power relations of British society. This expectation is reflected in the dominant norms and values which project how the world is characterized, analysed, portrayed and apprehended.

Trowler (1996) cites Hartmann and Husband (1974) as offering up two main thrusts for the biased reporting of minority ethnic groups in the UK media, the press more generally. Firstly, the representation of people of colour as a 'problem' converges with journalists' ideas of what they consider that the public will be interested in, i.e., their news values. Words such as fear, tension, conflict etc. arouse audience curiosity and make them pay attention. Words such as peace, harmony and coexistence are just not seen as good news copy, save for the Notting Hill Carnival with the duty-bound image of the smiling police constable participating in the good-humoured atmosphere, though even this introduces a fear factor provided by the ubiquitous threat of trouble. Secondly, by incorporating these images of people of colour in the media, journalists and those operating above them are merely producing again to society the unfavourable attitudes and symptoms concerning foreigners and people of colour which are intrinsic to British culture (Trowler,1996).

Hartmann and Husband therefore partly support the notion that the media don't influence society, they are influenced by it. Racism is etched onto the conscious awareness of Whites raised in a racist social setting. Their adopted way of thinking and feeling is permeated with archaic frames of reference passed down from centuries of imperialism and racism, and are thus tainted.

Countering racism

People have engaged and continue to engage in different ways to let nothing go unsaid about incidences that register as unfair and unjust in the press. Such challenges have chiefly been circumscribed to sensible responses to everyday events rather than making for part of an organized strategy. A number of attempts have been made, however, to lay down a framework for more protracted campaigning on this subject matter.

THE RIGHT OF REPLY

Dealing with racism in the media world is also part of the whole important bearing of the struggle for a 'right of reply', spearheaded by the Campaign for Press and Broadcasting Freedom (Gordon and Rosenberg,1989:68). The above right of reply would afford that any adult male/female or group who was at the centre of a distorted print media report would have a justified entitlement to reply within the structural arrangement of the newspaper. The foregoing distortion might present itself in ways not dissimilar to those seen in this chapter, through omission of evidence or through the inaccurate provision of evidence.

The advanced 'right of reply' has been cited by some as constituting a kind of censorship. To be specific, rather than censor, it seeks to extend press freedom to act, and extend the variety of views forwarded (Cohen and Gardner,1982; Gordon and Rosenberg,1989). To exemplify, then, had a right of reply been available in 1981, Black people and Black establishments who took exception to the press treatment of the Black People's Day of Action would have had the right to explain their grievances and present their take on events in the publications complained against.

Without the not-long-mentioned right of reply and to respond in kind to the patterns of racist reporting which have been considered in this chapter, Black people have drawn on their own newspapers to encounter accurate reporting and a fairer reflection of their plight. To exemplify, then, the weekly publication *New Life* can share the company of few other papers in the attention it pays to racialized broadsides, drawing up a regular litany of its occurrence in its 'Score of Shame' column (Gordon and Rosenberg,1989). In addition, and having the same importance, are newspapers like *Asian Times* and *Caribbean Times* that have highlighted topics of interest to Black people, like policing, the agency of immigration controls, education etc., and have thrown their weight behind the outlook of Black people.

The National Union of Journalists

In 1980, the National Union of Journalists (NUJ) chose to dissociate itself from the Press Council on account of its absence of real potency and impact. From then on, the union, which incorporates the greater part of Britain's journalists, has created its own system for enquiring into complaints of biased and invidious coverage, including complaints around press racism. The NUJ Code of Conduct admonishes pressmen/presswomen not to 'originate material which encourages discrimination on grounds of race, colour, creed, gender or sexual orientation' and complaints have rung in on numerous occasions that this has gone unheeded (Gordon and Rosenberg,1989:66). Take 1981, for example; numerous complaints were made of press treatment of the Black People's Day of Action, however, these complaints failed to lead to any punitive action against the journalists involved. There was a problem locating exactly which sub-editors were to blame for particular headlines, whereas other complaints were found unproven or the offending journalist was simply let off the hook (Gordon and Rosenberg,1989). In 1985, the union determined to establish a new Ethics Council to search into complaints against members and to conduct educational programmes on 'ethical issues' not excluding race. In 1987, the Ethics Council supported complaints that were at variance with the 'Angry Voice' feature of the *Daily Star* newspaper. A news story about the influence of new visa constraints on Black people intending on a sojourn to the United Kingdom was, the Council argued, 'a deliberate attempt to reinforce racial prejudice and an attempt to incite opinion against Asians on unfair, unfounded and spurious grounds' (Gordon and Rosenberg,1989:67). The article's author, Ray Mills, reciprocated by asserting that he regarded the adjudication – and the union – with the disdain of which it was worthy (Daily Star 23 June 1987; in Gordon and Rosenberg,1989).

The Press Council

Year on year, more than 1,000 people voice their concerns to the Press Council. This is an organization set up by officialdom in 1953 to police and safeguard journalistic standards. It is funded by the newspaper sector itself. The Council is required to look into complaints and to disseminate its decisions or 'adjudications', but power is not vested in its activity and can only urge newspapers to disseminate details of its decision-making and conform to its policy processes. However, newspapers tend, more often than not, to ignore such a suggestion. For example, the Press Council has repeatedly said that an individual's colour need not be raised in newspaper reports other than when this is strictly pertinent or where it might assist the police to track down or locate someone wanted for questioning. Notwithstanding this, some newspapers repeatedly mention that someone in police custody charged over an offence is Black (Gordon and Rosenberg,1989).

In May 1985, the *Daily Express, Evening Standard, Sun* and the *Daily Mail* were chided by the Press Council for announcing that a man found guilty for depredation of chastity and murder was Black, despite the fact that the man's colour was extraneous to the news reportage.

In the succeeding year, the Press Council advised that newspapers were at risk of encouraging or catering to racism by making unnecessary allusions to the race or shade of people in their news item features. Crime stories that tell of people being Black, the Council's chairperson stated, were highly selective and, more times than not, were encountered only in reports of instances involving 'grosser violence' (Gordon and Rosenberg,1989).

Direct action

Confronted with the above inadequate solutions for racism in the press, Black people and anti-racists have fallen back on more direct forms of struggle. The mid-1970s witnessed a group of media professionals in London who formed the Campaign Against Racism in the Media (CARM).

In its infancy, it interjected in the race reportage of two regional publications in north and east London. CARM also made an extremely popular video for the BBC's access programme *Open Door* entitled 'It Ain't Half Racist, Mum' which castigated television's handling of race issues (Gordon and Rosenberg,1989:67). This motley crew also played a pivotal role in marshalling resistance against media exploitation by fascist groups in the final stages of the 1970s.

Alternate groups and struggles have been organized around particular issues. In 1981, to cite as an example, the Black People's Day of Action filed through Fleet Street to demonstrate its ire at the press coverage of the New Cross Fire which incorporated the loss of life of 13 young Black people. In the same vein, in 1985, at the time at which the editors of the *Daily Mail* declined to cooperate with a group of people who took issue with the story about a 'Brides for passports' scandal, a 'Working Group Against *Daily Mail* Racism' was amalgamated (Gordon and Rosenberg,1989:67). This mobilized numerous pickets of the daily's Manchester office and spawned an exhibition putting the feature item into the frame of a chronicle of racist reporting through the *Daily Mail* and alternate mediums. The Group coordinated a condemnatory petition of the publication which drew in excess of 3,000 signatures. In 1987, those behind Viraj Mendis, a Sri Lankan who happened to get cornered into taking shelter in a Manchester church in seeking to avoid deportation, picketed the premises of the *Daily Star* newspaper holding the paper responsible for encouraging violent onslaughts on the church and on those in agreement with Mendis through its vile and antagonistic handling of the issue. In March 1987, for instance, *Daily Star* critic and deputy editor Ray Mills had urged the police to engage in swift action against Mendis and indicated that a 'couple of dozen should march right in, grab him by the tamils, and put him on the next plane to Sri Lanka. Now that really would be a jolly jape' (24 March 1987; in Gordon and Rosenberg,1989:68).

Conclusion

In this chapter, I have mapped some of the processes of newspaper reporting on 'race', and have shown that the media privilege events over causes as the 'race' riots of the 1980s serve to exemplify. Emphasis on events over causes has tended to show Blacks in a negative light consistent with the view held by the general public, though inconsistent with the balancing act that the inclusion of causes can bring to prominence and call attention to. The reporting of more recent riots could have been alluded to, but the 1980's riots sketch the contours of what the press inclines towards. I could have compared and contrasted the reporting of 1980's riots and twenty-first-century riots to evince whether anything has changed but when it comes to Black protest, the media outlook appears to remain the same. The 'racialisation' of the riots drew attention towards the leitmotif of law and order's rhetorical backlash, but seldom was there any mention of the inner-city deprivation, economic decline, the social disadvantage of African - Caribbean youth or the tension precipitated by high-intensity stop and search policing as contributory factors of the disturbances.

The media is not a moral nor rational place in which justice is dispensed. It often relies on distortions, myths and absolute lies that deflect critical attention away from the wealthy and powerful sectors at the pinnacle of society. The power and influence of media barons in newspaper output is extensive and wide-ranging, raising concerns about impartiality, objectivity and balance. Media bias favours the dominant establishment viewpoint and, to some extent, explains Rupert Murdoch's commitment to the status quo. As Hall et al (2013) argue, of the media industry in Britain, it is more complex than to conclude that there is a deliberate conspiracy to fail to represent marginalised groups' interests and experiences of structural inequality and perceived racism equitably.

Enoch Powell addressed national identity and the racisms therein were exposed. The newspapers sympathized with Powell and ignored the effect it might have on minority ethnic communities and race relations, even though his calls for repatriation were considered 'impractical'. I traced news stories of 'muggings' that created Black folk devils which led to moral panics and criminalized large sections of the Black population. Again, as with Powellism, the early 1970's spate of 'muggings' framed Black youth as a social 'problem' alongside the threat minority communities posed to British culture and the British way of life. The construction of communities of colour as social 'problems' is a matter that rests with White hostility and antagonism against minority groups born by their very presence, pure and simple. Black and minority ethnic groups are thought to represent a threat born of fear that this group's birth rate exceeds that of Whites, and this buys into 'fear of a Black planet' and is why entrenched racism makes radical change very difficult and unlikely unless the democratic material fabric of society in toto is undermined. The criticisms levelled at minority communities legitimated the treatment they receive (exclusion/discrimination) being a solution to their presence in these sceptred isles, and could be seen as a way of managing a so-called 'problem'. Subjecting these groups to repressive measures could be seen as a policy strategy to contain and manage a perceived threat. On the other hand, an additional way in which ethnic diversity has been managed is through race relations legislation.

I followed the incidence of racial violence and it becomes clear that White loss of life is more newsworthy than the loss of Black life and when it is covered, reporting lasts for only a temporary phase. Racist violence has an ideological basis upon which reporting takes place and newspapers are inclined to not feature the opinions and experiences of South Asian victims. Newspaper reporting was shown to contribute towards the perpetuation of racist attacks by the types of stories they covered, and how these news items were presented, helping to inflame prejudices and making prejudice seem respectable. We have seen that newspapers produce and reproduce racism; in a particular instance, the media supported and buttressed White hostility even though it was in contravention of UK race relations law. The press has been at pains to point out the wrongheadedness of trying to outlaw prejudice and acts as a partisan conveyance system of the majority ethnic communities' self-obsessed hegemonic agenda, but the moot point rests with majority ethnic hostility and antagonism towards a multi-ethnic reality. Media moguls are well known for influencing the content of news, and, if editors stand in their way, they remove them, so, therefore, we cannot expect mainstream opinion to be too far removed from newspaper bias.

Newspapers such as the *Sun* and *Daily Mail,* which exonerate the British public and deny that racism exists, live in a world where they are untouched by it and that racism is beyond their experience. They neglect, ignore and marginalize the interests and concerns of Black and minority ethnic people and explain it all away by blaming the victim. Such news mediums operate from a white bourgeois perspective that endorses the ideas that legitimate White group power. They are defending their own group interests and their own complicity within it, rendering the majority in a comfortable space and the minority in an uncomfortable space. Such communication media structures are also distorting or bending reality and projecting and reflecting a dominant, albeit conflicting viewpoint on the current state of human affairs and are being unthinkingly enthusiastic and eager when it comes to White privilege. 'Fear of a Black planet' is about fear of loss and it seems as though the predominantly shared White fear of accepting Britain's ignominious past and present with 'race' is somehow tantamount to admitting that a loss has been sustained (Eddo-Lodge,2017:129). The *Sun* newspaper's denial of racism is an example of where one's value system interferes with the deductive reasoning component of thinking, resulting in "partisan" or "autistic" cognition that serves to justify one's values (Sears,1988:75; cited in Katz and Taylor,1988). Research has come up with little support for the assertion that racism has now left us (Sue,1988; cited in Katz and Taylor, 1988 210).

Black journalists, on the other hand, would not venture to state such a case as they know it would contravene entirely everything they stand for and they would be denying a lived reality which they themselves know only too well. This leaves only White journalists to peddle these abhorrent and horrendous points of view which are out of step with reality. It is the media's stock-in-trade to bend or distort reality, and, if reader's lack critical insight, it is easily legitimated and internalised to feed and fuel anti-Black sentiment. There is a need for the media industry to employ more Black journalists if there is to be anything near a climate of change, but this is unlikely to change the mentality of those at the very top, the owners and controllers, because this is where it really counts since they are the ventriloquists and the newspaper the dummy. As McLuhan (1964) argues, the owners and controllers can make the newspapers reflect their particular views and White journalists are inclined to play up to the White middle-class male perspective. Since newspaper proprietors are committed to the status quo, this means the increased employment of Black and minority ethnic journalists will do nothing other than help provide equality of opportunity and also serve the purpose of a more authoritative and sensitive reporting quality around issues of 'race'.

However, not all newspapers are characterized by the same line of racist approach. Liberal and principled ideas, forbearance and flexibility are not infrequently found in the *Guardian*, the defunct *Independent* and the *Daily Mirror* which stand alongside the explicit racism on display in the *Daily Mail* and the *Sun*. However, racist values and beliefs have come to light and are not unheard of in the progressive 'quality' newspapers also. Stuart Hall considers this phenomenon by discerning an important disparity between overt and inferential racism.

Overt racism is when newspaper treatment of a storyline confers sanction and approval to explicitly racist ideas and propositions. Such treatment, Hall claims, has escalated over the past years. The corollary is to rationalize racist rhetoric and to advance the frontiers of readership audience toleration of racism. By way of rapid strides forward, what passes for 'acceptable' often soon is held to be 'true' and what is deemed 'true' comes to represent a racist 'common sense'. Widely interpreted stereotypes of 'illegal immigrants' or 'black scroungers' are the handiwork of the art and practice of the press.

Inferential racism is put across far less deliberately. In such instances, newspapers represent incidents in certain ways unbeknown of the racist premises or contentions on which these inscribed meanings might be based. Chauvinism is constructed anew here as a taken-for-granted system that is largely unseen by those who conceive Planet Earth in these terms. For instance, even the liberal press has members willing to voice concerns on the subject of Black immigration to Britain, and the value judgement that 'good race relations' ride on firm controls being organized around such immigration is the subtext to their analysis and approach. In more generalized wrangling over race relations, the value judgement of natural suspicion and conflict between various ethnic groups and their way of living similarly is the subtext of much liberal newspaper thinking. For instance, when forwarding an opinion on anti-racist agitation and proposed action, Guardian feature writer Jill Tweedie referred to the 'private fears and worries we have and the minor frictions we experience in getting along with other races' and 'human preference for the company of our own kind' (Guardian 24 January 1984; quoted in Gordon and Rosenberg,1989:64-65).

International news is permeated with inferential racism. Hall delineates the manner in which Third World people are portrayed: '... passive and waiting for the technology or aid to arrive, objects of our pity or of a Blue Peter appeal. They are not represented as subjects of continuing exploitation or dependency, or of global division of wealth and labour, but as victims of fate' (Gordon and Rosenberg,1989:65).

The difference between overt and inferential racism squares somewhat with the line dividing the 'popular' and 'quality' papers, but under greater 'Murdochisation' of sections of the second and the more politically strident tendency of the New Right, these lines come to be more and more hazy. At any rate, both varieties of racism emanate from a common source – the core theme in British culture today. However, it is important to recognize and consider this distinction because different approaches are appropriate to managing witting and unwitting racism. While overt racism is expressed in harsher, more contentious terms, inferential racism is more subtle, specifically 'because of its invisibility and because it has become so naturalised' (Gordon and Rosenberg,1989:65). Also, given the customer base of the quality press – chiefly business and professional types – the seemingly milder yet more subtle form of racism is being imbibed in large quantities by an influential public sector statistically smaller but much more powerful than that stratum being served with a cruder diet.

Orthodox interpretations of press racism with regard to personnel and preponderant commercial and news values are short of complete, partial interpretations which are, to a greater extent, symptoms rather than causes. Hall advocates a structural analysis that does not rest on newspapers being controlled or staffed by racists trotting out sensationalist news reports rousing racial tensions. Rather, he advances that the fourth estate, as a structure, is circumscribed within and shaped by the prevailing ideas of British culture and the unequal distribution of power between different groups of people in Britain on which that culture is founded. Hall's rational calculus highlights the indispensability, when deracinating racism by the roots, to cast doubt on this culture and these unequal relations at wide-ranging levels of thought (Gordon and Rosenberg,1989).

The idea that media output places in the minds of people concerning minority populations is that of a 'threat' and a 'problem', a thought pattern more conducive to the emergence of hostility levelled at them than acceptance. In the same vein, the sensational treatment frequently accorded to race-related news events is possibly just a reflection of a peculiar journalistic idiosyncrasy, but its consequences in amplifying racial tensions and maintaining exaggerated misconceptions render it an untenable indulgence. 'Racial stories should be advanced so as to dissuade simple racist inferences on the part of the consumer. It is crucial that the communication media should debate the context to conflict rather than confining itself to documenting the symptoms (Hartmann and Husband,1974). The problem with the news media and society generally is that disproportionate numbers of the White British take issue with and wholly discredit the facts. Whereas press racism is propaganda – since one can usually question the premises upon which it rests – this book asserts propaganda of the truth based on the 'battlefields of knowing' that racism has permeated the British way of life, ever since the dawn of the Black presence in this country (Shyllon,1977; Housee,2018:75). Since racism sufficiently permeates the newspapers as a commercial enterprise, it suggests that the press function to protect and continue the status quo, and the institutional culture of the press underlies this impediment.

Inequality persists between White and Black people because of factors that the press do not help but instead hinder. The press fail to edify their readers, fail to employ enough Black people, fail to report objectively on the Black experience and on issues that affect Black people and ethnic communities, and inextricably linked with this struggle is the struggle for racial justice throughout British society. Racism in the culture forms the cultural backdrop for the drip-drip effect of racism that is widespread in our newspapers. The difficult question to press racism is bound up with the bigger picture point at issue to racial inequality.

Chapter 7: Black Politics and the Campaign for Equality

In the previous chapter, we saw how Hartmann and Husband (1974) partially subscribed to the notion that the media don't have an effect upon society, they are affected by it, and it appears that the destiny of equality for people of colour both here and in the US is also shaped by White manipulation of the rules of the game in order to gain ground. The White man's rules can be seen to reflect how the Black man plays the game, yet by playing according to the rules, the Black man fails to find the faintest recognition of these very values in him. Linda Bellos identified the contradiction that is raised when Black activists succumb to the political game:

> White people always look for a way to undermine our credibility when we try to get into politics. To call us middle-class careerists is such a contradiction. On the one hand, if we, as Black politicians, are inarticulate, then we are authentic, but if we learn their language and use their rules then they say that we are not legitimate – we don't really represent the black community. So white people win both ways around. It's just a successful means of ensuring blacks continue to be disenfranchised (Sewell,1993:111).

The rules of the game are elusive as White people tend to change or contradict themselves to remain ahead. The struggle for freedom and equality is Black politics' objective goal and to appropriate or expropriate it from his oppressor is difficult to imagine in one's mind's eye but, it is futile to expect that it would be handed to him on a platter (Sivanandan,1982). Although Linda Bellos is correct to stress the operation of double standards here, the evidence suggests that the characterization of the Labour Party Black Sections as middle-class stand as well-founded in reality. Progressively, those who take part in the political *mise en scene* tend to be middle-class and scholastically fortunate, and therefore, untypical of the social grouping they rub shoulders with. The aggregate affiliation of the Labour Party has been veering along this route, so there is no reason to hope for activists in Black Sections to be any different. Indeed, one can be led to believe that the disparity extending across from Black political activists and the ethnically diverse community would be so much greater, given the unduly working-class composition of Black and minority ethnic communities (Sewell,1993).

The narrative of action and reaction, of attack and counter-attack, is self-evident: Whites act, Blacks react – and with reference to history, there is little doubt as to the order of events. To advocate, under the conditions, that violence is a question of choice, that it guarantees no special object, is to be resistant to the evidence that for some of the downtrodden peoples on Planet Earth – for the American urban dweller who happens to be Black, certainly – 'violence ... is not a matter of choice ... but a symptom of the fact that there is no other' (Sivanandan,1982:65). That an individual's scope of alternatives should be so minimized to this one unavoidable caveat is itself the scale of the violence perpetrated on him. Also, violence in the twenty-first century need not be openly expressed and flagrant to register as violence – for the antonym of wealth is violence and racism and the convergence of poverty and racism is enough of a violence as to be intolerable.

To advocate, also, that Black power entails a reaction to racism is inherently racist is to lose sight of the fact that racial bias is quintessentially the White man's problem. White oppression is at the root of one of the

West's greatest problems and it blocks the Black man from achieving his humanity which *inter alia* is basic to human life (Sivanandan,1982; Wilkins and Coleman,2005). To take up the option to oppress, the traditional assumption of racial superiority is itself the White man's burden. It is imperative that he choose not to pursue it. The Black man, to reiterate, has no choice.

Expressed differently, White racism is, on one hand, a question of choice, on the other hand, a question of privilege, but at all stages, an exercise in oppression. White racism engenders, somewhere along the process, the opposition to human dignity; Black 'racism' foresees the negation of such opposition. It is 'the rhetoric of abstracted liberalism' which affords them equal importance (Sivanandan,1982:66).

What is more, the liberal, fearful of a counter-response action, suggest that 'Black Power' itself is a conflicting, sympathy-sapping phrase. 'Coloured Power', conceivably, or 'Negro Power' would have been all the more acceptable to the White authority figures and less unsettling on the White persona. Yet this, to repeat, is the White man's problem – since the meanings of 'Black' introduced by the Caucasian male himself are so dire, so sinister, so primordial that to align it with power also is to elicit the nightmare scenario of divine retribution, of a Black doomsday (Sivanandan,1982; Eddo-Lodge, 2017).

The arrival and presence of Black and minority ethnic communities has seen a growing concern to serve minority community interests and this chapter is an attempt at chronicling the nature and influence of their development and the direction in which political interplay has taken matters. The main aim is to incorporate the fundamental modes of Black and minority ethnic mobilisation, the role of antiracist political organisations, the action of race and class acting on each other, minority political participation and how minority politics feeds into local political agendas. Before concluding this chapter, we shall consider what the future chances are for Black and minority politics hitting their mark, particularly from the standpoint of social change that is unfolding within minority communities in the contemporary political climate. Prior to engaging with the particulars at the heart of this chapter, however, it is *sine qua non* to broach certain general contentions about political participation and modes of mobilisation (Solomos,1989,2003).

Political participation and exclusion

Political participation and enterprise are vital elements along the continuum of political systems and structures, which traditionally has involved the amalgamation of essentially different collectives into the polity and the configuration of networks of participation and acceptance. In organized political state entities like Britain, the most conspicuous processes for enabling and minimizing participation are through elections, trade unions, parties, as well as pressure groups (Solomos,1989,2003). These processes and structures tend to consolidate identification with the conventions, procedures and assumptions of the society, they enable the representation of demands to promote consent and they reinforce acceptance of the reasonableness of the political order.

Needless to say, however, is that equal access to participate through 'legitimate' channels is not enjoyed by all groups (Solomos,1989,2003). As delineated by Katznelson and Weir (1985:204), distinct group formation may (a) be incorporated entirely and equitably into the political formal arrangement and possess the embodiment to affect the specifics of policy, (b) be incorporated entirely and equitably but have correspondingly little power to influence the political system, (c) be incorporated in the partial and structurally subordinate sense, but possess innate endowment to influence policy direction at certain times or (d) be structurally subordinate and unable to access the resources necessary to affect the business of the state (Solomos,1989: 142; Solomos,2003:193).

Therefore, assuming that individuals or groups manage to access pathways of political participation, they do not, as a corollary, hold sway where agenda-setting and drawing up policy procedure is concerned. Certain groups and individuals carry far greater weight over any advance towards what issues actually make the agenda. In fact, it has been furthered that certain kinds of problems and particular groups of people are systematically precluded from participation; namely, the fact is a mobilisation of bias exists whereby some bones of contention are organised into the business of state while others are organised out (Solomos,1989,2003).

Dominant social and political norms, as well as structural conventions, can also circumscribe the political agenda. The epitome of this is how the swing of the political pendulum to the right in the period of Conservative Party ascendency, from 1979 to 1997, caused demands for action to facilitate racial equality and positive action came to be marginalised politically. Since these demands do not chime with individualism and self-interested acquisitiveness of the Conservative Party, consecutive administrations systematically opposed the introduction of any important new measure to raise the political representation of diasporic populations. They also offered scant regard to calls to consolidate race relations legislation or to disseminate more resources to institutions responsible for advancing greater racial equality. However, what crystallizes is that such lack of attention to detail acted as a fillip to diverse minority communities to assert themselves towards a more amplified political voice (Solomos,1989,2003).

Racist political mobilisations, which apply in the case of Powellism or the exploits of extreme-right groups, tended almost always to attract considerable attention from the 1960s onwards. However, throughout this time, Black and anti-racist political mobilisations made an important political contribution in determining the politics of race in Britain. Mobilisations of this sort were, however, largely under-researched and unappreciated (Solomos1989,2003; Shukra1998).

The comparative failure of this significant aspect of the politics of race and racism with UK perimeters stems partly from there being, until the mid-1970s, the not infrequent assumption that there existed little and perhaps no political mobilisation by the minority ethnic population at the political level. This impression seemed to be substantiated by national research of electoral behaviour and regional political research exemplified in Newton's research exposition of Birmingham, which discovered no significant data of political mobilisation (Newton,1976 cited in Solomos,1989,2003).

A further variable that contravened the sober research exposition of Black and minority politics was the delicacy of research on political questions. Research on alternate items like the national or regional politics of race is likely to prove highly controversial hence there was a definite reluctance by social scientists to conduct research in the light of opposition from regional Black community groups and activists against outside researchers. The admixture of these two methods of working helped to create a context in which the political participation of Black and South Asian people during the 1970s and 1980s was under-appreciated or researched. A small number of studies did place the experiences of particular cities or minority ethnic organisations under scrutiny, but they remained as isolated data collection activity.

From the starting point of the mid-1970s period and advancing, however, the matter of Black and minority political participation came to be noticed by a number of researchers. While this research lacked a definite focus, it helped to explain certain aspects of minority political mobilisation and electoral participation, and the interplay of political parties and organisations to minority political behaviour (Solomos,1989,2003).

Among the central questions of several research studies has been what minority politics will look like in the future, particularly once Black and minority ethnic groups become more established and integrated into political processes. Such studies have identified three possible formations for the future political integration of diverse groups into the British political culture.

First, the argument has been forwarded that, in time, 'immigrants' and their successive generations would become integrated fully, albeit unequally, into Britain's political institutions, counting political parties, lobbyists and trade unions. Second, the suggestion has been furthered that migrant communities might be integrated into the political culture through their own ethnically or locally-based organisations. These organisations would attempt to forward the interests of specific ethnic groups through political means. Third, the argument was advanced that in answer to institutional racism and the political engagement about racial issues in British social configuration minority communities no matter what their ethnic background, could develop a mutual political identity as a precluded 'black' minority (Solomos,1989,2003).

Agreement was thin on the ground concerning the most likely trajectory that the political integration of minorities would assume, or about the measure of choice they might have in this, yet it was widely accepted by Marxists and pluralists that the various minority political participation was expected to shadow one of the foregoing courses.

For example, research by Phizacklea and Miles (1980), which was contingent on fieldwork in London occupying the late 1970s and applied a Marxist perspective, concluded that the apparent course of events in Britain involved a coalescence of class-based and 'race'-based political mobilisation (Solomos,1989,2003). By reason of their class orientation, minority communities showed a positive interest in established patterns of proletarian participation in the political order, expressed through their commitment to the Labour Party and participation in trades unions. However, on account of the extensiveness of racial exclusionism in all strata of society, they were also compelled to organise independently along racial lines to champion their interests. Generally speaking, this was also the contention advanced by Layton-Henry (1984) although he focuses more attention on the integration of minority politics into political institutions and electoral processes (Solomos,1989,2003).

Since the profile of research material is barely detectable on the political integration or independent political mobilisation among the diverse minority communities, it is far from easy to elicit firm prophetic thoughts on the horizon of minority politics within British shorelines without such in-depth analysis; therefore, in what this chapter has yet to disclose, we shall foreshadow some of the major dimensions of minority ethnic political commitment since the 1940s and, in passing, look at the possible prospects which lie ahead. In the line and direction this account takes, we shall elucidate again on the themes outlined in this opening section.

Early minority activism

The orientation of the newly arrived migrants during the 1940s and 1950s can be characterised by exclusion and disenfranchisement from the political orthodox configuration; as grassroots activists and associations, they lacked the resources to shape state delivery of action (Solomos,1989,2003; Sewell,1993). This is not to say that 'immigrants' took no part in politics; indeed, despite adverse circumstances, the period saw Black and South Asian people who still managed to cultivate their own political organisations, though on a regional level and limited in operation. The 'immigrant' activists never lost sight of their obligations back home nor did they experience impercipience when it came to the need for forming political partnerships in Britain (Sewell,1993). Teaming up with White workers, who themselves belonged to the labour movement, seemed a positive natural development. Organisations like the Caribbean Labour Congress and the Indian Workers' Association rose out of and prospered from the concerns of life in the countries from which they hailed and from the disappointment of life in England (Sewell,1993)

In the 1960s, several minority groups and individuals started to confront this exclusion and raise basic concerns about citizenship and equality. African-Caribbean and South Asian migrants established a set of local and national bodies that attempted in different ways to confront their exclusion from equal involvement in British society. These organisations included the by then operational Indian Workers' Association, the West Indian Standing Conference and additional ethnically based groups (Solomos,1989,2003; Sewell,1993).

The coordinated group that underwent the most public scrutiny during the 1960s was the Campaign Against Racial Discrimination (CARD), which was established in 1964-5 by a merger of Black political partnerships, White liberals and agitators against racism (Solomos,1989,2003). Its chief reason for being was to rid society of racial discrimination, oppose racially discriminatory legal decrees and coordinate the effort of regional and national organisations waging war against racial discrimination. Even though it folded following an ephemeral and highly controversial infighting power struggle during 1967, it participated in public debates concerning the denouement of initiatives to deal with racial discrimination and was useful as a catalyst for an extensive debate on the call for independent Black political organisations to combat the underlying basis of racial inequality in all strata of British society (Solomos,1989,2003; Sewell,1993).

Voting behaviour

We shall now examine who the various ethnic groups, not precluding the indigenous Whites, voted for in three different general elections, 1979, 1983, and 1987. It is worth noting that the CRE studies in 1979 and 1983 were largely carried out in inner-city locations where Labour Party allegiance is generally higher (Werbner and Anwar,1991).

During the 1979 general election, a cross-section of voters from twenty-four constituencies had been asked to log (on duplicate 'ballot' papers) who they supported in the polling stations. Similar 'ballot' papers were used to the ones in the actual election, save that they were distinguished in some way by the interviewers to register the voters' ethnic origin. The 'ballot' papers were deposited in a receptacle container by the voters on leaving the polling booth. From a total cross-section of 3,225 voting participants engaged in the process, 1,205 were from minority ethnic backgrounds. The outcome demonstrated that the majority of ethnic voters did in fact vote for the Labour Party in contrast with other parties. Whereas 50 per cent of Whites opted to vote Labour, 90 per cent of Caribbean and 86 per cent of South Asians in the test case voted Labour (Werbner and Anwar, 1991).

Between Whites in the sample, Labour acquired an 11 per cent ascendency over the Conservatives relative to a 78 per cent ascendency between South Asians and 85 per cent between African-Caribbeans. At the time when we compared the 1979 study results with another carried out in 1974, we discovered that in seven constituency wards where parallels of voting were prospective, it appeared that the Conservative option of choice among minority ethnics, particularly South Asians, had risen in 1979. The finding was that minority ethnic 'swings' to the right of politics were largely explained by the voting behaviour of South Asian voters in contrast with African-Caribbean voters. While African-Caribbean voters staunchly supported the Labour Party, South Asian voters allocated their votes between the two major parties to such an extent that higher proportions opted for the Tories in some constituencies as against others. In seven constituencies from the twenty-four we studied, above 15 per cent of South Asian voters made an election choice for the Conservative Party (Werbner and Anwar,1991).

The CRE's exit poll of the 1983 general election contingent on 4,240 voters in twenty-five constituencies demonstrated that 71 per cent of South Asians voted Labour, 5 per cent Conservative, and 11 per cent for the Liberal/SDP Alliance candidates (Werbner and Anwar,1991:50). It is important to appreciate that most of the twenty-five constituencies included in this survey were Labour-held during the 1983 general election and this bore some relation to these findings. On the other hand, a national exit poll undertaken by the Harris Research Centre (1983) for ITN also substantiates this trend. It demonstrated that the overwhelming preponderance of minority ethnic groups had voted Labour (57 per cent) however 24 per cent and 16 per cent of them had voted Conservative and Alliance respectively (Werbner and Anwar,1991).

The two CRE surveys, placed side by side, illustrate that South Asian commitment to Labour had fallen from 86 per cent in 1979 to 71 per cent in 1983. An additional survey demonstrated that 21 per cent of minority ethnic voters who had supported the Labour Party in 1979 shifted from Labour to alternate parties at the 1983 election (Werbner and Anwar,1991).

However, in relative terms, the Labour vote had continued to be at its most pronounced among African-Caribbeans. The Liberal/SDP Alliance was the sole party that had substantially grown in its basis of support in these constituencies between White and minority ethnic voters alike. The apogee of minority ethnic support for the Labour Party was in Bristol East (93 per cent), for the Tories in Croydon North-east (27 per cent), and for the Alliance in Rochdale (54 per cent), the final two with a largely South Asian electorate. This trend was consonant with the CRE survey of the 1979 general election alluded to above. Keeping these three constituencies under surveillance had shown that the special individual quality of the respective prospective spokesperson for these parties was among the key factors in compelling minority devotion (Werbner and Anwar,1991).

A research study for the Hansib group of papers, carried out by Harris Research Centre at the time of the 1987 general election campaign (25-9 May) on the voting intentions of African-Caribbean and South Asians, illustrated that 86.8 per cent of African-Caribbeans and 66.8 per cent of South Asians planned to support the Labour Party relative to 5.7 per cent and 22.7 per cent respectively for the Conservative Party. Seven per cent of African-Caribbeans and 10 per cent of South Asians planned to support the Alliance. There was no inclusion of White electors in the survey. Since these were only projected plans, we cannot suppose that we know whether these minority groups changed their minds come polling day (Werbner and Anwar,1991).

Another survey completed by the Harris Research Centre, in London on 8-9 June 1987, however, demonstrated that 64 per cent of minority ethnic voters planned to support Labour, 23 per cent Conservative, and 11 per cent Alliance. At the same time, 32 per cent of Whites planned to support Labour, 45 per cent Conservative, and 23 per cent Alliance (Werbner and Anwar).

The forecast of minority ethnic voting behaviours at the 1987 general election followed on from an ITN poll also completed by the Harris Research Centre. It revealed that 61 per cent of South Asians and 92 per cent of African-Caribbeans had selected Labour at the polls relative to 31 per cent of Whites. But 20 per cent of South Asians, 6 per cent of African-Caribbeans, and 43 per cent of Whites had selected the Conservative Party on polling day. The Alliance obtained 17 per cent of votes from South Asians, 24 per cent from Whites, and nadir from African-Caribbeans in the sample. It is worth noting that these findings are based on a finite sample of minority ethnic people (Werbner and Anwar,1991).

A Harris poll demonstrated that almost 60 per cent of the 542 minority ethnic respondents declared they voted Labour during the 1987 election and 62 per cent intended to vote Labour at the time of the next general election. Seven per cent indicated that they voted Conservative and would do so in the future. On the other hand, 27 per cent failed to vote at the last election and 16 per cent had no intention of voting in the next (Werbner and Anwar,1991).

The voting behaviours of minority ethnic groups rest on various factors, but what seems possible is that regular contacts extending across from political parties and minority ethnic groups, their organisation and political action at elections, whether the selected prospective spokesperson is an established figure in the life of minority electors, and their institutional action plans generally, and those of race and immigration concerns in particular, are significant determinant factors in the process of encouraging minority ethnic votes. Recent research indicates that minority ethnic groups currently vote along party lines and not along ethnic lines (Werbner and Anwar,1991; Anwar,1994). Such an account was substantiated in Birmingham Small Heath, which consists of an ethnic minority community of 55 per cent but nevertheless elected a White Labour candidate standing counter to a South Asian Conservative candidate (Anwar,1994). A similar scenario applied to Birmingham Sparkbrook (ethnic minority population 49%) which was instrumental in the election success of a White candidate with a 39.5 per cent majority standing counter to a South Asian candidate in a parallel constituency who gained 24.8 per cent of the vote. Bradford North, itself comprising a minority population of 20.7 per cent, steered the same course electing a White Labour candidate standing diametrically opposed to a South Asian Conservative prospective spokesperson at the 1992 general election. The bearing of the White candidates in these locations also saw the cultivation of good community links with minority ethnic people.

Minority ethnic political affairs

During the second half of the twentieth century, a range of community-based associations and groups have emerged within the broad remit of minority communities. In fact, a distinguishing mark of African-Caribbean and South Asian self-organisation is the variety of communal, religious, political and interest-inspired groups that have materialized. These organisations have often been of a regional or community-based feel, and have involved an array of forms of autonomous organisation in any number of contexts, as against unified ethnic movements (Solomos,1989, 2003).

Despite there being few systematic studies of the early vestiges and political ideologies of these groups, during the 1960s and 1970s, several studies of South Asian political and cultural organisations have been completed, specifically in connection with their political participation and belief system commitment. Studies on a narrower scale of Black organisations and associations were also conducted during that period, but these were scaled back in terms of scope and geography.

Integral to the neglect of this aspect of minority political mobilization may have been the premise that such organisations and collectives were not very effective at higher political echelons. Goulbourne (1987), however, advocated convincingly that without subjecting such groups activity to scrutiny, it would be inconceivable to understand the aggrandizing epiphenomenon of minority politics on the main political parties and established institutions (Solomos,1989,2003). He considered this as highly important in placing social issues like the education of Black children, the state of affairs between police and Black people, Black economic inactivity and racial attacks on the mainstream agenda at both levels of the geographical political divide.

Further scrutiny of minority community associations in the 1980s helped unravel how active self-organisation was a daily aspect of the political life of diverse minority communities. Cheetham (1988) detected that the crucial feature of ethnic organisations in Britain, as can be identified, was their 'extraordinary vitality, energy, and commitment' (Solomos,1989:149; Solomos,2003:198). She determined from her study of typical ethnic associations that two decisive factors were of particular value to more than half of the groups she subjected to analysis: questions of culture, everyday speech and ethnic identity, incorporating the politics of the country from which the associations' members hailed; and how to engineer greater democracy and become absorbed into British society without relinquishing traditions and values (Cheetham,1988:150-1, cited in Solomos,1989: 149;2003:198).

The salience of the instrumental functionality of community-based associations in the public affairs arena of larger minority ethnic structures is only currently being fully appreciated. There is a likelihood that this will result in more in-depth studies of the series of actions of political mobilisation and regional cooperation, both in connection with issue-centred politics and to the ballot box and party politics. The exemplification of this tendency is shown in the attention that has already been afforded to the expansion of political coordination among ethnically and religiously based regional groups. The two key examples in this connection are the Muslim and Sikh communities, which have agitated to raise the ante of political organisation and community-dependent action on issues concerning British politics and the politics of their ancestral origins. Evidence also suggests that formations of religious and ethnic mobilisation are becoming established in Hindu communities appearing within the country's built environments (Solomos,1989,2003).

The push for Labour Party Black Sections

The Labour Party Black Sections grew in part out of a response to the 1981 riots, but in particular, it confronted the frustration Black people faced within the political system and was a call for greater representation. The spark for the idea was provided by Ben Bousquet, Billy Poh and Ray Philbert in May 1982. The fact remains that from the very earliest stages of post-war immigration, Black and South Asian people had rallied behind the Labour Party and continued to do so. Yet, this was not bounced back in terms of party policies or first concerns and in the party hierarchical structure.

A second platform for the emergence of LPBS was a political atmosphere that encouraged intra-party activity and played host to the proliferation of issue-based associations and groupings among the party's left and right-wing ranks. The Campaign for Labour Party Democracy, the Labour Race Action Group, the Tribune Group and the Socialist Educational Association were but a few examples (Sewell,1993:101). The Party's Black members actively participated in the large majority of the *de rigueur* left-wing groups. To be sure, it was by way of the Labour Party Race Action Group that the revolutionary model resolution in 1983 was disseminated for Party conference: the impetus for Black representation from inside the Party had commenced.

The fact that there were other 'Sections' in the Labour Party represented irresistible early signs. 'How could they deny us the right to organise, when there [were] women's sections and youth sections, and even the Jewish Party members have an organised pressure group?' asked Diane Abbott, an initial advocate of the LPBS (Sewell,1993:101). The incentivizing spur for the campaign was, accordingly, that the Black electorate constituted an equally valuable voting public, and that the Party ought to be held more accountable to their needs.

The most important aim of the LPBS was to gain constitutional recognition by the Party alongside the same freedoms and resources had by the Women's and Youth Sections (Sewell,1993). They called for formal representation at each stratum of the party, particularly the privilege to nominate and appoint their own job-seeker for council and parliamentary vacant positions. Along with the ability to short-list, the LPBS also stipulated having a seat booked on the National Executive Committee (NEC) of the

Labour Party to serve their own ends. The decisive factor for LPBS activists was to play a part in and speak up for an issue-based programme (Sewell,1993).

The LPBS provided the springboard for announcing 'race-specific' demands and imposed a 'Black perspective' on the long-established class-based political programme of the party. In serving the purpose of Black representation, the LPBS also stipulated racial exclusivity. With accusations of creating internal party 'apartheid', Black Sections' activists asserted that Black representatives were best placed to voice the concerns of Black people. 'Only he who weareth the shoe, knoweth the pinks', Phil Sealy, former race relations advisor in Lambeth, declared. 'White people are always trying to map the road for us and they never think black people are capable of mapping their own road' (Sewell,1993:102).

With the concentration of these issues at stake, the establishment of a Black Section within the Labour Party became the focus of attention, which was construed as seeking enhanced leverage for Black and South Asian Party members surrounding policy-making and causing a magnetic draw to new minority people to enter into political activity. A resolution encouraging the official appreciation of a Black Section was deliberated during the course of annual conferences staged in 1983 and 1984, and at follow-up conferences. The Labour leadership, however, came out in open opposition to the suggestion of Black Sections, largely qualifying their decision on the basis that it could be construed as divisive and as a particular brand of apartheid. What the leadership seemed also to avail themselves to is a fear that elements of LPBS could become politically damaging if they were headed by hard left-leaning Black groups (Solomos,1989,2003). Consequently, the initiative to establish Black Sections was depicted as backwards for race relations and not as a forward-looking step.

The scathing official Labour Party line was conveniently offered for recommendation under the seal of approval of 'Party unity'. Roy Hattersley even ventured to call Black Sections on affront to socialism, announcing that 'it is, or ought to be, an article of socialist faith that all men and women are treated the same. We can't insist on this ... if we then choose to treat the races differently within the Labour Party itself' (Sewell,1993:103-104). The emphasis on unity was alarmingly suspect: given the mounting disunity that the Party was hitherto experiencing through the agency of its hard left, attaching responsibility for the cleavages on Black Sections activists was as much dishonest as it was unscrupulous.

Clearly, the real paradox was that (despite the leadership's justification) the Party had countenanced Women's and Youth Sections; however, it refused to officially approve Black Sections under the same conditions. Neil Kinnock rejected this accusation of inconsistency:

> No one could sustain the argument that history's precedent for a provision for women is parallel with racism. Black people suffer from different forms of discrimination which require a different response. It is discrimination felt by individuals, not by mass groupings (Sewell,1993:104).

Black Labour Party members could be excused, perhaps, for impercipience regarding Kinnock's separate treatment of women who were disadvantaged as a 'mass grouping' and Blacks who were disadvantaged merely as individuals. From the perspective of some Black activists, this shortfall to appreciate the systematic and institutional character of racism in the wider social sphere added up to clear evidence of the Labour Party's inherent racism. 'It's out and out bloody racism', Phil Sealy exclaimed. 'There is no other reason for the Party to provide special provision for women and not for us' (Sewell,1993:104).

Even though the LPBS failed to realize their objective of official recognition by the party, appeals for greater representation of minority concerns continued to have some import on political intra-party debates during the 1980s and 1990s (Solomos,1989, 2003; Sewell,1993). The motivation for the leadership's resolute sanctioning of the Labour left was a great desire to re-establish the Party's electoral future. With all the comparisons that were drawn of forming a 'ghetto' and an 'apartheid' within Party ranks, the Labour leadership's real bugbear was that a wholesale adoption of Black Sections would be a vote-loser. The matter was in the right-wing press's sights as well as that of other political parties for open exploitation. 'They are afraid that we might become an embarrassment to the Party', former Labour councillor, Andrew Carnegie admitted (Sewell,1993:106). Through its bearing with the 'loony left', the LPBS was construed as yet another bane in the life of the Labour Party. LPBS activist Diane Abbott threw Gerald Kaufman's words of apartheid right back at him, insisting:

> I'll tell you what is apartheid. All-white parties in multi-racial constituencies, that's apartheid. An all-white House of Commons, that's apartheid. We [Black Sections] are providing a remedy for this apartheid (Sewell,1993:109).

Although Abbott was stolen away by its intrinsic value, the LPBS faced persistent criticism from various sides of the political divide for lacking joined-up systematic policy decisions.

The above and other complaints about LPBS's saw the launch in 1988 of The Black Agenda, a document imparting structure to Black Sections' policy on subjects like education, unemployment and health. But the agenda failed to feature in the policies adopted by the Labour Party. Since minority representation has, to a greater extent, established itself in local and central government politics throughout the 1990s, pressure for minority inclusion into political institutions persisted and had, at any rate, some consequence on Labour Party strategy.

Minority politics, as from the 1980s, has been defined by the growing involvement of Black people in established structures. The stand-out examples of this were the desperately disputatious Labour Party Black Section (LPBS) during the 1980s and Black Socialist Society (BSS) innovation which was introduced in 1993. While the Labour Party leadership was dead against LPBS, it formally endorsed the construction of BSS. Extending the official stamp of approval for BSS gave rise to the question of what all the rigmarole over Labour Party Black Sections was really concerning (Shukra,1998). Various Black and minority ethnic politicians and activists who were not LPBS members during the 1980s and 1990s are applying pressure for enhanced minority representation in party structures and elected positions. Notwithstanding formal rivalry, this pressure is beginning to have good results, especially at local government level. Enhanced minority representation in local authorities like Birmingham and Tower Hamlets from the 1990s onwards is a prime example. John Solomos (1989,2003) and Terri Sewell (1993) are both seen to use the idea of LPBS as a 'movement' as though it is unproblematic; instead, LPBS was nothing other than a pressure group or a political merger of individual activists intent on instituting change in the Labour Party. This had ramifications for the definition of 'Black'. (Shukra,1998)

Minority ethnic parliamentary representation

The last element of Black and minority ethnic political participation that is worthy of exploration is the matter of representation in parliament. In the period before the Second World War, three MPs from the Indian sub-continent were voted into the House of Commons. The first, Dadabhai Naoroji, was elected as early as 1892 as a Liberal who captured a majority of five at Finsbury Central. The second, Sir Mancherjee Bhownagree, was, on two occasions, voted in as a Conservative candidate for Bethnal Green North-East, in 1895 and 1900. The third, Shapurji Saklatvala, was, on two instances, elected for Battersea North – as a Labour Party prospect in 1922 and as a Communist in 1924. In the House of Lords, there sat a single member from the Indian sub-continent, Lord Sinha of Raipur (1863-1928). But in the post-war era, there were no MPs of South Asian or African-Caribbean descent until 1987, compared to the presence of three members installed in the House of Lords, Lords Constantine, Pitt, and Chitnis (Werbner and Anwar,1991).

The first post-war minority ethnic prospect put forward by a leading political party for a general election was Sardar K.S.N Ahluwala, who fought the Willesden West seat for the Liberal Party in 1950. Dr David Pitt (now Lord Pitt) fought the Hampstead seat in 1959 and the Clapham seat in 1970 for the Labour Party. In 1970, the fact remains that three minority ethnic prospects also stood for the Liberal Party. In February 1974, the Labour Party selected a Pakistani, Councillor Bashir Mann from Glasgow, to do battle for East Fife. Dhani Prem (Coventry South-East) endorsed the Liberal Party cause. Not one of them had achievable prospects of winning. In the October 1974 general election, minority ethnic candidates numbered just one, Cecil Williams who was fielded for the Liberal Party. During the 1979 general election, the three major political Parties fielded five minority ethnic candidates: one Labour prospect, two Liberals and two Conservatives. This marked the first occasion since 1945 that the Conservative Party had put forward minority ethnic candidates. As it transpired, not a solitary candidate was elected as they fought seats where they had no achievable prospect of winning (Werbner and Anwar,1991).

When the 1983 general election took place, there were eighteen minority ethnic prospects who fought for the main (four) parties. Werbner and Anwar ask, how well did they run as candidates? Generally, they performed not unlike any other candidate for their parties. For instance, in 17 of the 18 constituencies in which battle was done, where a comparison with the hypothetical party position in 1979 was feasible, the party's position remained unchanged. However, in 1979, no minority ethnic prospect contested a winnable seat (save Paul Boateng who did battle over Hemel Hempstead, a hypothetically winnable seat contingent on the redrawn boundaries (Werbner and Anwar,1991).

The exegesis of the independent or fringe party minority ethnic prospects who campaigned in general elections between 1950 and 1983 reveals that their performance, in the main, had been 'poor' contrasted with those who campaigned for the major political parties. Werbner and Anwar ask, for what reason did these candidates fight in those elections? A measured audit of their campaigns indicates that some, like dissimilar fringe or independent prospects in elections, stood as they wanted to highlight certain issues, others fought for small parties, and yet others fought because they wanted to remonstrate against the scarcity of minority ethnic representation in parliament (Werbner and Anwar,1991).

During the 1987 general election, among the twenty-seven minority ethnic prospects for the four foremost political parties, four were elected. The quartet, each of whom represented Labour, were the late Bernie Grant (Tottenham), Diane Abbott (Hackney North and Stoke Newington), Paul Boateng (Brent South), and Keith Vaz (Leicester East). The trio of London MPs was jointly elected in 'safe' Labour seats. But Keith Vaz triumphed with a groundswell of opinion of over 9 per cent from the Tory prospect, Peter Bruinvels, compared with a groundswell of just over 2.2 per cent for Labour prospects in alternative seats in the East Midlands. The work rate of other minority ethnic prospects was, in overarching syllables, like that of separate party prospects in the same locations (Werbner and Anwar,1991).

However, it is important to appreciate that the marvel of the work rate of a minority ethnic candidate is not a simple or straightforward matter. Various factors influence such performances and these could vacillate according to individual party affiliation, the demography of the site of battle, the personal magnetism of the prospect, rejection by some White constituents on the basis of colour, and whether the vacant position is 'safe' or 'winnable'. Certain of these determinant factors could just as well have a bearing on a White candidate. Meanwhile, there is now sufficient evidence to show that minority ethnic prospects are progressively being welcomed into the 'party' fold as candidates. Local elections have spawned a profusion of triumphant achievements in recent years, not to overlook the 1987 general election. For instance, in the Greater London boroughs' poll in May 1986, in excess of 150 minority ethnic councillors were elected. Different candidates were elected in Birmingham, Bradford, and Leicester, to name only a few areas. In total, it is thought that there are in excess of 200 minority ethnic councillors distributed country-wide (Werbner and Anwar,1991).

The success of four minority ethnic Labour MPs in the 1987 general election was popularly portrayed as a major shift in British political life (Solomos,1989, 2003). At the 1992 general election, the number of minority ethnic Labour MPs expanded to five, and with the election of the first Conservative minority MP came the cry from all political parties that race presented no more an object in British political life. All of those who received a mandate in 1987 were re-elected, two of which significantly increased their majorities: Bernie Grant with a 9.4 per cent improvement and Keith Vaz with a 10.4 per cent improvement. Whereas Ashok Kumar, who received a mandate as Labour MP for Langbaugh in a 1991 by-election, lost his deposit, two new minority MPs received a mandate: Piara Khabra took charge of her Labour former incumbent's seat of Ealing Southall, and in Brentford and Isleworth, Nirj Deva assumed the mantle of first minority Conservative MP.

In toto, 23 minority ethnic prospects contested the 1992 general election: ten for Labour, four for the liberal Democrats and eight for the Conservatives (Solomos,2003). The mandate received by the Black and South Asian candidates was taken as proof that Britain was beginning to be a multiracial society. This was held up against what other European societies came into contact with where immigration was beginning to be raised as a conscious awareness issue and there was proportionately little minority coalescence into the political mainstream (Solomos,2003).

The motivating rationale for the widely dispersed interest in the mandate given to the minority MPs in 1987 was the cause célèbre around their nomination, which was popularly portrayed as the outcome of pressure by the LPBS and sections of the Labour left. Also, many of the Black and minority ethnic politicians given local and national mandates were characterized in the media and in widely publicised political discussion as either proponents of Black power and the hard left, or as proponents of specific faith and ethnic groups.

During the run-up to the 1987 general election, the Labour Party named a number of minority ethnic prospects for safe seats as there were unambiguous signs of fear about the possible ramification of minority representation in the House of Commons. The *Sun* implored that handing a mandate to minority MPs would not assist the greater number of the minority ethnic composition since they were 'all holders of loony left ideas which have shocked the nation' (Solomos,2003:202). Considering things more loosely, the naming of minority prospects became mired in the popular debate over the consequence of the 'loony left' on Labour Party politics and the exploits of left-wing borough administrations akin to Lambeth and Brent. The contention over the nomination and suspension of Sharon Atkin as the prospect for Nottingham East in the run-up to the election was an unambiguous illustration of how these matters coalesced in widely disseminated political debates. Sharon Atkin was suspended for applying the epithet 'racist' to the Labour Party (Sewell,1993; Shukra,1998).

In the aftermath of the 1987 and 1992 general elections, a great deal of attention was focused on the parliamentary work rate of the minority MPs and to their effect on deliberations in parliament and on committees. The evidence also clearly suggests that Black and South Asian MPs were experiencing unique pressures that were making their position not very unproblematic both as regional ward MPs and as minority ethnic politicians. On one level, they were under difficult demands to become incorporated into the ideals of parliamentary life, while on another level, they were expected to perform as spokespersons on a range of race and ethnic issues. The same circumstances confronted the rising level of minority politicians who were elected as regional ward councillors, and who were, more times than not, thought of as arguing for entire communities irrespective of ethnic, cultural or religious distinctions (Solomos,2003; Werbner and Anwar,1991).

At the May 1997 general election, 44 minority ethnic prospects stood for the established political parties – 14 for Labour, 19 for the Liberal Democrats and 11 for the Conservatives – yet just nine were successful, entirely for the Labour Party. The circumstances in the June 2001 general election were widely indistinguishable, though there was some expansion in the level of minority candidates contesting for the Conservatives, the Liberal Democrats and fringe parties. From the 25 Liberal Democrat, 16 Labour and 16 Conservative prospects, only 12 (from a variety of minority backgrounds) were victorious, all for the Labour Party. While this was scarcely a significant increase in minority representatives at Westminster, it symbolized the entrenchment of, at minimum, some level of minority political representation (Solomos,2003).

The rise of New Labour in the 1997 national polling decision caused heightened opinion that minority political representation might gain a more prominent position. Of course, during its first administrative term, the then Blair government touched on the need for further Black and South Asian models of excellence in political life, however, recent research has shown the limited and somewhat spasmodic advancement that minority representation has forged in both regional and national structures (Solomos,2003). As if there was not cause enough for concern, the evidence points to no consensus about the way in which this relatively slow incidence of progress can be dealt with, let alone policy processes for substantive reform.

Antiracist clamour and political alliances

The counteroffensive on racism in Britain has many more difficult years ahead. Among the national movements to emerge to fight this corner since the Second World War were CARD in the 1960s, which Heineman characterizes as 'an organisation representing a movement that did not exist' (1972:2) and the Anti-Nazi League alliance, alongside another organisation known as Rock Against Racism (RAR) in the 1970s (Heineman,1972 quoted in Werbner and Anwar,1991:29). CARD is the abbreviation for Campaign Against Racial Discrimination. Although CARD made little headway in tapping regional rank and file organisations and was exclusive throughout, it did propagate, during its short-lived period, a somewhat broad alliance with significant influence on the direction of anti-racist law-making in Britain. Conscious awareness indicates, as Heineman recognises, it rode in the slipstream of the American civil rights movement's momentum. When its legislative agenda was accepted, it fell into disarray, amid mutual mud-slinging and internal differences between Black Power revolutionaries and liberal/socialist reformers.

Rock Against Racism grew in counter position to Powellism and the rising electoral gains of the National Front. This anti-racism focused attention on the convoluted race politics of exclusively White pop music and appreciated the significance of the Black antecedents of even the most anglicized rock as a political negation for those who were gravitating towards racist conceptualization and interpretation of the crisis (Gilroy,1987). The initial issues of *Temporary Hoarding* carried montages, many promoting the Black and White musicians who had offered RAR their labour, alongside the catchphrases and slogans of the anti-racist mobilization: 'Love Music, Hate Racism' and 'Black and White Unite and Fight' (Gilroy,2002:166). Visual interaction with the audience at this level rather than in verbal format was a highly noteworthy feature of RAR's success.

It is rare indeed to find an account of RAR's achievements that does not acknowledge the visual aspect of their political attraction. Their configurations and montages made provision for the communication of convoluted and, at times, challenging ideas in an abridged yet exhilarating form which juxtaposed sharply with the dull, didactic announcements of their fascist opponents in the battle to win young hearts and minds. The organisation's success emanated from not calling it Rock against Patriotism, Rock against Royalty or Rock against the Nation, but in these initial stages, those were the challenges on which it spread and reproduced. In one way or another, racism symbolized and articulated the unacceptable modus operandi of all of the aforementioned and more (Gilroy,2002).

The interpretation of racism, which directed RAR's practice, was not limited but extensive. It acceded that racism had taken on a shortened symbology for all the beyond the pale social relations of 'Krisis Time 1977' and 'Labour Party Capitalist Britain' (Gilroy,2002:168). The Anti-Nazi League came into being on 10 November 1977. It acted to alter and re-direct RAR's ideological affairs and orientation. The League's inaugural statement focused attention on the electoral threat presented by the NF and their alliance partners. The League's sponsors attempted to organize 'on the widest possible scale' and prevailed upon 'all those who oppose the growth of the Nazis in Britain [to unite] irrespective of other political differences' (Gilroy,2002:171). Just as the League's title might suggest, its aims were uncomplicated and more clear-cut than RAR's heterogeneous commitments.

The notion that the British Nazis were just sham patriots who sullied the Union Flag by their tapping into it was a strong distinguishing mark of ANL leaflets. This disingenuous patriotism was laid bare and counter-positioned with the bona fide nationalist spirit which had been cultivated during Britain's defining moment – the 'anti-fascist' 1939-45 war. The neo-fascists sported the uniforms of Nazism under their exterior form of respectability and it is difficult to calibrate what made them more horrendous to the ANL, their Nazism or the manner in which they were hauling British patriotism through the mire. The league's pamphlets brought back the paraphernalia of war – concentration camps and Nazi servicemen – and were capped with the anti-fascist mantra 'Never Again'. One pamphlet, 'What would life be like under the Nazis?', warned future NF supporters that 'The NF says they are just putting Britons first. But their Britain will be just like Hitler's Germany' (Gilroy,2002:171). Another, 'Why you should oppose the National Front' made a more pointed challenge to the characteristic of NF patriotism: 'They say they are just patriots. Then why does Chairman Tyndall say: "the Second World War was fought for Jewish, not British, interests? Under the leadership of Adolf Hitler, Germany proved she could be a great power"' (Gilroy,2002:171-172).

The League then asked, 'To what extent could those who privately aped the fascistic practices of Britain's arch-rivals then pose as custodians of national culture and the body politic?' Its monetary funds were invested in materials that could be employed in anti-fascist campaigning for constituency polls and the expected general election. The effort to instigate the obliteration of Nazism as an urgent matter on the diverse and intricate political consciousness reified by RAR was a gross distortion of the truth. The literal translation of the problem of 'race' – as a feature of fascism – corresponded by a rapid expanse of the drive against it tapped RAR's impetus, punk and the residuum of anti-Jubilee sensibility. But this alteration inflicted a shorter life and multiple narrowed aims on the movement. The ideals of anti-racism were becoming redefined. The brainchild of Rasta endeavour for 'Equal rights and Justice' was being neglected, in the ANL and perhaps even RAR. These values were supplanted by the more demure aim of freezing out and nullifying the fascist parties through means of the ballot. While both campaigns still targeted young people, the piecemeal transition from anti-racism to anti-Nazism, which had been spurred by the expansion of the League, represented the onset of a concerted effort for older voters and entailed a direct connectedness to their recall of anti-fascism during the 1930s and 1940s. Ernie Roberts, a League Steering Committee member, articulated this change in weight:

> The success and strength of the league are based on the old who remember fascism and the 1939-45 war, on the young who see fascism as a menace to their freedom, culture and future and on the women who know the inferior position which fascism forces them to accept (Gilroy,2002:173).

On the occasion that the ANL did level its message at the young, it was highly dependent on the approach and political vernacular of both RAR and punk. An issue of its literature prepared for distribution amid school pupils, for example, combined the anti-fascist beliefs of John 'Rotten' Lydon, the Sex Pistols' vocalist, and Brian Clough, the football manager, beneath the title NF=No future (Gilroy,2002).

The League's magnetism to older citizens came alongside further alterations in its organizational approach. The single most outstanding of these was the development of a multitude of orbital satellite organizations which were to transport the anti-Nazis struggle from the dance halls and to transcend street corners through to the workplace and, therefore, supposedly into conventional working-class politics. Large numbers of people against Nazism and from all walks of life began to fracture the delicate harmony which had been forged by shared cultural antithesis to the nationalism, fascist thuggery and police persecution which RAR had discerned as the makings of racism and the critical signs of the domestic malaise (Gilroy,2002).

Rocking Against Racism had given occasion for youth to rally against the perceived vices of 'Labour Party Capitalist Britain'. The universal foreground tactics ushered in by the ANL put paid to it. Identifying with 'Anti-Nazi' situated the political problem presented by the spread of racism in Britain solely in the exploits of a narrow and eccentric, yet violent, group of neo-fascists. While they had a higher than usual profile in the 1976-9 period, and irrespective of whether they had the ability to make serious progress into the traditional support base of working-class constituents in the urban sprawl, Tyndall, Webster, Mclaughlin and their associates were only a narrow and minor part of the political priorities which had animated RAR youth (Gilroy,2002).

Temporary Hoarding's reportage of Front leader Webster's solitary patriotic demonstration through Manchester streets was inflamed by public outcry against the association between his fascism and the connivance of the racist state. The fact that manifold numbers of police directed the lone flag-bearing figure en route through the anti-fascist rally was evidence of continuity. In marked difference, the ANL made steadily more of the link between these fascists and those which had been defeated by Britain in 1945. Notwithstanding how much vitality the league could amass for the object of 'kicking out' the Nazis from whence they lurked, even the exemplary racist Britons did not inevitably see themselves as Nazis or associate their ideas concerning alien culture, mugging or repatriation, to follow from dogma authenticated by Hitler or Mussolini.

The league stressed the Nazis moral code of neo-fascist and chauvinistic public affairs without accounting for any other consideration. Such a strategy may have resulted in the unsuccessful election breakthrough of the NF, British Movement and their cohorts but this was accomplished ironically by breathing new life into the very components of nationalism and xenophobia which had assisted Britannia through the most worrying periods of the 1939-1945 war. This patriotism, briefly reflected to the anti-

Nazi ideal, was a rocky foundation. There is the likelihood of it working itself free from the anti-fascist allies at the very moment that the NF and like-minded groups began to throw aside calls of Nazism and set about presenting themselves convincingly as nothing other than trepidatious British patriots (Gilroy,2002).

The establishment of a popular anti-racist movement in this geographical and political boundary has gone largely ignored by left writers. It is worth noting that at the moment when RAR and the ANL hit their apogee, considerable rhetorical backlash was transmitted over their enterprises by socialist commentators. The perception was that the action plan of the League was at fault, giving, for example, inadequate importance to the question of setting up workers' self-defence groups or more notably, that anti-racism could be no more than a halfway stage in the evolution of a solid realistic base and complete range of political cognizance and organization. Pointing towards this orientation, Tariq Ali, then among the leadership of the International Marxist Group (IMG), a Trotskyist group whose members were participants of the ANL, described the Victoria Park Carnival which had attracted 80,000 people under the signage of RAR and the ANL with the outlined words: 'Lots of people will come along for Rock Against Racism today and see that it should be Rock Against the Stock Exchange tomorrow' (Gilroy,2002:175). The handiwork and organizational strategies taken up by the far right in the post RAR/ANL era were clearly influenced, other than by the approach which anti-racism had incorporated to fashion a mass movement but by an understanding of the significance of pop culture in establishing the political perspective of young people. This bore no comparison on the left. The *young nationalist*, youth outlet of the British National Party, informed its audience:

> The record and cassette is [sic] more powerful than the TV or newspapers where youth is concerned. Disco and its melting pot pseudo-philosophy must be fought or Britain's streets will be full of black-worshipping soul boys (Barber,1979; quoted in Gilroy,2002:176).

The NF's youth publication, *Bulldog*, regularly devoted expressive language to pop culture and, over a number of years, tried unsuccessfully to introduce a 'Rock Against Communism' campaign similar in style to that of RAR. As a result of the power of Black music as a vehicle other than for Black culture but of counter-positional and anti-authoritarian conventions, extreme right groups have undertaken their own informal struggle against local outlets which have, from their viewpoint, played a disproportionate amount of Black music thereby watering down the national will. For instance, London's Capital Radio was assailed by an organized barrage of calls to their switchboard protesting that the musical content by Black artists accounted for as much as a third of the station's output. The general public was made aware that up to thirty calls around this issue were being recorded daily. The voice of Capital Radio stated, 'The callers sound as if they are reading from a script and using the same expressions like "you're pandering to the latter-day immigrants instead of serving the traditional cockney"' (Gilroy,2002:176).

The initial stage of the ANL mobilization came to an end with the Conservative rise to power in 1979. For RAR, it was business as usual, championing the 'two-tone' trends and bands even given the gradual decline of its mass support base. The organization was not about to relinquish organizing nationwide gigs and *Temporary Hoarding* focused on the activities of regional groups in various areas. A 'Dance and Defend' extravaganza was put on to lend support to the anti-fascist demonstrators who were arrested and assaulted at some point in the course of a police riot at an NF popular vote demonstration in Southall (Gilroy,2002:176). The police were behind the killing of an ANL activist, and several RAR workers who had also played a role in a local area and music centre – 'People Unite' – sustained severe injuries when the venue was raided by officers from the Met's arms-bearing squad, the Special Patrol Group (SPG). *Temporary Hoarding's* tenth publication issue, in November 1979, featured column inches devoted to the Southall events, immigration control, mods, two-tone, ska, Northern Ireland, teenage sexuality and the thuggery of night-club doormen. The content of its leaves bore reports from RAR groups in

Stevenage, Dublin, Hull, Reading and also London. The fresh new Conservative government had decided to exploit the race issue as part of its design to appeal to the masses. This changed the arrangement of racial politics, rendering of little usefulness the purpose of the neo-fascist parties. Consequently, anti-racism had thrust upon it a party political hidden meaning. The League's first and last priority became harder to support and appeared to look misplaced when the then head of government asserted the claim around the British people 'feeling rather swamped'. Chastened in the elections, the neo-fascist groups assumed a lower profile, raised their work rate with youth applying many of RAR's convictions and adopted what they referred to as a strategy of tension which laid a greater weight on physical intimidation and persecution of Blacks. Towards a belated response to this, unsuccessful representations were made to breathe new life into the League throughout spring of 1981 (Gilroy,2002:177).

However this may seem, antiracist political alliances did not cease to exist. For instance, Ben-Tovim et al. (1986) discovered that locally based antiracist groups in Liverpool and Wolverhampton were working industriously to raise minority political concerns and mobilise public perception against racist organizations (Solomos,1989,2003). Out of this, they deduced that at the community level at least, antiracist political partnerships remained an important constitutive element of the policy formation of racism in Britain. Also, research conducted by Solomos and Back (1995) in Birmingham throughout the course of the early 1990s indicated that coalition politics was doing a great deal to influence minority political agendas throughout the course of this period.

On the other hand, single-issue campaigns on matters of fundamental regard to minority communities continued to be an important part of community and wider social-political mobilisation. A fitting example of this encircles the work done by the National Coalition of Anti-Deportation Campaigns, an interest group that developed out of local agitation on immigration and associated issues.

Throughout the 1990s, there were several different attempts to establish a national umbrella unit to amalgamate these local groups. The ANL regrouped for this reason, but it soon crystallized that interests had branched off and a number of competing bodies, namely the National Assembly Against Racism and the Anti-Racist Alliance, emerged to reflect the various camps of the now-ruptured anti-racist movement (Solomos,2003). The legacy of the Stephen Lawrence murder, inter alia, witnessed the establishment in April 1999 of the National Civil Rights Movement, which took its lead from the American Civil Rights Movement traceable to the 1950s and 1960s.

Politics, pressure groups and reform

Key questions upon which all interpretations of minority political mobilisation rest are what influence can minority ethnic communities exert on the political agenda, and what is the likelihood that effective defiance to racism can be launched in the current political climate? Such questions have doubtless become usual baseline criteria in debates on clearly defined policy issues like education and policing, which have emerged as matters of lively debate among the distinctive minority communities for a significant period of time.

Far from going unnoticed, however, is the prospect of there being no uniform solution to these problems. Solutions vary from deep pessimism about the likelihood of minorities having an important effect on the orthodox political agenda, to a modicum of hopefulness about the potential of minority politicians to reform political institutions (Solomos,1989,2003).

Possibly towering above all other political developments in the modern era has been the concern by minority politicians to reach positions of political support and power at both central government and constituency level. The inference beneath this strategy holds that only through the gateway of integration into the established pathway of political power and support can minority communities move outside the range of political exclusion and powerlessness to a state where they are included equally into the political process and have the wherewithal needed to initiate policy changes that respond to their needs.

Given how optimistic the above view is of the possibility of Black forward movement through the political system, it is not the general agreement of all commentators. The associated failure of the established political institutions to address the very origins of racial inequality and racism in British society is assigned to why some commentators look past the channels of conventional politics for a response to these questions (Solomos,1989,2003).

Gilroy (2002), for example, closes his account of inner-urban social change and Black community resistance in the 1980s by advocating that:

> In the representation of the recent riots, it is possible to glimpse a struggle, a sequence of antagonisms which has moved beyond the grasp of orthodox class analysis. Unable to control the social relations in which they find themselves, people have shrunk the world to the size of their communities and begun to act politically on that basis (ibid.:336).

Despite the difficulty of discerning a definitive political strategy in this somewhat general and cryptic formulation, Gilroy seems to be asserting that (a) the acknowledgement that minority people are turning out to be increasingly integrated into the established class-based political structure is inadequate, and (b) disadvantaged groups are likely to endorse political behaviour patterns that operate at the micro as against the macro level (Solomos,1989,2003).

This school of thought is diametrically opposed to the persistent effort made by other minority root and branch thinkers to prioritise the realization of more direct minority participation in central and regional political institutions. This paradox also resonated in the discursive struggle on the establishment of a Black faction in the Labour Party and the broader discursive struggle on enhanced minority representation in the conventional political institutions.

Solomos (2003) lets us know that in recent years, even the addition of twelve minority ethnic MPs and a large number of minority councillors in various local authorities is unlikely to produce an effect on the distribution of resources and political power. That this is so was implicitly recognised in the veritable Black Agenda issued by the pressure group Black Section throughout 1988.

Minority appeals for full citizenship face a difficult road ahead in the present political environment. Inner-city unrest that broke out in isolated instances during the 1980s and 1990s may meet a better-prepared response in forthcoming decades, but the root causes at the heart of the problem are not going to evaporate. Routine approaches to dispute resolution have hitherto proved incapable of addressing conflict with this scale of meaning and dynamic, and the future prospects do not look at all good (Solomos,1989,2003).

However, it is worth noting that this state of play is not likely to lead to wholesale withdrawal from all kinds of political activity. In this is possibly the best hope amid minority communities' long, dark-night struggle for equality and full citizenship. Thinking about the history of endeavours to establish a national body to fight the minority corner at the political level, Hall (1985) maintains that a monadic reason for the non-success of such endeavours is the lacuna between such organisations and the 'actual day-to-day experience of repression and exploitation which the black community has gone through' (Solomos,2003:207).

Race and class

We are interested in the structures which, operating within the prevailing 'logic' of capital, create and recreate the social circumstances of the Black working class, affect the social world and the productive universe of that class, and allocate its members and representatives to positions of structured secondariness within it. The structures which achieve this critical function of 'reproducing the conditions of production' for the British proletariat as a general rule also operate in a particular way as to shape that class in a racially segmented and fragmented form. Race is a crucial component of this reproduction of class associations, not simply because groups from one ethnic category have racially differential dealings with other groups, but because race is among the variables which provide the detail and social foundation on which 'racism' as a system of ideas flourishes. Race emerges as a key constituent in the given order of societies structures which each fledgling generation of the proletariat encounters as a feature of the 'given' material frame of its life. Black youth, from every generation, does not start out as a set of lone individuals who happen to be given the tools to live and work in particular ways, experiencing racial discrimination en route to adulthood. Black youth starts out in each generation from an established class orientation, produced in an existing structure, through processes which are discernible, not derived from their origins; and that class orientation is, in the same breath, a racial or ethnic orientation (Hall et al,2013).

However, race performs a binary function, and it is the major modality in which the Black individuals of that class 'live', go through, demystify and therefore come to an awareness of their structured secondariness. It is in the process of race that Blacks fathom, deal with and then raise opposition to the exploitation which is an actual feature of their class position. Race is consequently not merely a component of the 'structures'; it's a key component in the class struggle – and accordingly in the cultures – of Black endeavour. It is in the counter-weltanschauung of race, colour and identity that the Black proletariat becomes knowledgeable about the inconsistencies of its actual situation and takes the necessary steps to 'fight it through'. This is all the more now the case for Black youth. As it so happens, race provides the connecting link between the structured situation of subordination which is the 'lot', the 'plight' enshrined in the status of this division of the class, and the lived confrontation, the state of mind that comes with their being second-class citizens. It is through the process of race that those whom the social compositions systematically exploit, exclude and subordinate come to the realization that they are 'an exploited, excluded and subordinated class (Hall et al,2013:341). Accordingly, it is primarily during the process of race that resistance, hostility and rebellion initially put themselves across. On a basic, most obvious and perfunctory level, one can grasp this fulcrum of race for the arrangement of consciousness in the direct accounts and symbolic forms of young Black people themselves: how race makes up, viscerally, the full range of their lived experience. As an example, we have Paul, aged 18, conversing on work:

> You always get this thing like when I went for a job up the road and the man he says: 'You don't mind if we call you a black bastard or a wog or a nigger or anything because it's entirely a joke'. I told him to keep his job. Him say, 'I'm not colour prejudiced' and everything like this. But it's foolishness when a man asks a question like that straight away.

And Leslie, discussing Paul's experience:

> Paul here went for a job and the white man says, you've got an afro haircut and you've got to change your hairstyle. If it had been me, I'd have kicked him down. I'd have kicked him rassclaat down. I'd have kicked him in his c - . F – ing bastard. I don't want to work for no white man. Black people have been working for them for a long time. I don't want to work for them. I never used to hate white people. I still don't hate all of them. But it's them who teach me how to hate (Hall et al,2013:341).

Conclusion

This chapter has drawn attention to the role of minority and antiracist political mobilisation against the background of the racialisation of British political affairs since 1945. It makes an attempt to elucidate that, far from being hapless victims, minority communities have actively sought to squarely confront racism and injustice. What has transpired in recent years would seem to signal that the participation and engagement of South Asian and Black people in central as well as local politics is likely to multiply (Solomos,1989,2003).

The politics of antiracist structures have also made a valuable contribution at various moments since the 1950s and have drawn widespread sympathy and approval from quarters extending beyond minority communities. Up and down the country, attempts to create partnerships against racism have been essentially inconsistent and have proved incongruous, but the emergence of groups like Rock Against Racism and the Anti-Nazi League in the 1970s, together with various regional initiatives, seems to signal that the likelihood for political mobilisation against racism has shown itself. However, the revolutionary classes have much to achieve if they are to halt the march of inequality and, in turn, change the political landscape. The eradication of racial inequality has to be brokered to some extent with the dominant groups' permission.

In terms of the future, interest seems to bring into full focus young Blacks and other frustrated minority groups. To illustrate, Rose (1985:59) asks whether the national procedural process will succeed in producing wider social integration or the conjuncture where 'a small, politically alienated and active group will identify themselves as Blacks rather than Britons' (cited in Solomos,1989:158; Solomos,2003:208). Taking a somewhat different approach, (Gilroy,2002:338) argues that the instant prospect of metamorphosis from the present conjuncture is to be located among 'those groups who find the premises of their collective existence threatened' (cited in Solomos,1989:158; Solomos,2003:208). Similarly, Cedric Robinson (1983) argued that 'the black radical tradition', as opposed to a broader proletariat, is the engine of social change (Shukra,1998:41).

Possibly the most important information to be retained from the events of the 1980s and 1990s is that it is much too simplistic to put forward one paradigm of sable or antiracist political mobilisation. Alternatively, it is noteworthy to accept the volatile, and, to a point, unpredictable nature of political strife over race and to discover whether such strife has a chauvinist or an antiracist political purpose. When this is conducted, it becomes evident that the active participation of Black and minority ethnic residents must be a constitutive element of any realistic approach for running counter to the political agenda regarding race in British society (Solomos,1989,2003).

The struggle for equality will remain so long as Black and minority ethnic people fail to realize equal power relations between groups, which is the best fundamental foundation for equality of status. Since there is a White backlash awaiting all attempts to challenge the political agenda on race, equality may prove ever more elusive and far from an inevitable outcome. In other words, although White people have more progressive attitudes and beliefs about minority groups, they still present opposition to moves to remedy inequality. Despite there being the possibility of a consensus on the facts, there is deep dispute over the appropriate panacea. Black and minority ethnic groups face an uncertain future where the prospect of racial equality is concerned because White society shows no signs of relinquishing its privileged position over non-white people. The national will or collective identity gains a material advantage through differential treatment of minority people and the national will is complicit with the continuity of Black subordination even given the facts. It is difficult to envision equality ever emerging as racial inequality is so deeply entrenched in Britain today, and rather than racial equality being a foregone conclusion, the coming decades may only see it emerge as a subject that stimulates debate although unlikely to realize any change by way of it.

At the level of learning the practical lessons of history, a European-wide plan of action is needed to tackle racism with a sharp focus. Greater democracy can be advanced through the vehicle of education so far as distortion is not a factor (Luthra,1998). The hidden meaning of viewing racism in terms of a Black experience per se is that the answer is detectable in and through raising minority consciousness and resistance. What then follows is that if the negative influence of racism is converted into a positive influence of being Black, a sense of being can be achieved which can be geared towards the pursuit of equality. On that account, Sivanandan argued: 'We don't need a cultural identity for its own sake, but to make use of the positive aspects of our culture to forge correct alliances and fight the correct battles' (Sivanandan, 1982:11; cited in Shukra, 1998:42). If the standard by which society can be judged rests on the example set by government intervention in the form of racially discriminatory legislation, and where blaming the victim is indispensable to glossing over the real conflicts associated with the political culture, then it should not strike one as unusual that inequality rather than equality is the order of the day. Whether the Black population is disadvantaged and discriminated against in their quest for employment will be the centre of discussion in chapter eight.

Britain is famed and reputed throughout the world for upstanding principles such as freedom and justice, however, it shows a dismal and flagrant failure to live up to and reify these in actual reality, on either of the dual building block aspects of a decent and civilized society with regard to race. And, so long as there are disenfranchised, oppressed, and excluded human beings, Britain cannot be considered as "the citadel of democracy" (Perry,2015:155). Second-class citizenship is located in the shadow of inequality and exists in and is inseparable from race. It was an age before the monster of slavery was no more, and just as slavery was built on inequality, so too is capitalist liberal democracy which, unless something drastic happens, seems destined to run and run. However, the political participation of Black and minority ethnic communities necessarily is an important part of any balanced approach to challenging the political objective on race in Britain today.

Chapter 8: Racial Discrimination in Employment

This chapter aims to provide a summary of the main findings of studies conducted with minority ethnic groups in employment. In the process, what will be revealed is the extent and nature of racial discrimination in the labour market and I will attempt to update this evidence by considering more recent data in this specific field of enquiry. The basis for electing to look at this particular study is because racial discrimination features significantly in the lives of African-Caribbean and South Asian people and I wanted to see whether this 1970's study bore any contemporary relevance.

Racial Discrimination in Britain

As we have already seen, the Caribbean and Asian subcontinent responded to Britain's labour shortage after the Second World War by migrating in large numbers and the corollary has been the establishment of ethnically distinct community enclaves, and, in effect, has added an ethnically diverse dimension to contemporary British society (Pilkington,2003:39). This begs the question, what reception have these communities met with? Though most tend to agree that their reception casts a generally unwelcome trend, two different responses have been posited for this. One stresses the comparative newness of minority ethnic groups to British society, ordinarily described as 'immigrants' or children of 'immigrants'; the other stresses that minority groups differ in external appearance from the indigenous White population. The first response sees the newness of minorities as the single most decisive factor in their negative reception, whereas the second response sees the colour of minorities as the single most decisive factor in their negative reception (Pilkington,2003:40).

The PEP (Political and Economic Planning) report I have elected to examine is not an isolated piece of research but rather it had a forerunner and stands alongside further follow-up studies, such as Brown and Gay (1985). The report claims to be objective and the author asks as a start-up question, how far are the racial minority groups at a disadvantage compared with the rest of the population, and what are the sources of this disadvantage? (Smith,1977:15). Smith appears to summarize five different research enquiries in his book 'Racial Discrimination in Britain', and of these, I shall be concerned with racial discrimination in employment. The report itself was based on interviews with 3,300 South Asians and African-Caribbeans and White men were also interviewed for comparative reasons. In employment, these included a community-wide survey of 300 firms, in-depth case studies of fourteen business enterprises, interviews with twenty-seven of the forty major league employers at managerial level and interviews in the administrative centres of eight of the largest trade unions (Smith,1977:16).

Three fields of investigation

The PEP study had 'three fields of enquiry'; the first was concerned with the plight of individual South Asians and African-Caribbeans, and South Asians and African-Caribbeans as a group, compared with the majority population (Smith,1977:15). The most obvious analytical approach indicates, e.g., what are the occupational levels and remunerations of South Asians and African-Caribbeans compared with White people? More in-depth analysis will attempt to advance a theory of any differences (Smith,1977:15).

The second area of investigation examines the structure, aims and agency of key organizations, and to what extent these impact on the minority groups (Smith,1977:16). The degree to which this worked against the minorities' interests must issue from the contact between the migrants and the leading institutions in the areas of housing and employment. An investigation of the institutions is germane to showing how the disadvantages come to exist (Smith,1977:16).

The third investigative area is racial discrimination. It needs to be established how frequently a South Asian or African-Caribbean, when attempting to access jobs or housing, encounters less favourable treatment than a White person simply owing to his or her South Asian or African-Caribbean descent and for no additional reason. A way of establishing this is through controlled experiments. The term 'experiment' does not mean that the findings are mere theory; it means that conditions are constructed and no relevant factors are left uncontrolled, so that any variation in treatment between minority ethnic groups and White people must be because of ethnic differences: for instance, Black and White people with matching qualifications and experience can be delegated to seek the same jobs. A grand itinerary of controlled experiments fitting this description was undertaken in 1973-4 (Smith,1977:17).

Smith considered this research programme to be complementary, and that the various investigative outcomes tended to support one another. According to Smith, research with employers and trade unions sustains the main thrust that discrimination remains widespread, but more significantly, shows how it comes to light and what variety of anti-discrimination policy is likely to prove effective. David J. Smith offers a summary of how racial disadvantage in employment is seen:

> The minority groups are more vulnerable to unemployment than whites; they are concentrated within the lower job levels in a way that cannot be explained by lower academic or job qualifications; within

broad categories of jobs, they have lower earnings than whites, particularly at the higher end of the job scale; they tend to do shift work, which is generally thought undesirable, but shift work premiums do not raise their earnings above those of whites, because the jobs are intrinsically badly paid; they are concentrated within certain plants, and they have to make about twice as many applications as whites before finding a job (Fryer,1984:388).

The above findings point towards racial discrimination as a major factor in the plight of minority ethnic groups (Smith,1977:104). In the same breath, none of them records the extent of discrimination or so much as incontrovertibly demonstrates that discrimination exists. The best way to obtain an objective measure of the level of discrimination is, again, through controlled experiments (Smith,1977:104).

While substantial indirect evidence of discrimination was gleaned through analysis, opening up the subject of disadvantage further, 'a more direct and more precise measure can be obtained by arranging for White and for Asian and West Indian testers to apply in person, by telephone and by letter, in a set of carefully controlled situations, so that the success rate can be compared for the different 'racial' groups' (Smith,1977:104-105). The PEP project conducted in 1966-7 laid the foundations for personal and telephone testing; the correspondence method was endorsed by authors Jowell and Prescott-Clarke. These initial developments established the practicality of the methods; in addition, they make comparisons possible with the recent PEP work, enabling conclusions to be drawn about shifts in the extent of discrimination since 1967 and since 1969 (Smith,1977:105). The current tests were conducted in late 1973 and early 1974.

The testing included recruitment to unskilled and semi-skilled manual posts, skilled manual posts and a variety of six forms of white-collar work. The tests covering recruitment to manual positions were completed by a cohort of actors; job applications took place in person where unskilled and semi-skilled positions were concerned, and by telephone where skilled positions were concerned. The tests associated with white-collar job recruitment were conducted by correspondence (Smith,1977:105).

Controlled actor testing

These tests were conducted in London and Birmingham. Two sets of actors participated, each set comprising of an indigenous White British actor, an African-Caribbean, a Pakistani, an Indian and a Greek. Two actors participated in each individual test; a consistent feature of the pair was the White actor while his opposite number was one of four options (Smith,1977:105).

Where unskilled and semi-skilled jobs were concerned, the testers were assigned to districts where a not inconsiderable number of organizations could be found in close proximity to each other which offered the right calibre of work (Smith,1977:105). In the main, the tests were conducted at factory plants. The testers sought jobs whether or not advertisements existed, though employers frequently advertised vacancies on the premises. The testers approached the factory gate attendant, the minority one first followed by the other about thirty minutes later, and said they were seeking employment. In certain instances, they were rejected out of hand; in others, they were directed to the person responsible (Smith,1977:106).

The likelihood of the job being taken during the thirty-minute interval between the two liaisons was always present (Smith,1977:106). The minority tester was always sent first ensuring that the level at which this happened gave the minority tester all probability, leading, it seems, to an understatement of the incidence of discrimination against the minority tester (Smith,1977:106).

With applying for jobs came prescribed tester roles which were fully explained beforehand and the following two examples add clarity.

West Indian: Age 29. Educated in primary and secondary school in Jamaica. Came to Britain with his parents at the age of 16. Took a job as a bus conductor in 1963 and remained in that job for five years. He then moved to a canning factory working on the production line. He is now wanting to leave his present job because he no longer wants to work on permanent night shifts. Present wage about £30 net, including bonuses and overtime (this was late 1973). Married, with two children.

White British: Age 31. Born and bred in Glasgow. He has held three jobs in Glasgow in the past fourteen years; warehouseman in a distillery (1960-64), packer in a dairy produce firm (1964-9), production line in a cereals factory (1969-73). He is now moving to the London area. Present wage about £27 net, including bonuses and overtime (Smith,1977:106).

The above particulars were sufficiently disparate to avoid casting doubt among respondents; by the same token, the differences are inconsequential as far as a potential employer would be concerned.

The South Asian and African-Caribbean testers spoke good English with only traces of an accent.

Where skilled jobs were concerned, the tester responded via telephone to press advertisements (Smith,1977:106). The problem area here was fitting the actors with the requisite technical knowledge to hold a job-related conversation. This was leapfrogged in two stages. First, jobs approximating to expert knowledge were avoided while jobs such as fitter, bricklayer, carpenter were preferred. Secondly, actors and experimenter analysed a variety of advertisements in selected newspapers for similar types of frequently advertised skilled jobs, with the outcome that a good idea of the qualifications and experience necessary for these jobs was formulated (Smith,1977:107).

The background history of each tester was held constant in every sense as with the non-skilled tests. However, the actual positions held had to be altered to suit every single application. The occupational experience and qualifications of each minority tester intimated that, while his country of origin provided the education, he had gained the appropriate skill within this country's boundaries (Smith,1977:107).

The type of information testers were required to give over the telephone was seldom detailed. The respondent would tend either to sum up the job requiring answers to a number of straightforward and fundamental questions before requesting the tester to attend an interview, or he would disclose that the position had been filled before a conversation could develop (Smith,1977:107).

The testers invariably started the conversation by giving their names; where the South Asians were concerned, this was sufficient a tell-tale sign of their South Asian origin, though it was not always possible to know assuredly that the respondent realized whether the South Asian hailed from India or Pakistan. Where the African-Caribbean was concerned, the Christian name employed was Leroy, which to some extent points to the ethnic origin, but to make sure that the employer was fully cognizant, it was *sine qua non* for the tester to speak some patois. Where the Greek was concerned, the name was ample to indicate foreign-ness; a verbal slant was also used (Smith,1977:107).

Steps were taken to alter the input of the tester and the data given in the different tests, but because the testers functioned in pairs, the possibility remained for them to see to it that for each test they gave carefully aligned details. Records were kept of the details given, in order that the experimenter could subsequently verify that they had been suitably matched (Smith,1977:107).

White and minority actor pairings were controlled in order to ensure that, in each particular case, similar numbers of tests were conducted by a White and an Indian tester, a White and a Pakistani tester, etc. Where non-skilled jobs were concerned, all possible pairs were deployed, comprising of two White testers and two teams of four minority testers. This enabled researchers to make judgments around success rate variances between individual actors, to determine whether this could influence the final outcome of the tests (Smith,1977:108).

In the event, 102 tests were completed for non-skilled jobs and 76 for skilled jobs (a pair of applications constituted one test). Although the results

Findings of the actor tests

The findings of each test were classified on the basis of whether discrimination was evident or not. 'Discrimination is defined as a case where one tester was made an offer while the other was made none or one where a better offer was made to one tester than to the other' (Smith,1977:108). In certain cases, there was, what seems like discrimination against the native White tester and in preference for the 'immigrant'. While this could be for the reason that the 'immigrant' was always first to participate, researchers considered these cases as actual reverse discrimination. To incorporate them, researchers have reported the findings through the expression 'net discrimination' against the 'immigrant'. 'Net discrimination' is the overall instances in which discrimination was committed against the 'immigrant' minus the instances in which discrimination was committed against the native White tester. This guarantees that the isolated instances of reverse discrimination are incorporated into the final assessment (Smith,1977:108).

According to Smith, where non-skilled jobs were concerned, seven test results presented classification questions because a poorly remunerated job was extended to the 'immigrant' while no offer was extended to the White British tester. The likelihood, Smith asserts, is that these plants sought cheap labour; they may have judged that the 'immigrant' would consider such jobs and that it would be flatly declined by the White British tester. On Smith's authority, the jobs extended in these seven dubious instances were as follows:

- General handyman in machine shop at £25 per week
- Unskilled machine work (engineering) at £25 per week
- General labourer at £22 per week

- Cleaning and sweeping in a rolling mill at £20 per week
- Machine operator in electrical engineering at £20 per week (plus bonus of £3 to £5)
- Labourer at £19 per week (1977:109).

The financial reward, he adds, in each case, reached such a low that it seems as though extremely low-level jobs were extended to a South Asian or African-Caribbean which would not be extended to a White individual. However, the more cautious explanation, he maintains, that these were actual instances of reverse discrimination, appears just as likely, and so two different assessments of net discrimination will be carried into the two possible classificatory schemes.

Evidence indicates that the South Asian and African-Caribbean applicants for non-skilled jobs encountered discrimination in less than half of all cases (46 per cent) (Smith,1977:109). Given that the doubtful cases are put down to actual cases of reverse discrimination, then the percentage rating falls to 37 per cent. South Asian and African-Caribbean applicants for skilled occupations encountered discrimination in a fifth of cases. Such findings demonstrate conclusively 'that there is still very substantial racial discrimination against South Asians and West Indians when seeking manual jobs, and that discrimination is worse for non-skilled than for skilled job applicants' (Smith,1977:109).

It is possible to argue that employers discriminate against South Asians and African-Caribbeans not on grounds of colour, but on grounds that they are foreign. To show the extent to which the discrimination was predicated on 'race', Greek testers were involved in the experiment. Evidence intimates that discrimination against Greeks was relatively low. Where non-skilled jobs were concerned, it was 10 per cent (against 46 per cent for South Asians and African-Caribbeans); for skilled occupations, it was 9 per cent (against 20 per cent for South Asians and African-Caribbean (Smith,1977:110). Observations number at rather a low level here, but when the housing tests are included to boost the figures, the result remains scarcely dissimilar. This demonstrates that the discrimination against South Asians and African-Caribbeans is principally predicated on colour prejudice (Smith,1977:110).

Comparisons can also be drawn between the extent of discrimination against each minority ethnic group. To raise sufficient numbers for this comparison, results across all situations have to come together, including the housing situations. Accordingly, then, evidence shows that there is no salient dissimilarity in the extent of discrimination between African-Caribbeans, Indians and Pakistanis, though it was established earlier that discrimination against Greeks is significantly lower. This implies that discrimination is predicated on a non-specific colour prejudice, which fails to decipher much between people pertaining to different ethnic groups, having different faiths, speaking different linguistic codes and hailing from different countries. They are regarded en bloc as 'coloured people' (Smith,1977:111).

Summary of main findings

The findings of the actor tests demonstrate that South Asians and African-Caribbeans still face substantial levels of discrimination in pursuit of manual occupations; that the discrimination is more marked against applicants seeking non-skilled than seeking skilled occupations; that it is principally predicated on colour prejudice and not prejudice against foreigners; and that the extent of discrimination against African-Caribbean, Indians and Pakistanis is scarcely dissimilar (Smith,1977:111). I shall now consider more recent data concerning these principal conclusions.

Direct racial discrimination

The most prominent evidence emanates from three PSI (Policy Studies Institute) studies headed by Daniel (1968), D Smith (1977) and Brown and Gay (1985) (Pilkington,2003:41). Collectively, these studies provide, bridging two decades, these studies provide the most credible data information on the prevalence of discrimination in Britain. To establish the extent of discrimination and if it was predicated on newness or colour, Daniel completed a set of situation tests where actors applied for jobs, housing and commercial services in a set of carefully controlled development of events (Pilkington, 2003:41). In each case, a Caribbean or South Asian 'immigrant', a White 'immigrant' (Hungarian) and an indigenous White person of the same age and inseparable by occupational qualifications or housing needs applied (in the above order) for a job, a house, or a commercial service for public consumption. Discrimination was defined as an instance where one tester secured an offer or a much greater offer, and the other(s) came up with nothing or a worse one. Daniel found that the Caribbean or South Asian 'immigrant' was much more likely to experience higher levels of discrimination. Despite subsequent laws aimed at combatting racial discrimination, the studies done since show a continued trend towards the considerable and is based mainly on colour. While for Smith the extent of discrimination had fallen between 1967 and 1973, Brown and Gay – using both actor testing and something in the mould of the situation test developed by Smith, and termed correspondence testing, in which indistinguishable written applications were mailed in response to advertised vacancies – found no evidence to indicate that the extent of racial discrimination (ascertained in 1984-85) had shown a reduction since 1973. A baseline one-third of employers remained among those choosing to reject African-Caribbean or South Asian job applicants on grounds of colour (Pilkington,2003:44).

There has been no further comparable national test investigation into the level of discrimination since 1985 (Pilkington,2003:44). The 1994 PSI survey elected instead to study people's beliefs and attitudes. To determine both the extent and nature of discrimination, we need to look at other evidence.

The most up to date tests of discrimination at regional level (CRE 1996, Simpson and Stevenson 1994) continue to signpost racial discrimination (Pilkington,2003:45). Consider those completed in Nottingham in 1992. Replicating techniques used in a study between 1977 and 1979, which used traditional written applications, from three fictional candidates (White;

Asian; Caribbean) matched in terms of age and credentials, to potential employers, the authors learned 'that, much as in 1979, a white applicant's chances of getting an interview were twice as high as those of either the South Asian or Afro-Caribbean applicant' (Simpson and Stevenson,1994:15; cited in Pilkington,2003:45).

Another way of viewing racial discrimination is by studying whether people from diverse ethnic backgrounds, with the same academic qualifications, have equal prospects of reaching the most fortunate occupational destinations, for instance, managerial and professional occupations, and evading the least fortunate occupational destinations, for instance, unemployment (Pilkington,2003:45). If people from minority ethnic groups, with equivalent academic qualifications as indigenous White people, do not have similar opportunities, we can assume that they encounter an 'ethnic penalty'. An ethnic penalty is 'a broader concept than that of discrimination', as it alludes 'to all the sources of disadvantage that might lead an ethnic group to fare less well in the labour market than do similarly qualified Whites (Heath and Mcmahon,1997:91; cited in Pilkington,2003:45). Examination of the 1983-89 LFS (Labour Force Survey) showed 'the absence of ethnic penalties for the Irish and Chinese and their presence among Indian, Pakistani and West Indian men' which 'suggests strongly that discrimination along the lines of skin colour' is occurring (Cheng and Heath,1993:164; quoted in Pilkington,2003:45). This examination concentrated on minority ethnic members who hailed from overseas, the first generation, among whom were overseas qualification holders, and their English lacked fluency. More concurrently, Heath and McMahon have researched the 1991 Census to draw parallels between the plight of this generation and that of the succeeding generation, born and reared in Britain, who have been awarded British qualifications and speak fluent English. A parallel, drawn between the two generations, matched regarding age and qualifications, revealed that 'for both men and women ... the second generation experience the same pattern and magnitude of ethnic penalties in the British labour market as did the first generation' (Heath and Mcmahon,1997:108; cited in Pilkington,2003:46).

This emphatically announces, even more so than the analysis that came before, that racial discrimination is taking place. In truth, minority ethnic groups face different ethnic penalties, which intimates that discrimination in accordance with colour is not the full expression of what is going on, but curiously, in light of Modood's assumption that discrimination has religious overtones, it is Black Africans and not Pakistanis who incur the biggest penalty (Pilkington, 2003:46).

Together, the regional evidence, which entails testing if South Asians and Caribbeans encounter discrimination in employment, and the national study of ethnic penalties signpost continuity instead of change and intimate that the magnitude of discrimination has not made a significant turn-about since 1984-85 (Pilkington,2003:46). Moreover, the Nottingham study shows that African-Caribbeans and South Asians experience not dissimilar levels of discrimination, and research into ethnic penalties indicate an inscrutable quality, in which South Asian groups, Muslims as well, do not look in any worse a position than other minority groups. Given this, there seems no logical reason to doubt the main thrust of the vast research available, viz, that the discrimination minority ethnic groups face can best be explained in terms of colour, and not, as some entertained, newness, but Modood does seem to have a point about the inseparability of colour and religion in light of the recent 2001 September 11 bombings in the US, orchestrated by Muslims (Pilkington,2003:46).

Indirect racial discrimination

We have, however, considered just one form of discrimination – direct discrimination. Proceeding in a gradual, subtle way, however, is a form of discrimination otherwise known as 'institutional racism', but which can also be termed indirect discrimination. This describes institutional practices which, however inadvertently, have the effect of systematically working to the disadvantage of groups perceived as racially different. The following are but a few examples:

- A school uniform rule which has the effect of preventing the wearing of turbans;

- The practice of awarding apprenticeships with no formal procedures to the 'lads of dads', a practice which plainly disadvantages people who cannot access this network;

- The practice of recruiting workforce candidates from old universities, which have unfair amounts of White graduates, or through word of mouth which may restrict minority group access (Pilkington, 2003:47).

This is but a minor proportion of the examples available, yet they do suggest that indirect discrimination is widespread (Pilkinngton,2003:47). Still, ineluctably, when we consider specific cases, problems surface. Also, we discover that the dividing line between direct and indirect discrimination is blurred in practice. Much of these practices, common knowledge reveals, are indirectly discriminating and continue regardless. Moreover, close inspection may reveal that some of them are in place for racial considerations. However, the dividing line between direct and indirect discrimination still serves a purpose, and, when we consider both forms, it emerges that racial discrimination still remains extremely prevalent (Modood,2000:204; Pilkington,2003:48; Scott and Marshall, 2005:344).

Estimating the value of evidence, it is an inescapable and unavoidable conclusion that discrimination, either direct or indirect, personalized or institutional, still aggregates as a manifest force acting on the life-chances of Britain's minorities (Ratcliffe,2004:102). Occasionally this proves insidious, for example, direction from (say) careers officers. Under many other circumstances, it normally goes undetected, though revealed only by means of experimental testing programmes utilized by Brown and Gay (1985) or by the unravelling of informal recruitment as concerning the CRE official enquiry into the Massey Ferguson plant in Coventry (Ratcliffe,2004:102).

The material detail that discrimination on the grounds of 'race', colour, nationality or ethnic origin is now illegal since the Race Relations Act 1968 was written into the Statute Book has, in many instances, simply had the consequence of forcing matters into disrepute (Ratcliffe, 2004:102). More recently, the race relations (Amendment) Act was passed in 2001 which not only prohibited racial discrimination but also included indirect discrimination in the fight to combat levels of racial discrimination. Exclusionary aims and objectives have become covert as opposed to overt. This relates not only to recruitment processes but also to additional staffing level concerns, such as training, upward social mobility and disciplinary procedures (Ratcliffe, 2004:102).

Conclusion

Lastly, one of the aims of this chapter has been to reveal the extent and character of racial discrimination in the labour market. It comes as no surprise that the extent of discrimination still remains substantial and that discrimination is based predominantly on colour prejudice as the levels of discrimination between Caribbean, South Asian and White people demonstrate. Scholars who considered that the negative reception of Caribbean and South Asian migrants was about newness fail to account for the fact that African-Caribbean and South Asian people have a British settlement history predating post-war immigration as previously mentioned in the introduction. It is also of no surprise to find that discrimination is a powerful constraining force that affects the life-chances of minority ethnic groups and that ethnic penalties impact upon successive generations just as much as the first generation. The findings of the PEP report on racial discrimination in employment and the conclusions drawn in this chapter represents a confirmation of the fears that I held before producing this work; that it would illustrate a pattern of racial inequality. The fact that minority groups are often discriminated against overlaps with ideas related to the underclass discussed in the next chapter.

Chapter 9: A Black Underclass in Millennium Britain - Myth or Reality?

This chapter will consider the validity of the underclass concept in a way that makes it accessible. Some of the social factors which could account for underclass membership shall also be the focus of attention and individual insight will be brought to bear on the subject to acquire greater transparency. This chapter aims to critically analyse and consider the plight of Black and minority ethnic groups with a view to establishing whether they constitute an underclass stratum in contemporary British society. This chapter also constitutes the cumulative effects of social institutions' influence on Black aspiration.

To be precise, Black and minority ethnic people are discriminated against individually but the cumulative effects mean that they are discriminated against en masse and that has only to be evinced and seen in the supposed formation of an underclass. While there is evidence to suggest that Britain is becoming a multiracial society it is a long distance away from being a hotbed of racial harmony as we are divided by class, religion, 'race', region, generational patterns and so on. We may read or become aware of class war and of society being class-ridden or class-riven and reference to a classless society seems to smack of doing away with division along class lines which is an unlikely prospect. The fact that there is more than one religious faith, championing a version of God, yet there is but one humanity, suggests that religion is not of God but of man or man-made. If there is such an entity as a celestial being or higher power, responsible for the existence of humanity, it is incompatible with and called into question by scientific theory. The validity of religious faith facing a direct challenge really begs the question, which of the two alternatives represents the truth?

Large sections of society seem hopelessly disposed to the fear and hatred of Black and minority ethnic people. Institutional racism is an attempt to thwart, play for time, frustrate, impede and halt Black aspiration in its tracks, and, in the cold hard light of day, it is working. It is not as easily identified as a revealing immodestly dressed individual or Saint George's flag at an English Defence League march. It is shrouded in and covered over with respectability. The broad configuration of the north/south divide in Britain remains largely distinguished along economic lines. Teenagers tend often to be rebellious against their parents and adults generally and both generations experience a wide gulf between one another. A divided Britain is one thing but a fragmented and broken Britain is another, adding a new dimension that favours a different spin on things. By considering the structure of society, it begins to become easier to see that a substratum may exist beneath the working-class and that the social class scale is not all that we thought it was.

Margaret Thatcher's swamping statement, like Powell a decade earlier, defended the national will and rallied behind the cleavage of indigenous welfare and security while being distinctly fearful of a Black planet failing to realize that humanity is enhanced and enriched by diversity. Ultimately, we are all homo sapiens sapiens and essentially the same, only in Britain, 'race', class and culture matter. We are not just human, we are defined by these characteristics and they determine Black and minority ethnic entitlement to scarce resources, our social position and how we are treated by mainstream society. British culture valorizes those from a White middle-class background and White people generally, while often, the reverse is true for people from African-Caribbean and South Asian heritage. This racist bias helps structure society and runs counter to multiculturalism which is feared and censured by prominent right-wing commentators such as Roger Scruton in *The Times*, Peregrine Worsthorne in the *Sunday Telegraph* and John Vincent in the *Sun* to name a few.

It seems that in Britain, one's background is critical to whether aspirations are realized since being stymied or obstructed is a consequence of being born Black. The facts are ignored in relation to how racism appears to be woven into the fabric of society and is why change is scarcely foreseeable or, by any manner of means, inevitable. In other words, inequality seems destined to continue because White Brits believe that they should enjoy better opportunities than 'immigrants' and their successive generations. For the most part, then, in the struggle for life through natural selection, White individuals win out and Black individuals lose out. So, equal opportunities come to represent a mere tick-box exercise as policy fails to emerge, at all times, into practice.

Humanity should be able to celebrate that different human skin colour does not mean people of colour experience different treatment, that is, exclusion, exploitation and discrimination. Unequal distribution of the world's scarce resources is central to human division and is not the best way to respond to universal human needs. The reverse strategy would contribute to unifying the human race and help people feel that they have a genuine stake in society. Government policy action should always aim to make a positive difference to people's lives, but invariably, lip service or skating around the issue of racial inequality is all that we hear, and is as far as things are taken.

Charles Murray's 1990 underclass thesis distinguishes between the deserving and the undeserving poor. One class of the poor is distinguished by inadequate pecuniary means, and the other by their behaviour. Portraying himself as 'a visitor from a plague area come to see whether the disease is spreading', Murray (1990:3-4; cited in Devine, 1997:236) argued that, 'Britain does have an underclass, still largely out of sight and still smaller than the one in the US. But it is growing rapidly. Over the next decade, it will probably become larger'. Distinctive indicators of underclass behaviour, according to Murray, were high rates of illegitimacy, increasing levels of violent crime and labour market drop-out (Devine, 1997: 236). Murray saw liberal society as culpable – leniency on crime and the cancellation of social stigma linked to illegitimacy – and the welfare system which had spawned a dependency culture as central to the development of an underclass. For Murray, these social problems were connected, and that piecemeal changes would do little to solve them. He argued for 'authentic self-government if Britain is to escape an anticipated bleak future' (Devine,1997:237). Murray's thesis came under fierce criticism from academics such as Lister (1990).

According to Lister (1990), Murray's depiction of the 'underclass' is imprecise and also disturbing in that he uses the vocabulary of disease and contamination. Her argument is that he describes himself as 'a visitor from a plague area come to see whether the disease is spreading' (Lister,1990:194). She adds that his language fosters a pathological image of poor people as somehow dissimilar to other people and to be looked upon with trepidation. Because the 'underclass' concept is so imprecise, Lister argues, there is the danger that it gets extended to delineate those in poverty generally, and so value-laden and contentious that it taints their character and sets them apart. However, Murray is careful not to apply the term 'underclass' as a broad brushstroke for the poor generally, only to those defined by their undesirable behaviour, for example, drug-taking, crime, illegitimacy, failure to remain employed, deliberate absence from school and casual violence Green,1990:vi). By the same token, Murray's portrayal of the poor as pathological shows a failure to recognize the especially vulnerable positions or victim status of the Black and minority population in contemporary British society (Field,1990:38).

The British Angle on the Underclass Thesis

The British debate primarily concerns itself with the class position of minorities and the underclass concept has been used as part of a debate with Marx and/or Weber. Pilkington examines the evidence which points strongly towards a British underclass and Weberians and Marxists offer their support for this view. Furthermore, many British sociologists are aware of sound evidence suggesting that minority ethnic groups feature in an underclass, yet Pilkington cites two PSI surveys, the Census, and the LFS to challenge the notion that minority groups comprise a racialised underclass. Again, Moore (1999) examines the evidence which also indicates the existence of an underclass but he rejects the very idea out of hand. His rejection of the underclass concept, at best, amounts to a denial of the truth, and at worst, an expression of racism in its utter dismissal of unequal treatment for Black and minority ethnic people.

Runciman, on the other hand, argues that there exist seven classes in British society and the underclass is thought to appear below the working class. His concern to divest minorities of inclusion with those occupying disadvantaged stations in the economy, however, includes 'those members of British society whose roles place them more or less permanently at the economic level where benefits are paid by the state to those unable to participate in the labour market at all' (Runciman,1990:388; cited in Devine, 1997:239). For Runciman, many members of the underclass are minority ethnic, many are women (largely single mothers), and certain of these are both, but their ethnicity or gender does not ascribe class position. A person's ethnicity or gender does not equate to underclass status, however, minorities and women are more prone to joblessness and some may regard joblessness as a characteristic of the underclass (Hudson and Williams,1995:285).

Life in a post-industrial, metropolitan and technologically advanced society warrants no guarantee to a rise in the number of those living in poverty (Webster,1998:17). In the light of this, some sociologists have engaged in the production of theory heralding a new 'underclass' that ranks below the working class in the class system. The underclass is thought to be a category of people who either lack work or are extremely low wage earners (Webster,1998:17).

The underclass encompasses the unemployed, single parents, the disabled, unskilled workers, casual workers, part-time workers, women and minority ethnic groups (Webster,1998:17). That is not to say that all women, African-Caribbean or South Asian et cetera, make up the underclass. However, the chances of them being in it are far higher than for males and White people (Webster,1998:17).

The litany of people the press have tended to describe as underclass demonstrates that the term is either misused or means different things to different people. Also, the press prevails upon the public at large to believe that the underclass consists of joy-riders, football hooligans, ram-raiders, meths drinkers, people sleeping rough, single mothers, homosexuals, the unemployed, school-age parents, rioters, New Age travellers, Caribbean Youth, (all) people on benefits, homeless young people, drug addicts, hunt saboteurs and anarchists (Moore,1999:2). Since the British take on the underclass thesis concerns itself with a debate with Marx and/or Weber about the class position of minorities, it is therefore *sine qua non* to explore the cleavage that separates them.

Between the Marxist and Weberian schools of thought on class, the tendency for the latter has been to associate minority ethnic groups with the underclass (Pilkington,1997:255). This is consistent with Weber's view that the social hierarchy is much more than mere capitalists versus workers (Webster,1998:17). For Weber, stratification translated into three dimensions: economic class, social status and political power, racial inequality is regarded as a form of status inequality which may be as noteworthy as class inequality (Pilkington,1997:255; Weber,1998:17).

White people and minority ethnic groups are divided by status differential, with its associated belief in the supremacy of the former, developed to justify imperialism (Pilkington,1997:255). Division along racial lines continues and is consolidated when social groups (such as White working-class citizens) seek to maximise their entitlement by controlling the access of outsider groups, deemed racially different, to life chances and opportunities ... Were the effects of racial discrimination severe enough to restrict Black and minority ethnic groups to occupations that provide low pay, poor promotion prospects and unstable job security, status disadvantages are transforming class disadvantages and this would legitimise references to a Black and minority underclass (Pilkington,1997:255). Of course, this would not mean that all Black and minority ethnic members were part of this racialised underclass.

Marxist Critique of the Underclass Theory

The term 'underclass' is said to be an affront to the people who come beneath its banner (Webster,1998:18). A valid point, perhaps, but this is a slight upon the language, sparing the theory itself.

Marxists represent the theory's main critics (Webster,1998:18). For instance, Castles and Kosack have dismissed Rex's view that minority ethnic groups constitute an underclass. They argue that although African-Caribbean and South Asians experience racism and are particularly prone to unemployment or to occupy unskilled jobs, this scarcely suggests that they are a separate class. They make up the working class, despite facing distinctly worse conditions than their working-class counterparts. In addition, African-Caribbean workers are more likely to hold trade union membership.

Marxists consider the working class as all those who incur capitalist exploitation; they may be skilled or unskilled, office-based or manual, casual or permanent, full-time or part-time (Webster,1998:18). An affluent factory worker, a nondescript clerical worker, a part-time supermarket cashier and an unemployed person are all working-class according to the Marxist perspective.

Marxists regard the large majority of those who are termed the underclass by other sociologists as nothing short of working-class

(Webster,1998:18). Divisions within and between the working class, of course, exist: some are higher earners than others, and the capitalist establishment uses forms of unequal treatment to divide workers. However, since the working population are exploited, they could potentially come together in an uprising against the capitalists, forcing a changeover of power. The working class remains the majority and it remains the revolutionary class (Webster,1998:18).

For Marxists, the overall picture of the 'underclass' as a distinct contingent has been exaggerated (Webster,1998:18). The unemployed are mainly former job holders and at some stage will re-enter the labour market. Great numbers of women can only work part-time when rearing young children but revert to full-time posts when the children are school age. Pensioners are thought of as retired workers, and so forth.

According to Webster, Marx's treatment of the unemployed using terms like the 'industrial reserve army' or the 'reserve army of labour', did not translate into him seeing them as an entirely distinct class. They were, he continues, inseparable from the working class, at present lacking work, who would be pulled into the workforce and pushed out again relative to the changing requirements of the capitalists.

Lastly, the 'underclass' is not the same thing as Marx's contingent, the 'lumpenproletariat' (Webster,1998:18). Marxists consider the lumpenproletariat to be a marginal 'declassed' group which, in practical terms, is outside the class system, with no structural role for capital. In a first-world country such as Britain, it is a rather small group comprising of 'drop-outs', 'winos', small-time criminals and other 'outsiders'. During the nineteenth century period of British industrial expansion, Marx foresaw this group's potential to be used by the bourgeoisie as a counter-revolutionary strike-breaking force in opposition to the working-class (Webster,1998:18).

The underclass theory is fundamentally a Weberian one and Weberians would take issue with these criticisms. Firstly, minorities tend to be constrained by forms of direct and indirect racial discrimination, racism, unemployment, long-term unemployment and underemployment, all of which beset minority ethnic groups like no other, and thus separates and relegates them by status characteristics to the underclass. Minorities are the poorest section of the community for all of the five defining characteristics, yet Marxists fail to consider that this would lead to the development of essentially different interests distinct from the White British working-class. Secondly, just because trade unions are working-class institutions, with a large minority ethnic membership, does not make African-Caribbeans and South Asians affiliated members of the working class. For, after all, trade union treatment of African-Caribbean and South Asian members has been woeful, unions have actively worked against their interests in failing to back their strikes and have conspired with capital in constraining their promotion prospects (Fryer,1984:376,385; Phillips and Phillips,1998:151-2). This would suggest a status differential between minority ethnic groups and White working-class British which implies that the White working-class British do not consider them as equals. White British people facilitate the creation of an underclass and when sociologists like John Rex point it out, they find it very hard to accept.

Thirdly, minority ethnic groups are doubly exploited not only by the capitalists but also by the White working-class, so strictly speaking, they fall below the working class because of structured inequality that controls, checks and constrains them, and predominantly because of White prejudice towards colour, foreignness and religion. Minority ethnic concentration in the secondary labour market where jobs are characterised by poor promotion prospects, low pay, insecurity and unskilled work, suggests that status disadvantages are being converted into class disadvantages and then legitimate references can be made to a Black and minority ethnic underclass.

Fourthly, the depiction of the underclass as a distinct section of the population is anything but exaggerated. For example, most Black and minority ethnic youth, like an increasing proportion of their White counterparts, 'know, viscerally, that there will be no work for them, ever, no call for their labour ... They are not the unemployed but the never employed' (Fryer,1984:388). Moreover, minorities undergo unemployment and long-term unemployment to a far greater extent than the majority population (Moore,1999:5). Protracted unemployment may be inextricably linked with unemployment verging into loss of skills and progressively bars the way to work through employers' unreasonable recruitment practices. Consequently, the long-term unemployed can be where underclass membership is produced (Moore,1999:3). Rex demonstrated that racial discrimination edges a significant proportion of people from minority ethnic backgrounds into unemployment and the secondary labour market (Webster,1998:17). Pensioners are retired workers but, they no longer bear any practical purposes to industry and therefore come outside the mainstream of society, or fall into the underclass as a group of people said to be living in poverty. Of course, a percentage of pensioners are, in fact, wealthy and comfortably off.

Finally, Marx's description of the unemployed as the 'industrial reserve army' or 'reserve army of labour' can be, and has been, construed as the underclass, for example, by sociologists Cashmore and Troyna (1990), perhaps because the term refers to persistent unemployment. Marx's lumpenproletariat can also be construed as meaning the underclass as it consists of outsiders which would include pensioners, the severely disabled and the long-term sick. Labour market drop-outs were one of Murray's underclass indexes which is similar to what Marx called the lumpenproletariat. Although Marxists are critical of the underclass thesis, it is important to acknowledge their agreement with Weberians on four key questions, as will now be developed.

They see eye to eye on four key questions. Firstly, they appreciate that the economy produces low-level jobs in the class system, and racial discrimination enforces the continued minority ethnic restriction to such labour market positions. Secondly, they converge in regarding racism as extremely pervasive, influencing the position of the minorities both in the occupational sector and also elsewhere, particularly in housing. Thirdly, they agree that in locating minority groups in the social hierarchy or class system, due regard must be paid to their subordinate labour market status position. Finally, they are as one in recognizing that the unique position of minorities tends towards their development of unique consciousness levels and action (Pilkington,2003:63).

Social Factors that Determine the Underclass

The grave reservation that a firmly established underclass of Black inner-city occupants is emerging is a vestige of institutional racism that the moderate achievements of Blacks who have come to the fore in the middle-class does scarcely obviate. Also, the conviction that the woes of the Black underclass are pecuniary and not racial once more understates the accrued consequences of racism and their existing contribution in this human long dark tragedy. Restrictive immigration laws, discussed in chapter two, have reinforced in the collective consciousness the imposed inferior social status of Black and minority ethnic people and also as unwanted, unwelcome and undesirable. In short, Black and minority ethnic groups are deemed second-class citizens because of the regulatory controls imposed on them as a collective group and the actions of cross-party British politicians have not been lost on the White British public. Discrimination against groups of people deemed inferior, unwelcome, unwanted and undesirable pushes proportions of Black and minority ethnic members into unemployment and low-level jobs concomitant with the underclass.

The mid-1970s witnessed economic changes that resulted in class polarization (Pilkington,1997:251). Further clarity was given to this scenario by 1979 with the Conservative Party leadership in government, whose economic restructuring included substantial job losses and whose neo-Conservative weltanschauung justified welfare cuts. Although for the large majority, economic restructuring and burgeoning inequality have spelt an increase in living standards, a growing minority faced, in relative terms, the reverse effect. Some suppose that this stratum should be called an underclass. Mounting evidence suggests that Black and minority ethnic groups and women experience significant disadvantage. Continued discrimination based on 'race' and sex is severe enough for some to suggest that minorities and/or women form or feature disproportionately in an underclass (Pilkington, 1997:251).

Modood's PSI study revealed considerable evidence of labour market advancement – even if influence higher up the chain of command, in business, industry and government, still largely excludes minorities (Moore,1999:5). Gone are the 1950's and 1960's signs on the doors of rented accommodation stating 'No Blacks, No Irish', but then discrimination and racism went underground. However, over time, White British people have allowed doors that were once closed off to minorities to give somewhat open access, for example, African-Caribbean men have made significant advances such as Paul Boateng, first African-Caribbean cabinet minister, John Taylor became Lord Taylor of Warwick and African-Caribbean female, the Right Hon Baroness Amos of Brondesbury the first African-Caribbean leader of the House of Lords. South Asians have penetrated the office of mayor, such as Sadiq Kahn, Mayor of London.

The 5th of November 2008 saw the election of Barack Obama to the White House and this is a giant leap forward for the United States of America and the world. He was given a convincing mandate over the late senator John McCain and went on to complete two full terms in office. While it is easy to feel that his achievement symbolically elevated the status of African Americans and people of African descent the world over, it was for all but a temporary period. Obama's exit from office gave way to the rise of Donald Trump whose far-right leanings put a question mark over how far America really has progressed.

Since the underclass debate seldom finds articulation beyond the 1990s, it suggests that the debate has faded; however, further research is needed as the British economy now appears to have witnessed an increase in the gap between rich and poor, due to economic restructuring and, currently, a world recession which has put increasing numbers out of work. The numbers out of work can also be laid at the door of futuristic technology and those already in the long-term unemployed category face an uncertain future as jobs become more and more scarce. Yet, news stories suggest that there are more people in work presently than was the case in the 1970s.

Education is key to unlocking doors in the labour market and as long as schools continue to fail proportions of its roll, as referred to in chapter three, the underclass will be a permanent feature of contemporary British society. The solution to a burgeoning underclass appears to lie in a strong and growing economy that provides full employment, an education system that ceases to place emphasis on excluding its pupils, and increased international cooperation to rescue the world economy. Castles and Kosack suggest that the subordinate labour market position of Black and minority ethnic groups seems to be an economic necessity, and so, to some extent, a permanent feature of the class system, 'although upward social mobility might be possible for the most talented individuals' (1985:475).

Castles and Kosack's adoption of functionalist theory glosses over the fact that 'immigrants' were shepherded into performing subordinate labour market roles through means of employers' discriminatory recruitment practices and were here with expectations of a better life but were perceived as only good enough to fill low-level jobs. This demonstrates the exploitative nature of capitalism, the role of discrimination and racism, and the steepness of the struggle for full citizenship and equality. That minorities were discriminated against and had their aspirations dashed can hardly be described as 'an economic necessity'; this description begins to think of 'immigrants' as at the bottom of the economic pile and not equal to the White British. Castles' and Kosack's stress on lone individuals eschewing this plight still suggests that the large majority of minorities are seen as deficient and inferior. White social status offers clarity to and responsibility for Castles and Kosack's apparent resignation to Black social status being 'necessary', and enduring unequal labour market outcomes extends some meaning and some reality to underclass formation which is merely implied. The co-authors spare us the raw detail that in order to realize upward social mobility, Black and minority ethnic individuals have to outflank or be doubly better than their White opposite number.

Conclusion

This chapter has attempted to achieve several outcomes - to extend an understanding of the collective influence of social institutions on Black aspiration, to give examples of the underclass, to examine the cleavage that separates Weberian and Marxist schools of thought on class, to argue that the underclass is not a myth but reality and is determined, to an extent, by social factors which imply that underclass membership is not entirely of an individual's or collective group's own making. The concluding chapter picks up the threads and strands of previous chapters and describes and evaluates whether the press will ever change, and deals with the prospect that social reform-type change in the lives of Black and minority ethnic people is not necessarily inevitable but suggests that Martin Luther King's dream was not misplaced. Black aspiration is the locus of focus and some recommendations for the elimination of inequality are offered.

Chapter 10: Conclusion

The subtext of the preceding chapters has been that Black aspiration has a fervent hope and boundless desire that in the future, we will cease to be seen as inferior and treated accordingly but continuity rather than change seems likely. Current indicators suggest that in a recession labour market, positions are lacking and employers tend, in light of the downturn, to employ largely or exclusively White staff. In view of scarce resources, the first priority when it comes to promotion is usually not a Black or minority ethnic person. I have drawn attention to the problems Black and minority ethnic people face as regards career progression in this work (see Chapter 4). Even when qualified for a particular job, Black and minority ethnic people have to attend many more interviews than their White opposite numbers.

Although the tendency is for young African-Caribbean people to continue their education after school, there is now the added burden of debt attached to a university education. In the current climate, White middle-class young people may not see the accumulation of debt as a problem or obstacle to higher education and may still aspire in their droves, while for seemingly many Black and minority ethnic people, it appears to loom large as a deterrent. On a subjective level, I would always argue that education is worthwhile pursuing, but young Black and minority people will have to assess whether qualifications will secure entitlement to professional and managerial labour market roles, or will they have to settle for something other than their ideal job at the end of university life? In an economic downturn, it is a prospect which they will have to weigh.

Unless the economy improves and more jobs become available, Black people with aspirations will find it increasingly difficult to look forward to the future with an optimistic view of their prospects. The prime labour market positions are held by the dominant group, and as the economy declines, this appears much more likely to be the case. Take journalism, for example, a sought-after career involving the exercise of free speech. However, unless one is White and privately educated, the doors of opportunity remain largely closed, and the people to whom access is allowed are unrepresentative of the people at large. This calibre of person is more likely to be committed to the status quo as are newspaper proprietors, and more likely to be amenable to reproducing the dominant ideology in their chosen field of employment or at least less likely to challenge the skew and bias in the media world.

Black aspiration, for what it's worth, may be seen as unwelcome and unhealthy competition but the time is ripe for mainstream society to take a different view. The former point seems to encapsulate the plight of African-Caribbean and South Asian people and seems destined not to change anytime in the foreseeable future. This is no reason, nor is it the time, to down tools and surrender to what seems like the inevitable because where there is life, there is hope and Black aspiration is all about hope and optimism in the future; that one day, a further fresh push for justice will fly the doors free of their fetters and justice and fairness will come rushing through like a wild tempestuous wind to a brave new world. Until such time, Black aspiration must continue to live in hope because without hope, mountains cannot be moved.

As we saw in Chapter Three, schools appear to be veering towards insisting on conformity and control or else incur discipline or be shown the door to temporary or permanent exclusion. In addition, African-Caribbean pupils have thrust upon them unwelcome and humiliating identities in the way of stereotypes which teachers would never attach to White pupils and the African-Caribbean community tend to be blamed or denounced for the problems their children face at school (Mac an Ghaill,1988). African-Caribbean pupils come under disproportionate criticism and are subject to censure and allocated to lower streams, sets or bands regardless of cognitive ability as if preparing them for the world beyond the school gates where they will once again be seen as the bottom of the pile. Schools hamper Black aspiration and those male African-Caribbean pupils who succeed tend to pay a social cost as a sacrifice for success against the odds among their peers.

One pupil in Mac an Ghaill's (1988) study hit the nail right on the head by suggesting that the problem does not lie with Black and minority ethnic people but is a matter of hostile and antagonistic attitudes which minorities feel the effects of and it is White people who are the perpetrators and consequent problem. African-Caribbean pupils tend to have to run the gauntlet of these attitudes daily and end up doing less well relative to their peers in terms of collecting GCSE A-C grade qualifications as a result.

By side-tracking and parrying the call for reparations in their recent rebuttal, the then Liberal/Conservative coalition government can be seen as refusing to acknowledge the debt this country owes to African-Caribbean men and women whose ancestors' blood helped build Britain. Also, the then Liberal/Conservative coalition government can be seen to relegate the concerns of the Black African and Black Caribbean diaspora to the status of insignificant and not worthy of the political agenda-setting machinery, showing a cold, unfeeling and cavalier disregard for a legitimate proposal and call for economic *quid pro quo* for slavery and the slave trade, sending out the message to the world that they care just as little for, and think just as little of Black people as their antecedents did all those years ago when they awarded slave owners compensation for loss of human property. This is the latest reminder that Black people do not have a stake in society on a par with White people.

The prison building deal which Prime Minister Cameron offered instead of reparations served the purposes of Britain more than Jamaica as

Jamaica would have to fund its end of the bargain, saving Britain untold fiscal benefits each year once some of the island's nationals were shipped back to Jamaica to serve out their time there. This would send out, in turn, the message that the Black prison population is sufficiently large as to be a burden on the British tax-payer and it is clear whose interests the scheme served. Moreover, Cameron buys into the Black stereotypical image of the Black criminal element and the British public recognize and appreciate the subtext.

Historically, the British government perpetuated the myth that Africa had no arts or sciences and lifted not a finger to relieve Africans of the myth of inferiority. The fight against racism seldom featured on Theresa May's Tory government agenda. However, for the first time in what seems like living memory, the then leader of the Conservative Party, Theresa May – who claims to be 'government of the many and not the few' – has put racial equality on the political agenda intending to remedy it (Voice Newspaper, 12-18 October 2017). Is this a ploy to capture the Black and minority ethnic vote or is it a serious and concerted attempt at tackling the problem of racial inequality? Because let us not forget that traditionally, the Conservative Party are the party of private enterprise and capital, which are the interests of the elite few as opposed to the many they claim to represent.

As we saw in Chapters 3 and 4, schools stymie Black aspiration and so too does higher education. Higher education has hitherto operated in a climate unaffected by change in the form of policies developed in schools, the health service, local authorities and the police to combat racism and foster ethnic and cultural diversity (Law et al,2004). Higher education institutions primarily function in a 'colour-blind' fashion and seldom admit that beneath the façade of the liberal academy, there are underlying issues. Contemporary sociological inquiry has, however, pointed out that the liberal academy cannot in all possibility rest on its laurels. Major sociological expositions have pointed out key areas of concern. Among the things that stymie Black aspiration is racist discrimination in grading and assessment of written work which functions to maintain Black and minority ethnic *amour propre* at rock-bottom levels. The overarching function of schools and higher education, it seems, is to maintain the status quo.

My own personal case-study narrative is one of exclusion at the hands of racist admissions tutors and in Chapter 4, I rake over the coals of how each application proved to be another brick in the wall of exclusion. After applying to multiple institutions, I was failed and my hopes and dreams of achieving a Doctorate were dashed. Institutions report, in a callous and calculated manner, that they are unable to offer one a place yet giving no admissible reason for their decision. When a reason was given, it was implausible, did not chime with staff approval of one's decision to apply and smacked of a lack of professional expertise in staff composition. One particular university did not even respond to my online application; it was as blatant as that and I am left to assume that they suspected that I was Black and subsequently took evasive action. Two universities were utterly elitist even though I was qualified to progress further, in one case, implying that my overall standard was not good enough and, in another case, the high volume of applications was blamed, alluding implicitly to their popularity and prestige. This, however, was not an admissible reason as others may have been given priority over me, such as public school-educated and privileged types from the south of the country which the university favours over Black and minority ethnic students from the north as it is well known for this type of chauvinism.

Another university rejected me on two separate occasions and left the door open for a further application, knowing full well that they remove the suspicion of racism by this strategy and also knowing perfectly well that their second decision to exclude would be discouragement enough. Needless to say, perhaps, but the fact that I possess the credentials needed to proceed speaks volumes, and thus sees the institution for what it is and in the light in which it would much rather not be portrayed in, i.e., at best elitist and at worst decidedly, overwhelmingly and unconscionably racist. Predominantly, these institutions were 'old' universities known for excluding prospective African-Caribbean and South Asian candidates and from which employers have a preference for sourcing recruitment. The proportion of applications made suggests that this country's educational institutions had decided that I was *persona non grata* and that they could take me no further forward, and so, barred the way, despite how inescapably and unavoidably suspect the institutions in question all are.

Oxbridge; still too elitist

The latest up to date information on Oxbridge admissions policies is that they are still too elitist (Adams and Bengtsson,2017). One in three Oxford colleges failed to admit a solitary Black British A-level student in 2015, facing accusations of "social apartheid" by the former education minister, David Lammy. The indications are that 10 out of 32 colleges failed to grant admission to a Black British student with A-levels in 2015, although the 2010 figures were the last release of such statistics. Oriel college managed to offer just a single place to a Black British A-level pupil in six years. Corresponding data made available by Cambridge revealed six colleges did not even admit one Black British A-level student in the equivalent year.

Lammy initially asked for the ethnicity figures from Oxford and Cambridge in 2016. Although Cambridge provided theirs directly, Oxford drew matters out until October 19 2017 when they were made aware that the Guardian was making ready an article. Included in the data from the two universities was also a sharply defined regional and socioeconomic cleavage in their intake; the data highlighted that only 1.5% of overall offers from the associated universities to UK A-level students were extended to Black British applicants. Approximately 3% of the British populace are identified as Black according to the most recent UK census. Lammy reflected that the figures illustrated that many colleges at both institutions failed to mirror the UK's demographic composition. "This is social apartheid, and it is utterly unrepresentative of life in modern Britain," he opined (Adams and Bengtsson,2017).

Bringing published figures up to date since 2010, freedom of information calls by Lammy illustrate that Merton College, Oxford, had failed to offer scarcely any place to a Black British student in five years.

Whereas the data constitutes an increase from 2009 – when 21 Oxbridge colleges placed no Black students, set against 16 in 2015 – the figures give the impression that elite colleges continue to fail Black British school pupils, particularly from state schools.

A modicum of Black British students – an aggregate of 3.5 each year extending across from 2010 and 2015 – who have qualifications other than A-levels attain Oxbridge places. For the most part, independent schools are the driver to this alternative supply of pupils who they enter on obviative exams as exemplified by the international baccalaureate.

The latest figures also highlight certain parts of the country – particularly disadvantaged heartlands of the north-west of England and Wales – remain chiefly under the radar of efforts by the two institutions to widen their recruitment opportunities and recruit students from beyond the south of England (Adams and Bengtsson,2017).

A mere three Oxford colleges and six Cambridge colleges extended the offer of an undergraduate posting to a Black British A-level student in all six consecutive years between 2010 and 2015. The evidence forwarded by Oxford revealed an extra three Black students with alternate qualifications were granted places at Oriel.

"Difficult questions have to be asked, including whether there is systematic bias inherent in the Oxbridge admissions process that is working against talented young people from ethnic minority backgrounds," stated Lammy, the Labour MP for Tottenham at the vanguard of Black British Harvard Law School achievement (Adams and Bengtsson,2017).

Lammy recalled there being almost 400 Black students receiving three As at A-level or doing better still per annum, yet few were drawn to give Oxford or Cambridge an attempt.

To the aforementioned, an official agent for Oxford said correcting the problem would be "a long journey that requires huge, joined-up effort across society – including from leading universities like Oxford – to address serious inequalities" (Adams and Bengtsson,2017). Oxford said their intake of students from the Black and minority ethnic conjuncture comprised 15% of its 2016 UK undergraduates, raised from 14.5 in 2015 and twice as many as in 2010. This incorporates British Asian students and additional minorities. "We're also working with organisations such as Target Oxbridge and the newly formed Oxford Black alumni network, to show talented young Black people that they can fit in and thrive at a university like Oxford. All of this shows real progress and is something we want to improve on further," an official agent said (Adams and Bengtsson,2017).

An official agent for Cambridge said entrance decisions were based on academic considerations alone, and it funded £5m a year on access procedures including liaising with minority ethnic pupils. "The greatest barrier to participation at selective universities for students from disadvantaged backgrounds is low attainment at school. We assess the achievements of these students in their full context to ensure that students with great academic potential are identified," the official said. "Widening participation further will require government, schools, universities, charities, parents and students to work closely together. We will continue to work hard with all parties to raise aspirations and attainment to improve access to higher education" (Adams and Bengtsson,2017).

The latest Oxford documentation emerged following a lengthy impasse between Lammy and Oxford, in which the university offered stubborn resistance to publishing elaborate breakdowns of its entrance decisions by ethnic groups despite repeated requests, including Lammy taking matters into his own hands and formally approaching its vice-chancellor.

Lammy's first request for the evidence last year was declined by Oxford, even though Cambridge provided the breakdown of admissions and applications and yet Oxford had generated the same evidence in 2010. The ci-devant education minister remained disconsolate that Oxford negated to forward detailed figures indicating access to Black African and Black Caribbean students (Adams and Bengtsson,2017).

The initial evidence acquired by Lammy illustrated that just one Black Briton of Caribbean extract had been granted entry as an Oxford undergraduate in 2009. "I have been pressuring the University of Oxford to publish this data for over a year and they have only begrudgingly decided to partially publish it now," he said, nominating Oxford's decision as "defensive" and "evasive" (Adams and Bengtsson,2017)

"While I am pleased Oxford has backed down to avoid further embarrassment, I am disappointed that the university has combined all Black people together into one group – why should they be the only institution that doesn't break down data properly when you need granularity to understand different ethnic groups?" (Adams and Bengtsson,2017).

Accordingly, Oxford argued that it had extended the hand of cooperation to make public the limited evidence, aggregating Black students into a single category, last year.

"We made an offer to Mr Lammy in September 2016 to provide data about offers made to Black and White candidates, by college, in each year. To break the information down further would allow the specific ethnic background of some individual students to be identified," the university stated. "This is not information the Data Protection Act allows us to disclose without the consent of the student" (Adams and Bengtsson,2017).

Oxford and Cambridge continue to reek of regional disparities in those offered places and a privileged background appears key to a successful application to these national institutions which defy the appellation as the wealthier students from the south-east continue to be at the vanguard and cutting edge of Oxbridge recruits. I shall go so far as to add that I would not have included this news update had it not borne some relevance. Indeed, I wanted to show the elitism, bias and inequality of the Oxbridge admissions policy and process and I hope it has given the reader some insight. Cambridge is at ease with itself and unabashed at the findings whereas Oxford shows signs of being unwilling to be accountable to the public for their exclusivity and appears conscience-stricken at how biased they really are. All of this has huge ramifications and consequences for Black aspiration. If one is Black, Oxbridge may only be a pipedream but it should not deter young Black people from making an application.

The failure of Oxbridge to admit enough Black and minority ethnic students is part of the complex structure of what is meant by higher education functioning and operating to maintain the status quo. Oxbridge are not unique in this respect as many of the 'old' universities operate in a similar fashion while the former polytechnics are more open to Black and minority ethnic students. Indeed, this is where they are concentrated. The existing state of affairs is maintained by higher education because higher education reproduces inequality of status and employers prefer to source recruitment from 'old' universities hence Black Caribbean people tend to be a secondary alternative option when it comes to graduate recruitment.

The African-Caribbean community has long known to their cost that Oxford and Cambridge universities have been failing their like and recent revelations come as old news. The underlying message in all of this is that Black African-Caribbean people, in particular, are being continually and perpetually held back, and being told to form another queue elsewhere, and are prevented from progressing up the social ladder chiefly through no fault of their own. To give this point added meaning and significance, a Black underclass exists through social factors such as in the above, which implies that underclass membership is not entirely of an individual's or collective group's own making. To break this down and reconfigure it slightly, an underclass exists and, of course, there is some wastage, however, because of social factors flagging up as the denial of educational or occupational opportunities and consequently a tendency for Black people to gravitate towards baseline social strata, it is easy to see that the education system and the labour market are in some sense responsible and not the individual or collective group. Social institutions are knocking Black aspiration sideways and into reverse so that it occupies the lowest stratum of society from which few navigate their way out to a prosperous and successful state of being.

On the contrary, this is no surprise to African-Caribbean people and the newspaper headline might as well have read 'Oxbridge clamping down on Black aspiration' because that is the ill-effect that Black and minority ethnic students are facing and experiencing at the hands of White society. Not until Britain's social institutions improve and reform will there be any satisfactory strides forward in Black and minority ethnic social conditions and standing. In judgment of Oxbridge, David Lammy advances the point that 'if they can't improve, there is no reason the taxpayer should give them so much money' (Adams and Bengtsson, 2017).

Facing the Facts

Far from ignoring the evidence and facing the facts, many British institutions, or at least all those I have looked at in this study, do much less than operate in the interests of Black and minority ethnic groups, and, in the main, the motto of these institutions appears to be that charity begins at home. The definition of institutional racism describes the processes at work in the lives of Black African-Caribbean people and can be applied to South Asian groups to a lesser extent as they are doing relatively better and, in some cases, outperforming White pupils in schools, and it captures in a tightly compact nutshell the nature of institutional racism that is alive and unwell in our society. As we saw in Chapter 4, institutional racism functions to keep down Black and minority ethnic people and any form of oppression and discrimination is a waste of human resources.

Just as the current ethos of institutions and organisations is to ask for feedback on how they perform in order that they can improve the service they provide, so too, does this book feed back into society by holding a mirror up to it and exposing and highlighting those social ills which are system-deep, society-wide and structurally unsound and unsustainable so that a fresh look can be taken into the workings of the mechanisms of society's social institutions and reform cast. Books like this are written because of the tendency to do nothing and remain unchanged, but the feedback on society that is spread throughout and resonates beyond the pages of this book cries out to be addressed. It is only through positing critical feedback that matters can be looked into and changes and improvements instigated which is the lineality along which feedback is requested.

In previous chapters, I have drawn a detailed sketch of social institutions and organisations and their influence should now be clear to the mind. The Stephen Lawrence case suggests that Black people are hated by the police; schools exclude Black people even when White peers are participants in the same behaviour; employers discriminate against diverse communities; universities discriminate against Black people on grounds of 'race', as I found to my own personal cost; the British government has refused to be drawn, for as long as possible, on exposing the myth of Black inferiority as they also refuse to apologize for the slave trade and slavery and reject legitimate calls for reparations; indeed, the climate created by British organisations and institutions is a hostile one.

The influence of British social institutions and organisations on Black aspiration is ever-present and complex and its extent is such that paranoid bewilderment can sometimes be the by-product of an experience characterized by exclusion, exploitation and discrimination. That is not to suggest that racism is not very real; only its pervasiveness can at times leave a person bewildered and slightly knocked paranoid and, in some mainstream quarters, the experience is written off as paranoia. Those who make this attribution (usually White people) are in denial that racism exists and would rather blame the victim, running away with the notion that racism is all in the mind and has nothing whatever to do with a person's complexion. In this way, White people absolve members of their own group from the charge of racism.

Reni Eddo-Lodge (2017) talks about the 'emotional disconnect' and the sense that White people just want to say that you have got it wrong. However, one can be acutely aware of 'race' and not be paranoid because being White is universal and the norm and one can but notice this because one deviates from it. Racism by definition only happens to people of colour and there is no mistaking the harsh fact of the matter, and because racism is grounded in reality, one can dismiss thoughts of it all being a figment of the imagination and listen to one's inner man or woman, or that sneaky suspicion that a particular incident was a slight on one's reputation and personality.

The Black individual is made to feel that he or she has to be twice as good as his or her White counterpart before educational or occupational opportunities are extended, and even given that such standards are achieved, there are no guarantees that progress will be forged. Again, the influence of social institutions on Black aspiration is such that it undermines one's potential to do good and reduces a person's self-concept to a shadow of a person's former self and leaves one feeling that, if only one had lower expectations, things would not be as bad, but then no matter what one chooses to do in life the chains of discrimination are ever-present. There is, therefore, no good reason why expectations should ever be lowered. In essence, the influence of social institutions and organisations whittle away at the confidence levels of Black people and make people doubt their potential.

In the light of calls for more restrictive immigration controls, the Black and minority ethnic population feels the cumulative effect of being unwelcome, unwanted and social pariahs merely achieving the status of grudging acceptance. After being invited here to rebuild Britain's post-war economy, members of the Windrush generation are being threatened with deportation or have been wrongly deported. The 'unreachable bar' as the then Labour Party leader, Jeremy Corbyn puts it, is the inability of the Windrush generation to provide evidence of legitimate stay in this country, given the then deliberate Theresa May government ploy to clamp down on immigration. Theresa May's government measure affects large numbers of well-established UK residents who travelled to Britain in their formative years.

The threat of deportation, to countries they vacated as children and young adults some 50 years ago and have since not returned to, affects untold numbers of people. A proportion have been denied healthcare provision, lost jobs or been relegated to the status of no fixed abode as they cannot produce sufficient paperwork to confirm that they have the right of permanent residency in the UK (Gentleman, 2018).

This problem has arisen owing to newly tightened immigration measures that do not assume legal status in the UK, since in order to rent property, access employment, benefits and services, documented legal status to live in the UK would have to be demonstrated. This is Conservative government policy to enable effective immigration control.

Numbers of people moved before their homelands became independent, and thought that they were British. The Migration Observatory at Oxford University holds that some 50,000 Commonwealth-born people residing in Britain, who came here before 1971, may not yet possess the documentation of their legal right to live here.

Albert Thompson (who has asked for anonymity after taking legal advice) has been awaiting treatment for prostate cancer because last November he was informed he was not entitled to free NHS treatment if he could not satisfy that he was here legally. When asked to comment he said, "I'm very angry about this".

The whys and wherefores of this matter are an important point to consider because poisonous far-right symbolic forms on immigration made respectable a hostile environment for those viewed as outsiders. This latest debacle exposes the fact that many Black and minority ethnic people are mutually incompatible when it comes to being treated as equal citizens and accorded dignity and respect. It is a glaring example of a Tory government reflecting the message that they are being tough on immigration in order to garner support among the masses, without concern for how far-reaching its effects are on the Black community and reinforcing the message that Black people are not wanted in Britain.

The government under Theresa May was, in words and deeds, expressing straightforwardly and unceremoniously that, 'We do not like your brown skin. It offends us. We need to make Britain White again and nothing else will do' (Eleanor Louise in The Voice newspaper, 19 April 2018). The Windrush generation has made this country their home and, after serving a useful purpose, the powers that be have taken steps to send them back from whence they came. It is not only scandalous and outrageous but also down-right parasitical; having leeched off a generation then wanting to rid itself of that very same generation that according to Diane Abbot, "showed unparalleled commitment to this country, unparalleled pride in being British, and unparalleled commitment to hard work and contribution to society. It is shameful that this government has treated this generation in this way" (Gentleman,2018). For a government that previously put race equality on the political agenda, this just poses one question - whether their heart was really in it, or whether they were, in hindsight, only paying lip service and instead is symptomatic of deep-seated institutional racism and makes the then Theresa May government look rather ridiculous and ignoble. It explains why little came of the motion and how it seems as though it was political hot air or just talk. As regards racism, it is of the calibre that has the power to severely impact people's life chances.

The Windrush scandal undermines values Britain nurtures on the international stage, and of course, fails to nurture the 'moral imagination' to remain catholic to difference. Racist power relations extending across from Black and White people in society are reinforced and normalised in the Windrush scandal. Moreover, Windrush can be seen as opportunistic, insomuch as government is seizing on the opportunity that people may not have the right documentation to prove legal status. Windrush can also be conceptualised as a crucible within which individuals are negatively and unfavourably impacted on by the state through a dominant culture value system dynamic. This outcome of events operated in a climate where all moral sense was lost and irretrievably diminished, but racism is the struggle to remain closely aligned and affiliated to systemic power.

The Windrush saga is an example of state intervention on immigration by out-of-touch politicians and state administrators. This involved story meets at the axis of public opinion and is an attempt to win political expediency. The Windrush episode is founded on the principle that the fewer in number the Black presence, the better it is for race relations; albeit a fallacy that smacks more of Black people receiving a smaller slice of the cake while their White counterparts enjoy that much more economic advantage. It cannot be overstated how desperately woeful the Windrush news item has been in its effect upon certain sections of the African-Caribbean community.

This outrage is contrasted with the tendency for White people to be treated with dignity and respect in predominantly Black company and, on the whole, Black nations. Black and minority ethnic people are disadvantaged and this takes place practically on a day-to-day basis. It is important to appreciate that British institutions' routine and typical response to Black people give rise to feelings of disaffection and alienation in a country where there is a glaring and flagrant question mark over whether Blacks feel as if they belong. So long as British culture positions the man of colour as subordinate to the White man, conflict will invariably be the order of the day.

There is also the double-bind prospect that so long as White people remain envious of Black and South Asians possessing higher levels of melanin in their bodies, which is vital for brain and nervous system function, for the eyes to be the window on the world, and for the cells to regenerate, conflict will not disappear (Suzar,1999). Although humanity differs on the exterior with variations in skin colour, yet on the interior, they are all Black, all essentially and fundamentally African. The open-ended question which challenges all human beings is how to form a connective link with this Blackness. For change to take place, this requires first the core sensations or feelings and rarefied African knowledge as disseminated in ancient African universities. Nowadays, the racist is fearful of his/her Blackness, electing to distance themselves from the antecedent Black core. Contemporary reborn Black masters will embrace their Blackness, become at one with the universe and be motivated to create inventive innovations at levels that transcend the pyramids (Suzar,1999).

The tendency for Black aspiration to be thwarted and frustrated can only regularly be laid at the door of prejudice and ethnocentrism to a multi-ethnic reality. The domestic outlook is bleak. Research from a range of different sources illustrates how racism is sewn into the material of our world. The complete deconstruction of race is long overdue. This book makes some utopian and unrealistic demands but it warrants the need to aspire before actually setting out to acquire these ideals, rather than sanguinely resting on one's laurels, reproducing reality, and accepting the old established orthodoxy as it currently appears to stand. When all is said and done, utopian paradigms form the basis of objective ideas on a par with the political foundations of the social environment we currently inhabit. Yet it behoves us not to be as naïve as to think that those in power are remotely interested in impinging on their power so that the consequence is a fairer society. Moreover, even though working-class White people and people of colour have intersecting realities, we need to recognize that even though the experiences are very much alike, they are also quite different. Black and minority ethnic groups live in a hostile environment in which they are at risk.

While some cope with class prejudice, others cope with racialised class prejudice. It's this tangled web that needs to be negotiated successfully if we are to have a veridical understanding of what it is to be working-class in contemporary Britain. Racism, according to Lenny Henry, 'has no finish line' and will exist long after I die and once White people start to understand, it's even more discomforting for them to contemplate how their Whiteness has lubricated their passage through life. Racism unravels the anxieties, hypocrisies and faux-heartedness of Whiteness. It is a Gordian knot in the persona of Whiteness and it is for that humanity to take up the cudgels to solve. There is a limit to what one can do from the outside.

In a climate where churlish, obvious acts are simply the thin end of the wedge of racism, we need to encapsulate the invisible megalith (Eddo-Lodge,2017). Currently, racism can be determined in the manner a discursive struggle is framed. Currently, racism can be determined in coded terminology. Undermining racist frame, form, format and codes with an absence of words to encapsulate them can make it seem as if you are the sole being who comprehends the problem. It is essential to understand racism as structural so that it is possible to see its ability to proceed subtly, but with very harmful effects. It is important to appreciate how it permeates, like a mephitic vapour, into everything.

Below, Eddo-Lodge (2017) makes a point about structured inequality that is, at the same time, both glaringly obvious and profoundly obscure. Structures, she argues, comprise and consist of people. In the event of having a conversation about structured inequality, we are conversing about the amplification of personal prejudices of dominant culture hegemony. It is prevalent. However, she continues, rather than regarding the current state of affairs as an utter tragedy, we should grasp the opportunity to move in the direction of collective responsibility for social betterment allowing for the internal hierarchies and convergences along the way.

This state of human affairs need not be the case and the solution begins with us, she asserts. Racism's systematic scope is so universal that we must adopt the mantle of transforming our workplaces and network circles ourselves. There is a frequency in these conversations where someone will interject to say winning will require a united front, she further adds. She believes that if we are to wait for unity, an indeterminate amount of time will elapse. People will always find room to disagree over the finer details of progress. Letting time pass for unity's sake is simply fostering inertia, she maintains.

So, *on dit* to those who sense the burden of racism, who acutely sense the effects of the way in which it stifles potential, and compassion, and kindness; the way in which it is a restraining action on the world we reside in. While the past is part of the present, we can use the past to model and fashion a future. The late Terry Pratchett penned the words, 'there's no justice. Just us'. This is a fitting tribute to the circumstances we find ourselves in and the task that presents itself (Eddo-Lodge,2017:223).

It falls on yourselves and yours truly to deconstruct what we once internalised as true. It's our job of work. The present time is now the propitious time in which to prosecute this job of work through the use of whatever resources we have available. It is incumbent upon us to change narratives. It is incumbent upon us to change the frames. We need to assert that the whole of British history is our history (Eddo-Lodge,2017). We need to establish in people's minds that Black is British, and Brown is British, and despite everything, we are here to stay. Waiting for a hero to come along and make things better is not the question. Other than having little choice but to respond to biased agendas, we should categorically reject them and induct our own. More generally, we must weather the storm of misfortune by taking shelter beneath a refuge of hope and fortitude.

If what you read and hear disgusts you, and if you feel full of vim, vigour and fire, then it's contingent on your discretion. Whether you are the lead figure of a global spearheading campaign or a well-known name does not really matter. It need only be on a minor level such as beavering away to gradually reduce warped workplace cultures. The passing on of knowledge and skills to people who wouldn't access them normally is another. It can involve using imaginative powers. It can be without formal structure. It can be your occupation. The level at which you operate is unimportant, only that you are doing something (Eddo-Lodge,2017).

Prospects for the Future

The picture built up within this research study is of a Britain still not at ease with itself when it comes to the acceptance of Black African-Caribbean and South Asian people; a Britain that continues to be unable to accept people of colour for who they are, let alone English citizens – Enoch Powell inveighed on this very point all too clearly. 'The West Indian or Indian does not, by being born in England, become an Englishman. In law, he becomes a United Kingdom citizen by birth; in fact, he is a West Indian or Asian still … he will, by the very nature of things, lose one nationality without acquiring a new one. Time is running against us and them' (Olusoga,2016:14). South Asians seem some way further along being accepted for who they are. An indication of this is that they are able to wear turbans rather than helmets on motorbikes, and the inclusion into the physical built environment and proliferation of Sikh Temples, but also South Asians have gained the respect of financial institutions and are more likely than an African-Caribbean to be extended a loan for business purposes. South Asian cuisine is fast becoming, if not already, the most popular dish on the menu; curry, samosas and nan bread are readily consumed, enjoyed and indulged in by many from all walks of life on entertaining days or nights out.

Just as the media reminds us of Diwali, the South Asian festival of light, so too should they remind us of Black History Month. And, just as the African-Caribbean community holds annual carnivals, South Asians are allowed the freedom to march and congregate in the streets promoting their music and culture with official sanction from high office. This is also evidence of acceptance for who they are although full acceptance and equality are as far from the political agenda as ever. South Asian people tend sometimes to express themselves in an English Asian language variety which is as much criticized as tolerated, though is becoming less and less common, and there are those who believe that South Asians who cannot be understood should not be here and resident in this country. While Black English is recorded in dictionaries, which suggests that our contribution to the language is valued, yet it does not translate in the full light of day into acceptance and belonging. Integration, as we have already seen, implies that Black and minority ethnic people should adjust and adapt or make all the concessions in order to fit in, but Warsi and Fergusson (2017) suggest a "genuine two-way integration" (Times Literary Supplement, September 15 2017).

The Chinese community is also famed for its food, love of noodles and also its food shops or restaurants. This group often participates in the university system and is highly aspirational succeeding to become dentists, psychiatrists and doctors, etc. They are also successful business people, and, not unlike South Asians, they are inclined towards establishing their own businesses sometimes to avoid disadvantage in the labour market. The Chinese community, it would seem, would not want to be known by any other name and while their low-key approach seemingly presents no apparent threat, whether they are accepted for who they are is difficult to say. Incidentally, the Chinese cohort are an inward tight-knit community who have seldom been the subject of a sociological enquiry. In this analysis, I have endeavoured to make the distinction between Black people and

South Asian people as they prefer to assert their own particularity, but when it comes to the fight for equality, will they throw their hat into the ring of unity with Black people? The terms people of colour, minority ethnic groups and non-white people are used as terms that both unite and are inclusive.

Full acceptance is still some way off but long overdue for Britain's Black and minority ethnic people since mainstream society is only prepared to accept tokens whether that be in the form of Trevor Macdonald or Keith Vaz, negating the idea that the talent pool amongst Black African-Caribbeans and South Asians is vast. In other words, White people succeed and prosper because it is their own country and they are permitted access to valuable scarce resources, whereas the same in reverse tends to apply to this country's Black and minority ethnic population. While this implies social exclusion and racism which serves the purposes of the entire White group, it will, above all else, be of benefit to the power of the political oligarchies (van Dijk, 2017). Because the preponderant mainstream media and their belief systems are intertwined with these political, social, and cooperative oligarchies, and mediate, legitimate, or so much as openly support White oligarchical power, it is also to their advantage to play their central 'symbolic' role in the replication of the ethnic joined-up thinking and actually, to take part per se in its (pre) formulation. Independent and specific media authority in this instance is characterized by the textual detail that in contemporary societies, the mass media have almost absolute regulatory power over the symbolic wherewithal needed to construct popular consent, particularly in the field of ethnic relations. The sense in which this can be interpreted is that anti-racist belief systems can be successfully made light of and are, therefore, omitted from attaining respectable public reception.

A community of citizens and communities needs to be constructed from the lowest to the highest point which includes government action. Only when the mainstream media steers an alternate course by beginning to feature news items on racism, inequality and the experience of disadvantage will the tide be stemmed on prejudices becoming inflamed and anti-Black sentiment being fanned and fuelled, creating a climate for change in the mentality. Theresa May's Conservative government should have maintained the momentum on racial equality until a process of change came to light in every single district, shire, borough and city, and in every single organisation and institution; the fact that momentum was not maintained indicates that the drive for change was merely hot air. It is important that the government is seen to be leading by example in steering society towards change in a specified direction, and although we have learned not to trust politicians, we will now never know because of her sudden departure whether Theresa May would have stayed true to her word, that her government was the government of the many and not the few. Not only does the Westminster administration need to put measures in place, but also, the administrations in Cardiff and Holyrood, certainly though not in themselves necessarily sufficient.

I take the Oxford spokesmen's point that the problem of racial inequality is enormous and requires huge joined-up thinking across society in order that inequality is addressed leading to a radical transformation in the political landscape (Adams and Bengtsson, 2017). Racial inequality is a phenomenon we should be reminded of daily, serving the purpose that it becomes second nature that fair play is seen to be enacted.

Schools should counter racial inequality by teaching Black History and so too should higher education if it does not already. People should be re-educated and made to perceive the injustice of racial inequality on as many levels as is humanly possible so that people develop an aversion to racial inequality and feel positive about racial equality. Parekh (2000) stresses that there should be respect for equality and respect for diversity. The entire cultural system needs to embrace decency and fair play on a more concerted level and banish apathy, ignorance, thoughtlessness, discrimination and racist stereotyping of and towards Black and minority ethnic people. The re-education of society to combat racial inequality must address myths, lies and stereotypes that aim at liberating White minds of the vestiges of what they were brought up with.

Chapter 10: Conclusion

To set the tide of change running that is not just discussion for discussion's sake or political hot air, it has to involve sustained government effort to set the context and to ask the question of how government can start the trickle-down effect of people working together to combat racial inequality and to promote cultural diversity with a view to ultimately putting measures in place to ensure South Asian and African-Caribbean people have a greater stake in society; namely, social justice and equal opportunities. The fact that Theresa May has even begun to think about racial inequality is a sign of the times since Conservative party ideology incorporates a belief in natural inequality; the notion that hierarchy should be left alone and unhindered either because inequality is an essential prerequisite of culture and polite ideals, or because they have a deference for tradition and inequality is primordial (Scott and Marshall,2005). This includes an aversion to change and reform and a sense of conserving or 'keeping something intact' (Vincent, 1993:55). Theresa May's strategy seems to suggest that government of the many and not the few is an attempt to broaden the working-class support base while seeming to appeal to the 'Black vote'.

Will the Press ever change?

That the press operate in accordance with the denial of racism is a defence mechanism to which Whites have recourse when faced with an uncomfortable and unpleasant fact. For the media to feature stories about inequality, racism and the experience of disadvantage would be tantamount to admitting that racism exists, and going against the defence mechanism, instead of implying that Whites appear unable to stomach too much reality and prefer to bury their heads in the sand. Moreover, the press refuses to accept or to challenge their conscience that racism is alive and unwell so would rather marginalize anti-racist ideologies, and to leave it up to the press to reform would be rather like waiting until kingdom come. Also, because this type of journalism shapes perception and reflects society's attitudes, is it any wonder that the defence mechanism against racism is extremely pervasive? The print media appear to be releasing the type of data information the public like to read but it is a form of cultural imperialism on Black and minority ethnic groups and change for the foreseeable future is unlikely as the mentality has to change first. There appears no possible intervention against freedom of speech – even though it might incite someone to racial hatred – and against a press intent on attacking anti-racist strategies and inflaming White people's prejudices, apart from using the infrastructure presented above.

Just as the British National Party (BNP) had freedom of movement to establish themselves within the boundaries of a free country, and freedom of speech to act, within the limits of a liberal democracy, the press too has similar kinds of freedom which it mobilizes against multi-culturalism. The press represents the potential to turn the tide of public opinion and produce change across society but, instead, it is reinforcing and reproducing the dominant ideology. The reader might ask, well what does one expect? British values are based on decency and fair play but clearly, the press is not playing ball and refuses to purge itself of platitudes that are hostile and antagonistic to this country's Black and minority ethnic communities. And although one would rather be accepted than tolerated, tolerance being another value the British like to think they can aspire to, where does the interplay of tolerance feature in what the press tends to say or the positions the press tends to adopt inside its news story coverages? The prevention of future racist action or practice and the avoidance of putting racial equality on the table of people's hearts signposts the direction the press is headed. The press is cold and calculating and knows its art and craft where it concerns maintaining the status quo and working independently, though sometimes, it seems, in tandem with political elites.

Food for thought

If we can return to the idea that White people appear unable to digest too much reality and appear ostrich-like in their actions, the following is something one does not hear every day. 'You probably already know that Jesus Christ was a woolly haired Black man' ... drawn from the Bible itself, referred to as the "Lamb of God" with kinky, convoluted hair likened to lamb's wool, feet the shade of burnt brass (Rev.1:14,15) and an appearance befitting jasper and sardine stone (Rev.4:3) (Suzar,1999:1). Jasper and sardine stone (also referred to as sard/sardonyx), are routinely brownish and brownish-red. Three female antecedents of Jesus were Hamitic (African). Documented in Matthew's genealogy of Christ (1:1-16), their appellations were Tamar and Rachab (who were Canaanites), and Bathsheba who was probably a Hittite, as Uriah, her significant other, was a Hittite. The biblical Hittites originated from Heth, a son of Ham (Gen.10:15; 23:10) (Suzar,1999).

The first pictures of Christ resoundingly portray him as Black

In the subterranean world of Rome where the first recorded images of Jesus are manifest, black paintings and graven images of Christ, the Madonna, and biblical dramatis personae still survive from the dawn of Christian worship. In the difficult to search out classic, *Anacalypsis*, historian Godfrey Higgens elucidates on page 138, "the God Christ, as well as his mother, are described in their old pictures and statues to be Black. The infant God in the arms of his Black mother, his eyes and drapery white, is himself perfectly Black ... the whiteness of the eyes and teeth, and the studied redness of the lips are very observable" (Suzar,1999:1).

Not infrequently arousing the establishment with his propensity to make a great show of heretical truth, the talks and tomes by the no-nonsense scholar, Kersey Graves, were often suppressed and sometimes prohibited. Originally made public in 1875, one such tome, *The World's Sixteen Crucified Saviours*, remained a clandestine blockbuster for almost a century, despite all-out suppression. On page 56, Kersey writes: "There is as much evidence that the Christian Saviour was a Black man or at least a dark man ... and that evidence is the testimony of his disciples, who had nearly as good an opportunity of knowing what his complexion was as the evangelists, who omit to say anything about it. In the pictures and portraits of Christ by the early Christians, he is uniformly represented as being Black. And to make this the more certain, the red tinge is given to the lips; and the only text in the Christian bible quoted by orthodox Christians as describing his complexion, represent it as being Black". [emphasis added] (Suzar,1999:2). Kersey asks what the outcome would be in the event of Christ making a second appearance on earth as Christians expect, "and that he comes in the character of a sable Messiah, how would he be received by our negro-hating Christians ... ? Would they worship a negro God? Let us imagine he enters one of our fashionable churches ... what would be the result? Would the sexton show him to a seat? Would he not rather point to the door, and exclaim, 'Get out of here; no place here for niggers?' What a ludicrous series of ideas is thus suggested by the thought that Jesus Christ was a 'darkey' (Suzar,1999:2).

An ancient Roman coin illustrates Christ's African identity

The British Museum houses an ancient gold coin depicting Christ as an African with closely compact, woolly hair featuring a cross behind him (Suzar,1999). This coin was produced under the second governing rule of Roman Emperor, Justinian II, who governed at two distinct times, separated by a decade (685-695 and 705-711 A.D.). Throughout his first governing rule, the gold coins he had produced portrayed Christ as a lank-haired European. Throughout his second governing rule, he changed the symbolism of Christ on the coin to an Africoid symbol so as to ensure that this portrayal was more congruent with the early cultural traits of the Byzantine Church, which routinely represented Jesus as an African. The opposite side of the coin depicts Justinian with a cross in the background as well. The Cambridge Encyclopedia set down: "Whatever the fact, this coin places beyond dispute the belief that Jesus Christ was a negro. The coin is of otherwise great historical interest, for it was the cause of a war between Justinian and Abdul Malik, 5th caliph of the Umayyads, the former demanding tribute to be paid in these same coins and the latter refusing." (Suzar,1999:2).

Christ's Mother, "The Black Madonna" is worshipped throughout Europe, of all places

The most highly prized symbols of the Catholic Church are the Black Madonna and Christ child, which can be found in Europe's most revered shrines and cathedrals (Suzar,1999:3). Annually, hundreds of thousands of European followers ritually submit themselves on coming into contact with the image of Black Mary and her Christ progeny at Black Madonna locations throughout Germany, Spain, France, Belgium, Italy, Portugal and further additional Catholic countries. Numerous Black Madonna icons undergo black paint removal through the action of kissing their hands and feet. In Poland, the Church urges believers to supplicate to the Black Madonna of Częstochowa each new morn before rising. It has been made known that Pope John Paul abides by this ritual. Time Magazine (June 11, 1979) covered Pope Paul II's visit to Częstochowa's most sacred shrine, which strikingly exhibits "The Lady" known throughout the ages as the Black Madonna. At our Lady of Koden (Poland), there are icons of White saints bearing portraits of Black Madonnas. Pilgrims for centuries have paid homage to Black Madonna sites and left enthused, self-assured, unburdened, or had their physical ailments ministered to. In contemporary France, there are more than 300 listed Black Madonna locations! On occasions, they are hidden from public view in vaults, while made available to the public are Madonnas with European characteristics.

In the classic, Anacalypsis, historian Godfrey Higgins sets out, " ... in all the Romish countries of Europe, in France, Italy, Germany, &c., the God Christ, as well as his mother, are described in their old pictures and statues to be Black. The infant God in the arms of his Black Mother, his eyes and drapery white' is himself perfectly Black. If the reader doubt my word, he may go to the cathedral at Moulins – to the famous chapel of the Virgin at Loretto ... the whiteness of the eyes and teeth, and the studied redness of the lips, are very observable ... There is scarcely an old church in Italy where some remains of the worship of the BLACK VIRGIN and BLACK CHILD are not to be met with. Very often, the Black figures have given way to white ones, and in these cases, the Black ones, as being held sacred, were put into retired places in the churches, but were not destroyed ..." (Suzar,1999:3).

To begin with, all the Black Madonnas had Africoid features preceding a time when most of them met their end at the hands of iconoclasts. At the time they came to be replaced, the artists resolved to keep the dark skin colour, however, not knowing what real Africans looked like, gave European attributes to the paintings. In instances in which originals have survived, one may discern Africoid features on Mary and her son Jesus, like the Black Madonna of Nuria, Spain – named "the Queen of the Pyrenees" (Suzar,1999:3). Russia's extraordinary legacy of Black Madonnas and further additional Christian statues of dark skin is documented in the volume, *Russian Icons* by Vladimir Ivanov, subsuming the news item coverage of the Spring 1994 edition of *Russian Life* magazine, adorned by a Black Madonna on its foremost page.

The Turin Shroud, a Hoax

Heralded as the burial raiment of Jesus, the Turin Shroud has been confirmed to be a false alarm. Carbon dating suggests the Shroud's authenticity does not date back as far as the Fourth Crusade 1204 (Suzar,1999:2). The feature is comprehensively dealt with in *Turin Shroud* by Picknett and Prince, who put forward, "there is no historical evidence that the Shroud is older than – at the very best reckoning – 650 years" (Suzar,1999:2).

In fact, the veneration of the virgin, Black "Mother of God". With her celestial being begotten son, far exceeds Christianity and endured throughout ancient civilisation.

Historians accept that the image of the Egyptian Goddess Isis with her son Horus in her arms constituted the original Madonna and Child. The names Mary and Jesus were attached when Europe came under pressure to be Christianized. The veneration of Isis and Horus was particularly common in ancient Rome. "Roman legions carried this figure of Black Isis holding the Black infant Horus all over Europe where shrines were established to her. So holy and venerate were these shrines that when Christianity invaded Europe, these figures of the Black Isis holding the Black Horus were not destroyed but turned into figures of the Black Madonna and Child. Today, these are still the holiest shrines in Catholic Europe" (Suzar,1999:4). Appellations like Our Lady, The Great Mother, are not dissimilar appellations attributed to Isis. The word "Madonna" per se is from mater domina, an appellation used for Isis! The month of May, which was devoted to the heathen Virgin Mother, is what's more the month of Mary, the Christian Virgin (Suzar,1999:4).

Disbelievingly, many contemporary White commentators appear unable to see or accept the Black Madonna's sable shade with her African origin, while their forebears did without even as much as a second thought. Some categorically deny any racial association. Rather, they raise other contentious issues and nuanced understandings (the "dark" phase of the moon, fecundity of the earth, etc.) – any obviating claim save for melanin – to reason why the Lady is put across as Black. This is apparent in certain books penned by White scholars on the subject of Black Madonnas. Maybe Whites have come to be so caught up in the network of false history spun by their forebears that many cannot see the wood for the trees, unable to grasp or discern even monumental evidence of African age-old influence. Whether today's White authors are indeed this myopic – or feigning myopia – of the Black Madonna's African root source, then they are invited to read the endeavours of certain rare truth-seeking White erudite academics who predate them, such as Godfrey Higgins, Kersey Graves, Gerald Massey and T.W. Doane. These writers enquired after the truth and set it in writing. What makes this all the more remarkable is the ne plus ultra overtly racist age in which they lived. However, at present, official White controlling authority does not and is unlikely to accept the African origin of their whitewashed religions. In *Bible Myths*, T.W. Doane consigns to paper a chapter on *The Worship of the Virgin Mother*, in which he openly states, "The whole secret of the fact of these early representations of the Virgin Mary and Jesus – so-called – being black, crowned and covered with jewels, is that they are of pre-Christian origin; they are *Isis* and *Horus* ... baptised anew" (Suzar,1999:4). The relevance of this section is to show that God created the Black man in his own image and some would say that Black people are sculpted in the likeness of God. Need I say anything of what this means?

Black aspiration and parent power

Black aspiration is tending to fall by the wayside because needs are not being met, opportunities are not being granted and primarily and substantially, Black African-Caribbean people are being left to their own devices to muddle through and eke out a living while often not reaching the position in society they aspired to. It has been at a point of crisis for some time and has reached a moment of great importance, the acquisition of a favourable stake in society, that is the hunger and appetite, not to mention the expected status of Black African-Caribbean people. With burgeoning inequality and an expanding underclass, it seems like never before more decisive for Black aspiration to secure a greater share in societies dealings. More often than not, Black aspiration faces frustration, disappointment, exclusion and spanners being thrown into the works in the enterprise of self-determination, self-advancement and self-actualization towards self-dependence. Don't let us deceive ourselves; there is no legitimate justification for the wholesale and needless oppression of a primarily and substantially African-Caribbean people. Since South Asian people do not bear as destructive a stereotype as African-Caribbean people, they get the green light of forward advancement in schools and tend to be given favourable opportunities beyond the school gates, as do some Black African-Caribbean people, but not nearly enough.

Chapter 10: Conclusion

The way for Black aspiration to begin to thrive and flourish is located in the schools as education can change lives and opens a whole new vista of hope and aspiration on which one can build. When education really does matter, Black aspiration is beset by problem factors such as unconscious bias in teachers who see Black African-Caribbean pupils not as potential A* GCSE success stories but as sources of trouble. The matter may be more complex than this, but the problem appears to lie in the likelihood that Black pupils respond to being goaded, and take no nonsense from teachers who tend to insist on conformity and control, and are seen to come down harder and stricter where African-Caribbean students are concerned. This may go some way towards explaining the high exclusion rate among African-Caribbean males. Moreover, the tendency for African-Caribbean culture to produce an uncompromising hard man exterior – coupled with having thrust upon them humiliating identities instilled within teachers – is a volatile mixture. The macho peer group culture of Black youth tends to not be helpful for teachers nor the youth themselves, and the more controlled behaviour of Black females is something young Black male individuals can learn from, so as to survive the worst effects of their school career.

Black African-Caribbean parents are key to the successful navigation of their children's school careers. They should admonish and thoroughly brief their children about teachers who reflect society's value system where it pertains to Black African-Caribbean people, and for their children to not become involved in peer-group dynamics as played out in the classroom. Black African-Caribbean parents should interact with and take an interest in their children's education and emotional wellbeing, letting them know that they are not alone by offering support and advice whenever needed. Parents should be proactive in guiding their children through the process of school life and should not hesitate to demand an appointment with the headmaster should a problem arise. They should not be intimidated by teachers who are just as fallible as themselves and should also attend every parents' evening and let the school know that they are full square behind their children's education. Parents should consult with their children on matters arising in school life on a daily basis and ensure the healthy personal development of their children.

Parents have a crucial role to play in their children's developmental stages and long-term goals and a good parent-child relationship can make the difference between a school career that is dull and lacklustre and one that is satisfying, fulfilling and rewarding. For boys, the social cost of academic success against the odds amongst their peers seems a solitary route but, a solid and strong parenting role can offer comfort and compensation in the face of adverse personal circumstances. The underachievement of Black youth in secondary schools is partly due to complex contributing factors and also because macho Black boys tend to see schoolwork as effeminate or gay and Black African-Caribbean parents can help break this misconception.

The West and the rest

Black aspiration or the wishes and desires of Black people face many obstacles, some of which I have attempted to call attention to, and outlined, with some sketching in, throughout the preceding leaves of this book. Despite the prerequisite of race relations laws, discrimination continues unabated, and we are no closer to the colour-blind society that is sought, which is a situation where greater happiness would exist and prevail. It links into and intersects with Martin Luther King's dream, that is to say, it is the hope and optimism that one day, the Black man and woman will be judged not by his or her skin colour but by the content of their character, and the freedom that stems from what appears to be freedom from all forms of subordination: oppression, discrimination, inequality, prejudice and racism, and such a conjuncture constitutes, and is tantamount to, a state of true democracy. Democracy is a government for the people, of the people, by the people and also a government committed to the principles of social equality. Under such conditions, then, and only then, will this country live out the true meaning of its creed. If Black African-Caribbean people can realize equal power relations between groups, then this is the best fundamental foundation for equality of status (Hartmann and Husband,1974: 213-14). Individual Black aspiration is all well and good, but collective Black aspiration facilitates the individual and ensures that Black aspiration, in a general sense, is well lubricated in order to achieve and succeed without a spanner being thrown into the works as so often tends to transpire. Egypt was not built in a day; Blacks in Egypt excelled because collectively, they could stand strong and build a civilization unsurpassed by any other of its day; the first in recorded history because they were unhindered and free from a social system that undermined them constantly.

Preceding Chapters highlight the concerns that the mainstream dominant culture would often like to forget and stays silent on. These are the concerns the education system tends to thwart and even dash; these are the concerns higher education tends to devalue and discredit and is not colour-blind towards, while inclined to use unnecessary manoeuvres to play for time; these are the concerns the labour market ignores when it comes to career progression and in finding excuses to turn able Black people away from jobs. While the media seeks to influence public opinion against Black aspirational concerns, the British government offers only lip service on Black aspiration and is historically known to do nothing and remain unchanged on key Black aspirational concerns. The governing elites, in whose interests these institutions seem to operate, can be seen as the puppet masters of actions and processes that serve their purpose but which blight Black and minority ethnic lives. The fact that Black people are portrayed as a 'social problem' belies the fact that the reverse is true and people of colour are more often victims than anything else; more sinned against than sinning. This could be the aetiology or answer to why Black and minority ethnic crime has created a moral panic and is why minorities have a reason to be angry at the system in which they live and where they are forced to accept constant criticism.

Despite our common human heritage, we live in a time, place, and space riven with division, whether by region, class, religion, gender, disability, sexual orientation or race. Does it have to take a fight for human survival on a catastrophic scale before all of humanity comes together as one? Or will it always be that society predestines the survival of one group over others? We see the former in the movies with the invincible alien creatures; capital is making vast profits from a twist on the existing order, for these films are based on the reverse of reality where only a threat to human survival enables an unyielding resolve of the human spirit that revolutionizes and turns things around. The underlying theme and subtext of Black aspiration is the hope and optimism that one glorious and magnificent day, humanity will come to a moment of sudden and great revelation or realization, the like of which will take some reckoning. At present, the dominant group's first priority is its own interests and that is how humanity is seen to be getting its priorities in the correct order. The demands of global needs and desires constantly exert pressure on the consciousness of Western European governing elites, and daily, there is resistance to such demands.

Division fractures and fragments society and all because the wealthy and the powerful are committed to the status quo. The elite may argue that society is not broken so therefore it does not need fixing, but a fractured and fragmented society is broken, as clearly as a vessel that haemorrhages fluid, yet there is a failure to see or an uncaring apathy to face the truth as the elite remain unaffected by a broken society. It is practically only those at the bottom of the pile that experience the effects of a profoundly and devastatingly corrupt conjuncture that is modern-day broken Britain.

The west is guaranteed food supplies all year round despite the changing of the seasons, while regions of the African continent are tormented and ravaged by hunger and starvation. In the 1980s, the conscience of western societies was pricked. The famous Band Aid campaign to relieve Africa of hunger and starvation is an illustration of this awakening to the needs of a country that continues to be exploited. The role of Europe in the underdevelopment of Africa could not have helped matters and is responsible for a whole range of the miscellany of problems Africa faces. The image in the media of ravaged African bodies torn by hunger is enough to move one to tears, portraying a side of Africa that is corrupt and helpless and if it is not representing a form of subordination on a global level and scale, then, it remains to be seen what is. These images on our newspaper covers portray an Africa that cannot help itself out of a crisis and needs Europe to bail it out with food aid.

Meanwhile, the British people cry out that their first concern is with the people in need of help domestically, as the 'Children In Need' fundraising campaign points up, and the high-profile charity focus shifted away from Africa as it gets left out in the cold. Moreover, we also hear through the grapevine that Africa is itself to blame for its own problems and difficulties as African mothers bring into the world children they can neither feed nor look after. Here, there is a failure to perceive that life carries on no matter what the circumstances. Because we are influenced by the media on subjects we know little about or are influenced by people who are themselves influenced by the media, given media bias, all we see in the media should be put through a critical filtration process or taken with a pinch of salt or judgement suspended (Winter,2007).

World leaders need to meet periodically to rescue the world economy and Africa ought to be tabled as a motion for the redirection and redistribution of wealth and resources so that Africa can be insulated and saved from the ravages of drought and all the other reasons why they tend to face one crisis after another. World leaders should lay selfish self-interest aside for once and give a thought to those at the very bottom of the food chain who so desperately need to be considered in world affairs and the general scheme of things. The west is often seen to separate itself from the rest - as in fortress Europe and America's obsession and preoccupation with immigration - and should be pro-active about the existence of others and the plan to live active and useful lives which is intrinsic to and dovetails with the fact that each of us belongs to the human family. In the event of such action, democracy's leading lights can take intrinsic and extrinsic reward from helping others less fortunate than themselves. The west should remember the rest for the rest of humanity are just as important and not mutually exclusive, yet equally deserving of the right to an honourable and dignified natural life.

Division versus unity

At the very heart of the issue, humanity has a vast reservoir of resourcefulness and is a community of citizens and a community of communities, but also, humanity should not let that which destructively and perniciously divides us interfere with, or come between, the powerful all-embracing entity that unites us. Beyond what has been said and when it comes to the specifics, culture divides, race divides and so does religion, along with living in a country divided by class, gender and region. However, let us not forget that we are all part of the rich and indivisible tapestry that is humanity. To be sure, we all have common shared needs and desires; however, to all intents and purposes, division is a spanner in the works that stops us from uniting, albeit dwarfed by the shared towering kaleidoscope that unites humanity. Put differently, we are united by what we have in common rather than by what sets us apart. Bias creeps into human behaviour in the light of scarce resources resulting in inequality and a lacuna between groups. Division between human groups tends towards conflict and although a device for rule ultimately is anathema to the universe, unity, on the other hand, inclines towards the cosmos. Some may see no further than what divides us, hence, the bigger picture is the dominant culture's desire to maintain and reinforce a political, economic and social edge and hegemony over all those considered as outsider groups.

Is there any wonder why W.E.B. Du Bois, in his analysis "The Souls of Black Folk", asserted that the major problem of the twentieth century would be the colour line? While Du Bois correctly predicted this, its validity seems destined to continue for some time to come, yet, degrees of change, however slow and painful, are creeping forward. Although change is not taking place rapidly enough, the wheels move in fits and starts, rarely gathering momentum, but there are some glimmers of hope, some of which I shall make brief and passing reference to below. Given the various descriptive terms that have been applied over time and how, to incorporate people of colour into the British political landscape, posits scope for hope as the current designations Asian, Black and Muslim arose out of complex interactions and struggles, signposting that humanity is fluid and mutable and a work in progress.

As well as being the year when the Windrush docked at Tilbury, 1948 was the year of the UN Declaration of Human Rights. Partly owing to the declaration, the long-established and frequently religious tradition of human equality applicable to all races and classes – the theory that each human individual was as innately valuable as the next – came to filter through into the broad range of public affairs of the western democracies of the First World. On the other hand, it had yet to become part of the cultural mores of the general population, especially in a geographic and political unit such as Britain where it was a widely distributed and centuries-old idea to feel superior to people of colour (Goodhart,2013:139). This feeling of superiority or hubris appears to interlink with the need to feel confident in, for example, a public-speaking role and there are ways and methods to build confidence in order to carry out such an occupational practice.

In this context, there is a need to feel superior and thus confident. Optimum levels of confidence appear to underlie the feeling of superiority and the two tend to feed off one another. It is difficult perhaps to feel supremely confident without also feeling superior to other people. This need not adversely impact others but, needless to say, it sometimes does. Martin Luther King appeared to give credence to the notion of an intellectually superior class of individuals and associated with this is a certain level of confidence in one's own abilities and the two things appear to run parallel.

However, the feeling of superiority among the White British public can be traced back to the years preceding the emergence of racist ideology simply because the British were disgorging Africa of its natural resources and sought to justify slavery and the slave trade. These obsolete ideas are being renewed in the minds of a generation, and for over 200 years, these ideas have been central to the Black experience whereby people are beset by their subordinate labour market position, unemployment, long-term unemployment, under-employment, discrimination, racial inequality, prejudice and racism.

The damaging effects of superior versus inferior races felt during the Second World War precipitated the United Nations Educational, Scientific and Cultural Organisation (UNESCO) to charge a commission of doyens with the aim and purpose of drafting a scientific statement alluding to the nature of 'race'. The outcome of this was put in the public domain in Paris in July 1950. The UNESCO statement is outlined in Chapter Two of this work making three additional statements in the 1950s and 1960s. The UNESCO statement on race signifies and denotes landmark evidence through which optimism can be expressed in humanity's tendency towards gradual and piecemeal organisational structural transposition. The Race Relations Acts of 1965, 1968, 1976 and the Race Relations (Amendment) Act 2000 are beacons of hope and evidence of the slow grind of the progress towards protecting minority ethnic groups.

At the contemporary level, Black and South Asian minority groups can vacillate from feeling that significant progress in race relations and in their daily lives has occurred for the better, but beneath that change is the sudden reminder that there is stubborn resistance, in some quarters, to change in the form of incidents which minorities suspect to have been racist, and in the form of race equality disappearing from the radar of institutions and the political agenda; and also, White authority's reluctance to want to know or hear about equality and influential types higher up the chain of command. On the other hand, if freedom, justice and equality breaking out and raining down like a mighty torrential flood of cascading waters were to become evident and apparent, then I, for one, would rue the outburst of changes as having not played out in the proceedings much sooner.

Whether such a state of change will ever transpire is difficult to foresee; it is rather similar to enquiring whether Britain will ever elect a Black Prime Minister; if John Taylor's bid to become Cheltenham's first Black Conservative Member of Parliament in a safe Tory seat is anything on which to base an opinion, I would have to say that the British public does not openly welcome the prospect because John Taylor lost his deposit and, more recently, senior Labour figure Diane Abbot was unsuccessful in her bid to secure the Labour leadership position.

One thing is certain, justice delayed is justice denied and if Martin Luther King back in 1960's America could claim that the time was ripe for change, then, going forward in the present epoch. minorities here and in America seem to be losing out or indeed are being robbed of their birthright as freedom, justice and equality seem a distant and far from tangible reality. Equality of opportunity tends to be the articulated mission statement of most, if not all, British institutions, yet, according to Gilroy (2002), inequality is increasing. Laws and legislation are all very well, but on the ground and at grassroots level, little has changed and, of course, Gilroy (2002) suggests that this has been the case since his book first came out in 1987. Black aspiration looks forward to the day when a change will come, transforming the moral and social landscape and breaking out and rolling down from the hillsides and mountain tops and flowing into and settling within the valleys below with a lively hope that the cascading waters will never cease from flowing.

At present, Black aspiration is at the wrong end of being buffeted from pillar to post and for evil to succeed, all it takes is for good people to just stand by and do nothing. To turn the tide, Black aspiration would be in a better position if a great source of support came from good people. This is Britain, however, but it would help if other language varieties aside from standard English were valorised and not made the subject of uproarious laughter as this denigrates and belittles all things pertaining to that ethnic community. For example, patois can be used to indicate Black identity, Black solidarity and Black pride and so, therefore, linguistic acceptance has its place and significance.

Will change always prove elusive?

As a practice and system of ideas, racism is so entrenched and society so deeply anti-Black that the possibility of change is very difficult or unlikely.

That impercipience is bliss is the universal language, but it is important to recognize that White society will always tend to expect privileged preferment over other social groups recently arrived in Britain and their British-born children, and will always tend to perpetuate a divide between those indigenous to the country and those seen as 'the outsider within' (Troyna,1981; Gordon and Rosenberg,1989). Black and minority ethnic groups live parallel lives with the majority ethnic group but are separate and incompatible regarding equality; that hangs in the balance and so long as this continues, each group will always play host to different interests and actions.

According to Triandis (1988), 'the way to reduce conflict is not for one side to lose what the other side gains, but for both sides to gain' (in Katz and Taylor,1988:42). Operationally, the gaining of equality by minority ethnic groups could be one gain, but where the scales of advantage are tipped into balance, White society can claim a moral victory by finally living out the principles of democracy. Another way in which to view this is that Whites, schematically, have a real motive in the maintenance of racial inequality as it benefits White social status and so is no better off in terms of benefit gains by introducing equality initiatives. This is why equality may never be extended to Black and minority ethnic groups. In the main, it is the assumption of a belief system that Whites, as representatives of the in-group, will tend to devise and incorporate attitudes and beliefs that legitimate their privileged, hegemonic social status. Such stultifying insularity, however, emerges and operates within the constraints set by the existing social structure and cultural environment (Bobo,1988; in Katz and Taylor,1988).

The fact that people of colour are not indigenous to this sceptred isle is partly why we are expected to make all the integration concessions while Whites remain unchanged and this is unlikely to become a two-way process. However, it can be, since the dominant culture can be bolstered and boosted by considering the opinions of the few minority cultures that live in Britain rather than putting pressure on these minorities to assume a monolithic, impoverished, narrow perspective that may, over the long term, diminish creativity and the possibilities of effective adjustment in a rapidly developing world. These targets are equally practicable for minority and majority individuals, provided we respect one another's cultural identity (Triandis,1988; in Katz and Taylor,1988). Whites should not ask Blacks to put on a culturally White mantle. Whites should not ask Blacks to divest themselves of their identity. The term integration as in becoming like them signifies by definition that our culture is inferior. Alternatively, what behoves us is to locate more common superlative goals and methods of inter-reliance that give self-worth to all. We must be adaptable if we are to chance upon such methods (Triandis,1988).

'Fear of a Black planet' goes some way to explaining why change is unlikely. This entrenched property and prospect is seen in the notion that many White people reject racial injustice, in theory, but are reluctant to accept the measures needed to eliminate racial injustice (Bobo,1988; in Katz and Taylor,1988). Martin Luther King Jr offered a similar observation as early as 1967 and Bobo (1988) noted a gap between "principles and implementation", or more broadly, pointed up the constraints imposed on racial progress. The lacuna between principles and implementation implies that racial attitudes possess both positive and negative tendencies, a set of features that, on its own, pose questions for a prejudice interpretation. The symbolic racism commentators have taken two somewhat different angles on this problem. Kinder and Sears (1981) observed that "since the explicitly segregationist, White supremacist view has all but disappeared, it can no longer be a major political force" (p.416; in Katz and Taylor,1988:106-107). They claimed, however, that prejudice continues to be operating albeit in some mutated form. The challenge, then, is to understand and evaluate the new reifications of prejudice – hence the concept of symbolic racism. As Kinder and Sears (1981) maintained, "what has replaced [segregationist, White supremacist views], we suggest, is a new variant that might be called symbolic racism" (p.416; in Katz and Taylor,1988:107).

As far as this standpoint is concerned, approbation for racial principles is of limited contemporary political importance. McConahay et al (1981) insisted on an elaboration of this point. They advocated that Whites can identify the racist content of research enquiry on racial principles and therefore attribute the socially acceptable response. New-fangled, contemporary racism items do not succumb to this contamination, McConahay et al, asserted, because people do not discern the racist content of accepting, for example, that Blacks have disproportionate political influence. In each work, the main thrust is that prejudice has become more nuanced (Bobo,1988; in Katz and Taylor,1988).

While pointing up an important mutation in the nature of racial attitudes, both expositions are problematic. No exhaustive analysis of the reasons for this change in attitudes transpiring is provided. If the problem stems from a form of prejudice, in that case, it is difficult to see why the pressure for any variation from segregationist attitudes to a nascent, more pertinent form of articulating an unreasonable hostility toward Blacks (Bobo,1988; in Katz and Taylor,1988). And it is not at all accurate to consider segregationist beliefs and attitudes as purely a simpler, more advanced in years form of prejudice (though various commentators have done so). The rise of White supremacist activity and ideology, particularly the rise of segregation, although partly the product of prejudice, can further be traced to a coalescence of political necessity (e.g., increased Black suffrage and the democratic movement), cultural conventions (e.g., social Darwinism), and the practical defence of group interests. According to Cell (1982), "Segregation is at the same time an interlocking system of economic institutions, social practices and customs, political power, law, and ideology, all of which function both as means and ends in one group's effort to keep another (or others) in their place within a society that is actually becoming unified" (p.14; in Katz and Taylor,1988:107). Whichever fresh set of opinions said to emanate from segregationist opinions may also reveal a group-interested ideology adapted to new circumstances. Bobo (1988) suggests that a primary contributor to the increased convolutions of racial attitudes is the involuntary process of a prevailing group's explicating social events and motions for change in a way that permits the continuity of its hegemony beneath and within very different structural (economic and ideological) and cultural conditions.

American background experience and culture do render at the disposal, however, an unenviable image of Blacks as indolent and dependent slaves, cavalier minstrels and potentially pernicious vagabonds. Such an image may even incorporate a deeply held fixation with colour that extends throughout Western society. It is important to appreciate that this cultural form, though not at the forefront or everywhere as in a previous age, is still vaguely intertwined in the racial attitudes of Black and White Americans (Bobo,1988). From this particularly narrow angle, the concept of symbolic racism aptly admonishes us that prejudice has a lasting quality that scarcely relinquishes its grip on people. However, the concept may exaggerate the seriousness of prejudice as such, specifically insofar as attitudes directed at Black political activism are classed as key pointers of this concept.

In the absence of a civil rights movement or urban unrest, or had these events not received media coverage and inexorable elite attention, then, attitudes in the direction of Black activists and activism might clearly amount to a *laissez-faire* racial resentment. Neither of these alternatives gains. Quite the opposite; the mass media afforded intensive reporting of Black protest, the general public developed fairly unambiguous assessments of the objectives of civil rights protagonists, and political main characters and institutions helped centre public conscious awareness on Black grievances. To be sure, some have argued – and have made available particulars from national surveys that indicate – that the general elections of 1964 and 1968 were useful to make 'race' among the main constituent of established partisan political allegiance and political punditry among the general public.

The recent branding of Martin Luther King's birthday as a calendar date vacation has also served to drive home more firmly in American culture a perception of Black protest as a catalyst for social reform (Bobo,1988). The above discursive struggle acknowledges the true global dimension of the 'race' issue and bound up within it is clear relevance pertaining to Britain. A complex web of cultural and political alignment mediates Blacks here to Blacks in other places (Gilroy,2002). By the same token, they are part and parcel of the social relations of the United Kingdom and America.

Also, the idea of racism elucidated by Bobo (1988) argues that White approbation for the rational calculus of racial justice is real but amounts to lip service. The term lip service assumes that full commitment is not extended in that it often falls short of being converted into approbation for concrete policy change to the extent that Blacks are seen to represent a competing body for the resources that Whites value and have dominion over. Bobo (1988) informs us that these kinds of analyses are not mutually exclusive (offering Allport,1954; Williams,1965 as examples), nor are they entirely comprehensive as concerns the likely factors influencing contemporary racial attitudes.

In light of this, Black aspiration can continue to look to the skies as there is no restriction on dreaming of scaling seemingly impossible heights. Before the advent of the slave trade and slavery, Black aspiration soared, and this event in history is a basis upon which a firm foundation can be built predicated on past glory from which there is a potential to excel. Just as inspiration can be drawn from Black History, so too can Black music fire the imagination and motivate Black people to strive in the face of adversity. Black aspiration tends often to be the result of a set of circumstances and experiences which Blacks have little control over and renders us social products that long for and dream of the good life, meaning that one day, Black aspiration hopes to be free of external influences such as inequality, discrimination, prejudice, racism and oppression, that are themselves the complete antithesis of the good life.

This book has attempted to outline and highlight the many obstacles in the way of Black aspiration and the great hope and dream is that most of these barriers can be lifted and overcome. This implies that although the odds are stacked against Black aspiration reaching its preferred destination, the reason this is the case tends to be through no fault of, or not entirely the responsibility of, an individual or collective group's own making. Black aspiration has, in common with all social groups, the pursuit of the good life, and that it is so often thwarted, frustrated and disappointed is a great pity, an imitation of the real and an unfortunate travesty. The pursuit of the good life is an uphill struggle anyway, but if you are Black, you are more likely to experience difficulty and spanners being thrown in the works. It remains a problem to build a social environment that includes all of us in all spheres of civilized society. A lot of the way people think and act does not happen in a vacuum, therefore, society should intervene to save society from itself.

Such a conclusion is unlikely to be adopted by society at large because Whites are unlikely to act in a way that might jeopardize their future prospects and they always seek to legitimate their advantage, so, therefore, can be subject to the charge of being idealistic and utopian. However, wherever it is found wanting as a conclusion, it more than makes up for by being well-founded, credible and a logical argument that holds its own and an adequate amount of water. Society is at fault by poisoning itself against itself and only society can be the remedy for its ills. The actions of Whites ensure that change will be difficult and unlikely. They entertain a different approach such as presenting the argument that society is not broken, so why on earth attempt to fix it, knowing full well that it works in their favour so why change things to accommodate others who don't even belong?

I have already mentioned a few reasons why change will be very difficult or unlikely but there are more besides. The African connection to the success of this country is massive and the past and the present are inextricably linked and the world is run using African inventions (Suzar,1999). The African contribution to world civilization is colossal, yet, the British government fight shy of contrition for the slave trade and slavery – it is about taking responsibility for an accursed apocalyptic sin and atoning. If the British government cannot even apologize, then, the slave trade and slavery was not an abomination, but all very well and good, as it made this country what it is today, in large part through the exploitation of people of colour. It appears that an apology will not be forthcoming because along with such contrition should come reparations to back up and support the words, but again, this is what the British government backs away from.

The British people do not fail to notice this and this is partly why racism continues. They see a government holding out on Black African-descended people while the Jews were compensated for the Holocaust as were slave owners for loss of human property, by the Germans and the British respectively. The slave trade was big business in this country and far worse a harm and injury than the Holocaust ever was, yet, as far as the British government is concerned, it does not even warrant an official apology; expressing 'regret' as then Prime Minister Tony Blair did, is far wide of the mark. The fact that the Jews were extended the olive branch of conciliation suggests that Black people are not only undeserving of respect but should be scorned for even asking. It is as if the word reparation is like a red rag to a bull for the British state. If the British government can discount and deny Black people as it has done, what change is on the cards other than entrenched racism? In this case, the British government has sanctioned a trickle-down effect of how its people should read their actions and it is the go-ahead to the continuation and perpetuation of racist oppression and there is no end in sight of differential treatment.

The British government is not the only institution that hampers change – Chapter 6 showed that with an adversarial press that works against the interests of Black and minority ethnic groups, little if anything will change. The indications are that every institution and organisation in Britain has work to be done if Black and minority ethnic people are to have a fairer crack of the whip. On the authority of Alexander Cockburn,

> Murdoch offers his target governments a privatized version of a state propaganda service, manipulated without scruple and with no regard for truth. His price takes the form of vast government favours such as tax breaks, regulatory relief (as with the recent FCC ruling on the acquisition of Direct TV), monopoly markets and so forth (Winter,2007:7).

Rupert Murdoch, the Australian/American media tycoon is, as I write, scaling down his global potential audience exposure of 4.7 billion, in a sell-off of most of his assets in a $66bn (£50bn) deal with Walt Disney (Sweney,2017; Winter,2007). He retains 21st Century Fox and News Corporation, the controlling arm of the Murdoch publishing enterprises, encircling book publishing, the Wall Street Journal, the Times and the Sun. He disposes of 20th Century Fox, Hollywood's fourth-largest film studio, Fox assets incorporating its TV studio, Star India as well as a 30% stake in Hulu and a 39% share interest in Sky which has 22.5m subscribers spanning the UK and Ireland, Austria, Germany, Spain and Italy. All of this is said to signal the end of a media empire reign for Murdoch (Sweney,2017).

For newspaper readers in the UK, the influence of Murdoch will remain since the *Sun* tends to outsell all other tabloids, while it matters little that the Times lags a long way behind proportionately (Gordon and Rosenberg, 1989). Since media ownership sees no change in Britain of the ventriloquist and his dummy, we will continue to be in receipt of journalism based on Murdoch-type prejudice. The potential audience reach of this ventriloquist with no regard for truth allows little scope for White group power and ideologies to alter any time soon and implies a drip-drip effect of more of the same in an ever-unchanging social, economic and cultural landscape. Murdoch may have contributed to Brexit and the rise of Donald Trump beneath which is the rise of far-right politics that cannot be said to be a good or propitious thing. Indeed, far-right politics are an indication of a downward spiral of things getting worse and not better and there should be no place for the toleration of political extremism. Murdoch's raison d'être is to capitalize on his business enterprises and where he can give the government a good press, his price is tax breaks in return, or so it seems.

Successive British governments have been party to the message that people of Black-African descent do not, in the scheme of things, count or matter. However, it is important to acknowledge that Black lives clearly do matter and this point cannot be stressed enough. The fact that the British government finds no fault with British ancestral malfeasance is one thing, but to effectively show approval is another thing entirely, and this is the cumulative effect of withholding an official apology to the African-descended diaspora. This begs the question, will the British government ever capitulate to the Black diaspora on this matter? This may be an age-old concern but it is entirely that because successive British governments have allowed it to be, by resisting the call for justice in which it can be seen and in which it can be seen to be done.

The topic of discussion can give rise to strong adjectives or verbs, but those to whom justice is due possess no monopoly on truth. For Sertima (1991), there is no single indisputable mode of knowing; there are modes of knowing. It will take a terrific and seismic climb-down and would not be a vote-winning exercise but justice is what we all hold in high regard. White people speak with a forked tongue because on the one hand, they decry racial injustice and on the other hand, are reluctant to support the remedy to tackle racial injustice. The great paradox is that Blacks are seen as a 'threat' and a 'problem', while also, are disenfranchised members of the underclass, yet, the White British public sees no reason to relent nor contain themselves in their hostilities towards Blacks. Society should never be preordained to live in denial of its true creed. The economic enrichment of Black people through the extension of reparations would be too much to bear for this country's indigenous population and is, therefore, a highly unlikely prospect indeed, and is why racism is destined to continue. Yet, back then, Africans had to accept that with their freedom came former slave master enrichment through the extension of government compensation.

Two other things suggest that change is very difficult or unlikely. Firstly, major change takes place only within political realities, or when political realities allow change to be countenanced by the state and, secondly, change only takes place once the state ceases to believe that good race relations are dependent on restricting Black immigration. These issues only suggest that change is nigh on impossible.

Whose world is it anyway? The British used to preside over a vast empire, but that is no longer the case. Since Africans are the parents of humanity and established a civilization on Planet Earth long before the Europeans even drew breath, then, by rights, Africans have a birthright claim on the planet that far exceeds that of any European claim. White British people may *de facto* be indigenous to this corner of the universe, but Black people are heirs to it also; they say, that we (Caribbeans and South

Asians) are here because you (the British) were there, but that does not account for the fact that Africans were here (in Britain) before the English came here, and are the very people being excluded from it on racially discriminatory grounds. We share the planet and each generation has a role to play but it is a White man's world because the Black diaspora experiences forms of subordination and exploitation that Whites could be said to be responsible for. White European control of goods and resources on this side of mortality is the world and means everything.

The Roman conquest gave way to the legacy of Roman roads and a contribution to how the British live in this sceptred isle but the African contribution to this nation's development is huge, from slavery through to colonialism, and the first wave of immigration was a response to this country's call to rebuild post-war Britain, and so Black and minority ethnic people have as much a right to be here as anybody. Just because this country's people can identify more readily with overseas White nationals such as the Falkland Islanders is an impoverished excuse for privileging them with access to this country over non-white minority groups. The same argument can be applied to Black and South Asian people being seen as an intractable 'race problem' as White prejudice and hostility seems closer to the mark and the reason why minority ethnic groups are denied access to enter and settle in this country. Rumours abound of this country becoming overcrowded but the truth is that at the turn of the century, 11,000 more people vacated Britain than came to settle here and above half of those granted work permits hailed from America (Zephaniah,2001). Minority ethnic people are 'blamed for the very problems that affect them most severely' (Gordon and Rosenberg,1989:62; Trowler,1996:220; Troyna,1981:58, 60).

Humanity has a shared and common economic goal, with few exceptions, to strive for the good life, and, as human beings, we are shrouded in the same veil of mortal fate and destiny, and if only we were united in our quest for the good life and not divided, then the world would be a much better place in which to live. The UK is riven by the lacuna between affluence and poverty and this only serves the purposes of capitalism and the ruling class, but when the 'race' dimension enters the equation, we see unemployment among Black people far outweighing and exceeding that of their White opposite number. Certain organisations and institutions do not even have a workplace environment that reflects the demographic composition of the UK; the media is just one example, Oxford and Cambridge Universities are another. However, striving to at least represent the minority demographics of the country in our workplaces and institutions is only the start; attitudes towards division, in a holistic and rounded sense, need remedying and society should begin to apportion opportunities and share the economic slices of the cake more equitably.

Since we do not live in a colour-blind society and bias creeps into the workaday world, how is it that the right man for the job is almost always a White man or woman when the potential to achieve great things is within us all, minority ethnic groups included? Hence, favouritism or clannishness should really and veridically be thrown out with the baby and the bathwater. What people tend to miss is that we are all homo sapiens sapiens with universal needs and the reason why we are disunited in our struggle for the good life is that competition for scarce resources underlies conflict. In several different ways or respects, this tends to illustrate the essential self-interest of the in-group cultural imperialism. The humanitarian aspect of social organisation is the matter that I have attempted to highlight and substantiate and to show that social inequality is coterminous with, and overriding of, that reality.

However, as the implicit evidence of the text points up, majority populations in their practical everyday lives have difficulties in being of the persuasion that a wide variety of minority populations are in every sense their equal and deserving of equal respect. Specifically, as the text suggests, the historical construction of racial categorization makes reflexive equal recognition problematic. A political mechanism that has been found to be a highly successful device for bridging the divide between the value system of equal recognition and coming into contact with minority ethnic groups has been the principle of tolerance. Tolerance is universally held as an

Chapter 10: Conclusion

unambiguous subjective virtue and an expedient political resource (Downing and Husband,2005).

I would be more than mistaken to consider that this book will amount to or count as a catalyst for change since persecution, oppression, racism and discrimination will never cease as long as White society perceive Black and minority ethnic groups as posing a 'threat' to British national culture and as long as the British government find it anathema to apologize for the slave trade and slavery; nevertheless, I recognize the power that language has to transform reality. White people are also afraid that our birth rate exceeds that of the indigenous population. A further concern that obfuscates change is the immigration issue, where there is a system founded on a discriminatory principle of 'patriality', in which millions of White people throughout the world with antecedent kin in Britain have eligibility to enter and seek residency, while far fewer Black and minority ethnic people, who attempt to enter legally, are often denied access rights (Gordon and Rosenberg,1989).

An urgent claim requires the widespread acceptance that racism is very different from being a 'thing' outside the wider social sphere and ushered in by non-white minority groups. Our attention should find a focus on a nuanced understanding that ideations of racism and their reifications are in a state of flux vis-à-vis specific historical and ideological provisos (Bhavnani et al,2005:152).

So far, in Chapter 4, we have only touched on there being not one racism, in the singular, but multiple racisms (Bhavnani et al,2005:150). Politicians express racisms and so indeed do the press aided by immigration laws, which evens up the balance to laws targeted at combatting discrimination. The power of certain of these racisms outweighs others. The disputations over connotations and context of these efficacious racisms must be shed light upon. There remains also the racisms of executives and administrators in gainsaying racism, or considering it insignificant and situating it in localities where there is a denser population of Black and minority ethnic dwellers. Extant are the racisms conveyed through proletarian young men's woe of masculinity in the background of diminishing state resources. Racisms are continued and sustained through legislation, on, for instance, the prerogative for jury trial, which unduly affects people of colour in the criminal justice procedural arrangement. Racisms are made manifest within 'cultural' assumptions; for example, that each individual bearing the label Muslim must somehow fall under a ray of suspicion. Another of the racisms is the consideration of young African-Caribbean-heritage men as 'lawless and threatening' (Bhavnani, 2005:150). There are further racisms that imply that all young women of South Asian heritage are liable to repression behind closed doors. To these racisms is the visceral racism of minorities which is articulated against other racialised social categories, and also through 'identity' crises. We might add the racism of British or English, Welsh, Scottish and Irish national identities.

Racisms are articulated on an interpersonal level; for instance, in the form of impromptu remarks, jokes and discursive struggles. There is also the silent transmission through White middle-class withdrawal from racialised areas, through non-verbal cues, and through informal group relations. They are transmitted through portrayals in media communication. They are reflected through failing to recognize and denying racism. They are evinced through racist onslaughts and murders (Bhavnani et al,2005).

Everyday racist patterns of behaviour are produced and located within current sets of ideas and structures. These everyday forms of behaviour include hating and harrying Black neighbours, unequal local authority housing distribution policies and openly racist immigration procedures of dispersal and internment. They are symbolic of and inspired by the root causes of racism. These origins of racism have developed over centuries of social and intelligence-led imperialism (Bhavnani et al,2005).

Both elite and local racisms need carefully devised interventions. But white-collar policy interventions in racism have had little effect in dealing with the causes of racism. By the latter, we mean two things; the roots or origins of racism, and the techniques by which it is replicated in the daily round. White-collar interventions, for the most part, tackle the effects of racism (Bhavnani et al,2005).

A further reason for why change is very difficult or unlikely is because newspapers centre on a market of White opinion and interests, and thereby marginalize Black and minority ethnic interests, voices and opinion. For example, rather than construct symbolic forms around immigration per se, columnists have focused almost entirely on Black immigration and have carried this out as if they were dealing with a monocultural White audience with a shared 'White' interest (Gordon and Rosenberg,1989).

All professions have their mythologies as regards the nature and consequence of their role, and journalism is little different. The extraordinary thing with regard to journalism, however, is that more significantly than most other professions or institutions, it regulates the discursive struggle about itself. We consider that in a democratic social milieu, research of the type elucidated on these pages is the vital antidote to this. It is scarcely a matter of seeking to tell journalists how to carry out their job of work, for we have no qualification here. But it is an issue – a vitally important issue – of intimating that if journalists knew more as regards the communication process, and more in relation to the nature of the social milieu and its institutions, and if, also, they were more equipped and conscientious about the ramifications of what they were contributing towards, then they would be able to make a more favourable input to the evolution of agreeable relationships in a multi-racial social milieu than they are enacting currently. Research has a far-reaching role to play in this connection – notably in relation to the training of journalists (Halloran,1981; in Troyna,1981). One such journalist, John Whale, has put forward the following argument:

> The press is predominantly conservative in tone because its readers are. If any substantial number of people seriously wanted the structure of society rebuilt from the bottom, the Morning Star would sell more copies than it does (Trowler,1996:80).

This illustrates that the dominant hegemonic ideology is so entrenched in society's material fabric or society's double helix that people really rather fear radical change and are immutably preoccupied with the media's White monolithic one-sided view of apprehending and explicating the world. Rupert Murdoch has been referred to as Britain's phantom Prime Minister and it is with good reason, as he wields the type of influence that elects political leaders to office, and is sometimes responsible for their political turn of events and is considered by governments to be a force that they would rather have on their side than in opposition. Furthermore, the influence Murdoch can discharge routinely is a force of considerable reckoning and the British government recognize its potent effect upon the general public to the extent that the media are considered dangerous to cross.

To bring things into sharp focus, the communication media is societies guardian against radical change ever occurring and change will only occur at the presses' behest or say-so, or in other words, until the press changes nothing else will, as the press consistently serve to reinforce racism and continue to do so (Gordon and Rosenberg,1989; Downing and Husband,2005). By doing this, it is being constantly reinforced that change is very difficult or unlikely and that White society recognizes that press racism serves their interests. Press racism benefits the majority and guarantees or ensures that Whites are not at the bottom of the social status hierarchy. Trowler (1996) confirms this outlook by arguing that readers would quickly switch allegiance if the *Sun* or the *Star* had long and detailed analyses of discriminatory practices in employment and housing. The fact that the White British public are reluctant to hear or read about the Black experience suggests they are in denial of racism and that press racism reflects their prejudices. It is important to note that press reporting on race has to be in keeping with what the public wants and is identified by news editors, demonstrated by newspaper sales and declared by public opinion survey.

Chapter 10: Conclusion

Is Black aspiration a chimera?

The achievement of an academic degree may at first seem impossible but persistent effort and perseverance moves success within striking distance. The impossible remains impossible until it is achieved; Mount Everest remained unconquered until man scaled its summit. On the one hand, those people of colour who utter Black aspiration and chimera in the same breath are twice defeated as they have already relinquished on what they believe deep within and fail to see beyond their present circumstances. On the other hand, Black aspiration can be characterized as illusory and impossible to achieve simply because it remains to be achieved and is heavily dependent upon the will of White authority figures. The mountain to climb resides with those who tend to stymie progress and the onus of Black aspiration is to put the case forward. In this enlightened and technologically advanced age, technology appears to be outpacing enlightened progress while Black aspiration is yet to be settled and is contingent on factors beyond its control. In the current political climate, enlightened self-interest appears the scheme and order of the day.

The 5th of November 2008 saw the election of Barack Obama to the White House and this constituted a giant leap forward for the United States of America and the world. His election victory over Senator John McCain was largely predicated on merit and was a convincing electoral mandate. Barack Obama went on to complete two terms in the White House. I, for one, feel that his achievement has symbolically elevated the status of African Americans and people of African descent the world over and refutes the first idea that Black aspiration is a chimera. Given the likelihood that the racial divide is more accentuated presently in the USA than most other places, this augurs well for the UK to produce African-Caribbean leaders within their own fields of specialism and suggests that to everything – including impossibility - there is a season beyond which anything can happen in relation to individual and/or collective Black aspiration. Before giving this the nod, we must first consider that mainstream media, unlike various ultra-rightist media, tend not to encourage individual violence, but they provide a network structure coterminous with easier ultra-rightist media intervention, a kind of shared value system of negative, fearful and unfavourable perceptual combined meld and extremely incomplete and fallacious information regarding communities of colour, out of which the ultra-right can further its 'policy panacea' to 'the problem' (Downing and Husband,2005:81).

Downing and Husband (2005) regard this, along with a range of other factors, as nothing short of a pogrom, if applied in a direct sense, but on account of its prevalent occurrence across nations, its time-span approaching half a century or so, and its level of effect, the term 'ongoing low-intensity pogrom' seems apt (p.81). It entails relatively few actual killings vis-à-vis the scores, hundreds, or still more who perish in 'conventional' pogroms – and so much as those horrors are irregular, they are not consistent events. At any rate, almost throughout the OECD countries, the general pattern of racist oppression and violence from the civil agencies of law enforcement and ultra-rightist groupings, either accommodated or simply marginalized by various mainstream media, is serious, has been cumulative, and any indication of some let-up is far from obvious. The perception of the prison-industrial network as 'social death', of which the established media silence on prison life as a key element, is an important facet of coming to accept as real the linkages between all these tentacles of power. Once more, perceptions vary widely even over collective measures from within the prison-industrial network, which is a non-homogenous entity, although HoSang (1999-2000) maintains that the disparate police reform measures over the past ten years and longer symbolize an attempt to overhaul the system as opposed to substantively transforming it (Downing and Husband,2005).

The circumstances and Downing and Husbands' (2005) proposition require more detailed enquiry and it is, of course, likely that the crisis is considerably more marked currently in America than any other geographical and political boundary. Having said that, it is a highly pernicious and frightful tendency, one which undermines the bedrock of life chances, freedom and social justice, in line with extracting the rich kernel that is citizenship and democracy. Whether there remains a more fitting term to describe this set of characteristic signs than 'ongoing low-intensity pogrom' we determine that it has not been found (Downing and Husband,2005:82).

The above is a serious bone of contention in relation to Black British aspiration and needs to be considered in light of present-day occurrences and the state of human affairs within the political economy. Certainly, it could be held to account for why there are so few prominent Black leaders in Britain today. Nonetheless, if this syndrome is considerably marked in the USA and under such conditions they elected a Black president, then surely, this suggests a glass-half-full prospect; however, Britain shows no signs of electing a Black Labour or Conservative Party leader, and, in fact, failed to elect a Black candidate in a safe Tory constituency; so, what happened in the US seems less likely, for the foreseeable future, to take place in Britain.

Although I believe that Barack Obama elevated the image of African Americans and people of African descent across the world, law enforcement agencies, particularly in the US, continued to treat Black people with hostile aggression and show scant regard for their civil liberties, which suggests that the stereotype did not undergo any radical transformation by virtue of the idea that Barack Obama was seen as the exception that proves the rule. Stereotypes have the potential to change over time as, for example, the Irish in America who had a stereotype equivalent to the African, though now, have the same status as White Americans. However, the stereotype of Blacks shows stubborn resistance and obstinate opposition to change. Thus, in essence, the Obama administration did hold the image of the Black man up in the ascendancy but perhaps only momentarily as the stereotype's stolid resistance to change demonstrates that he was merely seen as a one-off model exemplar and his achievements did not, for many, cast a long shadow over global 'race relations' situations.

Addressing tolerance

Earlier in this chapter, I stressed the importance of acceptance over tolerance even though in social science commentary and political reflection, tolerance has been ordinarily seen as the direct antithesis of prejudice, and below, Downing and Husband (2005) illustrate the problem with the idea of tolerance. As Charles Husband argued in a previous publication:

> For tolerance to be necessary, there must be a prior belief that the person to be tolerated has an intrinsically undesirable characteristic, or that they are not fundamentally entitled to the benefits which are to be allowed them. Those to be tolerated, by definition, possess some such social stigma.
>
> Tolerance is the exercise of largesse by the powerful, ultimately on behalf of the powerful. It is the generous extension of forbearance toward someone who is intrinsically objectionable or not deserving of the privilege being allowed (Husband,1994:65; Quoted in Downing and Husband,2005:197).

On the condition that a response to give credence to the media needs and eligibility of minority ethnic enclaves within the political unit is dependent on a guiding principle in the essential forbearance of the majority group, then the minority enclaves are implicitly expected to cheerfully consume the crumbs from the master's table. Since considering tolerance is an arbitrary power practised by the majority, it ineluctably negates the validity of minority community assertions that they are entitled to the wherewithal they look to attain.

Moreover, sovereign territories appear to be uncritically satisfied with the assumption that there is an innate perimeter to their tolerance; that they attain not to be driven beyond bounds in inclining towards equal recognition. In their research of the Belgian engagement with ethnic diversity, Blommaert and Verschueren (1998) make mention of the development of a theory of 'the threshold of tolerance' (Downing and

Husband,2005:198). In total, this maintains that there is an innate perimeter outside which it is unconscionable to expect majority inhabitants to countenance their 'normal' degree of tolerance. They maintain that:

> The threshold of tolerance is an objectifying socio-mathematical concept that defines the conditions under which the all-European tolerance and openness may be cancelled without affecting the basic self-image. The European does not become intolerant until this threshold, i.e., just reduce the number of foreigners again and the good old tolerance will return. In other words, even in moments of intolerance, the European is still tolerant at heart, and the observed behaviour is completely due to the factual circumstances which render it impossible to exercise this essential openness. Needless to say, the threshold of tolerance is not an exclusively Belgian notion. It is commonly used in other European countries (1998:78; in Downing and Husband,2005:198).

The sublime political usefulness of the idea of the threshold of tolerance resides in its capacity to champion the assertion that forbearance is a constraining capacity of the moral majority, whilst simultaneously providing scope for conditions in which it has an innate limit owing to unconscionable external pressures. The emergent corollary is that a proper community-wide politics of diversity resides in creating the social milieu in which tolerance gravitates towards perhaps being guaranteed. To be sure, this may mean drastic border controls, institutional methods to contain the 'unreasonable' exertions of communities of colour and the creative manipulation of majority distinctiveness means they emerge unscathed. The regulation implicit in the superficial capabilities of the Sami Parliaments, or the Australian Aboriginal and Torre Strait Islander Commission (ATSIC), and the 'partial' allegiance of media industry equal opportunity initiatives is semiotic of this belief system of equal recognition (Downing and Husband,2005:198).

However, it has, in addition, been the self-interested resource of tolerance that has been manifest as a problematic feature in the ideology of equal recognition. Concomitant parallel power and pertinence have been basic criticisms of the universalism that occupies the centre of this paradigm. From a radical contradiction to liberal universalism, Young (1989) has cogently argued that in the backdrop of universalist provision for ethnic diversity, it is the business and the primacy of the majority that describe the matter that are the normative needs and social mores that should be dealt with via equal provision (cited in Downing and Husband,2005). In this sense, universalism is not a distant relative of paternalism.

In a past period, an alternative thinking pattern of structuring an approach to managing diversity has been established through what Taylor has termed the 'politics of difference'. He has furthered the view that:

> The development of the modern notion of identity has given rise to a politics of difference. There is, of course, a universalist basis to this as well, making for the overlap and confusion between the two. Everyone should be recognised for his or her unique identity. But recognition here means something else. With the politics of equal dignity, what is established is meant to be universally the same; an identical basket of rights and immunities. With the politics of difference, what we are asked to recognise is the unique identity of this individual or group; their distinctiveness from everyone else. The idea is that it is precisely this distinctiveness that has been ignored, glossed over, assimilated to a dominant or majority identity (1992:38; in Downing and Husband,2005:199).

According to Taylor's elegant explanation, the failing in the universalist cultural system of recognition lies directly in the adoption, indeed stipulation, that people be dealt with, quite literally, equally (Downing and Husband,2005). This prevents any substantive acknowledgement of individual and communities' entirely different requirements and prime concerns. Rather than minimizing equality to similar resources and allocation, the politics of difference preserves the fundamental acknowledgement of personal worth, whilst tenaciously preserving an acquaintance of unique individual requirements. Framed in a different way, the politics of difference effectively insists that if you intend to grant me equal treatment, you most probably will have to address me differently. It calls for a large helping of equal rights rolled out in a suitable array of particularistic responses. This, for instance, is precisely the question at the centre of appropriate transcultural health care praxis (Downing and Husband,2005).

The silent dignities of a liberal culture of recognition have quite reasonably served a state strategy revolving around an axis of benign universalism. The two things have the capacity for continuous expression with the humanistic assumptions of equivalence integrated into a wide spectrum of theisms, and in political ideals incorporating liberalism and socialism. It was an inaugurated political theory and practice that has, at the same time, nurtured the egotism of the socially advantaged and powerful, and the reliance and obedience of the powerless. The essential contradiction of the politics of difference has severely upset the apple cart of this hegemonic bundle.

This has, among other things, followed from the inherent challenges of the politics of difference, but additionally, because the advent of this ideal has been juxtaposed by a powerful organisation of identity politics by itself. Given the dislocation, albeit not final exit, of class politics and the fractured state of gender politics, political units across continents have experienced a powerful upswing of identity politics articulated within, and outside, conventional political frameworks. It is somewhat uncertain that such identity politics contribute towards the production of an anchor in the highly charged waters of globalization and social reform (Downing and Husband,2005).

For diverse populations, the overlap of identity politics and the world view of the politics of difference have unbridled and intensified a pre-existing negation of the paternalism and minimalistic blanket equality extended by majority groups. They omit or decline the tolerance of the majority and instead, lay claim to their rights.

Diasporic communities who have learnt to repudiate the homogenizing philosophy of White liberal society are everywhere repudiating assimilation into the domestic conventional standard. In maintaining this stance, they uncritically feed into a national identity which apportions them a subordinate, and/or inferior rank position, while it is a rights-based legal obligation of citizenship that minority ethnic communities display allegiance to the state (Downing and Husband,2005). The Baudrillardian admixture is not restricted to outlining ethnicity with gender and generation: it remains a practice that raises wide open the aperture of possibility and viability, of fresh, joined-up national associations. Directly discernible in the functioning of diasporic communities, and uniformly evident in the identity politics of domestic minorities and native populations, the politics of difference calls for the essential mutual tolerance of a common duty to participate in social affairs as equals, and a loyalty to negotiating political co-existence.

The transparency and expressiveness with which the substantiveness of the politics of difference are not infrequently presented by minority ethnic politics readily produce a reaction where the majority community conceptualize that the logic of their privileged position is challenged and endangered. As regards the resolute xenophobe and reactionary bigot, this challenge is encountered as an outrageous articulation of minority-ethnic haughtiness and avaricious greed. (The picture the media paint is one of an unreasonable threat to the capital and *modus vivendi* resources of the majority). Correspondingly, avant-garde liberals from within the majority-ethnic demographics may feel perplexed and apoplectic when what they apprehend with the mind through the senses as their tolerant altruism is fed back as minimalistic, paternalistic and self-centred. Periodically cited as 'the victimisation of the majority', this defensive reaction gives rise to renewed efforts to re-establish the 'limits of tolerance' as natural and understandable and necessary for the seamless cohesion of the body politic (Downing and Husband,2005:200).

With these adversarial political vectors, it is hardly unforeseen that across continents, the explicit meaning and praxis of multiculturalism has been inordinately contested and widely varied. Multiculturalism has been downgraded as leftist demagoguery. It has been questioned for its sweeping statements and essentializing of differentness and it has been criticized as tending to polarize opinion in the direction of national cohesion. The subtitles of a few of the recent publications on the subject reveal a shade of these agendas: for example, Robert Hughes (1994) *Culture of Complaint: The Fraying of America*; Brian Barry (2001) *Culture and Equality: An Egalitarian Critique of Multiculturalism*; and Gertrude Himmelfarb (2001) *One Nation, Two Cultures: A Searching Examination of American Society in the Aftermath of Our Cultural Revolution*. However, particular policy approaches framed by a 'multicultural' logic have been criticized by minority ethnic populations, members of national minorities and native peoples, for having been imagined and motivated by investments that are impercipient of their way of life, political prime concerns and methods of organisation (Downing and Husband, 2005).

Within the Canadian landscape, Juteau provides an edifying note on the heterogeneous nature and influence of multiculturalism. She argues that:

> In hindsight, one can also see that multiculturalism served as mobilizing ideology for a heightened participation in public institutions. It allowed for the definition of a more inclusive discourse on the participation of minoritized groups within the political community ... and fostered the erosion of the myth of national homogeneity founded on nature or on culture. Former conceptions of Canada have been altered and its Waspish core challenged. The acceptance of ethnic pluralism opens up a space for public debate, as exemplified in the critique of the folklorizing and essentializing aspects of multiculturalism, and the growing emphasis on material as well as on ideational interests (1997: 108; in Downing and Husband,2005:201).

An acknowledgement of ethnic pluralism is scarcely a standpoint that can be adopted without question in the constitutional liberal democratic politics of the contemporary age. It has been an approach that has noticeably grown in visibility and prominence across a wide spectrum of states over the preceding six decades. On the other hand, it remains an ethical principle and a political custom that is very different from being consensual and is inordinately resisted in certain sectors. The meaning of this in relation to our analysis of diversity and the communications industry is double-edged. It signifies the absence of a controlling combination of theory and praxis that can be called upon to inform our ambition for media policy. Further, as a natural consequence of this, it signifies that we must individually be prepared to state, clearly and in detail, the emotional and rational foundation for our own approach around the management of diversity.

The thread running through this discussion of 'addressing tolerance' is to suggest that there is more to tolerance than meets the eye. In whichever national context, it is certainly easy to absorb an implicit national model on citizenship and identity. In immediately moving to a principled critique of particular incidences of the (mis)representation of minority ethnic people and communities, we are, on quite rare occasions, challenged to lucidly reveal the macro-paradigm of 'multiculturalism', and the dependent politics of difference that are taken for granted within the terms of this judgement. However, as the anti-racist agitation of times past has revealed, underlying and unacknowledged differences in fundamental belief systems all too easily threaten attempts at working together to eliminate inequality. Where media industry professionals, affiliated associates of minority communities and affiliated associates of majority communities aspire to transpose media systems for progress' sake, it is sine qua non to recognize prospectively profound differences in 'where you are coming from' (Downing and Husband,2005:202).

Moral values

"Manners maketh a man" and so also a civilized society, and moral values are widely disseminated and transmitted through the agency of family, the education system and the workplace. The working activity can be conceptualized and analysed both as personal knowledge expansion and as cultural proliferation by the community at large. Polities reproduce their political norms and values by introducing new generations into conventional forms of thought and conduct – through the educational system, the media industry, the workplace environment, the neighbourhood forum, and also through political establishments themselves. In opinion poll surveys, values are ideas internalised by people about righteous conduct or appropriate conduct, what is right or wrong, favourable or deplorable. In a similar manner, philosophers treat values as consisting of ethics, aesthetics, and political philosophy (Scott and Marshall, 2005).

Concerning values as a form of social data, conclusions are often formulated between values, which are in the affirmative, semi-permanent, unexpressed, and sometimes indirect dispositions; and opinions, which are superficial, weakly maintained, and highly divergent views and approaches. Civilizations can usually tolerate extremely dissimilar attitudes, whereas they need some level of homogeneity and consonance in the values internalised by people, providing a universal investment of mutual values which shape social and ideological consensus. It is routinely considered that the sociological theories of structural functionalists (or consensus theorists) in most cases, and of Talcott Parsons especially, overemphasize the value of shared ethics in maintaining social stability (Scott and Marshall, 2005).

And, in the main, all sociology is connected with value issues, and with few exceptions amongst classical authors – not least among their number Emile Durkheim and Max Weber – wrote about the role values play in social research in some detail. At this intensified epistemological level, the issues concerning sociology would appear to be binary. First, considering that society itself is shadily established by law through values, the exposition of sociology is somewhat of a piece with the exposition of values. Second, considering that sociologists are themselves constituents of a social milieu and presumably subscribe to values (religious, political, and so on), sociological endeavour may become involved in matters of ethics – or even (as Marxists might phrase it) matters of ideology. To be sure, some have argued that, hence, sociologists may be beyond the scope of the value-neutrality looked for in scientists more customarily (Scott and Marshall,2005).

By its very nature, these epistemological debates concerning the role of ethics in social science can impact sociological inquiry on three levels: first, on settling to study a particular subject area like religion or homosexuality, in which issues of value-relevance are floated; second, in the actual prosecution of a study, in which the questions of bias, value-neutrality and objectivity come to the surface; and finally, in the implications of particular theories or investigative inquiry for society, in which the question of 'value effects' is floated. Operationally, most sociologists cannot easily be individualized, and the numerous value issues intersect (Scott and Marshall,2005).

Among the defining characteristics of theoretical positivism is that it necessitates the sciences (subsuming the social sciences) to be value-neutral or freestanding – the assumption being that scientists will (or clearly should) eradicate all biases and special interests at all gradations of their studies. Value-neutrality is thus necessary if we are to talk of scientific sociology. Correspondingly, sociology is deemed to have no more than a technical character, documenting findings that convey no logically given consequences for guideline plans or the prosecution of particular values. In sharp contrast, Marxists advocate that every juncture of sociological analysis is pregnant with political and ethical concerns and implications, such that sociology *ipso facto* is undoubtedly an ideological exercise. But most sociologists position themselves partway between this continuum of extremes, advocating (for example) that while the election of study areas must raise issues of value, the prosecution of an exposition should be as freestanding as possible, and the outcome presented neutrally, at which stage the way such conclusions are put into effect by others will once more raise value (namely, policy) issues. A not infrequently encountered practical solution to the intractable epistemological issues floated by the subject of values is the advancement that sociology is invariably closely connected with ethics, politics and values, and because it cannot rid itself of them, it behoves sociologists to make the underlying debates transparent (Scott and Marshall,2005).

If majority ethnic groups had a greater sense of right and wrong then the world would be an entirely different place, but as it stands, they deliberately or unthinkingly discriminate against minority ethnic groups and apparently think no more about their despicable deeds; however, if called to account, the probability is that they would justify their actions. However, this is not to put minority ethnic populations in the clear because humanity is fallible, therefore, we can hardly expect society to be perfect as imperfection begets imperfection. We can only hope and aspire that society does its level best to deracinate injustice and seek fair and equitable treatment for all concerned. The consequences of a world without a heightened sense of moral decency are far-reaching and wide-ranging.

One in four people in Britain suffer from mental illness at some point in their lives and although it proceeds in a subtle, piecemeal, and gradual manner, it may never reach crisis point and sometimes occurs due to moral issues in people's lives, which can have negative consequences. Such quantitative data constitute those that have been diagnosed as there are people who fall beneath the radar of mental health services and escape detection. Indeed, it can be argued that at some time or another, the large majority of us may to some extent experience mental health issues and the trigger could be among the following: pressure at work, a marital breakdown, drug misuse, or something as traumatic as a death in the family; even the onset of winter is said to trigger melancholy and depression in some people.

The overrepresentation of Black Caribbean people in mental health services means the scarring of racism and discrimination cannot be ruled out. Downing and Husband (2005) argue that this scarring effect may mean that, 'if you enfranchise the oppressed, they will bite the oppressor' (p. 216). Mental health difficulties and moral issues in people's lives appear to bear inextricable correlation with one another. For example, marriage partnerships that become adulterous can potentially lead to depression on either side of the partnership and can have consequences for children of the family break-up, if not immediately, perhaps, later in life. With the growing number of one-parent families, this takes into account a potential time bomb of a future dysfunctional generation. Socialization inducts new generations to racist thought patterns and ways of behaving so that the replenishment of a racist element is neither natural nor normal but socially constructed. Just as mental ill-health and morality are closely tied, so majority group and minority group attitudes are unavoidably linked because majority group feelings result in minority group sentiment, and the same applies in reverse. The claim could almost be posited that one side obtains its identity from the firmly established phenomenon of its rivalry with the other.

There should be no shame in admitting that one has experienced mental health difficulties as life is sometimes fraught with traumatic twists and turns. On the other hand, the stigma associated with mental ill-health is often why many people do not come forward for help and treatment because the stigma is like an accusing finger that apportions blame to the sufferer. Recognizing that the challenges in life can lead to a mental health collapse and that it can happen to anyone should help eliminate the stigma, but the universal nature and resilience of the stigma means organizations and institutions need to back the drive for recognition in order that the above is not seen as mere wishful thinking.

The arrangement of special educational provision for remedial children has led to significant proportions of Black Caribbean children being directed to institutions for the educationally subnormal by the use of culturally biased intelligence tests, applied, we can but suppose, by people who are misguided as to the Black child's cognitive ability. The essential nature and character of many British establishments are such that people of colour have been likely to experience the deleterious effects even without any evidence of active hostility raising itself against them. Hate and vituperation are, however, universal and make the situation of diasporic groups particularly difficult (Hartmann and Husband,1974).

It cannot be overstated the many people who rallied behind Powell's stance on immigration even though they may not have agreed with the impractical solution of repatriation. And, as if this was not by itself sufficient, the press describe the British people as owing a great debt to Powell for addressing and reflecting the nation's anxiety over race and national identity. The press was instrumental in glorifying and sensationalizing his significance in the numbers game and aimed to influence an up-and-coming generation to close ranks with the heightened collective consciousness that minority ethnic communities have interests that are not necessarily coterminous with the position and opinion of the majority ethnic population.

Research showing high percentages of majority ethnic people expressing the opinion that people of colour are inferior to themselves and expressing majority ethnic preferment over people of colour as well as expressing a low register of attitudes towards minority ethnic people underestimates the true prevalence of majority ethnic hostility and suggests that calls for equality will be met with firm and robust rebuttal and opposition (Hartmann and Husband, 1974:18). This fundamental difference of opinion between groups has far-reaching consequences and is deeply divisive implying turbulent waters for future race relations and a nation divided upon itself unable to see and progress beyond entrenched majority ethnic privilege or a country locked into a stultifying insularity.

This concise outline should serve to underscore several vital details of the current state of affairs. First, the fact remains that diverse ethnic groups in Britain occupy contrastingly disadvantaged rungs in the British class system. Secondly, it dawns brightly that their comparatively low status is partly due to them being beset by active discrimination. The evidence also speaks for itself pointing in the direction of hostility towards them arising from the White population, hostility to their crossing into this country and, on past occasions, a drive has been staged for their repatriation. Finally, there is the suggestion that prejudice and disadvantage are linked to their colour, and not exclusively to their underclass status and ethnic background (Hartmann and Husband,1974).

British culture

In Chapter Two, I referred to British culture without thoroughly investigating the elements which constitute this ideological concept and although the analysis was not too far removed from reality, a close inspection will reveal a more detailed insight into the concept. British culture is held up as something which must at all costs be defended against the onslaught of a 'threat' from African-Caribbean and South Asian people, but it is only under 'threat' because it comprises a negative response to these groups of people who aspire to be treated on equal terms. The demystification of British culture is what I hope to show through looking into various aspects of the idea.

British colour prejudice, regardless of opposing schools of thought, became an important part of British culture towards the close of the nineteenth century (Hartmann and Husband,1974). The core feature of this prejudice is that White superiority and Black inferiority are taken as given. This idea became part of the tapestry of British tradition, British culture and British global ambition as Britain's colonial commitment intensified, and was a veridical analogy of the typical interrelation between the White British and non-white peoples; a relationship of conqueror and conquered, colonizer and colonized, master and servant, citizen and foreigner and employer and employee. Before the advent of slavery and the slave trade, Whites did not always have it all their own way. Presiding over Southern France, a large proportion of Scotland, Spain and North Africa for a 700-year period during the Middle Ages, the Black African Moors bequeathed Europe a civilization of remarkable note (Suzar,1999). The term Moor means Black, obtained from the Greek mauros, signifying scorched. The African polities Morocco and Mauritania are also derivatives of this term. Throughout the Middle Ages, Africans and Moors were one and the same thing.

In the preface of The *Story of the Moors in Spain* by Stanley Lane-Poole, John Jackson comments: "Eurocentric historians argue that Europe gave civilization to Africa, which is a complete inversion of the truth. The first civilized Europeans were the Greeks, who were chiefly civilized by the Africans of the Nile Valley. The Greeks transmitted this culture to the Romans, who finally lost it, bringing on a dark age of five hundred years. Civilization was restored to Europe when another group of Africans, the Moors, brought this dark age to an end ... During the Golden Age of Islam, the Moorish Empire ... was the most advanced state in the world ... Cordova was the most wonderful city of the tenth century; the streets were well-paved, with raised sidewalks for pedestrians ... Public baths numbered in the hundreds ... at a time when cleanliness in Christian Europe was regarded a sin ... Moorish monarchs dwelt in splendid palaces, while crowned heads of England, France, and Germany lived in big barns, lacking both windows and chimneys, with only a hole in the roof for the emission of smoke" (cited in Suzar,1999:43).

However, colour prejudice was greater in degree than the mere acquiescence of colour as a r true pointer of subordinate rank position – which it has been, and, on the whole, remains. Racial prejudice – or racism – has an objective reality when colour stands to represent a reduced entitlement to the use of power and resources (Hartmann and Husband,1974).

By the onset of the twentieth century, colour-related status inequalities had come to be seen by Whites not only as actual reality but as normal and even compulsory. In addition, it came to appear natural that Blacks necessarily assumes second place to Whites, and that an alternative scenario might be the case seemed unnatural, preposterous or inane. The reasoning behind this situation being either clarified as God's will as rendered a consequence of the non-white man's intrinsic baseness or innocent naivety, or on some other basis, is not vitally important; various legitimations were devised across the centuries. Provided that the idea of unequal entitlement is privileged, the particular justifications that encircle it may transpose as one loses authority and others seem to carry more force. Regardless of what you argue, that, under apartheid, for instance, South African Blacks were deemed naturally inferior to Whites, were regarded as not meeting the criteria to govern their native lands, or some other persuasion, it is relatively immaterial provided that the argument affords a cogent reason for withholding their political rights. As the nineteenth century drew to a close, the assumption of unequal entitlement on the basis of colour was expressed through each and every aspect of British culture. The key principle was, as it were, most economically captured in the ever-present lines of Kipling, for whom the trusteeship pattern of prejudice was:

Take up the White Man's burden –

    Send forth the best ye breed –

Go, bind your sons to exile

    To serve your captives' need;

To wait, in heavy harness,

    On fluttered folk and wild –

Your new-caught sullen peoples,

    Half devil and half child.

(Fryer,1984:187).

The world defines people of colour by their skin colour attribute but we do not define each other by colour alone; we are greater in degree than a colour, as unique and individual and possess all aspects of humanity whether that is the capacity to do something positive or negative, good or ill. Is there any wonder British culture is said to be under 'threat' when it governs a chief element waging and wielding itself against non-white people embodying dead outmoded ideas which should no longer occupy a place and space in a multi-ethnic society? These dead ideas continue to blight Black and minority ethnic lives and all of this because White society cannot purge itself of colour prejudice.

It appears that White groups will, for some time to come, be unable to bury the hatchet as people of colour will still be seen, at best, as 'outsiders', 'the other' and, at worst, 'the enemy within'. This simply illustrates that White society is persistently determined to be a fly in the ointment against

Chapter 10: Conclusion

Black and minority ethnic interests and aspiration and are determined to guard against all processes fashioned to root out colour prejudice. British culture's adherents seem to most heavily criticize notions of multiculturalism and if it is not an initiative geared towards change and eliminating colour prejudice or chauvinism, then many people would suggest that it is entirely that. There is no avoiding the fact that British culture bears all the hallmarks of a way of life that incorporates an approach that is unbecoming, unconscionable, and unreasonably hostile towards people of colour and is, thus, a close cousin of and akin to racist ideology; masquerading as a cultural bastion operating on a routine quotidian basis on levels of bias, one can only barely begin to touch. Rather than diasporic populations posing as a 'threat' to British culture and the British way of life, it is completely and quite the antithetical reverse and continues to be in the current contemporary political culture.

The Nation of Islam, among whom Muhamad Ali, Malcolm X and Elijah Muhamad were their most famous acolytes, cast Caucasian people in the mould of 'White devils' and, certainly, there is no escaping the fact that their actions, past and present, give credence to why they referred to White people in this way. Moreover, that a full-grown adult Black male can be, and sometimes is referred to in the States as 'boy' by White people, makes a nonsense of a common-sense adult approach to matters and when such an attitude is taken, it is indicative of a racist sleight of hand on the part of the name-caller. However, not all White people are evil vicious racists. White people are human beings who appear to stop at nothing to remain top dog. Generalisations are useful for what Whites do collectively and British culture has a good deal to answer for; conversely, it is important to appreciate that not all White people believe what they read or hear. In other words, if the shoe fits, wear it, and one size does not fit each and every White person.

So much as at the standard stage of factual daily features in the press, the symbolism of colonialism and stereotypical attitudes are floated periodically. Far from being the major trait of the press inclusion of race and ethnic diversity, its existence points towards an underlying standpoint in British culture which furnishes a ready interpretive structure on questions of race and colour. Despite decolonization, the firmly held assumptions and image of White superiority appear to have common currency in Britain and reflect a widespread propensity to accept the comparatively disadvantaged social situation of Blacks as natural, and to the point of being necessary (Hartmann and Husband,1974).

It is crucial to understand the link between those long-established cultural assumptions and the contemporary social situation of non-whites, both here and overseas. Although such attitudes persist, to the point of being in minimum and diminished mode, so too will it happen to appear normal to encounter Blacks mainly in low-grade employment in the domestic market, and malnourished and miseducated abroad. And, for the duration of time that Third World poverty and unjust race relations in South Africa continue and Blacks remain subject in Britain, so also will the thought patterns of White superiority and Black inferiority appear to be corroborated by the same social relations that are the cultural commensurate. Furthermore, it is difficult to envision a society in which race is no longer an active indicator of expedient advantage, where this is masked by the unmistakable social phenomena. Prejudice props up injustice, as injustice shores up prejudice. While Britain is the concern here, due consideration should also be given to the fact that to discuss matters of colour prejudice and disadvantage solely as expressed by social and political proceedings within this political unit is disingenuously to set apart the incidence from its true international magnitude (Hartmann and Husband,1974).

Focusing on colour prejudice

While the public declaration of racial prejudice is likely to be formally met with disapprobation in Britain, racist beliefs and values remain a feature of the prevailing cultural system of British society. There is a significance in transparency by what I mean here. I do not mean that direct racist ideology is supported by all White Brits; merely, it is widely recognized as standard for Whites to pin their hopes upon preferment over Blacks. This is the case even of those who effectively frown on and reject racial prejudice and discrimination (Hartmann and Husband,1974). From this angle, colour prejudice represents a normative stance in twenty-first century Britain. The state of affairs remains unchanged by the detail that colour prejudice is at variance with other values. The standards of freedom and equality, for example, are held by many people simply to not relate to people of colour simultaneously as they do for Whites, and the role of the different excuses of colour prejudice – namely, the assumption of biological or cultural inferiority – is quite literally to uphold such principles while precluding minorities from their areas of activity. Racist assumptions and the state-sanctioned values of freedom and democracy coincide in British culture. Racist thought patterns and symbolic representation are culturally ever-present and the historical ramifications of skin colour, which is among the cultural inheritance of all Britons, amount to a potential basis of opinion and action. This is the reason for which it can be entirely misleading to designate people as intolerant or tolerant as though intolerance were a purely subjective characteristic, present in certain people and non-existent in others, and generally a matter of personal virtue or pathology. Prejudice is located in the culture. Individuals vary in the extent to which prejudiced cultural ideations rather than egalitarian ideations enter into their lexicon on the world and reasoning behind their actions; but the elemental ideations are the familiar feature of all (Hartmann and Husband,1974).

An additional point needs to be furthered. The notion of white ability and black incapacity, which is pivotal to colour prejudice, is the matter that differentiates it from various other types of inter-racial attitudes. Feelings of hostility have not only been levelled at minority groups but there has been and continues to be a significant level of anti-German prejudice, for example. This perception may comprise elements of derision, disdain, malice, fear and even vituperation but it does not possess as its central property the impression of the inadequacy of the German in contrast to the Briton, and it scarcely arose in conditions through which the Germans were enslaved or underwent colonization. Similarly, it may be stated of anti-white intolerance on the part of minorities, which, no matter how intense, is not contingent on any traditionally normative ideation of inferiority. Prejudices of this kind never served the civic role of maintaining a class of people in a state of subordination to another. An important exception to these declarations is the instance of Anti-Semitism which merges many aspects with colour prejudice, from biblical legitimation to the civic role of maintaining a social category in a pariah condition in Western societies (Hartmann and Husband,1974).

The indispensable assumption of inferiority which is the distinguishing element of White racial prejudice is something that has tended to go unsaid by commentators on the subject (Hartmann and Husband,1974). Where the purpose in mind is to appreciate the mental processes underlying prejudice – stereotyping, over-generalization, inflexibility, projection and so forth – it may be fair to treat all inter-racial attitudes as psychologically similar. Where the purpose is to appreciate the association between social categories in a specific historical situation, it comes to be crucial to identify the distinctive elements of the attitudes and to view them having regard to the relative standing of the groups, traditional and modern-day. A prejudice conflicting with a previously enslaved social category is more or less likely to diverge from a prejudice conflicting with a conqueror or an imperial opponent, both in the material detail of its justifying assumptions and in its significations for inter-racial relations (Hartmann and Husband,1974).

Managing diversity

However one may see the situation of Black and minority ethnic people in this country, it is a predominantly White country and White people are more likely to set the rules of the game. The fourth estate tends to set the terms of the debate on multiculturalism and how ethnic diversity is portrayed in the media, which mirrors directly their economic and political marginalization, or efficacy. In other words, economic forces within an unequal and multi-racial society will scarcely of themselves produce an equal multi-ethnic media environment. Furthermore, change takes place only in a structure where the press undergoes change. The press's negative, unfavourable and disparaging response to the non-white presence has a regulatory effect on ethnically diverse communities.

The government refuse to say the 'S' word ('sorry') on slavery and without this, White perceptions toward diasporic populations will not begin to change and entrenched racism will not begin to be overcome. Reparations are, unto some White groups, like a strong adjective or verb but should as a point of principle follow from an apology which would influence and impact on the standing of Black people in the eyes of Whites – even though an element of this may be resentment and anti-Black feeling. So long as these two issues remain unmet and unaddressed and so long as assumptions of White preferment over Blacks and White advantage and Black disadvantage as well as where colour comes to represent a lesser entitlement to the benefits of power and resources, equality is as far distant as it has ever been and the result can only be an increased sense of alienation and a climate of simmering racial tension. It could also be seen as a method by which government is containing the so-called unreasonable demands of communities of colour.

Globally, Black aspiration is struggling for our recognition as a people and to be extended the same rights and opportunities as everyone else. In the US, the position of Blacks is accentuated by differential treatment towards them, especially by White law enforcement officers. In America, a Black man is more likely to be shot or brutalised by White police officers than in most other places in the world. In comparison, equality in Britain is as far from being enacted now than at any point in history and the escalation of such undue treatment in the USA took place under President Barack Obama's watch and therefore the battle is with the 'survival strategy of systemic power'. African-Caribbean people dying in the custody of the police authorities is at an alarming rate and figure in Britain and is indicative of Downing and Husband's (2005) phrase 'ongoing low-intensity pogrom'. The world over, Black people face obstacles to their welfare and security and this feeds the attentions of those who look for a vindication for discriminatory practices and seems to push the drive for equality that much further backwards in the overall scheme of things.

Over the decades, the management of diversity has been tended and tilled by the introduction of race relations legislation to protect minorities and their interests, but what will equality look like and how will it be enacted or phased in, if at all? If equality incorporates the absence of prejudice, then prejudice will only be eradicated through a deep-seated cultural change where the language and symbolic meaning of superior versus inferior 'races' is abandoned and the fact of possessing White skin covering ceases to be a reservoir of esteem, and Blackness ceases to be a blot on one's escutcheon that it is presently arousing, in different measure, contempt, hostility, pity or fellow feeling in the White seat of the emotions. Not being able to envisage how this kind of reverence for non-white people, in contrast with tolerance, will emerge in not inconsiderable proportions until ethnically diverse populations are enabled to gain full equality in this social environment rather than the illusory equality and tangible and systematic discrimination that defines their current situation (Hartmann and Husband,1974).

The press has managed diversity with a dismal and appalling record of highly critical rhetoric about a multi-ethnic Britain, from calls for more restrictive immigration controls to dictating the terms of what minority groups should be governed by, and meeting calls for cultural pluralism with the audacity and arrogance that such groups are undermining and pose a 'threat' to British national culture. Firstly, a fresh understanding reveals an important new insight. In Chapter Two, I argued that 'immigrants' could hardly be a threat to British culture and the British way of life merely by their very presence, when, in fact, it would be mistaken and impercipient not to revise this position now. Since colour prejudice is central to the culture, it is only fair to say that African-Caribbean and South Asian people do present opposition to such a culture; if only because British culture is in conflict with and in opposition to the man and woman of colour simply because they seek to be treated on equal terms with indigenous White people. Secondly, the assumptions and beliefs on which British culture rests are absurdly flawed and unnatural concepts that are predicated on colour prejudice and pose a threat and undermine any possibility of equality ever emerging and witnessing the shimmering daybreak of future beginnings. To put the matter into some perspective, it is only mandatory to petition why there is not a similar breadth of social resentment and antagonism against the 'immigrant' Irish and other (White) 'immigrant' groups.

The struggle to be recognized as a people and to be extended equality and equal opportunities alongside the right of freedom from the fetters of discrimination is Black aspiration's long-held dream - to break free from these chains and manacles. Because Whites assume that the Black man should be subordinate to the White man, change is very difficult or unlikely and despite recent attempts to put equality on the agenda, by the time of Theresa May's Conservative government, such attempts had petered out and subsequently been overshadowed by Brexit talks and there has been a return to the condition of business as usual. Implicitly and explicitly in the above is my emotional and intellectual approach to the management of diversity made meaningful as opposed to the mismanagement of it. Martin Luther King, Jr. referred to the idea of freedom from discrimination by waxing mellifluously on freedom to stress its primacy and I leave the following words of the great man himself to illustrate my point:

With this faith, we will be able to work together, to pray together, to struggle together, to go to jail together, to stand up for freedom together, knowing that we will be free one day. This will be the day when all of God's children will be able to sing with new meaning – "My country, 'tis of thee; sweet land of liberty; of thee, I sing. Land where my fathers died, land of the pilgrim's pride; from every mountainside, let freedom ring" – and if America is to be a great nation, this must become true.

So let freedom ring from the prodigious hilltops of New Hampshire.

Let freedom ring from the mighty mountains of New York.

Let freedom ring from the heightening Alleghenies of Pennsylvania.

Let freedom ring from the snow-capped Rockies of Colorado.

Let freedom ring from the curvaceous slopes of California.

But not only that.

Let freedom ring from Stone Mountain of Georgia.

Let freedom ring from Lookout Mountain of Tennessee.

Let freedom ring from every hill and molehill of Mississippi, from every mountainside, let freedom ring.

And when we allow freedom to ring, when we let it ring from every village and hamlet, from every state and city, we will be able to speed up that day when all God's children – black men and white men, Jews and Gentiles, Catholics and Protestants – will be able to join hands and to sing in the words of the old Negro spiritual, "Free at last, free at last, thank God Almighty, we are free at last".

(Washington,1991:219-220)

The above is not only inspirational, but also systematically goes about stressing the plan of freedom from the chains and manacles of discrimination in a way that cannot be ignored because it is so emphatic, and certainly King's dream is, far from any stretch of the imagination, a misplaced visionary cause.

Signs of the times, prospects and futures

Circumstances and relations between Black and White people have not changed by a tremendous amount in the last thirty to forty years; there is still a power relations differential though racism is not as overt as it once was. Overt racism has, in the light of race relations legislation, become improper and frowned upon, but has mutated and is still as pervasive and widespread as ever before. Whether White groups hail from a privileged background or not, they are still privileged in a society that venerates whiteness and stigmatizes Blackness and the distinction does not end there; Blacks tend to occupy an underprivileged rung of the social hierarchy and tend to be at a disadvantage to Whites. Unemployment among Blacks is significantly higher than that of White unemployment, thus racial distinctions draw on expectations of labour market opportunity that favours Whites while opportunities are closed off or restricted if one is Black. Even Black graduates have to apply for more job vacancies before they secure a post, and even then, it may not be their most preferred position whereas Whites make far fewer applications for jobs and sometimes succeed against their Black counterparts who, in certain instances, may be more qualified academically. This can still transpire even though in grading and assessment, the written work by Black and minority ethnic students tends to be marked down, ultimately affecting the final award category of the qualification they receive. South Asian groups tend to be owner-occupiers and are more likely to be self-employed. Compulsory and higher education tend to replicate and reflect the social hierarchy, so then, again, the winners tend to be White and we need only look at Oxbridge to see that they enrol predominantly White candidates while Blacks tend to be a token gesture and seem to lose out in finding themselves in less prestigious institutions. Nowadays, the old adage of, if you are White, you're alright, if you are brown, stick around and if you are Black, get to the back, still bears germane relevance even in this enlightened and technologically advanced age and appears stubbornly as if it will remain so for some time to come.

The implications for where this leaves Black aspiration are clear. This leaves Black aspiration with the prospect of drawing strength from Black History and modelling a foundation on which new futures can be built. Black History Month should apply all year round as Black people do not disappear at the end of October and it is as much a part of British history and a part of the historical narrative as anything else, so why should Black History be anything other than ubiquitous? New ideas can drive change; if Black people can think of new ways of contributing to the economy without dependence on employers, therein lies independent economic activity. Barack Obama proved that Black aspiration can achieve high office so Black people should approach their dreams with rose-tinted spectacles and persistent tenacity. Also, Black aspiration should seek to unravel his or her full potential in whatever field of endeavour. Education is key to unlocking doors in the labour market and so long as schools continue to fail proportions of its roll, the underclass will be a permanent feature of contemporary British social life. The solution to a burgeoning underclass appears to lie in a strong and growing economy that provides full employment – if that is now possible with robots and technology replacing humans – an education system that ceases to place emphasis on excluding its Black pupils, and increased international cooperation to rescue the global economy.

Castles and Kosack suggest that the subordinate labour market position of Black and minority ethnic groups seems to be an economic necessity and so, to some extent, a permanent feature of the class system, although for the most able members, upward social mobility is always possible (1985:475). (See Chapter 9 for a critique of Castles and Kosack's view.) I would applaud further research into Black aspiration as I believe that this volume falls short of turning over all the stones. It appears that Black aspiration is under-researched and little understood. This book does not claim to be an exhaustive guide and exposé of the influence of British social institutions on Black aspiration even though there appear few gaps left under-researched and untouched here.

Although there are gaps in this analysis, the Stephen Lawrence inquiry speaks volumes where Black aspiration is concerned. Since the findings show that all major institutions and organizations in Britain are characterized by institutional racism, there is little more that the nerve of Black aspiration needs to be alive to when it comes to relations between the ethnic majority and people of colour. If I have said it before, it is worth repeating, institutional racism is the pathological problem at the heart of a society that has deep and adverse effects on Black aspiration. So long as Black and minority ethnic people are seen as a 'threat' and a 'problem', and the bipartisan British government shows an unwillingness to apologize for the slave trade and slavery, so institutional racism and conflict will be the order of the day because the masses will not see a change in the type of conduct the British government approves of.

'The survival strategy of systemic power' and the desire to control the 'other' is also part of the problem which is unlikely to undergo a sea change unless the democratic material fabric of the aggregate of society is undermined (Eddo-Lodge, 2017:64). The media and central government can be the drivers for change and set an example by showing the initiative as opposed to political expedience and opportunism. These agencies possess the power to re-educate and re-orientate society towards the full acceptance of people of colour. The redistribution of wealth that would come with reparations would tend to mean power relations and racial inequality would be destabilized but would appear not to change totally.

The incidence of racism in the lives of Black Caribbean people contributes to their over-representation in the mental health services, though this is sharply contrasted with under-representation of Bangladeshi people. In this, we can see the devastating influence of a nation and its people working on complex levels to produce poverty, unemployment, educational underachievement, outcomes in criminal justice, poor health and even premature death. And this is what is meant by pointing up that British culture functions to hinder, frustrate, disappoint, and block Black aspiration. This begs the question, how can all of this be brought to an end without causing considerable adverse White backlash in the process? How can White society break a centuries-old habit, when racism operates to their overall benefit? The domestic institutional and organisational culture must change if Black aspiration is to enjoy a fair share of resources, a fair share of opportunities, and a fair share of the cake.

The two seemingly behemoth institutions, the government and the media can promote this change in policy intervention by drawing attention to humanitarianism; the fact that regardless of skin colour, we are all shrouded in the same mortal destiny and have universal needs; also, the human family should work together in the interest of human progress and human development. But when did we last hear of government or the media having to justify their actions? Usually, they just act and then wait for the people to react. Come to mention universal human needs, the unemployment rate amongst Black school-leavers is four times the national average (Hall et al,2013). Black and minority ethnic unemployment registers at 6.3% contrasting with 3.6% for White people (Booth and Mohdin,2018). Can this symptom of inequality be justified or explained without being explained away? Does this unequal conjuncture stem from racial discrimination?

Whereas once a widely held view, many now do not think so. "When we talk about discrimination today," Nathan Glazer declared, "we really do not have in mind discrimination; we have in mind inferior economic status which is the effect of many causes, among which may be discrimination" (Glasser,1988; in Katz and Taylor,1988:343). What is more, the Black economist Thomas Sowell (1984) purported that "skills, education and work habits" are the solution, not civil rights intervention or court-imposed answers (Glasser,1988; in Katz and Taylor,1988:343). This smacks of the notion that Black people should pull themselves up by their own bootstraps. To some extent, these critics are not barking up the wrong tree. Skills and industry are relevant. And the kind of discrimination Blacks encountered in the 1950s and 1960s is not what it once was.

However, scholars like Glazer and Sowell buy into the new "blame the victims" movement, partly because they appear to undervalue the impact and continuity of the less apparent but still effective impulse of racism, and partly because they fall short of recognizing the link between discrimination and aspiration. Part of what motivates people to hone and polish their skills, and to strive, is to second-guess that opportunity will emerge. At the time that opportunity is non-existent, or is very limited, or is seen to be very limited, ambition is rained on and the fire of hope extinguished. It is every bit acceptable and reasonable to encourage the oppressed to strive harder, but the sharpening of skills will not come about in a climate where there is little hope of economic activity and forward progression.

Race, in terms of White racism and Black resistance, is among the most volatile of political forces in our times. A Black underclass is symbolic of Black aspiration undergoing control by forces that are not of its own making; it is a result of the adverse effects of social institutions on Black aspiration.

As social institutions are an integral part of the social fabric and are inextricably tethered to the past and shaping and reshaping the world in which Black aspiration is subject and no stranger to, hence the status of Black aspiration will, for the foreseeable future, remain embattled. It is important to recognize that part of why minorities are oppressed is because of the 'survival strategy of systemic power' and conscious and unconscious bias working up and down the chain of command in social institutions and organisations. The structure of social institutions is its manpower and for Black social status and self-image to not lag behind this structure then social attitudes need to change profoundly because in almost every aspect of life, the likelihood is that operating at the most esoteric levels, joined-up adverse action and reaction await Black and minority ethnic people in their dealings with White society in Britain today.

While Whites tend to live in a near-perfect state of happiness, Blacks live in an entirely counter dimensional sphere which is why there is reference to Black America and White America. In Britain, since we live in a liberal democracy where government plays politics with people or supports the utilitarian dream asserting the greatest happiness of the greatest number, this indicates the unlikeliness of and little room for radical change ever emerging. It is, therefore, no great leap to see that almost invariably, White British interests are served while the concerns of people of colour are subordinated and submerged beneath political priorities to gather much dust. What are deemed political priorities sometimes need not take precedent over longstanding basic human rights, if Black and minority ethnic lives are to matter as well.

Nothing in the push (poverty, unemployment and underemployment in their homeland) and pull (availability of jobs in Britain and avenues to social mobility) could stop Caribbean migrants from pursuing their mission to come to these shores, even though some may have been forewarned to brace themselves for the conditions of life in the 'mother country'. As news of Kelso Cochrane's racist murder filtered back to the then British Caribbean in 1959, fear of walking Britain's streets at night may have gripped actual and potential migrants (Perry,2015:141). We should all be working for a world as it should be not the opposite way about and Britain is all the poorer as a result. Similarly, we all have a unique and important contribution to make for justice to rain down like a cascading waterfall. But as the unemployment statistics indicate, in the case of minority groups, opportunities are not as readily extended when put alongside the majority ethnic population.

The sword of Damocles can best describe and highlight the status of the struggle for equality and full citizenship even though, at present, the numbers of Black and minority ethnic MPs and councillors operating at a local and/or national level make little difference to resource allocation and political influence; yet, it is through political activity that the drum can be beaten for freedom, equality and justice in a climate where the prospects for upcoming outcomes are not good. Further, to the paucity of social status, the Black and minority ethnic orientation within a social structure regulated by majority interests plays into the maintenance of non-white people on the periphery of power.

Historically and recently, bipartisan British government has been supine on the issue of racial injustice thereby giving the nod to ancestral malfeasance, hate crime, differential treatment and the marginalization of people of colour. A brief overview of our systematic examination of the influence of social institutions on Black aspiration reveals the following highlights and details.

This study places social institutions such as the education system, the labour market and the media, *inter alia*, under close scrutiny and examines their policies and practice and investigates the position of Black and minority ethnic people within these institutions and how they fare as a result of their contact with what are essentially White institutions. Because it has been written that White people are superior to Black people, the consequences are still being felt. This fundamental idea underlies conflict between White British people and people of colour, whether consciously or unconsciously derived. The study explores British culture to discover race prejudice at its core being responsible for adversely and disproportionately affecting Black and minority ethnic lives and aspirations.

The study concludes that mainstream institutions are all devastating and catastrophic to Black aspiration. By Black people, I mean people of African descent, though people of colour are subject to the same influence. The father of racist ideology, Edward Long, legitimated White supremacy and the institution of slavery and the slave trade, the former and the latter being culpable for present and future circumstance. The study is essentially about how minorities are continually and perpetually oppressed and seek solutions.

The main thrust of the above overview does not so much tap into and feed off 'fear of a Black planet', but instead, states the facts and shows the need for change and reform. The survey of main points assumes that 'otherness' and not belonging help contribute to the influence of social institutions on Black aspiration and illustrates continuity rather than change.

Saying no to reparations now

George Santayana may have had a point in putting forward the argument that those who fail to learn from history are destined to repeat it (Nakanishi,1988; cited in Katz and Taylor,1988). The history we should never repeat is man's inhumanity to man, by which I mean the African enslavement holocaust that had a life far longer and with appreciably millions more lives lost owing to avarice and greed than the Jewish encampment holocaust. Also, America seems never to learn lessons from the police killings and brutality of Black Americans and so is destined to repeat these crimes. Despite the point made earlier, instead of the emphasis being placed on contrition and atonement, the Black diaspora are callously told to put it behind them and see past it whereas the European Jews are urged to never forget. Meanwhile, the British educate their young that slavery transpired in history and is part of their heritage. Moreover, the Jews are in receipt of billions in reparations and the African and African ancestral lines hitherto haven't received a cent in reparations. The message this transmits is that the dominant group could not care less about Black people, only their own kind, and that slavery was not all that bad, but something slavery dwarfed and put into the shade was. Furthermore, when it boils down to it, the dominant group seem not to respect the dignity of Black people as fellow human beings which harks back to the days of slavery.

The lesson the British government appears to have learned from slavery and the slave trade is that it is scarcely appropriate to apologize for something that happened nearly two centuries ago. In other words, anything approaching reparations is not on the table for discussion and this means that they will never admit that the real victims of the institution of slavery were Black people. While White slave owners were compensated handsomely as they were seen to have sustained a loss in human property which was not theirs to claim ownership of in the first place, in practical terms, they have learned never to apply the past to the present or to compensate as that would rather defeat the object of the exercise.

As things stand, the British empire was built on forced unremunerated labour and the bipartisan British government refuse to see that they owe the Black man and woman an outstanding economic and psychological debt, yet, are among the very people who stigmatize and turn the tables on the innocent party. Moreover, because the British character is essentially flawed or elements within which display unreasonable hostility towards people of colour, it follows that the British character will not miraculously turn good overnight. Trowler (1999) offers support for this outlook and designates White people as "untrustworthy". It is because of the past that the British find themselves in a favourable position in the present, and the historical arc of time gone by can be called to account for much of their present-day conduct and action.

This is the picture on the face of it, however. The bipartisan British government are aware of their culpability but resolve to maintain their position out of sheer economic and political expediency. The British government of past and present would rather be in the wrong and retain its world ranking position among the wealthiest of nations than be in the right and see that position slip. It is worth pointing out that the lessons of the past have been quietly learned but reparation is not anywhere close to being on the table and this is bipartisan British government policy. If almost two centuries is anything to set store by, the struggle for reparations can be likened to trying to get blood out of a stone and is an ill-fated struggle. This is, of course, the view of a realist and not a pessimist. There needs to be a total shift in political will if anything approaching reparations is to see the light of day.

Black aspiration will continue to have a vision but whether it will continue to dream the same dreams is contingent as much on Black people as it is on White society. Even though injustice has its own reward, the universe is consonant with and inclines towards justice, whose cause for optimism is eternal in the human breast. And, this is consistent with Good and Evil being bound up in a metaphysical discursive struggle across space and time. We owe it to ourselves and subsequent generations to build a more just and humane world, accepting that humanity does not display and express its full and unadulterated bounty. Why is it that the British government can recognize racial injustice, yet, at the same time, heed the call for reparations with dispassion?

Since racial inequality and the withholding of reparations is a non-minority group injustice, it reflects a dismal picture of inertia and apathetic torpor, whereby matters of utmost importance are left submerged beneath the political agenda, and only recently has it been exploited to broaden Conservative Party political appeal, and nothing else besides. And notwithstanding the possibility of a consensus around the facts, there is considerable dissonance over the appropriate universal panacea. After an age of saying no to reparations, it would take a significant climb-down for the bipartisan British government to apologize for slavery and the slave trade because as they know only too well, they would have to prove how genuinely sorry they really were and for delaying and procrastinating over the decades.

In the struggle to change reality, none of the various remedies has created such a stir as affirmative action. In addition, affirmative action failed to come up with anything like the moral consensus enjoyed by the nonviolent campaign for civil rights some 60-70 years ago, it is the view of some who championed that cause to be itself styled on discrimination or racism. Paradoxically, at the very time when the democratic moral consensus for affirmative action appeared to be lost, the institutions of American society seem to have taken it on board. The U.S. Supreme Court has pragmatically agreed to affirmative action by approving numerical goals and timetables, which some construe as quotas, and Congress has unequivocally refused to pass laws against such remedies.

Furthermore, on the say-so of a relatively recent exposition in Fortune magazine, more than 95% of major American organizations would continue to apply numerical objectives in the engagement and progression of minorities even if it was not a requirement. Therefore, the establishments that were once opposed to civil rights legislation and remedies now appear at ease with them, even as conventional support has waned and conventional opposition has grown. Such divergence cannot continue indefinitely, which is exactly why it is key to get a handle on the concept of affirmative action from a moral perspective rather than just as a legal one (Glasser,1988; in Katz and Taylor,1988).

In what remains of the available space, we shall focus mostly on a discussion of affirmative action where it relates to and impacts upon Black Americans, partly because the issues are rather different as compared with other minority ethnic groups and women, and partly because we intend to concentrate, in the space left available, not on affirmative action of itself, but on the rather narrower subject of anti-Black discrimination and the remedies necessary to stop this discrimination.

Etymologies and definitions

Since affirmative action has emerged to become an indistinguishable code word for both those in favour and those against, it behoves us to explain our

Chapter 10: Conclusion

terms. The *idée reçue* of affirmative action, as mutually exclusive from the term, possesses two distinct, though related etymologies. Beneath one definition, affirmative action assumes a general kind of moral reparation, a variant of temporary compensatory opportunity, developed to make amends for past injustices and to even up the balance once more before seeing the race resume on relatively equal material conditions. Beneath the second definition, affirmative action assumes a narrow, if draconian legal remedy, temporarily enforced or countenanced by the courts in certain cases to redress the particular effects of past or present-day discrimination, where such discrimination is found unfair.

Also apparent is a third strand of thought, which explains affirmative action as an attempt to achieve fair observable representation for minorities on grounds of social or political efficacy. Beneath this definition, to exemplify, police forces in urban districts should reflect an adequate proportion of Blacks not simply because that may constitute a solution for individual discrimination or a *quid pro quo* for previous exclusions, but additionally because society will have gained an improved police service when Blacks are adequately represented, especially if a significant proportion of the general public is Black. Such a contention has also been directed at teachers and other employment sectors. The contention has been made in seminal fashion with reference to political representation on steering groups such as regional legislatures and school boards (Glasser,1988; in Katz and Taylor,1988).

Those who further such contentions claim that such a statement in leadership roles is not just a legal extension of the franchise of suffrage itself, but, in addition, a reification of full citizenship and an important indicator that, finally, historic racial exclusions from the franchise of citizenship have ended. Also, certain political scientists, not least Philip Green (1981), have asserted that only the development of leadership classes that dynamically demonstrate the natural potential in the excluded population can begin to undermine the internalized belief attributed to many in the excluded section that somehow, they are at fault (Glasser,1988; in Katz and Taylor,1988).

While this line of contention provides a convincing justification for affirmative action, it is scarcely that, as no one contends that such a statement should be authorized where there is no discriminatory exclusion or autonomously of whatever yardstick of merit in other respects apply. Objectively, therefore, affirmative action is often seen to mean either the general, if temporary, compensatory opportunity for group affiliates that have faced enduring disadvantage in sharp contrast to the dominant social group or the more specific legal remedy to particular discriminatory exclusion. Each of these definitions will be discussed later under affirmative action as legal remedy.

Affirmative Action as Compensatory Opportunity

More complicated than affirmative action as legal remedy is the broad condition of compensatory opportunities or rights, special advantages given based on race to compensate, in a wide sense, for disadvantages that were enforced on the grounds of race. The first instances of such compensatory opportunities and rights occurred following the Civil War when Congress devised certain fiscal and educational plans to which only freshly freed slaves and additional Blacks in the South were eligible. The dominant group were expressly excluded (including impoverished Whites), and certain Blacks were subsumed who arguably had not privately experienced discrimination.

However, the criterion was outlined that Blacks as an aggregate had sustained a special disadvantage – slavery – and thus required certain special countervailing forces to operate in order to realign things. In the event, the special countervailing forces weren't enough and scarcely made amends for the disadvantages, both historically and developing. On the other hand, the rationale appeared just; indeed, it appeared the only moral posture (Glasser,1988).

In non-racial situations, the same rationale has been used without *cause célèbre*. The GI bill and many other special advantages for war veterans after World War II did not necessitate that each veteran demonstrate personal

Chapter 10: Conclusion

disadvantage. Not once did such advantages permit non-veterans to claim based on any disadvantages they might have sustained as a consequence of the war. Instead, society came to the decision that, because all veterans, collectively, had been required for active service, by being conscripted to do battle in an overseas territory, all veterans, collectively, were entitled to a range of economic and educational benefits to redress the balance.

Such plans were generally held to be morally just. Therefore, isn't there reason enough that similar plans be justified in the interests of Blacks, who as a cohort certainly have, to a greater extent, been deeply and broadly disadvantaged by government processes than returning veterans? (Glasser,1988). Yet from the outset, unlike special plans for veterans, special plans for Blacks were not perceived as morally just – indeed, they were often thought immoral as being a kind of "reverse racism". Since the problem is conceptualized from this perspective, it is reasonable to assume that the apparent divergence in opinion between affirmative action plans for veterans and affirmative action plans for Blacks is itself symbolic of race discrimination.

Way back in 1963, at the zenith of the civil rights struggle, this idea was given a very public airing. Guichard Parris, an assistant to Whitney Young of the National Urban League, broached the matter thus:

> It's time to discriminate in the Negro's favour for five or ten years …. The veterans of World War II got a break – the GI bill and extra points in Civil Service examinations – because they were out of the mainstream of the economy for three or four years. Negroes have never been in that mainstream (Newsweek, July 15, 1963, p.69; quoted in Glasser,1988:347).

Martin Luther King, Jr., made a similar point on national television around the same time:

> Temporary special provisions for Negroes are urgently needed to bring about a greater racial balance …. Discrimination in reverse [is] a good idea ("Protestant Heritage", 1963; quoted in Glasser,1988:348).

The mental picture of compensatory opportunity was not an argument only being endorsed by Black leaders. In a ground-breaking book published in 1963, John H. Fischer, then president of Teachers College, Columbia University, declared quite clearly that equal opportunity did not go far enough (Glasser,1988). He identified that the idea of considering Black children in a special manner was nothing new: "The American Negro youngster," he wrote, "happens to be a member of a large and distinctive group that for a very long time has been the object of special political, legal and social action". The outlined special actions, Fischer asserted, were deeply destructive extending across a long time-span. To take direct action "as though any child is suddenly separable from his history is indefensible. In terms of educational planning, it is also irresponsible". Also, while he was at pains to identify that every child, among their number every Black child, is worthy of being regarded as an individual, he also stipulated that "Every Negro child is the victim of the history of his race in this country. On the day he enters Kindergarten, he carries a burden no white child can ever know". He concluded his analysis by petitioning and addressing the key question:

> Is it not a reasonable contention – and a just one – that to compensate for past injustice, we should offer these children educational services beyond the level of what might be called standard equality? Could it be that to achieve total equality of opportunity in America we may have to modify currently accepted ideas about equality of opportunity? ... We may need to substitute for our traditional concept of equal educational opportunity a new concept of compensatory opportunity (p.295; quoted in Glasser,1988:348).

These initial ideas, and others, began to intimate the undoubted fact and need for a temporary imbalance in preference of Blacks if we wanted to realize true equality of opportunity. The important thing to stress here is that all these advocates were referring to temporary plans, and all withstood any notion of lasting, institutionalized preferential processes. To be sure, they were deeply hostile to permanent preferences predicated on race and were making a strenuous effort, in some cases putting their lives at risk, for a colour-blind polity where individuals would be scrutinized and perceived through the standard measure of merit and not skin colour.

However, they were coming to realize that the disadvantages that were foisted on Blacks collectively could not be surmounted by acting as if the race was equal or that everyone had begun on a level playing field. They were coming to appreciate that, in a political unit that had been so negatively race-conscious for a very long time, the pathway to a colour-blind society called for a changeover period of positive race consciousness. They foresaw that it could only be temporary and the idea did not sit perfectly well with them. Not nearly did they know the precise detail of how the idea was to be implemented. The rationale, however, had started to take effect and it seemed as much moral and necessary.

At this most embryonic of stages, however, chasms appeared to become apparent. In a soliloquy to the U.S. Senate on June 27, 1963, Senator Abraham Ribicoff, apart from on this occasion an ardent sympathizer of the civil rights movement, raised his objection to the idea:

> Those who claim that X number of jobs or Y percent of jobs must be set aside for Negroes are not favouring equality of opportunity. They are saying that opportunity doesn't matter, that merit doesn't matter, that only arbitrary numbers and percentages matter. That point of view will undermine the whole effort to achieve equality in this country (Glasser,1988:348).

However, the idea had taken hold – and came to be consolidated. By 1965, it echoed in the White House. In what has become a much-publicized speech at Howard University, President Lyndon Johnson hailed:

> Freedom is not enough. You do not wipe away the scars of centuries by saying: Now, you are free to go where you want, do as you desire, and choose the leaders you please. You do not take a man who for years has been hobbled by chains, liberate him, bring him to the starting line of a race, saying, "you are free to compete with all the others", and still

justly believe you have been completely fair. Thus, it is not enough to open the gates of opportunity (Glasser,1988:348-349).

Since it was not adequate to improve the life chances of Blacks, no one knew precisely what was adequate. In 1965, Lyndon Johnson appeared to be pointing in the direction of some sort of Marshall Plan for African American families. Owing to a number of reasons, that Marshall Plan failed to materialize. Yet, the rationale upon which it rests was clear: Equal opportunity was short of being adequate. In 1965, this moral principle was one American society seemed ready to accept. In fact, it seemed to set the parameters of the civil rights movement.

Currently, that moral principle falls under a hail of criticism. William Bradford Reynolds, Assistant Attorney General of the United States, has stated that "the use of racial preferences, whether in the form of quotas, goals or any other numerical device [is] morally wrong" (New York Times, January 30, 1986, p.89; quoted in Glasser,1988:349). Before looking into the basis of such moral objections, we shall consider affirmative action as legal remedy.

Affirmative Action as Legal Remedy

The troubled situation that most readily illustrates this mental picture is jury discrimination. Think of a southern town with Black adult proportions numbering 40%; not one among them has ever been engaged on a jury panel. A civil rights case is brought, and following a trial, the judge adjudicates that the urban district has discriminated on the grounds of race and that such discrimination is unlawful. An edict is issued requiring the urban sprawl to desist from discriminating.

Twelve months later, the plaintiffs wind up in court. Their grievance is that the urban area is continuing to discriminate, despite the court order. The urban neighbourhood defends itself by demonstrating that 10 Blacks have appeared or have been summoned to appear on juries in the past year. However, the judge determines that 10 Blacks constitutes only one-tenth of the electorate. Since all adults are entitled to serve and are subject to random selection, it is impossible to accept that so few Blacks came under selection unless racial discrimination was persisting and enduringly practised. The town extends other explanations, but not one of which is found to be convincing. The judge directs that discrimination is still a problem and, for the second time of asking, orders the town to desist, and to launch a new procedure for selecting jurors that will secure non-discrimination (Glasser,1988).

Six months on, everyone finishes up in court again. On this occasion, the plaintiffs seek an edict requiring the town to satisfy a goal of 40% African Americans in the pool inside the next 3 months. The town repeats its claims that discrimination is in the past and says that it is working extremely hard to include Blacks. However, the facts illustrate that only 10% of the jury pool are African American – a significant improvement, but still falling short of the expected figures had there been no discrimination. The judge looks closely at the processes employed by the town in addition to its reasons for why only 10% of the jury pool is African American when 40% of the available adult population is African American when the selection process is supposed to be arbitrary (Glasser,1988).

The judge then takes account of the history of deep-rooted racism within the town and the specific influence that that racism has on jury selection. Following the trial, the court determines that, despite substantial improvement, the only cause for the consistent exclusion of Blacks is discrimination. The urban neighbourhood claims that it can now consign its intention to discriminate to the past, but intent is difficult to prove, and provided the long history of direct discrimination, the court glances towards the impact of the procedure for selecting jurors and discovers that it still excludes undue numbers of adult Blacks. Consequently, the court now requires a more drastic solution to rectify the persistent exclusion: the town is required to adopt a technique that leads to roughly 40% Blacks in the jury pool, add or subtract 3% inside 6 months. Furthermore, a self-governing monitor is engaged by the court to rethink the town's advancement and to occasionally feed back to the court (Glasser,1988).

There is a difficulty in understanding why anyone would find this sort of specific solution objectionable, under the situation described. And, in spite of that, all the aspects of affirmative action that people frequently find objectionable are extant in this example. First and foremost, the solution is race-conscious, not colour-blind. It enumerates people contingent on race and calibrates the extent to which discrimination has stood still by comparing the proportion of Blacks assigned a place to their proportion in the qualified pool. Second, the solution includes a numerical goal (40% add or subtract 3%) and a timetable (6 months, with occasional monitoring), or what some label quotas. The goal is set as a way of calibrating whether discrimination has stood still; the timetable is established to coerce the town to stop procrastinating.

Adversaries of affirmative action frequently argue for a colour-blind conjuncture, not race-conscious, and that goals and timetables reflect a "reverse discrimination" (Glasser,1988:345). They disparage such goals and timetables by branding them "quotas" so as to identify this kind of solution with past systems that were applied to place man-made restrictions on the incorporation of minorities. However, in an instance like that described above, to what extent can we fairly calibrate progress against the fundamentally flawed exclusion of Blacks aside from enumerating Blacks? Further, if 40% of the adult population is Black, for what reason is it unconscionable to expect that something approaching 40% would be incorporated in the jury pool if the option were made fairly, and with the absence of discrimination? (Glasser,1988).

Jury discrimination is an instance one can readily put one's hand to, of course. In instances of employment discrimination, the values just established are that much more difficult to apply. The whys and the wherefores are somewhat obvious. There is no difficulty distinguishing who is entitled to appear on a jury: anyone who has come of full legal age. Provided that 40% of the adult inhabitants are Black, then 40% of the qualified inhabitants are Black. To estimate the value is more difficult and intricate in the sector of employment. Supposing 40% of the adult demographic is Black; it does not inevitably correlate that 40% of those qualified to teach in schools or to be firefighters will be Black. However, it is feasible to identify reasonable credentials for these posts and to calculate the percentage of the certified labour pool that is Black. Consider, for instance, that painstaking studies demonstrated that 20% of the inhabitants qualified to be firefighters were Black, but as little as 3% were ever appointed. Does this not present a similar problem and call for a similar solution as the jury discrimination instance? (Glasser,1988).

Needless to say, the assessment of the proper proportion is much more problematic in the sector of employment. Specifications of what represent proper qualifications for particular jobs differ, as also do their methods of assessing those qualifications. However, more often than not, "qualifications" in times gone by were not really genuine qualifications in line with job performance; rather, they were limitations designed to preclude people for inadmissible reasons. Hence there were literacy tests in order that the vote could be exercised, or university degree conditions for many manual labour posts, or weight-lifting conditions that ruled out women even though such conditions were not consistent with the post (Glasser,1988).

The undeniable point is that, in the past and present day, the specification of qualifications for given jobs in addition to the methods for estimating the value of the applicants have themselves frequently been reflections of discrimination as opposed to fair tests of on-the-job qualities. Affirmative action lawsuits have compelled everyone to consider, more cautiously and precisely, the extent to which qualifications are actually needed for a particular job, and to ascertain better ways of assessing those qualifications. This way of working has undoubtedly scaled discrimination down and rendered hiring fairer.

At any rate, it is ordinarily possible, for any job sector, to ascertain, within an acceptable range, what proportion of the available entitled labour pool is Black or female (Glasser,1988). Imagine again, taking our, for the sake of argument, town, that 20% of the inhabitants qualified to be firefighters was Black, yet as little as 3% Blacks were ever appointed.

Suppose that the statistic of 20% is plausibly correct and that the urban neighbourhood has a past record of racial discrimination and, despite the prevailing circumstances, hires a maximum of 3% Black firefighters. For what reason isn't that situation, ethically speaking, precisely similar to the jury discrimination case? (Glasser,1988).

Imagine, for instance, that several Blacks, who have the required credentials for the position of firefighter but who were not accepted, take the town to court claiming racial discrimination. Imagine again that, after the case had been heard, the court establishes that the town has a lasting link with racial discrimination in public job placement and, more specifically, in the placing of firefighters. Lastly, imagine the court determines that the tests now being used by the district to qualify firefighters unreasonably exclude Blacks and are not true indexes of job performance. The court consequently abrogates the use of such tests and directs the town to create a process of estimating the value of job candidates that is non-discriminatory (Glasser,1988).

Similar to the jury case, twelve months pass and the percentage of Blacks taken on as firefighters barely increases and does not come anywhere near the estimate of 20%, which is the percentage of procurable qualified Blacks in the labour market. The district neighbourhood defends itself by demonstrating that it currently uses non-discriminatory tests and has gone out of its way to recruit minorities. It then maintains that its failure to take on more Blacks is not indicative of discrimination since it has acted with honest intention to recruit and employ on a non-discriminatory basis (Glasser,1988).

Supposing that, having heeded both sides and looking analytically at the evidence in addition to what the experts say, the court bestows faith in the town's apology, then the case will be declined further hearing. Honest intention efforts to employ on a non-discriminatory basis are sufficient. Supposing that, on the obverse, the court judges the town's defence specious and a masquerade for continued, if more insidious, discriminatory acts, or supposing that the court judges that the town's current arrangements are not enough to overcome the consequences of past discrimination, it follows that the court may direct to achieve a goal of something in the region of 15% Blacks in its firefighter unit within 2 years.

Similar to the jury case, this goal would be set depending on the court's judgement that, without discrimination, there would be a roughly 15% representation of Black firefighters. While the percentage used in real terms may well be a moot point, the fact that other Blacks would have been taken on save for discrimination is hard to dispute. Despite persistent discriminatory exclusion, for what purpose is it unreasonable, far less unethical, for a court to direct the infringing employer to desist from discriminating and then to evaluate compliance with that direction by setting a reasonable goal?

I have focused on examples that are relatively straightforward. Cases exist and come to light which are much more convoluted and render the solution of goals and timetables a great deal more difficult to deploy fairly. However, the principle never changes: If qualified Blacks are looking for work but are not being taken on as a consequence of past or present discrimination, it follows that they should be taken on. Moreover, the solitary way to evaluate whether they are being employed on a non-discriminatory basis is to enumerate them and compare the proportion hired with the proportion of certified people among the available inhabitants. To gainsay this sort of solution in cases of proven discrimination, and where racial exclusion is unrelenting, is to utter that in the face of fundamental rights being violated, we will be supine to act in order to resolve such violations. Such an outcome seems deeply flawed (Classer,1988). In the following discussion, we shall examine the basis of moral criticisms surrounding affirmative action.

Justifications and Criticisms
Fairness

A key counter-argument of affirmative action – a counter-argument endorsed by a substantial number of White workers – is that action warrants employers to discriminate at variance with better-qualified, or just as qualified, Whites who themselves shoulder no burden for discrimination. The foregoing is, in some cases, referred to as reverse discrimination. Based on this counter-argument, if, in a hypothetical factory, there are 100 jobs, all in White hands, and the affirmative action goal warrants 20% Blacks, then ultimately 20 Whites who, under one circumstance would be employed, though under another, unemployed, even though they, as separate entities, were not to blame for past discrimination (Glasser,1988).

The question of blame is one of concern, but it fails to consider and begin to deal with the fact that, although such White workers fell short individually of blame for excluding Blacks, they doubtlessly benefited from that prohibition. And they benefited inequitably. Each discriminatory act to keep Black workers out unfairly benefitted a White worker. At present, the dominant group is destined to profit from all forms of Black subordination. The contention that such unjust benefits need to be perpetuated is a contention for the persistence of anti-Black discrimination, at least in an environment where job vacancies continue to be finite and smaller than the numbers of people competing for jobs.

For instance, when Jackie Robinson smashed through the colour line in baseball, there were roughly 400 major league openings for baseball players (Glasser,1988). All were in the clutches of Whites, because Blacks were entirely excluded. Given that Blacks were permitted, in a non-discriminatory *de rigueur* style of approach, to compete for these postings on the basis of merit, doubtless some Blacks would have shown more merit than some Whites. Supposing that 100 Blacks had secured jobs, 100 Whites would have faced an unemployment spell. However, those Whites were hired for the reason that Blacks were ruled out. Save for racial discrimination, they would not have measured up to standard to hold those jobs. The derived employment utility for those 100 White players was a straightforward outcome of discrimination. These positions were unjustly allocated. Less certified Whites were hired whereas more certified Blacks were not. For what reason, then, should it be deemed reverse discrimination to resolve the situation by introducing a process of non-discrimination? (Glasser,1988).

In baseball, it occurred in the absence of affirmative action goals and timetables. However, what would result if, following the achievement of Jackie Robinson, the Brooklyn Dodgers had been the solitary team willing to employ Blacks? (Glasser,1988). What would result if a number of teams remained defiant on the employment of Blacks? In the end, wouldn't it have been justified for Black ballplayers to engage in legal proceedings against those teams and cite them with discrimination? Moreover, on condition that discrimination was ascertained, wouldn't it have been just for a court to establish the percentage of Black ballplayers throughout the community and set that percentage, alongside a timetable for accomplishing it, as a goal to bring pressure to bear on ending discriminatory hiring? (Glasser,1988).

In baseball, however, several teams did pursue the route of Black exclusion for a period of time and the enforcement of such a court-administered remedy proved needless. Discrimination came to a close without it (at least insomuch as players were concerned). However, in many other areas of economic activity, discrimination was not at an end. And, as a consequence, legal proceedings were actioned and, where discrimination was uncovered, remedies were sought.

Of course, where job numbers are restricted, fewer Whites will access jobs, just as fewer men will hold positions if women are free to stand rival on a non-discriminatory basis. But when too few are available, the ones whose lap those jobs fall into cannot morally be decided on the grounds of race or sex. The reality that the allocation of jobs was decided for time immemorial on the grounds of race and sex gave rise to an expectation between Whites and males. That that expectation is no longer what it was may contemporaneously seem unfair to them. However, the expectation was the opposite of fair from the very beginning. Fairness demands an end to discrimination, which is not the same as perpetuating it, and that subsumes ending the benefits that Whites delighted in as the outcome of anti-Black discrimination (Glasser,1988).

But even though individual Whites were on the favourable side of this discrimination, in various instances, they did not, as separate entities, cause it. The onus for employment discrimination rests with the employer, who may shoulder certain responsibilities to Black and White workers alike, during the conversion to a non-discriminatory method of working.

For instance, say a worker in a plant is unfairly sacked. He opposes the sacking by complaining under his union contract. During the complaint procedure, the employer engages a replacement. Six months transpire. Conclusively, an independent body awards a decision firmly in sympathy of the employee and directs his reoccupation with back pay. The employer capitulates and dispenses with the services of the replacement, who has now acquired 6 months experience. The employee who is now left without a job was not accountable for the unjust sacking of the initial employee. However, he took full advantage of it and now he finds himself bereft of a job as a straightforward outcome of the remedy decreed by the arbitrator. Fairness wins the day, but the replacement employee loses access to a job (Glasser,1988).

The *prima facie* point to render is that no individual would maintain that the replacement manpower was unfairly dismissed. His job was thanks in the first place to a vacancy generated by illegally prohibiting the original employee. As a consequence of the fact that the illegal preclusion has been corrected, he is deprived of the benefit. Precisely the homogenous moral analysis is pertinent to racial discrimination cases. Job opportunities were generated for White employees as the clear outcome of unlawful exclusions of Black workers. At the time when those unlawful exclusions are remedied, the benefits unjustly acquired are ended.

Ordinarily, the enforcement of an affirmative action solution does not lead to White workers getting sacked (Glasser,1988). The solution is prospective. Therefore, White candidates will, at the present time, have to vie with Black candidates for the available jobs. Furthermore, as Whites have, for time immemorial, enjoyed an unfair edge, Blacks have a good deal of ground to make up. The conditions of the competition, warped uninterruptedly towards Whites, will now be momentarily reversed. A necessary requirement of the employer is to employ a certain number of Blacks within a certain time frame in order to eliminate discrimination. Throughout this temporary phase, the conditions of competition may not be level. Blacks may enjoy the advantage. That hardly denotes or should not denote that unqualified Blacks get the jobs. The meaning that does attach itself is that, where qualifications are observed and are approximately equal, Blacks will be accorded preference, not only because it is the one single alternative to break the employer's penchant for Whites but also because it is unjust to have buttressed biased conditions of competition for an indeterminate length of time without turning the tables on bias. (Glasser,1988).

Turning the tables on bias, of course, is dangerous for it may institutionalize the reasonableness of bias and render it more difficult in the end to accomplish a colour-blind, non-discriminatory world. To be precise, it is a danger that exponents of affirmative action must face head-on and resolve to eschew. The plan of affirmative action procedures is a fair and principled panacea for institutionalized racism, but the remedy must be ephemeral and measured. Adversaries of affirmative action remedies understand the danger but lack sufficient sensitivity to the obduracy of discrimination and its consequences and to the call for draconian remedies. Chemotherapy is a draconian solution for cancer. It has awful side effects. Used imprudently, it can fatally injure the patient. However, used prudently and with knowledge of its side effects, it can put an end to cancer (Glasser,1988).

Like a cancer, racial discrimination is the single biggest social ill. Its steady progress in the social parameters has endured over a long period. The danger of affirmative action measures is real, but the contention that such measures should be axed and the cancer left to do its worst before it is totally annihilated is immoral (Glasser,1988).

Some opponents of affirmative action measures now argue that it is time to axe the temporary enforcement of affirmative action goals and timetables for the reason that the procedures that warrant fairness have, in considerable part, been institutionalized. As for what these critics mean to say, not a great deal would occur in the way of change if affirmative action measures were ended forthwith. As Robert J. Samuelson (1984) wrote:

[The aggressive uses of anti-discrimination laws, including affirmative action,] have changed the way labour markets work. Many firms have overhauled personnel policies. Recruitment has been broadened. Tests unrelated to qualifications have been abandoned. Promotions are less informal. When positions become open, they are posted publicly so anyone (not just the bosses' favourite) can apply. Formal evaluations have been strengthened so that, when a manager selects one candidate over another (say, a white man over a woman), there are objective criteria. Equally important, women and blacks, increasingly, are plugged into the informal information and lobbying networks that remain critical in hiring and promotion decisions (p.8) (quoted in Glasser,1988:353).

While this description is clearly accurate in certain cases, it does not legitimize a general rejection of affirmative action measures for two reasons.

Firstly, the conjuncture Samuelson outlined is idealized and fails to describe every employer. Affirmative action measures are never imposed save for when discrimination has been shown, and a court, or case between two conflicting parties, agrees that such a measure is needed to end discrimination. In certain rare instances where non-discriminatory hiring has been resolutely institutionalized, it may be constructive to begin a discourse on relaxing the temporary measures of affirmative action processes. But in that, all due care and attention should be exercised as also should it be monitored, treating each case according to the circumstances.

Secondly, a great deal of the conjuncture that Samuelson outlined is the clear outcome of demands applied by affirmative action objectives and timescales. It would be premature to believe that the incline towards discrimination and preferential procedures for the hiring and progression of Whites, maintained and normalized for an epic period, would not recommence, at least in degree, if affirmative action pressures were withdrawn. The realization of a colour-blind social system of non-discrimination has come short of being accomplished. It is no word of a lie that the strongest exponents seeking an end to affirmative action remedies in late 1980's America are those who withheld supporting them from the very beginning (Glasser,1988). It is not the time to begin a broad relaxation of the demands that have just begun to undermine the mores of racial discrimination.

Legitimations and Counter-arguments

Merit

A key counter-argument of affirmative action is that it loses sight of merit in its inexorable drive to achieve the necessary percentage of Blacks. As claimed by this line of counter-argument, individual merit and nothing but individual merit should be what establishes whether a person acquires a particular post or is accepted by a particular school. Based on the first impression, this would seem to be an incontrovertible standard. Was it not the aim of the civil rights movement to arrive at a society where individuals would be judged, as Martin Luther King, Jr., declared, by the content of their character and not by the colour of their skin?

However, "merit" is a slippery issue, hard to clarify and even harder to justify in regard to established practices. In reality, a decision about who acquires a particular post and who gets accepted by a particular school have invariably been made, and carry on being made, on the foundation of criteria not commensurate with individual merit.

As we mentioned earlier, veterans receive preference at the time that they apply for some civil service jobs. This preference spanned the entire spectrum of veterans, whether they were called up or not, whether they experienced combat or not, whether they can point out particular disadvantage caused by their term in the military or not. Those non-veterans are discriminated against even though, as individuals, they may be seriously disadvantaged in some form or arguably more educated. This well-organized tendency towards the mainstream, which is not founded strictly on personal merit, has not been discerned by American society as unjust or unprincipled. The line of thought was carried that veterans were, as a section of society, disadvantaged and that fairness thus required us to grant them special, if ephemeral, benefits as a category (Glasser,1988).

Alternate preferential systems fail even to seek to justify compensatory advantages predicated on fairness. For instance, schools often plump for applicants who dwell within the state in which the school is situated, even if these applicants display not so much merit as out-of-state applicants. And, schools often go for the children of former students, even if other children exhibit greater merit as individuals. Preference along these lines not only detracts from the value of individual merit, it also extends past discriminatory advantages. If previous patterns of admission to a given school reflected discrimination, it follows that a system that inclines towards the children of former students perpetuates such discrimination. However, such preferential processes have not caused an outbreak of public anger among those who defend the merit approach, nor have such preferential processes been mostly seen by Americans as unjust or unprincipled (Glasser,1988)

Seniority entitlements in employment present another example. The extent of activity in a particular employ determines certain benefits pertaining to promotion, protection from layoff, training opportunities, and so forth. These advantages mount up regardless of individual merit merely because of extent of service. Such a system may of course be justified on a number of grounds, but individual merit falls short of being one of them. Furthermore, in a system famed for producing discriminatorily excluded people predicated on race historically, the seniority system extends the disadvantages of this discrimination and takes forward its effects into a future trajectory. Yet, regularly those – especially labour union leaders – who pontificate about merit at the time that affirmative action programs are being considered, manage to banish from memory the concern of merit when seniority systems are being considered.

Lastly, those who rail against affirmative action in practical conditions, that it is a distraction from the merit system, must recognize, if they have an ounce of regard for facts whatsoever, that factors alien to merit have traditionally regulated access into various professions. Philip Green (1981) captured the point:

> To make their case consistent, these opponents [of affirmative action] would also have to explain what "merit" has been possessed by those professionals who have enjoyed the rewards of restrictive rules of entry to their professions (e.g., lawyers and doctors), by businessmen, bankers and brokers who were privileged by virtue of coming from an acceptable social background, public employees who belonged to the right ethnic group in the right place at the right time, craftsmen whose acceptance by a trade union has been contingent on their recommendation by members of their own family and academics who, through most of their careers, have engaged in neither productive scholarship nor innovative teaching but have rather been "good old boys", expertly mimicking the values of their superiors (p.79) (quoted in Glasser,1988:350).

The real truth is that even though everyone recognizes the idea of merit, factors extraneous to merit regularly and routinely determine who acquires what jobs. "Only in the most technologically advanced and abstruse careers are factors extrinsic to any true ranking of skills totally discarded," Green concluded. "Most of the time, the question is not whether other facts ... are going to be taken into account by us, but which ones" (p.80) (quoted in Glasser,1988:350).

People clearly do discriminate. They are guided by certain characteristics, which they hold to be proxies for merit, though, in most cases, are not. For vast numbers of Blacks who, from one generation to the next, lived with knowing that despite the level of individual merit they might have to hand, they would be systematically ignored, and that others, displaying alternative skill-sets, would be chosen, the latest preoccupation by critics of affirmative action regarding the idea of merit appears to be not much more than an attempt to change the rules while the game is underway (Glasser,1988).

Closely linked to the mental picture of merit is the sublime wonder of the super-black. It was an age before Blacks were allowed to participate in major league baseball. At the time that Jackie Robinson was engaged by Branch Rickey to compete for the Brooklyn Dodgers in 1947, he did not have to match up to the common or garden White player; he had to be head and shoulders above them. Furthermore, for a long time after Robinson's breach of the discriminatory habit, only phenomenal Black ballplayers were hired. For years, time seemed to come to a standstill before baseball players at a top-flight level displayed the same array of skills – from execrable to middling to exceptional – paraded by White players.

No committed exponent of affirmative action renounces merit or maintains that employers should be bound to employ unqualified applicants, or that measuring rods should be lowered in order to satisfy affirmative action goals. Still, we do argue that the regulations should be similar for Blacks as they have consistently been for Whites. Principles need not be raised out of all proportion when measuring Black applicants. Merit need not be thrown up in a novel way to render it harder to bring discrimination to an end. Non-discrimination suggests applying the same benchmarks to each individual regardless of race. If such benchmarks are high, let them continue to be high. However, they should not be raised as a reciprocation to affirmative action.

On condition that Jackie Robinson had hit .230 or fielded his position inconsistently, he would not have succeeded in the major leagues. Yet, in that time-space, White players hitting .230 or fielding their positions inconsistently were employed. Merit is substantive, but when higher measuring gauges exist for Blacks and bear no relation to Whites, that's known as discrimination.

Affirmative action is a way of bringing such discrimination to a close. It does not run counter to high standards, but it does run counter to double standards. In addition, it does accept that employers, who have, for time and a day, discriminated in the process of building a workforce by using criteria extraneous to merit, cannot be depended on all of a sudden to end such social mores without some prompting. Goals and timetables reflect such a prompting, and they are fair.

There is also a danger in them, since, although they are designed to be brief remedies to end the social mores of discrimination, there is the likelihood of them being transformed into perpetual quotas that normalize discrimination. Committed exponents of affirmative action accept that danger and are alive to it. However, the fact of there being a danger does not legitimize casting the remedy aside (Glasser,1988).

THE INTERNALIZATION OF INFERIORITY

The outstandingly inconsistent counter-arguments of affirmative action remedies claim that such remedies undermine Blacks themselves and impede their economic progression. This pitch takes various forms.

For instance, Charles Murray (1984) claimed that affirmative action remedies, which he termed "preferential treatment", perpetuate a thought process of inferiority between Blacks. This thought process, he implied, originates from the feeling by numerous Blacks that they obtained their jobs not through dint of their own merit but for the simple reason that they were Black, and additionally, from the personal shortfalls that were the product of being catapulted into positions for which they lacked the paper documentation.

The second point is insubstantial and of little value (Glasser,1988). Achievement undoubtedly begets confidence, and failure, in particular revisited failure, just as undoubtedly shatters confidence. But not a solitary human being advocates placing people in stations for which they lack the paper documentation. Also, no one is prepared to give people employment they cannot do. Provided that that is occurring as a consequence of affirmative action, it ultimately must stop. But catapulting people into employment for which they lack the necessary credentials is not an essential ingredient of affirmative action, nor can it be thought of as a phenomenon restricted to affirmative action (Glasser,1988).

Political support has eternally been a method for placing unqualified individuals in prominent jobs. Relationships between people and business connections are also important. In my experience, the phrase "It's not what you know, it's who you know" resonated as an expression of life as it is lived in reality, involving unwelcome as well as welcome experiences, as distinct from a fictional world. This reality clearly troubled those who were, by that social process, filtered out of certain life chances, but one never assumed that the recipients of such networks spent many restless nights in a blind panic about it.

There is no doubting the fact that, where affirmative action employment goals are satisfied in unsophisticated and cobbled-together ways, the recipients of those employment goals may well consider whether they were employed on their own unique qualities. More often than not, however, minority applicants will think, as we all do, that they are competent people who, if exposed to a fair prospect, will be able to measure up to the required standard. Also, they will comprehend affirmative action goals as indispensable to giving them a fighting chance, or in Philip Green's words (1981), "to force their prospective employers to recognize and reward their abilities", (p.80), quoted in Glasser,1988:354). Despite everything, most Blacks know perfectly well, as do most Whites, that jobs routinely rest on who you are friends with and on what your status level is as contrasted with natural abilities. As Green's work indicates:

> Do all those corporate directors, bankers, etc., who got their jobs for extraneous reasons – first, because they were somebody's son, second, because they were male, third, because they were Protestant and fourth,

because they were white – feel demeaned thereby? It would be interesting to ask them – or to ask the same question of those doctors who managed to get into good medical schools because there were quotas keeping out Jews, the skilled tradesmen who were admitted to the union because two members of their family recommended them, and so on. Clearly implicit in this standard critique of affirmative action is a notion that whereas it's never painful to be rewarded because you are in the majority, or the established elite, it's always painful to be rewarded because you're in the minority, or a marginal group (p.79) cited in Glasser,1988:354).

A second pitch of counter-argument suggests that Black economic advancement cannot be formulated through legal channels and that the attempt to do so via the enforcement of affirmative action objectives actually reinforces the conceptual picture among Blacks that mastery and diligence aren't foremost and that their poor state of progress is attributed to society.

Thomas Sowell (1984), an economist who is a Black group member, has been largely associated with this view:

Is it possible to din into the heads of a whole generation that their problems are all other people's fault; that the world owes them an enormous debt; that everything they have yet to achieve is an injustice; that violence is excusable when the world is flawed – and yet expect it all to have no effect on attitudes? Is the arduous process of acquiring skills and discipline supposed to be endured for years by people who are told, by word and deed, that skills are not the real issue? (sec.B, p.4, col.4) (cited in Glasser, 1988:354).

Thomas Sowell quite likes castigating liberals for their inattention to underpin their rhetorical contentions with concrete evidence, but he has offered no evidence to underpin his own rhetoric. No committed exponents of affirmative action even suggest that mastery and industriousness are not foremost, nor does there appear to be any evidence that shows that Blacks' volition to devote themselves to "the arduous process of acquiring skills" has been undermined by affirmative action remedies. To be precise, I would counterclaim that the reverse is the case (Glasser,1988:354). Through dismantling the discriminatory blockages to employment, affirmative action remedies foster the expansion of skills.

There was no disputing Sowell when he declared that skills will face a development shortfall if people are told, by word and deed, that skills are not the actual concern of the day. The reality of racial discrimination exacted such a development. It urged Blacks, by actions and words, that whatever skills they developed, however hard they worked, life-chance openings would not follow and certain jobs would simply be unattainable. By itself, discrimination, not the drive to end discrimination, accounted for depriving ambition of oxygen and obliterating hope. The absolute certainty of being denied access to employment, not the logic of inclusion, rendered hard work a straw man.

Affirmative action programs should certainly not be put into practice in an approach that lowers standards or the value of skills. The amount to which some affirmative action plans have relegated the value of skills, their just deserts ought only to be criticism. However, the mental image of affirmative action per se cannot be diminished by alluding to those instances in which it has failed to function to its strengths, or where it has abrogated some of the standards that justified it from the very outset.

Affirmative action programs, correctly formulated and implemented, lead themselves to establishing opportunities for the expansion of skills, opportunities once closed either by crude racial discrimination or by the social mores that thrived in a racist society.

Sowell also wallowed in the inability of affirmative action plans to service every economic problem Blacks faced. He advocated that affirmative action has a dismal record in establishing opportunities for the most impoverished Black Americans and inferred that it should henceforth be abandoned:

> The truly disadvantaged – those with little education or job experience, or from broken families – have fallen even further behind during the

era of affirmative action. As in other countries, the benefits of preferential programs go disproportionately to those already more fortunate. It may help a black professor get an endowed chair, but it is counter-productive for the black teenager trying to get a job ....

This is not unique to the United States. A number of studies of preferential programs for untouchables in India have concluded that little or no benefit actually accrues to these poverty-stricken people. Yet it is precisely the poor untouchable who suffers from the backlash against the great privileges he is thought to be enjoying. Violence against untouchables doubled in less than a decade during the 1970s, amid rising denunciations of preferential policies on their behalf. (sec. B, p.4 col. 4) (quoted in Glasser,1988:355).

However, provided that affirmative action plans cannot service the problems of impoverished education and institutionalized destitution, that does not suggest they should be rubbished. To be sure, not one exponent of affirmative action has argued that it is a universal medicine or a cure for the whole bundle of racial and economic woes we face. Affirmative action is only a means of penetrating a reified structure of inequality and of providing people, who have abidingly been disadvantaged by that structure, a temporary helping hand.

What is more, with the amount to which Black children growing up need to be aware that opportunities are accessible and that industry matters, it is vital to have tangible examples. (Glasser,1988). To draw on the Jackie Robinson example once again, the practice of racial exclusion, extant in baseball prior to 1947, was enforced partly by visceral constraints: most Black children at different stages of development knew that, regardless of what they did, any ambition they harboured of becoming a major league baseball player would not be realized. They could see that there were no Black faces. When Robinson broke that mould and others succeeded him, perceptions changed and prospects became brighter. An argument that exponents of White baseball used to trot out is that these jobs lacked Black applicants. Predominantly, they were not wrong. Why on earth should they have made an application when rejection was guaranteed? However, once opportunities were rolled out, and once the results of these opportunities became apparent, ambition was fortified and hope renewed (Glasser,1988).

It beggars belief that the same isn't true of additional jobs in additional spheres of economic activity. Sowell decried the achievement of a Black professor securing a post to an endowed chair as certain as to suggest that that official position of authority had no correlation to the ambitions and aspirations of poor Black families. He had plumbed the depths of depravity. Affirmative action is today an unlikely gateway to opportunities for the cash-strapped, the unrefined and the inexpert. However, it will change the way in which they see the world, and it will symbolize, by theory and practice, that hard work has its rewards and that skills really do matter. Affirmative action plans may not directly solve every problem. However, in the absence of such plans, the cruelly crushing influence of discrimination will persist.

In the above, I have attempted to show that there is moral reasoning behind the concept of affirmative action.

As I have already mentioned, affirmative action remedies must be temporary, must not lead to diminishing the value of skills, and must not be managed in a way that sees standards fall or institutionalizes, however inadvertently, unfair practices. It is hard to believe that a moral general agreement behind these principles cannot be recovered (Glasser,1988).

The challenges facing Black aspiration

The aftermath of slavery and a protracted period of legal discrimination still plagues our society and largely limits the life chances of a significant number of Black children. Justice on a daily round requires that those of us falling short of being affected by the disadvantages caused by historic and present-day racial discrimination – who may indeed have gained from it – do not eschew the struggle to establish reasonable remedies for people who do. That said, white liberal credence for such remedies, subsuming affirmative action, has mostly evaporated since the apogee of the civil rights movement, now approaching six or seven decades ago. There is a danger of Blacks becoming alienated again, and this remains a principal moral concern in American social life. Affirmative action hardly qualifies as the single component of this moral concern, but it has emerged as a major dividing line characteristic for it. One way or another, the moral concern must regain its general accord and its high priority on our social to-do list, until the various shades in our complexions stop being a marker for where we live, what school we attend, where we work, and whether we are extended favourable treatment (Glasser,1988).

It seems important to clarify the main thrust of this text on affirmative action, and that is that the influence of social institutions on Black aspiration is such that Black and minority ethnic groups are experiencing direct and indirect racism through their interaction with social institutions, on complex levels, and the influence on Black aspiration is catastrophic. As Glasser (1988) indicates, the influence deprives ambition of the oxygen Black aspiration needs and destroys hope. There are exceptions to this general aphorism but scarcely every White individual subscribes to and agrees with racist ideology; however, for satisfactory change not to have taken place, this suggests that the majority are consciously or unconsciously card-carrying believers of racist ideology, and the influence of this on Black aspiration is devastating and disastrous. Social institutions or White society are not constructive towards Black aspiration but destructive. Put slightly differently, the influence of social institutions on Black aspiration is a toxic meld. And affirmative action is compensation for the disadvantage of slavery so minority ethnic groups would not benefit. Although affirmative action is inadequate compensation for slavery, Glasser (1988) avoids the very mention of reparations. What is to say that the two forms of compensation cannot complement and supplement one another?

While there are some exceptions to the rule, Blacks tend to have lower aspirational expectations of career-level positions for several reasons: as a result of the lack of role models engaged in prosecuting certain jobs; as a result of the deliberate and unthinking attempt to keep Black people from obtaining educational and occupational opportunities; as a result of the influence social institutions have on Black individual and collective thought patterns, and as a result of labour market glass ceilings which affect members of minority groups. Any other reading would not speak to the Black experience.

The evidence of blighted Black aspiration is seen, for example, in the scarcity of Black leaders in this country and in the formation of a Black underclass where jobless Blacks outnumber their majority ethnic counterparts. The limits placed on Black academic careers is something I can vouch for (see Chapter Four), and in this connection, the system of rule down the White male line has a penchant for recruiting and supporting those like themselves, without a care for diversity, and are nothing other than highly suspect and wholly disreputable. A further example is that there are few Black football managers in this country, even though there are many successful Black football players.

Oxbridge have tended to exclude Blacks because they know perfectly well that Oxbridge credentials do not fail to impress prospective employers and have the potential to take the holder of such awards from opportunity to opportunity, opening doors where such gateways would otherwise be closed. Most of the old established universities, in my experience, follow Oxbridge's lead because they also know that employers source recruitment of personnel from universities of their calibre. Further evidence of blighted Black aspiration can be seen in the two-tier university system of new and old institutions and, of course, the only institutions that tend to welcome Black and minority ethnic groups are the new universities, where such social categories are concentrated. Notwithstanding other reasons, this is why I argue that higher education functions to maintain the status quo. It is all tantamount to the fact that Whites, the length and breadth of the country, are mobilized to Enoch Powell's prescient warning and join forces in complex ways to hinder, impede and stop Blacks and minorities from achieving positions of influence and power. Moreover, underlying this fact is that Whites do not countenance being told what to do by a person of colour. Since the colour of knowledge and power is predominantly White, those aiming to present a different picture, it would seem, are destined to have barriers erected and racism heaped upon them, and even persecuted for daring to tell the truth which, according to Plato (2007), no self-respecting individual has the right to be offended by.

Meanwhile, affirmative action may never happen in Britain, as a means of penetrating a reified structure of inequality and of providing people, who have abidingly been disadvantaged by that structure, with a temporary helping hand. History has had a bearing on the contemporary state of modern Britain and dead ideas continue to grip the minds of a nation and its people, consistently dealing Black people a bad hand, dealt because of anachronistic and current relations. Blacks in Britain today are a reminder to Whites of empire and their indebtedness, and because compensation may never be brokered for slavery and the slave trade, and because oppression continues unabated, Blacks are, in so many ways, at their mercy, to do with as they please because of being seen as a so-called threat and a problem.

For centuries, Whites have been a threat to Black lives and Black aspiration. Racist murders, racist attacks and blighted lives are testament here. We need only look to history to see why Whites ought to play a fairer game and affirmative action remedies would be a step in that direction. That the past is inextricably linked to the present cannot be denied and is at the root of problems concerning 'race'. That the British are a backward-looking people suggests that conflict may always be with us because the historical memory of most White Brits evokes not sorrow and contrition at human misery, suffering, and torment, but all-consuming pride, and this is where the problem lies, suggesting that they will never get behind reparations and what bodes ill, and seems in store, is more of the same unfavourable treatment rather than change and reform.

Historically, the government set the *Zeitgeist* for contemporary Britain; for example, the construction of the 'race/immigration equals problem' theme, failing African-Caribbean and South Asian people outright and doing them no favours, and we continue to live under the long dark shadow cast over us by the post-war British bipartisan government who set an example for the nation and its people to follow. Consequently, the effects of such an example have a devastating and catastrophic impact on the individual and collective minority psyche and are still being felt today.

Blacks seem to have done little to court this deep-seated anti-Black vibration: 'fear of a Black planet', the relentless drive of the survival strategy of systemic power, accounts for why Black people receive poor treatment through social institutions and at the hands of the dominant group. White society has to develop and grow a considerable amount more before Black aspiration is to truly realize anywhere near its full potential. We have made a substantial amount of progress, but there remains a significant distance to traverse. Better holding true to the ways we are human may lead to mutual respect, unity and understanding.

There's a world of difference between this being theory and being practice in objective reality. The cynic may argue that the above statement is all very well in theory, but in practice, it is unrealistic and will not work. However, if we take it that the universe inclines towards justice, it is consistent with and coherent to the human condition and searches for something better which we can all have a share in. On paper, at least, it is quite possible that if we all embrace the ways in which we are all similar, it may lead to a better world.

Black aspiration and the vision that belongs to it long for dominant mainstream abandonment of injustice, inequality, inhumanity and oppression. For Martin Luther King, Jr., the universe inclines towards justice and this belief is echoed and confirmed in the British commitment to fair play, but it is the responsibility of us all to ensure that this pressing concern is done and seen to be done in relation to national and international race relations. For Britain to work for everyone and everybody would seem to mean hard-won minority acceptance, on the one hand, though it may for a moment destabilize society which rests on inequality, and on the other hand, it would require a seismic shift in British political culture, and would, therefore, be a crucial starting point towards a fairer, more inclusive society.

Chapter 10: Conclusion

As I write, 6 June 2019, the world commemorates the 75th Anniversary of the D-Day landings in Normandy. What is striking about all of this is that we must never forget the scale of sacrifice of the British and their allies in the name of liberty, democracy and peace, but on an equally sombre note, I doubt whether these great ideals have been perfectly realized by Britain's Black and minority communities despite their contribution in both world wars. The ability of global sentient beings has been desensitized and anaesthetized for centuries to the wonders of African genius; so why should this not surprise us? The issue in this country is that White people in prominent positions are busily engaged in making White Brits as great as they possibly can be while tending to undermine, subjugate and marginalize the rest.

If an estimated £24 billion is being lost to the UK economy per annum because Black and minority group individuals are being stymied from progression in the workplace simply because their skin colour does not correlate, this merely shows the scale of the problem Black aspiration is confronted with. Social institutions make up society and they reflect its structure; thus, social institutions need to be overhauled and made more accountable to a newly modernized government concerning how and what they are doing in the direction of making their organisation a colour-blind zone in the recruitment and career progression of Black and minority ethnic individuals. Given that successive governments have not done anything vaguely resembling this demonstrates that there is no political will and no political capital to be gained from it by UK political parties.

The White British public are the sticking point here because they are inclined not to extend a mandate to the party with such a political will. The British government is shaped by vote-winning and not vote-losing policies. The British government are the people's representatives and if the people articulate change, such as in the above, and in sufficient numbers, the government would be urged to implement change, but until such time, the White electorate are the sticking point as policies of this colour are vote-losers. This is the case because it appears to threaten White social privilege which is fiercely contested.

To eliminate institutional racism, by which all major organisations are characterized, and for the British economy to grow by an estimated £24 billion – roughly the same as 1.3 per cent of gross domestic product (GDP) per annum - change has to be enforced across the country by a newly modernized government that reaches into the workings of every social institution making them accountable for matters concerning race, recruitment and career advancement with the effect that it changes the national institutional convention. Black aspiration is indeed 'a different hunger'; however, to consider that there is a dominant group conspiracy to do the man and woman of colour down calls for more soul-searching because it is more complex and problematical than that. Still, the past continues to affect the present and the future of our world. And, so long as White society or social institutions show a reluctance to revise their opinion of Black people and only incline towards thinking the worst, then the status quo will remain unchanged and the wider political conjuncture unaltered.

The frantic despair that gives expression to no change ever occurring can be seen through the view an African-Caribbean organisation in Handsworth is reported to adopt by one of its associates: 'History shows that the whites have never done the blacks any favours. They organise their whole system so that, even when they're doing them good, they're really keeping them down. What reasons can you give me for thinking this will ever change?' (Cashmore and Troyna,1982:29). A perfect example of the above quote is ethnic monitoring for recruitment to educational and occupational opportunities which is purported to be a good development for Black people but really is just another way of keeping the numbers of Blacks in certain positions down. Ethnic monitoring should be scrapped as it is masquerading with positive assumptions for Black people when, in fact, what is really happening is that the doors are being left wide open for admissions officers in universities and employers to discriminate, exploit and exclude Black candidates. If institutions and organisations are truly serious about being colour-blind, they should do away with or abandon ethnic monitoring as it only serves the purpose of functioning to maintain the status quo. However, ethnic monitoring to identify the numbers already in post would seem an appropriate way to supplant the practice. To be fortunate enough to be employed is one thing, but to then be passed over for promotion is quite another thing entirely, which correlates to and squares with the Caribbean organisation's view.

The past helped shape the present and the present contorts the past; therefore, some of today's developments may be destined to shape the future. How can the Black man and woman hope for deliverance from the chains and manacles of oppression when racism is enshrined in this country's very laws and deep within the national psyche? While progress and change move at a grindingly piecemeal pace, it is so because the White British obstinately resist change, and, in particular, change in favour of Blacks. Where the survival strategy of systemic power is the end, and racism is the means, it makes clear that the end does not justify the means and thus illustrates the wrong-headedness of racism.

Black people are the consummate antithesis of 'free at last' since justice has not rained down like a mighty torrential flood of cascading waters and come to our rescue; its action sipping into every institution and organisation; into every urban and rural district, and into the seat of the emotions of every White man and woman. The future is firmly in the province of the dominant group, yet, among that group's weaknesses and failings appear to be the inability to parade the best interests of Black people at heart, which, as sure as eggs is eggs, suggests that the future bodes ill for Blacks in Britain today.

A vitally important strand which this conclusion should not be without, and if I am to learn anything from my experience, is that British social institutions and organisations function to maintain and perpetuate the status quo, and, in so doing, the sectors I have examined tend to commit the cardinal sin of conscious or unconscious bias, or direct or indirect discrimination against people of colour. How White society keep Black and minority people at the bottom rung of the social hierarchy can be witnessed here and in various stages of this study. The purpose of this book has been to raise awareness of the power relations between and across groups and how this affects Black aspiration which is situated and positioned within this complex dynamic.

Although the universe inclines towards justice, when we unpack justice, we discover that, according to Plato, there will never be, or we can never hope there to ever be, a state of true justice on earth; that says an awful lot about whether reparations will one day become reality and whether discrimination, exploitation and exclusion will ever stop. But this does not mean that society cannot evolve and grow because the current conjuncture cannot be any farther removed from a satisfactory state of evolution or development – an idea the dominant group opposes and negates, and is not full square behind. On the other hand, the avoidance of extremes and justice "is the surest way to the highest human happiness" (Plato,2007:366).

The simple truth and direct consequence of the influence of social institutions on Black aspiration is akin to the White policeman's knee on the neck of a Black individual and it suggests and begs the question that, for over 400 years, the catalogue of oppression has seen very little in the way of progress and change and is quite simply because all of society's institutions are contributory determinant factors - as we have attempted to illustrate in this book - in exerting pressure through the action of their processes and procedures. So then, when will White society get their knee off the neck of Black people? Despite their contribution to civilization and stellar achievements in various fields of endeavour, minority groups are threatened, yet, Whites feel that Blacks are a 'threat' and a 'problem' and if world populations were not largely Black, we would now be concerned about the global depopulation of Black people. It is worth noting, pointing out and highlighting again that isn't it, once and for all, about time that White society got their knee off our necks? Is society predestined to never learn the lesson that Black Lives Matter also?

What brings the above observation to light is the 25 May 2020 killing of George Floyd where a White American police officer held his knee on the neck of George Floyd for 8 minutes 46 seconds, despite repeated gasps from George Floyd saying that he could not breathe – this was a senseless and merciless killing of a Black man who did not deserve to die. The killing was filmed and news networks circulated it around the world and it came to be known as the killing that shook the world. In the aftermath of the news event, riots in the US city of Minneapolis were sparked and there were demonstrations around the world around Black Lives Matter. This prompted the arrest of the offending police officer and his collaborators who now face criminal proceedings.

As I have already mentioned, in America, it is not unusual for Black males to be killed or brutalized by the police, and notwithstanding the distressing footage of George Floyd's killing and the furore that was stirred, American police killed another Black man who was fleeing from them just days after. What will it take for American police to learn that Black Lives Matter just as much as the White lives that they manage not to harm every single day? In spite of this, some White people claim that George Floyd's killing was not racial. How can they take this position if White people are not subject to police brutality? So, therefore, this contention is seriously flawed, mistaken and in denial of the existence of racism and is indeed a defence mechanism suggesting that the police were only doing their job. Black Lives Matter, and this contention is a deep-seated wish to sweep George Floyd's murder under the carpet. It is shocking to know that despite the facts, White people have no sympathy for Blacks and rate their lives cheaply.

Ultimately, Some White people are incorrigibly cold and heartless and no amount of counterclaim to their view will sway or convince them – just like George Floyd's killer himself - of that very mentality. The US and the UK need to correct and improve their dealings around Black Lives Matter: social inequality, social conditions and social justice all cry out to be addressed and UK ministers need to measure their words rather than laying themselves open to the charge of being socially insensitive. Black Lives Matter, and it has taken over 400 years for this to come to a head and to say enough is enough, and the fact that George Floyd's murder was filmed left no scope for justifying police action. Will the future repeat the past or will change come and usher in a bright new dawn? As repression is the archrival of progress and civilization and makes a mockery of and trivializes Black lives, so it is consequently profoundly important to understand that the statement Black Lives Matter needs to be stated and restated whereas the status of White lives is implicitly and explicitly stated from day-to-day, and so, I need not say that the lives of all members of humanity matter, although, of course, they do.

Black Lives Matter seems to mean equal treatment and that it's time to take a stand against a deeply racist society, whereas the straightforward backlash is the proposition White lives matter which is an implicit and explicit given that goes without saying; e.g., Whites experience preferment over Blacks and are regarded as superior to Blacks, therefore, this proposition need not be made as freedom, justice and equality are not experienced in the same ways by Whites and Blacks alike. Again, because Black life is rated cheaply and White life held dear, this is why we have the statement, Black Lives Matter. Also, the assertion White lives matter diametrically opposes and shows intolerance towards repeated cries of Black Lives Matter and should be roundly condemned as right-wing political extremism at work. Furthermore, the proposal that White lives matter attempts to steal the thunder and upstage demonstrations and protests around Black Lives Matter.

Finally, it seems the easiest and basest instinct is to become Black racists, since ahead of us rest generations of White expertise in the material area. Considering our march forward day after day, week after week, month after month, year after year and decade after decade, the blackest thing about the interaction between the Blacks and the Whites need not necessarily be the Black people. In this Chapter, among other things, I have sought to stress the unifying quality of Black and White people as human beings. Black people in their interaction with Whites have fought for everything that is honourable and virtuous and human. Racism is an insanity, an outrage to humanity, and a contravention of man, and this should be observed and recognized by Blacks and Whites consistently. It is worth noting that there can be no finer nor nobler ideal goal that is humanly imaginable - in a global system of capitalist economic relations - than for humanity to work together, struggle together, and strive together, in this enlightened and technologically advanced twenty-first century period, in the interests of peace, understanding and unity.

Bibliography

- Abercrombie, N, Hill, and Turner, B.S (1988) Dictionary of Sociology, 2nd Edn, Penguin Books, London.

- Abercrombie, N and Warde, A et al. (2000) Contemporary British Society, 3rd Edn, Polity Press, Cambridge.

- Adams, R and Bengtsson, (2017) 'Oxbridge still failing Black British pupils', The Guardian, London.

- Adebayo, D (2018) 'Call a spade a spade', The Voice Newspaper, April 19-25, London.

- Anwar, M (1994) Race and Elections: The Participation of Minorities in Politics, Centre for Research in Ethnic Relations, Coventry.

- Armor, D. J (1988) 'School Busing: A Time for Change' in P.A. Katz, and Taylor, D. A. Eliminating Racism: Profiles in Controversy, Plenum Press, London.

- Aronson, E and Gonzalez, A (1988) 'Desegregation, Jigsaw, and the Mexican-American Experience', in P.A. Katz, and Taylor, D.A, Eliminating Racism: Profiles in Controversy, Plenum Press, London.

- Bagilhole, B (1997) Equal Opportunities and Social Policy, Longman, London.

- Barker, M (1981) The New Racism, Junction, London.

- Bell, J (1999) Doing Your Research Project: A guide for first-time researchers in education and social science 3rd Edn, Open University Press, Buckingham.

- Berthoud, R (1999) Young Caribbean men and the Labour Market: A comparison with other ethnic groups, Joseph Rowntree Foundation, York.

Bibliography

- Bhavnani, R, Mirza, H.S, Meetoo, V (2005) Tackling the roots of racism: Lessons for success, The Polity Press, Bristol.

- Bilton, T, Bonnet, K, Jones, P, Stanworth, M Sheard, K, Webster, A, Introductory Sociology, 2nd Edn, Macmillan Education LTD, London.

- Bird, (1996) Black Students and Higher Education: Rhetorics and Realities, The Society for Research into Higher Education, Open University Press, Buckingham.

- Bobo, L (1988) 'Group Conflict, Prejudice and the Paradox of Contemporary Racial Attitudes' in P.A. Katz and D.A. Taylor, Eliminating Racism: Profiles in Controversy, Plenum Press, London.

- Boffey, D (2018) 'Colonialism Belgium starts to address the legacy of its 1958 Congolese 'human zoo', The Guardian, April 16, London.

- Bonechi, C E. (2010) Art and History: EGYPT 5000 Years of Civilization, Centro Stampa Editonale Bonechi, Sesto Fiorentino, Italy.

- Booth, R and Mohdin, A (2018) 'Racism in Britain: the stark truth uncovered', The Guardian, 3 December, London.

- Bourne, J and Sivanandan, A (1980) 'Cheerleaders and ombudsmen: the sociology of race relations in Britain', Race and Class xxi 4 :331-351.

- Brand, R (2014) REVOLUTION, Century, London.

- Brewer, M.D and Miller, N (1988) 'Contact and Cooperation: When do they work?' In P.A. Katz and D.A. Taylor, Eliminating Racism: Profiles in Controversy, Plenum Press, London.

- Briscoe, C (2006) Ugly: The true story of a loveless childhood, Hodder and Stoughton, London.

- Bubeula-Dodd, J (1997) Nubian Jak's Book of World Facts Volume 1 : The Ultimate Guide to Black Entertainment History and Achievement, Nu Jak Media Publishing, London.

- Buckingham, A (1999) 'Is there an underclass in Britain?' British Journal of Sociology, vol.50 No.1 pp49-75.

- Butler, D (2018) 'Check your legal status', The Voice, April19-25, London.

- Campbell, E (2015) 'Time to Move on', The Weekly Gleaner, October 8-14 London.

- Campbell, E and Pears, E (2015) 'Cameron Arrives In Jamaica To Controversy', The Voice newspaper, October 1 – 7, London.

- Campbell, E et al. (2018) Windrush 70 and Beyond: Intergenerational Reflections, Kingsway Project.
- Carter, J, Fenton, S and Modood, T (1999) Ethnicity and Employment in Higher Education, Policy Studies Institute, London.
- Cashmore, E, E (1988) Dictionary of Race and Ethnic Relations, 2nd Edn, Routledge, London.
- Cashmore, E and Troyna, B (1990) Introduction to Race Relations, 2nd Edn, The Falmer Press, London.
- Cashmore, E, Troyna, B (1982) 'Black Youth in Crisis', in Cashmore, E and Troyna, B, (eds), Black youth in Crisis, George Allen and Unwin, London.
- Castles, S and Kosack, G (1985) Immigrant Workers and Class structure in Western Europe, 2rd Edn, Oxford University Press, Oxford.
- Cheung, S.Y and Heath, A.F (2007) 'Nice Work if you can get it: Ethnic Penalties in Great Britain' in A. F. Heath and S. Y Cheung Unequal Chances: ethnic minorities in Western Labour markets, (eds), Oxford University Press, Oxford.
- Clark, K and Drinkwater, S (2007) Ethnic minorities in the labour market: Dynamics and diversity, Policy Press, Bristol.
- Coard, B (1971) How the West Indian child is made Educationally sub-normal in the British system, New Beacon Books Ltd, London.
- Cohen, C. J (2016) 'Blackman in the White House Midwifing Trump: Race, neoliberalism and the Obama legacy', TLS, December 23, London.
- Cohen, P and Gardner, C (1982) It ain't half racist, mum: Fighting racism in the media, Comedia Publishing Group, London.
- Cook, Stuart W. (1988) 'The 1954 Social Science Statement and School Desegregation: A reply to Gerard' in P.A. Katz and D.A. Taylor, Eliminating Racism: Profiles in Controversy, Plenum Press, London.
- Cottle, S (2000) 'Media Research and Ethnic minorities: Mapping the field', in S Cottle, Ethnic Minorities and the Media, Open University Press, Buckingham.
- Creasey, S (2016) 'Is unconscious bias holding your pupils back?' TES 19 February, TES Global LTD, London.
- Grerar, P and Gentleman, A (2018) 'UK Citizenship for Windrush generation', The Guardian, April 24, London.
- Crow, H. (2007) The Memoirs of Captain Hugh Crow, Bodleian Library, Oxford.

- Curran, J, Ecclestone, J, Oakley, G and Richardson, A (1986) Bending Reality: The State of the Media, Pluto Press, London.

- d' Ancona, M (2018) 'Let's be honest about what's really driving Brexit: bigotry, The Guardian, 3 December, London.

- d' Ancona, M (2018) 'Enoch Powell's hateful tricks are still with us', The Guardian, April 16, London.

- Darwin, C (2014) On the Origins of Species By means of Natural Selection, Arcturus, London.

- Degraft-johnson, J, C (1986) African Glory: The Story of Vanished Negro Civilizations, Black Classic Press, Baltimore.

- Dennis, N, Erdos, G, Al-Shahi, A (2000) Racist Murder and Pressure Group Politics: The Macpherson Report and the Police, Institute for the Study of Civil Society, London.

- Denscombe, M (2003) The Good Research Guide, 2nd edn, Open University Press, Maidenhead.

- Devine, F (1997) Social Class in America and Britain, Edinburgh University Press, Edinburgh.

- Devlin, H (2018) 'Cheddar man had dark skin and blue eyes, DNA tests reveal', The Guardian, 7 February, London.

- Devlin, H (2018) 'Unconscious bias: Psychological tool to tackle a taboo', The Guardian, 3 December, London.

- Diop, C A. (1974) The African Origin of Civilization Myth or Reality, Lawrence Hill Books, Illinois.

- Downing, J and Husband, C (2005) Representing 'Race', Racisms Ethnicities and Media, Sage, London.

- Du Bois, W.E.B (1998) The Souls of Black Folk and Related Readings, McDougal Littel, Evanston, Illinois, Boston.

- Eddo-Lodge, R (2017) Why I'm no longer talking to White people about Race, Bloomsbury Circus, London.

- Elam, A M. (1989) The Status of Blacks in Higher Education, National Association for Equal Opportunity in Higher Education Research Institute Publication, London.

- Ellison, J (2018) 'Revelatory history of the League Against Imperialism', Morning Star, April 30, London.

- Torrington, A, Mclean, R Osborne, V, Grosvenor, L (2007) Equiano: Enslavement, Resistance and abolition, The Equiano Society and B'ham Museums and Art Gallery.

- Ericson, R, Baranek, P Chan, J (1997) 'Visualizing the news, in A Giddens (ed) Sociology: Introductory Readings, Polity Press, Cornwall.

- Evaristo, B (2017) 'Check Your Privilege: A Provocative argument about race relations', The Times Literary Supplement (TLS), July 7, London.

- Field, F (1990) Britain's Underclass: Countering The Growth, in C Murray, The Emerging British Underclass, IEA Health and Welfare Unit, London.

- Finch, C.S (1999) Echoes of the Old Darkland: Themes From the African Eden, Khenti, Inc., Georgia

- Finch, C S. (2007) The Star of Deep Beginnings: The Genesis of African Science And Technology, Khenti, Inc., Georgia.

- Foot, P (1964) The Rise of Enoch Powell, Cornmarket Press, London.

- Foster, P (1990) Policy and Practice in Multicultural and Anti-Racist Education: A case study of a multi-ethnic comprehensive school, Routledge, London.

- Foster, P, Gomm, R and Hammersley, M (1996) Constructing Educational Inequality: An Assessment of Research on School Processes, Falmer Press, London.

- Fryer, P (1993) Aspects of British Black History, Index Books, London.

- Fryer, P (1984) Staying Power: The History of Black People in Britain, Pluto Press, London.

- Fuller, M (1982) 'Young, Female and Black', in E Cashmore and B Troyna, (eds) Black Youth in Crisis, George Allen & Unwin, London.

- Gamble, A (1990) Britain in Decline: Economic Policy, Political Strategy And The British State, 3rd Edn, Macmillan, Basingstoke and London.

- Gayle, D and Marsh, S (2018) 'Inherent Racism: From dating sites to mental healthcare, inequity is rife', The Guardian, 3 December, London.

- Gentleman, A (2018) 'What took so long? Rudd and May try to distance themselves from policy', The Guardian, April 24, London.

- Gentleman, A (2018) 'Talks rejected on 'shameful' treatment of Windrush generation', The Guardian, 16 April, London.
- Geraghty, C (1997) 'The Appeal of Soap Opera' in A Giddens (ed) Sociology: Introductory Readings, Polity Press, Cornwall.
- Gerard, Harold B. (1988) 'School Desegregation: The Social Science role', P.A. in Katz and D.A. Taylor, Eliminating Racism: Profiles in Controversy, Plenum Press, London.
- Gibson, A. and Barrow, J (1986) The Unequal Struggle, Unwin Brothers, London.
- Giddens, A (1997) Sociology: Introductory Readings, Polity Press, Cambridge.
- Gillborn, D (1990) 'Race' Ethnicity and Education: Teaching And Learning in Multi-Ethnic Schools, Routledge, Falmer, London.
- Gilroy, P (2002) There Ain't No Black in the Union Jack, Routledge Classics, London.
- Glasser, I (1988) Affirmative Action and the Legacy of Racial Injustice, in P. A. Katz and D.A. Taylor, Eliminating Racism: Profiles in Controversy, Plenum Press, London.
- Goodhart, D (2014) The British Dream: Successes and Failures of Post-war Immigration, Atlantic Books, London.
- Gordon, P and Rosenberg, D (1989) Daily Racism: The Press and Black People in Britain, The Runnymede Trust, London.
- Green, D. G, (1990) Foreword in C Murray, The Emerging British Underclass, IEA Health and Welfare Unit, London.
- Grint, K (2000) Work and Society: A Reader, Polity Press, Cambridge.
- Hall, S, Critcher, C, Jefferson, T, Clarke, J and Roberts, B (2013) Policing the Crisis mugging, the state and law and order, 35th Anniversary Edition, Palgrave Macmillan, Hampshire.
- Haley, A (2007) The Autobiography of Malcolm X, Penguin Books, London.
- Harris, J (2018) 'Forcing Schools to abandon inclusion leaves us all poorer', The Guardian, April 16, London.
- Hartmann, P and Husband, C (1974) Racism and the Mass Media, Rowman and Littlefield, Totowa, New Jersey.
- Hawking, S (2016) A Brief History of Time: From the Big Bang To Black Holes, Bantam Books, London.

- Willis D Hawley and mark A. Smylie (1988) 'The Contribution of School Desegregation to Academic Achievement and Racial Integration', in P. A. Katz and D. A. Taylor Eliminating Racism: Profiles in Controversy, Plenum Press, London.

- Heath, A, F. (2007) 'Cross-national Patterns and Processes of Ethnic Disadvantage' in A. F. Heath and S. Y. Cheung, Unequal Chances: Ethnic Minorities in Western Labour Markets, Oxford University Press, Oxford.

- Heath, A. F. and Cheung, S.Y. (2007) 'The Comparative Study of Ethnic Minority Disadvantage' in A. F. Heath and S. Y. Cheung, Unequal Chances: Ethnic Minorities in Western Labour Markets, Oxford University Press, Oxford.

- Hesse, B (2004) 'Discourse on Institutional Racism, the genealogy of a concept', in I Law et al. Institutional Racism in Higher Education, Trentham Books, Stoke on Trent.

- Hirsch, A (2018) 'Bias is alive and well. Now we have proof, we need to act', The Guardian, 3 December, London.

- H.M.S.O. (2006) Social Trends, 36. London.

- Holt, J (1984) How Children Fail, Penguin Books, London.

- Housee, S (2018) Speaking Out Against Racism in the University Space, UCL Institute of Education Press, London.

- Hudson, R and Williams, M (1995) Divided Britain, 2nd edn, Wiley, Chichester.

- Humphry, D and John, G (1971) Because They're Black, Harmondsworth, Penguin.

- Husband, C (2000) 'Media and the Public Sphere in Multi-Ethnic Societies' in S Cottle, Ethnic minorities and the Media, Open University Press, Buckingham.

- Jaffer, N (2017) 'Notion Within a Nation: On Britishness and Islam', The Times Literary Supplement (TLS) September 15, London.

- Jones, J. M (1988) 'Racism in Black and White: A Bicultural Model of Reaction and Evolution' in P. A. Katz and D.A. Taylor, Eliminating Racism Profiles in Controversy, Plenum Press, London.

- Jones, O (2016) 'Broken Britain', in O Jones, Chavs: The Demonization of the Working Class, Verso, London.

- Jones, O (2015) The Establishment: And how they get away with it, Penguin Books, London.

- Joshi, S. and Carter, B (1984) 'The role of Labour in the creation of a racist Britain', Race and class xxv, 3: 53-70.
- Kavanagh, D (1990) Thatcherism and British Politics: The End of Consensus? 2nd Edn, Oxford University Press, Oxford.
- Lacey, C (1988) Foreword, in M Mac an Ghaill, Young, Gifted and Black, Open University Press, Milton Keynes.
- Lammy, D (2011) Out of the Ashes: Britain After the Riots, Guardian Books, London.
- Law, I (2002) Race in the News, Palgrave, Hampshire
- Law, I, Phillips, D, Turney, L (2004) Institutional Racism in Higher Education, Trentham Books, Stoke on Trent.
- Layton-Henry, Z (1984) The Politics of Race in Britain, Unwin, London.
- Lazenby, P (2018) 'Avoiding healthcare, avoiding travel: the black Britons terrified of deportations', Morning Star, April 30, London.
- Lee, D and Newby, H (1989) The Problem of Sociology, Unwin Hyman, London.
- Leigh, D. (2018) 'It's the moment we lost trust in the system', The Guardian, April 16, London.
- Levy, S, Hafner, K, Rogers, A (1997) 'The Internet and Global Communications', in A Giddens (ed) Sociology: Introductory Readings, Polity Press, Cornwall.
- Lister, R (1990) 'Concepts of Poverty', Social Studies review 6(5) May.
- Livingstone, D. W (1998) The Education-jobs Gap: Underemployment or Economic Democracy.
- Louise, E (2018) 'Government Forcing Us Out', The Voice, April 19-25, London.
- Lowi, T.J and Mink, G (1998) Losing Ground, Gaining Power, in C Murray Required Reading Sociology's Most Influential Books (ed) D Clawson, Amerst: University of Massachusetts Press.
- Luthra, M (1997) Britain's Black Population: Social Change, Public policy and Agenda, Arena, Aldershot.
- Mac an Ghaill, M (1988) Young, Gifted and Black, Open University Press, Milton Keynes.
- Mac an Ghaill, M (1998) The Making of Men: Masculinities, Sexualities and Schooling, Open University Press, Buckingham.

- Mackie, L (2001) The Great Marcus Garvey, Hansib, London.
- Mandela, N (1995) Long Walk to Freedom, Abacus, London.
- Mandela, N (2010) Conversations with Myself, Macmillan, London.
- Marx, F (2018) 'What is Fascism', Morning Star, April 30, London.
- Massey, G (2007) A Book of the Beginnings, Volume 1, A & B Publishers Group, Brooklyn, New York.
- Massey, G (2007) A Book of the Beginnings, Volume II, A & B Publishers Group, Brooklyn, New York.
- McLuhan, M (2001) Understanding Media, Routledge Classics, London.
- McNeill, P (1990) Research Methods, 2nd edn, Routledge, London.
- Miles, R (1993) Racism after 'race relations', Routledge, London.
- Miles, R and Brown, B (2003) Racism, 2nd edn, Routledge, London.
- Miles, R and Phizacklea, A (1984) White Man's Country: Racism in British Politics, Pluto Press, London.
- Milner, A (1999) Class, Sage, London.
- Modood, T (2000) 'Race and Ethnicity: Employment' in K Grint, Work and Society: A Reader, Polity Press, Cambridge.
- Modood, T and Acland, T (1998) Race and Higher Education, (ed) Policy Studies Institute, London.
- Modood, T, Berthoud, R, Lakey, J, Nazroo, J, Smith, P, Virdee, S Beishon, S (1997) Ethnic Minorities in Britain: Diversity and Disadvantage, Policy Studies Institute, London.
- Mooney, B (1986) 'Living with the Media – two views', in J Curran, J Ecclestone, G Oakley and A Richardson, Bending Reality: The State of the Media, Pluto Press, London.
- Moore, R (1999) 'The Underclass', Social Science Teacher vol. 29 No 1.
- Moore, S (2018) 'The Windrush Scandal is no accident – it is Tory policy', The Guardian 2, April 24, London.
- Morris, G (1982) 'Employment, training and the work of the Black Media Workers' Association' in P Cohen and C Gardner (eds) It ain't half racist mum, Comedia/CARM, London.

- Motune, V (2018) 'Government forced to act on Windrush injustice', The Voice, April 19-25, London.

- Mullard, C (1982) 'Multiracial Education in Britain: From Assimilation to Cultural Pluralism', in J Tierney (ed) Race, Migration And Schooling, Holt, Rinehart and Winston, East Sussex.

- Murray, C (1990) The Emerging British Underclass, LEA, Health and Welfare Unit, London.

- Nairn, T (1977) The Break-up of Britain: Crisis and Neo-Nationalism, NLB, London.

- Nakanishi D, T (1988) 'Seeking Convergence in Race Relations: Japanese-Americans and the resurrection of the Internment' in P. A. Katz and D. A. Taylor, Eliminating Racism Profiles in Controversy, Plenum Press, London.

- Neal, S (1998) The Making of Equal Opportunities Policies in Universities, The Society for Research into Higher Education & Open University Press, Buckingham.

- Obama, B (2007) Dreams of my Father, Canongate Books, Edinburgh.

- Obama, M (2018) Becoming, Viking, Random House, UK.

- Ojo, W (2007) 'Teachers are unwittingly racist', The Voice, March 19-25, London.

- Olusoga, D (2017) Black and British: A Forgotten History, Pan Books, London.

- Onibada, A (2014) 'Cameron blasted over Jamaican prison plan', The Voice Newspaper, October 8-14, London.

- Parekh, B (2000) The Future of Multi-Ethnic Britain: The Parekh Report, Profile Books, London.

- Perry, K H (2015) London is the Place for Me: Black Britons, Citizenship and the Politics of Race, Oxford University Press, Oxford.

- Pettigrew T F (1988) 'Integration and Pluralism', in P. A. Katz and D. A. Taylor, Eliminating Racism Profiles in Controversy, Plenum Press, London

- Phalet, K (2007) 'Down and Out: The Children of Migrant Workers in the Belgian Labour Market', in A. F. Heath and S.Y. Cheung (eds) Unequal Chances ethnic minorities in western labour markets, Oxford University Press, Oxford.

- Phillips, M and Phillips, T (1998) Windrush: The Irresistible Rise of Multi-racial Britain, HarperCollins, London.

- Pilkington, A (2003) Racial Disadvantage and Ethnic Diversity in Britain, Palgrave Macmillan, Hampshire.
- Pilkington (1997) 'Is there a British Underclass?' in A Giddens, Sociology: Introductory Readings, Polity Press, Cambridge.
- Pilkington, A (2011) Institutional Racism in the Academy: A case study, Trentham Books, Stoke on Trent.
- Plato, (2007) The Republic, 2nd edn, Penguin Books, London.
- Poyser, A (2015) 'Cameron faces backlash in Kingston', The Weekly Gleaner, October 8-14, London.
- Procter, A (2018) 'Museums are still in denial about their imperial past', The Guardian 2, April 24, London.
- Rangasamy, J (2004) Understanding Institutional Racism, in I Law et al. Institutional Racism in Higher Education, Trentham Books, Stoke on Trent.
- Ratcliffe, P (2004) 'Race, Ethnicity and Difference: imagining the Inclusive Society, Open University Press, Berkshire.
- Rattansi, A (2007) Racism: A Very Short Introduction, Oxford University Press, Oxford.
- Reid, P T. (1988) 'Racism and Sexism: Comparisons and Conflicts', in P. A. Katz and D. A. Taylor, Eliminating Racism: Profiles in Controversy, Plenum Press, London.
- Rice-Oxley, M and Kalia, A (2018) 'What is Populism and Why is it such a potent force?' 3 December, The Guardian, London.
- Richards, V (2008) Poetry Trilogy "Streets paved with Gold", AuthorHouse, Central Milton Keynes.
- Richardson, B (2005) Tell it like it is: How our Schools fail Black children, (ed) Trentham Books, Stoke on Trent.
- Richardson J E. (2004) (Mis) Representing Islam: The racism and rhetoric of British broadsheet newspapers, John Benjamins Publishing Company, Amsterdam/Philadelphia.
- Rogers, J.A. (1996) World's Great Men of Color, Volume 1, Touchstone Books, Simon & Schuster, London.
- Rogers, J. A. (1996) World's Great Men of Color, Volume II Touchstone Books, Simon & Schuster, London.

- Ruddock, G (2018) 'Standing up for our rights', The Voice, April 19-25, London.
- Runciman, W G (1990) 'How Many Classes Are There In Contemporary British Society?' Sociology, Vol. 24, No 3, 377-396.
- Sabin, L (2018) 'People Power: Anti-racists take on Tories over Windrush chaos' Morning Star Newspaper, April 30, London.
- Scott, J and Marshall, G (2005) Oxford Dictionary of Sociology, Oxford University Press, Oxford.
- Sears, D O (1988) 'Symbolic Racism', in P.A. Katz and D. A. Taylor, Eliminating Racism: Profiles in Controversy, Plenum Press, London.
- Sertima, I V (1991) Blacks in Science: ancient and modern (ed), Transaction Books, New Brunswick (U.S.A.) and London (UK).
- Sewell, T (1993) Black Tribunes: Black Political Participation in Britain, Lawrence & Wishart, London.
- Sewell, T (1997) Black Masculinities And Schooling: How Black boys survive modern schooling, Trentham Books, Stoke on Trent.
- Sherwood, H (2018) 'Stephen Lawrence Day to be created as annual tribute to murdered teenager', The Guardian, April 24, London.
- Shakespeare, W (1980) Hamlet, Penguin Books, London.
- Shukra, K (1998) The changing Pattern of Black Politics in Britain, Pluto Press, London.
- Shyllon, F. (1977) Black people in Britain 1555-1833, Oxford University Press, London.
- Sissay, L (2017) Gold from the Stone, Canongate Books Ltd, Edinburgh.
- Sivanandan, A (1982) A Different Hunger: Writings on Black Resistance, Pluto Press, London.
- Skellington, R (1996) 'Race' in Britain Today, 2nd edn, Sage, London.
- Slattery, M (1991) Key Ideas in Sociology, Macmillan, Basingstoke and London.
- Smith, D J (1977) Racial Disadvantage in Britain: The PEP Report, Penguin Books Harmondsworth.
- Solomos, J (1989) Race and Racism in Contemporary Britain, Macmillan Press, Basingstoke and London.

- Solomos, J (2003) Race and Racism in Britain, 3rd edn, Palgrave Macmillan, Basingstoke and New York.
- Stoll, L C (2013) Race and Gender in the Classroom: Teachers, Privilege, and Enduring Social Inequalities, Lexington Books, Plymouth.
- Sullivan, W (2018) 'A Time to Remember', The Voice, April 19-25, London.
- Suzar (Dr S Epps) (1999) Blacked Out Through Whitewash, Volume 1, A-Kar Productions, U.S.A.
- Swinford, S and Wright, O (2020) 'Home Office is racist, said report into Windrush', The Times, London.
- Thompson, J B (1997) 'Mass Communication, Symbolic Goods and Media Productions', A Giddens Sociology: Introductory Readings (ed) Polity Press, Oxford.
- Tierney, J (1982) Race, Migration and Schooling, Holt, Rinehart and Winston, London.
- Tivey, L and Wright, A (eds) (1989) Party Ideology in Britain, Routledge, London.
- Torrington, A, Mclean, R, Osborne, V and Grosvenor, I (eds) (2007) EQUIANO: Enslavement, Resistance and Abolition, The Equiano Society and Birmingham Museums and Art Gallery.
- Triandis, H, C (1988) 'The Future of Pluralism Revisited', in P.A. Katz and D.A Taylor, Eliminating Racism: Profiles in Controversy, Plenum Press, London.
- Trowler, P (1999) Investigating Mass Media, HarperCollins, London.
- Troyna, B (1981) Public Awareness and the Media: A Study of Reporting on Race, Commission for Racial Equality, London.
- Troyna, B (ed) (1987) Racial Inequality in Education, Tavistock Publications, London.
- Van Dijk, T A. (2000) 'New(s) Racism: A Discourse Analytical Approach', in S Cottle (ed) (2000) Ethnic Minorities and the Media, Open University Press, Buckingham.
- Van Dijk, T A. (2016) Racism and the Press, Routledge, London.
- Vincent, A (1992) Modern Political Ideologies, Blackwell, Oxford and Cambridge.
- Walker, R (2008) Before the Slave Trade: African World History in Pictures, Black History Studies Publications, London.

Bibliography

- Walker, R (2006) When We Ruled: The Ancient and Medieval History of Black Civilisations, Every Generation Media, London.

- Walvin, J (2007) The Trader, The Owner, The Slave, Jonathan Cape, London.

- Warmington, P (2014) Black British Intellectuals and Education: Multiculturalism's hidden history, Routledge, London.

- Washington, J M (ed) (1991) A Testament of Hope: The essential writings and speeches of Martin Luther King, Jr, HarperCollins, New York.

- Webster, P (1998) 'Underclass Theory', Social Science Teacher vol 27 No 2.

- Werbner, P and Muhammad, A (eds) (1991) Black And Ethnic Leaderships: The Cultural Dimensions of Political Action, Routledge, London.

- Wilkins, L (2005) The Moral Media: How Journalists Reason About Ethics, Lawrence Erlbaum Associates, Publishers, London.

- Williams, M and Henry, A (2003) Black Scientists and Inventors, Book II BIS Publications Ltd, London.

- William, Z (2018) 'Turn our anger into action with a summer of solidarity', The Guardian 2, April 24, London.

- Willis, P (2000) Learning To Labour: How working-class kids get working-class jobs, Ashgate, Farnham.

- Wilson, A. N (2003) The Victorians, Arrow Books, London.

- Winter, J (2007) Lies the Media Tell Us, Black Rose Books, London.

- Wright, C (1987) 'Black students – white teachers', in Racial Inequality in Education, B Troyna, (ed) Tavistock Publications, London.

- Wright, C (1992) Race relations in the Primary School, David Fulton Publishers, London.

- Wright, C, Weekes, D and McGlaughlin, A (2000) 'Race', Class and Gender in Exclusion from School, Falmer Press, London.

- Young, G (2018) 'How a rebel leader was lost to history', The Guardian 2, April 4, London.

- Yu, S & Heath, A (2007) 'Inclusion for all but Aboriginals in Canada', in A. F Heath & S.Y. Cheung (eds) Unequal Chances : ethnic minorities in Western labour markets, Oxford University Press, Oxford.

- Zephaniah, B (1992) City Psalms, Bloodaxe Books Ltd, Northumberland.

- Zephaniah, B (1996) Propa Propaganda, Bloodaxe Books Ltd, Northumberland.
- Zephaniah, B (2001) Too Black, Too Strong, Bloodaxe Books Ltd, Northumberland,

Milton Keynes UK
Ingram Content Group UK Ltd.
UKHW041901010224
437131UK00005BA/12/J